R00132 15907

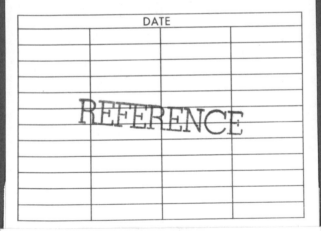

QUALITATIVE EVALUATION

Concepts and Cases
in Curriculum Criticism

■

George Willis, Editor

University of Rhode Island

McCutchan Publishing Corporation
2526 Grove Street
Berkeley, California 94704

©1978 by McCutchan Publishing Corporation
All rights reserved

Library of Congress catalog card number 77-23647
ISBN 0-8211-2257-6

Printed in the United States of America

FOR
NANCY, ELIZABETH, AND KATHRYN

Contents

Foreword

A new climate appears to be developing in the field of educational evaluation, one that could have significant consequences for the ways in which inquiry into educational problems is conceived. I am referring here to the growing interest in the use of the qualitative methods and nonscientific approaches to the study and evaluation of educational practice. This book—the first reader of its kind—is devoted entirely to the use of qualitative methods in educational evaluation and is symptomatic of that interest.

Although quantitative methods of research and evaluation have a long history (as far as the systematic empirical study of education goes), qualitative procedures are comparatively new. American educators in particular have been enchanted by the prospect of developing specific and replicable methods that will ensure that students have learned what they were taught. It was not too long ago that a great deal of research was conducted to discover the best method of teaching reading, mathematics, handwriting, spelling, and other school subjects. Given a belief in the existence of the one best method, it appeared reasonable to try to evaluate what students learn through one standardized test. If content is regarded as common to all students, and if method is regarded as common to all teachers, then why not develop a standardized set of procedures for evaluating achievement? Such a view of education and evaluation is, of course, alluring. It presents no dilemmas, it suggests no difficulties, it is straightforward and appears reasonable to a great many people, particularly lay people.

This book does not participate in that tradition. Instead, it makes a contribution to the development of another tradition. By recognizing the need for a book that links together significant practical and theoretical examples of qualitative approaches to evaluation, George Willis has contributed to the tools with which professors and their students can learn to think more clearly about the theory and methods of qualitative evaluation.

As I see it, the motives for the developing of qualitative methods in educational evaluation emanate from three major sources. First, there are those whose interest stems from political motives. These individuals view the schools as an institutionalized conspiracy to keep children dependent, ill-informed, and tolerant of mindless tasks so that when they become adults they will fit into the existing social order. To such individuals the feckless character of schools is not indicative of failure but of success. Schools, they believe, were and are intended to be a mindless experience. Because the research establishment and the testing industry participate in this subterfuge, they are important targets to attack. Critical methods, particularly those that illuminate the kind of experience that teachers and students have in schools, hold promise for raising the level of critical awareness among the public. In addition, such methods have a kind of emotional impact in revealing what really goes on in schools, which might lead the public to seek significant changes in the structure and goals of schooling. For many of those politically motivated to use qualitative methods, a socialist society or Marxist-socialist philosophy is more compatible with the kind of schooling they prefer. Qualitative methods of evaluation, they believe, might make a significant contribution to the realization of such ends.

The second motive for the development of qualitative approaches to educational evaluation is methodological. Many of those interested in the use of such methods regard laboratory research methods associated with educational psychology as inappropriate for the study of classroom life, and desire a more flexible and naturalistic approach to inquiry. For such individuals, ethnography, for example, provides a more desirable and more appropriate alternative. By attending to the context as a whole, by observing what naturally transpires without intervention by experimenters, a more valid picture can be secured. With more valid data, the likelihood of developing theory that is effective for understanding classrooms, teaching, and schooling is increased.

It should be noted that the motives here are not necessarily political in character. What those people who wish to extend social science methods to education seek is not necessarily the radical reform of schools or society, but the widening of legitimate procedures for research and evaluation. They frequently find the dominant view of research parochial and the methods for evaluating what students learn superficial.

A third motive for the development of qualitative approaches to evaluation is, at base, epistemological. Those moved by this ideal regard scientific epistemology as inadequate by itself for articulating all that needs to be known about schools, classrooms, teaching, and learning. Scientific and quantitative methods are important utilities for describing some aspect of educational life and its consequences, but they are far too limited to be the exclusive or even dominant set of methods. To complement these methods of evaluation, evaluators must look to the qualities that pervade classrooms, the experience that students have in schools, and the character of the work that children produce. To see these qualities requires a perceptive eye, an ability to employ theory to understand what is seen, and an understanding of educational values so that an appraisal of the *educational* significance of what has been seen can be determined.

But what is equally as important as perceiving the qualities that constitute classroom life is the ability to convey those qualities to others. For this to occur, the methods used must be artistically critical. The educational critic must be able to create, render, portray, and disclose in such a way that the reader will be able to participate empathically in the events described. The language of the critic using qualitative methods capitalizes on the role of emotion in knowing. Far from the ideal of emotional neutrality so often aspired to in social science, the educational critic exploits the potential of language to further human understanding. The language she or he uses is expressive, so that the kind of understanding the reader can secure is one that reaches into the deeper levels of meaning individuals in schools experience. To provide such meaning, art is a necessity.

I am pleased that samples of each of these motives for the use of qualitative methods appears in this volume. One will find articles that attack the culture for providing schools which encourage children to become obsequious and docile, articles which focus on the need for new, more appropriate methods, and perhaps most importantly, articles that present the fruits of qualitative evaluation so that the reader may get a taste of what such methods have to offer. Their epistemology inheres in the work itself.

To attempt to alter or expand methods of evaluation that have dominated the field for three quarters of a century is not an easy task. Professionals in the field of education already have a large investment in the methods now employed. To question existing methods—indeed, to point out their limitations—is often to pose a threat to the status quo. This threat is often resisted by asking the qualitative evaluator to demonstrate the validity and reliability of his claims, to demonstrate the generalizability of her findings—in short, to meet the same criteria that the social sciences use to evaluate educational research. What is often not understood is that the criteria that one considers appropriate for quantitative, scientific work in education are not those that are necessarily appropriate for work that rests upon different assumptions, uses different methods, and appeals to different forms of understanding. There is plenty of room in the field of education for both quantitative and qualitative methods—methods that are artistic as well as those that are scientific. What the field does not need is narrow-minded parochialism that assumes that only one set of criteria or one kind of method of inquiry is valid. I believe that this book will contribute to the legitimization of a wider set of methods to educational evaluation; this is no small achievement.

The doing of qualitative evaluation is a difficult task. Unlike the straightforward application of observation schedules or achievement tests, qualitative evaluation offers no recipe-like devices or procedures that one can employ. What theory regarding qualitative evaluation can provide are concepts, considerations, and desiderata that the inquirer can use. But the inquirer is the major "instrument," not a procedural prescription, and in this task a high degree of sensibility and intelligence must be employed. The inquirer needs to know when to shift purpose or focus, how to recognize what is real and what is feigned, how to interpret the meaning of the events observed, and what to make of them from an educational point of view. The task is one that requires not only a tremendous degree of sensitivity but an ability to understand and apply social science theory to the phenomena being observed. One needs a high toleration for complexity and an ability to synthesize material that comes from various fields.

Doing qualitative evaluation is difficult in another way as well. Because it has a personal quality about it, the inquirer puts himself or herself on the line whenever something is written and shared. Unlike the application of standardized tests, which purport to be objective and pose little risk to the test administrator, the individual doing qualitative evaluation has a personal stake in the work that is being done. This can be threatening. Indeed, it is far easier to talk and write about qualitative evaluation than to do it. I am particularly pleased, therefore, that such a substantial proportion of the material in this book is samples of such work. To be sure, all of the samples could be further refined; the last word has yet to be said. But the use of qualitative methods in educational evaluation is only just beginning. There are, for example, very few schools of education that offer courses on such methods to graduate students and no schools or departments of education whose variety of courses in methods of qualitative inquiry approximate the number offered in quantitative methods. Yet for graduate students, the need for such courses is crucial for at least two reasons. First, the existence of such courses provides tacit acknowledgment that qualitative methods of inquiry are legitimate and that graduate students wishing to use them in their own research can do so. Such courses contribute to the catholicity of climate as far as method is concerned.

The second reason such courses are important is because graduate students need more than to know that certain methods can legitimately be used; they need training in their use. Courses on qualitative methods can provide such training and, if I may say so, they may do as much for the instructors as for the students who enroll in their courses.

It is significant that such a large number of the contributors to this volume are people at the beginning of their careers in education. These are individuals who have twenty to thirty years ahead of them in the field and who are helping to open up some new vistas and develop some new approaches to educational evaluation. Several of them will, I am confident, provide much of the leadership in the field. And their students will develop even further the work that they helped to advance. In the last analysis, the forms that can be used to conceptualize, express, and understand the world are limitless, since human capacity itself seems to be shaped by the fruits of the imagination as they influence culture. Up to now we have barely scratched the surface of possibility. But scratch we have, and I believe some new leads have been found. This book provides one of the tools we can use to help us get on with the digging.

Elliot W. Eisner
Stanford University

Preface

Evaluation is a critical activity depending on context and meaning. It is critical in two senses. First (and more obviously), it analyzes and judges an object of criticism. The critic should have reasons to support these judgments. Second (and less obviously), it analyzes and judges the process of criticism itself. The critic should also have reasons to support choices about critical methodologies. In both these senses good criticism requires considerable reflection by the critic, whether reflection is on object or process.

The context and meaning on which critical activity depends also exist in two analogous senses. One context is external to the critic: the object of criticism itself and the social, cultural, political, and economic milieu in which it is embedded. The second context is internal: the value system and personal perceptions of the critic. Similarly, meaning may be of the external world or of the internal processes of the critic in reacting to and valuing externals. Ultimately, any critical activity depends on the meanings constituted within both external and internal contexts. Judgments flow from meanings so constituted; social consequences, from judgments.

This volume, therefore, is based on the assumptions that educational evaluation is essentially reflection about context and meaning in both these senses; and that external world of educational "object" and social milieu, internal world of personal values and perceptions, and resulting judgments and social actions are inextricably linked together. For instance, even those chapters which most emphasize internal ("personal") contexts and meanings assume these to be linked, on the one hand, with external contexts and meanings and, on the other, with judgments and actions. Even when meaning is treated from a highly personal perspective, it is still regarded as also a function of other contexts: of how it arises in part in the external world and of how resulting judgments influence that world. While the volume suggests that in many ways qualitative and quantitative evaluation are complementary processes, it further suggests that the two can be differentiated in terms of how they treat these linkages, qualitative often being, in fact, the more powerful mode of evaluation precisely because qualitative methods tend to emphasize these linkages whereas quantitative tend to treat contexts and meanings as isolated.

This volume purports to be neither definitive nor exhaustive. In dealing with qualitative evaluation and curriculum criticism it offers suggestions about the basis for and the current dimensions of the field, descriptions and examples of methodological techniques, and explanations of related topics and issues. It does not, however, assume that the field cannot be conceived in other ways nor that it will no longer continue to evolve. It does not attempt systematically to catalog all qualitative techniques. It does not extensively discuss all issues which it raises. For instance, several chapters suggest that qualitative techniques encourage educational evaluation by practitioners themselves, mostly teachers, or that experience as a teacher may be extremely important in the development of an insightful educational critic. However, many of the questions which surround such suggestions simply cannot be addressed fully in this volume. Most readers will develop their own agenda of topics for further consideration.

The volume begins with an introductory chapter which outlines the general topic of qualitative evaluation within contemporary education. The remainder of the book is divided into three sections. The first of these sections, entitled "Concepts," provides both background on the basis for qualitative educational criticism and several closely related views of how educational criticism functions. The second section, "Cases," provides specific examples of applied educational criticism, many of these case studies also including theoretical discussions of the principles and methods they employ. The third section, "Comments," provides retrospective analyses of some of the major issues raised in the book and, in chapter 21, direct commentary on many of the case studies in the preceding section.

I am grateful to all those people whose names are listed in the table of contents of this volume. Many have made contributions far greater than their listings as authors of individual chapters can indicate. I am grateful, also, to Elliot Eisner, Barry MacDonald, Edmund Short, Robert Stake, and David Purpel for suggestions which have helped me identify and locate many of the contributing authors. Without these suggestions the book could not have been assembled.

Contributors of original essays have been encouraged to write chapters for this volume which express their own points of view, and they have done so. While all contributors in some ways share certain common assumptions, they do not, of course, necessarily subscribe to all other statements in this volume. Individual authors are responsible only for their own chapters. Weaknesses in the organization of the book or in its overall treatment of the topic are my own responsibility.

Contributors

Anthony J. Allen is assistant professor of education at the University of Rhode Island. He has published articles on creativity, classroom use of test results, teaching of composition, and educational evaluation. His current interests include literary responses of students, pupil observation techniques, and nontraditional evaluation schemes for inservice programs.

Michael W. Apple is professor of curriculum and instruction at the University of Wisconsin-Madison. He has written numerous articles and monographs on ideology and curriculum, the hidden curriculum, and student rights. His most recent publications include *Educational Evaluation: Analysis and Responsibility* and *Schooling and the Rights of Children.*

Leonard Davidman is assistant professor of education at California Polytechnic State University at San Luis Obispo. His current projects include designing naturalistic inquiries into the influences of high-quality questioning and listening on learners, of television viewing on learning style and school behavior, and of sociodrama on patterns of ethical reasoning.

W. Dwaine Greer is program area coordinator, Fine Arts, at SWRL Educational Research and Development. His interests include

arts curriculum design and development and educational criticism. He has published articles and reviews in art education
journals. He exhibits textile works, and recently had a one-man
show in Los Angeles.

Madeleine R. Grumet is a doctoral candidate at the University of
Rochester. She has written a number of papers on curriculum
and, with William Pinar, is the author of *Toward a Poor Curriculum.*

David Jenkins is professor of education at the New University of Ulster, Northern Ireland. He has worked in curriculum development at Keele, in curriculum evaluation at the University of
East Anglia, and with the Open University central academic
team.

Daniel Kallós is currently professor of education in the Department
of Educational Research at the School of Education in Uppsala,
Sweden. Among his publications in English are papers dealing
with educational research and the study of curriculum in *British
Journal of Educational Psychology, Educational Studies,* and
Journal of Curriculum Studies.

Edward F. Kelly is associate director for research and evaluation at
the Center for Instructional Development, Syracuse University.
He has contributed numerous articles on topics in curriculum
and evaluation to books and journals.

Nancy King is assistant professor of education at Wheelock College.
She has written about ideology and educational research for
such journals as *Educational Theory.* She is now engaged in a
research project dealing with a comparative analysis of the hidden curriculum.

John S. Mann has taught at Goddard College, the Johns Hopkins University, and the University of New Mexico. He now lives in
Springfield, Massachusetts, where he is active in social causes
and writes about class, politics, economics, and education.

Gail McCutcheon is assistant professor of education at the University
of Virginia. As a generalist, she is interested in many sorts of
curriculum questions. She has written several methodological
articles exploring different facets of qualitative approaches and
case studies using methods of educational criticism and ethnography.

W. Lynn McKinney is associate professor of education and director of the Curriculum Research and Development Center at the University of Rhode Island. He is a contributor to the book *Case Studies in Curriculum Change.*

Edward W. Milner has taught and developed courses at several colleges and universities, currently Johnson C. Smith. He holds degrees from Davidson, Columbia Theological Seminary, the University of Chicago, and the University of North Carolina at Greensboro, where in 1976 he completed his Ed.D. dissertation, "Myths, Morals, and Models; Implications for Special Education."

Bridget O'Toole is lecturer in English literature at the New University of Ulster, Northern Ireland, where she specializes in American and Anglo-Irish literature. Her school teaching experience includes a spell in an inner-Liverpool secondary school.

William F. Pinar is associate professor of education at the University of Rochester. He has written *Sanity, Madness, and the School* and, with Madeleine R. Grumet, *Toward a Poor Curriculum.* He edited *Heightened Consciousness, Cultural Revolution, and Curriculum Theory* and *Curriculum Theorizing: The Reconceptualists.*

Thomas Popkewitz is associate professor of curriculum and instruction at the University of Wisconsin-Madison. He is concerned with the development of research approaches that focus upon the social and political functions of educational reform and with general philosophical questions about the nature and character of social science.

José Rosario is assistant professor of education at the State University of New York College at Geneseo. He has written on topics in aesthetics and curriculum and is co-author of the chapter "Morality, Science, and the Use of the Child in History" in *Schooling and the Rights of Children.*

Francine Shuchat Shaw is assistant professor of education at New York University and a filmmaker. Her writing has focused on conceptions of knowledge and expressive dimensions of teachers and students. She is currently investigating the place of filmmaking in education, conceiving it as a mode of inquiry and criticism.

Robert M. W. Travers is Distinguished University Professor at Western Michigan University. He edited the *Second Handbook of*

Research on Teaching and is the author of several books which, through numerous translations, have had a worldwide circulation.

Elizabeth Vallance is director of curriculum planning for the University of Mid-America (Lincoln, Nebraska), a regional postsecondary open-learning project. She received her Ph.D. from Stanford University, has worked in educational research, planning, and curriculum design, and does photography. She is co-editor of *Conflicting Conceptions of Curriculum.*

George Willis is associate professor of education at the University of Rhode Island. He has contributed articles on curriculum to a number of journals and books, including *Curriculum Theory Network, Journal of Curriculum Studies,* and *Curriculum Theorizing: The Reconceptualists.*

Look not too long in the face of the fire, O man! Never dream with thy hand on the helm! Turn not thy back to the compass; accept the first hint of the hitching tiller; believe not the artificial fire, when its redness makes all things look ghastly. To-morrow, in the natural sun, the skies will be bright; those who glared like devils in the forking flames, the morn will show in far other, at least gentler, relief; the glorious, golden, glad sun, the only true lamp—all others but liars!

Herman Melville, Moby Dick

Introduction

1

Qualitative Evaluation as the Aesthetic, Personal, and Political Dimensions of Curriculum Criticism

George Willis

Quantitative Evaluation, Qualitative Evaluation, and the Times

There are two principal ways to differentiate quantitative and qualitative evaluation in education. Both ways suggest what all forms of educational research and evaluation have in common, as well as how the quantitative and the qualitative differ. The first way is to examine the differing logics of inference employed in the two types of studies. As Robert M. W. Travers points out,[1] both types of studies begin with observation of phenomena and their characteristics, and in this sense, both are empirical. But whereas in quantitative studies the logic of inference is one of classification and seriation, resulting in numerical comparison, in qualitative studies the logic of inference is one of direct comparison, resulting in new insight and reclassification.

The second method of differentiation is to examine the ways in which evaluators apprehend the world. Quantitative studies often consider only the most easily observed and empirically verifiable *characteristics* of the environment. Qualitative studies usually attempt more fully to consider both observed characteristics and specific qualities perceived as personal forms of meaning. In this sense, the evaluator in quantitative studies tends to see the world as largely determinate and nonproblematic, although personal choice is still necessary in deciding what characteristics to enumerate and how to value them. In contrast, the evaluator in qualitative studies tends to see the world as largely indeterminate and problematic; hence, its qualities are seen more directly as functions of the perceptions and personal meanings the evaluator brings to the situation. These two ways of apprehending the world are not always distinct; at times they tend to blend into each other. Still, to the extent that qualitative evaluation includes the personal determination of the qualities of an indeterminate world, it can be considered as involving a process of qualitative thinking or qualitative problem-solving.[2] Further, this process of perceiving and valuing in a qualitative way largely determines the quality of the evaluator's own experience and may, in turn, influence the quality of life of other people.

Both of these ways of differentiation underline the importance of the individual within the work of educational evaluation and call into question ordinary distinctions between subjectivity and objectivity. Personal perceptions, meanings, and value systems underlie both types of evaluation, for even the most apparently straightforward observations of empirically verifiable characteristics of educational environments are made selectively, in tune with the particular perceptual orientation and value system of the observer. For instance, observations of results on a standardized achievement test deflect attention from observations that might be made about freely chosen actions of students. A decision to compare test results quantitatively to socioeconomic characteristics of students interprets the reasons for the actions of individuals as being determined largely by the environment. Yet the use of such comparisons in making educational judgments inevitably devalues the significance of more ephemeral but more powerfully felt qualities of the environment. There are many other and far different observations and decisions that *could* have been made by the evaluator. Considerations such as these apply to both quantitative and qualitative forms of evaluation.

Since both forms of evaluation depend directly (although to different extents) on the personal and idiosyncratic funds of meaning brought to them by individual evaluators, there is no such thing as "objective" educational evaluation. There are no conclusions that are strictly warranted by the "facts" of any case, for the "facts" themselves, their meanings, and their significances are always and inevitably in doubt. The best that can be hoped for in either form of evaluation is that observations be careful and discerning, interpretations be full and insightful, and that judgments be justified and wise. Still, these considerations do not mean that the complex and individualistic personal bases from which education must be considered make educational evaluation a socially irresponsible enterprise. Rather, they may strengthen an enlightened social commitment.

To illustrate this last point, consider first a highly personal ("subjective," if you will) perspective by James B. Macdonald, personal in the sense of insisting that individual perceptions, meanings, and values be brought to bear on education. Addressing himself to the curriculum field and specifically to the question "Why be concerned about curriculum?" Macdonald affirms:

Curriculum, it seems to me, is the study of "What should constitute a world for learning and how to go about making this world?" As such, it is in *microcosm* the very question that seems to me to be of foremost concern to all of humanity. Such questions as "What is the good society?" "What is the good life?" and "What is a good person?" are implicit in the curriculum question. Further, the moral question of how to relate to others or how best to live together is clearly a critical part of curriculum.

Thus, "Why be concerned about curriculum?" can, for me, be expanded to "Why be concerned about life?" For me, the school setting is a potentially manageable microcosm of a rather unmanageable macrocosmic society. Schools lack none of the elements found in the larger context, and they do provide, for me, concrete entry points for thought and action growing out of my own experiences. Thus, for example, I have experience with politics *in* schools that gives me a concrete referent for generalizing beyond that context.

If, on the other hand, I felt that curriculum talk and work were only specific socially available roles limited in their meaning to concrete processes and situations in schools, they would hold little interest for me. It is the human intentions embodied in curriculum making and the micro-macro relationships that bring curriculum work alive and create processes and situations that become more than technical problems. . . .

It is here that I shall express what values I feel ought to undergird curriculum talk and work; I suppose to illustrate the point, although hopefully to convince someone also. Here I am afraid I am rather parochial, rather American in my makeup, for I believe that a kind of religious socialism should be that central core. These are in other words two fundamental value questions that inform and form the human condition. They are a) What is the meaning of human life?, and b) How shall we live together?[3]

Macdonald does not expect anyone else to think *quite* as he does nor to supply *quite* the same answers to the questions posed about education. His statement stands as precisely that—a "statement," a personal assertion of meaning, all the more interesting and powerful because in a few words it links personal, political, and religious convictions with a view of humanity, the quality of life, and how the schools should be valued. From it one could not tell exactly what observations Macdonald might make about any specific educational environment, what particular perceived qualities he might choose for disclosure of meaning, or how that disclosure might be organized; but one could be relatively certain of what might be emphasized, of why Macdonald thought these emphases important, and of the value bases upon which his judgments would rest. As such, the passage stands as a basis for, and indeed, a condensation of, qualitative evaluation that clearly exemplifies both a highly personal perspective and a lucid social commitment.

In contrast, consider next a generalized example of some major efforts to conduct educational research and evaluation on a non-personalistic basis in order to achieve socially beneficial results. While few people might question the basic impulse, one of the least desirable consequences of direct efforts during the last two decades by politicians and social scientists to improve American schools has been the intensification and perpetuation of the belief that research and evaluation in education are defensible only when their methods lead to quantifiable results.[4] On a national scale the impulse for social commitment has merged with an aura of science, objectivity, consensus, and social responsibility. Efforts to use the schools directly in ending deep-rooted social inequities, to implement standardized curricula, to increase performance on academic achievement tests, or to usher in an era of statistical accountability have all helped to create on a large scale a comparatively new class of professional, the social scientist as educational evaluator, who tends to accept this belief. Usually better trained in statistics and probability theory than in philosophy and history, and more insightful about the nuances of research designs than the nuances of classrooms, this professional has actually become so influential that even many educators themselves now identify all research and evaluation in education solely with techniques of quantification. The pervasiveness of this example now tends to obscure thoughtful consideration of the strengths and limitations of these techniques and their alternatives. And whether or not the schools have actually improved in recent years, there is no reason for supposing that the bulk of quantitative research and evaluation has been helpful, as the trials undergone by the National Institute of Education in recent years ironically suggest.

In this general vein, consider further the kind of issues taken most seriously by this new professional and the way these issues have been approached. Since the middle 1960s America has endured solemn debates in many forms on the general topic of "Do schools make a difference?" Failure by social scientists to find demonstrably different effects among various forms of schooling has usually been taken as indicating that society has overestimated the value of formal education. Yet any educator (and virtually anyone who has spent any time at all in school) is profoundly aware at some level of consciousness of the very powerful and pervasive differences schools do in fact make on the quality of individual lives, particularly in terms of how individuals perceive and act to change their environments. Failure by social scientists through techniques of quantification to demonstrate such patently obvious differences is clearly evidence of the limitations of such techniques or how they have been applied, not of lack of influence or limitations of value of formal education. Similarly, debates on such topics as the genetic versus environmental determination of intelligence and whether school busing works have largely been in-house debates on technical issues and thus have been without genuine educational or social significance, whatever their impact on popular or professional opinion.

The belief that only the use of supposedly objective techniques of quantification provides a sound basis for research and evaluation in education or for the shaping of social policies is not thus based on any demonstrated superiority of quantitative techniques. No doubt the belief has been encouraged by the sociopolitical climate of the times and by the basic value systems of Americans. Such things as the social revolutions of the 1960s, the political changes of the 1970s, the Vietnam War, Watergate, the energy crisis, financial stringencies, changes in family life, and the growing recognition of the fragility of the environment in sustaining life have all acted on such conflicting American faiths as individual initiative and social conformity and have helped heighten a search for immediate and dependable answers and technical solutions in many phases of life. But for whatever reasons, many people seem in recent times to have found the questionable assumption that quantitative techniques are more rigorous and more nearly value-free than qualitative techniques an acceptable notion. In point of fact, the assumption is mistaken, for any kind of evaluation depends upon the perceptions of the evaluator and by its nature is heavily value-laden, and both kinds of techniques can be applied with considerable rigor or with considerable slovenliness.

One limitation of quantitative evaluation is that the value assumptions often tend to be obscured by the techniques themselves. For instance, assumptions are built into the instruments (such as tests, questionnaires, personality scales, etc.) from which quantified results are obtained. These results may appear to speak for themselves, to be relatively objective, scientific, or free from personal biases. However, assumptions and biases have gone into the creation of the instruments, and additional assumptions and biases have gone into their selection by the evaluator. In qualitative evaluation the value assumptions of the evaluator may be transparent or opaque, clearly or inarticulately stated, but since conclusions seem to stem directly from the personal discernments and insights of the evaluator, the fact that assumptions and biases are inherent in the process is rarely forgotten altogether by the reader of the study.

For the most part, quantitative evaluation aims at *general* understanding. Starting with a number of cases and identifying and quantifying a limited number of factors, a typical study might ordinarily derive statistical correlations between factors and statistical probabilities that such correlations occur or do not occur by chance. While correlation and statistical significance are particularly useful in inferring causation and, beyond that, in providing insight within certain limits, the causal influences inferred remain those between general factors only. These generalizations may or may not hold for any of the individual cases that went into formulating the collective quantification of each factor. For instance, a characteristic that is true of a group collectively, such as the mean score on an achievement test, may not be true of any individual member of the group. While quantitative techniques are thus useful in dealing simultaneously with a large number of cases, their basic value in any particular study depends on the significance and explanatory power of the factors identified, the degree to which statistical significance corresponds to other forms of significance, and the worthwhileness of the derived generalizations.

In contrast, qualitative evaluation aims at *particular* understanding. Starting with specific characteristics of individuals and environment and including qualities perceived personally as meaningful by the evaluator, such a study ordinarily seeks to disclose a variety of meanings, hence to generate a variety of insights of potentially limitless kind and number, directly about these particulars. Why did a child misbehave on a certain occasion? Careful observation of the occasion may have made the reasons completely clear to a discerning parent or teacher, but since neither occasion nor misbehavior recur, the explanation, even in most simplified form, is not quantifiable and admits of no statistical significance. Depending on the insightfulness and skill of the evaluator, qualitative techniques may or may not focus on the most significant characteristics and qualities of an unfolding situation and may or may not generate perceptive or even adequate meanings and explanations; nonetheless, they permit personal engagement with and direct understanding of a full range of highly specific characteristics and qualities, including those not amenable to quantification. In this sense, qualitative techniques are particularly useful since they focus on specific events in process rather than on the numerical representations of events past. Recommendations entailed in qualitative evaluations may thus be based on direct perceptions of causality and meaning, which may in time prove to be the basis needed for substantial improvement of American schools.

Given these fundamental differences between quantitative and qualitative techniques of evaluation and given the prevailing national climate that has effectively recognized and honored only the quantitative, Robert Stake has observed that while professional educational evaluators now occupy privileged and influential positions in society, the ordinary forms of quantitative evaluation remain but cogs in the social machinery. Much has been expected from and promised by the newly burgeoning educational evaluation industry, but little has been delivered, especially of the sort that questions *status quo* assumptions about the business of schooling. As part of this observation Stake has suggested that an essential part of the evaluation of educational programs should be the direct, qualitative judgments of insightful evaluators based on their personal experience and personal acquaintance with the programs.[5]

The thesis of this volume is that quantitative evaluation, due both to its inherent limitations and to the aura that now surrounds it, neither asks nor answers many basic educational questions dealing with personal meaning and social significance. Educational evaluation in the United States will not develop into a mature and socially responsible enterprise until it widely adopts artistically developed and skillfully employed techniques of qualitative evaluation that directly confront both the significance of and the qualities of personal experience within education.

Qualitative Evaluation as Curriculum Criticism

Qualitative evaluation in education, in the most general meaning of that phrase, is as old as education itself. Anyone who has observed educational processes, events, or materials and then formulated opinions about what has been observed has been engaged at least informally in educational criticism: the parent observing a child's classroom, the school committee member perusing a sex education text, the old grad considering a Black Studies program. More often than not, informal evaluation has proceeded without use of techniques of quantification. Only when the observer-evaluator has become sufficiently self-conscious about this task, usually by attempting to supply reasons for opinions as well as opinions themselves, has he become an educational critic in a more formal sense. The self-conscious critic of American education, whether or not he relies on techniques of quantification, has a long and time-honored, if also somewhat checkered history ranging from Joseph Mayer Rice to Charles Silberman and beyond. Among the most accomplished of those who have been qualitative educational critics on a grand scale during this century are John Dewey and Boyd Bode. Only during recent decades of the century have techniques of quantification become sufficiently sophisticated so that quantitative evaluation has emerged as a separate (although potentially stunted) branch of educational criticism, the branch now often identified with educational evaluation as a whole.

As a reaction, in recent years a movement has been developing to refurbish qualitative evaluation generally and to educate both the public and professional educators as to its virtues and to the uses of its specific forms. This movement is in some measure traceable to the essay "Curriculum Criticism," by John S. Mann,[6] published originally in 1968. Mann has suggested that a curriculum can be considered as a literary or, in a broader sense, an artistic object, and that the task of the curriculum critic is, thus, much like the task of the literary or artistic critic: for instance, to disclose meanings inherent in the design of the object, particularly meanings inherent in the choices made by the creator of the work. Moreover, especially when a curriculum is considered broadly, as the educational environment itself, curriculum criticism becomes educational criticism of the fullest kind and may employ not only techniques of literary and artistic criticism, but also critical techniques derived from any area of study intended to illuminate the way humans constitute meaning.

Curriculum criticism, then, is a major branch of educational criticism and evaluation. It has developed self-consciously in the last decade by appropriately applying to educational situations forms of criticism similar principally to literary and artistic criticism, but also to other forms of critical understanding of how meaning is constituted. For the most part its techniques are similar to those of the humanities (as opposed to those of quantification of the natural and of some social sciences), and its techniques tend to deal with particular cases, especially those that are not amenable to quantification. For practical purposes the terms "curriculum criticism" and "qualitative evaluation" are synonymous, although the former is more frequently used to indicate specific cases and the latter to indicate the general movement. While Mann originally popularized the former term, the most active spokesman for the movement during the 1970s has been Elliot Eisner,[7] who has urged the development of qualitative forms of educational criticism as an alternative to quantitative evaluation. Beyond the potential impact of the movement for qualitative evaluation on educational evaluation in the United States, the movement has distinct parallels with current efforts to reconstitute the curriculum field. For instance, the "Reconceptualists"[8] among curriculum theorists have been concerned with reorganizing the field around human consciousness and political action. These are also two of the currently dominant themes among many qualitative educational critics. The 1975 Yearbook of the Association for Supervision and Curriculum Development[9] is fully developed qualitative educational evaluation organized around the latter theme.

The Processes of Criticism

Since the curriculum can be considered broadly as the educational environment, qualitative evaluation in education is curriculum criticism in its fullest sense. For it to be fully developed and well articulated, it therefore must include a series of interrelated processes inherent in all critical activities. While these processes may be broken down in a number of ways, they are here considered as description, disclosure of meaning, and judgment.[10]

Description is a way of recreating what is observed by the critic. In educational criticism observations might be of numerous things: the physical environment of a classroom, curriculum materials, actions by a teacher, and reactions by students, to list but a few. In describing for others what has been observed, the critic must be selective. No critic can observe everything that might be observed, nor can a critic describe for others everything that has been observed. In this sense, description in educational criticism of any kind is a selective rendering of those characteristics the critic considers most significant. Still, both quantitative and qualitative forms of criticism are empirical; description in both begins with direct observation. In quantitative evaluation the critic tends to describe only characteristics that seem easiest to verify through simple observation—those characteristics that require the least complex interpretation to receive wide assent ("age," "sex," "behavior"). In qualitative evaluation the critic is ordinarily more free to include description of characteristics discernible or verifiable only through a more elaborate process of observation and interpretation ("atmosphere," "strategem," "gesture"). Ordinarily, then, in qualitative evaluation the critic has a greater range of observed characteristics from which to select for description, and the critic may even extend description sufficiently to include perceived qualities of the situation that are personal forms of meaning not subject to public verification.

Disclosure of meaning is the pointing out of qualities and characteristics described in ways that permit a variety of comparisons leading to inferences about meanings. For instance, in analyzing the events of a classroom the critic may assert that these events fall into certain patterns that, in comparison with other patterns—actual or potential—imply certain meanings for, say, teacher, students, or society. The critic therefore asserts either directly or indirectly that these patterns have meanings different from patterns of characteristics observed in a different classroom. This, of course, is what Mann meant in asserting that the critic's basic task is to disclose meaning. Such disclosure, however, depends upon the critic's skill in selecting and applying a variety of constructs. "Socioeconomic class" is a construct upon which agreement is reasonably easy, "bureaucratization" is more difficult, "oppressiveness" more difficult still. Clearly, not all inferences about meaning are equally logical. The best are usually those that are the most warrantable, the most incisive, and the most powerful in creating significant insights. Ordinarily, in quantitative evaluation most inferences are in terms of statistical significance, whereas in qualitative evaluation inferences about meaning tend to focus on broader kinds of educational and personal significance.

Judgment is the assertion of worth of what has been observed and described and about which meaning has been disclosed. Such judgment may be in terms of the intrinsic worth of what has been observed or its value in relation to an extrinsic goal or purpose. Also judged may be the worth of the purposes themselves, the wisdom of their selection, and the skill by which they have been carried out in practice. Here the critic's value system may become most explicit. Often the best critic at this point is one who can supply the fullest reasons for the judgments rendered and the most coherent, appropriate, or clearly articulated basis for those reasons. Unfortunately, quantitative evaluation on the whole has been notably deficient in this regard. Comparatively few quantitative studies carefully describe the value bases of the evaluator.

Educational criticism is not a casual art, although it has often been practiced casually. Much depends on the skill of the critic in carrying out the tasks of description, disclosure of meaning, and judgment. Not all critics are equally perceptive or insightful in making observations, nor wise in selecting observations to be described. Not all descriptions are constructed equally well, nor all meanings equally warranted or profound. Not all judgments are equally appropriate. Contrary to somewhat common belief, then, qualitative evaluation in education is far more than the exchange of mere opinion, although it does include a personal basis for meaning. As do all forms of fully developed criticism, it embodies rather rigorous standards. A piece of curriculum criticism may itself be judged in terms of several principal criteria: its accessibility and credibility to intelligent readers, its consistency and internal coherence, the accuracy or the adequacy of its representations of what is specifically being criticized, the appropriateness of its judgments, and the power of its disclosures to generate meanings beyond those immediate meanings explicitly disclosed.

More directly, more obviously, and perhaps more fully than in all but rather rare examples of quantitative evaluation, curriculum criticism depends on the insightfulness and skill of the critic. In this sense it begins in the perceptions and personal insights of the critic and educates its audience by enhancing the skills necessary to achieve a well warranted and expanded range of personal meanings. Often this educative process proceeds through the critic's identifying the most pervasive or significant qualities of a classroom and relating them to external social and political qualities. In this way curriculum criticism encourages personal and aesthetic responses to both the natural and the artistically arranged configurations of educational environments or their specific qualities, but these responses include social and political insights, which lead to public consequences. Thus, qualitative evaluation in education, as embodied in specific forms of curriculum criticism, is the highly focused and selective rendering of the critic's perceptions and his experience of specific characteristics of the educational environment. By emphasizing certain qualities of experiencing that occur in response to that environment, it both illuminates the environment and discloses meaning by evoking similar responses in its audience. These evoked responses, while largely influenced by the environment and by the critic's perceptions and skills, constitute personal meanings from which flow social consequences.

Aesthetic, Personal, and Political Dimensions

The essays in this volume are basically of two types: those that outline general concepts about the nature of qualitative evaluation and curriculum criticism or discuss issues concerning their use, and those that exemplify curriculum criticism in practice. The essays of the former type are included in the sections titled "Concepts" and "Comments"; those of the latter type, in the section titled "Cases." Since qualitative evaluation is an emerging field, this volume provides neither a conclusive set of concepts that define it nor exhaustive discussions of all issues and implications. Rather, the various essays present a variety of points of view, although on a common theme and based on common assumptions. The reader will gain definite ideas of both the general outlines of the field and the specific characteristics of its distinctive features.

The essays in the "Cases" section are, of course, case studies in curriculum criticism. They have been intended by their writers as careful critical works, and most have been written expressly for this volume. They exemplify a variety of methodological techniques drawn from such areas as artistic, literary, and social criticism and applied to education. They reflect the three dominant interests within the work of contemporary curriculum critics; hence, they reflect the major dimensions of the field. These dominant interests are the aesthetic, the personal, and the political.

The aesthetic interest has thus far been the most closely associated with curriculum criticism. In a general sense, the development of meaning of virtually any kind is largely an aesthetic process. More specifically, the aesthetic interest is concerned primarily with how people develop meaning in response to the particulars of the external world as embodied in individual and collective forms. Are parts harmoniously related? Can a person respond holistically to them? For instance, in considering a specific classroom one might look first at the physical surroundings. Is the room attractive? What associations and reactions is it likely to evoke? Does it invite the student to become an active participant in shaping the educational process or a more passive recipient of whatever is offered? Turning next to the contents of instruction, one might ask: Are the ideas dogmatic? Are they hackneyed, or novel and exciting? Are materials abundant or sparse? Are materials, taken as a whole, self-consistent or self-contradictory? And in assessing the methods of instruction and the social relationships in the classroom, one might consider: Is the teacher accessible or aloof? What tone of voice prevails? Do the teacher's ideas contradict those of the texts? Are students encouraged to work cooperatively or competitively? In asking any such question one may find certain meanings inherent in the classroom. In asking a series of such questions one builds up the overall pattern of meanings that the classroom conveys, and one may discern its consistency, its pervasive qualities, and the extent to which its parts have been artistically related. The aesthetic interest is concerned principally with the integrity of form and meaning.

The personal interest is also concerned with the development of meaning, but here emphasis shifts away from meanings about the external world and toward meanings about how the individual self responds to its own perceptions of the world. Since different individuals may respond with integrity to the same characteristics of the external world in different ways, and thereby formulate different meanings, the personal interest in curriculum criticism deals quite literally with personal insights. One might ask the same kinds of questions about a specific classroom as would be asked by the person with aesthetic interests, but rather than answering in terms of the way the environment itself evokes meanings, one might now answer in terms of the way the perceptions, attitudes, and values of specific individuals cause different personal meanings to be evoked. Why does one individual respond differently from another? Are all personal meanings equally justified? How do differences in biographies affect perceptions of meaning? What common patterns emerge within distinctly individual variations? Can one self-consciously alter the way one constitutes personal meaning? The personal interest in curriculum criticism is concerned primarily with how an individual develops meaning as a function of his experience of the world.

The political interest, while also concerned with meanings developed by individuals in response to both external forms and internal processes, emphasizes the uses for which meanings are intended and the uses to which they are put. Do meanings inherent in the external world lead toward individual liberation or toward social control? Do personal responses develop new forms of social meaning? In considering a specific classroom one might here be concerned not only with specifics of the physical environment, materials, and methodology, but also with the general view of society and of the role of the school purveyed by them. Should society honor cultural pluralism? Does society require obedient workers? Is the school's role to train such workers? To provide career education for jobs that may exist only in the future? To develop individuals to create a better social order or simply to demolish the old? The particulars of any classroom convey answers to these and many other such questions, and these answers, sometimes intended and sometimes unintended, tell students about the nature of their society and how they should live their lives. When are the meanings intended in the classroom actually those conveyed? What is the social significance of both kinds of meaning? The political interest in curriculum criticism is principally concerned with the relationships between individual meanings, collective meanings, and social action.

These three interests are three modalities of experience that blend closely into one another. They are illustrated in detail by the case studies in this volume. While the case studies have been arranged to reflect a progression from the aesthetic to the personal to the political, many of the studies explicitly reflect two or more of these interests. In fact, in none of the studies is any one of the three interests totally absent, although an interest may remain unacknowledged or undeveloped. Attempting to keep separate responses to the external world, personal insights, and social consequences is ultimately futile. Because these modalities of experience blend so closely, no effort has been made beyond the general sequence by progression to separate the studies into three sub-sections, each devoted to one interest only. The short introductions that preface the case studies discuss the dominant interests present in each.

Whether or not in the future new and different interests will develop within the work of curriculum critics or new and different ways of considering present interests will come into being are matters for speculation. This volume illustrates a number of the varied techniques now prevalent in curriculum criticism and qualitative evaluation. It does not purport to represent the relative importance of specific techniques nor the relative numbers of active critics of differing interests. It is by no means exhaustive of the valid techniques that are or can be skillfully used. Therefore, in this sense the volume is not an effort prematurely to define or to delimit curriculum criticism as methodology or qualitative evaluation as contemporary movement. Movement and methodologies are emerging and in time will further create and define themselves. In this sense the volume is not an effort to create new orthodoxies but is an invitation to reconsider old.

Future Uses of Curriculum Criticism

In the hands of a skillful educational critic the complexity of an educational environment is not deprived of its richness or the variety of its nuances, and this point in itself should be sufficient reason for the widespread use of qualitative techniques in the evaluation of educational programs of all kinds. Put simply, qualitative techniques get at things that are inaccessible to quantitative methods. But for qualitative techniques to be widely used in the United States, they must be recognized and valued. In effect, this is the reason for the current movement for qualitative evaluation, of which this volume is a part. However, the success of the movement does not necessarily depend solely upon its first being recognized as a movement. Just as it is possible for individual critics to develop their perceptions and abilities through experience, perseverance, and discerning criticism of their own work, it is also possible to encourage and develop increasing numbers of intelligent and skillful new educational critics. For such progress to occur, both formal and informal networks of communication among curriculum critics must become better established and new programs for the training of critics should be begun. Since the critic's role is largely the reeducation of the perceptions and the values of his audience, increasing numbers of curriculum critics practicing skillfully can serve to educate a widening audience to the value of techniques of qualitative evaluation.

Despite the wide variety of techniques that may be used and insights that may be developed by curriculum criticism, qualitative evaluation is based on extremely commonsensical assumptions. They are the assumptions honored by most people as they come to value in a variety of ways the richness of their own experiences and the experiences of others. They evolve from the discovery that the value of experience depends mostly on its specific qualities. They center on the idea that direct personal engagement in the autonomous activities of making a world for oneself and for others enhances the specific qualities of living. To the extent that schools are treated as means only to other ends, such commonsensical assumptions are not now widely used in the United States in evaluating educational programs, which is quite remarkable. That they should be widely used in the future is not. While in many ways qualitative and quantitative evaluation are compatible, the former is in its own right a very powerful alternative. Its principal strength is that it creates what Macdonald has called a "self-reflective" form of evaluation,[11] one in which participants develop not only personal implications for themselves and others, but political and moral implications as well. Such self-reflectivity seems an essential quality of autonomous living and moral participation in creating a better world. Qualitative evaluation in education, therefore, has a very substantial impact yet to be realized on individuals, on classrooms, on schools, on the professional educational community, and on society. Its use in providing increasingly adequate modes of thought and practice in education is extremely commonsensical as well.

Notes

1. See chap. 2.

2. For a more detailed explanation of qualitative problem-solving, see the article by W. Dwaine Greer (chap. 8).

3. James B. Macdonald, "Value Bases and Issues for Curriculum" (Paper delivered at the Curriculum Theory Conference, University of Wisconsin at Milwaukee, November 1976).

4. For a history and a critique of the development of curriculum evaluation in both the United States and Great Britain (including an assessment of the dominant statistical research methodologies), see David Hamilton, *Curriculum Evaluation* (London: Open Books Publishing Limited, 1976), especially chap. 2, "Evaluation as Quality Control," and chap. 3, "Evaluation as Informing Decision Makers: Old Roots, New Routes."

5. Robert Stake, "An Overview and Critique of Existing Educational Evaluation Practices and Some New Leads for the Future" (Paper delivered at the annual meeting of the American Educational Research Association, San Francisco, Ca., April 1976).

6. See chap. 4.

7. Elliot W. Eisner, "Emerging Models for Educational Evaluation," *School Review* 80, no. 4 (August 1972): 573-90; idem, "The Perceptive Eye: Toward the Reformation of Educational Evaluation" (Paper delivered at the annual meeting of the American Educational Research Association, Washington, D.C., March 1975); idem, "How Can Curriculum Evaluation be Reported Artistically?" (Paper delivered at the annual meeting of the American Educational Research Association, San Francisco, Ca., April 1976).

8. For an interpretation of these efforts collectively and for specific examples, see William Pinar, ed., *Curriculum Theorizing: The Reconceptualists* (Berkeley, Ca.: McCutchan Publishing Corp., 1975).

9. James B. Macdonald and Esther Zaret, eds., *Schools in Search of Meaning*, 1975 Yearbook of the Association of Supervision and Curriculum Development (Washington, D.C.: ASCD, 1975).

10. Gail McCutcheon originated the delineation of the processes of educational criticism into three parts, identified as "description," "interpretation," and "appraisal." For her own perspective and for detailed explanations of these processes, see McCutcheon, chap 9; idem, "The Use of Ethnography and Criticism as Methods for Disclosing Classroom Settings" (Paper delivered at the annual meeting of the American Educational Research Association, San Francisco, Ca., April 1976); and idem, "The Disclosure of Classroom Life" (Ph.D. diss., Stanford University, 1976). For still another perspective on criticism and a different delineation of the processes of criticism, see chap. 6.

11. James B. Macdonald, response to Eisner, "The Perceptive Eye" (Paper delivered at the annual meeting of the American Educational Research Association, Washington, D.C., March 1975).

Concepts

Chapters 2-6 discuss from a variety of perspectives some of the conceptual bases upon which approaches to qualitative evaluation and curriculum criticism rest. Collectively, these chapters address a series of issues concerning the personal basis for meaning, the embodiment of meaning in form, and the relationship of meaning to and the uses of meaning in the world.

Robert M. W. Travers's essay examines several of the issues most fundamental to the use of qualitative methods in educational research and evaluation, particularly the essential difference between quantitative and qualitative methods and the extent to which both methods are based upon personal ("phenomenal") experience of the world. Travers explains that qualitative methods are consistent with scientific methods in general (since scientific methods are rooted in phenomenal experience) and points out what the next steps may be in advancing qualitative evaluation. The essay thus presents a basic rationale for the use of curriculum criticism.

Travers suggests that the essential difference between quantitative and qualitative methods is not measurement, since both involve observation and inference. Rather, inference in quantitative studies depends on a logic of enumeration of observed characteristics, while inference in qualitative studies depends on a logic of direct comparison of characteristics. Moreover, the essence of a science is the ability to think logically in formulating conceptions of the universe. Sciences, therefore, include conceptions formulated through qualitative inference, and many such conceptions have advanced modern science.

20

Still, not all observations are equally accurate nor all inferences equally logical, so knowledge tends to be considered objective or scientific only when it has received wide agreement. On this point Travers accepts Kant's position, suggesting further that complete agreement is extremely difficult, if not impossible, since reality is not known directly. An individual must first personally, or phenomenally, experience the world and then use constructs developed out of that experience in order to interpret and to give meaning to experience. Many of the ways in which individuals apprehend the world are qualitative. Thus, the basis for wide agreement about knowledge depends on commonalities within the phenomenal experience of different individuals. The extent of such commonalities is not known, although, as Travers concludes, even in such presently murky areas as moral, affective, and aesthetic development much may yet be discovered about the existence of commonalities.

If this conclusion should prove to be prophetic of future discoveries, its significance is immense. It means that even the most personal insights a curriculum critic may use to disclose meaning about and to judge all areas of educational experience, once soundly made, can be assented to with increasing confidence by any other discerning observer. Even if the commonalities within the phenomenal experience of individuals should prove to be less than the universals asserted by Kant, Travers's essay suggests, at the least, that qualitative methods of evaluating education can be soundly based on what is still known about phenomenal experience and can be particularly useful in uncovering how common perceptions and meanings develop within educational environments.

2

Some Comments on Qualitative Approaches to the Development of Scientific Knowledge and the Use of Constructs Derived from Phenomenal Experience

Robert M. W. Travers

Introduction

The essays in this volume cover a great range of problems, but many share an approach to knowledge different from the conventional American scientific approach as manifested in modern educational research literature. The approach of the essayists is typically qualitative, an approach frowned upon by most research journal editors. Quantitative research is academically respectable in modern America, but qualitative research is not, which may make us wonder whether this is just a reflection of prejudice or whether qualitative methods are inherently inferior. Many of the essays also place heavy emphasis on constructs derived from phenomenal experience. Here again one must raise the issue of the utility and justifiability of the use of such constructs. These are the problems that will be considered briefly here. First let us consider the role of qualitative methods in the history of scientific research.

Qualitative Methods in Scientific Research

Measurement and mathematics have become, in our society, the prestigious marks of a mature science. Although there can be no doubt that measurement and the quantitative method have produced dramatic discoveries, the prestige of these methods derives from a number of factors, only one of which is their success in achieving knowledge. The modern American scientific community, nevertheless, bestows enormous prestige on methods that involve measurement and mathematics. Scientists point to the fact that until Antoine Lavoisier was able to demonstrate that chemical equations could be written, there was no science of chemistry. They also point out that Albert Einstein began his work by puzzling over the fact that the measured velocity of light was constant regardless of whether one was approaching or receding from its source. Such a fact could not have been established without very precise methods of measurement. Once this had been established, it required the mathematical genius of an Einstein to develop an explanation of what appeared to be an extraordinary phenomenon. The work of both Lavoisier and Einstein was, beyond any doubt, epoch-making, and it is easy to see in such work a quantitative model for all worthwhile scientific work. However, such extraordinary scientific developments may blind us to the fact that other, qualitative, approaches to the development of knowledge have also produced revolutions in thought. Quantitative aspects of science are so highly regarded that they tend to overwhelm the public, and even the professional scientist, with admiration, which leads to a disregard of achievements attained by other means.

The thesis of this paper is that much of the development of a scientific conception of the universe has not depended upon measurement and mathematics but has evolved from the human capacity to think logically.

In the nineteenth century, as well as in our own, mathematics was viewed as having a special mystique. It was not until Whitehead and Russell published their *Principia Mathematica* (the second edition, published in 1925, is available in paperback) that a modern view of the relation of logic to mathematics emerged.[1] In that massive work mathematics was viewed as simply a branch of logic, that is to say, a subdiscipline within a broader discipline. This is the modern view of the place of mathematics in a theory of knowledge. I cannot claim to be an expert on the *Principia*, but I am familiar enough with it to understand the general message it conveys in this context. Jean Piaget has developed this view of the nature of mathematics and science within his theory of how knowledge develops, a theory he identifies as genetic epistemology.[2] Piaget was obviously deeply impressed with Russell and Whitehead's analysis of the nature of mathematics, differing with them in only minor respects, such as the nature of number. Piaget views the human as having evolved as a logical system, with the capability of extending that logic into the mathematical area. He argues that the development of the human intellect, as a logical system, permitted man to survive. He also argues that the intellect evolved as an adaptive response to the environment that permitted man to understand his environment. A logical-mathematical universe could be understood only by a logical-mathematical intellect. Piaget sees a basic similarity, within limits, between the nature of the human intellect and the nature of the universe that the intellect was able to master. The logic of the intellect was readily extended into the form of mathematics, because mathematical thinking is a form of logical thinking.

Piaget does not assume that the human has innate logical abilities. Man is assumed only to have the capacity to invent logical tools for the solution of problems—tools that must be reinvented by each generation. Piaget does not seem to be willing to concede that culture progresses through the transmission of these logical tools from one generation to another, yet to some degree this seems to take place. For example, since the days of Isaac Newton and Gottfried Leibniz generations of students have been taught calculus, which is the tool for solving a vast range of problems. Such a tool is handed down from generation to generation. Piaget would argue that each generation must reinvent the logic on which an understanding of calculus is based, even though the algebra of the calculus is culturally transmitted.

The history of science provides examples of how forms of logic other than the mathematical have made their contributions to the building of systematic knowledge. One might be tempted to conjecture that qualitative reasoning is the basis for scientific advancement in the early stages of a science, and that quantitative methods represent the more advanced stages, but this certainly does not seem to be so. Astronomers used quantitative methods long before Copernicus provided his reconceptualization of all of astronomy. As a matter of fact, the Alexandrian astronomers had estimated the size of the earth, with an error of only a few miles, before the Christian era had even begun.

Qualitative Contributions to Scientific Knowledge

Although one may think of the physical sciences as essentially quantitative and mathematical in nature, many of the most important discoveries were not of this character at all. Consider, for example, Newton's demonstration that sunlight could be separated into components of different colors, called the spectrum, and then recombined into white light. This was an immensely important demonstration in the history of the development of our knowledge of light. Although Newton was the most eminent mathematician of his time, the demonstration was not quantitative and did not involve mathematical theory. Later developments in the theory of light, of course, did involve mathematics. Another important discovery in the field of the spectrum was the accidental, nontheoretical demonstration of X rays by Roentgen.

The whole field of biology advanced, until recent times, through the application of logic in nonmathematical forms. Perhaps the most superb example of such work is that of Louis Pasteur. There was little that was quantitative about the work of Louis Pasteur. His great scientific principle that living things come only from living things has no quantitative measurements to support it, yet the evidence he provided for it was overwhelming. Today the principle seems so obvious and axiomatic (except in the case of very fundamental sources of life) that we might well ridicule even an adolescent who thought living creatures could be produced from the slime of rivers or the rotting humus of plants. Most of Pasteur's other great discoveries, which led the way to the development of immunization techniques, were also based on qualitative observations. The basis of the latter work was the statement of a man who claimed to have been bitten so many times by snakes that he was no longer harmed by them. The qualitative work of Pasteur, sometimes supplemented by crude measurements, as when he slowly increased the doses of toxins given to patients, remains one of the foundation stones of modern biology. Not all biologists of Pasteur's era were working in qualitative terms, of course; the great Gregor Mendel was quantitatively oriented, and his discoveries depended upon predicting that certain theoretical ratios would be actually found. His discoveries were of immense importance, but who can say that they are more or less important than those of Louis Pasteur?

One can point to many other lines of work in biology, of fundamental importance, that depended upon qualitative observation. All
of the extraordinary work on life cycles undertaken in the last century was necessarily qualitative in nature. There were no quantitative
methods employed in the discovery of the life cycle of the mosquito,
with its impact on understanding the way malaria is communicated.

The qualitative and the quantitative conceptualizations of the
physical world have often been intermixed. When Dmitri Mendeleev
discovered the periodic law, he did so by arranging the elements in
terms of their atomic weights, but each group of elements thus produced represented a group that brought together elements having
common qualitative properties. Copernicus's reconceptualization of
the solar system had been preceded by a massive accumulation of
data, yet the reconceptualization provided a simplified way of looking at the data. He built a new model of the solar system, but his
model had simplified mathematical properties. Although Copernicus
was a mathematician of repute, his lasting contribution was not in
the collection of data, nor in any mathematical theory, but in a qualitative theory of the nature of the solar system.

Although we think of the physical sciences as being entirely
quantitatively oriented, much of the early development was a result
of qualitative observation. Perhaps the exception to this is chemistry,
for the predecessors of the modern chemist seem to have made no
progress until Lavoisier showed that chemical equations could be
written, and the use of equations required measurement. Nevertheless, Rudolf Clausius's famous statement of the second law of ther-
modynamics was made in a qualitative form. "Heat cannot pass from
a colder to a hotter body," he said, linking his statement to the phenomenal experience of one object being hotter or colder than
another.

Differences between Qualitative and Quantitative Studies

To say that the one group of studies involves some form of measurement and the latter does not is a gross oversimplification that is
almost misleading. Both involve similar logical processes. In both
forms of research, facts are collected, and inferences are made from
the facts. Darwin collected observations on the wildlife of the Gala-
pagos Islands and inferred that differences within the same species
could be attributed to differences in the environments offered by the

particular islands. The Darwin observations can be forced into the hypothesis-testing paradigm of conventional American behavioral research, but Darwin made no attempt to measure the attributes of the same species on different islands. The differences were obvious to Darwin the observer and would also be evident to any modern biologist. The animals could be classified in terms of their characteristics, as could their environments; the core of the discovery, however, was not that such a classification could be made, but that the characteristics of the animals reflected adaptations to environmental conditions.

In quantitative studies, the logic of inference is closely tied to the logic of mathematics. Number is a result of the combined use of the logic of classification and seriation, and some problems can be clarified by the application of logic within such a framework. In qualitative studies, the logic of inference is based on a logic of classes that does not involve the logic of a number system. Darwin, for example, simply related classes of species characteristics to classes of environments. If he had been educated in modern America he would have, through habit, tried to circumscribe his problem of species variation by measuring characteristics of the animals, measuring characteristics of their environment, and attempting to show a statistical relationship between the two. Of course, he might well have undertaken such a quantitative study without ever recognizing the evolutionary implications of his data. Indeed, the whole idea of evolution might have escaped him, since the mathematical relationships would not have been likely to show the adaptive nature of species variation in relation to the environment. Clearly, quantification does not necessarily improve a study. (I wonder how often we force a doctoral student into undertaking a quantitative study that hides the essential facts a qualitative study would have so clearly brought out.) This should not be taken to mean that we should abandon quantitative studies in education, but rather that quantitative studies should not be held up as the only model to follow. There are quite obviously some areas in which the logic of quantitative methods is appropriate and areas in which it is not.

Phenomenal Interpretations of Environmental Events

The view that has been taken up to this point is that logical interpretations of the world around us can assume either a mathematical or a nonmathematical form. Both these forms may constitute the essence of a science. The interpretations of such a science require that there be close agreement between the conclusions of different observers, for there must be agreement on what the relevant observations are and what conclusions can be drawn logically from them for science to exist. Such empirical-logical interpretations of the environment have reached a high degree of perfection only in the physical sciences. All too often in the behavioral sciences there is disagreement on what the important observations are, and even when there is agreement, there is usually controversy on how the observations should be interpreted. Thus the classical conditioning described by Pavlov is viewed as a trivial phenomenon by B. F. Skinner, though the Pavlovian type of observation is considered to be very important by modern clinical psychologists. The observations of B. F. Skinner and his operant school are viewed as trivial by Jean Piaget and his school of genetic epistemologists, and so the controversy goes on. There is little agreement on the observations, or *experiences* if one wishes to be phenomenalistic, that should constitute the core of a science of behavior. This is in contrast with the physical world, where we can agree that such phenomena as falling bodies, heat and heat exchanges, electricity, light and how it is bent and changed are all phenomena of basic importance.

Yet there are areas of experience (using the term in a phenomenalistic sense) in which there is some agreement that phenomenal experiences are of vital importance. Immanuel Kant long ago pointed out that logical operations interpret experience but do not account for experience being the way it is. Knowledge is preconditioned by the forms of our sensibility. We understand that we live in a world in which events take place in space and time, because they could not be perceived as being otherwise. We also understand the world as involving a complexity of causal relationships, with our own direct experience of being the cause of our own actions at the core of our understanding of this causal network. This thesis that our own *experience* of being a causal agent is the basis of our whole concept of cause has been expounded in recent times by De Charms, who has been a lone voice in this respect in the field of psychology.[3] De Charms points out that our only direct understanding of the nature of causal relations derives from our own personal experience of being the cause of certain events. We are hungry, so we go to the refrigerator and find something to eat. In doing so we have the direct experience of being the cause of our actions, not just a passive observer. We are the agents who initiate the entire sequence of actions. Without such experiences, we could not derive the idea that one event is the cause of another event in the world around us. Indeed, we project our own personal experience of causality onto the world we experience. We may, through the application of analysis and logic, extend our conception of causality and incorporate in it a number of different conceptions, as Thomas Aquinas and others have done; nevertheless, our basic conception of causality remains firmly rooted in phenomenal experience, not in the universe.

Kant took the position, accepted here, that it is our logic acting on our phenomenal experiences that permits us to acquire a scientific conception of the nature of the universe. The nature of phenomenal experience limits what we can understand about the nature of reality, for reality is not known directly but only through the way that it is structured in phenomenal experience.

Behavioral scientists who believe that they are studying reality directly have beliefs that are on the order of myths. When operant psychologists say that it is, in some sense, unscientific to hold the belief that the phenomenal self can be a cause of behavior, they are neglecting the fact that our only direct understanding of causal relations is achieved through our experience of being the cause of our own behavior. There is nothing in the universe that can give us any direct knowledge of cause and effect, as David Hume long ago pointed out, but we can escape Hume's difficulties by following the Kantian view that causal relations are a necessary category of experience.

There are obvious limits on the extent to which our understanding of the environment, reached through the applications of logical operations to our phenomenal experience, can produce knowledge that is widely agreed upon. (We refer to such knowledge as objective knowledge, despite the fact that much of it is what it is because of the nature of phenomenal experience.) The limits to such knowledge become apparent as soon as individuality is introduced into our phenomenal experiences. Although we all experience space, time, and causality in the same way, our experience of the aesthetic properties of objects and events shows great individuality. Our aesthetic experiences can be communicated only to *some* other individuals, not to all other individuals, because only some other individuals have aesthetic experiences similar to our own.

There is much controversy as to where the limits to achieving knowledge rooted in the nature of personal experience are set . Consider the case of moral judgment. The Kantian view is that there is a universal moral element inherent in the common experience of all of us. Piaget, long impressed with Kant's viewpoint, has given it a special twist. His view is that all individuals, given the opportunity, eventually construct the same set of moral principles, because their way of thinking and the development of thought is such that moral progress can take place in only one direction. This is a radical view, accepted by only a minority of scholars at this time, but it is thought-provoking. If it does prove to be an acceptable view in the area of moral development and related aspects of affective development, then the possibility that aesthetic development might have a uniform and necessary sequence of development, with a corresponding set of universals of experience, may come to be accepted as well. This is, of course, a matter for conjecture. If it turns out to have some truth to it, then it opens the way to giving artistic and literary criticism a foundation far more solid than the whims and feelings that are commonly believed to be the basis of what one can know in these areas.

Summarizing Comments

I have attempted in this paper to point out that there can be many approaches to the development of knowledge related to education. The traditional quantitative approach is just one of many. All approaches share a common dependency on logic, with mathematics being a special branch of logic. All knowledge about events in our environment is also a function of the nature of our experience. Some aspects of phenomenal experience are shared by all individuals, and such shared elements are readily accepted as representing a component of what is called objective science. We do not quite know the limits of the aspects of experience that we share, a fact that places limits on what we can be sure that we know and what will become universally accepted as knowledge. We fall into difficulties in those areas in which we cannot be sure that all share the same experiences. Although we can be sure that all have the experience of being the cause of certain events, we cannot be sure that all will have the same emotional responses to a particular component of a curriculum. The area of moral judgment is one in which issues related to whether there are universal common experiences has recently become a focus of great interest. In other areas the extent to which there are common attributes of experience that can form the foundation for what can be called knowledge is even less certain.

Notes

1. Alfred North Whitehead and Bertrand Russell, *Principia Mathematica,* 2d ed. (Cambridge, England: Cambridge University Press, 1925).

2. Piaget has written about his view of the knowledge of the nature of behavior in a number of different articles and books, all of which cannot be mentioned here. The main sources of information are his short monograph, *Genetic Epistemology,* trans. E. Duckworth (New York: Columbia University Press, 1970); his book entitled *Biology and Knowledge* (Chicago, Ill.: University of Chicago Press, 1974); and his recent book *Insights and Illusions of Philosophy* (Ft. Meyers, Fla.: Wolfe, 1974).

3. Richard De Charms, *Personal Causation* (New York: Academic Press, 1968).

The essay by George Willis and Anthony J. Allen investigates the use of techniques that they describe as "phenomenological analysis." These techniques are among those of curriculum criticism, for they deal directly with how individuals develop personal meanings in response to their environments. The essay describes and comments upon common patterns of personal meanings considered specifically as phenomenological responses to educational environments. However, it also includes some quantitative methods, stops short of fully interpreting or explicitly judging either the responses described or the environments, and focuses principally on broader issues, including those related to the nature of qualitative evaluation and its uses. In these senses the essay is not itself a piece of curriculum criticism. Rather, it logically follows Travers's essay as an explanation of the extent to which commonalities exist within the phenomenal experience of different individuals and as a setting forth of some major implications.

A basic question raised by Travers is whether there exists what can be considered a common "syntax" of how individuals constitute meaning. The existence of such a "syntax" would provide an ontological basis upon which certain principles of qualitative evaluation could be firmly established. Willis and Allen suggest that there may indeed be common patterns of response to educational environments and that from these patterns common meanings, based upon commonalities in phenomenal experience, can be inferred. Knowledge of common patterns may be useful in understanding the relationships between the structures of the external world and the dynamics of inward experience. Still, just how closely the responses observed actually correspond to personal meanings at the deepest and most inward level remains mysterious, and inferences are far from certain. Moreover, the most striking characteristic of the particular patterns observed is their wide variability in details. Therefore, the discovery of something as invariant as a universal "syntax" of the way meaning is constituted seems unlikely, and further investigation through techniques of phenomenological analysis will probably tend to confirm wide variations in the phenomenal experience of different individuals, although within certain general patterns.

Given these observations, Willis and Allen suggest that the ideology within which research and evaluation in education are conducted is significant. The nature of phenomenal experience seems inconsistent with an ideology that considers education to be a means of individual or social control. Phenomenal experience seems individualistic enough so that neither quantitative nor qualitative methods can be established with complete certainty upon its general commonalities, although these commonalities can be most useful. On them, methods of educational evaluation can be grounded firmly enough to lead properly to the development of insight and understanding but not, logically, to lead to direct control.

In exploring the nature of phenomenal experience the essay principally uses qualitative methods, particularly in those places where it interprets observations. A future step in the development of qualitative evaluation is the inclusion within such methods of ways of more fully disclosing meanings about particular phenomenological responses and of more adequately judging both the outward environmental and the inward personal contexts within which responses occur. Such a development will help do justice to the complexities of educational contexts that are more accessible to qualitative methods than to quantitative.

3

Patterns of Phenomenological Response to Curricula: Implications

George Willis and Anthony J. Allen

Phenomenology

The world itself is not the same as our immediate apprehensions of the world, nor are our immediate apprehensions the same as the deep structures of our experience. We live within an external environment that we are experiencing immediately, but we also live within an inward world in which we constitute meaning by ultimately experiencing experience. Yet the curriculum field historically has treated variations in immediate apprehensions or in inward experiencing (when it has treated them at all) as if they were directly reflected from variations in the external world.[1] It is a notorious fact that the world is often changed by how we perceive it, and how we perceive it is always influenced by how we have previously constituted meaning. The curriculum field, therefore, has two massive tasks before it: to take adequate cognizance of these two neglected levels of experiencing and to create curriculum rationales that do justice to the importance and complexity of these levels.

Perhaps a major reason for the neglect of these tasks lies in the

An earlier version of this paper was presented at the annual meeting of the American Educational Research Association, San Francisco, Ca., April 1976.

complex nature of experiencing itself, for experience at either level is neither unified nor stable. It consists of varying measures of feeling, thinking, and doing within a constantly changing situation, and countless formulations as diverse as Aristotle's view of catharsis, Dewey's *Art as Experience,* and the ideas of modern existentialists are witness to the variable nature of such characteristics as its intensity, pleasurability, and quality. The curriculumist is thus faced with some extremely difficult problems in coming to grips with the nature of experiencing.

Fortunately, the development of phenomenological methodology may offer some aid. Phenomenology is often considered as the study of one's immediate apprehensions of a situation as they present themselves to one's consciousness. So considered, phenomenology is confined largely to the immediate or surface level of experiencing, although variations or patterns within one's immediate responses to a situation have a great influence on variations in the characteristics of one's general experience. However, in "Phenomenological Methodology and Understanding Education," which may become a landmark essay, J. Gordon Chamberlin suggests that phenomenology must be considered as extending into both levels of experiencing and that a methodology has been developed that elucidates "the structure of consciousness" at the deep level and, therefore, "the way meaning is constituted."[2]

Chamberlin contrasts phenomenological methodology with the deductive procedures employed by most philosophies and sciences, procedures that attempt to derive hard or objective knowledge from invariant first principles. While Chamberlin asserts that "there is no orthodox procedure which can be held up as the authoritative phenomenological method," all such methods begin by examining the consciousness the individual has of whatever objects or processes enter his field of perception, move through analysis of "how meanings develop in the continuing reconstruction process of the consciousness," and thus end in the individual's "critical re-viewing of both his experience and his present philosophical commitments."[3] The objects, processes, and structures of the external world may or may not be regarded as fixed, but all phenomenological methods attempt to take seriously the individual's own particular perceptions of them and his own process of moving from the surface level of experiencing to the deep level of experiencing experience.

The particular methodology Chamberlin explicates is derived from Husserl, and it is very much an active skill one can acquire, like learning to read. One attends to the external world, but one also moves into exploration of the depths of experience and thus becomes aware of personal meanings one would remain unaware of through attending alone. No matter how one perceives any object of consciousness, that perception is among many other perceptions that are possible. Furthermore, one cannot attend simultaneously to all objects of perception. Ultimately, therefore, one perceives selectively, only within a context made up largely of the constituted meanings of previous experience. Chamberlin points out that Husserl used the term "intentionality" to refer to the bridging of the gap between an object of consciousness and the consciousness of the object. He summarizes these ideas as follows:

To discern the meaning of an object (idea, process, person, house) one does not respond to one's perceptions of that object from one perspective only. Such a view may be a profile, but the consciousness is aware that a house can be viewed from many other perspectives, and that all the different perceptions are still of the same object. Intentionality refers to the total meaning of the object which is always more than what is given in the perception of a single profile or perspective. Husserl used two Latin terms, *noesis* and *noema*, to indicate the intimate relationship between intentionality as total meaning (*noema*) and particular acts of perception (*noesis*) of the object. In this way he discerns how consciousness, in dealing with what is given in perception, does so in the light of data that are not perceived.[4]

The methodology Husserl describes (sometimes called "bracketing") rests on this basis, and it is most simply the careful and conscious setting aside of ordinary, commonsense assumptions about surface level experiencing in order to work through and to make explicit at the deep level of experience all meanings (*noema*) which were implicit at the surface level of immediate apprehension and perception (*noesis*).

Chamberlin suggests that a principal value in using phenomenological methodology in education is that it encourages the individual to engage not only in self-analysis but also in analysis of all the commonalities within the structure of the external world. In this sense it becomes a means of communicating meaning, for the personal meanings of different individuals inevitably become part of the context within which other individuals formulate their own meanings. Chamberlin points out that in using phenomenological methodology educators may fail to grasp "the futility of designing educational programs and methods as though the meaning which a person has constituted in his experience is easily accessible."[5] The complexity of establishing common meanings, he contends, should challenge ordinary assumptions about learning, about teacher training, and about the development of programs.

Phenomenological methodology, then, is directed toward generating knowledge about the deep structures of experience, and in this respect it has much in common with psychoanalysis and with other techniques intended to create heightened consciousness and clarified understanding in the individual about his own meaning and his own relationship to the external world. While phenomenological methodology shares all the difficulties inherent in such techniques, all such techniques also share the same therapeutic purpose: they are ways of fostering mental health and creativity. Ultimately, social consequences flow from individual prophylaxis. In these respects phenomenological analysis has much in common with all studies dealing with perception and meaning and can thus in some ways be regarded as a confluence of insights drawn from such areas as semiotics, psychiatry, aesthetics, existentialism, and religion.

Precedents

Chamberlin has helped establish a precedent and an example for increasingly widespread use of phenomenological methodology in education. There are also precedents for the use of phenomenological analysis in the curriculum field itself. While descriptions of phenomenological reactions of groups and individuals at both the surface and deep levels of experiencing exist in varied writings within many cultures, and while work has been done relating phenomenology to the curriculum field in a general way,[6] the first effort to pull together the basic elements of such descriptions within a truly comprehensive theoretical framework for curriculumists was probably not made until 1974 in a symposium presentation at the annual meeting of the American Educational Research Association. In remarks titled "A Phenomenological Research Method for Knowledge Generation in Curriculum," William Pinar pointed out that since the relationship that exists between a piece of literature and the literary experience of a reader is analogous to the relationship between a curriculum and the educational experience of a student, the structural elements used in analyzing literary experience can be used in analyzing educational experience. These elements are: (1) the literary text, or curriculum; (2) the place of the text, or curriculum, in history; (3) the response of the reader, or student; and (4) the broad psychological and biographical context brought to the exchange by the reader, or student.

Pinar has published these remarks in a slightly different version, and in several other recent papers he has begun a systematic pursuit of the line of inquiry he has demarcated.[7] Basically, he has chosen to focus on the third and fourth structural elements and in so doing has developed a technique for analyzing the individual's educational experience (which Pinar calls *currere,* the Latin root of "curriculum") in terms of the individual's own psychological and biographical makeup. This technique begins by asking the individual to pose to himself and then to record his responses to the question: what has been and what is now the nature of my educational experience?

By taking as a hypothesis that I do not know the answer to this question, I take myself and my existential experience as a data source. The method of data generation is the psycho-analytical technique of free association. I take a particular question, like why am I involved in the research project I am involved in? and I record, by pen or recorder, all that occurs to me, regardless how esoteric and hence unrelated the information *apparently* is. . . .

My hunch is that by working in the manner I will describe, I will obtain information that will move me biographically, and not only linearly, but multidimensionally. If I take my current perspective, and try to put parentheses around it (so to speak) by recording it, then I have moved to another vantage point. I have found this to be so. If I write about my biographic situation as I see it (not as I *want* to see it, although this can be included) then it is as if I have escaped from it. It is *there,* on the paper in a way, and I am still here, at the typewriter, looking at the print and the conceptualization of the perspective that *was* mine, and so the place is new. I have in Sartre's language, totalized my situation, and the new sum is where I conceptually and (more inclusively) ontologically am now.[8]

Quite clearly, this technique of recording free associations is very much what Chamberlin describes as Husserl's method of bracketing, a way of attending to the world but then of moving beyond immediate apprehensions of it to the deep level of experience where meaning is constituted.

The technique, however, includes a second step, one which is important lest the meaning constituted by the individual be solely personal. Pinar suggests that if we consider the technique of recording free associations as a way of telling stories about our experience, then next

we can try to generalize on the basis of the stories we tell and the ones we hear others tell, taking them as evidence of a sort, and attempt to formulate in general terms the broad outlines of past, present and future, the nature of our experience, and specially our educational experience, that is the way we can understand our present in the way that allows us to move on, more learned, more evolved than before.[9]

While this explanation emphasizes the personal uses we can make of generalizations drawn from our own and from others' experiences, it is also clear that these generalizations within individual experience do appear, that they are responses based in part upon the commonalities within the structure of the external world, and that they can be made public. Through attending at the deep level of experience to our own experiencing of the world and to the experiencing of others, we can learn something about both the nature and structure of the world and the nature and structure of experience. Pinar, therefore, has directed himself toward gathering data and discerning generalities about the third and fourth structural elements he has identified, the response of the student and the psychological and biographical context of the student. This work is an excellent beginning, and it should be pursued at length. Nonetheless, it needs to be supplemented by additional ways of gathering data about all four structural elements, by ways of discerning various commonalities within all such data, and by ways of interrelating all such commonalities. Only through work of such proportions will the curriculum field represent a disciplined effort to come to grips with the complexities of both individual and collective educational experience.

The potential of phenomenological methodology both to shape long-term basic disciplinary inquiry in curriculum and to yield more immediate advantages and insights has been described by Grumet:

[The] reply [of phenomenological analysis] to the traditional empirical paradigm is a return to the experience of the individual, respecting all those qualities which disqualify it for consideration in the behavioral sciences: its idiosyncratic history, its preconceptual foundation, its contextual dependency, its innate freedom expressed in choice and self-direction. . . . The path of reconceptualized inquiry leads us inward, to individual experience and outward to meta-theory. . . . [It] reaches back first to the pre-predicative encounter, the lived sense that is a sine qua non for a conceptual hability. It then reconstructs the pathway to the present choice by digging back under the layers of one's biography to identify the encounters that led to it. . . . This is to say, we . . . attempt to describe educational experience in its most particularized incarnation, the history and response of the individual, and in its most general expression, the interpretations of human experience that characterize the conceptual frameworks of the disciplines that shape educational research.[10]

Basically, Grumet is suggesting that insights derived from phenomenological methodology require the curriculum field to abandon ordinary assumptions borrowed from such fields as psychology and sociology in order to develop different and more adequate assumptions of its own. While not identifying explicit assumptions that might define the curriculum field so reconceptualized, Klohr has identified nine "themes" that characterize the writings of advocates of phenomenological analysis in curriculum:

1. A holistic, organic view is taken of man and his relation to nature.
2. The individual becomes the chief agent in the construction of knowledge; that is, he is a culture creator as well as culture bearer.
3. The curriculum theorist draws heavily on his own experiential base as method.
4. Curriculum theorizing recognizes as major resources the preconscious realms of experience.
5. The foundational roots of their theorizing lie in existential philosophy, phenomenology and radical psychoanalysis, also drawing on humanistic reconceptualizations of such cognate fields as sociology, anthropology, and political science.
6. Personal liberty and the attainment of higher levels of consciousness become central values in the curriculum process.
7. Diversity and pluralism are celebrated in both social ends and in the proposals projected to move toward those ends.
8. A reconceptualization of supporting political-social operations is basic.
9. New language forms are generated to translate fresh meanings—metaphors, for example.[11]

There are, then, recent precedents for the use of phenomenological methodology in the curriculum field. These precedents describe the methodology, the structural framework within which it can be used, and the potential impact of its use in subsequently reconstituting the curriculum field.

Precedents for the use of phenomenological analysis itself are recent and have thus far been confined to a few members of the field; however, there is increasing interest among curriculumists in how meanings are constituted within a number of forms of educational experience. Such interests no doubt represent additional and perhaps more numerous precedents for use of methods designed to illuminate the dynamics of experiencing.

Take, for example, recent attention given to aesthetic interests in curriculum. Rosario has identified four basic aesthetic constructs, each of which has a definite history of use by curriculumists and each of which can be considered a different mode of conceiving and analyzing the aesthetic component of the student's more generalized educational experience.[12] Mann has suggested that a curriculum can be considered as a "disclosure model"; that is, a curriculum is pregnant with implicit and nonliteral meanings intended (and sometimes unintended) by its creator, and the task of the curriculum critic, much like the task of the literary critic, is to disclose or to make explicit those meanings.[13] Willis has described how portions of any curriculum necessarily embody nonliteral and poetical components of language and nonverbal communication and how, therefore, they must be regarded as evoking at least partially an aesthetic response in the student.[14] Kelly has outlined a "rhetoric for the curriculum," which consists of "metaphor," "point of view," "plot," and "theme," four concepts "originating in literary criticism that can be used to develop curricular critiques," and has pointed out how such rhetoric evokes personal meanings but within a range governed by a context and by the nature of the rhetorical figures.[15] Eisner has suggested that all educational evaluation might be conducted in terms of artistic assumptions (since scientific procedures do not address phenomena that cannot be measured) and that such evaluation depends on "educational connoisseurship," the appreciative art of becoming aware of characteristics and becoming discerning, and on "educational criticism," the public art of disclosing meanings and reeducating perception.[16] Willis has described four focal points traditionally used in literary criticism and how analogous focal points can be used in curricular criticism.[17] These focal points are similar to the four structural elements used by Pinar in analyzing educational experience through phenomenological methods and closely correspond to what Westbury and Steimer call "the commonplace curricular elements."[18] Perhaps significantly, these four focal points are remarkably similar to those used by a number of aestheticians, such as Berleant, in describing aesthetic transactions generally and in elaborating the nature and characteristics of the phenomenology of aesthetic experience.[19]

These precedents for a growing interest in the aesthetic dimensions of curriculum are not the same as the precedents cited for the use of phenomenological analysis; however, they all suggest that curriculum can be considered as a form of human experiencing. Therefore, they suggest that whatever methods illuminate the dynamics of experiencing and how meanings are constituted are within the province of the curriculumist. Clearly, the techniques for "bracketing" experience described by Chamberlin and Pinar are among these methods, as are similar methods drawn from related areas that can be regarded as reaching a confluence within phenomenology. All such methods share similar heuristic and therapeutic purposes and are organized around similar structural elements. While such methods uncover idiosyncrasies, the unique character of each individual's experiencing, they also press toward and help uncover commonalities in the structure of the external world and commonalities in the structure of various forms of experiencing at both the surface and deep levels. Information about both commonalities and individual differences can be used to inform differing areas of interest within curriculum. For instance, descriptions of general aesthetic experience at the level of immediate apprehension and at the level of constituting meaning can be used to inform descriptions of aesthetic experience within curriculum, which, in turn, can be used to inform descriptions of the dynamics of general educational experience.

Patterns

The literature of many areas that deal with various forms of human experiencing (such as aesthetics) contain speculations and descriptions that are essentially phenomenological, descriptions of feelings or states of mind and of how these evolve within a changing situation. One of the most striking features of such descriptions is that there do seem to be commonalities within reported feelings and states of mind. In other words, phenomenological responses to a wide variety of situations, despite real differences between situations and among individuals, seem to fall within some generally discernible patterns that comprise generally discernible clusters of characteristics.[20] For instance, Berleant lists the dominant characteristics of any aesthetic experience as active-receptive, qualitative, sensuous, immediate, intuitive, noncognitive (primarily), unique, intrinsic, and integral. Investigations of such characteristics within aesthetic responses to curricula are open to curriculumists. Open, also, are investigations into the basic patterns within which individuals immediately apprehend and constitute meaning in response to variations in basic curricular patterns. Such investigations may be informed by previous speculations and descriptions of patterns of phenomenological response in related areas.

Since curriculum does have an aesthetic component, reports of patterns of phenomenological response in aesthetics may be a fruitful place to begin. One such report by Ingarden deals with the general phenomenological structure of aesthetic experience in relation to aesthetic objects.[21]

Ingarden suggests that all aesthetic experiences are processes extended in time, with various phases, and "composed of many acts of consciousness differing from one another." Any aesthetic experience is, then, a number of connected experiences, usually (but not necessarily) beginning with sense impressions of some kind of empirically real object, but not identical with these sense impressions. Such an experience is, according to Ingarden, "a *composite process having various phases and a characteristic development* which contains many heterogeneous elements." Despite the "characteristic development" of any aesthetic experience, differing experiences have differing qualities, such as duration and complexity, because they are often picked up in the middle or broken off, because they depend in part upon the complexity and the type of the aesthetic object that evokes them (and which can be imaginative), and because they depend "on the psychic type of person who has the aesthetic experiences, *e.g.,* on his aesthetic susceptibility, his emotional and intellectual type, his aesthetic as well as general culture, etc."[22]

The general pattern or characteristic development of an aesthetic experience contains what Ingarden terms "essential moments." These begin when one is in some way struck by the qualities of an aesthetic object, so that the object evokes a "preliminary emotion," which is at first passive and fleeting. But in some way astonished or excited (though not necessarily pleased) by the qualities of the object, one finds that the preliminary emotion becomes one of "eagerness for satiation." This eagerness may include an element of disagreeableness if one has not yet attained a direct intuitive relationship with the aesthetic object. The preliminary emotion itself and the response to it constitute a transition from an ordinary attitude assumed in everyday life to an investigating, aesthetic attitude, which, Ingarden suggests, enriches and confers a new sense on life.

As a consequence of this transition, one's stream of normal experiencing is checked and one's field of consciousness is narrowed to focus on the aesthetic object itself, although one never loses altogether an intuitive sense of the presence of the rest of the world. Ingarden notes that if the check is not strong, one's ordinary experiencing of the world returns, although with some disorientation, which demonstrates that a check did occur. This "phenomenon of return" is common, Ingarden thinks, and it involves in itself a fresh orientation and change of attitude toward the world. Nonetheless, within a strong check a new present forms a secluded whole, which is to be included into the course of one's life only after the aesthetic process is over, although this seclusion is not characteristic of aesthetic experience alone, being felt in many forms of strong or concentrated experience, such as abstract research. However, the main consequence of the preliminary emotion is to direct one's attitude toward "*an intuitive intercourse with qualitative essences,*" and the search for such essences is basically an active, intensive, creative process carried on for its own sake, with the most active phases alternating with phases of more passive experiencing and, at times, moments of contemplation.[23]

The search for essences is in itself the next of the "essential moments" within aesthetic experience. The preliminary emotion leads to an intuitive perception or grasp of the qualities that evoked it; these qualities are first perceived most fully as an object of perception itself apart from its background within the overall aesthetic object and the rest of the world. Initially, one attempts to satiate oneself with these newly discovered qualities; one is pleased with the "presence" of the qualities. But, as Ingarden suggests, "becoming satiated with something almost always includes a germ of new longings and desires," so one is recalled from preliminary emotion and perception of attracting qualities to perception of new and perhaps more essential qualities now appearing as details against the background of the overall aesthetic object.[24] Now one notices "deficiencies," which invite completion, and the search for essences moves into a more long-term phase in which one attempts to impose new details into the aesthetic object. One may succeed easily, but when details which "improve" the object are not readily apparent, one may have to make a laborious and painful effort to find them. In fact, at this point the aesthetic experience may terminate with a negative response if the object appears simply to "shock" or to "fall short" of expectations or because of the emotional dissonance resulting from initially viewing the object as having harmonious qualities and later viewing it as containing uncorrectable deficiencies.

Usually, however, the object suggests new details; then one re-experiences the preliminary emotion and actively re-searches for details and qualities that enable one to grasp an overall harmony to the object. As Ingarden points out, during this process the aesthetic object must be perceived attentively, from many points of view, in a way that takes both time and effort. In effect, this process consists of three kinds of elements: the emotional reaction to one's perception of an object; the active, reconstitutive engagement with the object in which one projects oneself into the qualities and the "community of experience" contained within the object; and the passive perception of revealed or harmonized qualities. These elements may many times recur and many times alternate in dominating the process. Eventually one grasps two kinds of qualities: the categorical structures of the object and the qualitative harmony within those structures. Eventually, therefore, this process leads to perception of an overall or dominant quality, a "harmony quality," which unveils underlying qualities, which themselves may act as a diverse ensemble changing within certain limits imposed by the integrating "harmony quality." Ingarden contends that the whole process is characterized by a "searching disquietude."

It is only at this point that aesthetic experience reaches its final phase. "In contrast with this [searching disquietude], in the final phase of an aesthetic experience there ensues an *appeasement* in the sense that, on the one hand, there is a rather quiet *gazing upon* (contemplating) the qualitative harmony of the aesthetic object already constituted and a 'taking in' of these qualities."[25] Ingarden suggests that in this final phase one achieves a direct intuitive relationship with the aesthetic object, and this relationship includes a vivid emotional response to the harmonized qualities, an acknowledgement of the value of the object, and the basis for judgment of the object through a linking of the emotional and the cognitive components of the experience. Ultimately, a positive aesthetic experience serves to confirm and to enhance one's conviction of the connection between one's experience and the existence of the rest of the world.

The "characteristic development" and "essential moments" of

an aesthetic experience that Ingarden describes are, then, indicative
of a complex process and a complex pattern of phenomenological
response. While there is considerable room for individual variation,
there are still discernible commonalities within the general pattern. If
Ingarden is correct, one begins with an emotional reaction to some
qualities of an aesthetic object, but then in a recurring cyclical pattern alternates attention from emotion, to object, to reconstituting
the qualities of the object, until finally reaching an intuitive relationship with the object and its harmonized qualities. Within this pattern
one moves between involvement and disengagement with the object
and with one's perceptions, between feelings of pleasure and disagreeableness, between actively constituting and passively contemplating, and between the surface and the deep levels of experiencing.
Perhaps most interesting is that the general cyclical pattern Ingarden
describes contains within itself any number of small epicycles, each
containing movements very similar to those comprising the larger
general pattern.

As we have suggested, consideration of such descriptions leads
directly into phenomenological concerns, for phenomenological
methods and techniques of analysis can perhaps help verify the existence of such patterns and therefore help elucidate the dynamics of
experiencing. Furthermore, descriptions such as Ingarden's are of
concern to the curriculumist, for phenomenological patterns within
aesthetic experience are applicable to curriculum, since, as the precedents demonstrate, a curriculum contains aesthetic components.
Beyond such considerations, however, lies a more important question: to what extent is the general pattern of aesthetic experience
described by Ingarden indicative of a general pattern of phenomenological response within any kind of self-focused and unified experience?

Let us consider the phenomenological characteristics of another
kind of experience that is seemingly of increasing concern to contemporary educators, the experience of happiness. While not describing a
pattern in nearly as much detail as Ingarden, perhaps because happiness itself (apart from the pursuit of it) is in part like the final phase
of aesthetic experience, Strasser describes in some detail the characteristics of the attainment of happiness and suggests that the path
leading to it may be a kind of recurrent pattern.[26]

Strassser rejects as incomplete ordinary characterizations of happiness as a mode of contentment, chance, harmony, rapture, or deliverance. He thinks these modes contain only elements of true happiness and another more encompassing mode includes these elements and more. This encompassing mode of happiness Strasser calls "transcending anticipation." In ordinary experience one often discovers truths or acquires goods and derives some satisfaction and refreshment from them, however fleeting and imperfect. Nonetheless, these interludes are important, for they are genuine, they indicate that there is some end or "terminus" for one's acts, and they point the way toward a more complete fulfillment. The experience of such "transcending moments" within otherwise ordinary experience begins to distinguish the encompassing mode of happiness from other modes. "In every genuine experience of happiness something transcendent is there to be apprehended, however inadequately. Insofar as the happiness of this world lets us glimpse a certain infinitude, it is not a mere phantom of the senses . . . but a revelation of the deepest reality."[27]

Strasser is suggesting, therefore, that there is an existential or "transcendent ground" for all modes of one's experience of happiness, but that it is only within the encompassing mode of "transcending anticipation" that one can become as fully aware as possible of this ground. He suggests that it is principally the metaphysician who is able to glimpse "the possibility of an absolutely positive infinite happiness," but it is clear that what he means by metaphysics is basically the moving beyond the ordinary and immediate apprehension of the world to the deep level of experience and careful effort to constitute meanings.[28] This movement thus seems to rely at least in part on what Chamberlin, for instance, considers phenomenological methodology." Furthermore, within the alternations between the ordinary and transcendent phases of one's experience, this movement would seem to form a cyclical pattern of recurrent phases very similar to Ingarden's description of the general pattern of aesthetic experience.

Strasser considers the mode of transcending anticipation to be a characteristic style of human experiencing. One initially intends to achieve only a fleeting happiness in the world, but through this transitory goal one is directed toward the intransitory; by some kind of happy accident one can receive "an imperfect foretaste of the ultimate completion of one's own existence."[29] Although Strasser does not conceive of this completion in a religious sense only, he terms it "beatitude," which, he suggests, in its infinite, intransitory face is peaceful, unique, undisturbed, and "eternal," while in its concrete, transitory face is full of rich contents providing occasions for joy, love, and renewed possessing.[30]

The experience of happiness is, then, for Strasser, a concrete although imperfect and fleeting foretaste of transcending fulfillment and the ground of existence. He summarizes as follows:

The conviction that we already possess beatitude as a prospective grasp of the most sublime possibility of our existence is likewise the expression of a typical basic attitude. This attitude consists in regarding joy, rapture, and happiness, but also disappointment, pain, and sorrow as moments of a necessary, value-realizing, and meaningful dialectic. They all count as "stations" for the human "wayfarer" on his journey to the unknown—only vaguely anticipated goal. "But, as long as we are still seeking, and yet not satiated by the fountain itself—to use our word—by fullness—we must confess that we have not yet reached our measure," says Augustine. . . . Thanks to the oriented character of his experience, the seeker will grasp the further reference implicit in every contentment, every pleasure, every joy. And thus he will not seek permanent rest in any of them, nor cling to any particular form of the experience of happiness. Instead, he will regard them as a sample and—a test. Never will he confuse the resting places along the way with the ultimate goal. Gratefully accepting what the way brings, but never lingering there—that seems to us the most essential trait of the Christian attitude toward human happiness."[31]

This passage very probably suggests an attitude toward happiness that is considerably broader than that of any one religion or any one culture, and it describes in roughly phenomenological terms at least one phase within the on-going and "meaningful dialectic" of human experiencing. Apart from that, it illustrates a link between the experience of happiness and another form of experience, religious experience.

Thus far we have pointed out some of the basic characteristics of phenomenology and phenomenological methodology, identified some of the precedents for the inclusion of such considerations in the curriculum field, and attempted to describe a general commonality or pattern within human experience, illustrating this pattern and variations in it in some detail within aesthetic experience and the experience of happiness. Let us conclude this section by briefly attempting both to broaden and refine what we have already described as a general and recurrent pattern and by linking it with several other forms of human experience.

Perhaps more than any other American writer, Ralph Harper, the existential philosopher-theologian-poet, has devoted himself to such a task. In his first book (*Existentialism: A Theory of Man,* 1948) he set out to compose a theory of the dynamics of existential experience, or an "existential syntax," and he has developed his ideas in subsequent works until he has come to regard himself as "a specialist . . . in the themes of interior experience."[32] He has thus been concerned with the radical phenomenology of all human existence and also with its various forms.

Not having pursued this task simply as an academic exercise, Harper has fallen heir to and has extended the tradition of Augustine, Pascal, and Descartes, the tradition of passionate, meditative reflections that define a "history of consciousness," as Macksey observes in his Foreword to Harper's *Nostalgia: An Existential Exploration of Longing and Fulfillment in the Modern Age,* and "suggests that all modern ontologies can be comprehended within the original experience of nostalgia; for authentic being is first certified in its absence, in the anguished experience of separation, the search for that 'other place' . . . of the *Phaedo.*"[33]

Harper uses the idea of nostalgia as a key element in what can be considered his phenomenology of being.[34] For Harper, nostalgia is not only a harking back to the past but also a pointing toward the future, and as such it is a way both of providing some warrant for the ontological basis for existence and of leading toward the fulfillment of existence. Put very simply, Harper suggests that existence, a feeling or experience of being, is a kind of first fact, an ontological given, but in a personal sense so that in intuitions of early existence one develops a sense of self. During the course of living, many events, such as suffering or being isolated, may cut one off at least in part from one's ontological roots, so that the sense of self is weakened and one develops feelings of separation, even despair. However, in this "dark night of the soul" a sense of nostalgic longing for what one once was provides a glimpse of hope for what might yet be and compels a seeking for reunion with one's undivided self. Ultimately, then, in all experiences that do not end in complete destruction of the self, one may persevere long enough until at last, perhaps by some graceful accident, one experiences "presence" (a state much like Strasser's "beatitude"), a fresh recognition of a return to what previous intuitions of existence had promised, a recognition attended by feelings of fullness and unity. This journey toward "presence," Harper suggests, may be spiritual, but it may also be a paradigm for any form of redeeming human, existential experience. As Harper observes, this pattern is similar to the traditional stages of religious experience (purgation, illumination, union), only our initial intuitions of existence form a kind of preliminary unitive stage that precedes the purgative, and the intermediate purgative and illuminative stages are often mixed within experiences ranging from unease to despair, but experiences tinged with nostalgia and its feelings of loss but also of "presence."[35]

Harper has devoted two of his early books to outlining this general phenomenological pattern.[36] In other works he has described how the pattern applies to more specific kinds of experience: to educational experience; to literary and religious experience; to the experience of isolation; to the experience of love and to religious experience; to the experience of tragic suffering, in literature and in life; and to literary experience within a particular genre.[37]

In his last book he has returned to elucidation of the general pattern, but with extreme skepticism about his early belief in an "existential syntax," an unalterable structure of categories defined with sufficient precision to predict the specific phenomenology of any individual within a given situation. Yet, Harper concludes, basic "themes of interior experience" are still discernible and still have some coherence within a general pattern:

Nevertheless, I believe that there are a few areas of interior experience that one can focus on and that, as one moves one's eye from one to the other, one can achieve a fuller understanding of the nature of man. I also believe that this is done best when one moves in a certain order, from the simplest and most inescapable intuitions of self to the more elusive and yet more desirable experiences.[38]

For Harper, then, intuitions of existence and the experience of "presence" are the beginning and ending points of all coherent and redeeming human experiences. Between these points, in individual variations of interlocking fragments and patterns, fall common purgative and illuminative themes: of restlessness, isolation, and despair; of nostalgia, striving, and insight. In moving between the surface and the deep levels of experiencing within this general pattern, commonalities and variations in individual patterns of phenomenological response are both possible and likely.

Possibilities

The foregoing discussions give us some basis for predicting the response of a student within an educational situation, for despite the wide variations that are likely among the reactions of individual students to situations of similar external structures, we now have some inkling of what commonalities may occur and what kind of very general pattern of response may characterize any healthy, educative experience. We also have some basis for explaining both the commonalities and the variations that might occur. Whereas educators have traditionally attempted to focus on rather narrow ranges (i.e., "outcomes," such as cognition *or* affect, or both reduced to overt behaviors) of what actually happens to students and to treat these ranges as if comprised of isolable and discrete components (i.e., "learning"), very few systematic efforts have been made to treat what happens as an unfolding and holistic process with both external and internal dimensions and with a characteristic development. What we have been describing as one's phenomenological response to a situation, a composite of both one's immediate apprehensions at the surface level of experiencing and one's awareness and assessment at the deep level of those apprehensions, is perhaps as nearly a holistic view as possible, and it may be one means of overcoming the patent shortcomings of traditional approaches to the nature of educational experience.

Furthermore, despite a body of speculative literature concerning phenomenological response in a variety of situations, virtually no efforts have been made, aside from the recent precedents we have described, systemically to assess phenomenological patterns within distinctly educational situations and to point out the implications of these findings for educators. In this light, this study has four purposes: (1) to establish the efficacy of a procedure for empirically determining patterns of phenomenological response; (2) to determine whether the most general pattern of phenomenological response described in philosophical and imaginative literature and in other forms of thought of Western civilization obtains in educational situations; (3) to determine general norms and individual variations within this pattern; and (4) briefly to describe the potential impact that systematic phenomenological analysis may have on the curriculum field. Because the first three purposes are rather ambitious and could be fulfilled completely only by massive long-range studies (which the authors have yet to mount), findings are necessarily tentative, although quite promising and consistent with the scope of this study. The fourth purpose is discussed throughout the study, although primarily in the concluding section.

Procedures

We assume that educational experience can be analyzed within the four structural elements described by Pinar: (1) the curriculum,[39] (2) the place of the curriculum in history, (3) the response of the student, and (4) the psychological and biographical context of the student. Presumably, a reasonably complete analysis of all four of these elements is necessary for explaining the dynamics of any educational experience. Nonetheless, careful analysis of a large number of cases of the third element, particularly among students of widely differing biographies and to widely differing curricula, may at times for practical purposes constitute a sufficient explanation. Analysis of a smaller number of cases within reasonably uniform curricula may also be predictive.

The procedures described by Pinar and Grumet are clearly meant to generate knowledge about the third and fourth structural elements, particularly about mutual influences between these elements, and eventually to relate this knowledge to knowledge about the first and second structural elements. These techniques of phenomenological analysis are directed primarily toward the deep level of experiencing and are clearly akin to psychoanalysis. The scope of this study is somewhat more modest; it is meant to generate knowledge about the third structural element only and to focus primarily on more immediate reactions to the environment, whether these reactions be at the surface level, the deep level, or both. Whereas it is of extreme importance for the curriculum field to develop techniques of analyzing and appraising the deepest levels of educational experience, we think it also important for the field to develop techniques for monitoring the flow of educational experience at more immediately accessible levels. For instance, a physician's understandings of psychoanalysis and of brain wave patterns are by no means mutually exclusive; in fact, they may be mutually reinforcing for both heuristic and therapeutic purposes.

Within this framework, the hypothesis we have chosen to investigate is a composite drawn up from the precedents and patterns we have described. Phenomenological methodology suggests that individuals move between the surface and deep levels of experiencing. Ingarden suggests that within an aesthetic experience we are first struck by some quality of the aesthetic object, that we must then reconstitute or harmonize additional qualities of the object through a difficult process of repeatedly engaging ourselves with and disengaging ourselves from the object, but that this process may sometimes be broken off or exist in attenuated form. Strasser suggests that the final phase of the most positive experiences finds us at the deep level of fully experiencing constituted meaning and provides the promise of reexperiencing this phase. Harper suggests this kind of phase may be the logical beginning and ending points of any positive human experience and may frame individual patterns of negative and positive, of surface and deep response.

Taking Harper especially as representing perhaps the most common pattern of experiencing described by Western philosophers, religious thinkers, and other serious commentators on living, we hypothesize that any reasonably self-focused and positive experience of more than very brief duration must have either some kind of grounding or a definite beginning comprised of a generally positive engagement with the experienced situation and must conclude with a similar positive engagement. Between these frames, periods both of engagement and disengagement and of positive and negative character will alternate in highly idiosyncratic sub-patterns as individuals react to and constitute meaning within the situation.

To the best of our knowledge, investigations of such a hypothesis have not been undertaken within the curriculum field. However, we have identified two modest research traditions in somewhat related areas that seem particularly germane to our investigation. Purves and Beach have summarized and commented upon studies devoted to response to literature, and these studies are useful to the extent that the analogy holds between curriculum and literature, between curricular experience and literary experience. They suggest that response to literature is a complicated psychological process involving attention to the text, ability to grasp verbal and human complexities, critical judgments, and reappraisal of one's self.[40] For instance, Shrodes reports that it involves the identification of the reader with the text, the projection of the reader's self into the text, an emotional purging or catharsis, and a resulting intellectual or conscious insight.[41] Purves and Beach further suggest that many studies of the process of response have developed techniques to tap the changing mental states of readers and that these changing states display certain commonalities across diverse groups.[42]

Nowlis has similarly summarized and commented upon studies of mood, defined basically as the individual's somewhat subjective disposition or state of mind. He points out that mood tends to fluctuate naturally, often without any discernible changes in an individual's external situation, and that "within intervals of minutes, hours, or rarely days, mood involves some constancies in behavior and subjective experience."[43] Nowlis suggests also that the individual's overall mood may be comprised of several sub-moods that vary independently of each other and that the most promising ways of determining mood combine traditional self-reports by individuals with simultaneous monitoring of physiological processes, such as EEG patterns. Allen and Potkay describe a traditional and useful way of assessing mood over long periods of time, through checklists of adjectives, and report that the moods of individuals tend to vary quite considerably from day to day with peaks and valleys in mood ordinarily occurring in close proximity.[44]

We suggest that both areas of research provide useful insights into the nature of educational experience. Whereas fluctuations in mood seem largely to occur spontaneously, without changes in the external environment, and whereas varying responses to literature seem largely to occur as a result of a carefully contrived external environment (for instance, a poem), what we have been describing as phenomenological response to curriculum no doubt falls between these two cases, varying in somewhat balanced measure between changes in both the internal and the external environments. Ordinarily, students bring their own biological and psychological rhythms to the classroom, which itself is only loosely contrived to modify feelings or states of mind.

In order to investigate our hypothesis, but particularly to begin to ascertain what patterns of phenomenological response might occur normally within reasonably ordinary educational situations not contrived directly to modify them, we developed a checklist of thirty-eight adjectives that describe feelings or states of mind. A large list of adjectives was generated by asking students in an undergraduate educational psychology course to read a short story and respond at specific points in the reading of the story by completing the sentence, "I feel _____," with an adjective that described their feelings at the particular point in the story. At a later class session the same students were asked to record an adjective each time their feelings changed in response to that particular class session itself. This large working list of adjectives was next refined somewhat to eliminate duplication, and the remaining adjectives were then rated on two dimensions: levels of involvement and elation. Each dimension was viewed as a continuum, the first ranging from a very low level to a very high level of involvement with the external environment and the second ranging from depression to joy.

To accomplish this rating the list of adjectives was given to several colleagues who were asked to rate each adjective on a scale of one to ten in terms of low to high involvement and in terms of low to high elation. The authors further ranked the adjectives relative to each other on each dimension regardless of numerical score and in this way generally verified and refined the numerical ratings supplied by colleagues. Next, we selectively eliminated adjectives where exact duplication of ratings occurred or where large numbers of adjectives clustered closely together on ratings in both dimensions. Finally, we added several adjectives with ratings not closely approximated by any other adjectives on the list. In this way we arrived at a list of thirty-eight adjectives more-or-less evenly distributed across the range of possible ratings on both dimensions. The adjectives and their ratings are presented in table 1.

Figure 1 represents a graph showing the relationship between the two dimensions on which the adjectives were rated. By dividing the two axes at their midpoints, four quadrants are obtained. Each adjective can therefore be located in one of the four quadrants: quadrant 1, low involvement-low elation; quadrant 2, low involvement-high elation; quadrant 3, high involvement-low elation; and quadrant 4, high involvement-high elation. The exception is the adjective "neutral," which was arbitrarily rated at "5" on both dimensions and which is therefore located at the intersection of the axes. For the purposes of this study "neutral" is considered the conjunction of all four quadrants and is designated as quadrant 5.

Applying our hypothesis to these quadrants suggests that students who obtain a generally positive experience from a course will

Table 1
Adjectives and Their Ratings

	Involvement	Elation		Involvement	Elation
1. amused	6	7	20. glad	7	7
2. angry	9	1	21. helpless	3	1
3. annoyed	7	3	22. indifferent	1	3
4. anticipatory	8	6	23. indignant	9	2
5. apprehensive	7	2	24. inquisitive	7	6
6. bored	0	3	25. interested	6	6
7. calm	4	6	26. involved	9	7
8. complacent	2	4	27. joyful	9	9
9. concerned	6	4	28. liberated	2	9
10. content	4	6	29. lonely	2	1
11. depressed	1	1	30. meditative	2	6
12. despairing	9	0	31. neutral	5	5
13. detached	1	4	32. satisfied	6	7
14. disappointed	6	2	33. serene	2	8
15. disturbed	6	2	34. somber	3	2
16. ecstatic	10	10	35. still	1	6
17. elated	10	9	36. terrified	10	0
18. exasperated	8	2	37. tranquil	3	7
19. excited	8	8	38. uneasy	4	3

probably both begin and end the course in quadrant 4, perhaps moving from moderate to somewhat more pronounced levels of high involvement-high elation. But, the hypothesis suggests, between beginning and end, in attempting to constitute meanings or harmonize the overall qualities of a course, students will very probably move in reasonably individualistic ways among the other quadrants, returning occasionally to quadrant 4. While the hypothesis does not directly suggest a typical pattern for students who do not obtain a generally positive experience from a course, for students who find their experience broken off or a course unusually difficult or generally distasteful or unengaging, it seems clear that such students will probably neither begin nor end in quadrant 4 and that they will probably spend relatively more time as the course progresses in other quadrants, particularly quadrants 1 and 3.

Subjects for the initial testing of instrument and hypothesis were students in two five-week courses in educational foundations, one at the undergraduate level and one at the graduate level, offered during the summer of 1975. At the beginning of each course all stu-

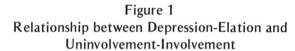

Figure 1
Relationship between Depression-Elation and
Uninvolvement-Involvement

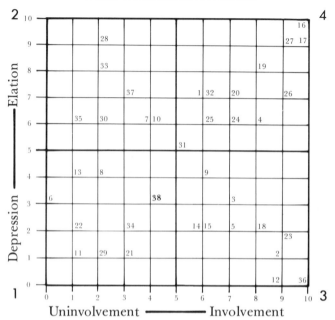

dents were given the list of adjectives and were invited to participate in what was described as a survey intended to assess "normal" series of reactions to "ordinary" educational situations, something about which educators had little dependable knowledge. The instructor stressed that the survey was in no way meant to be evaluative of either course or students, nor was the course contrived to shape students' reactions in predicted ways. Most students indicated willingness to participate, and participants were requested to record at the close of each class session one adjective that most nearly approximated their reactions to the course for that day. No adjectives were recorded on days of examinations, and on the last day of class each participant also recorded an adjective that summarized his reactions to the entire course. Through this procedure relatively complete sets of data were obtained from nine students in the undergraduate course over nineteen occasions (including the summative occasion) and from ten students in the graduate course over twenty occasions. Throughout both courses the instructor endeavored to hold methodology and material relatively constant day by day and to minimize dramatic or provocative events that might have had unusual influence on responses to a particular session.

Instrument and hypothesis were further tested in similar classes with the same instructor during the fall semester of 1975. During this second testing, procedures were adopted to ensure anonymity of subjects, and subjects were requested to record adjectives that summarized reactions to the entire course at the time of recording. (In this sense all occasions were summative.) Unfortunately, during the fall semester data could be collected from each class no more than once a week, and due to absences and vagaries in the university calendar data could not be collected uniformly throughout the semester. Only twelve occasions for the undergraduate class and eleven for the graduate class were recorded, and few subjects were present for all of these.

Because of differences in procedures and in calendar and because of the few occasions recorded during the fall semester, we do not consider data from the summer and fall testings to be directly comparable. We consider the data from the summer to be considerably more reliable and usable as an indicator of evolving patterns of response. Therefore, the remainder of our discussions will focus on the summer data, although we will refer to the fall data primarily for illustrative purposes.

Gleanings

Group means for involvement and elation for both initial and final occasions for all classes (summer and fall) were recorded. All changes in elation were positive; changes in involvement were mixed. The results of t-tests showed only the increase in elation for the two summer classes to be statistically significant at the .01 level. These findings are not surprising, since class sessions were intended neither to increase nor to decrease scores. Far more important for our purposes is what seemed to happen day by day to both groups and individuals.

The daily mean scores for the undergraduate summer class are plotted in figure 2. On the first occasion involvement is relatively

Figure 2
Mean Score for Undergraduate Class, by Occasion

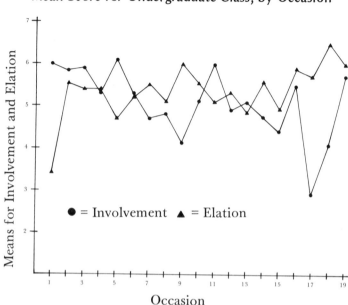

Occasion

high but elation is low, indicating that collectively the group is in quadrant 3, actively involved but also concerned or slightly apprehensive about the course. However, this concern seems to give way to a more positive involvement or interest (indicative of quadrant 4) during four of the next five occasions, returning slightly only on the fifth occasion. On the seventh occasion a new phase begins, which is henceforth to dominate (seven and one-half of the last thirteen presummative occasions) the group's collective reactions; here the group means enter quadrant 2, indicative of calmness or contentment and, at more pronounced levels, of tranquillity and meditativeness. This phase reaches extremely pronounced levels on the seventeenth and eighteenth occasions, before the summative occasion indicates a strong high involvement-high elation (quadrant 4) group reaction to the course as a whole. Of the eighteen presummative occasions, seven group means were in quadrant 4, three in quadrant 3, seven and one-half in quadrant 2, and one-half in quadrant 1.

The daily mean scores for the graduate summer class are plotted in figure 3. Once again on the first occasion involvement is high but elation low (quadrant 3). On the second occasion the group moves

Figure 3
Mean Score for Graduate Class, by Occasion

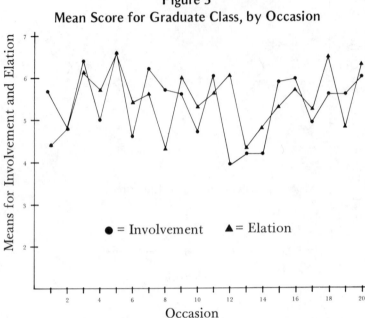

very slightly into quadrant 1, indicating slight uneasiness, before entering a series of occasions dominated by high involvement-high elation (quadrant 4, indicative of positive interest). Intermittently quadrant 2 and quadrant 3 occasions displace strong quadrant 4 occasions during the presummative series. The summative occasion indicates a very strong high involvement-high elation (quadrant 4) group reaction to the course as a whole. Of the nineteen presummative occasions, eight and one-half group means were in quadrant 4, four were in quadrant 3, five were in quadrant 2, and one and one-half were in quadrant 1.

These results seem to bear out the perceptions of the instructor, who believed both classes went unusually well, both in terms of students' engagement with the course material and in terms of their personal satisfaction with the courses. All but three of the nineteen subjects reported summative adjectives in quadrant 4; these three reported summative adjectives in quadrant 2. Interestingly, contrary to expectations only one subject reported an initial adjective in quadrant 4 and none in quadrant 2. Twelve reported initial adjectives in quadrant 3, three in quadrant 1, and three in quadrant 5 ("neutral"). However, eighteen reported at least one adjective in quadrant 4 during the first three occasions, and eight reported adjectives in quadrant 4 on both the second and third occasions. It appears, then, for a student to summarize his reactions to a course in terms of high involvement-high elation, he need not react this way initially; nonetheless, all who so summarized their reactions also reacted in terms of high involvement-high elation early in the course. The one student who did not report an adjective in quadrant 4 during the first three occasions (not reporting one until the sixth occasion) reported a summative adjective in quadrant 2.

Why were most initial reactions in quadrant 3, indicating involvement with a course but at a moderately low level? The explanation may be that this is a typical reaction to the presentation of any course outline that embodies a series of challenging tasks for the student. Initially, the student may be more concerned with soberly appraising his prospects for meeting these challenges than with appraising and developing some interest in the course material itself. On the other hand, this kind of initial reaction may be typical only in response to curricular elements of certain kinds. For instance, the instructor may have initially emphasized difficult or challenging characteristics of the courses rather than more immediately stimulating or engaging characteristics of the material. Also, this kind of initial reaction may have been at least in part a function of the fourth structural element, the psychological and biographical context of the student. For instance, students may have had certain expectations about the courses which were initially either met or violated. The typicalness of initial reactions in quadrant 3 can be further tested.

Why was there a tendency for group means to move into quadrant 2 as courses progressed? (This tendency was extremely pronounced in the undergraduate summer class but was also true to a lesser extent in the other three classes.) Again, the explanation may be simply that this is a typical or normal tendency under most sets of circumstances. Or it may have been a function of the characteristics of students, or of characteristics of the curriculum. For instance, the

instructor of the classes reports both valuing and encouraging reflective thinking, thoughtful intellectual and personal engagement with
course material. Is this encouragement a necessary part of any curriculum within which reactions in quadrant 2 become common? Do
these reactions themselves indicate a movement from the surface to
the deep levels of experiencing? Are they typical, even necessary, in
any sequence of reactions within a self-focused and positive experience? Such questions can be investigated further.

While the patterns of individual students display some commonalities, some interesting differences also emerge. As noted, students
typically responded initially in quadrant 3, moved on the next several occasions pronouncedly into quadrant 4, and reported a summative adjective in quadrant 4. However, between the third to fifth
occasions and the summative occasion considerable variation in patterns emerged. While quadrant 4 responses were the most common in
both courses (98 of 188 recorded responses in the graduate class, 56
of 152 in the undergraduate class), on only one occasion (the third
day of the graduate class) did all students in the same class respond
in any one quadrant. Responses of individual students were not confined largely to one or two quadrants as courses progressed. Excluding quadrant 5, responses of thirteen students were in all four quadrants, and responses of eighteen students in at least three quadrants.
Only one student responded in just two quadrants.

The sequence of responses by quadrant of the student displaying least variability follows. Dashes indicate absences; the final
numeral is for the summative occasion.

3 4 4 4 4 5 4 – 4 4 4 4 – 4 4 4 – 4 4   4

We have raised the possibility that responses in quadrant 2 may be
indicative of a student's moving from the surface to the deep level of
experience. While this possibility remains very much a hypothesis
only, what may be indicated about a student who reports continuous
responses of high involvement-high elation? Perhaps this student is
responding on the surface level only. On the other hand, the student
whose sequence is represented above is an unusually mature, competent, and self-possessed woman in her late thirties. Perhaps she has
developed some skill in bracketing her experience and habitually
responds to many situations at the deep level, quite intentionally

attempting to constitute meanings. Does this indicate that habituated response at the deep level of experience encourages continuous high involvement-high elation responses to a course? Does this provide reason for educators to develop techniques based on phenomenological methodology? As yet we do not know.

The sequence of responses by quadrant of the student displaying perhaps the most typical sequence follows.

3 4 4 1 4 — 4 1 5 1 4 2 4 1 4 3 1 4 2   4

Note that after the initial preponderance of quadrant 4 responses on early occasions no clear-cut pattern emerges. Quadrant 4 responses do recur throughout the sequence with some semblance of regularity, but these responses are interspersed with responses in all other quadrants. Nonetheless, we think that what we have described at some length earlier provides some powerful ways to explain what we see here. Basically, both group and individual patterns can be conveniently explained in terms of movement between surface and deep levels of experiencing, in terms of harmonizing aesthetic qualities, in terms of Harper's phenomenology of experiencing, and in terms of ordinary variations in mood. Between characteristic beginnings and endings of high involvement-high elation are individualistic patterns encompassing the high and low range on both dimensions.

We think, then, that the sequences of responses we have recorded that culminate in high involvement-high elation strongly support our hypothesis and may represent a typical general pattern of phenomenological response within a self-focused and positive experience of some duration. What, however, of sequences of response that did not culminate in a summative response in quadrant 4?

Only three students did not so summarize their reactions to the courses; all of these reported summative adjectives in quadrant 2. Of these three, two reported sequences of responses very similar to the most typical sequence (displayed above), with the exception of the summative adjectives.[45] The sequence of responses by quadrant of the most atypical student follows.

3 3 2 2 2 4 2 1 1 4 — 1 4 — 2 2 — 4   2

We have no convenient explanation of why quadrant 2 responses are preponderant in this sequence and in no other sequence, except to suggest that such differences can be attributed to differences in students themselves, particularly their psychological and biographical makeup. Still, we are by no means ready to suggest that a sequence dominated by responses in quadrant 2 does not constitute a highly positive overall experience.

No student reported a summative response in quadrant 1 or 3. However, results in similar classes during the fall semester were more mixed. Group means and individual sequences for the undergraduate class were similar to those of the summer, although of more neutral values. Group means for the graduate class began in quadrant 3, moved on several occasions into quadrants 2 and 4, but also ended in quadrant 3. Differences in procedures making each occasion in the fall a summative occasion and substantially reducing the number of occasions probably account for some of the differences noted. Most of the shorter and flatter individual sequences reported in the fall are still similar to sequences reported in the summer. Although, as we have suggested, results obtained in the fall are not directly comparable to those obtained in the summer, we offer for comparative purposes examples of sequences by quadrant concluding in quadrant 3 and in quadrant 1.

$$3 \quad 3 \quad 4 \quad 3 \quad 1 \quad 5 \quad 4 \quad 5 \quad 5 \quad 2 \quad 3$$
$$3 \quad 1 \quad 3 \quad 2 \quad 4 \quad 1 \quad 4 \quad 3 \quad 3 \quad 2 \quad 1$$

Interpreting these sequences is extremely difficult, particularly since few similar sequences were recorded. However, they are probably representative of generally negative overall experiences and may prove to be predictive of basic phenomenological patterns within an incomplete, mixed, or undesirable experience.

Next Steps

We believe we have fulfilled our first three purposes to an extent consistent with the scope of this study: the procedure for determining patterns of response seems to work, the most general pattern of response described in our hypothesis seems to obtain, and we seem to have made a modest but perhaps promising beginning at determining general norms and individual variations within this pattern. Clearly, a number of next steps need to be taken.

The most obvious of these is to conduct future studies using similar procedures on population samples large enough to wash out the effects of variations in individual psychological and biographical contexts and in individual curricula. In this way sufficient data can be obtained and analyzed to discern with increasing confidence and sophistication perhaps several basic general patterns in educational experience and individual variations within these patterns. Further, more specific studies can be done to correlate differences in patterns of response with differences in curricula and with differences in various characteristics of students. Eventually, norms can be established with regard to major differences in such things as subject matter, instructional methods, age, previous educational history, and expectations of students. Also needed are studies of a different sort that attempt to correlate patterns of response with long-range educational and experiential effects. For instance, what patterns of response seem to be associated with beneficial educational results or with productive and satisfying living?

The primary use of such next steps will be to provide an additional way of helping the individual student find his way through his educational experience. The study suggests that even experiences that seem overall to be highly positive ordinarily contain phases perceived as diminished or disillusioning levels of experiencing. Perhaps, therefore, some disillusionment or disorientation is inevitable and even beneficial under many circumstances. However, if the disorientation is unusually pronounced, or of unusually long duration, or unusually disproportionate to the objective circumstances, or especially unusual or unprecedented for a particular individual, then the overall situation may be unhealthy, and as we have suggested, the educator should very probably move to change it. But aside from the educator, what of the individual student often striving but grappling alone with the meaning of his experiencing? We think it might represent considerably more than cold comfort to him to know that other individuals have coped with similar situations, to know how they have found their way through these labyrinths, and to know what satisfactions they may have eventually obtained.

Implications

Several questions deserve further brief examination, for they help illuminate the implications of this study for the curriculum field.

What was being measured? We think the adjectives reported by students are indicative of something, but we cannot be entirely sure of what. For instance, we do not know to what extent the reported feelings and states of mind are indicative of the surface or the deep level of experiencing, although both levels are very probably present in some way. Whereas the adjectives are probably reasonably good indicators of immediate apprehensions of a course, we cannot be sure how closely or how loosely they may approximate the very complex processes going on at a more inward level. It is clear that the adjectives are approximations, but perhaps they are consistent approximations that can be used reasonably.

Were students responding emotionally or intellectually? Were they responding to the content or the form of a course? Again, we cannot be sure of answers to such questions. We have suggested that students at the deep level of experience probably are reacting analytically, and analytic responses are probably good, for they may indicate that students have developed some skill in using the environment selectively as a means of changing themselves. But whether this kind of selective, analytic responding is primarily conscious or intellectual is another matter.

Nor is it certain that content and form can be kept separate. Anonymous interviews conducted by the nonteaching author with several students about the midpoint of the fall semester suggested that these students recalled the initial instructions to respond to the course itself rather than to extraneous influences, and for the most part they were doing so. However, one student reported that she had once responded extremely, due to an emotional reaction to somewhat passing references in class to the topic of child abuse. For the most part, adjectives with very extreme values (in any quadrant) were rarely reported, and in no case was a very extreme adjective reported again on the immediately following occasion. Most such reports seemed associated with specific and unusual events in the course, often occurring the day before an examination or the day of an individual's oral presentation, although, as the example just cited points out, some were no doubt connected with personal and emotional reactions to specific course content.

Now all this may suggest, quite logically, that life itself has more power to move us than has life encapsulated in the curriculum. But here we must note a finding of Squire.[46] In appraising how individuals respond to literature, Squire observed that immature readers often react personally but inappropriately, their range of response extending beyond that reasonably suggested by the literary text. This indicates a lack of development of the ability to read critically. The same kind of thing happening in the phenomenological responses of students may thus indicate lack of skill in how to "read" critically the educational environment. The most obvious implication for curriculumists is that critical discernment and judgment may be developed by making courses both laboratories within which and materials upon which criticism is exercised. Perhaps courses focusing on certain issues or subject matters in curriculum might provide more powerful or worthwhile ways of developing critical abilities than would courses in other areas.

How typical is the general pattern of response described by this study? How well does the study substantiate that pattern? The most general purpose of the study was, of course, to provide this kind of description and substantiation. We think that, consistent with its scope, the study has done this. Nonetheless, we cannot be sure that the pattern was not specific to a certain kind of curriculum or to certain kinds of students. Without considerable further substantiation of patterns within a variety of educational circumstances, this study proves very little. Without linking knowledge about how students respond with knowledge about the other three structural elements used in analyzing educational experience, the knowledge generated by this study explains only tenuously. However, we think the study may directly suggest quite a lot.

Among the most far-reaching implications for the curriculum field is the suggestion that studies of phenomenological response can provide a new and integrating focal point for curriculum research. Such studies can be regarded as representing a confluence of insights drawn from all areas that deal with human experience, areas such as aesthetics, religion, semiotics, and psychoanalysis. Linked with insights drawn from more traditional forms of educational research, such as classroom analysis, such studies may provide a means of reordering and integrating a number of powerful perspectives heretofore brought to bear on curricular problems only piecemeal and separately. Focusing this integrated perspective on distinctively curricular phenomena may provide some basis for the development of the kind of distinctively curricular research that Walker thinks the field has been lacking.[47] Research of this kind may help provide increasingly dependable knowledge not only about student response and its relationship to curricular characteristics, but about many related topics, such as student evaluation of instruction, the process of curriculum development, and the utilization of curriculum studies.

Beyond this, the study implies a basic reorientation in thinking about curriculum. This reorientation is consistent with the growth of the kind of educational ideology described by Macdonald and with which we are in agreement. Basically, this "transcendental developmental" ideology is a way of linking and doing justice to the structures of both the inner and outer world, although neither of these is regarded as linear or fixed. Macdonald suggests that in this view the curriculum becomes a means of facilitating the kind of implicit understanding he describes as "indwelling."[48]

To the extent that this study is consistent with this ideology, the study suggests that any norms developed for patterns of phenomenological response will be misused if they are used as a means of control. But, used otherwise, they can provide the curriculumist with a new diagnostic tool and an alternative way of viewing and evaluating curricula. In this sense they become an integrating center for many humanistic concerns and may thus herald a further shift among curriculumists away from the technological assumptions and solely utilitarian values inherent in the Tyler rationale. Such norms must be used in an open, diagnostic, facilitating way. Rather than attempt to predict and control highly specific outcomes, the curriculumist would use such norms to monitor the pattern of reactions within a healthy but individualistic flow of experience. Knowledge of the commonalities within experiencing becomes diagnostic in the sense that students in difficulty can be aided in redirecting their efforts to constitute meaning within their own experience. Curricula can be altered to enhance this process. Ultimately, then, assessment of phenomenological patterns can be used not only to modify educational environments directly but to modify conceptions of such things as mental health, classroom analysis, and educational purposes.

The greatest danger in the kind of work this study describes is that some will seize upon it as evidence that each individual's experience is like every other's, or, worse yet, that it should and can be made like every other's. Nothing can be further from the truth. The

fact that on only one occasion in a total of thirty-nine in both summer courses did all nine or ten students in each class report responses
in the same quadrant is particularly noteworthy. It indicates that
within a discernible common pattern and to common external curricular structures, individuals still respond with individuality. If,
then, work of this kind is likely to demonstrate anything, it is how
mysteriously unpredictable, how variable and rich, the individual's
experience can and should be. And it should help celebrate that fact,
particularly by helping the curriculum field move away from sterile
and outmoded beliefs such as the conviction that norms provide a
justification for uniformity and an occasion for control.

Nor does this study give educators an excuse for carelessness.
Clearly, low points within educational experience may be inevitable,
but they need not be perpetuated by the curriculum. Neither, however, can education be a perpetual high. But it can be redeemed from
meanness, from being conceived, carried out, and analyzed in petty
terms. Perhaps this is the least we can ask—and the most. We can all
thus hope for moments akin to "transcending anticipation" or "presence" in our educational experience, as in our lives. But if we wish to
have them in full measure, we must be aware of the richly variable
path by which they are approached.

Notes

1. George Willis, "The Concept of Experience in Major Curriculum Literature: 1918-1970" (Ph.D. diss., The Johns Hopkins University, 1971).
2. J. Gordon Chamberlin, "Phenomenological Methodology and Understanding Education," in *Existentialism and Phenomenology in Education*, ed.
David E. Denton (New York: Teachers College Press, 1974), p. 128.
3. Ibid., pp. 126, 136, 124.
4. Ibid., p. 129.
5. Ibid., p. 133.
6. See Maxine Greene, "Curriculum and Consciousness," *Teachers College
Record* 73, no. 2 (December 1971): 253-69.
7. William Pinar, "Search for a Method," in *Curriculum Theorizing: The
Reconceptualists*, ed. William Pinar (Berkeley, Ca.: McCutchan Publishing Corp.,
1975); idem, "The Analysis of Educational Experience," in ibid.; idem,
"*Currere*: Toward Reconceptualization," in ibid.; idem, "The Method of
Currere" (Paper delivered at the annual meeting of the American Educational
Research Association, Washington, D.C., April 1975).
8. Pinar, "The Method of *Currere*," p. 2. Emphasis in original.
9. Ibid., p. 15. Emphasis in original.
10. Madeleine R. Grumet, "Existential and Phenomenological Founda-

tions of *Currere*: Self-Report in Curriculum Inquiry" (Paper delivered at the annual meeting of the American Educational Research Association, Washington, D.C., April 1975), pp. 18-19.

11. Paul R. Klohr, "Response of Discussant" (Response to presentations in the symposium "Toward Reconceptualization of Curriculum Inquiry" at the annual meeting of the American Educational Research Association, Washington, D.C., April 1975), pp. 5-6.

12. José R. Rosario, "Harold Rugg and the Aesthetic Tradition in the Curriculum Field" (Paper delivered at the annual meeting of the American Educational Research Association, Washington, D.C., April 1975).

13. John S. Mann, "Curriculum Criticism," *Teachers College Record* 71, no. 1 (September 1969): 27-40. (This article appears as chap. 4 of this volume.)

14. George Willis, "Curriculum Theory and the Context of Curriculum," *Curriculum Theory Network* 6 (Winter 1970-71): 41-59.

15. Edward F. Kelly, "Curriculum Evaluation and Literary Criticism: Comments on the Analogy," *Curriculum Theory Network* 5, no. 2 (1975): 89. (This article appears as chap. 6 of this volume.)

16. Elliot W. Eisner, "The Perceptive Eye: Toward the Reformation of Educational Evaluation" (Paper delivered at the annual meeting of the American Educational Research Association, Washington, D.C., March 1975).

17. George Willis, "Curriculum Criticism and Literary Criticism," *Journal of Curriculum Studies* 7, no. 1 (May 1975): 3-17. (This article appears as chap. 5 of this volume.)

18. Ian Westbury and William Steimer, "Curriculum: A Discipline in Search of Its Problems," *School Review* 79, no. 2 (1971): 243-67.

19. Arnold Berleant, *The Aesthetic Field: A Phenomenology of Aesthetic Experience* (Springfield, Ill.: Charles C Thomas, 1970).

20. This, of course, is an assumption upon which a number of approaches to mental health, such as psychoanalysis, rest. Furthermore, no communication whatsoever would be possible without some commonalities within the patterns of past experiencing of the communicators.

21. Roman Ingarden, "Aesthetic Experience and Aesthetic Object," in *Readings in Existential Phenomenology*, ed. Nathaniel Lawrence and Daniel O'Connor (Englewood Cliffs, N.J.: Prentice-Hall, 1967).

22. Ibid., p. 303; ibid., p. 308 (emphasis in original); ibid., p. 323.

23. Ibid., p. 312. Emphasis in original.

24. Ibid., p. 313.

25. Ibid., p. 319. Emphasis in original.

26. Stephen Strasser, "The Experience of Happiness: A Phenomenological Typology," in *Readings in Existential Phenomenology*, ed. Lawrence and O'Connor.

27. Ibid., p. 299.

28. Ibid.

29. Ibid., p. 301.

30. Strasser writes: "Great thinkers—Christian and non-Christian—have given expression to this experience" (ibid., p. 301). He cites examples from Nietzsche, Rousseau, and Aquinas, among others.

31. Ibid., p. 302.

32. Ralph Harper, *The Existential Experience* (Baltimore, Md.: The Johns Hopkins University Press, 1972), p. x.

33. Richard A. Macksey, Foreword to Ralph Harper, *Nostalgia: An Exis-*

tential Exploration of Longing and Fulfillment in the Modern Age (Cleveland, Ohio: Case Western Reserve University Press, 1966); Harper, *Nostalgia*, p. 10.

34. Harper, *Nostalgia*.

35. Ralph Harper, *Human Love: Existential and Mystical* (Baltimore, Md.: The Johns Hopkins University Press, 1966).

36. Ralph Harper, *Existentialism: A Theory of Man* (Cambridge, Mass.: Harvard University Press, 1948); idem, *Nostalgia*.

37. Ralph Harper, "Significance of Existence and Recognition for Education," in *Modern Philosophies of Education*, Fifty-fourth Yearbook of the National Society for the Study of Education, pt. 1 (Chicago, Ill.: University of Chicago Press, 1955); idem, "The Dark Night of Sisyphus," in *The Climate of Faith in Modern Literature*, ed. Nathan A. Scott, Jr. (New York: The Seabury Press, 1964); idem, *The Seventh Solitude: Man's Isolation in Kierkegaard, Dostoevsky, and Nietzsche* (Baltimore, Md.: The Johns Hopkins University Press, 1965); idem, *Human Love*; idem, *The Path of Darkness* (Cleveland, Ohio: Case Western Reserve University Press, 1968); idem, *The World of the Thriller* (Cleveland, Ohio: Case Western Reserve University Press, 1969).

38. Harper, *Existential Experience*, p. 12.

39. Curriculum is here conceived in a broad sense, as the arrangement of the educational environment.

40. Alan C. Purves and Richard Beach, *Literature and the Reader* (Urbana, Ill.: National Council of Teachers of English, 1972), p. 35.

41. Caroline Shrodes, "Bibliotherapy: A Theoretical and Clinical Experimental Study" (Ph.D. diss., University of California at Berkeley, 1949), p. 21.

42. Purves and Beach, *Literature and the Reader*, p. 21.

43. Vincent Nowlis, "Mood: Behavior and Experience," in *Feelings and Emotions*, ed. Magda Arnold (New York: Academic Press, 1970), p. 264.

44. Bem P. Allen and Charles R. Potkay, "Variability of Self-Description on a Day-to-Day Basis: Longitudinal Use of the Adjective Generation Technique," *Journal of Personality* 41, no. 4 (December 1973): 638-52.

45. These three summative adjectives in quadrant 2 are "meditative," "content," and "calm." The latter two fall close to the border of quadrant 4.

46. James R. Squire, *The Responses of Adolescents While Reading Four Short Stories* (Urbana, Ill.: National Council of Teachers of English, 1964).

47. Decker Walker, "What Curriculum Research?" *Journal of Curriculum Studies* 5, no. 1 (May 1973): 58-72.

48. James B. Macdonald, "A Transcendental Developmental Ideology of Education," in *Heightened Consciousness, Cultural Revolution, and Curriculum Theory*, ed. William Pinar (Berkeley, Ca.: McCutchan Publishing Corp., 1974), p. 113.

The essay by John S. Mann was originally published in 1968 and since has been widely reprinted and cited. It has been the single most influential essay in giving definition to the term "curriculum criticism" and in bringing to the attention of educational critics both the aesthetic dimensions of curriculum and the use of critical methods similar to those of literary criticism. As such it presents a conception of qualitative evaluation in education that has received widespread assent.

Mann believes that educators have been generally naive in neglecting the extent to which advances even in the physical sciences depend upon the imaginative use of personal knowledge. Although their quest has been laudable, educators have unwisely succumbed to a myth of "objectivity," often adopting formal methodological procedures that deal only with the products of education and developing a technological language that is inadequate to talk about educational situations. As a way of talking about aspects of education other than the technological only, Mann suggests "curriculum criticism," which, he asserts, combines elements of aesthetics and science.

In the type of curriculum criticism Mann describes, a curriculum can be considered as a piece of literature, a symbolic commen-

tary upon life in which its creator has embodied a series of choices about what to represent and how to represent it. By focusing upon the curriculum itself, the curriculum critic can explain the choices embodied in its design. The function of the curriculum critic is thus the disclosure of meaning abiding in the selections made by the creator of the curriculum. However, since no critique can be exhaustive, the critic must also be selective, acting much as did the creator of the curriculum, artfully choosing new propositions that reveal meaning and are based upon what Mann calls the critic's own "personal knowledge" and assumptions about "ethical reality." Ultimately, Mann suggests, even the student shares this common task with both the creator and the critic: the artful discernment and disclosure of personal meanings through living in the world.

The critical methods Mann urges in this essay are very similar to the techniques known to literary critics as the "new criticism," in which the critic deliberately ignores the biography of the author or effects on readers but carefully explicates the meaning inherent in the overall structure of the work and in its component parts as representing the author's intentions. However, in suggesting that the curriculum critic carries out this task ultimately on the basis of personal knowledge and ethical assumptions, the essay at least indirectly extends the disclosure of meaning in qualitative evaluation beyond the aesthetic dimension of meaning to the personal and the political dimensions. While the essay thus defines one specific type of curriculum criticism, it opens up the possibilities of other types as well.

4

Curriculum Criticism

John S. Mann

> The mind is like a bat. Precisely. Save
> That in the very happiest intellection
> A graceful error may correct the cave.
> —*Mind* by Richard Wilbur

This paper takes as its premise the assertion that the language we use to talk about educational situations is inadequate. I share with many people the view, most cogently and most insistently developed by Dwayne Huebner, that our current mode of discourse is an instrumental language structured around assumed means-ends, cause-effect relations, and is thus convenient primarily for regarding a curriculum in its technological aspect.[1] Just as most educators would agree that this is an important aspect, so too I am sure they would agree that it is not the *only* important aspect. In this paper I want to look at a different way of talking about curricula—a way that combines elements of aesthetics and science. I shall call it curriculum criticism.[2] When I talk about what one might consider curriculum to be, I shall be stressing the aesthetic elements. Specifically,

This article originally appeared in *Curriculum Theory Network* 2 (Winter 1968-69): 2-14. Reprinted by permission.

I will ask what is involved in talking about curriculum as if it were a literary object. When I ask how one may proceed to talk about curriculum so regarded, certain elements of scientific thought enter in. It is surprising only at first glance to find how well scientific and aesthetic talk get along together.

Curriculum and Fiction

For the purposes of discovering what may be involved in talking about a curriculum as a literary object, I will use as an exemplum—to be guided but not bound by—Mark Schorer's lucid treatment of the story.[3] And the first point to note is that in his criticism Schorer focuses neither on the biography of the author nor on the effect of the work on the reader, but firmly on the literary object itself. The function of his critique is to disclose meanings in the object. It seeks to help the beholder come close to, or even touch or enter into, the object, to know its meanings well.

Schorer says, "Fiction is, or can be, an art, and art, if it is about anything, is about life. But exactly because it is about it, it is a different thing from it."[4] In fiction, a boy, let us say, who has a real name and "looks" like a real boy, runs around the corner in pursuit of a balloon. There may or may not "really" have been such a boy, and for fiction this is not important. What matters, for this paper, is that this particular boy in this particular circumstance was selected for representation from a universe of possibilities. This selection is fixed in a complex set of other choices, both about what to tell and about how to tell it. The selection made, considered against the infinite background of selections passed over, constitutes an assertion of meaning.

I would like to propose that a curriculum can be regarded in the same manner. Like fiction, a curriculum can have a story, a set of facts which on the surface purport to represent life. In a curriculum, a scientist precipitates a salt or notes the effect of X rays on a photographic plate. It matters here, more than in fiction, whether there "really" was such a scientist. But putting this fact aside for a while, it matters very much in a curriculum as well as in a story that this scientist was selected for representation from a universe of possibilities. And note that the scientist is not *presented* but *represented*. It is not a chunk of raw life a curriculum contains, but a film maker's or a text writer's representation of life or selections from life. And this particular selection, like that of the boy and the balloon, is fixed in a complex set of other choices about what to represent, how to represent it, and in what context to represent it. In both cases, the curriculum no less than the story, the network of selections constitutes an assertion of meaning—a symbolic commentary upon life.

Limit and Possibility

To regard a curriculum as a literary object, then, means first of all to think of it as a set of selections from a universe of possibilities. The statement embodies some complex conceptions which may best be approached through Goethe's succinct observation that "Art exists in limitation."[5] The point has been made by many others that raw life is formless, chaotic, and without meaning until man-the-artist creates meaning by bounding it. Thus the artist whose raw material is the undifferentiated totality of life, actual as well as imaginable, possible as well as fantastic, by choosing this rather than that instant to tell and this rather than that feature to leave unstated, creates a shape and a meaning for life. I read somewhere that Stephen Mallarmé stood in terror before the blank page; while it was blank it was infinite possibility, but to write a word upon it was to limit the possible meanings of the page. The blank page was, in a sense, his perfect poem. By the same token, however, the blank page is precisely nonart, for by selecting nothing it bounds nothing and affirms no meaning. To listen to a chaotic infinite universe and then to answer with form, finitely, is to order chaos and assert meaning. Such answering is the hallmark of man-the-artist: his answers are his works of art.

If you turn this proposition around and look at it from the other side, it discloses something important—the unconditionedness of the curriculum as art. His answers are his works of art, but in addition, his works of art answer to the conjunction of his human gift of seeking forms truthfully with his human habitation of chaos. This is the artist's commitment, and his work of art is art only insofar as it unconditionally fulfills this commitment. To whatever extent a work of art answers to something else—say the desire to sway or influence or even to teach—to that extent does it fall short of art-fullness. It is something-else-and-art; perhaps propaganda-and-art. And this explains why technological talk cannot comprehend a curriculum-as-art. For technological talk is precisely talk about conditions, conditioning, and the conditioned. It is talk locked in a means-end cause-effect structure which cannot be bent to describe curriculum as unconditioned immediacy.

One might well ask whether there is any such thing, really, as an "unconditioned" curriculum. Clearly there is not. Nor can it be said of any other work of art that "this is unconditioned." A work of art—a curriculum, story, painting, or song—is not art but a work of hands by man-the-artist. It aspires to art-fullness, to unconditioned-ness. The primary assertion of any work of art is the exuberance over partaking of unconditionedness—the discovery or creation or achievement of a piece of freedom. But it is a partaking of freedom and not a being free. Art is unconditioned, but the art-object, like man-the-artist, is both conditioned and unconditioned. Thus to regard an object-of-art, or a curriculum-as-art, as unconditioned is not to forget that it is also conditioned, but merely to look at it and talk about it in its art-fullness. And surely a curriculum, which cannot be art, can be artful in some degree, and can be considered not only in terms of how it conditions and is conditioned by man, but also in terms of how it answers man's listening and seeking.

The Forms of Meaning

As with literary critique, the function of the curricular critique is to disclose its meanings, to illuminate its answers. If meaning is expressed as unconditioned selection from a universe of possibilities, then the form of the meanings asserted is the design, or patterns of relatedness, of the selections. A single selected item is not meaningful by itself, but only in its relations to other items. As E. E. Cummings points out, nouns create no movement. It is, as he put it, the poet's "ineluctable preoccupation with the verb"[6] that gives him power. Or, as someone else once noted, only an unsubtle mind sees no difference between an elephant in the White House and an elephant in the zoo.

Meaning, then, abides in the design of selections. A later section of this paper will consider tools the critic might use to get at meaning through design. For the moment I would like to propose a very general formulation: the critic discloses meaning by explaining design.

To explain something is to account for it, to point to something at a high level of abstraction in terms of which the thing to be explained can be seen to "make sense." In just this sense, D. H. Lawrence's concern with the ramifications of sexual power "explains" the emphasis he gives to physical descriptions of the men and women in many of his stories. And in this same sense Boyle's Law "explains" the cork coming out of a heated bottle and Snell's Law "explains" the oar's foreshortening. To find an explanation, then, is to find what accounts for things being as they are. Yet there are differences between the kind of statement that accounts for the behavior of a gas and the kind that accounts for the behavior of a story or a curriculum-as-art, and these differences are instructive. The expansion of gas is not (save from an unorthodox theological point of view) chosen in the sense that intense and prolonged physical description is chosen in a Lawrence story. What is explained in the comment about Lawrence, it must be remembered, is a set of choices. And if the choices are to be regarded in their artfulness, they must be regarded as chosen not for an extrinsic purpose but simply for what they themselves mean. To say what they mean, therefore, is to account for their being chosen. Their meaning *is* their reason for being chosen. Thus to account for the choices in a work of art is precisely to discover what the choices mean. Explanation of the design of choices and disclosure of meaning are logically identical, a single thing come at from opposite sides. When the relations among selections that constitute the designs of a curriculum have been explained, the meanings of the curriculum have thereby been disclosed.

Since a single curriculum, like a single story, has many designs to be explained and thus many meanings to be disclosed, no single critique is exhaustive. The critic, therefore, must be selective.

Against Dichotomy

The problem of selection among styles may be approached by noting at a somewhat superficial level the argument over "objective" and "subjective" knowing and the common tendency to associate the former with science and the latter with art. Long before the point was formalized in "creativity research" literature, artists and scientists alike recognized that the objective-science, subjective-art scheme was inadequate if not wrong. The various selections in Gheselin's collection of essays on the creative process,[7] for example, almost without exception call attention more to the similarities than to the differences between artistic and scientific work. Albert Einstein asserted that at the heart of theoretical physics was the free play of the imagination,[8] just as convincingly as the classical and classically inclined poets have asserted that the foundation of art is the objective imitation of nature.[9] More thorough and sophisticated treatments of the problem, such as Michael Polanyi's,[10] have shown that the dichotomy between objective and subjective, while possessing some logical validity, is not really a very adequate device for describing man's creative activities in science or in art.[11] Instead Polanyi suggests that science and art alike, both of which have aspects that are formal and rule-bound and independent therefore of individual perceptions, are nevertheless directed by an all-pervasive and dominant "personal" component. The "personal" component, however, while neither rule-bound nor convention-bound, nor tied to formal logical operations, is not "subjective." The one necessary and sufficient constraint that separates it decisively from subjectivity is what Polanyi calls its "universal intent." The scientist's commitment, like the artist's, is to universality of statement; and this commitment assures, within the limits of human fallibility, that his intellectual freedom from other constraints is not self-serving. At every point of his inquiry, from the selection of problems to the drawing of conclusions, the scientist's work is a combination of formal rule-governed procedures and "heuristic leaps" beyond the constraints of such procedures. These leaps are what make science go into the unknown from the known; they are guided by the scientist's intuitively held "personal knowledge."

Personal Knowledge

The purpose of this parenthesis is to introduce an approach to the critic's problem of selecting from an inexhaustible realm of designs and meanings those he will study; and in introducing this approach, it seeks to forestall the objection that this first step or any other step of the critical technique proposed is merely "subjective" as compared to the "objective" accounts of curricula given by the more customary tools of research. Indeed, just as the paper has suggested that science and art are less dissimilar than is often assumed, it will now suggest that the "aesthetically" oriented critique and the scientifically conceived research program are less different than may be imagined. In the first place, after all, the research project, like the less customary forms of criticism,[12] must begin with a decision about what to select for study. And what one selects in either case is a matter of what one's personal (not subjective) knowledge leads him to see as valuable and fruitful. The ground of these judgments is different in different cases, however. The personal knowledge that figures in the physicist's choice of a problem or a range or set of phenomena to study is knowledge about physical reality. The personal knowledge of the educational psychologist that figures in his selection is probably knowledge about psychological reality. The personal knowledge in which the curriculum critique is grounded is principally knowledge about ethical reality.[13]

This means that personally held and universally intended knowledge about good and evil or right and wrong stands as a valuable guide to the processes of the curriculum critique, including the initial process of selecting a focus of attention. In the absence of a thorough analysis of this proposition, it may be helpful to think of it as suggesting that one approaches the phenomena to be examined not with the wholly impossible "open mind of the scientist" but with a set of predispositions which are forms of designs that it would be of value to discover. The content of these models is knowledge of ethical reality, and the form of the models is the form of that ethical knowledge. It is crucial to understand what this does *not* mean. It does not mean that the *content* of what one will disclose in a critique is fixed in advance by prior personal knowledge. It does mean that the dimensions in terms of which content will be sought are so fixed. The ethics-based models do not determine what meanings will be disclosed in a curriculum but they suggest the ethical dimensions which, if found in a design, will incline one to regard such a design as worth examining.

Returning, then, to the critic's problem of deciding which designs he will study, the following summary statement may be made. The critic's choices have their origin in his personal knowledge of ethical reality. The form and content of this knowledge serve together as a heuristic model; they direct the critic's attention to those designs which may be expected to have meaning within the context of his ethical knowledge.[14]

The grounding of the critique in personal ethical knowledge gives it a range of deployment that in principle is very broad compared to the range of research grounded in empirical methodology. Whether it can have the precision of the latter is another question, and whether it ought to is still another. The point I should like to make, however, is that a critique thus conceived, particularly when it can take the form of conversation among interested persons, presents the possibility of continuous discovery of new meanings in educational situations.

The Critic's Stock in Trade

To Einstein's assertion that the theoretical base of physics is founded not in experience in the laboratory but in the free play of the imagination, Toulmin adds a cautionary note. "We must not go too far," he argues. "This is not work for the untutored imagination. It may be an art, but it is one whose exercise requires stiff training. . . . Theoretical physicists have to be taught their trade and cannot afford to proceed by genius alone."[15] The same point has been made innumerable times about the artist. Without argument, and recognizing the apparent fact that untutored geniuses sometimes do accomplish great things, it seems likely that Toulmin's caution would be well taken by the curricular critic.

Thus we come to the problem of delineating the curriculum critic's trade. And the first question to be faced is whether he has one. What is there, for example, in the jargon of scope and sequence, learning experience and grade placement, objectives and articulation, that can serve as stock in the trade of discovering meaning? The answer I shall pursue here is that these and other concepts can be a part, but not all, of the critic's stock in trade provided they first undergo a transformation in logical status. The nature of the transformation may be demonstrated through a few important examples. As one might gather from earlier remarks, the basic direction of the transformation is from a technological to an esthetic mode; from a framework in which the curriculum is input in a production system to one in which it is regarded as an environing work of art that conveys meaning.

The term *learning* is a suitable first example. It is given a variety of uses, but most of them have certain properties in common. Thus it is almost always used in reference to a process that has knowledge of some kind as an end and a purpose. Almost always, too, the process is regarded as a means to be controlled in order to achieve a given end. Thus the term directs attention to aspects of schooling construed as "learning situations," and its subsumed concepts serve heuristically in the pursuit of data bearing upon the technological progress (progress by controlled means toward prespecified criterion ends) of "learners."

As data for the critic, however, the emphasis is not upon the phenomena subsumed by the concept "learning" but upon the role in the school of the concept itself. The critic's task is not the same as that of the curriculum developer's. His work, for example, does not involve calculating what arrangement of curriculum variables will, according to a given learning theory, bring about certain learning results. Rather he is interested in the fact that a given learning theory making certain assumptions is employed by teachers as a criterion for their behavior. And he is interested, to carry the example further, in the limiting conditions under which learning theory as a criterion is discarded in favor of other criteria. He may be interested in the extent to which an aspect of school activity can be said to be entailed by a conception of learning, and the relations between such activity and other activity that may be entailed by other conceptions. Or he may be interested in the different language uses of the concepts of learning theory, focusing upon its use for legitimation, explanation, prediction, or control.[16] The critic, in short, uses learning theory not to explain or control learning, but to explain patterns of events that may be regarded as resulting from convictions about learning theory. Or, to restate this in terms more nearly parallel to the discussion in section 3, certain designs or patterns of choice in a school situation may be explained by regarding them as entailing assumptions and principles of a given theory of learning. Or, to state it still another way, the critic may express the meaning, say, of certain patterns of teacher behavior in terms of the premises about human nature required to explain those patterns.[17]

A second, related, example involves "knowing." The school practitioner seeks answers to such questions as what is known and what should be known. These questions concern the critic not because he seeks answers to them but because the fact that they are asked, as well as the processes the practitioner employs in seeking answers to them and the character of answers accepted, all constitute data for him. These fall into designs which it is the critic's task to analyze. Thus he will seek, for example, to discover what ideas about (1) the nature of knowledge, (2) the processes by which knowledge is acquired, (3) the values associated with knowledge, and (4) the status of knowledge in relation to other intellectual attributes, are entailed in the designs he observes. For instance, whereas the science teacher may be interested in discovering whether a pupil knows Boyle's Law or in how to get a pupil to know it, the critic is interested in discovering what meanings of "knowledge" may account for both the teacher's analysis of the problem and his teaching behavior with respect to the problem. The critic may discover, for example, that teachers vary considerably from each other and from established epistemologies in their understanding of the meaning of the scientific assertion that something is known. They vary, that is, in their understanding of the logical status of something regarded as known. And these observations in turn may account for or explain similarities and contrasts between different science instruction situations.

The point of these examples is to demonstrate the kind of transformation required to turn the material of the practitioner into material for the critic. Whereas the practitioner employs his material in the context of discovering means and ends, the critic may employ the same material as data for his analysis of the designs of educational events. Where the practitioner seeks solutions to problems, the critic seeks meaning in the manner in which problems are posed and solved. Where the practitioner may customarily evaluate his practices by examining their consequences, the critic construes practice as falling in designs that may be accounted for as expressions of meaning.

Choice and Transformation

This transformation is applicable to the bulk of the practitioner's stock. "Scope," "sequence," and "continuity" may be readily transformed from techniques employed to achieve certain ends to patterns of choice expressing beliefs about the function of schools, the nature of knowledge, or the ethical relation between teacher and student. Likewise, where the practitioner attempts to be rational about the selection of "objectives," the critic seeks to discover meaning in the fact that the need for statements of objectives is often a

controlling feature in the emergence of designs in school phenomena.

The conclusion to be drawn here is that the critic's stock in
trade includes knowledge of the practitioner's, as well as the ability
to transform it into appropriate data for his task. But these constitute only the simpler part of the critic's stock. Even transformed in
the manner described here, the familiar language of the schools is
insufficient for the critic's task. And so too is the erroneous understanding of the relation between explanation and data which is sometimes associated with this language. Toulmin's examination of the
explanatory statements of physics elucidates this point, and in so
doing shows the way toward the more complex aspects of the critic's
trade. He writes: "It is not that our theoretical statements ought to
be entailed by the data, but fail to be, and so assert things the data
do not warrant: they neither could nor need to be entailed by them,
being neither generalizations from them nor other logical constructs
out of them, but rather principles in accordance with which we can
make inferences about phenomena."[18] Then again he asserts that:
"There can be no question of (a given physical principle) being de-
ductively related to these data, nor any point in looking for, or
bewailing the absence of such a connection. The transition from the
everyday to the physicist's view . . . involves not so much the deduction of new corollaries or the discovery of new facts as the adoption
of a new approach."[19]

The explanatory statements of the critic, like those of the
physicist, are not formally derived by deduction or any other logical
process from the data themselves, but rather are the result of adopting a "new approach." And by "new approach," Toulmin makes it
clear that he means new techniques for representing phenomena.
Thus he shows that the enormous explanatory power of geometric
optics is a result of the discovery that light could be represented as
traveling in straight lines from a source to an illuminated object. And
this discovery, which was initially used to explain not new data but
data that had been puzzled over literally for centuries, clearly was
not produced by the performance of operations upon the data.

So too, critical discovery requires proper and inventive techniques for representing phenomena. This concept of representing,
however, has difficulties.

In what sense, for example, does a straight line in the models of geometric optics "represent" a light "ray"? Is it in the same sense that an equation "represents" the motion of a particle, or in the same sense that "child-centered" "represents" a particular type of classroom or a given score "represents" achievement? What about Rutherford's billiard ball atom, and what about Wordsworth's description of woods near Tintern Abbey or E. E. Cummings's statement that "spring is perhaps hand (which comes carefully out of Nowhere)"?

It is beyond this paper to examine these various instances of representation and to answer questions about them. An assumption is that fruitful representation in science as in art conforms more or less to the characteristics which Ramsey ascribes to what he conveniently calls "disclosure models," in contrast to the characteristics he ascribes to "picturing models."[20]

Disclosure Models

To be very brief about a complex distinction, a picturing model is one thought of as being as much like the phenomena as possible. The disclosure model is thought of only as bearing certain key structural similarities to the phenomena. The picturing model is thought of as derived from detailed observation of phenomena, much as the artist bases a portrait on careful study of a face. The disclosure model is studied for its own intrinsic qualities and this study gives rise to propositions, originally about the model, which are then superimposed upon phenomena and tested for goodness of fit. When the fit is good, then the model has potential for disclosure. Where the picturing model is judged for its static accuracy, the disclosure model is judged for its capacity to continue generating new propositions that reveal the phenomena. Thus disclosure models lead without end to the unfolding of a world. Where the picturing model closes the world, the disclosure model discloses, opens, the world. The building of disclosure models as new modes of representation, then, is to be part of the critic's trade.

Of the many unanswered problems about the use of disclosure models in criticism, three in particular require attention. The first problem concerns the source of disclosure models. If they are not constructed out of observed curriculum events, what are they constructed out of? The second problem concerns the content of the models, and the third concerns the relationship between models and data. If models are not built out of data, are they then data-free?

The answers I will propose to all of these are related to points discussed earlier in the paper. It will be useful first of all, then, to recall the approach taken to the problem of choosing designs to study. It was suggested that what a critic finds worth attending to depends upon "highly abstract models" grounded in "personal knowledge of ethical reality." In the light of the subsequent discussion it should be clear that this earlier problem was a subproblem in the one now being considered, and that the "highly abstract models" of that section are the "disclosure models" of this. Here, as there, the problem originates in the observation that the data themselves do not logically entail the constructs we place upon them. And here, as there, the models are to be regarded as grounded and entailed in personal knowledge of ethical reality. That is to say that the models employed to disclose meanings in phenomena are not the result of operations upon data, but are rather the result of extensions, transformations, and deployments of intuitively held personal knowledge.

The relation of such models to data is very simple, and should allay fears that the sort of criticism being described here is "data-free." For if the function of the models is to disclose meaning in the world (and data are selected representatives of the world), then a model is useful if it does disclose meaning and useless if it does not. The Greek model of light as an antenna from the eye did not reveal or explain light phenomena; the modern model of light as "rays traveling in straight lines" does. The point is that disclosure models originating in "personal knowledge" must reveal a world and in so doing explain it, or be modified to do so, or be abandoned. In observation of phenomena, then, lie the object and the proof of the model but not its source.

Finally, something must be said about the content of the curriculum critic's disclosure models. The key to this problem lies in the so far unexplained assertion that the curriculum critic's relevant personal knowledge is personal knowledge of *ethical* reality.

Ethical Reality

Curriculum, to select one of the most important views, is a form of influence over persons,[21] and disclosures of meanings in a curriculum are disclosures about the character of an influence. What one sees as important about the influence of a magnet on iron filings depends upon one's personal knowledge of magnets and filings and the structures used by physics to describe what is formally known about these. Thus it was said above that a physicist's heuristic leaps are grounded in his personal knowledge of physical reality. But what one sees as important about the influence of a curriculum over persons does not in the same sense depend upon one's personal knowledge of persons. It is a different sort of matter entirely. The curriculum critic, unlike the physicist, must regard himself as responsible to that influence, and must consider that influence from the perspective of his responsibility. This perspective certainly must be grounded in what the critic knows about right and wrong or good and bad—that is, what he knows about ethical reality—because only if it is so grounded can it, in fact, provide appropriate content for his models; that is, content that will enable him to answer his responsibility. His commitment is to disclosing those meanings that impinge upon his ethical knowledge, and he fulfills this commitment by deriving disclosure models from this knowledge.

The meanings the curriculum critic discloses, then, are meanings about which he believes ethical judgments are to be made. An appropriate final problem to be considered here, then, is whether or not his critique should include these judgments. The point could be argued well either way. If the judgments are included, there is a danger that the critic's commitment to disclosing may become a commitment to persuading, and his criticism become advocacy. Certainly this has characterized much of the curriculum literature of the past that has started out with the intent to be "theoretical."

The danger if the critic does not make ethical judgments of the meanings he has disclosed is that the judgments may never be made, or may be made improperly. Still, considering the extent to which curriculum literature is dominated by advocacy and the frequent failure of the most enlightened advocacy to bring about enlightened reform, this second danger seems small next to the first. My tentative conviction is that the critic would do well to write his critique in dimensions that to him are of ethical import, thereby giving tools to the practitioner, and allow the latter the freedom to employ the critique, or the many critiques, as he and his colleagues who design curricula see fit.

Toward a New Language

In this paper, I have tried to outline some assumptions and techniques which I believe would be helpful to people who want to talk about curriculum but who find the common forms of curriculum talk inadequate. I think that there have been two unorthodox propositions underlying all the arguments in this paper, and these I would now like to state. One proposition concerns technique. It states that the educator, in a laudable quest for a scientific approach to his problems, has allowed himself a somewhat naive view of what a scientific approach entails. In particular, he has succumbed to the myth of "objectivity" which suggests that his problems can be solved through the refinement and application of formal procedures of measurement, analysis, and interpretation, without any messy turning inward. I have proposed here that critical discoveries in education, as in the physical sciences, depend, along with good formal procedure, upon the critic's ability to draw upon knowledge that is uniquely his and is not part of any formal discipline, and to use that knowledge in a disciplined and imaginative way. While the phrase "turning inward" may be guilty, by association, of confusion, the sort of use suggested here of intuitively held unformalized knowledge is not messy, nor can formal knowledge progress unless it is considered. New understanding of what is involved in curriculum will come from those scholars who can make the heuristic leap from the data they must know well to the ethical roots of their concern.

The second proposition concerns an assumption some educators tend to make—the assumption that the measure of education is solely its products. That the product is a measure of education I cannot deny, but for two reasons the matter does not end there. The first reason is best expressed in terms of what I should like to call the premise of ethical continuity. This premise asserts that education is properly concerned with the ethical aspects of its product; that exceedingly little is known and is likely to be known (people being as complex as they are) about controlling this aspect of education's product; that the very best the educator can do, therefore, is to rely on the general tendency for good to produce good and pay very careful attention to the ethical qualities of the process of education.

Secondly, concern over the product of education seems somehow to obscure the fact that the world the educator creates through the curriculum is a world inhabited by actual children as well as by potential adults.

Why then are educators often so willing to judge educational institutions by the characteristics of their pupil-products, and so unwilling to judge or even note the qualities of the situation itself? The philosophical problem of rendering an ethical judgment of a future entity is at least as complex as the problem posed by a present entity. Is it possible that the educator's preoccupation with products involves an escape, by removal in time, from the responsibility to see and value education in ethical terms altogether? The world we create through the curriculum is a real present world, a lived-in world, and a meaning world. Ought not the educator to know and respond to its meanings?

My second proposition, then, is that curriculum is to be thought of not only as producing but also as meaning and as lived in. It is a mortal thing, and Gerard Manley Hopkins writes of mortal things:

> Each mortal thing does one thing and the same:
> Deals out that being indoors each one dwells;
> Selves—goes itself; *myself* it speaks and spells;
> Crying *What I do is me: for that I came.*[22]

Notes

1. See, for example, Professor Huebner's "Curriculum Language and Classroom Meaning," in *Language and Meaning,* ed. James Macdonald and Robert Leeper (Washington, D.C.: ASCD, 1966).

2. Professor Dwayne Huebner has spoken about "critiquing" the curriculum; it is from his remarks that the idea for this idea developed. His thinking has helped me in this paper in ways that cannot be acknowledged by notes alone.

3. Mark Schorer, *The Story* (Englewood Cliffs, N.J.: Prentice-Hall, 1950).

4. Ibid., p. 3.

5. Cited by Schorer, ibid., p. 4.

6. Foreword to "IS 5," in E. E. Cummings, *Poems, 1923-1954* (New York: Harcourt, Brace, 1954).

7. Brewster Gheselin, ed., *The Creative Process* (Berkeley: University of California Press, 1952).

8. Albert Einstein, *Relativity,* trans. Robert W. Lawson (New York: Crown Publishers, 1961).

9. See Abrams's discussion of the transition from the classical to the romantic attitude in poetry, in M. H. Abrams, *The Mirror and the Lamp* (New York: W. W. Norton, 1958).

10. Michael Polanyi, *Personal Knowledge* (Chicago: University of Chicago Press, 1958).

11. Writing from a psychoanalytic point of view, Lawrence Kubie arrives

at a very similar conclusion. He too sees the creative process as ubiquitous in its general characteristics; creative work in science and art is subtended by the same psychological operations. See Lawrence S. Kubie, *Neurotic Distortion of the Creative Process* (New York: Noonday Press, 1961).

12. Huebner has (quite correctly, I think) referred to research as "a vehicle of empirical criticism." Dwayne Huebner, "The Tasks of the Curricular Theorist," mimeographed.

13. The reason for "ethical" reality is developed in the next section. Briefly, it has to do with the fact that curriculum is an environment for persons (Dewey, Macdonald), and the curriculum critic is responsible to these persons.

14. More will be said to this point in the next section.

15. Stephen Toulmin, *The Philosophy of Science: An Introduction* (New York: Harper & Row, 1960).

16. The different purposes served by school talk are analyzed by Dwayne Huebner in "The Tasks of the Curricular Theorist," mimeographed.

17. This should not be taken to imply that the teachers "intend" these meanings. The question of intent is complicated, and beyond the scope of this paper. For arguments on the question in the context of literary criticism, see the following: Rene Wellek and Austin Warren, *Theory of Literature* (New York: Harcourt, Brace & World, 1963); William K. Wimsatt, "The Intentional Fallacy," in *The Verbal Icon* (Lexington: University of Kentucky Press, 1967), pp. 3-21.

18. Toulmin, *Philosophy of Science*, p. 42.

19. Ibid., p. 64.

20. Ian Ramsey, *Models and Mystery* (London: Oxford University Press, 1964).

21. "Influence" need not be understood technologically, that is, as a means to an end. Rather it is to be taken here in the sense of "under the influence of," to describe a present relationship. The example below in the text of a magnet and filings illustrates the usage intended.

22. Gerard Manley Hopkins, "As kingfishers catch fire . . ." in *Poems by Gerard Manley Hopkins* (New York: Oxford University Press, 1948).

*The essay by George Willis is in part a commentary on the pre-
ceding essay by Mann. Willis explicates Mann's principal ideas and
explains why Mann's position, albeit a central one, is necessarily still
one among many alternative positions about curriculum criticism and
the critic's role. The essay describes means for identifying and judging between alternatives and points out some implications for curriculum as an area of thought and study and for those who do practical
curriculum work. The essay is basically an overview of issues and of
broad outlines in the development and uses in qualitative evaluation
of many specific techniques of curriculum criticism.*

*Willis suggests that the curriculum field itself incorporates as-
pects of both art and science and that for the field to develop fully it
must be self-consciously self-critical. Therefore, there are distinct
analogues between major aspects of the field and the humanities, and
the health of the field depends on the ability of curriculumists to
develop and to understand a variety of critical principles and methods. Careful scrutiny of analogous developments in the humanities
may inform the development of appropriate critical principles and
methods in curriculum.*

Mann's position that the critic's role is to disclose meanings embodied in the selection of those possibilities that in fact constitute the form a curriculum takes is, the essay suggests, one position among many for a basic reason that Mann himself provides. Specific pieces of criticism necessarily embody the choices made by specific critics about methodology and about what to focus on. In this sense, no one critical methodology can be considered "best," although differing methodologies may be appropriate for different critical tasks. Still, methodologies can be judged principally in terms of what Willis calls their "focal points," and the four principal focal points of literary criticism have distinct analogues in curriculum criticism. These focal points are the "work," or the curriculum itself (conceived narrowly as subject matter or broadly as environment); the "author," or the creator of the curriculum; the "world," or the overall educational and social milieu or environment of which the curriculum is a part; and the "audience," or those for whom the curriculum is intended. Methodologies may in fact include foci on more than one of these points, but in considering "work," the critic usually discloses meaning about form and implied intentions; in considering "author," meaning about biography and stated intentions; in considering "world," meaning about the nature of the universe or its parts; and in considering "audience," meaning about influences and modes of recognition. The introductions to the essays included in the "Cases" section of this volume identify the focal point(s) of the methodology employed in each case study.

The essay concludes by asserting that the aesthetic perspective it describes is not a simple alternative in educational evaluation, one which may or may not be chosen. Rather, it must be chosen to assure a full view of the complexities of educational environments. In adopting it a curriculum worker reorients practical perspectives on objectives, methods of curriculum development, curricular effects, and sources of values. In doing so, the curriculum worker may gain professional autonomy, become a discerning moral agent, and foster mental health.

5

Curriculum Criticism and Literary Criticism

George Willis

1. The Curriculum and the Humanities

The curriculum field is multidimensional for at least two powerful reasons.[1] First, insofar as the curriculum is a practical enterprise, it is an art as well as a science. While it is well for the curriculum worker to know the scientific principles, the empirical data, and the technological applications that inform much of his practice, it is equally well for him to be conversant with those aspects of art which come into play when what happens with a curriculum or in a classroom inevitably spills out beyond those scientific constructs he has chosen to employ. Second, insofar as curriculum is a theoretic enterprise, it must be self-conscious and self-critical. The curriculum theorist must be aware of and able to judge between competing rationales and canons of excellence for how curricula should be developed or practice carried out. He must use logic and discretion—in short, informed intelligence—in this task. The curriculum field, then, is multidimensional since it exists on two levels, the practical and the

This article originally appeared in *The Journal of Curriculum Studies*, May 1975. Reprinted by permission.

theoretical, since the practical employs aspects of both science and art, and since the theoretical must judge between competing theories.

If this basic assumption is correct, then clearly the principles and methods of either the natural or the social sciences do not exhaust those principles and methods which come into play in many of the dimensions of the curriculum field. Curriculum thought and practice, therefore, have much in common, in terms of subject matter, principles, and methodology, with the humanities. In fact, the author thinks that one of the most pressing, yet comparatively unrecognized, questions facing educationists is the extent to which education generally and the curriculum field particularly can and should be considered as a branch of the humanities rather than solely as a natural, social, technological, or professional science.

While ends and justifications for sciences, technologies, and professions can be found most usually in direct practical applications, the justifications for the humanities are more remote from practice. To be sure, practical applications there are, but the major justifying ends for the humanities are not found in directly demonstrable results, but rather in the quality of the inquiry they evoke and in the subsequent effect of this inquiry on the freeing and development of mind, imagination, creative potential, and sensibility. Presumably, the humanistically well-educated person may intelligently work out his own utilitarian applications, but these applications in themselves are largely extrinsic to the educational process, which in itself becomes a source of intellectual, social, emotional, and aesthetic values.

The humanities have traditionally proceeded, therefore, on the assumption that open inquiry of the highest quality will have beneficial effects on the perceptions, feelings, thoughts, and actions of the individual and perhaps ultimately on society at large, but that the proper procedure for fostering inquiry of high quality is by concentrating on what can be considered the subject matter of the humanities and on the development of principles and methods by which this subject matter can be put to humanistic uses. As the literary critic R. S. Crane puts it, the issue of quality in the humanities is largely a problem of critical scrutiny which "... depends upon the existing intellectual state of the art itself, that is to say, upon the sufficiency of the principles and devices in vogue among its practitioners to a full discovery of the values that lie within its scope."[2] The principles and methods of humanistic studies depend, therefore, on constant critical reappraisal. Additionally, the humanities have traditionally dealt with subject matter within which philosophical, ethical, religious, social, and scientific ideas have been embodied, and with methodology intended to assess the quality of these ideas, to place them within historical contexts, to understand differences in the various symbolic media through which they are expressed, and to analyze the symbolic structures through which they are presented. The humanities, then, are multidimensional for basically the same reasons that the curriculum field is multidimensional. The humanities exist on two levels, being concerned on the practical level with the artistic or aesthetic aspects of the representation of ideas and on the theoretical level with critical judgment about how this task is carried out.

Many of the problems of the curriculum field and the problems of the humanities are thus largely the same problems, for both areas focus on similar kinds of subject matter, apply similar kinds of principles and methodology, and both need subject themselves to similar kinds of critical self-scrutiny. Therefore, developments within curriculum have—either directly or potentially—distinct analogues within various branches of the humanities, and acquaintance with events in some of these branches may be most useful in informing critical appraisal of the curriculum field itself. For instance, many recent events in curriculum theory, development, and evaluation indicate that the curriculum field is currently undergoing a series of major conceptual changes. Basically the field is expanding the conceptual basis from which it draws theoretical models and the main modes of practice which subsequently follow. In doing so, it appears to be moving away from exclusive reliance on the now-classical technological curriculum model embodied in Ralph Tyler's famous rationale.[3] Within this process the field has begun to take increasing cognizance of the aesthetic as well as the scientific and technological dimensions of the curriculum, redefining and expanding the roles of both curriculum theorists and curriculum workers in ways consistent with considerations drawn from the humanities in general and from literary criticism particularly.

2. Curriculum Criticism

A major contribution to knowledge about the aesthetics of curriculum practice and to the relationship between curriculum theory and an analogous branch of the humanities, literary criticism, has been the paper "Curriculum Criticism" by John S. Mann.[4] In this paper Mann contends that the curriculum can be considered as a literary object and, hence, can be treated in many of the same ways that a literary critic treats a literary work. On this basis he outlines a function for the curriculum critic and differentiates it from the function of the practitioner.

Mann bases his work on two major assumptions: that education cannot be measured solely by its products and that educators have naively adopted a supposedly "objective" or "scientific" language which is instrumental and technological, but which is thus inadequate to describe everything which is important about educational situations. He suggests that educators develop a more adequate method of describing and appraising curricula, one which combines aspects of aesthetics and science, and this he describes as "curriculum criticism."

Accordingly, Mann asserts that a curriculum can be treated as a literary object and that criticism can focus on the "object" itself (the curriculum) rather than on the biography of the "author" (the curriculum developer or, perhaps, the teacher) or on the effect of the object on the "reader" (the student). The task of the curriculum critic, in this view, is to analyze and to explain what Mann calls the "design" of the object, especially to disclose the meanings of the author which are embodied in his selections of those possibilities which in fact constitute the form his work takes.

In this view of the nonscientific side of curriculum, the author is artist, symbolically representing a commentary upon life, the curriculum is art, the symbolic medium, and the curriculum critic is commentator upon the process, interpreting the symbolic representation. But what is especially important to keep in mind about this view is that the author as representer and the critic as interpreter and commentator are each faced with the same kind of methodological task and are each bound by the same kind of methodological limitations.

As Mann points out, when the artist sets out to make a symbolic commentary upon life, he is faced with a virtually limitless number of possibilities; and in his selections of what to represent, how to represent it, and in what context to represent it, he creates an assertion of meaning. But the critic, too, is faced with perhaps as limitless a number of possibilities in making his own selections of how to interpret and to convey the author's meanings, as well as how to convey his own. Clearly, the critic's own choices about these matters represent his own assertion of meaning as well. Just as no work of art exhausts all possible meanings, no critique is exhaustive; the critic *must* be selective about his own subject matter and methodology, for he must delimit a virtually limitless universe of possibilities.

The critic's statements, therefore, are not logically derived directly from the data before him, but are the somewhat artful result of his adoption of a methodology entailing his own critical principles and assumptions and a pattern of selection constituting his choices about subject matter and imposed on the data. In point of fact, the curriculum critic's task is more complex than the literary critic's, for whereas a literary object is static and solely artistic, a curriculum object combines both scientific and artistic considerations and, as applied in a classroom, does not do the critic the courtesy of holding still.

Nonetheless, as Mann describes the curriculum critic's role, it is to explain certain designs or patterns of choice within a school situation primarily by identifying the assumptions and principles which the designs entail. The critic's role includes consideration of the data used by the practitioner but tends to transform the practitioner's technological modes of conduct to aesthetic modes.

Whereas the practitioner employs his stock in the context of discovering means and ends, the critic may employ the same stock as data for his analysis of the design of education events. Where the practitioner seeks solutions to problems, the critic seeks meaning in the manner in which problems are posed and solved. Where the practitioner may customarily evaluate his practices by examining their consequences, the critic construes practices as falling in designs that may be accounted for as expressions of meaning.[5]

In short, the curriculum critic needs to be aware of (and perhaps able to employ) the practitioner's subject matter and methodology as well as to be able to use his own, just as the literary critic needs to be aware not only of the principles and uses of criticism but also of the subject matter and methodology of the author.

This brief summary does not, of course, do justice to either the complexity or the range of Mann's paper. Nor should it be construed, on the other hand, as indicating that "Curriculum Criticism" offers a final or exhaustive word on the aesthetics of curriculum or on the relationship between curriculum and literature. For instance, Mann does not deal directly with philosophical problems concerning intentionality. Nonetheless, "Curriculum Criticism" is both a cogent and a timely contribution to the professional curriculum literature, first because it firmly establishes the notions that curriculum people can deal with aesthetics, that they can do so by treating a curriculum as a literary object, and that the curriculum field can be informed by developments and methodology derived from humanistic studies; and secondly because it establishes these notions at a time when events in the curriculum field can be interpreted perhaps only in the light of the kind of conceptual apparatus it identifies. Despite these contributions of "Curriculum Criticism," the present author knows of no direct efforts in the subsequent professional literature to refine or to extend Mann's work, and he feels that this lack is unfortunate. Consequently, part 3 of this paper places Mann's view of curriculum criticism in a metatheoretical framework, part 4 identifies some of the implications this conceptual framework may have for assessing theoretical developments in the curriculum field, and part 5 suggests how use of curriculum criticism may influence educational practice.

3. Criticism of Criticism: For Pluralism

The fact that the curriculum field is multidimensional is perhaps sufficient in itself to justify a pluralism in subject matter and methodology within curriculum inquiry.[6] For instance, the problems and scope of the humanities are sufficiently broad to incorporate a wide variety of methodologies. Yet, this point is also true of various branches within the humanities, including literary criticism. In point of fact, literary critics have developed over a long period of time a number of alternative theoretical positions. Therefore, insofar as "Curriculum Criticism" identifies a function which is drawn from and which, in effect, corresponds to one general theoretical position in literary criticism, it represents only one of the alternative positions from which analogous positions in the curriculum field can be drawn. The present author thinks that much of the confusion attending the present expansion of the conceptual basis for curriculum theorizing can be in part dispelled by recognizing this point.

These issues are, however, to raise the question of whether differing theoretical positions become competing or complementary alternatives, be they in the humanities generally, in literary criticism, or in the curriculum field. There is, of course, no easy answer to this question, but perhaps the most satisfactory one can be found in the considerations introduced in part 2. Since a theoretical representation of any set of phenomena is necessarily an abstraction of some—not all—of the qualities the phenomena embody concretely, any maker of theory is also necessarily a maker of choices about what to represent and how to represent it. Theory making is therefore in its own right an artistic pursuit, the theorist making choices from a virtually limitless number of possibilities. In effect, then, all theories and, hence, all critical positions are based upon a series of assumptions and principles which can be thought of as embodying the theorist-critic's methodology and even his selection of what constitutes his subject matter.

While this point does not imply that all theoretical or critical utterances are equally valid, it does imply that at least the critic's choice of subject matter and methodology is something of a personal and a practical decision and, furthermore, that no particular methodology can be fixed as "best," for differing methodologies necessarily deal with differing critical problems or emphases. R. S. Crane describes this view of literary criticism as "pluralistic" and "instrumentalist," pointing out:

> ... it would appear that the only satisfactory approach to the existing diversities of criticism must be one that recognizes a plurality of distinct critical methods—each of them valid or partially valid within its proper sphere—and that insists, consequently, upon ascertaining, in methodological terms, what a given critic is doing, and why. . . .[7]

Despite the kind of relativism a pluralistic view of criticism provides, there are, nonetheless, two general ways of judging between differing critical positions. First, given a critic's choice of subject matter and methodological principles, one can assess the degree of consistency between various critical utterances and the methodology adopted. In other words, one can assess the degree of self-consistency within an individual critic's position.[8] Secondly, one can assess what can be considered the scope or the explanatory power of a critical position. A curriculum, just as a literary object, is doubtless the result of a large number of causes, most of which operate through the "author." In general, the most adequate critical position is the one which provides the means for explaining the greatest number of these causes while retaining sufficient flexibility to determine which causes are the most important in each individual case. In other words, a critical position can be judged in terms of its ability to determine significance and to explain meaning—in short, in terms of its ability to illuminate the critical enterprise.

If all or most of the foregoing remarks about the nature of the humanities, of literary criticism, and of the curriculum field are correct, then a number of tasks are indicated for curriculum researchers. While the field should, of course, continue to function on the practical level and to develop schema for assessing practice as it now does in a somewhat naturalistic way, it must also perform the essentially metatheoretical task of becoming increasingly self-conscious and self-critical about the pluralistic subject matters and methodological principles which it does or can employ. These metatheoretical tasks can be well accomplished perhaps only by a careful comparative analysis of principles—past, present, and future—within curriculum and within related disciplines in which definite analogues exist. Furthermore, these efforts will be particularly timely if the curriculum field is in fact broadening its conceptual basis to include aesthetic and humanistic concerns along with technological and scientific. More specifically, these tasks include the following kinds of things: continued debate on the necessity for pluralism in subject matter and methodology; critical appraisal of the history of the curriculum field and of its current principles, with an eye toward developing new (or reviving old) principles and formulating criteria for judging comparative merits and demerits of these principles[9]; development of some kind of classificatory or taxonomical arrangement of actual or potential subject matters and methodologies; and assessment of analogous developments in related fields.

4. Focal Points in Curriculum Criticism

While Mann has established the notion of curriculum criticism within the professional literature, he has chosen to limit himself to a subject matter which, of course, does not exhaust the range of subject matters with which literary critics have traditionally dealt. In choosing to focus critical attention on the literary or curriculum object itself, he is, in effect, also choosing *not* to focus on other critical subject matters. In choosing to develop methodological principles appropriate to his subject matter, he is also choosing *not* to develop methodological principles appropriate to other subject matters. Yet, if the arguments for pluralism in part 3 hold good, clearly the field needs to develop a pluralism of critical approaches to the curriculum and a metatheory which permits and makes rational this kind of pluralism.[10]

Let us now assume that in directing the curriculum critic's attention to the curriculum object itself, Mann is suggesting that the critic focus on what literary critics have often called the "work." Mann suggests that the critic examine the pattern of choices inherent in the design of the "work" and through a process of inference thereby disclose meaning. This is very similar to what the advocates of the New Criticism, for instance, have suggested as the task of the literary critic: analyze how meaning is embodied in the form and even the content of the "work" itself. In the hands of an accomplished critic this approach is a powerful tool; inferences are tight and all kinds of speculations—especially about influences on and motivations of the author—can be avoided.

However, if we ask the question, "Whose meaning?" (as eventually we must), we find that attempting to confine inferences totally within the evidence provided by the "work" itself is strictly impossible. For instance, the meaning could be the author's intended meaning, or more diverse meanings suggested somewhat unintentionally to various members of his audience, or a meaning read into the "work" by the critic or one he himself in part creates and in part reveals through his criticism. In fact, the meaning might even be considered a kind of pattern immanent in the structure of the world and manifesting itself in the "work." The point, of course, is not that all these potential sources of meaning are equally plausible or equally deserving of attention at any one time, but that they cannot be totally excluded from critical discourse.[11] When a curriculum critic or a literary critic chooses one focal point as the subject matter for his considerations, he neither does nor can commit himself to excluding all considerations of alternative focal points, but he does commit himself to employing methodological principles which are appropriate to the focal point he has chosen. Focal points serve to center inquiry around certain areas, not to exclude other areas from investigation.

If the curriculum field can be schooled by developments and methodology in literary criticism, then curriculum criticism may eventually adopt either the same or a similar pattern of focal points. In addition to the "work," subject matters which literary critics have traditionally chosen to center their methodology around can be described as "author," "world," and "audience," although some critics have developed methodologies directed to the relationships between two or even more of these focal points. In general, however, it is safe to say that even when the most accomplished critics have shifted their attention from subject matter to subject matter, they have found it necessary to develop alternative methodological principles and that, therefore, not even the most accomplished critics have developed a single methodology appropriate to all focal points within the range of critical discourse. Basically, the best critic is the one who has the largest number of flexible, explanatory methodologies at his disposal and the intelligence to know how and when to apply a methodology for appropriate humanistic purposes.

Turning back to the "work," it is clear that Mann's approach to this focal point is similar to the approach of the New Criticism to literature. However, not all literary critics analyze design or structure in order to disclose certain kinds of meaning, but rather in order to classify properly the literary object as a type or within a genre. In other words, within this focal point widely differing analytic methodologies can and do exist. Just as the curriculum field needs further efforts similar to Mann's, it also needs to develop schema within which curriculum objects can be classified according to their designs. The extent to which a curriculum makes provision for its own modification in practice according to the interests and purposes of students might provide some basis for classification, for instance.

The "author" is a focal point in literary criticism within which a very complex set of problems has generated a wide variety of approaches; perhaps as complex a set of analogues will eventually be developed within curriculum criticism. Literary critics have employed a wide variety of means to assess what can be loosely considered as the biography of the "author." These means have included the consideration of events within his life; all manner of outside influences upon him; his place within a community; his philosophical orientation; his personal, psychological, or phenomenological make-up; and his attitudes and intentions, especially toward his artistic function and, on the one hand, his observing of the "world" and, on the other, his making of his "work." In curriculum criticism, problems in dealing with this focal point are compounded by the fact that a curriculum as developed and applied is often created by a group, its members thereby jointly becoming its "author." Clearly, a great number of approaches to this focal point are warranted, and while a vast amount of work remains to be done, much has already been accomplished. Basically, studies within this focal point can be directed at such topics as the philosophies, intentions, motivations, personalities, and techniques of curriculum people; the roles these people play and the relationships between these roles; and the economic, political, and social considerations which influence curriculum development and practices. For instance, the curriculum field appears currently to have renewed interest in investigating the process of curriculum deliberation, and some promising work in this area can be represented by a paper by Decker Walker, "A Naturalistic Model for Curriculum Development."[12] In it Walker outlines a descriptive model which provides assessment of the decision points, assumptions, and principles with which the "author" creates a curriculum object.

One of the fundamental questions in literary criticism is the extent to which literature can and should be a matter of a writer's self-expression or a matter of reflecting the outside "world" itself. Educators, of course, must pay considerable attention to how accurately data representing the "world" are reflected in curriculum objects. (Note, for instance, the current criticism of books which reflect diminished or stereotyped roles for minority groups or women.) The question ultimately is metaphysical, but insofar as the curriculum is concerned with knowledge, it becomes for the curriculum critic an essentially epistemological one. To what extent is knowledge a priori and intellectually discovered? To what extent is it a posteriori and personally or socially created and reconstructed? Many studies dealing with philosophy, especially with epistemology, or devoted to the structures of knowledge or to the structures of the disciplines are directed to this third focal point, the "world."

The fourth and final focal point in literary criticism, the "audience," has in the curriculum field a very distinct analogue, the student, to which considerable attention has been devoted. Since at least the time of Aristotle, critics have been concerned with how

literature has affected its readers. They have not, however, been primarily concerned with the uniformity of the effect of a piece of literature on all members of its "audience," generally recognizing the
complexity of the considerations which literary and aesthetic response entails. Unfortunately, this has not been the case in the curriculum field, and in recent decades the dominant modes of thought
and practice have been devoted to how narrowly defined responses
can be efficiently evoked in members of the "audience" as nearly
universally as possible. For instance, within this focal point the curriculum field has made extensive use of the Tyler rationale. Whereas
for technological purposes this rationale has served the field well, for
aesthetic and humanistic purposes it has served abominably, corresponding to the kind of Marxist criticism which maintains that the
only "artistic" considerations of any importance are the directly
propagandistic results that a work of art achieves. Literary critics
have ordinarily avoided patently technological assumptions in dealing
with the "audience" perhaps because response to a highly symbolic
medium is so obviously cognitive, inward, and personal. For instance,
it makes no sense to judge the "correctness" of a response to a piece
of music. It often makes no sense to judge the "correctness" of a
response to a piece of literature. Correspondingly, it may make no
sense to judge the "correctness" of a response to a symbolic or representational portion of a curriculum. Literary critics have, therefore,
paid considerable attention to such things as the modes of recognition and the conventions employed by the "audience" in interpreting
or simply reacting to the "work," including the "audience's" place
within a community, and its philosophy, attitudes, and psychological
or phenomenological makeup. Clearly, much significant work in curriculum has been done in some of these areas,[13] but while nonetheless recognizing the real differences between literature and curriculum, the author looks forward to the day when the rationales most
widely employed in the curriculum field can treat the "audience"
with even a modicum of the sophistication currently within the range
of literary critics.

5. Practical Uses of Curriculum Criticism

Thus far the paper has dealt primarily with the theoretical uses
of curriculum criticism. For instance, part 4 has suggested that focal

points drawn from literary criticism may be useful to curriculum theorists as ways of organizing the subject matter of the curriculum field and of determining the appropriateness of varying methodologies. The theoretical uses of curriculum criticism, then, concern the reorientation of theoretical perspectives. But what of the practical perspectives of the curriculum worker? What does it mean to a curriculum worker to look at a curriculum as he might a literary object? Of what use are the focal points of curriculum criticism in organizing practical concerns? Such questions are not idle, for a reorientation of practical perspectives perhaps implies direct changes in practice itself. The concluding section of this paper sketches a brief answer to these questions.

First, it is well to establish that there is an ontological basis as well as a metaphorical and heuristic basis for the use of the focal points described above as ways of reorienting practice. Ian Westbury and William Steimer, in a passage suggesting how curriculum practice might be considered, provide some indication of this basis.

The study of Curriculum *as means* should become an enquiry into the devices and modes for actualizing the interactions of the commonplace curricular elements: subject, student, milieu, and teacher. Education in and for curriculum research becomes a training in this quasi-discipline; education in and for Curriculum becomes a study of curriculum research *and* a practical study of the application of the fruits of curriculum research to real and educative ends.[14]

"Subject," "teacher," "milieu," and "student," what Westbury and Steimer call "commonplace curricular elements" or "subject matter elements" and what may well comprise the primordial stuff of curriculum, clearly correspond to the "work," "author," "world," and "audience" of the literary critic. The apparent soundness of this correspondence adds substantial warrant to the belief that the focal points of the literary critic are quite compatible with the material of the curriculum worker and, therefore, that they can and perhaps should be adopted into the curriculum field without dislocation of patently curricular considerations.

The author agrees with Westbury and Steimer's suggestions about practice. Yet there is some categorical blurring between their "elements" and the literary critic's focal points, and the former's terminology has the advantage of being readily identifiable with distinctly curricular problems. Nonetheless, certain objections can be raised against the eventual adoption of the former's more practically rooted terminology as descriptors for the focal points in curriculum. For instance, "subject" and "teacher" (as opposed to "work" and "author") eliminate much of the implication that the creation of a curriculum is at least in part a self-consciously artistic process, while "milieu" (as opposed to "world") perhaps invites analysis of the particular environment within which a curriculum is put into practice, rather than of how a broader environment is represented by that curriculum. In any case, for the time being at least, the influence of differing terminology on the reorientation of the practical perspectives of curriculum workers remains an open question.

But aside from problems of terminology or of a basis in ontology, and bearing in mind that this paper has asserted curriculum practice includes aspects of both science and art and has argued for a pluralism of valid approaches to art, consider, finally, how a curriculum worker might reorient his practical perspectives as he shifts from scientific and technological modes to aesthetic modes of considering curriculum. His considerations would probably include the objectives of a curriculum, the methodology employed in curriculum building and implementation, the effects of a curriculum, and the sources of value that underlie these concerns.

Put rather simply, the curriculum worker thinking scientifically and technologically might well adopt the curricular elements identified by Westbury and Steimer and might even focus on the interactions between them rather than consider them as unitary phenomena. However, the dominant emphasis, as Mann suggests, is on the solution to practical problems. For instance, what specific curriculum will increase a particular student's ability to read and, therewith, his potential usefulness to society? Curricular objectives are rooted directly in these solutions. The process of building the curriculum consists of discerning and validating the relationship between means and ends, in part analytically but largely through considering the results of empirical surveys of results previously obtained with as nearly identical curricula and students as possible. The effects of the curriculum are judged in terms of the observed degree of fit with the effects predicted as useful solutions to the practical problems. While engaged in this process, the curriculum worker attempts to use as many scientific constructs and data sources as feasible (for instance, an analysis of his own characteristics as a teacher or of the salient characteristics of the milieu) and to gather information pertinent to the future modification of the curriculum, but throughout the entire process strong emphasis clearly falls on the efficiency of the practical solution. In short, the dominant source of value within all of these concerns is utilitarian.

In contrast, the curriculum worker considering the curriculum as a literary object not only commonly thinks of the teacher as author, of subject or curriculum as work of art, of the milieu as world, and of the student as audience, he also necessarily thinks of the relationships between these focal points. For instance, the author, in reacting to his experiences of and his view of the world, selects and reorders for representation portions of the world and of his reactions to them. This representation exists first primarily as ideas within the author's mind, but he embodies it in a form that becomes the work. The work, therefore, is a selective representation of a portion of the world and a portion of the author's experience of it, and it leads the audience to a partial recreation of the author's ideas and experiences, as well as to the creation of new ideas and experiences. The author, therefore, through the work causes the audience to recreate and to experience his own world view, but also to create a new set of experiences comprising a world view at least partially new. The audience, therefore, sees the world doubly, through its own pristine, literal vision and through the representational vision of the artist, and this bifocal vision creates a new and heightened vision of the world.

The curriculum worker thinking this way considers his task as one of selecting and representing within an appropriate curricular form elements of subject matter drawn from the world itself and also from his own interpretation of them in order to reorder the experience of students at least partly in unpredictable and new ways. In contrast to the technologically oriented curriculum worker, he is concerned principally with problems of how to represent meaning for both literally accurate and nonliterally imaginative and novel interpretation. In being thus concerned he doubtless considers a virtually limitless number of problems about the relationships between vision, world, form, and outcomes. He considers curricular objectives not as the solutions to practical problems, but in their potential for evoking a wide range of literal and imaginative responses. He considers the process of building a curriculum not as the validation of the relationship between means and ends, but in the selection of a coherent form, which is in itself a source of intrinsic value. He considers the effects of the curriculum not in their degree of fit with the effects predicted as useful, but principally in the breadth and depth, in the explanatory, emotional, and ethical power of the responses evoked. The dominant source of value that underlies his concern is not utilitarian; it includes intellectual, social, emotional, aesthetic, and ethical sources of value as well.[15] In short, whereas the technologically oriented curriculum worker asks questions about the usefulness and efficiency of replicating literal portions of the world, the aesthetically oriented curriculum worker asks questions about the evocation of multiple responses to representational portions of the world and about their multiple uses within an ethical framework as the student-as-audience reconstructs his personal experience of the world.

While these two perspectives toward practice are not, of course, mutually exclusive, there are certain advantages for the curriculum worker in at least partially incorporating the focal points, the methodology, and the values of the aesthetic or literary perspective immanent within the idea of curriculum criticism. These broaden the range of considerations which enter into curriculum practice, particularly the range of choices which the curriculum worker may make, and this form of pluralism may in itself be a source of intrinsic value. They increase the flexibility and fluidity of the decisional context within which these considerations may be applied. They increase the tentativeness with which the teacher-as-author's views are to be accepted by the student-as-audience, but they also, therefore, increase the potential for significantly changing the audience, since the members of the audience become discerning and autonomous moral agents within the process of change. They make possible a similar kind of change for the curriculum worker himself, for in his role as maker of artistic choices he is also heightening his own moral vision. And, lastly, they increase the professional autonomy of the curriculum worker, for he makes choices about representational and ethical matters as well as about literal and applied.

The professional autonomy of the curriculum worker is a significant practical matter. One of the often unrecognized sources of tension in the curriculum worker's role is a tendency to be pushed toward the scientific and technological perspective toward practice alone, to accept the notion that a curriculum should be judged solely in terms of its directly applied results, usually in a narrow sphere, rather than in terms of the humanistic possibilities it opens up. Often the curriculum worker resists this push but does not know why. The practical uses of curriculum criticism to reorient the practitioner's perspectives include his explicit recognition of the full range of possibilities within his role. This recognition is itself important not only because it directly influences practical choices, but because it eliminates a source of professional tension, perhaps improving the practitioner's mental health and certainly creating necessary conditions for him to perform his practice as an autonomous professional. The final reason, then, for raising the issue of the practical uses of curriculum criticism is to enable the curriculum worker to see the limits of using solely scientific and technological reasoning and values to guide his practice, to enable him to see differences—especially ethical differences—between teaching predetermined subject matter and engaging in a professional discipline involved in teaching curricula considered as works of art. The change from a solely technological perspective on practice to a disciplinary professional perspective, for which there is an ontological basis, is desirable, therefore, for professional, ontological, and humanistic reasons.

This paper as a whole points to why curriculum is as complicated as the humanities. A specific curriculum, therefore, is never purely literal; it shares the same functions of any work of art. In this case, the aesthetic perspective on curriculum is not simply an alternative perspective which may or may not be chosen, but one which must be chosen (at least in combination with the more literal perspective) in order to assure a comprehensive and full view of curriculum as a theoretical discipline and as a practical art.

The author believes that examination of the foregoing considerations by the curriculum field can help to dispel confusion and generally to increase knowledge about the aesthetic and humanistic uses of the curriculum. This paper has offered considerations drawn from the humanities and has provided a brief overview of focal points within literary criticism. It has suggested that the curriculum field further examine subject matters and methodologies drawn from literary criticism and from other fields within the humanities where analogues may exist. It has suggested that the practical uses of these considerations lead to the broadening of the curriculum worker's perspectives and, hence, to more adequate modes of practice.

What is not important is that curriculum people adopt precisely those focal points and methodologies which this paper has described, nor that they attempt to reach universal agreement on critical subject matters and methodological principles. What is important is that curriculum people develop subject matters and methodologies appropriate to both the theoretical and the practical dimensions of the field, that they know what they are about, and that they communicate effectively when differences exist. This task may require the development of new conceptual apparatus and of what in effect is a new language of curriculum criticism, or it may simply require putting our present but imperfect concepts and language to an increasingly generous and clarifying range of uses.

Notes

1. A number of the ideas presented in parts 1 and 3 of this paper are drawn from R. S. Crane, ed., *Critics and Criticism: Ancient and Modern* (Chicago: University of Chicago Press, 1952). See especially pp. 1-12.

2. Ibid., p. 4.

3. Ralph W. Tyler, *Basic Principles of Curriculum and Instruction* (Chicago, Ill.: University of Chicago Press, 1949).

4. John S. Mann, "Curriculum Criticism," *The Record* 71, no. 1 (1969): 27-40. The essay is chap. 4 of this volume.

5. Ibid., p. 35.

6. A short paper urging this kind of pluralism is Morris Finder, "Justification for Pluralism in Curricular Inquiry" (n.d.), mimeographed.

7. Crane, *Critics and Criticism*, p. 9.

8. For examples of this kind of technique, see George Willis, "The Concept of Experience in Major Curriculum Literature: 1918-1970" (Ph.D. diss., Johns Hopkins University, 1971).

9. See n. 8.

10. Joseph Schwab has addressed himself to this problem in *The Practical: A Language for Curriculum* (Washington, D.C.: National Education Association, 1970). While Schwab indicates that the curriculum field should increasingly direct attention toward practical and away from theoretical concerns, he himself is, nonetheless, building a metatheory that permits and encourages pluralism in both practice and criticism.

11. Mann does not suggest that they should be excluded. He suggests the development of critical methodology directed toward analyzing meanings inherent in the "work." This kind of methodology is currently sparsely represented in the curriculum field.

12. Decker F. Walker, "A Naturalistic Model for Curriculum Development," *School Review* 80, no. 1 (1971): 51-65.

13. For instance, work which has increased the awareness of educators that a student's responding to a curriculum in unanticipated ways may be a func-

tion of inaccurate anticipation of the student's modes of recognition, rather than of a deficiency in those modes.

14. Ian Westbury and William Steimer, "Curriculum: A Discipline in Search of Its Problems," *School Review* 79, no. 2 (1971): 243-67.

15. For a discussion of these sources of value in educational practice, see John Walton, *Introduction to Education: A Substantive Discipline* (Waltham, Mass.: Xerox College Publishing, 1971), pp. 119-24.

The essay by Edward F. Kelly deals with three principal tasks. Kelly outlines a brief description of criticism in general; develops what he calls "a rhetoric for the curriculum" (basically a way of critically interpreting the curriculum); and explains how critical judgments are formulated, justified, and made credible. In accomplishing these tasks the essay develops a reasonably comprehensive view of the nature of qualitative evaluation in education and of the specific "language" of curriculum criticism.

As does the preceding essay by Willis, Kelly's points out that there are some distinct analogies between curriculum evaluation and literary criticism and that both forms of criticism are characterized by diversity. Still, any form of criticism consists of common, interrelated processes, and Kelly identifies four principal ones, which he calls "description," "analysis," "interpretation," and "evaluation."

The "rhetoric for the curriculum" examined in the essay is a group of concepts that can be borrowed from literary criticism and used in curriculum criticism as "a basis for investigating the manner of a curriculum evaluation." These concepts include "metaphor," "point of view (voice)," "plot (order)," and "theme." At its most basic, metaphor is a way of saying one thing but meaning another,

112

and in this broad sense the concept includes all forms of figurative language that might in fact be included in a curricular critique. The essay gives examples of curriculum evaluations that contain figurative language and points out that the assumptions embedded in such language often go unnoted. Point of view, or voice, is the manner in which something is related: for instance, the psychological frame of reference from which a story is told. Once again, the ordinary forms of quantitative curriculum evaluation are written as if "personalness" were absent, and the attitudes and values of the evaluator remain largely undisclosed. Plot, or order, is basically the way incidents are ordered in time to show causal relationships. In curriculum criticism, plot is closely tied up with description, and much depends on what the critic observes, how he makes inferences, and what he chooses to emphasize. Theme relates point of view and plot, resulting in what can be considered as the idea (actually a composite of many major and minor meanings) of the work. Curricular themes, then, are expressions of meaning embodied in the choices which comprise the curriculum itself.

The essay discusses at some length the relationships between description, judgment, and prescription, and the process of inference used by the critic in dealing with these relationships. Judgment is central to the critical task. It grows directly out of description and leads directly to prescription. In this sense judgment is the expression of rational preferences manifest in making choices, and the critic must be aware of how specific judgments may be justified and of what may make them seem credible to different audiences. Kelly suggests that for a judgment to be made publicly reasonable it should contain three statements: of the judgment itself, of the reasons for the judgment, and of the norms that show the reasons to be good ones. A judgment can then be justified in terms of whether the norms were reached and in terms of whether the norms were appropriate.

The introductions to the essays included in the "Cases" section of this volume identify the way many of these case studies use the rhetorical concepts Kelly has explicated and how some reach critical judgments.

6

Curriculum Criticism and Literary Criticism: Comments on the Analogy

Edward F. Kelly

Implicit in Ian Westbury's review of the literature on curriculum evaluation was a belief that the traditional perspectives on curriculum evaluation were narrow and could profitably be expanded to include concepts, methodologies, and strategies from other fields.[1] Westbury noted the relevance of the writings of Mann and Olson and said that the analogies relating curriculum evaluation and literary criticism "seem to be worth explicating."[2]

Before I begin that explication, some background is necessary. Literary criticism and curriculum evaluation have a number of characteristics in common. One of the most striking is diversity. For example, the changing social and scientific forces of the past two thousand years have provided literary criticism with a variety of perspectives. The ancient Greeks believed that art could be judged by fixed criteria—music by rules of harmony, drama by Aristotle's three unities. So did the heirs of the classical tradition—Samuel Johnson, to name one example.

Modern criticism originated with the romantic view of art,

This article originally appeared in *Curriculum Theory Network* 5, no. 2 (1975): 98-106. Reprinted by permission.

which gained wide acceptance by the late eighteenth century. Kant, for example, held that art was founded not on rules but on genius, and that beauty was consequently a matter of taste rather than the satisfaction of some external set of criteria. As an outgrowth of Kant's concern with the internal aspects of a work of art, Walter Pater and George Moore began to develop the rationale for impressionistic criticism. Both saw the critic's true function as an artful, suggestive, and above all, sympathetic response to the genius of art and literature.

Classical and impressionistic criticism have parallels in curriculum evaluation. Look, for example, at the different points of view from which a test score may be interpreted. According to what might be termed "classical test theory," the observed score contains a certain amount of deviation or error that separates it from the unknown "true" score. (Similarly, classical criticism assumes a discrepancy between a work of art and an idealized conception of artistic truth.) Generalizability theory, on the other hand, is analogous to the romantic theory of criticism. It seeks not to identify the error component of an observed score, but rather to express how well that score may represent a universe of possible scores. Both generalizability theory and the romantic theory of criticism view their objects not in a discrepancy model, but in a relational or dispositional one, preserving the organic unity of the score and the work of art.

The professional critic of the arts and the curriculum evaluator hold as one of their primary goals the description of the phenomena they observe. My use of the term "description" follows Smith, who distinguishes four principal, yet overlapping phases of critical activity: description, analysis, interpretation, and evaluation. Smith defines description as "naming, identifying, and classifying, a kind of taking stock which inventories cognitively established aspects of a work of art."[3]

The difficulty of maintaining the descriptive intent of a passage without employing some analysis, interpretation, or evaluation is illustrated by the following excerpt from the report of a site visit to an Elementary and Secondary Education Act (ESEA) Title III project in Illinois. The project consisted of a nature study center designed for students from local school districts. The following passages were intended to describe the Center building and the surrounding area:

One is immediately struck with the isolation of the location . . . from communities, from schools and homes, from mass urban environments. The location is a "natural" . . . forested, birds, river, unpaved access road, nearby cornfield, limited public facilities . . . rural, pastoral. In contrast, the Center building is a beehive of human activity . . . bright colors, materials and equipment, files and desks . . . neat, clean, orderly. Indoor space with a tile floor, chairs in rows, tables in their places, museumlike exhibits . . . ready for the day's activity. Displays, models, cages, instruments to provoke, to interest, to entertain, perhaps to distract. A classroomlike space for multiple tasks . . . for orientation, for inclement weather, for follow-up, for meetings, for laboratory work, for in-service, for talking and looking out for emergencies, for testing.

Some forty-five acres of the site are across the river from the Center building. An absence of signs that tell you do or don't, no labels, no tricky gimmicks to call your attention to this or that, no printed words to invade the privacy of your thoughts and feelings. A solid structure to cross the waters to the larger site area . . . massive posts and timbers, firm and solid, not shaky or swaying, engineered to last. Like the entrance to another world . . . away from the familiar and commonplace in a child's life, outdoor space with design, rhythm, texture, freedom from restraints, unschoollike, a retreat.[4]

Through a mixture of description, characterization, interpretation, and evaluation, the passage reveals the atmosphere of the Center in addition to detailing the factual characteristics of its structure and surroundings. Not only does the passage establish the isolation of the area; it also suggests dimensions that are more aesthetic than factual: "Like the entrance to another world . . . away from the familiar and commonplace in a child's life . . . rhythm, texture . . . a retreat." Rich in language and evocative in intent, the paragraphs show a wide spectrum of rhetorical and figurative devices including contrast, understatement, metaphor, simile, personification, and hyperbole.

The audience of an evaluation requires a sound basis on which to decide whether the judgments and conclusions that have been made are sensible in view of the type of program that was in effect and the conditions under which it existed. Description, then, is vitally important; for it is through description that the evaluator reconstructs his object.

A Rhetoric for the Curriculum

My comparison of curriculum evaluation and literary criticism will focus on language. The term "rhetoric for the curriculum" refers to a group of concepts originating in literary criticism that can be used to develop curricular critiques. As initial elements for a critique, they have two uses. First, they will provide a basis for discussing and conceiving of curriculum according to concepts that are more commonly thought of as the property of literature and its criticism; second, a basis for investigating the manner of a curriculum evaluation. I will offer examples to illustrate the application of the concepts to curriculum evaluation. The four concepts discussed are metaphor, point of view (voice), plot (order), and theme. The role of metaphor is given precedence, since it colors much of what follows.

Metaphor

A way of saying one thing and meaning another, metaphor allows what Frost called "the pleasure of ulteriority" as it joins unrelated notions together.[5] Richards saw metaphor as composed of a literal "vehicle" and an affective, allusive "tenor." His conception is a useful one. The vehicle of a metaphor is the succession of images that compose it, while the tenor is "the underlying idea or principle subject which the vehicle or figure means."[6] Through the play of tenor against vehicle, the writer invents, startles, and freshens language. But as Frost warned, he cannot exercise his imagination too freely without obscuring his meaning. It is indeed a challenge to be original, but it is equally challenging—and equally important—to employ the discipline that wards off confusion.

The interpretation of metaphor is also subject to certain restraints. One might ask, doesn't the reader's personal response determine the tenor? To some extent, yes. But the range of response to any metaphor is limited both by context and by previous use. The contextual limit is provided by the images, figures, and implications surrounding a metaphor. For example, in a poem about revolution, courage, and death, the tenor of "terrible beauty" carries an air of fear, sacrifice, and wondrous sorrow that is in part the product of images and supportive figures surrounding the phrase. In another context, the same words would assume a different "meaning."

Most people recognize metaphor as part of poetry. In fact, everyday language is full of metaphor. The child who once told me that my lesson was "a real waste" may have meant a waste of talent, money, energy, presence, or all of those things. The point is that by employing a figure as one of his descriptors of the classroom, the child identified a relationship that he inferred between one thing and another. Critical discourse, too, is often filled with metaphor. But curriculum evaluators seldom utilize metaphor effectively, as Clive Barnes does in this excerpt from a drama review: " 'Subject to Fits' . . . is a mad, mad play that is a joy to encounter. It is a cerebral play of dazzling intellectuality, manic wit and calm literacy. . . . It is a young man's play, bubbling with talent, almost arrogant in the joy it takes in hearing itself speak. It is an intricate play that is poised perilously on its own cleverness, its literary conceits and elegant stagecraft, but it balances and it works."[7]

The passage is filled with figure. Barnes could have sought out the specific structural components that composed the "balance" of the thing and expressed them in a literal fashion. He could have been extended and literal in his summary of the play, yet he chose principally metaphor to convey not only his observations on the play, but also his judgments on its effectiveness. Further on in the review, Barnes wrote that "The result (of the above) is something absolutely thrilling—a soul trip, an adventure of the heart and mind." What has occurred, from one point of view, is that the tenor of the metaphors of the introductory paragraph has been stated as emotional and intellectual thrill.

Metaphor in Curriculum Evaluation. Whether it has occurred as a result of a quest for precision, the application of a particular technology, or some other factor is unclear, but curriculum evaluators have characteristically employed a limited set of metaphors, principally from the realm of measurement, when they have built descriptions. The problem is not so much that we have done this, but that we may not have realized that we were doing it. Insofar as this occurs, we lose control of the tenor of our descriptions. Consider, for example, a passage from *Evaluation as a Tool in Curriculum Development,* a monograph by Lindvall and Cox. In their discussion of the need for criterion-referenced tests, the authors rely heavily on metaphors of measure.

Given that the IPI curricula are based in sequences of behavioral objectives organized into areas, levels, and units, it becomes the task of the test constructor to provide instruments that allow for placement of pupils at proper points in these sequences and that facilitate the continuous diagnosis of pupil achievement. If the instruments are to be used to help make decisions about pupils in reference to specific instructional objectives, then criterion-referenced measures are required. Criterion-referenced measures are designed so that they yield scores which can be interpreted in reference to the instructional objectives and give rather exact information as to where a pupil is in a learning sequence.[8]

Even though the metaphorical units may be unclear, it is apparent that the language is specialized and that several very powerful assumptions have been made about the people ("pupils") in the program. The obvious ones are that "achievement" or "progress" can be viewed and measured in a linear fashion, and that the outcomes of a curriculum can be prespecified in a behavioral fashion and "progress" toward (or away from) these objectives measured in an exact fashion. Furthermore, the passage itself suggests a metaphor for a curriculum that is structured in a microscopic fashion, and that structure implies that efficiency and its increase have strong relationships to worth.

A similar language typifies the report of a formative evaluation conducted by the Biological Sciences Curriculum Study (BSCS) on life science materials for the educable mentally handicapped. The following paragraph is taken from the discussion of the results of that evaluation.

The data indicate that age, WISC, total IQ, race and cerebral dysfunction are not significant predictors of success on the reduced post test. The pretest, however, is a highly significant ($p < .01$) predictor of success on the post test. Sex is also a significant ($p < .05$) predictor of success on the post test. These results indicate that prior knowledge of the concepts measured by the test instrument was the best determinant of whether or not the E.M.H. student attained a high score on the post test. Test analysis shows that 2/3 of the items were aimed at baseline information, hence this conclusion is not surprising, especially since achievement items were for the enabling objectives and were at a low cognitive level.[9]

Although it may be unclear exactly how each of the above examples qualifies as a metaphor of measure rather than of research or statistical inference, the point remains that the language of some curriculum evaluators is marked by a highly specialized figure. Just as Frost warned against letting metaphor get out of control to the point that meaning is obscured, the curriculum evaluator could profitably reexamine the influence that the metaphor of measure has had on his way of examining and describing curricula.

Point of View (Voice)

Although definitions of the term vary across traditions and theories, point of view has generally been taken as the manner in which the action[10] of a story is related. Sometimes referred to as the angle from which the author views a work, it is more appropriately construed as the psychological frame within which the narrator speaks.

What role has point of view played in curriculum evaluation? The angle from which an evaluator considers the nature and value of education, learning, and knowledge is the consequence of point of view. Similarly, point of view is reflected in the way the evaluator generally describes the program—attending to some aspects, dismissing others. Usually, though, the point of view remains undisclosed.

When he developed his theory of descriptions, Bertrand Russell understood that logically, an adequate description of an object would require collecting an infinite number of descriptions, each representing one of the infinite number of points from which an object could be seen. Clearly, the evaluator will never seriously consider such an effort, any more than Russell did. But if point of view is to be a concern, what the evaluator will have to consider is how he can best select an appropriate point of view, and when he will want to present divergent points of view.

Another aspect of point of view is suggested by Hastings, Wardrop, and Gooler as they present a model for evaluating geography courses. In reference to point of view, they said that after a systematic evaluation had been conducted to consider a wide range of complex costs, interests, and benefits, "the evaluator would then present a summary of these costs and benefits in such a form that his audience would be able to make judgments about the value of the program, from any of a number of points of view."[11] The implication is that not only can the evaluator adopt and present a wide range of points of view, but the audience can also choose to interpret the information from an equally diverse range of perspectives.

The evaluator's decisions about focus and design, about what he will attend to and dismiss, necessarily limit the applicable points of view that an audience may take on the story. In literature, if an author chooses to place the point of view in a child, the reader perceives a portrayal that is framed by that child's perspective. If the evaluator chooses to consider only program outcomes, for example, the points of view available to the audience are limited. The evaluator, like the author, must remember that the selection of a point of view can void alternative ones.

It is through the development of a "voice" that an author establishes part of the tone and humanity (or the lack of it) of his narrative. Moreover, it is partially through a sense of voice that critics and reviewers of literature have been able to establish themselves as meaningful and believable people who have responded to a work, felt it, and assessed its worth. *One thing that is absent from most curriculum evaluations is the sense that the evaluation was conducted by a real person who had some stake in the matter and who actually responded to the performance.*

The concept of voice tells how the narration of the action sounds. Much as one can speak of the tone of the remark, one can consider the tone or attitude reflected by a narrator. Hardy's voice in *Tess of the d'Urbervilles* is at times sympathetic or brooding, at others, sarcastic and mocking. Hemingway's omniscient voice in *The Old Man and the Sea,* on the other hand, is more matter of fact; yet it also betrays a deep concern and understanding of the old man's loss and foolishness.

It is through the voice of the narrative that the attitudes and values of the narrator are disclosed. His biases, his descriptive preferences, and the tone of the presentation are suggested by this term. While the angle from which the narrator views the object limits the range of things that he can say about that object, the voice that he adopts limits the range of attitude and value (tone) that will be reflected in the narrative.

The idea of voice seen as a way of expressing the person of the speaker, of letting the reader know where the narrator stands and how he feels about the subject, is a device that some evaluators have used with effectiveness.[12] The following quotation from a student-developed volume of teacher-course evaluations illustrates the presence of a voice that reflects an attitude toward the instructor.

The 362 students who deigned to tell all about History III left this unanimous and clear-cut opinion of lecturer [Smith]. He is a slightly weird and genuinely enthusiastic teacher with a sharp wit that everyone was too tired to catch as he rambled in circles like an unorganized, mousey inspiring revival minister with a cold.

What that means is that this was the usual survey course with the usual bell-shaped student reactions. Smith was just adequate for most of his students. He loves his subject and shows it, but most students just didn't respond well.[13]

Plot (Order)

In *Aspects of the Novel* E. M. Forster distinguishes between "plot" and "plot-line" according to incident, time, and causality.

Plot, as a series of incidents ordered in time showing a causal relationship, is distinguished from plot-line, a simple ordering of incidents over time. As a paradigm for plot-line, Forster suggests, "The
king died and then the queen died."[14] As a paradigm for plot, he
suggests, "The king died and then the queen died of grief." Forster
makes it clear that plot is intimately tied to characterization. One
begets the other.

Just as an author creates plot as he builds character through
dialogue, activity, and description, the curriculum evaluator's effort
to reconstruct the plot of a curriculum is based on his ability to collect pieces of it and to rebuild it by telling what people have said and
done. Understood as a reconstruction of experience, those aspects of
the curriculum that the evaluator chooses to depict mold the plot
that will appear in the evaluation. As different evaluators attend to
different elements, shifting their emphasis from what people said to
what they did, from what was observable to what was inferable, the
picture of the plot that is suggested also changes.

The question of adequacy has to haunt the evaluator. Faced
with the realization that it is hard enough to decipher the plot and
subplots that are embedded in a curriculum, he has the additional
worry of whether or not the evaluation of that curriculum has been
able to capture sufficient complexity. To say that the king died and
then the queen died is probably a great deal to say about a curriculum. To say, moreover, that the king died and then the queen died of
grief is to have unraveled mystery.

Some evaluators seem to assume that there is a mystery in curriculum and that it is the evaluator's responsibility to unfold it. Some
feel that the curriculum evaluator ought to be more concerned with
causality, with the "why" of the queen's death.[15] In order to do so,
in order to infer causality, the evaluator must borrow from science
the designs for causal inference.[16] But in so doing, he rarely has the
control, the budget, and wisdom, or the tenacity to pursue causality.
Audiences for curriculum evaluations, much like audiences for literary criticism, are frequently not concerned with the why of the
thing. Many times they want to know what happened next, and
whether it was worthwhile.

There is still another important sense in which concern with
plot or order may be seen as a similarity between criticism and evaluation. Both the critic and the evaluator are sometimes bemused by

the proper designation of the object under consideration into units or parts. For the evaluator, a language principally from the research tradition has brought the use of metaphors like "the unit of analysis" (meaning the student, the class, or the school, usually), and for the critic, it has brought terms like "incident," "episode," and "period." Whether the attempt has been to evaluate a work of literature or an educational program, the analytic effort has pressed for the designation of the object into a subsystem of components. In literature, analysis and grouping of related incidents can lead to the identification of secondary orderings or subplots that can be related. Thus terms like "loose" and "tight" can be applied to a narrative's plot and structure.[17]

Gagné has used the idea of a "unit of content" as the basis for a definition of curriculum. He said, *"A curriculum is a sequence of content units arranged in such a way that the learning of each unit may be accomplished as a single act, provided the capabilities described by specified prior units (in the sequence) have already been mastered by the learner."*[18] Thus a "unit of content" becomes *"a capability to be acquired under a single set of learning conditions,* among these conditions being certain specified prerequisite capabilities."[19] Based on this conception of curriculum, Gagné shows how a system of task analysis can be employed to construct and monitor a curriculum. He was probably correct when he wrote that such a methodology for "specifying a curriculum by deriving a hierarchy of capabilities beginning with educational objectives that described human performance, seems to have some important implications for research."[20] Considered as a technique for curriculum evaluation, Gagné's strategy raises all the questions and reservations inherent in the problem of specifying curricular outcomes in a behavioral fashion.[21]

Forster's concept of plot has clear limitations in literature, and these are reflected in its analogue in curriculum. Conceived as a causal ordering of incidents over time, it is easy to understand the confused dismay that met the publication of *Ulysses,* not to mention *Finnegans Wake.* The literature of free association or stream of consciousness, for example, does not readily submit to an analysis that seeks linearity and chronological ordering. The role of cause (and, consequently, of change) receives an alternative conception that does not anchor its referent in some evident logical reference. Rather, the rendition of action is based in the phenomenology of the individual and his alternative perceptions of the environment. Analogically, the search for curricular plot, best identified possibly with concerns over the "scope" and "sequence" of a curriculum, may prove somewhat inapplicable when these terms are imposed on a package that is not ordered through time or cause, but rather seeks an ordering that lies in the responsive psychology of the individual. For the curriculum evaluator, the search for logical contingency, for example, may be inappropriate in some alternative or "open" curricula where the ordering and contingency lie primarily in the principals' perceptions of the motifs and meanings of experience.

Theme

Theme is usually defined as an idea. Some clear voices from the realm of literary theory and poetry have encouraged the cessation of the search for answers to questions like, "What's the theme?" and "What does the story (poem) mean?" To this question, MacLeish concluded, "A poem should not mean / But be."[22]

To clarify the concept of theme, it is best to begin by employing the word in the plural form, since it is more accurate to seek the themes of a work than it is to search for a single one. Just as it is possible to discuss the major and minor plots of a story, its principal and minor actions, and its surface and underlying structure, it is appropriate to speak of primary and secondary, or major and minor themes. The identification of alternative themes within the same piece has long been a delight and a debate for the literary critic.

Theme relates point of view and plot. Residing in plot, evidenced by action, and supported by the structure of the work, theme works as a cohesive force. Like plot, it lies implicit in literature. With the exception of those instances where a hortatory or didactic emphasis is chosen by the author, the statement of theme is rendered as part and parcel of the work. The theme may be experienced in a series of related images, symbols, or figures. It may be represented by some incidents of plot, supported by others, and in turn, set in contradiction to itself by others. It can be twisted, played with, expanded, and compressed. As attempts to declare one of the themes of a work, the précis, the paraphrase, and the summary are inadequate to the task.

In curriculum evaluation, Stake identified the statement of educational goals as judgmental data.[23] The case is similar for theme. Its statement represents an inference, an effort to draw a conclusion from experience. The concept of a goal or higher level objective is no less abstract than that of theme. Broadly conceived, goals are statements of intent, statements about events planned for the future. In a curriculum, the search for themes suggests that to consider statements of goals or objectives as one basis is to place them outside the realm of action and experience and be forced to consider the "intended themes" of the curriculum. The notion seems somewhat contradictory to the analogical concept in literature.

This focuses the traditional point of view of the curriculum evaluator and the potential contribution of criticism. Where the conventional role of the evaluator has been one of verification, an attempt to evaluate practice by an examination of consequence and a comparison of intention to outcome, criticism suggests that the materials and practices of the curriculum be seen as representative of a series of *choices* reflected in point of view, plot, and structure. To account for these as expressions of meaning, or what is better called curricular themes, is a task for curriculum criticism.

Such an effort will not be an easy one, for metaphor, point of view, plot, and theme are mutually dependent. They are meant to be understood and used together. It is in the search for themes, as they appear in plots and metaphors and as they are emphasized through point of view, that the evaluator can maintain a holistic approach to the experience and avoid the danger of simplification.

John Mann was reluctant to say that any one critique or interpretation of a curriculum will be sufficient to capture or disclose its alternative themes. His discussion of curriculum criticism is concerned with the elucidation of curricular themes as part of an evaluation. Developing the concept of a disclosure model, Mann builds a case for saying that alternative themes are present in the curriculum and that one of the jobs of the critic is to extrapolate them. He implies that the curriculum will present a rich object for the critic and the evaluator to interpret.[24]

Stake adopts a similar position in his proposal for the evaluation of the Pilot-Demonstration Phase of the Follow-Through Program.[25] Realizing that programs contain a multitude of themes, and that the importance of some of them is possibly emergent rather than evident, Stake made it clear that any number of a broad range of ideas

suggested by Follow-Through might become a subject for sum-
marization.

Description and Judgment

Not only will the evaluator or critic have to be concerned with
locating the alternative points of view, plots, metaphors, and themes
that lie in the curriculum; he must also bear the equal burden of
wondering whether the descriptions and judgments he presents as an
evaluation will maintain a sufficient resemblance to the curricular object. Failing this, his becomes an exercise in delusion.

A lot of description and judgment goes on in theater alcoves.
My experience convinces me that these conversations have close
counterparts outside the auditoriums and classrooms of schools.
Maybe we can begin to understand something further about description and judgment by imagining two conversations that might occur
after a performance of Arthur Miller's *The Death of a Salesman.* The
chap from down the block might say, ". . . and what an unfortunate
set. It was an interesting play about a social loser. I'm getting rather
tired, really, of Miller and O'Neill and their stories about social
losers. Sure, I enjoyed it. But a play about a fat old man who kills
himself because he has become a terrible salesman. . . ."

But consider another man deciding what to write about the play
for the morning press: ". . . and the creative use of the set. Maybe
something about Cobb's portrayal of Loman—what the guy is able to
do with a line is brilliant. Loman, something of the antihero all right.
Miller's got himself a good, sensitive script about a man overcome by
his past failures and surrounded by a technology he can neither control nor understand. He was a man who should have worked with his
hands, not his mouth. People ought to see it."

There's more going on here than a naming of parts, a description of the action. There's more than an analytic attempt to separate,
to dismember. Both statements carry judgments, judgments of worth
at that. They are rather the same in the elements of the play that are
used as evidence to support the conclusions of "interesting" on the
one hand and "brilliant" on the other. What happened on that stage
was pretty clear to both of those "critics." Some would venture that
it was self-evident; certainly beyond the call of justification. One
might want to ask in reply, evident to what person?

I might believe parts of what they've said, all of it, some of it, none at all. There's a question of credibility in all judgments. We rarely accept the entire review or the entire report. Most audiences are rather selective in what they choose to accept, dismiss, or possibly overlook entirely. When I examine my experience, I see myself returning to the critics and men next door whose judgments have had the greatest similarity to mine. They have agreed with me, would be another way to put it. But then I wonder how much arrogance, bravado, wit, and style have to do with it.

It matters little whether it's the man next door or the critic, since, when they come to judgment, the process is the same although the outcomes may differ. Judgment is a central likeness. Their points of view and standards may be their central differences. The case is the same for the critic and the curriculum evaluator.

The Centrality of Judgment in Criticism and Evaluation

I've already mentioned Smith and his inclusion of evaluation as the last phase of the critical process, and I have described, as he did, how the four phases rarely remain discrete, but rather overlap in practice. In his discussion of the evaluative phase, Smith points out that evaluation "implies some kind of summation or assessment of the merit of the work of art in question. The simplest kind of verdict is one saying that the work is good or bad, based on an examination of its aesthetic qualities, say, its degree of unity, complexity, intensity, or some combination of these."[26] Describing the function of evaluation within education, one is struck by the similarity of the following definition from Scriven: "It's his [the professional evaluator's] task to try very hard to condense all that massive data into one word: *good* or *bad*."[27]

In remarks prepared as a critique of the Phi Delta Kappa volume on educational evaluation, Scriven reaffirmed his position by suggesting that one of the shortcomings of the volume was its failure to stress the necessity that evaluators conduct evaluations not only so that a judgment of the relative match between a set of intents and outcomes is accomplished, but also so that the worth of the intents themselves is judged. He suggested that such judgments of worth be rendered at both the beginning and end of a development process (this in view of the fact that programs frequently alter their intents while under development).[28]

Scriven's more recent development of the goal-free evaluator position presents an intriguing parallel to the position of the literary critic.[29] Much as Scriven would have the evaluator remain free of constraint by purposely avoiding any certain statement of intent on the part of the program under examination, the critic rarely has or seeks a preperformance statement of literary or theatrical intent.

Imagine the displeasure some would feel if the Broadway critic or local film reviewer never got around to saying whether or not the production was worth seeing. Possibly even without the broader awareness that there do exist legitimate, complicated, and useful critical points of view that do not necessarily eventuate in a judgment of worth, the public has developed the expectation that critics and reviewers ought to judge. Scriven would make the same case for evaluators, and would press for this type of evaluative responsibility.

What is notably absent from Scriven's evaluation suggestions (despite titles to the contrary, i.e., "The Methodology of Evaluation") is a delineation of the steps to follow in coming to and defending such a judgment of worth. It may have been partly as a result of the realization that such a judgment, rendered by an individual evaluator, could be so idiosyncratic as to be easily dismissed, that Stake suggested curriculum evaluators set about the task of collecting alternative judgments. Stake expressed his hesitation about whether or not evaluators would accept the challenge of judgment offered them in the form of an imperative by Scriven.[30]

In order to exhibit the range and number of problems involved in a judgment of worth, and to suggest some practical guides for the curriculum evaluator to use when he encounters them, the remainder of this paper considers the following:

1. Description: its relationship to judgment and prescription
2. The publicly reasonable expression of judgment
3. The justification of judgments
4. Credibility

Description: Its Relationship to Judgment and Prescription

Consider these three statements that exemplify the relationships between description, judgment, and prescription.

1. Mr. Becker talked 33% of the time his class was in session.

2. Mr. Becker's limited amount of talk is consistent with his expressed philosophy and goals.
3. Mr. Becker should continue to minimize his teacher-talk level.

Statement 1 is a descriptive proposition that denotes, in a summary fashion, one aspect of Becker's verbal interaction with his class. It states the percentage of the total class period that he talked. Statement 2 is a judgment based in part upon the descriptive observation given in statement 1. In statement 2, the use of the terms "limited" and "consistent" denotes the judgments that have been appended to the descriptive statement. Implicit in the statement are at least two standards that have been used as comparison bases: one to judge the "talk" as "limited"; the other to judge the congruence between a set of intents and a practice as "consistent." Statement 3 represents a move from description and judgment to prescription. The use of the term "should continue" is an indicant for future behavior that implies a rule or principle for practice. This means that the use of the term "should continue" is based on some other rule or principle such as "A teacher's behavior should be consistent." On the other hand, it might just as well be based on empirically generated evidence suggesting that such a prescription would have utility. Prescriptions may be justified in essentially two fashions: by showing how the prescription follows from some more inclusive set of principles or rules; by showing empirically that the prescription, when followed, leads to desired results.

Statements like "Mr. Becker is a good teacher," and "That was a wonderful lesson," exemplify a descriptive-judgmental problem which has been widely debated in the philosophical literature. On the one hand, some have held that statements of judgments are based on value terms that are primarily the *expression* of desires, attitudes, or feelings rather than the *assertion* of anything. They are taken to have emotive meaning but little else.[31] For example, to summarize a lengthy and complicated proposal, Ayer held that statements such as "Mr. Becker is a good teacher" are simply emotive expressions that do not assert anything.[32] Consequently, Ayer would argue, it is not possible to demonstrate empirically the truth or falsity of such statements. Similarly the idea of beginning with a set of value statements and then generating prescriptions for practice has been opposed. R. W. Burnett's warning that "there is simply no formal way by which the philosopher of education can logically deduce specific educational practices from metaphorical, epistemological, or axiological premises" is a case in point.[33] Sidney Hook has referred to this type of deductive behavior as eventuating in "garrulous absurdities."[34]

Dewey held, on the other hand, that there are "distinctive valuation-propositions" that can be empirically examined.[35] Similarly, Scriven has argued persuasively that value claims in the social sciences are legitimate and that they can be empirically examined.[36] I agree that the examination of value-oriented statements can be conducted if they are considered as taking the form of an "if-then" statement. In other words, the examination of the statement "Mr. Becker is a good teacher" would consider the question "If Mr. Becker is a good teacher, then what can be expected of Mr. Becker?" Dewey's instrumentalism was, in part, an expression of what that expectation might be.

In regard to the relationship of value judgment to prescription, few summaries better represent my own point of view than this one by Phenix:

The clearest case of prescription is the imperative, which discussion shows to be a close logical kinsman to the value judgment. The irreducible logical difference between statements and commands is that the former are indications of *believing* something, while the latter are attempts to induce action. Moreover, because of this logical difference, no amount of factual information can ever by itself add up to an imperative conclusion. Every imperative conclusion must be justified in part by reference to some imperative premise.

This analytic insight about the irreducibility of prescriptives to indicatives is of fundamental importance for moral instruction. It suggests that responsible moral persons can never be nurtured by being taught only facts. No accumulation of information can tell anyone what he ought to do. The ideal of the teacher as one who remains uncommitted and adheres to objective facts without involving himself in judgments of value or affirmations of obligation thus proves to be far from ideal. Sound moral judgment requires not only knowledge of the facts but a substantial stock of well-tested moral principles (prescriptions) for the guidance of conduct.

Important as principles are, they are not sufficient for moral growth. The other essential element is practice in making deliberate choices. The centrality of choice making comes out with particular force in Hare's analysis of the meaning of the term "good." He argues that "good" is not an indefinable quality like "yellow," as G. E. Moore and other intuitionists held, but that "good" is to be defined with reference to the act of choosing. One regards a thing as the "best" among several alternatives if it is the one he would choose to fulfill the function for which it is intended. That is to say, the choice is guided by some standard of preference. This holds both for nonmoral efficiency, and for moral choices, where nonfunctional standards of virtue apply. In every case, the essence of evaluative judgments is rational preference manifest in making choices.[37]

The Publicly Reasonable Expression of Judgment

I remember trying to convince a childhood friend that Roy Campanella was a better catcher than Yogi Berra. And I recall that when we got down to arguing, the words went something like:

Why?
Just because.
Well, because why?
Just because he is; that's why.
But because why?

Children seemed to know that to ask "why" was to ask a powerful question. Somehow, every child on the block had a pat answer —"just because." That was all. (No one would be caught dead saying, "Because my father said so." You only said a thing like that once and then you knew better.)

It's not hard to turn a discussion of justification and judgment into a polysyllabic nightmare that can become less instructive than the childish "just because."

One way to begin a discussion of justification is to say that it's mostly an effort to develop a "because" and then a "because why." Much as the child can drive you dumb in his irksome quest for cause, the process of justification can be seen as an irksome quest for "why?" I say irksome because it seems to be the case that we rarely ever know the answer for sure, or for long, after a certain number of whys. What also seems to occur is that after a time, some seem to lose their fear of saying, "Because my father said so," or something of that order, some suggestion of authority or evidence that warrants assent.

To speak of justification without remaining sensitive to credibility is to be unrealistic. There is a certain ease with which a questioning process of the "Why / Because why?" order leads toward infinite regression, a process that has no stopping until it has probed back to what appear to be first principles. In the pages that follow, I hope to indicate how we can avoid some of the problems of infinite regress by utilizing the factor of credibility.

A publicly reasonable expression of judgment consists of three parts: (1) a statement of the judgment or verdict, (2) a statement of the reason or reasons for the judgment, and (3) a statement of the norm or set of norms that shows the reasons to be good ones. A simple example of such an expression of judgment would be: "Jackson High School's English curriculum is an excellent one because it stresses talking, reading, and writing as the three avenues to self-expression and awareness, and these were the recommendations of the Dartmouth Conference." More realistically, the form of such an expression might cover several pages or chapters of an evaluation report. What is gained through the use of such a form of expression is that three important components of the judgment are made initially explicit, and it is possible to begin probing for further reasons and norms, if desired.

It's probably important to say "if desired," since in the case where all parties are in agreement on the judgment, there is little likelihood that a request for justification will arise. However, even in these cases, rare as they may be, it would be unfortunate if either judge or audience were to accept a verdict without having plumbed some of its implications.

The Justification of Judgments

Some of the implications of an expression of judgment can be made explicit through a verbal probing process.[38] In those instances where there may be less than agreement on the reasonableness of the judgment, the demonstration of the justification will focus on the two claims that every normative judgment makes. These claims are, in the first place, that the object either met or failed to meet a particular norm or set of norms, and, in the second place, that these norms were themselves appropriate to the judgment. It is the demonstration of the veracity of this "double claim" that is the object of the probing process.

Taylor has summarized the focus of this effort nicely.

The aim of the evaluation process is to arrive at a judgment in which we make the claim that the evaluation (object) either fulfills or fails to fulfill the norms. . . . [Evaluation] is the logical method which a rational person *would* follow if he were trying to come to a careful, reflective decision about the value of something. . . . Every process of evaluation and every value judgment contextually implies that the norms being used are appropriate and valid. By "contextually implies" I mean that anyone who understands that an evaluation is being carried out, or that a value judgment is being made, considers it legitimate and proper to question the appropriateness of the norms, and expects the evaluator to be able to give reasons showing that they are appropriate. . . . A double claim is involved whenever we evaluate something. First there is the claim that the evaluation fulfills or fails to fulfill the given norms, a claim explicitly made when we utter a value judgment. Second, there is the (contextually implied) claim that it is valid or appropriate to apply the given norms to the evaluation. Unless good reasons can be given in support of both of these claims, a value judgment cannot be justified.[39]

The first of these claims, that the object fulfills or fails to fulfill a norm, denotes the level at which most curriculum evaluations have labored.[40] The evaluations are usually partial—partially explicit, partially implied. They rarely move beyond the level of verification, the level of saying whether the object meets or fails to meet a standard.

Credibility

Credibility means believability. It becomes important in evaluation when evaluators want their audiences to believe that the evaluation has something to say, sometimes even to believe that it is worth doing in the first place. To speak of credibility is to speak of being credible to somebody, about something, within some circumstance.

To speak of a reasonable publication of judgment is to speak of credibility. To suggest that there is such a thing as a reasonable publication is to suggest that it is possible for two individuals wrapped in a normative dialogue to achieve a degree of exposure that both elicits their standards and rules and yet allows them to maintain their credibility before each other. Yet I began with the suggestion that there are times when we do not want to disclose that Campanella was better because our fathers said so. To be reasonable, to give reasons for the judgment, is not necessarily to be credible.

Within the process of probing for the justification of judgment and the achievement of publicly reasonable expression of judgment, the evaluator will come close to tampering with credibility. To disclose the reasons for a judgment is to reveal the evidence of the verdict. Different people, indeed different evaluators, appear to accept some types of evidence as more credible than others. Reasons become a question of evidence in the case of verification, and insofar as there are differences in belief systems, there will be a range of greater and lesser credibility in evidence.

The case is somewhat different with norms. When the dialogue and the disclosure get to validation, there is little credibility in evidence. To probe for validation and to seek a reasonable expression of the norms that give merit to the reasons is to question the very basis on which people value. Where verification may have recourse to evidence, validation is unrelenting in its confrontation with principle. As the alternative norms and counterevidences are uncovered, it is the evaluator's task to determine inconsistency, contradiction, and subterfuge, and then to render his own verdict. In order to do this wisely, he must balance many things. One of these will certainly be his own credibility against the ease of pleasantry and efficiency. I have wondered how much bravado, wit, and humor have to do with credibility. To this trinity I would add humility.

The processes of judgment and justification that have been examined here seem to force attention on the question of criteria. Where do they come from? How are they to be found? In his discussion of education's perpetual search for criteria, Harry S. Broudy once commented that "It is perhaps not too much to say that our search for criteria is impeded far less by their elusiveness than by a vague and persistent dread of finding them."[41]

Used indiscriminately, the process of probing for reasons and criteria can force the adoption of positions that are not representative of the person. Mr. Sammler, the principal character in Saul Bellow's *Mr. Sammler's Planet*, said it nicely. Thinking of explanation, he mused,

You had to be a crank to insist on being right. Being right was largely a matter of explanations. Intellectual man had become an explaining creature. Fathers to children, wives to husbands, lecturers to listeners, experts to laymen, colleagues to colleagues, doctors to patients, man to his own soul, explained. The roots of this, the causes of the other, the source of events, the history, the structure, the reasons why. For the most part, in one ear and out the other. The soul wanted what it wanted. It has its own natural knowledge. It sat unhappily on superstructures of explanation, poor bird, not knowing which way to fly. . . .

A Dutch drudgery, it occurred to Sammler, pumping and pumping to keep a few acres of dry ground. The invading sea being a metaphor for the multiplication of facts and sensations. The earth being an earth of ideas.[42]

Sammler may be right—"in one ear and out the other." That may be the greater part of explanation and of justification.

Sometimes there is little opportunity for justification—as, for example, when the *Montgomery County Sentinel* used its front page to publish its gradings of the county's twenty-two senior high school principals as either "outstanding," "good," "poor," or "unsuited." Public response from school board members, staff, and community spokesmen was swift and angry. The paper was criticized for being "presumptuous," "shallow and inaccurate" in its evaluation of a complex institution. "Other critics of the grading claimed that such judgments required more specific criteria and the expertise of professionals." The *Sentinel* replied that "principals, like other public officials, are subject to evaluation by the public, and declared that one 'does not need a Ph.D. in education to opine whether a principal is good or bad.' "[43] The *Sentinel* was right about what it takes to opine. Certainly one does not need a Ph.D. The question is better asked, "What does it take to satisfy people that judgments are sensible?"

One way to tell someone that you don't believe is to ask for criteria and standards. One way to start the debate going is to put these criteria on the line and make a public judgment. I have suggested some of the problems in that debate—and have indicated, I hope, how concepts borrowed from literary criticism may enable evaluators to describe and judge curricula without distortion or oversimplification.

Someone has said of literature that it presents not life lived, but life framed and identified. It would be unfortunate and a contradiction to my purpose if such a conclusion were suggested here. Much to the contrary, the plots and themes of the curriculum exist in a world of real people. Children and adults live there. As Mann said, "Curriculum . . . is a form of influence over persons, and disclosures of meanings in a curriculum are disclosures about the character of an influence."[44] My development of curriculum as based in experience and the exposition of a rhetoric for the field have been presented as some first thoughts on how the curriculum evaluator can attack the problem of curricular disclosure.

Notes

1. Ian Westbury, "Curriculum Evaluation," *Review of Educational Research* 40, no. 2 (April 1970): 239-60.

2. John S. Mann, "Curriculum Criticism," *Teachers College Record* 71, no. 1 (September 1969): 27-40; Elder Olson, ed., *Aristotle's "Poetics" and English Literature* (Chicago, Ill.: University of Chicago Press, 1965); Westbury, "Curriculum Evaluation," p. 247.

3. R. A. Smith, "Aesthetic Criticism: The Method of Aesthetic Education," *Studies in Art Education* 9, no. 3 (Spring 1968): 22.

4. T. Denny and E. Hoke, "Appendix to a Final Report, Illinois State ESEA Title III Evaluation Project" (Center for Instructional Research and Curriculum Evaluation [CIRCE], Urbana-Champaign, University of Illinois, 1969).

5. Robert Frost, *The Poems of Robert Frost* (New York: Random House, Modern Library, 1930).

6. I. A. Richards, *The Philosophy of Rhetoric* (New York: Oxford University Press, Galaxy Books, 1965).

7. Clive Barnes, "A Review of Robert Montgomery's *Subject to Fits*," *St. Louis Post-Dispatch*, 21 February 1971, p. 4H.

8. C. M. Lindvall and Richard C. Cox, *Evaluation as a Tool in Curriculum Development: The IPI Evaluation Program* (Chicago, Ill.: Rand McNally, 1970).

9. Biological Sciences Curriculum Study, *A Formative Evaluation of ME NOW, Unit One, Digestion and Circulation* (Boulder, Colo.: University of Colorado, 1970).

10. Ferguson has defined the Aristotelian concept of action as the whole working out of the motive of a plot to its end in success or failure. In the sense that action is motive, it may be distinguished from activity which is instrumental to the working out of the motive (*Aristotle's "Poetics,"* New York: Hill and Wang, 1961).

11. J. Thomas Hastings, James L. Wardrop, and Dennis Gooler, *Evaluating Geography Courses: A Model with Illustrative Applications* (Washington, D.C.: Association of American Geographers, Commission on College Geography, 1970).

12. See, for example, Denny and Hoke, n. 4 above.

13. I. P. Hansen and R. M. Simon, eds., *The Advisor* (Urbana: University of Illinois Press, 1970).

14. E. M. Forster, *Aspects of the Novel* (New York: Harcourt, Brace, 1927), p. 130.

15. J. Thomas Hastings, "Curriculum Evaluation: The Whys and The Outcomes," *Journal of Educational Measurement* 3, no. 1 (Spring 1966): 27-32.

16. J. L. Wardrop has suggested how a concern with "most probable causes" can be of help here, in "Determining 'Most Probable Causes': A Call for Re-examining Evaluation Methodology" (University of Illinois at Urbana-Champaign: Center for Instructional Research and Curriculum Evaluation, 1971).

17. The concept of structure in literature has been widely debated. The term has also been applied differently to the poem (see Richard P. Blackman, *Form and Value in Modern Poetry* [Garden City, N.Y.: Doubleday, 1946]) as compared to the novel (Dorothy Van Ghent, *The English Novel: Form and Function* [New York: Harper and Row, 1953]). In curriculum, it has been identified as scope and sequence and defined as "The parts of an object and the ways in which they are interrelated" (G. W. Ford and Lawrence Pugno, eds., *The Structure of Knowledge and The Curriculum* [Chicago, Ill.: Rand McNally, 1964]).

18. Robert Gagné, "Curriculum Research and The Promotion of Learning," in *Perspectives of Curriculum Evaluation,* ed. Ralph Tyler, Robert Gagné, and Michael Scriven, American Educational Research Association Monograph Series on Curriculum Evaluation, no. 1 (Chicago, Ill.: Rand McNally, 1967), p. 23. Emphasis in original.

19. Ibid., p. 22. Emphasis in original.

20. Ibid., p. 38.

21. See, for example, the excellent discussions in James W. Popham et al., *Instructional Objectives* (Chicago, Ill.: Rand McNally, 1969).

22. Archibald MacLeish, "Ars Poetica," in *Collected Poems, 1917-1952* (Boston: Houghton Mifflin, 1952), p. 41.

23. Robert E. Stake, "Objectives, Priorities, and Other Judgment Data," *Review of Educational Research* 40, no. 2 (April 1970): 181-212.

24. Mann, "Curriculum Criticism."

25. Robert E. Stake, "An Outline of a Program Evaluation Plan for Evaluating the Pilot Demonstration Phase of the FOLLOW-THROUGH Program, Academic Year 1967-68" (University of Illinois at Urbana-Champaign, Center for Instructional Research and Curriculum Evaluation, 1967).

26. Smith, "Aesthetic Criticism," p. 26.

27. Michael Scriven, "Evaluating Educational Progress: A Symposium," *Urban Review* 3, no. 4 (February 1969): 22.

28. Ibid., "Critique of the Phi Delta Kappa Volume on Educational Evaluation" (Remarks prepared for the symposium on the volume at the annual meeting of the American Educational Research Association, New York, 1971).

29. Ibid., "Prose and Cons about Goal-Free Evaluation," *Evaluation Comment* 3, no. 4 (December 1972): 1-4.

30. Robert E. Stake, "The Countenance of Educational Evaluation," *Teachers College Record* 68, no. 7 (April 1967): 523-40.

31. See, for example, Alfred Jules Ayer, *Language, Truth and Logic* (New York: Dover, 1952); Rudolph Carnap, *Philosophy and Logical Syntax* (London: K. Paul, Trench, Trubner, 1935); and Charles Leslie Stevenson, "The Emotive Meaning of Ethical Terms," *Mind* 46, no. 181 (January 1937): 14-31.

32. Ayer, *Language, Truth and Logic.*

33. J. R. Burnett, "Some Observations on the Logical Implications of Philosophic Theory for Educational Theory and Practice," *Proceedings of the Fourteenth Annual Meeting of the Philosophy of Education Society* (Lawrence: University of Kansas Press, 1958).

34. Sidney Hook, "The Scope of Philosophy of Education," *Harvard Educational Review* 26, no. 2 (Spring 1956): 145-48.

35. John Dewey, "Theory of Valuation," in *International Encyclopedia of Unified Science,* ed. Otto Neurath (Chicago, Ill.: University of Chicago Press, 1939). The following summary of "Theory of Valuation" is taken from *Philosophy of Education,* ed. Hobert W. Burns and Charles J. Brauner (New York: Ronald Press, 1962), p. 208: (1) People do in fact prize, desire, or value certain existential situations; these can be said to constitute (under certain conditions) ends in view; (2) Ends in view serve as plans or guides to behavior so that prized existential situations (ends) can be realized; ends in view are thus means to ends; (3) Propositions about values are thus propositions about existential means and ends; they are "if-then" in nature and, being hypothetical in nature, are no less susceptible to the empirical test than any scientific if-then generalization.

36. Michael Scriven, *Value Claims in the Social Sciences,* Publication no. 123 of The Social Science Education Consortium (Lafayette, Ind.: Purdue University, 1966).

37. Philip H. Phenix, "Curriculum and the Analysis of Language," in *Language and Meaning,* ed. James B. Macdonald and Robert R. Leeper (Washington, D.C.: Association for Supervision and Curriculum Development, 1966).

38. In his *Normative Discourse* (Englewood Cliffs, N.J.: Prentice-Hall, 1961), Paul W. Taylor presents a method of justification that assumes the exis-

tence of a hierarchy of standards and rules, a subsumptive system, up and through which the process of justification must proceed. Such assumptions of higher and lower order standards and rules are not implied in my discussion.

39. Ibid., pp. 4-5.

40. In "The Justification of Curricula" (Paper delivered at the annual meeting of the American Educational Research Association, New York, 1971), L. B. Daniels goes to great lengths to support the position that the preponderance of curriculum evaluations has been directed at questions of verification rather than validation.

41. Harry S. Broudy, "The Continuing Search for Criteria," American Association of Colleges for Teacher Education Evaluative Criteria Paper no. 3 (1967), p. 12.

42. Saul Bellow, *Mr. Sammler's Planet* (New York: Viking, 1969), pp. 7-8.

43. *Phi Delta Kappan* 1971, p. 635.

44. Mann, "Curriculum Criticism," p. 12.

Cases

Chapters 7-19 are case studies in curriculum criticism. They exemplify some of the variety of approaches and methodologies which can be used in qualitative educational evaluation. The short introductions to these chapters discuss each study in terms of "processes of criticism" and "dominant interest" (described in chapter 1), critical "focal points" (in chapter 5), and "rhetoric" (in chapter 6).

In her case study Elizabeth Vallance concentrates on the critical description of curriculum materials. The materials described are two pilot units of "The Great Plains Experience: A Cultural History," a multimedia course developed by the University of Mid-America for study by students at home and at a system of learning centers throughout a six-state region. Pointing out the basic similarities between curriculum materials and works of art, Vallance creates a vivid description of "The Great Plains Experience" intended to capture the pervasive and salient qualities of the materials and to illuminate the experiential qualities they provide to the student. In doing so her principal critical focal point is the "work" itself. The dominant interest of the study is aesthetic: How do the form and specific qualities of the curriculum color the experience that it provides? Nonetheless, as Vallance suggests, since critical description is a way of re-creating for an audience the critic's experience of the work, which itself is a re-creation of the artist's experience, much of the vividness of the description depends upon the critic's personally feeling and personally describing experiences. Despite the inevitability of such personalness in good critical description, the aesthetic experiences of artist, critic, and audience must still have much in common.

The portrayal of "The Great Plains Experience" exemplifies several prominent rhetorical features, particularly in developing a distinct "point of view," in freely using figurative language to disclose the "theme" of the curriculum materials. The portrayal emphasizes the critical process of description, but even in those places where disclosure of meaning and judgment remain implicit, the description is sufficiently vivid so that meaning and judgment are present to the reader. Especially in the latter portions of the portrayal Vallance makes many direct inferences about meaning, and disclosure and judgment become completely explicit. The study, therefore, illustrates the power of critical description to embody other fundamental critical processes.

Vallance concludes her chapter with a brief discussion of how her critique has illustrated the functions of the six pervasive characteristics of critical description that she had identified through an analysis of art criticism. In this discussion she suggests that, in the criticism of any work of art, several different and equally legitimate perspectives are possible; different critics will see different things in the materials. The adequacy and usefulness of any piece of criticism is judged by the reader, who must make his or her own comparisons between the description and the work itself. And she stresses that the final judgment of curriculum materials cannot be made by the critic alone, but must be shared by the teacher or student, who will see the materials in their real context of classroom use. The critic provides a set of insights which can begin the process of fully appreciating the experience the materials provide. The end of criticism, then, is to enable all of us to see more carefully; Vallance thus invites the reader to become a critic rather than to rely solely on the perceptions of any one critic.

7

Scanning Horizons and Looking at Weeds: A Critical Description of "The Great Plains Experience"

Elizabeth Vallance

Introduction: Rationale and Notes on Method

In a general sense, of course, the criticism of curriculum materials is in many ways not at all new. School superintendents, curriculum committees, publishing houses, parents, teachers, PTA subcommittees, and numerous other interested parties have been engaged in the assessment of curriculum materials for as long as there have been schools (and, some would argue, much longer). These assessments are made from different viewpoints, depending on the needs and interests of the critic and on the nature of the subject-matter at hand. More often than not, the materials are assessed on their own merit, out of the context of classroom use. (Consider, for example, the deliberation of textbook adoption committees or of PTA groups. Most of these refer to the books themselves rather than to the teaching methods or larger content.) Quite often, first-level judgments are made not even on the basis of the materials themselves but on the basis of written descriptions of them.

Adapted and reprinted by permission of John Wiley & Sons, Inc. from Vallance, "The Landscape of 'The Great Plains Experience': An Application of Curriculum Criticism" in *Curriculum Inquiry* 7, no. 2 (1977), copyright © by the Ontario Institute for Studies in Education.

Depending on its subject, a textbook may be analyzed for its readability, its objectives, its fit with existing parts of the curriculum, its political and moral content, its timeliness, the thoroughness and usefulness of the accompanying teacher's manual, the range of ability for which it is appropriate, and its cost. A number of curriculum-assessment and information services may help the teacher cope with the need to see these various curriculum sequences as a whole. The *Social Studies Curriculum Materials Data Book* is one excellent example of an effort to consolidate pertinent information about curriculum materials into one easily accessible source, and *Social Education* has published some systematic assessments of existing curricula in the social studies.[1] These descriptive aids to curriculum assessment provide a standardized body of information about the materials and allow them to be compared on the basis of some common criteria.

Another contribution to critical judgments about curriculum materials lies in curriculum evaluation. Evaluations of curricula or programs can tell us how well those curricula "worked," as measured against some predetermined criteria and compared to other curricula that claim similar outcomes. Formative and summative evaluations provide us with our most systematic and most carefully controlled information about the effectiveness of curricula. And if we are astute judges, we will also bring to bear the findings of educational research, most probably those of educational psychology and learning theory, which are beginning to provide us with guidelines about what sorts of teaching strategies work (or should work) with what sorts of students to achieve what sorts of goals. We can, if we bear in mind all the variables and qualifiers, dare to generalize and incorporate these generalizations into our judgments about particular materials. If we have been diligent in our homework, our judgments about the probable effects of the materials can be extremely well informed.

The problem with all of the above, to my mind and in the minds of numerous contemporary critics of curriculum discourse, is that neither the informational/descriptive data nor the evaluations of curriculum effectiveness really get at the heart of the matter. Rather, they deal either with the superficial structure of the curriculum materials (i.e., reading level, number of pages, and topics covered) or with their after-the-fact characteristics (i.e., their effectiveness). Both of these ignore the whole question of what experience the curriculum materials provide to the student. The question is not a trivial one. It is significant in schooling simply because, as Mann observes, curricula not only produce effects (measurable or otherwise) but they are also "lived in"—they structure and provide the flavor of a very hefty hunk of the child's daily life for quite a number of years.[2] Thus, while curriculum materials (and the interactions woven around them) may be teaching, creating effects, meeting objectives, and so on, they are also coloring the child's experience. They are, at least potentially, creating a personal environment that is unique for each child encountering them, much as a painting on a gallery wall provides a constant and relatively unchanging structure (allowing for shifts in daylight patterns) that affects each viewer slightly differently, depending on what that viewer brings to the setting.

The language of educational research and curriculum evaluation, with its predilection for identifying causal relationships generalizable across settings, cannot begin to account for (or "portray") this personal "lived-in" quality of curriculum materials. Nor can the impersonal descriptions in curriculum catalogs. A method of talking about curriculum materials in a way that can convey and illuminate the experiential qualities should provide rich and vivid descriptions of these materials, descriptions communicating the pervasive quality of the experiences they invite.

The language of art criticism is a language that deals in these qualities, and without stretching the comparison too far, it is easy to see some basic similarities between curriculum materials and works of art that justify our approaching curricula from an art-criticism perspective. I have summarized these similarities elsewhere but sketch them briefly here. (1) Both curricula and, for example, paintings are products of human construction: they are "artifactual." (2) Both are a means of communication between the originator (developer or artist) and an audience (users or museum-goers). (2) Both are a transformation of the knowledge of the originator into a form that is accessible to the audience (Langer's view of art as a transformation of nondiscursive knowledge into a physical medium articulates this view most clearly).[3] (4) Both are, in different senses, the product of a problem-solving process. Ecker's description of artistic work, as a series of meeting and resolving problems of form and expression, has a clear parallel in the kinds of deliberations engaged in by curriculists in determining the form and content of a curriculum.[4] (5) In both, the meaning depends on the encounter with the audience: both provide a situation in which the audience's response is invited and virtually demanded. (6) Both provide a set of "brackets" or boundaries around the audience's experience: both curricula and works of art present selections from the total realm of experience, organized and formulated in a way that structures one's perception of that experience. Both do this deliberately. (7) Both can be placed within a tradition of history and style change; both are participants in an ongoing development of style and a cumulation of tradition. Both may be revolutionary, superseded, or eventually both. (8) Both invite criticism and assessment.[5]

A perusal of the literature of art criticism—a glance through a few issues of *Art News* or *Artforum,* for example—will reveal that the language in which critics talk about the subjects of their criticism can be a delightfully evocative and vivid one. What I refer to as the "critical descriptions" of works of art constitute, as it were, the data on which judgments are based; to be convincing, these descriptions must capture the most pervasive and salient of the qualities of a painting if the judgment is to be plausible to the reader. Some of the most crucial characteristics of effective critical description are discussed below.

The argument of the effective critic is, first of all, coherent: it meets the standards of "structural corroboration," where the structure of evidence and observation clearly supports the interpretation or conclusion offered. This is a mode of corroboration most frequently applied in law, where evidence and coherence alone must argue the interpretation, since the criminal act cannot be replicated. It stands in opposition to the "multiplicative corroboration" used in most educational research, where multiple measurements of an act or situation corroborate the investigator's perceptions.[6] The argument of the effective critic is, in addition, "referentially adequate": it describes the work with enough accuracy that we can recognize the work from it.[7] The description matches our own perceptions, if not our interpretation, of a painting. Thus, effective and evocative critical description does more than simply identify the constituent parts of the work. The critic describes the patterns they create, the balances or imbalances produced, the relationships among colors or compositional areas, the richness or brilliance of tone—in short, the critic describes the work's effect on the viewer/writer. The critic renders into ordinary language the experience that particular work creates for the viewer. It is a personal experience, but it is subject to the proof of comparison with the artifact itself. Thus, whatever conclusions the critic may offer concerning a particular work, the critical description of that work reflects the immediacy of the experience it provides.

For example, here is Dore Ashton on Matisse's *The Red Studio*:

The composition of forms assumes the same elliptical shape around a central void. This circular sensation is reinforced by Matisse's arabesques, the coiling line of the vine flaring out from the green vase and the twist of the wicker chair. The off-center green vase is the nearest thing to a vertical axis around which objects (images in Matisse's own paintings) glide in a circular unit. Red from floor to ceiling, the room is at once flat—a marked plane surface—and deep. It is a room. A room in which Matisse, and we the spectators, reign calmly from a central, invisible position. The wheel of space, carefully punctuated with forms that in their similarities echo and re-echo, turns and creates a totality. . . it becomes the universe, the one-world perceived first in its mysterious harmony and only later as a subject.[8]

And here is Elizabeth Baker on Hofmann's "Renate Series":

By all odds, the most fascinating single work in the "Renate Series" is *Little Cherry*. Its means are most radical: the largest canvas of the group, it bears a thinned-down, poured, puddled wash on an empty white ground. Areas of darkness—a kind of sediment, apparently—have settled within the wash. The picture appears virtually untouched by the brush except for a couple of clusters at brown vertical strokes under the disconcerting "cyclops eye" area at the upper right. This brings up its other quality: it has an almost calamitous evocativeness, including its rather sinister dried-blood hue. It should seethe with all the associations one is supposed to draw from a Rorschach blob. Yet ultimately it is a calm image, perhaps because of its faint grid, which looks as though it results from pressure against the stretcher bars between which the poured liquid collected, as the canvas when wet became slightly slack. This grid is not a systematizing grid; rather, it seems to have been coincidentally arrived at—a welcome ghost, perhaps, of the rectangle which dominates so many of his other paintings. . . .[9]

The approach to curriculum criticism developed here focuses on this notion of vivid description. The issue here is not so much "How does the critic arrive at artistic judgments?" as, more simply, "How does the critic portray what he/she knows about a work?" How does the language of criticism create so vivid and immediate an impression? What does the critic *do* in creating a verbal portrait of the data at hand? Ultimately this question boils down to the more fundamental issue of what the critic sees in the artifact, how he or she examines it, what details are selected to be reported, the components of the portrait written in words. I begin, however, at the most immediate level, with the techniques the critic uses in creating the portrait of this experience. The assumptions required, the patterns disclosed, and the questions raised by this analysis should provide guidelines for further work in the area of critical inquiry.

At least six techniques of critical description can be distilled from vivid critical descriptions of paintings. These techniques can be translated into guidelines for writing critical descriptions of curriculum materials. I have analyzed this translation and the resulting guidelines at length in a 1975 publication; the techniques are summarized below.[10]

Through *selective emphasis* the critic selects one or two of the most salient qualities of a painting, such as color or composition, and builds the description around these perceptions. Few critics ever attempt an exhaustive analysis of every aspect of a painting; selection of the salient qualities is an important process in qualitative inquiry. In the examples above, for instance, Ashton focuses almost exclusively on the composition of Matisse's painting, and Baker emphasizes the relationship of paint to canvas in Hofmann's *Little Cherry*.

Many evocative pieces of critical description rely heavily on images created through the use of *simile* and *metaphor,* which connect qualities of a painting with qualities outside it. Simile and metaphor effect the connection between what the artist sees in a work of art and our own everyday experiences, and many make unexpected connections between elements within a painting. It can make the work of art more immediate to the reader. In the selections above, Ashton compares Matisse's room to a "wheel of space . . . the universe"; Baker provides a clearer example by comparing Hofmann's paint surface to a Rorschach blob. Occasionally, too, a critic will make a comparative reference to another work of art in order to highlight the qualities of the one under discussion. This technique is what I have called *incidental comparison*. Baker uses it here in alluding to other works by the same artist. Again, this is a connection between the work of art and something outside it. It defines a context.

Critics often describe the qualities of a work of art in terms of the technique that seems to have been used to create it. The use of implied technique can be very vivid in evoking the pervasive qualities of a work of art. Baker talks about the "thinned-down, poured, puddled wash" of *Little Cherry,* "untouched by the brush." Whether these are accurate descriptions of how the painting actually was created is less important than their effectiveness in portraying the visual impact of these elements. This descriptive technique can infuse the description with a feeling of life and dynamism; it allows the reader to see the relation among the elements in a painting and to feel their physical, experiential reality.

Critics are notorious for their use of action verbs (or *implied movement*) to describe what might otherwise be considered static two-dimensional surfaces. They may refer, for example, to "colors straining to merge," colors "blazing out," shadows "creeping," and so on. Ashton speaks of objects that "glide" across Matisse's room, a room that itself "turns" in space. The vine coils, flares out from the green vase, and so on. Vivid action verbs emphasize the salient relationships in a composition and convey them in a kind of shorthand that summarizes the effect they produce. It is a way of communicating the experience that the art work provides.

Finally, the language of art criticism is perhaps even more notorious for its use of *logically unnecessary adjectives*. That is, critics and others engaged in artistic discourse often render a particular quality of a work through a series of descriptive terms that overlap in meaning. This rhetorical device plays an important role. It adds a quality and a tone to the description that noticeably heightens the vividness of the impression it produces. Baker, for example, refers to Hofmann's painting as "calamitous," "sinister," having "a dried-blood hue," all in the same sentence. Her "thinned-down, poured, puddled" wash falls into this category as well. The technique of overlapping adjectives has the effect of forcing us to focus on the obvious qualities in the work, allowing us to linger and to notice the role they play in creating the total effect.

These techniques are devices used consistently by art critics, usually unconsciously, to enhance the vividness of their descriptions. Description, of course, is not the all of criticism. In a sense the description of the work is only the beginning, the data on which interpretations are based and judgments rendered. But it is the special province of art criticism that description involves judicious selection; it is an argument of perceptual and experiential data. It presents the work in terms vivid enough and evocative enough that the reader can visualize the work (or recognize it when it is encountered, actually or in reproduction). The critical description must portray the essential qualities in a way that communicates the uniqueness and the special value of the work, and it must do so in a language accessible to the public. The critical description says more than what the average viewer would initially see. It helps us to see below the surface. It communicates an experience.

Background: The Curriculum Materials of "The Great Plains Experience"

The materials portrayed here are two pilot units of a distance-learning course entitled "The Great Plains Experience: A Cultural History," which is being developed by the University of Mid-America. UMA is a consortium of nine state universities in the Mid-west dedicated to providing at-home study courses for college credit. The courses developed by UMA are integrated multi-media packages (generally including a television component, text, student's guide, and audio cassettes), designed to provide "distance learners" with the full complement of content, instructional strategies, practice activities, review, and feedback necessary to master the objectives of the course. Contact with campus faculty is available through WATS lines in the six states through a system of learning centers that provide video cassettes of the programs as well as additional resource materials.

The course materials themselves, however, are designed to stand alone if necessary. They are, in this sense, the purest example of curriculum-material-as-artifact: the "lived-in" experience provided by the materials and the student's interaction with them is in many cases the only experience deliberately provided by the course. Thus the critical description of these materials should, if it is thorough and attentive to the integrated nature of the package, portray the essential character of the experience that the student is offered through the materials. (The separate unique qualities of that experience for each student will, of course, vary greatly.) The description below is an attempt to capture the experiential qualities of the materials using the techniques of vivid description summarized above.

The author worked on the course during its very early design stages, serving primarily as brainstormer and critic; contrary to what the credits indicate, she had scarcely any influence on the form or content of the final version of the pilot materials and was involved in

another project when the final version was drafted. Her first complete reading of the printed materials was done for the purpose of
writing the critique. She is, in this case, a disinterested but informed
outsider, a role quite appropriate to the critic.[11]

"The Great Plains Experience: A Cultural History" is a one-
semester course designed for adults with no prior academic training
in either Great Plains history or cultural analysis. It is introductory.
At the time the pilot materials were done, the design of the course
called for fifteen half-hour television programs (to be aired weekly),
a reader (an anthology of new and existing essays), a study guide
(coordinating all the components and providing preview questions,
review questions, sample answers, and synthesis and analysis activities), and audio cassettes where appropriate. The course design called
for four major "units," or topic areas, each of these broken down
into three to five week-long "lessons" (fifteen lessons in all); a UMA
information sheet describes the course as follows:

Description: "The Great Plains Experience" course deals with the cultural history of the Great Plains from early Indian cultures through modern-day man. It
will utilize a new interdisciplinary approach to regional history, attempting to
define the culture of the region through the interaction of its peoples and environment over time. Although the course is specifically regional in scope it will
study the region in its national and international context, thereby broadening its
interest for students from outside the Great Plains region.

Course Components: The course will consist of nine units which will be designed
for use over a 15-week period. The home-study materials will include a student
study guide, a book of essays, 15 half-hour broadcast television programs, 15
newspaper articles, a set of audiotapes coordinated with the student study guide,
and an optional local delivery component designed to secure direct student involvement with the course materials.

The two pilot lessons (lessons 1 and 2 of the first unit) were
developed under a grant from the National Endowment for the
Humanities as the core of a later proposal for a major grant to complete the project. Thus, the materials described here are the first two
lessons of a fifteen-lesson sequence that had not been completed:
they are taken, if not out of context, then prior to their context.
This "pre-contextual" nature of the pilot materials is itself appropriate, for two reasons: (1) it is this small portion that is evaluated
by the funders considering the full proposal, and (2) it is selected
portions such as these that are sent out to the participating univer-

sities in the UMA consortium for accreditation approval. Critical judgments on these incomplete materials are, then, necessary for very practical purposes. Generally these judgments would be made using the traditional course-evaluation criteria familiar to the funders or to the campus departments. The description below portrays the materials using some of the techniques of vivid description typically applied by art critics.

A Portrayal of "The Great Plains Experience"

The Package

It is an appealing package, even at first glance. There is a slick self-conscious quality to it. It is distinctly a *package,* its various parts clearly coordinated by typeface, format, and by the student's guide, which makes all these things explicit. The packaged quality of it is solid, it is reassuring, it lets you know immediately that the lovely television sequences are purposeful and substantial as well as inviting and tantalizing; there is no fluff. And it is solid in its sheer substantiality as well as in its apparent tightness—there is a wealth of text material, both in the reader and in the student's guide, although one might normally fear that the "student's guide" would consist of little beyond assignments and review questions. These materials are conceptually thick; they do not look easy; there is clearly a lot to work through. But they are inviting. Let us examine, then, more closely why this is so, and whether these first impressions are borne out.

The course materials are multi-media. More correctly, with the exception of one audio-tutorial activity in the second lesson, they are bi-medial: video and print. This is hardly revolutionary, particularly in light of the nationwide trend toward "TV colleges" and courses tied into television series ("The Adams Chronicles," "The Ascent of Man"). "The Great Plains Experience" is unabashedly part of that trend. What makes this bi-medial course especially interesting is that the video and print components have rather obviously been developed in synchrony with one another—the developers would tell us this if we asked, but it is evident simply in the fact that what we have here are the first two lessons only; there *is* no television series awaiting a wrap-around. It is part of the package. Complete lessons in the course are developed one by one, with a coordination that is not the least bit fortuitous. The cast of thousands who produced the package have evidently worked hard at making it coherent. Intentionality lurks around every corner.

Each of the two pilot lessons consists of a study guide unit, a set of essays in the reader (both volumes are sprinkled with illustrations), and a lush, half-hour color television program. The study guide and reader are no-nonsense; they are printed in reasonable, non-fancy type, in two columns, with white space designed to identify pauses and breathers but not to overwhelm with empty artsyness. The television, on the other hand, is visually poetic; its colors are gorgeous, its music creates a mood, there are birdsongs and Indian drums, there is a sonorous male voice narrating (or appearing, either as trustworthy professor leaning against a sod house in sunshine and wind, or as an obviously successful and educated native American speaking poetically from a hilltop). There is, in the television segments, an atmosphere, an awareness of pace, a carrying-along of the viewer into flashbacks and nostalgia, the intention of gripping and holding; by all these devices the viewer is grabbed easily by the shoulders and exhorted, "Look here, listen to this story and learn from it. There is more."

The materials do, together, tell a story. Rather, they tell the beginning of a story; the context makes it clear that this is just the prelude to an accelerating pace. It is preamble. It sets the stage for a story that we already know ends up in the present day. We sit back, then, and look for the drama of our own history here on the Plains.

The Shaping of the Story

The story is thorough, we sense, and the lessons to be drawn from it are carefully premeditated. We sense that it is thorough because it gets off to a dramatic but ponderous start. We don't exactly jump into a roaring torrent; no, rather a methodically moving deep river. We must take it slowly; that is the message. The volume of print that caught the eye on first perusal is for real. The introductions (two of them in the study guide, one for the whole course and one for its first unit) are careful, scholarly, not something to be raced through. The outline of course components, which appears between these two introductions in the study guide, is again careful, almost too detailed, solicitous that we know exactly what we're getting into before we get into it. The study guide describes the structure of the course; it not only outlines the roles played by the various components, it also spells out the objectives of each and provides exercises in which to practice their mastery. It tells us what the course is doing. It tells us why, in effect, the subject matter is exciting. We grow a little impatient but assume that the background will be pertinent later on. Perhaps it will even be more exciting than the "describe, identify, and discuss" objectives suggest; Great Plains cultural history has got to be more exciting than that.

It is. When the course materials finally get on with telling their story and teaching their lessons, they do it with a passion, a commitment, and a focus that pull us along and make even the context-setting fun. The essays in the reader were clearly written by scholars who care; they attend to facts but they sparkle with the author's passion for even the most trivial of details. These become relevant; the details about prairie dogs or river drainage patterns do not get in our way as we might expect; we pick up these facts (or at least the most salient of them) and carry them with us. The matter-of-fact and decidedly nonlyrical subheadings ("Creation of the Rocky Mountains," "Characteristics of the Great Plains," "Climate"), if they don't inspire us to greatness, do help us in the sifting process. We are gathering the basics.

This same background (and then some) is then presented visually in the first of the two television segments. It is called "The Land." It includes panoramas, close-ups of weeds, the white-haired professor at his sod hut remembering the old days, some animals running, a thunderstorm rendered by a series of still photos and crashing cymbals, a modern ranch family. In many ways it tells us nothing we don't already know, especially if we live on the Plains; but that, we sense, is not entirely its point. This program is not informational, though it does inform; it is not a regional sales pitch. It creates a mood of appreciation, and it adds an element not yet encountered in the printed material, the theme of cultural perceptions. The Plains, we learn here for the first time, were perceived (by white people) first as a great desert, then as a passage to India, later as the Garden of the West, and finally to many people simply as home. Same place, different reactions. "Why?" we ask.

We are not told why, actually, but we are gradually shown how, or simply *that*. The theme of differing cultural perceptions is shouldered more sturdily by the printed material to which we now return. Both the essay and some literary excerpts in the study guide lead us through this exploration; we read and answer questions. We come to see, if we are astute, that our own views of the Great Plains are greatly shaped by our own culture and technology.

And so the story is shaped. We are led through essays and study questions and analysis activities and on to another television program, all of which gradually make the point that everything on the Plains has had to adapt to the unique geography and climate of this land, and that the native American culture was the first of a series of human adaptations to the whole setting. We have moved, by the end of the second lesson, from background into genuine cultural history, and the momentum of the saga is established. It is not so gripping a momentum as that of Michener's *Centennial,* but it is solid.

That, then, is the structure of the materials so far. The relationships among the components are clear and plainly marked: the study guide functions both as soloist and as conductor, directing the student hither and yon in the sequence deemed right by the designers, and providing, on occasion, substance of its own as well.

A Question of Rhythm, and Its Message

But is the course doing what it says it is? Does the momentum carry to fit the parts neatly together, is it an aesthetic whole? Let us look at the materials again, from the point of view of rhythm.

The pattern of grand sweep and detail is reflected in the rhythm and pacing of the materials. An energetic and moving rhythm is established by the study guide, which, we can gather, is the first component the student embarks upon. The energy is conveyed by the strong sense of purpose and commitment of the introductory sections here; the text portions of the study guide provide grand sweep, they define the broad contours, they establish the outlines of a bold and complex pattern and allow us to see where we are going. They establish a sense of anticipation. They invite. That is the job of the guide, and it does it well, at least insofar as the outlines are defined by course themes and content.

But the energy level even within the study guide drops shortly after that, when we step into the welter of details on the mechanics, components, their purposes and interrelationships, and all the rest. This section is slow, intimidating; surely, we think, if we do not memorize all these details we will never make it through the materials. But we move through this and on to the real content; the pace picks up again as we at last prepare to begin unit 1, called "The Land and the People," and the first of its four lessons, called simply "The Land." Here we encounter a sequence of study, a calendar of activities broken down day by day, which is called "How to Approach the Lesson." We breathe a sigh of relief: all those details fall into place here; it is quite simple. Why didn't they say it this way in the first place? We start with the first day's assignments and keep moving. Another halt for "learning objectives for students," which are dry and commanding (they are phrased as imperatives), but finally (and it is now page eighteen of the study guide) there is a genuine assignment. It is a reading assignment, succinctly introduced and outlined with guiding questions. We turn to the reader and its first essay.

It is in this potentially dry and informational essay that we first get a sense of the passion that has gone into this course. The essay opens with two very moving excerpts from a book called *Love Song to the Plains* by Mari Sandoz. Sandoz (whom we may or may not be familiar with) makes details come alive, she brings poetry to this place that we now know was once considered a desert. And the essay is exciting; it explores a territory that, we realize, is virtually unknown in many respects; it opens grandly with a dramatic overview but moves rapidly to a pattern of details, details that tell a story millions of years old, details that sparkle, details of a place we may have lived in all our lives but never really noticed. It is like taking a magnifying glass to the tiniest of flowers, or discovering the complete little world that exists in tide pools. It reveals. Clearly the author of the essay delights in this scrutiny of details; but after a time it goes too far, and the details and information begin to pile up. Just as we begin to wonder where we are going, we arrive at the section on living things and the point of the essay is made clear. All these details of land and climate are the context in which living things survive and thrive. We remember that adaptation is a theme of the course; it begins to come together. We are prepared now for the professor at the hut, the vistas, and the openness that we see in the first television program.

So after this careful and fully documented introduction to *what* was adapted to, the theme of adaptation gains stronger momentum. The course materials move us through a television segment, readings, and activities on human perceptions of the land over time; the second lesson carries us through to the different kinds of adaptations the different Indian tribes made to this land. The very moving television program on the Lakota is a poetic study of a tribe; it manages to make the case study representative of something grander. The momentum is slowed periodically when we dive into particulars, as in the details of the explorers' trips or in case studies of Indian tribes. The audio-tutorial exercise on Indian art is vivid, alive, concerned, and quite detailed. The "broad sweep of history" that opened the course might be more fun, more pulsating, more inviting than some of the closer looks, but these details are gripping if we let ourselves be reached by them. They make a point.

There is, then, a tension in these materials, a tension between the dynamism and drama of the broad sweep, of grand patterns, of conclusions on the one hand, and the slower-moving, methodical, and sometimes dry examination of facts on the other. It can be bewildering. We can lose the forest for the trees quite often. We want to rise from the bottom of the river and ride along on top for a while, enjoying the view. We do, from time to time. It is a constant to and fro, and since there is no one around to talk to about this course (perhaps the professor is on lunch break at his WATS extension), we are very much at the mercy of the materials. And since they are all we have, and they clearly seem to know what they are doing (the study guide spent seventeen pages telling us just that), we return to them. We look at the grand patterns and we reexamine the details; the copious review questions appended to each give us some clues as to what to look for.

Well, there is a lesson in all of this, of course, though the study guide has nowhere alluded to it as an objective of the course. The materials themselves, simply in their rhythm of conclusions and details (a rhythm nearly paralleled in the relationship of television to print, and again in the relationship of essays to analytical activities) are telling us something more than the story of cultural adaptation to the Plains, and even more than the uses of artifacts as historical document. They are telling us something—not a great deal, and not fully developed by any means—about the uses of data in history. They are telling us about the rigor and complexity of historical analysis, a counterbalance to the excitement and drama that first draws us in. They are telling us that the study of history is not only the learning of a marvelous story, it is the painstaking study of small details and the search for justifiable relationships between them. Again, the materials do not tell us this terribly clearly; they do not make a point of it; at times the trees have a way of overshadowing the forest so as to lose that point altogether. It is not a course in historiography. But the message is there; it can be distilled.

A last word, then, on the visual appearance of these materials in this context of rhythmic tension. The rhythm of drama and detail, of grand to minute, of story to data, is quite neatly reflected in the visual qualities of the course components themselves. The television segments are by far the flashiest, slickest, most enticing, and most dramatic of the components; they are done in soft, rich colors, and they move from vast panoramas to intricate details; they narrate a story, they exploit the mood-setting capabilities of music and background sounds; they use details (sometimes too thickly) to create a totality. They set their respective stages. It is in the print materials that the methodical attention to detail is the greatest, though as noted earlier it is also print—the introductory essays and orientation—that establishes the mood of drama and grandeur. The print is scholarly; visually, the text is broken up and balanced with photographs, illustrations, and white space, but it is clearly work; it demands careful attention; it balances the drama of the television.

These first two lessons only begin to identify the thematic content of the course. Cultural adaptation seems to be a theme that will be carried across the units and interwoven through the primary and secondary sources used there. We cannot tell, of course, how this course will conclude or what its messages ultimately will be. But it is an inviting, dramatic, and careful beginning. It seems worth exploring, even without a professor to guide us.

Discussion

Comments here are kept to a minimum, for readers will have had their own reactions to the critique above and my purpose is not the criticism of criticism, particularly my own. But it may be helpful simply to point out the uses of the various techniques of critical description outlined earlier. Not all were used equally, and some were more salient in the above example than others; a different critique of the same materials might have focused on different qualities of the experience they offer, using a different configuration of descriptive techniques. The discussion highlights the use of the descriptive techniques in the order they were presented earlier.

The technique of selective emphasis is evident in this description. Though the description covers a range of qualities and characteristics of the course materials, it focuses largely on the tension and rhythm in the relationship among the components and content areas covered. It is by no means an exhaustive examination of the materials, for it has selected the features most salient to the critic; the portrayal is based primarily on the experience of movement and rhythm. Simile is used sparingly and always through images drawn from nature. There is the comparison to the slowly moving river and the roaring torrent; there is the dual comparison to examining flowers with a magnifying glass and to discovering the details in familiar-looking tide pools; there is forest and trees, and the need to ride along the surface of the river for a while. Although these images are not central to the structure of the description, they supplement it. Incidental comparison is used only twice in this case study, in the faint hint of alternative course structures in the last sentence ("without a professor to guide us," as a comparison to other courses), and in the reference to *Centennial*.

Technique is implied: the course materials have "obviously been developed in synchrony," by a "cast of thousands," and the essays reflect a "passion, a commitment" on the part of the writer. References to movement, however, are numerous and are central to communicating the effect of the materials. We jump into rivers that are slow and methodical (and not roaring), we move slowly, pace picks up, we breathe sighs of relief, we halt, we skip, we arrive, the materials move us along, we dive and surface. It is through the technique of implied movement that the description tries to convey the experiential qualities of the course materials, qualities defined by the rhythm of the relationship among the parts. Finally, there is some use of overlapping adjectives, though probably less than there would have been had the description focused on the visual rather than the rhythmic quality of the course. The slowness of the "river" is well established: the essays are "careful, scholarly"; we linger on the "grand sweep, broad contours, bold and complex pattern." Overlapping adjectives here function more to set the stage than to invite a long lingering over details.

More could be said, of course. More (or less) could have been said in the critical description itself. A different critic might have seen different things in the materials and portrayed them differently;

both portrayals could be referentially adequate, and both could communicate aspects of the "lived-in" quality of the curriculum. The important point in critical description is, of course, ultimately not really the language the critic uses but the experience he or she has with the materials. The language of art criticism is a vehicle for communicating these experiences; it is a bridge between the critic's perceptions and appreciations of the work and the reader. In the end, then, it is the experiential qualities of the materials, and not the language per se, that matter. It is the experiential quality of the materials that will color the student's encounter with them. And it is on the basis of the quality of the student's encounter (or our own best estimate of what that is likely to be) that the decision to adopt (or to take) the course would be made. Thus, one major function of the critical description of curriculum materials is to portray them in a way that allows informed decisions to be made about them. Whether the critical description is ultimately more "useful" than a standard catalog description will depend largely on the reader's purpose in reading *about* the materials instead of reading the materials themselves. Critical description makes a far greater use of details, and presents a more personal point of view, than does a standard catalog or brochure presentation. It invites a close look, and it allows a decision founded on rather different grounds.

It seems clear that if educators are to know and appreciate the quality of the experiences offered to students as a result of curriculum decisions, these decisions themselves can be richly informed by a knowledge of the aesthetic and experiential qualities of the materials that form the most standard core of the curriculum. Reading critical descriptions, if these are available, would be one way to bridge the gap. Learning to look at materials themselves from this point of view, however, would be far more rewarding, just as it is more rewarding to learn to view a painting, see its aesthetic qualities, and make one's own judgments about it than it is to read even the most evocative criticism of it. For if we are more interested ultimately in the experiential quality of the curriculum materials than in the language used to communicate that experience, we are also more interested in the development of critical perception in educators than in merely generating a body of critical writing. The critical description developed here is one example of the perceptions allowed by this approach.

Notes

1. Social Science Education Consortium, *Social Studies Curriculum Materials Data Book* (Boulder, Colo.: S.S.E.C., Inc., 1971).

2. John S. Mann, "Curriculum Criticism," *Teachers College Record* 71 (September 1969): 27-40. (Chapter 4 of this volume.)

3. Susanne Langer, *Problems of Art* (New York: Scribner's, 1957).

4. David W. Ecker, "The Artistic Process as Qualitative Problem-Solving," *Journal of Aesthetic and Art Criticism* 21 (Spring 1963); Decker F. Walker, "A Naturalistic Model for Curriculum Development," *School Review* 80 (1971): 51-76.

5. Elizabeth Vallance, "The Application of Aesthetic Criticism to Curriculum Materials: Arguments and Issues" (Paper delivered at the annual meeting of the American Educational Research Association, San Francisco, Ca., April 1976).

6. Stephen C. Pepper, *The Basis of Criticism in the Arts* (Cambridge, Mass.: Harvard University Press, 1945).

7. Elliot Eisner, "The Perceptive Eye: Toward the Reformation of Educational Evaluation" (Paper delivered at the annual meeting of the American Educational Research Association, March 31, 1975).

8. Dore Ashton, *A Reading of Modern Art* (Cleveland, Ohio: The Press of Case Western Reserve University, 1969), p. 17.

9. Elizabeth Baker, "Tales of Hofmann: The 'Renate Series,' " *Art News* 71 (November 1972): 40.

10. Elizabeth Vallance, "Aesthetic Criticism and Curriculum Description" (Ph.D. diss., Stanford University School of Education, 1975).

11. John Dewey, *Art as Experience* (New York: Putnam's, Capricorn Books, 1958).

The dominant interest in the essay by W. Dwaine Greer is aesthetic. Considering teaching as an artistic process, Greer outlines a model for teaching as an art and adapts some methods of criticism within the arts in developing a critique of a series of acts of teaching.

The model outlined is based upon David Ecker's explanation of the artistic process as a form of "qualitative problem-solving." Applied specifically to teaching, the model suggests that teaching is a series of qualitative problems and their resolutions. Basically, the teacher thinks in terms of qualitative relationships, attempting to modify what transpires between himself, student, subject matter, and environment in order to create some kind of coherent whole characterized by a controlling, pervasive quality. While reminding the reader that qualitative problem-solving is seldom a neat progression of steps, Greer nevertheless suggests that a complete act of teaching will include Dewey's stages of reflective thinking. An aesthetic view of teaching, then, considers teaching as including characteristic stages within an overall process. The stages outlined in this chapter by Greer can be compared to those characteristic stages of aesthetic experience described by Willis and Allen (chapter 3).

The critique describes the development of skill over a period of

161

months by a student-teacher of secondary-school art. In illustrating the foregoing model, the critique maintains a dominant interest that is clearly aesthetic: how do people order and respond to patterns of meaning or pervasive qualities largely in the external world? But Greer also deliberately creates a personal tone by writing in the first person and by vivid description. The critique is very much like a narrative story, with description of the unfolding action interspersed occasionally with direct disclosures of meaning. The story builds to a calm and nicely understated climax and concludes with some mild but directly stated judgments by the first person narrator. The critique itself incorporates the rhetorical devices of "point of view," "plot," and "theme" while at the same time illuminating how these may be embodied in the process of teaching. The principal critical focal points in this case study are "work" and "author." In this study, however, the latter is, literally, artist.

8

A Model for the Art of Teaching and a Critique of Teaching

W. Dwaine Greer

The Model

Within each of the social sciences we can find writings that present structures upon which to base a study of teaching. Such writings are useful to the extent that teaching as a profession involves the aspects revealed by adopting a particular stance.

For instance, the sociologist might well be interested in studying the extent to which teaching involves the socialization of children to particular norms and values. Even though we might argue for the separation of such functions into a category called schooling, as distinct from education, we must still acknowledge the value of insights gained by adopting such a frame of reference. Jacob Kounin's *Group Management and Discipline in Classrooms* is a good example of such writing.[1] It does an excellent job of describing teaching in terms of group processes, but because of that focus must neglect such important aspects of teaching as individual development or knowledge of subject matter.

This chapter is based on the author's doctoral dissertation at Stanford University, *The Criticism of Teaching* (Ann Arbor, Mich., University Microfilms, 1974, No. 74-13, 632).

What we have is a kind of mosaic made up of different partial views of teaching. Of course the teacher does not view his activities in these various ways except at particular times and for a short while. Somehow we must combine the knowledge gained from considering teaching in a number of different lights into a single system upon which to act.

This he does, more or less successfully. The problem is not the teacher's; rather, the problem lies with those who would study teaching. What is noteworthy by its absence is writing that helps us to understand this teacher's view.[2] There does not appear to be a ready theory that helps us to comprehend the more holistic and action-oriented view necessary for understanding the process as the teacher sees it. Like other artists, teachers are to be held accountable and judged in terms of their products. Thus much of what might serve as an exposition of the process serves rather as the vehicle for the promulgation of a particular orthodoxy: not that "this is the way teaching is," but rather "this is the way it should be." A. S. Neill's book *Summerhill* is a good example.[3] Such works seek to persuade rather than explain.

The impression we get from the literature about teaching is that the closer one gets to the classroom, the more appreciation one has for techniques and problems of working in this kind of situation. Conversely, the further we move back to view the role of teaching in society and education in civilization in general, the more the observer becomes concerned with the ultimate result of educational experience.[4]

Thus the model presented here does not cover the whole range of activities and knowledge available from the various disciplines drawn upon when teaching. The development of curriculum, meetings with parents, or the teacher's continuing scholarship, all of which bear upon teaching, will not be understood through using this model. What we will try to understand is an act of teaching—that time of engagement with students and subject matter in a special setting that the teacher sees as teaching. Furthermore, and perhaps more importantly, the model attempts to present teaching from the teacher's vantage point. It helps us move teaching as an art away from being a concept fraught with a mysterious alchemy toward an understanding of it as a controlled process of problem-solving.

What we will be concerned with is teaching as a controlled process. Using Ecker's terminology, we assign a label to this process—

"qualitative problem-solving."[5] Our method will be to adapt Ecker's model and his writing about art to apply to teaching, proceeding on the assumption that this adaptation will serve teaching as Ecker's has served the arts; it will function as a theoretical framework that describes a teaching act.

We contend that if we examine what teachers do when ordering their educational means and ends as well as what is said about this process, in the way Ecker looked at the artist, it will improve our conception of the act of teaching. If it is possible to deal with teaching as a series of qualitative problems and their resolution, the model may be useful.

Like an artist confronted with a blank canvas, a teacher confronted with teaching may begin at several places. Sometimes the process is one in which no definite problem seems to be present. The teacher begins with a kind of get-acquainted session and out of this some direction becomes apparent. Sometimes the teacher begins with ideas arising from a subject matter around which he builds interrelationships to bring about changes in a learner, or he may begin by posing a problem and helping the learner to its solution.

We will suggest that the teacher thinks in a qualitative way. We might conceive of the teacher's medium as being the learner's thoughts. The teacher tries to work within the thought processes of his pupils. His goals are not entirely preconceived, but at some point a direction becomes apparent and the situation takes on a tone that holds until it is over. Interestingly, this might be true at various levels of complexity. There is a kind of general character to any particular lesson, to a teacher's courses, and to a whole school. And we value what is presented metaphorically in this qualitative aspect. (For example, the Harvard accent implies so much more than simply a way of speaking.)

Addressing this qualitative aspect that teachers often talk about but is often ignored in the literature on teaching, we find it expressed in terms of common problems. Teachers historically have faced a group of learners who are to be educated. Sometimes the means have been partially spelled out as subject matter, but usually the general process has been left in the hands of the teacher. Thus we might trace the historical progress of teachers gradually building the solutions to the problems of definition of teaching and methods of dealing with a group of learners.

If viewing the central problem in teaching (teachers confronted with learners) in historical perspective helps *us* to understand the nature of teaching, much of the shoptalk between teachers is verbal evidence of the way *they* view the problem. For shoptalk is largely a by-product of their mutual problems. The words incorporated into this talk have commonsense meanings to fellow teachers.[6] That is, the words refer to the shared qualities of their work. Consider: "That class just didn't move into the poem." "That announcement coming over the loudspeaker when it did destroyed the concentration I had going with the class and the point I was making about the sum of the squares." The language deals with the means and ends of the teaching process, what we would define as qualitative relationships among the commonplaces of education that teachers create, orchestrate, and modify in solving the problems of teaching.[7]

Given this kind of description it seems plausible to make the following inferences:

1. As they work, teachers think in terms of qualitative relationships, the feeling of the class. They are likely to proceed on the basis of this general feeling.

2. Thought is exercised on behalf of the construction of other qualitative relationships, or of modifying or improving existing ones.

3. Teaching problems are theoretical abstractions derived from practice. Problem-solving involves a projection into the learner's place. The teacher attempts to see the world as his pupils would.

4. Teaching problems can be described in terms of an awareness of possible modifications of the learner within a range of general qualities with attention given to some desired end-in-view or pervasive quality. Thus, problems can be described in a way that would make them available for study and modification.

5. The means for the resolution of teaching problems are the qualitative relationships among the commonplaces of teaching.

6. While language may be of help in the definition of a teaching problem, that is, assessing its location and dimensions, the ability to describe it verbally is not a necessary condition for having a problem.

7. Critical judgment does not necessarily precede the establishment of qualitative relationships, nor does it necessarily come after educational experience is complete. It often occurs as a part of the ongoing processes of action and interaction that result in learning.

8. None of the formal laws of logic as such seems directly appli-

cable to the qualitative thought process that the teacher uses to order the act of teaching. While attempts have been made to describe the teaching process using models derived from science, this approach does not seem to have resulted in an understanding of the phenomena labeled good teaching.[8]

Here we reach the point in a description of the artistic problem-solving process that is a major reason for using this approach. Here is an answer to the question of how direction of this whole process is achieved. Ecker says of achievement of direction in art:

Artistic thinking, then, occurs when present and possible qualities are taken as means, or ways of proceeding, toward a qualitative end-in-view, a total quality. The pervasive quality directs artistic behavior from stage to stage until a coherent whole is realized. This purposive activity may be conducted entirely in qualities—component, pervasive, and total. However, there *may* be ordering of theoretical symbols which may not be found as elements of the art work itself, but which are, nevertheless, helpful and in some cases demanded for the solution of a qualitative problem.[9]

Susanne Langer says this kind of feeling has an "act-like" quality. It has an amorphous beginning, rises to a peak, and finally achieves resolution. This gives an indication of the power of this approach to teaching.[10] The teacher moves to establish a pervasive quality that will lead in a particular direction. Problems may arise, of course, because this process is open to abuse, which means that the question of good versus bad teaching, education versus miseducation, remains to be examined.

For the moment, let us look at the procedure that the teacher follows when thinking of learning in these qualitative terms. The teacher is presented with a learner or learners in a particular environment. The teacher assesses the situation as a series of interrelated qualitative relationships. He moves to make some change in the relationships among the component parts. This action is based upon a fund of experience that tells the teacher that the results will probably be a positive modification of the learner or majority of the group of learners. Like the artist, the teacher may well seek a coherent whole—a mature person—as the primary focus of her efforts; therefore, the process of education is often seen as forever incomplete. The teacher strives for a limited end-in-view, realizing that as subsidiary foci many other experiences will go into achieving some kind of completeness. The process of changing the relationships among components usually involves subject matter, and here words and other symbols play a role, though sometimes they are not directly involved in the qualitative relationships. For example, the diagrams and notes used to illustrate a point may be an important part of the learning experience, but not necessarily an integral part of the qualitative relationships.

Ecker cites Dewey, and the quotations he applies to art apply equally well to teaching. Problem-solving that is qualitative is "not a neat progression of steps but a single, continuous means-ends progression, sometimes hesitating, halting, groping; it may be rethought, move forward again, or start over...."[11] In other words, the teaching process does not involve simply setting a goal and then moving directly to its realization. As the teacher proceeds he may realize that his assessment of the need for modification was wrong, and go back and start the whole interaction and interrelation process over again.

Translating Ecker's definition of qualitative problem-solving into a definition in terms of teaching gives us the following: it is the controlled process of instituting qualitative relationships among the commonplaces of teaching as a means to the achievement of modifications in the learner, modifications judged in qualitative terms as characteristic of a whole.

In the process of developing the qualitative problem-solving model, Ecker based the stages of the process on Dewey's stages of a complete act of reflective thinking. Using Ecker's stages as a base, we will examine the stages in an act of teaching. Not all of the steps or stages are to be taken in the order presented, but all will be present in a complete act of teaching.

A Presented Relationship. In the first phase of a teaching situation the teacher explores relationships among the commonplaces of education. This process is one of perception, selection, and discrimination of the component and/or total qualitative relationships present in the situation. It is the determination of the qualities of those aspects that are candidates for reconstruction or change in order to bring about modifications in the learner. These qualities, of course, vary with variations in the learner, the teacher, the subject matter, and the environment. As an example to follow through these steps we will examine the teaching of a poem. During this phase of the process the teacher must decide upon the particular poem to be presented to a particular class at a particular time for some set of reasons. Once we begin to consider these problems we can easily see how complicated and involved these decisions can be to a sensitive teacher.

Substantive Mediation. This is the action phase. The teacher acts in some way to change relationships among the components, thus achieving a change, however subtle, in the quality of these relationships. As this happens some of the new relationships become, however hazily, candidates for means whose status as means is dependent upon having an end-in-view. The choice of a particular set of relationships rather than some other set conditions succeeding choices among qualities. A future choice, however, may involve the destruction of a previous choice in the sense that another quality appears to compete with the initiating quality. Having made some choice about the reason or reasons for the learners to read and hear poetry in order to appreciate it, the teacher begins to act. He may simply set the stage for examining the poem or he may begin to read the poem.

Determination of Pervasive Control. The controlling pervasive quality may emerge at any time during the process of development. It results from components interacting with one another and is a product of the qualities emerging from these respective relationships. The pervasive quality of the experience of reading and discussing a poem may be the result of a conscious decision on the part of the teacher beginning to strive for a particular atmosphere. It might also arise during the initial reading or as a result of the reactions of the learners. It may also be built as discussion develops.

Qualitative Prescription. Once the pervasive quality is established, future actions follow according to patterns of qualitative relatedness. Components of an experience will only be identified and allowed to intrude into the situation if they contribute to the pervasive quality. However, during the act of teaching this quality is sometimes a very tenuous thing. Any powerful alteration of the relationships among the components may destroy it. Once again using our poetry lesson as an example, if an announcement over the loudspeaker interrupts a lesson, this quality may be destroyed. In general though, if the teacher and learners achieve this kind of quality of experience, actions or comments that do not enhance the pervasive quality will be ignored while contributions that make it more powerful will be rewarded.

Experimental Exploration. As every action takes place it is tested to see its relation to the general pervasive quality that is present. The teacher and every learner within the experience participate in this kind of process. At any time one or the other may move to change the direction of the experience, but the initial pervasive quality acts as a reference point. This reference may be as broad as the general tone that usually pervades a particular classroom or as specific as the connotations arising from a particular word. Even if the decision is made to abandon a particular set of relationships because the pervasive quality is no longer right for a particular situation, there is still the function of a reference point. The teacher may begin to feel that the learners are losing interest and further investigation of the poem under study would be useless. He then decides to act to change the situation, but this decision is based upon a change in the total feeling quality. We have all experienced a situation in which the teacher was not sensitive to this change in tone and can describe the resulting boredom or frustration.

Conclusion: The Total Quality. The situation is judged as a whole—the pervasive acts as a control. But the accomplishment of an end-in-view makes this single judgment a tentative affair. Much of what has been accomplished must be assessed in light of past achievements and future possibilities. If the end-in-view for this particular experience with a poem happened to be insight into the way a poet uses language, then the teacher will judge the whole accordingly. But there will be other outcomes that will also be taken into account, and the particular results will be compared with the long-range effect of this one teaching act upon the student. Consideration will also be given to different effects for different learners, making this final phase even more complex. Once more a synthesis takes place and the qualities of the interrelationships among the commonplaces will be assessed for further action. The continual and continuous nature of the process of teaching and learning becomes apparent.

To summarize the view of teaching developed by following Ecker's model for qualitative problem-solving, it may be said that teaching is an endeavor involving the use of qualitative relationships among the commonplaces of education to bring about modifications to improve a learner. To choose this kind of description is to deal with the practice of teaching as an art. The acceptance of this stance has profound implications for the study and understanding of teaching. It means that it should be possible to adapt the methods and tools of criticism developed within the arts for use in teaching. Thus we arrive at a point where we can begin to consider the development of critical tools for teaching.

The Critique

Criticism, as a "rendering" of the critic's encounter with a work of art, does not lend itself to rule-governed evaluation.[12] Like other art forms, criticism must stand or fall upon the insight it brings to its readers. It is a particularly difficult undertaking in that criticism requires both a developed sensibility in relation to the work observed and skill in the presentation of the resulting insights.

To make matters even more difficult, any theoretical position developed must stand the test of presentation in a way that may be quite unrelated to the soundness of the argument. There is no guarantee that, having developed the theoretical position that gives rise to the critical view of teaching, an author will be able to demonstrate the power of such an approach. Still, we must consider some example of what criticism would look like when applied to teaching as an art. What follows, then, is an attempt to present those "renderings" of the author's encounters with the works of one budding artist-teacher. They are presented in the belief that further refinement of method and insight will follow as we recognize the need for the rounding out of technical description. The training of the best of teachers calls for attention to the subtle nuances of mood and expressive quality that mark the differences between the competent and the outstanding. Only as we attempt to preserve and study our insights in particularly telling examples of teaching practice will we move to the fullest understanding of what teaching is about.

Because what follows is different in character from a theoretical discussion, the method of its presentation will differ. The rendering of an encounter with the work of a teacher requires a more intimate and personal touch than does theory; therefore, what follows will be presented as an account in the first person singular.

Like any other critic, I confronted a series of individual works. The insight gained from these separate incidents is the basis of what follows. Such interactions between a teacher, a pupil, and a class are not often preserved, yet I believe it is just these little critical moments that accumulate to make a teacher. It is here that the first impressions that go to make up a final critique begin. Like Kozloff, we must begin with a set of particulars, and these will be used to arrive at a critique.[13]

I have chosen an organicist view, and the overall description that follows could be analyzed using a set of questions derived from Pepper's work in criticism.[14]

As a trainee in Stanford's teacher education program, Miss M. was assigned to teach two classes of introductory art in a nearby high school. As her supervisor and instructor I saw her for instruction, individually as a counselor, and in her classroom. I visited her practicum room once every two weeks early in the school year, then gradually less and less frequently toward the end of the school term. What follows is a rendering of the developing style of a neophyte who has since fulfilled the promise evident in her early "works."

As I drove up to the school in which I was to observe the work of Miss M. I was struck, as I have been since, by its air of forced modernity. This rigid boxlike mound of steel and glass looked like thousands of others that dot those vast stretches of suburb that house the "silent majority."

Just a few blocks off a freeway, the school serves one of those many stretches of development that characterize the outskirts of many major cities in California. Five architectural plans repeated over and over for blocks on end, only slightly varied in color, each sporting a shiny new camper or boat proudly parked beside an equally shiny family car, marked this as a solid bastion of middle America. "The children from these homes should not be lacking in material goods," I thought. Going hungry wasn't likely to be a problem.

The school itself, like many of its counterparts, looked new. The parking lot looked just rolled, and the shrubs and trees planted in neat little borders and large concrete planters were not yet fully grown. They huddled together in sharply defined little clumps around the outskirts of buildings that looked like nothing more than ill-disguised fugitives from a nearby industrial park. The blank walls facing the street were expanses of sandy brick, unbroken except for double doors marking the end of a walkway. This neat stretch of concrete marched up to the doors between two large squares of grass manicured so carefully that it looked like green carpet.

Beside these doors a signed declared with the emphasis of large, black, block letters, ALL VISITORS MUST REGISTER IN THE MAIN OFFICE. As I proceeded through the doors, I passed into a short hall with the caged windows and impersonal air of a bank. Signs were posted to identify a dean's office and a counseling department. They were just doors, however, and I followed the large arrow pointing to the main office around the corner and into another hall.

As I turned the corner I entered one of those long corridors that Deborah James describes so well in *The Taming*.[15] Here in California, though, there was a slight variation. The school as a whole forms a giant letter E with extra horizontal bars added as the school population increases. The intervening spaces are often open to the air rather than being closed. Still, the walls of these patios are blank, broken only intermittently by a classroom door. The surfaces are hard, and if benches are present they have the stolid squat look of utility.

It was hardly the mecca of open air and "open" schooling I had expected when I came to California. Rather than the happy throngs of "Room 222," no students were visible, except for the occasional pass-carrier scurrying from door to door clutching that important slip of paper on the way "to" or "from."

"Wait," I reminded myself, "don't make snap judgments. Appearances can be deceiving." I found the door labeled Main Office.

Still, the room I entered hardly impressed me as an island of concern. The door opened into the inevitable institutional foyer; waxed, polished, orderly, and smelling faintly of Dustbane. Despite my years as a teacher, I still reacted with that slight sinking feeling in the pit of my stomach: "I've been sent to the principal's office."

And I am convinced that the room was arranged to bring on that twinge of awe. The whole of one side of the room was cordoned off by a counter, for beyond this barrier was the land of authority. Rows of teachers' boxes, a bulletin board, and a corps of gray filing cabinets surrounded the lady in charge.

Steel-gray hair, as carefully trimmed as the lawns outside, a muted dress, and that faint network of lines around her mouth and eyes left little doubt about her severity as she advanced to ask, "May I help you?"

I explained the purpose of my visit and the mention of supervision and Stanford provided the necessary reassurance and legitimation. I was given directions and set out to find the art room in that

labyrinth of halls and patios that spread out from the main office for
a city block in either direction.

Because the rooms were numbered and the arms of the *E* were
lettered it was easy for the first few corridors. Then the J-3 that I
was looking for didn't appear after corridor *I*. Instead I came to the
end of a hall and an open court. A separate building? Yes, there
across the court, undifferentiated by size or decoration, showing the
same blank brick walls, high windows, and numbered door, was the
object of my search.

I gave a light tap on the door, and stepped from the white sunshine of the court into the soft shade that sheltered Miss M. and her
students. Music, Bob Dylan, blasted out at me as I moved into the
room. There were groups of tables arranged to form islands of work
surface filling most of the available floor space and nearly every chair
around the tables was full. I thought, "We always seem to follow the
line that the newcomer should begin where it's toughest." And I was
to find that this was the case once again. The class had been created
as an "extra" to relieve overcrowding. As is so often the case, this
class had a high percentage of those who couldn't "make it" in other
classes.

As I looked for Miss M. I saw that she wasn't at the teacher's
desk up near the blackboard. Some of the students nearest the door
had seen me enter and, having given me a curious stare, turned back
toward the room. As I followed the direction of their gazes I saw
Miss M. near the far corner of the room. She was bent over, talking
to a pupil.

While I waited for her to become aware of my presence I sur-
veyed the environment in which she was to work. Storage cupboards
lined the wall to my immediate right and behind me, blackboards the
wall to my left and ahead to sinks below high windows opposite me,
and display boards covered the fourth wall to my far right. There
were two other doors, one open to my left led to another classroom,
the other farther up the blackboard wall was marked as the entrance
to a storeroom. Just above this second door I saw the speaker giving
off the waves of sound that swished over and around me.

The students, whose glances were even now sizing me up, were
the mixture of sizes, shapes, and types I had come to expect in the
typical classroom. A few wore the regalia of one or another group I
had come to expect as well. Some of the boys had the slicked-back

hair and leather jackets that said "greaser" in student terms, others wore the ragged jeans, castoff army clothes and long hair that showed a hippie influence. The girls, too, were similarly grouped. For some, heavy makeup and a back-combed bouffant hairdo was the look. Others wore long dresses and straight hair and tended to sit with their male counterparts. The far corner of the room was reserved for the short-haired "straights" that I later came to know were the "E.H.'ers" (educationally handicapped students) in this particular class.

There was a general air of busy activity, except for small clumps of people here or there who seemed to be engaged in that sort of aimless chatter so important in the who's-going-with-who world of early adolescence. My being there did seem to trigger the class cutup to perform, and his antics attracted Miss M.'s attention. The mechanist requirement of general interest and enjoyment seemed well taken care of. I made a mental note to discuss her "antennae" with her after class. Concentrating on one child while still being tuned in to the general tenor of class activity was one of those tricks that take some practice. For just a moment or two Miss M. had tuned out, and that is when problems develop.

As she looked up and saw me there was a fleeting moment when she had the startled expression of an animal interrupted when drinking. As she tuned back into the class activity and found nothing amiss, she looked relieved. No drastic problems were apparent and she gave me a wan smile and a slight nod as I walked over to say good afternoon.

She seemed rather apprehensive as I spoke to her and only as I talked to her later did I discover the cause. My appearance was different. Gone was the comfortable, casual appearance of a fellow student, and in his place she saw a rather severe, authoritative figure.

Having made myself known, I sat down at the side of the room in a student's desk and began to take the notes which were to form the basis of our later discussion—and this critique. While I did use some of the techniques borrowed from more formally objective observation systems, I relied more heavily on anecdotal notes that would serve to remind me of a particular incident. I did tune in to the tone of activity and I tried to record this general flow of activity as well as critical incidents of greater or lesser import. If an important event did occur I focused on its course, following the ripples and eddies such happenings occasion rather than monitoring general tone. Still, to the extent that I could focus on a particular event, and stay tuned in, as the teacher was expected to do, this critique is a critique of a class's activities.

On this particular day there was a timetable shift that I was not aware of and the period was over almost before I was settled. A buzzer sounded and cleanup began. Students moved about returning tools and putting away material and their work. Bustle and banter were added to Bob Dylan as the class trooped out into the sunshine and only music echoed around the room.

Just then the cutup darted back through the door and began breathlessly to tell Miss M. a story of yesterday's after-class adventure. Where he'd been and what he'd done were so exciting that they made him fairly sparkle. And he did a sort of jig as she gave him her full attention. A soft gladness came through the stern reminder that followed. Miss M. had trouble suppressing a smile as she let him know that he should be in another class. He was reaching out for recognition in a more constructive way than his usual class-disrupting antics and Miss M. responded happily. She liked people and seemed to recognize instinctively that this nuisance was simply asking to be noticed. To go to his next class he would need a late pass, of course, and I watched carefully to see what would happen. P. was watching too, for he shot me a calculating glance to see if I would interfere. "This time you may have one," was the answer given, "but another time you had better save your story until after school."

"That was well handled," I thought, as Miss M. and I were left alone to discuss what I had seen that day.

She began by fussing about, tidying a desk here and putting away materials there. I was concerned at this nervousness. Miss M. had always been very open in her approach and I felt that the relationship we had established over the preceding summer, both in class and in my observing her teaching, would allow me to attack the problem quite directly. I asked her how she felt about my visit and we shared a laugh over her misapprehension of my appearance.

I felt then that attention to the form of what I had seen was of secondary importance for this first visit. Rather, I tried to find out what purposes Miss M. saw for her teaching and the way in which she perceived the rather stark institution through which I had just come. I was seeking the general relationship between purpose and style that marks an organicist view. We just sat and chatted as I tried to get a feel for her reactions.

She did see the school as formal and restrictive, and like many of her fellow beginners she wanted to rebel. She wasn't sure of just how she should move, though. Neither was she willing to accept the school as she found it. Her class was crowded, and the addition of the E.H. students to an already difficult group hadn't helped. Many students, she told me, had indicated that the class was a time-filler. She had taken a survey of backgrounds and interests among her students, keen to find ways in which she could reach them more effectively. Unfortunately what emerged was quite different from her expectations. Few students had indicated that they were motivated to come to the class by an interest in art. They seemed burdened with many other problems, and the school did not offer a way out. Miss M. saw this concern for answers to social problems as the focus of her efforts as a teacher. Still she realized that her assignment was that of teaching art. She seemed determined to find that special project that would somehow jolt her pupils out of their lethargy and air of ennui.

I did mention her "antennae" in relation to the incident of my entry. She picked up on the remark very quickly and realized how startled she'd been when she became aware of the whole class once more. She asked for suggestions of projects she might do. I suggested one or two she might consider and we agreed to discuss the matter further in our next class meeting.

At this point she had to leave to catch her ride and I headed back through the labyrinth to drive back to Stanford. As I sped along the freeway in the late afternoon sunshine I felt comfortably sure that Miss M.'s beginnings were good ones. I resolved to talk to her more fully about the form of her presentation the next time I returned.

Two weeks went by very quickly. In the intervening university classes we had discussed various projects that students might do as well as exchanging anecdotes about classes and their activities. Once again I signed in and found Miss M.'s classroom. This time I had come early in order to see the beginning of the lesson and to check the sequence of what followed.

Miss M. arrived early to prepare the materials her students would need. As I talked to her I learned that she was working on a unit of drawing and that today's lesson would aim at introducing variety into the lines students were using.

As the bell rang the students trooped in and gradually settled into their seats. There followed a short (about five minute) introduction to the notion of variety in the use of line with Miss M. illustrating her talk as she went along. After demonstrating the use of India ink and a straight pen she assigned the students to draw a fellow student using the techniques she had just presented. At the close of this introduction, which was marked by some muttering among the students, they were invited to get their materials. Up they charged with tongues and feet flying. Five minutes of general uproar followed as hassles over pens, paper, and ink were gradually settled. Another five minutes were devoted to settling who was to draw whom and all began to draw a neighboring classmate using the materials provided. The noise level gradually went down, to be replaced with the strident sounds of rock.

For the next twenty-five minutes students worked individually as Miss M. moved around talking to this one and that one in turn. General fun was the order of the day as inexperienced artists showed their efforts to their neighbors. Here was the perfect opportunity to show off, and one or two of the caricatures of "that horrible girl" at the next table were both very funny and very pointed.

P. was in his element, and soon a cowboy sporting P.'s long hair and standing in an exaggerated guns-ready pose convulsed his table-mates. Miss M. came and spoke to him. He sheepishly tossed it into the wastebasket. He had had his fun and went back to work on what was eventually to be quite a sensitive self-portrait.

There were some who complained about the problems of controlling the ink and others who tried too hard for a likeness. These were cajoled into further efforts and the soft giggles and exclamations of enjoyment continued until the warning bell.

Once more there was an explosion of students and materials. Pushing to the cupboard to put away drawings in portfolios, back to the desk to return a pen and ink, they all moved and talked at once. The final bell rang and the turmoil passed out of the door, leaving yet another trail of papers, pens, and ink.

As I looked around rather pointedly at the mess, Miss M. seemed to become more aware of it. At her rather embarrassed comment, "And after my careful preparation, too," I couldn't help laughing at the helplessness teachers so often feel in the face of the high spirits that had just spilled out into the courtyard.

Once more we sat and talked about what had just transpired. At this point my concerns were very much the sort of thing addressed within the first set of questions devised from the mechanist view. Was the presentation interesting? Was there variety in the lesson? Where I had been able to do so I had made observations that would focus on a more directly individual level. Miss M.'s enthusiasm for her subject matter gave her demonstrations a particular power. She seemed to say, "Here is a powerful means of expressing what moves you. It is a moving power in my life and it can be in yours."

Not that her presentation was overly serious. Her manner was quiet rather than loud, yet she liked a lively, even noisy, classroom. As she presented her material she asked the pupils to imagine many of the qualities she sought. At the same time she had pointed out the textures of hair and the patterns of clothing that they would use in the drawings they produced.

As the lesson developed the students had been eager to begin their work and during the work time the pace had kept moving toward a close. Miss M. had been sensitive to the ebb and flow of attention and difficulties throughout the activity period. She was quick to move to help those pupils who had problems and kept the laggards moving. She planned to bring the various problems together in her discussion group, and indeed she did so. However, the same focus on the problems and restrictions the children brought with them to the room dominated Miss M.'s part of the discussion. She wasn't concerned about any of the hijinks. She considered them a healthy part of the natural behavior of these early teens. Their problems were of a different sort, she felt, and she had decided to institute a series of Friday afternoon critique and rap sessions. I expressed an interest in these sessions and asked to be invited to one when she felt comfortable in doing so. I did suggest that a word or two about the mess might be in order. Miss M. said that the department chairman had mentioned the problem and she would speak to the class the next day.

As I left the class this time I wondered how much of a burden this beginner was asking to shoulder. How much was her concern for students' personal problems leading her away from the contribution that her subject might make? Were these problems things she could really help with? These questions were to remain for some time.

The pattern that I had just seen continued to characterize most of the lessons I observed until well into the spring. As I came back, the contextualist focus on the emerging likenesses among the lessons was my concern. I was interested in the long-range effects of Miss M.'s strategy and I looked for the increasing artistic expression in the work of her students. An introductory talk, followed by a studio session and a short cleanup, became the routine procedure. The pattern became familiar and comfortable and the problems were few. The students liked Miss M. and she liked them in turn.

Any storm clouds that marred this tranquil existence rose only when Miss M. had to grade her students' work. Somehow the quality that results from deep commitment just wasn't there. The expressiveness that Miss M. found so satisfying in her own work was often lacking in that of her students. This she found unsettling and we continued to look for a cause and a remedy.

One result of these attempts was an invitation to attend one of the Friday afternoon rap sessions. Surely the last period on a warm afternoon at the end of the week is often a difficult time for both teacher and pupils. The weekend beckons and the evening's movies are often the most serious subject many students want to discuss. As I drove toward San Jose the warm sunshine and Friday afternoon made it necessary for me to push to get there. "How would Miss M. fare?" I wondered.

As usual, she was early, moving around the room putting up the students' work for the critique session. They were the self portraits that had been the culminating activity of the drawing unit. She was happy with the results of this lesson and eager to proceed with the session.

The students came in with less of the horsing around I had noticed earlier. They quickly settled in and there was an air of eager anticipation as the discussion began. Each student was given a few minutes to talk about his own work, presenting both what he liked best about it and what he saw as needing improvement. The class was then allowed to make positive statements about the particular work and ask questions of the artist.

There was a surprisingly adult and professional tone to what followed. Certainly, some like P. the cutup, enjoyed their turn at center stage. His verbal characterization of his portrait was witty and to the point. Having had a rather good beginning, as so often happens with beginners, he had kept on working and reworking his drawing. The final result I can only describe as blotchy. There was still a face but overworking had almost obliterated it.

"Notice the power of that big black blob!"

"What power there is in the black and white contrast."

P.'s comments were offered with a twinkle in his eye and a small smile playing around the corners of his mouth. And everyone caught the point of his exaggerated praise. Miss M. prodded him toward a more realistic appraisal. Suddenly with a sheepish grin he suggested that the whole thing was a colossal failure. "But what a grand failure!" was his implication.

Miss M. agreed that the portrait was indeed a grand failure. She suggested that every attempt with any medium was open to failure. The important point was to learn from the failure and do better the next time.

"An important lesson that presented the struggle of the artist," I thought to myself. But what was happening? Certainly the point wasn't being endorsed by the class.

"That's not what happens in school."

"You only get punished for mistakes."

"What about getting busted for possession?"

These and similar remarks tumbled out one on top of the other. The conversation began to take on a new tone. The injustices of a world insensitive to the real needs of youth was the theme, and the students played every variation.

Miss M. was hard put to maintain a position that allowed her to deal with the problems in some detached fashion. There was an attempt to create a we-they situation. Miss M. must choose, was the implication, to side with her virtuous students or with the cruel adults.

"What will her reaction be?" I wondered. Miss M. expressed her concern for their problems but insisted upon a special place for herself as a teacher. She would help but there could be no real rift between teacher and other adults. After all was said and done they would become adults. This was in a sense their special task as students.

At this point the bell sounded to end the session and with a final sally or two the gang thundered out into the sunshine.

I was drained after the tension of the interchanges I had just witnessed. Miss M., too, was weary. It had been a tough lesson. Despite the difficulty of such teaching, however, she still felt that the trouble was worthwhile. The personal problems of the students must take precedence over what she wanted to do.

As we talked about the discussions and moved into a more general consideration of what had been happening in these sessions Miss M. seemed less enthusiastic about her "adjustment" approach. "So much of teaching is giving," she said. The weight of student problems meant that she wasn't dealing with art. Her satisfaction and sense of fulfillment were coming from her own art work rather than from her teaching. She had taught before and felt that this just shouldn't be the case. I tried to rephrase her dissatisfaction for her.

"Should your primary concern be with the area you are trained to teach?"

"What is the relationship between the child's insight into his problems and what you can give him in art?"

"Which of their problems can you do something about and when can you only offer sympathy?"

It was hot and late and those questions were not going to be answered easily. That was enough for that day. We were both tired, and the weekend was more important for the moment. I was concerned that the larger organicist view be available to Miss M., and my questions were presented in the hope that she would consider the effects of her teaching beyond simple pupil enjoyment. We ended the session with a chuckle over P.'s little performance and my offer to drop into the office to talk further about the class's problems.

We were moving toward the end of the term and I didn't see Miss M. for a couple of weeks after that encounter. Then, late one afternoon, Miss M. appeared to ask me to come to see the class's kite flying. During the series of lessons she had asked one of the men in the science department at the high school to talk about aerodynamics, gone to the library for books, and built a kite of her own. The emphasis had been on design. The choice of project was a good one. Those things were to fly. "But what had happened to the problems?" I wondered.

I asked, and Miss M. related the following incident. She had been trying to extend the drawing techniques she had given the students to more complex and difficult subjects. The pace seemed sluggish, so she had taken special pains to find materials and prepare what she thought would be an exciting lesson. It seemed to get started quite well when one of the girls interrupted to recount the latest of a series of fights at home. The others picked up the theme and the discussion was off again.

"Suddenly," Miss M. said, "I realized there was no purpose other than getting it out served by such talk." This was the students' way of diverting her lesson. "They're dumping on me!" was Miss M.'s way of putting it.

She saw that her well-meant concern was being used simply as an excuse to goof off. The art that should have given meaning to her time with her students was being subverted. A new emphasis upon making visual statement was her resolve and the kites were the result.

After this incident Miss M.'s classes seemed to go even better. She was happier and so were her students. They wasted less time steering discussions into battles over the cruel adult world. More effort was given to art. The realization that her ability to guide others to insights within the discipline of art was what teaching was about was an important milestone for Miss M. She had come through a series of "works" that had set her well on the way toward becoming a mature artist-teacher. After completing her Stanford training she became a special visiting art teacher. Her concern for her students' problems continued. Now, however, it was tempered by an emphasis upon helping through the insights of artistic experience.

The foregoing critique is not particularly startling. It simply records the making of a teacher in terms of the qualitative dimensions of that process. Allowing the neophyte to find her own method of absorbing the techniques she learns to a point where they become habitual moves is like learning to pilot an airplane. You can describe the moves and even attempt to characterize the feel of the plane. Yet, like the new pilot, the beginning teacher, in the long run, must assume the controls and make the moves that will result in pupils learning. One hopes that a critic, sensitive to the results of the moves she makes, will be there to help her over the rough spots. One hopes, too, that these attempts to preserve some of one critic's reactions will be of help to others who face the same sort of situation. If such writing proves helpful others may be encouraged to do the same and we can begin to develop the criticism of teaching to the level of a useful art.

If what has just been presented were sets of empirical findings, it would now be appropriate to give some indication of their contributions to the field of teaching. Questions that arose in the course of the investigation would be raised and directions for further research suggested.

The results of the present critique are of a different order. The verification of criticism is accomplished as it is used. While it is a fact that Miss M. became a successful special art teacher, further study of the relationship between criticism and her competency needs to be carried out before any claims are made. As a direction for further study we would suggest that the practice of criticism in relation to teaching might be studied in a comparative way. A videotape could be made and critics' reactions written from the viewpoints suggested in the study with these presented to the teachers to test their effects upon further practice.

Notes

1. Jacob S. Kounin, *Discipline and Group Management in Classrooms* (New York: Holt, Rinehart and Winston, Inc., 1970).

2. The paucity of this kind of writing is noted in Ronald T. Hyman, ed., *Teaching: Vantage Points for Study* (Philadelphia, Pa.: Lippincott, 1968).

3. A. S. Neill, *Summerhill* (New York: Hart Publishing Co., 1960).

4. An example of this kind of teacher concern is found in Jonathan Kozol's *Death at an Early Age* (Boston: Houghton Mifflin Co., 1967). The more general view is found in Jerome Bruner's work; see, for example, *The Process of Education* (Cambridge, Mass.: Harvard University Press, 1960).

5. David W. Ecker, "The Artistic Process as Qualitative Problem-Solving," in *Readings in Art Education*, ed. Elliot W. Eisner and David W. Ecker (Waltham, Mass.: Blaisdell Publishing Co., 1966).

6. Descriptions of teaching in this mode can be found in books like Deborah James's *The Taming: A Teacher Speaks* (New York: McGraw-Hill, 1969).

7. These are identified by Schwab as the teacher, the learner, the subject matter, and the environment, in "The Practical: A Language for Curriculum," *The School Review* 78 (November 1969): 1-23.

8. A. Simon and E. G. Boyer, *Mirrors for Behavior*, 13 vols. (Philadelphia, Pa.: Research for Better Schools, Inc., 1967).

9. Ecker, *Readings*, p. 65.

10. Susanne Langer, *Mind: An Essay on Human Feeling* (Baltimore, Md.: The Johns Hopkins Press, 1967).

11. Ecker, *Readings*, p. 67.

12. The term "rendering" is taken from Kozloff (see n. 13), who suggests that the critic should give an account of the interaction between critic and a work of art.

13. Max Kozloff, *Renderings: Critical Essays on a Century of Modern Art* (New York: Simon and Schuster, 1961).

14. The term is taken from Stephen Pepper's *The Basis of Criticism in the Arts* (Cambridge, Mass.: Harvard University Press, 1956). The focus of organicist writing will be the coherence or relatedness of the many individual incidents observed.

15. See n. 6.

The case study by Gail McCutcheon is a very precise and systematically developed piece of curriculum criticism. In her introductory section McCutcheon briefly presents a highly focused but comprehensive explanation of the three part delineation of the processes of criticism ("description," "interpretation," "appraisal") which she has originated, including specific explanations of types of interpretations, of criteria for considering the truthfulness of interpretation, and of how appraisal may be carried out and justified. The remainder of the essay is a criticism of a particular fourth-grade classroom in which description, interpretation, and appraisal are blended.

The case study is a highly balanced exemplification of criticism, and, as such, no particular aspects of criticism seem especially emphasized, at least to the extent of deemphasizing other aspects. For instance, the principal critical focal point is probably the "work," with focus on how the classroom environment and activities are organized and how meanings are thereby embodied, but McCutcheon also deals with the intentions of the teacher ("author"), the individual and collective reactions of students and their own interpretations of meaning ("audience"), and the possible inadequacies of the classroom in reflecting the complexities of the outside "world."

186

In this study interpretation and appraisal often center around what McCutcheon considers the "social meanings" of classroom events and how these events are related to "external factors." Basically, meaning is disclosed and becomes the basis for judgment only as it is made public. To the extent that the study deals with individual meanings and depends on the perceptions of an individual critic, the study embodies the personal dimension of curriculum criticism. To the greater extent that it deliberately moves interpretation and appraisal into a public domain, the study embodies the political dimension. However, the dominant interest in the study is the aesthetic. Description of the classroom environment and activities is intended to evoke in the reader a sense of what being there is like, its "ambience," a distinctive trait of aesthetic criticism. Interpretation is often of configurations or patterns within what has been described. In short, the critical perspective that McCutcheon explicates and illustrates is similar primarily (though not exclusively) to critical methods in the arts.

9

Of Solar Systems, Responsibilities, and Basics: An Educational Criticism of Mr. Clement's Fourth Grade

Gail McCutcheon

Introduction and Methodological Notes

The case study related in this chapter is based upon six weeks of field work done in the winter of 1976. The focus of the study was Mr. Clement's class of twenty-six fourth-grade children in a suburban middle-class neighborhood. Information was obtained in several ways. Observations were recorded in field notes and on videotape. Informal chats held with the teacher, children, parents, and principal were also recorded in field notes. Additionally, student work was examined, as were Mr. Clement's plans.

Following methodological notes, the classroom will be described in order to re-create for readers its ambience, environment, and activities. Additionally, aspects of the classroom will be examined from several interpretive perspectives. Finally, the events will be appraised. Generally, the questions addressed in the chapter are: What is going on here? What are children likely to learn as a result? Is this worthwhile? And for what reasons?

Grateful acknowlededment is extended to Ron Comfort for his thoughtful comments on an earlier draft of this chapter.

Description, interpretation, and appraisal constitute the processes of educational criticism. Description involves re-creating the
classroom to evoke in the readers a sense of what it is like to be
there. The first three paragraphs of the following case study are descriptive in nature.

Another process, interpretation, is comprised of three perspectives. One interpretive perspective utilized in this chapter concerns
the examination of the social meanings of events in the classroom.
While we could merely recount the physical behavior of participants,
little would be learned, for many aspects of human behavior must be
interpreted to be understood. Gilbert Ryle coined the term "thick
description" in reference to the reporting of the social meaning of
activities.[1] What, for instance, does it imply if children say they are
"learning to be interdependent," but do not know what "interdependent" means? And what does it mean if children nod during a
class presentation? Are they following the teacher's train of thought
or agreeing with the teacher? Evincing an interest that isn't there?
Nodding because they know the teacher calls on children who don't
appear to be listening, hoping to catch them? The meanings of such
behavior are accounted for in this perspective.

Turning now to a second interpretive perspective, we will consider the relationship of activities and events to external factors. In
this instance, particulars are related to general theoretical principles
from education and the social sciences, to practices elsewhere, and to
the general context of schooling. For instance, a lesson in one classroom may exemplify behavior modification, which requires that
interpretation draw upon psychological theory. In another we may
observe a manifestation of the contemporary concern for the so-
called basics, requiring us to relate a specific classroom to current
trends in schooling. In this perspective, a dialectic occurs between
the particulars and the general, for theory is illuminated through the
examples, and specific events are understood in light of their relationship to large considerations. By this I mean we are likely to
understand a theory through the example and we can understand the
specific phenomena occurring in a classroom by referring to the
theory. Each provides a richer understanding of its counterpart.

Yet a third interpretive perspective consists of explaining affiliations that classroom events have with one another in terms of configurations. In this perspective discrete facts and events are related to

one another in the formation of patterns. Clearly, events in a classroom do not occur haphazardly; they have their own rationale. A
structural skeleton underlies the discrete events. This skeleton is
formed of customs, rules, and habits of the teacher and class in terms
of their relationships to one another, to the work, and to the environment. This does not mean that I embrace structuralism; I do not
mean that the structures or patterns underlying specific events are
the same across classrooms. On the contrary, I believe the structures
to vary as different groups of people form different ways of interacting with materials, the curriculum, and each other. As with theory
and specifics, a dialectic occurs between patterns and specific events.
That is, the patterns revealed in a classroom provide an understanding of specific events in it. Simultaneously, an understanding of the
patterns is provided, for the specific events exemplify patterns. Clifford Geertz put it nicely when he said they "render one another
intelligible."[2] As an example of this perspective, after observing a
reading class for several days, we may notice children only actually
reading when the teacher is nearby. The pattern may also be evident
in children's only putting books into the bookcase neatly if the
teacher is watching. This pattern of "teacher as watchdog" and children's responses to it may be apparent in other situations as well.
The first perspective concerning the social meaning may afford us the
vehicle to consider why the pattern is there. Through the second
perspective, research about children's reactions to authoritarian
teachers may be brought to bear on the incident. And through the
third, we may form the pattern to explain the particular events.

These three interpretive perspectives, then, will be employed in
helping to provide an understanding of Mr. Clement's classroom: the
social meaning of events, the relationship of classroom events to external factors, and the patterns of events in the classroom. As demonstrated in the most recent example, these perspectives overlap. Furthermore, they probably do not form an exhaustive set of the types
of interpretation of classroom phenomena. Readers are urged to consider other types to contribute to the list of interpretive perspectives.

In deciding upon the truthfulness of interpretations, I have used
three general criteria. The first concerns the amount and quality of
evidence supporting an interpretation. This is largely a question of
whether sufficient evidence is present for a particular conclusion to
be drawn. Evidence is usually cited from several converging sources

rather than repeated observation of the same phenomenon. Stephen Pepper referred to this type of substantiation through various bits of evidence as "structural corroboration."[3]

A second criterion is the relative likelihood of an interpretation. In other words, given the particular nature of the evidence, are other interpretations possible or even more credible? Casting about for a variety of possible interpretations is a crucial step here.

The third criterion relates to the usefulness and importance of an interpretation. Basically, the question is whether it makes a significant contribution to understanding classroom events and patterns of events.

We walk a thin line in doing educational criticism. On one hand, we may interpret with too much trepidation, not pushing an interpretation far enough, and descend into in the realms of the obvious, the banal, and the unimportant. On the other hand, we may push interpretations too far, leading us to consider important issues but not grounding our analysis in the reality of the classroom being critiqued. These excesses may be avoided in educational criticism by using the three criteria just discussed. Underinterpretation may be guarded against through the third criterion of usefulness and importance. Overinterpretation may be guarded against through the first criterion of sufficiency of evidence in terms of quality and quantity and the second criterion of credibility.

In addition to the description and interpretation of Mr. Clement's classroom, practices and activities will be appraised. Here we will consider whether the activities he arranges are worthwhile and whether he performed well in arranging them. Generally speaking, the two questions of appraisal are "Was it worth doing?" and "Was it done well?" Both questions are important, for they reveal two sides of a situation when considering the merits of a lesson. For example, stringing colored macaroni on a Friday afternoon may not be considered worthwhile on a number of counts, given all the other things children could be doing on a Friday afternoon. But the teacher may have presented the activity very artfully. This teacher has a content problem, not a pedagogical one. Consider now another teacher presenting a lesson about metrics. Surely we agree that children should be knowledgeable about using the metric system, since it appears the nation will eventually be using it. But this teacher may present the lesson poorly, confusing terms, not providing for practice, and so forth. Unlike the first teacher, this teacher has a pedagogical problem rather than a content problem. In appraising lessons, then, both questions are important.

While the three processes of description, interpretation, and appraisal can be treated separately in educational criticism, in this case study they are interwoven. Each process casts different light on the nature of classroom life. Description reveals the nature of a particular classroom, while through interpretation and appraisal we can consider a classroom and the potential consequences of what is taught there in a broader context, relating it to classrooms elsewhere and to theory. It is hoped that both the approach—the ways of thinking about this classroom—and the substance of this case study—the considerations and issues raised and conclusions drawn—may help teachers, supervisors, evaluators, administrators, and other educators in looking at classrooms elsewhere.[4]

In this case study of Mr. Clement's fourth grade, we will first look at the environment and consider how it supports his main emphases in schooling. Then we will examine the activities of the classroom. Throughout the case study, description, interpretation, and appraisal are used, although a concluding section is primarily devoted to appraisal.

The Classroom Environment

Myriad sounds, smells, and sights greet the newcomer to Mr. Clement's room. The squeal of a guinea pig and the scrabbling of rats in their wire cages mingle with the voices of children as they discuss their private lives and schoolwork. Penny wants to know whether Maria and Freddie like each other because they sit together. Laura asks Mr. Clement if she may go to the library as another girl returns triumphantly, holding up *Mrs. Piggle Wiggle,* apparently a treasure. The smells of guinea pigs, rats, clean wood shavings, school disinfectant, and a freshly peeled orange intermix. Randy is eating raisins.

Tables, desks, bookcases, orange crate art supply bins, filing cabinets, couches, and large pillows fill the carpeted room compactly, providing an intimate, informal ambience. An extra partition juts out into the room, turning the floor plan into a tight *U.* Even the ceiling seems close. One leg of the *U* is a cosy reading corner with soft pillows, a lumpy, inviting couch, and a low table with three chairs. Tables of varying character provide alternative places to work around the room. One is a rejected telephone company wire spool; another is a scant fourteen inches tall so children can sit on the carpet while they work.

Colorful walls gently enclose the room. A bookworm wriggles around the top; its segments advertise the books read by class members and it grows weekly. Materials line the shelves within easy reach of pupils: paperback books, guinea pigs, rats, a science kit, dictionaries, musical instruments, Sears catalogs, dominoes, math games, crossword puzzles, phonics games, and mazes. A milk carton mailbox and a container hold messages and supplies for each of the twenty-seven deskless students. Most children have found comfortable places to work, usually with a friend or two. While they may freely change seats, they seem to work in the same spot from day to day.

Many classrooms are institutional in appearance, with rows and columns of formica-topped steel desks, linoleum floors, metal book cases, rolled-up maps, and alphabet letters marching around the room in the thin strip of bulletin board just above the blackboard that seems to have been tacked up for just such a display. But this room is not institutional. Its soft surfaces, casual furniture and arrangements, varied work areas, and colorful displays at first seem jumbled and disorganized, perhaps because we expect schoolrooms to be hard-surfaced, uniform, and somewhat bland. In fact, this room seems more like a home than an institution. Children move more freely and relate to one another, to the teacher, and to the room itself less formally than in many classrooms, as they quietly joke, prod, sprawl, and work.

By providing this sort of environment, Mr. Clement has created a situation in which children must make many choices—where to sit, which friends to work with, whether to chat about last night's televised *Mystery Movie* or do the phonics chapter. Many things, friends, and places beckon for attention. Such choices require children to decide upon a course of action, to follow it, and to accept responsibility for it. In less informal settings teachers make many of these choices for children with seating plans and rules about when they may talk. But in Mr. Clement's classroom, children, being responsible for the choices and for behavior within the choices, are provided with the opportunity to practice and to experiment with responsibility for choice-making and behavior several times a day. The physical environment supports Mr. Clement's emphasis on these responsibilities.

Also reflected in the physical environment is Mr. Clement's concern for interaction among students. While children work individually on skills he deems important at some times during the day, most of the time they work in small groups in many spots around the room. They converse freely while they work, and a friendly atmosphere pervades the room. With the widespread interest in individualization, many teachers do not seem to be as concerned with the social processes of their groups as Mr. Clement is, so their children work as if encased in glass boxes, rarely going beyond their confines to interest with classmates. But Mr. Clement believes "it is important for children to learn how to get along with each other" and his concern is reflected in the quiet corners and furniture groupings conducive to working together.

The Activities of the Classroom

But what are the teacher and children doing? Generally, they work on one of two types of activities: a group activity requiring cooperation, or an individual activity aimed at practicing a skill Mr. Clement believes is important. The science lesson considered here is a group activity reflecting Mr. Clement's interest in having children practice making choices and working together.

Mr. Clement stands in front of a homemade chart of the solar system and a list of words on the blackboard. A mound of boxes, balls of string, black paper, silver stars, and modeling clay wait promisingly to one side. The children sit on the carpet in front of him, wigglingly expectant. They know they will make something—the materials bear silent testimony to that. But for now, they direct their attention to Mr. Clement's questions. They define, discuss, and become parts of the solar system in a quick ten-minute group meeting. Mr. Clement elicits information and directs demonstrations as Kenny becomes the earth revolving around Alan/sun. Chris suggests Kenny should also be rotating, anticipating Mr. Clement's next demonstration. Then Mr. Clement directs their attention to the chart on which he placed the sun, planets, and moons (while watching the Monday night football game, he confides). Children have a reason to look at it and to listen, for the chart is to act as a reference for their activity of building a solar system in a box. Reminding Penny to put something away, he checks whether they know how to read the chart. Which planet is closest to the sun? "Mercury!" they call out. "If you know, I'll call on you," he reminds them. (How could he discern whether they know the answer before calling on them?) They raise their hands and someone answers: it is still Mercury. Charlie suggests using science books for additional information. Mr. Clement picks up on the idea, asking children for the names of reference books, although he hadn't planned to.

"Okay," he says, "I'm gonna give each group of three a box to build a solar system in. Using the chart, I want you to decide what goes where and how big it should be." He says he will provide twenty seconds for children to find three people for a group. With a minimum of confusion (by fourth-grade standards) they seek their friends and form triads. In slightly over a minute they are sitting on the carpet with hands up to indicate their readiness. They seem eager to begin as they quiet one another. Mr. Clement lists the materials he will provide, although if they have another way of making a solar system, such as using crumpled paper, he says they may do so. He calls upon threesomes by name to get materials and they find places to work on the couch, behind bookcases, in corners, on the floor or under tables.

At this point group decisions must be made. Where to work? What materials to use? How large to make the bodies? Who is to do what? They start to discuss these problems.

But all is not well. Kenny argues about a box. Rachel's materials are grabbed out of her hand. Mr. Clement calls the group back to the carpet for a town-meetinglike discussion about how they should work. They list behavior in need of improvement: they were too noisy, misusing materials, grabbing, fighting, and teasing. Mr. Clement seems genuinely concerned about how students are behaving. The students respond in an equally concerned fashion. He asks for possible solutions, which are offered. Then he summarizes them: children should make the best of what they have, should simply stop grabbing, and be more orderly and patient. As a final statement of the meeting, Rachel declares heatedly, "Every box is as good as the other one. No one is a whole lot better than another. Kids should be more fair about materials and about what they say so they don't hurt feelings."

During the meeting, children are attentive. Perhaps they want to continue with the constructions. Perhaps also, they know that during such a meeting misbehaving is not a good idea. If they don't pay attention or they fool around, Kenny reports, "Mr. Clement gets real mad." Randy agrees: "Sometimes we can't even work on this any more." They may perceive Mr. Clement's concern and act as concerned to maintain peace. At any rate, group meetings are apparently not a good time to fool around. But the children also seem interested in continuing their constructions.

Mr. Clement says he is pleased with some students and wants them to get back to work—first, Chris, Randy, and Lindsay, then others. This rewards them publicly, perhaps reinforcing their good behavior (not always easy for Chris and Randy), and may also publicize Mr. Clement's standards.

Three boys remember a box of science materials in a cabinet. Bill wants to use a styrofoam ball from it for the sun. Fred believes it's the right size for Mars, but Bill exclaims "Think how big we'd have to make Jupiter and the sun!" "Oh, yeah," says Fred. They wonder how to suspend the balls they found in the science kit from the top of the box. No one boy acts as leader of the group continually; they shift the role.

Penny begins to cut the flaps off a box. Nearby, Clara says "No!"—she does not want Maria to help her cut planets, and she later perceives Penny as encroaching on her territory. "Move! Wanna get your face marked up?" she threatens. Penny and Maria plan together, leaving Clara to cut the planets alone. Penny and Maria accept Clara's threat and plan the remainder of the project, perhaps hoping to avoid a difficult argument.

Three other boys are intent on solving the problem of how to keep the string from showing on one side if they cut a circle of construction paper and glue the string to it. They decide to cut another circle and place the string in the middle.

Charlie lines a box with black paper, then puts his head all the way inside to look around. Alan wads up a paper Mercury, but Charlie says, "It's too big. How about chewing gum size?" Alan complies.

Sally, Janet, and Alice have divided the work, but when they meet to assemble their solar system, they find Sally's Mars is bigger than Alice's Jupiter, and Janet's sun is smaller than Jupiter. They salvage their work by renaming the spheres they made, working collegially on the problem rather than having one person tell the others what to do as Charlie's group does. Alice's Jupiter becomes the sun and Sally's Mars becomes Jupiter. Kenny takes Alice's glue. Clara yells at Penny again. Penny puts her hands over her ears.

Children solve problems as they arise, remember where materials are, invent ways of doing things, use names of planets and other astronomical terms in their work. Their work is not superficial, but has an intensity to it. After forty-five minutes of constructing solar systems, several groups have almost finished. Mr. Clement calls them all to the carpet again, for he has observed many types of unacceptable behavior and he believes another discussion is in order. Tomorrow they will finish the constructions, but he believes "they have been getting less and less thoughtful about each other for the last two weeks and this can't go on," so they meet to reflect about their behavior.

What did the children have an opportunity to learn in this activity? In order to build their solar systems, children had to attend to certain relationships among the sun and planets—relative distances among them, size, and position. This is a form of visual problem-solving, which may not be too out of place in elementary schools, although it is not frequently employed, to my knowledge. After all, we may recall, when Watson and Crick solved the puzzle of the structure of DNA, they built models to fit together certain known information. Eventually they arrived at a model of the double helix structure, accepted today by the scientific community, and the model also revealed new understandings of the way DNA replicates. It appears, then, that at times people can solve through constructions what they cannot solve solely by abstractly envisioning something. In this case, children learned about the solar system through visual problem-solving.

Most children's difficulties were primarily engineering or construction problems: how to suspend the sun, how to keep the string from being too obvious, and so forth. Other children's primary difficulties were those of self-control, which prevented them from even considering the relational or engineering problems. This problem was coupled with the fact that solar system construction as assigned by Mr. Clement required group cooperation. As a result, work had to be divided, concessions and decisions made, leadership and followership practiced, all of which are important skills for working socially. Groups developed different ways of dealing with these social processes, from shifting the leadership responsibility (as with Bill's group), to complying with the demands of one child (as with Penny's group), to following the directions of a strong leader (as with Charlie's group), to working collegially with no one acting as a leader (as with Sally's group).

While some activities in Mr. Clement's room require only self-control, this one also required social skills. Clara's lack of self-control kept her from working socially on the engineering and relational questions and consumed the energy of other group members whose work was affected. In fact, the other two members of Clara's group functioned as a pair and did most of the work. Kenny also suffered from problems of self-control and interfered with several groups.

Four types of problem situations that could lead to children's learning could be encountered in this assignment. (1) Relational problems concern the academic content of the lesson, such as how far away from the sun Pluto is and how much larger the sun is than Jupiter. (2) Engineering problems concern the medium of expression and involve construction difficulties such as how to make and suspend planets. (3) Social problems concern working together in a group. And (4) self-control problems encountered by a few children concern individual behavior. Mr. Clement is aware of the fact that several children are unable to experience the relational, engineering, and social problems because of their behavior. That is, children who had difficulty with behavior could not control themselves sufficiently to address themselves to learning how to work socially and to the content and engineering questions. Mr. Clement believes learning self-control has a higher priority; in fact, he believes it is the basis for other learning. To provide an opportunity for children to practice self-control, the environment and activities are structured in such a way that children must exercise it. Because the environment and activities require self-control, and because this teacher does not control children in an authoritarian way, we may see a bit more misbehavior in this classroom than in one where activities are more controlled by the teacher. As Mr. Clement says, "You can't expect them all to be responsible and controlled all the time, and some have more difficulty with it than others. Unfortunately, there isn't any other way to get them to become responsible for their own actions than to provide a freer setting."

In this lesson, then, children had the opportunity to learn many things—things about the solar system, construction, visual problem-solving, self-control and social interaction. We might wonder, though, whether responsibility for decision-making, planning socially, and self-control are worthwhile lessons. It is reasonable to believe that children who are afforded the opportunity to practice these responsibilities are more likely to acquire them than children who are controlled by a teacher in such a way that they do not practice them. Clearly, in every classroom, children learn to cooperate with peers to a certain extent. A continuum could be drawn to represent different types of cooperation. At one end we would have rather narrow cooperation of two children teaching one another number facts or spelling words. Here, little problem-solving and decision-making need occur beyond determining whose turn it is first and how to proceed. At the other end of the continuum, I suppose, would be a case in which several children decide together what to study, how to learn about it, where to work, and so forth. Here, every decision would be in their hands. Mr. Clement's brand of responsibility obviously resides somewhere between the two extremes, for triads of children are responsible for their behavior, for decisions about where to work, which materials to use, the scale of the model, and so forth. However, their product and the content of their activity is defined by the assignment.

But don't children learn these responsibilities anyway—in the home, the community, and school without so much emphasis being placed upon them? Not all children may be afforded the opportunity. In many homes, parents may not know how to foster responsibility. Additionally, many children's lives are managed so that they have Scouts on Monday, music lessons on Tuesday, swim club on Wednesday and so forth, leaving them little opportunity to learn how to be autonomously interdependent—that is, to learn how to plan and act cooperatively in a social setting, yet to be individually responsible for behavior. And in some classrooms, the responsibilities are probably more narrowly conceived. Here, children are given the opportunity to experiment with ways of dealing with the responsibilities and to practice them.

Similarly, we might wonder about the academic content of the lesson. Isn't it likely that fourth-graders know the relative size and position of planets already? Indeed, during the discussion preceding the activity, it seemed they already had a great deal of sophisticated information about the solar system. Chris, for example, anticipated the rotation demonstration. Could a more challenging activity have been designed? A more complex assignment seems possible, one that would still account for social interaction, self-control, visual problem-solving, and construction learnings, yet would expand their knowledge about the solar system.

The second major type of activity Mr. Clement provides is aimed at teaching individual skills to children, generally in writing, mathematics, reading, and spelling. Children have an hour of this type of work in the morning and another forty-five minutes consisting solely of math skills in the afternoon. At the beginning of the day, Mr. Clement gives each child a personal notelike contract stating what to do during the day. Children are free to choose where to work and the order in which to proceed. As a result, children are engaged in different activities at any given time during the work period. During the morning, they work on dittoes, read, write stories, practice cursive writing, and so forth.

Trainlike, some children make the stops at stations one, two, three, and four to work on materials while Mr. Clement circulates to help. "When we start a new sentence, how do we begin it?" he quietly asks Penny, who changes the small letter to a capital. Eliciting the information from Penny rather than merely pointing to the error and telling her how to change it causes her to recall the already-known rule. On other occasions, he may say "How do you need to change this sentence?" requiring students to spot the error as well as to recall the rule to apply.

While some children answer questions on worksheets at the stations, others read. Alan and Mr. Clement sit beside each other on two low chairs. They hold a paperback book between them as Alan reads a page softly. They seem informal, comfortable, and close. "Are you enjoying this story? You seem to be enjoying it an awful lot." Alan nods vigorously, his face breaking into a wide, partly toothless grin. "Tell me a little bit about the first chapter you read." Alan softly but earnestly retells the story to Mr. Clement, who gently interrupts with a question once in a while. "Who did you say that was? . . . Oh, have you ever felt like that?"

When discussing stories individually with students, Mr. Clement's questions tend to focus upon retrieving information, summarizing, and making personal connections with the story. Given Mr. Clement's approach of individualizing reading by having personal conferences, he might consider widening the types of conversations he has students address. For example, he could ask students to interpret a story, to analyze the author's use of language, or to consider their reading tastes to permit children to develop an awareness of them in addition to only building skills of retrieving information, summarizing, and personal connection-making. As it stands now, children may be learning how to decode words and to retrieve information, but they may be missing the appreciation of literature and its critical analysis. In many classrooms, it seems, teachers emphasize how to decode words through linguistics or phonics at the expense of the appreciation of literature. "Word-calling" may become such a chore and a goal that teachers and children forget about the content and style of a work of literature. When reading is a chore, we might wonder whether children are likely to do it unless they have to.

We may also wonder whether only talking about a story individually is as effective an approach as having small groups discuss a story. Together, a group can deliberate, wonder, and help each other reach an understanding of difficult aspects of a story on a more sophisticated level than individuals can operate on alone. The practice of holding small group discussions of a particular book or genre would conform to Mr. Clement's concern for social interaction and might expedite the learning of interpretive, analytic, and critical reading skills.

Phonics, linguistics, and dictionary use are presented on dittoes and workbook pages at the stations, requiring children to apply certain concepts. Mr. Clement notices difficulties as he walks around the room and helps individuals, or they signal a need for help by raising their hands. But not all students may be able to learn phonics and concepts from them. The difficulty with the written materials is this: if children can read the rather wordy directions, they do not need to practice the simple phonics and linguistics skills provided on the paper. And if they cannot do the phonics and linguistics exercises, how can they be expected to be able to read the directions? On other dittoes, if children can apply the required concept, they do not need to practice it; if they need to practice the concept, they cannot do the ditto. Perhaps these materials are really meant to keep children occupied while Mr. Clement works with others. But I believe he thinks that they will teach children skills and concepts he believes to be important. Children seem to enjoy working at their own pace, in their own places, but (as with the science lesson) more thought should be given to what they should be doing—to the substance of the lesson. Assigning papers they cannot do because they don't know a skill, or worksheets requiring them to apply skills they already have seems to be a waste of time for every one involved, both the children doing them and the teacher correcting them.

While others are working at stations or reading to Mr. Clement, Chris and Randy are reading comic books. Randy, reading to the guinea pig, is a comic book *maven*; he knows which issues are valuable, the life histories of Superman, the Fantastic Four, and Wonder Woman, and other essential information. Chris is also reading a comic book and is drawing and writing his own comic book about Putty Man. Permitting children to pursue their own interests through reading may help them understand its value and make connections between their own lives and the reading.

Amy has a shoe box house for a tiny, furry toy mouse. She made a telephone, bowl, penny bank, and cup for the mouse out of seashells, a bed and television out of small boxes, a chair out of a slice of apple wood, and a toybox out of a small plastic pillbox. As she works on her ditto from station four, she talks to the mouse about the assignment. Mr. Clement does not make Amy put the mouse away, nor make Chris cease to write about Putty Man. Instead he occasionally enters the fantasy—"How's the mouse today, Amy? Any new furniture yet?"—or Chris's personal comic book writing— "What's new with Putty Man, Chris? Is he able to leap tall buildings in a single bound?" Recognizing children's personal lives and admitting them to the classroom may partially eliminate the split between the real world and school. When school is seen as an integral part of children's lives, children may be more likely to apply school learning and to consider doing schoollike things at home. A more unified life may make schooling seem more relevant. The less formal setting of this classroom and Mr. Clement's acknowledging the existence of children's personal interests may work toward this end.

Just as responsibility was fostered in many ways in the science lesson, it is also fostered during these work periods in a variety of ways. For one thing, Mr. Clement writes personal contracts, and although he assigns the work on each contract rather than allowing students to choose it, they are held responsible for the work without being nagged about it. Additional provisions for nurturing this self-responsibility are numerous. Students file their stories, spelling, writing, and station work in their own folders, providing evidence of accomplishments and things remaining to be finished. Furthermore, Mr. Clement converses with students privately about their work and behavior. They also maintain diaries in which they reflect on their day. And after group meetings he asks each one whether he or she understood a social commitment, new rule, or whatever was discussed. In these ways, he personally contacts each student about particular responsibilities so children may be aware of them and believe the responsibilities to be important.

What is going on in this classroom? Clearly, several of Mr. Clement's concerns are reflected in the activities he plans and the environment he arranges for children.

As we have seen, he is concerned with building a sense of responsibility for actions and control over them. By providing opportunities in which children are free to exercise their self control, Mr. Clement arranges for children to practice responsibility for decision-making when they choose where to work, in what order to do things, and so forth.

Additionally, he is concerned that children learn how to interact with one another. This relates to his concern for responsibility, because children examine their actions in group meetings, discuss their behavior, its possible consequences and effects on others, and alternative courses of action. Children have the opportunity to learn both when they are disturbing others and when they are behaving in a congenial way. There seems to be a personal commitment to this enterprise and to the group. Mr. Clement demonstrates his concern about how children behave, and they seem to work conscientiously to get along together, addressing problems as they arise. The classroom seems to be viewed as a microcosm of society by Mr. Clement, who tries to help children learn how to get along in it.

Another concern reflected in the classroom is that school should not be separated from the real world. As a result, the room looks less institutional as children flow around the room easily, curling up in corners, draping themselves over pillows, huddling around materials on the floor, or lounging back on the couch to read the guinea pig a story. They seem comfortably occupied. Blurring the line between home and school may make schooling seem more relevant. Permitting children to pursue personal interests like Putty Man and a toy mouse may provide a sense of worth and meaning about what children do by allowing them to be interested in it. Additionally, he volunteers information about his own life, such as his making a chart while watching football on television. Perhaps partly as a result of school being a great deal like the real world, and the personal commitment children seem to bring to group meetings, this is a classroom in which children appear to be vitally involved in activities instead of being passive. They struggle with problems, exclaim about success, and are usually involved in their experiences. The social environment—its chatty and collaborative nature—may also seem like a real-life setting rather than an institutional one. It may afford children the opportunity to experiment with ways of interacting and to practice social relationships in the relatively safe environment of the classroom. As pointed out earlier, Mr. Clement seems to view it as a microcosm of society. Such a setting could conceivably aid in preparing children to enter society as effective members, an aim of schooling frequently advanced by social reconstructionists.

But Mr. Clement is not only concerned about learning how to work socially. He is also concerned that children learn how to decode and encode information in a variety of ways, reflected in the assortment of materials and media. In these lessons, for example, children solved problems through three-dimensional constructions, they read and worked on dittoes, and they expressed themselves out loud.

But these concerns are not accompanied by a concern for constructing complex or difficult enough assignments. Learning is active, but the academic content (phonics, solar systems, or whatever) is not rigorous enough for these children. Children knew the relative size and position of bodies in the solar system before they constructed them. And phonics may not be as effectively taught as it could be, for if the child can read the directions on the phonics ditto, clearly the drill is superfluous. Yet if the phonics drill is needed, the child would be unable to decode the directions. Additionally, discussions about stories between Mr. Clement and an individual student tend to focus upon personal reactions and retrieving information, but are less likely to consider interpretation, appreciation, literary criticism, or analysis, which are also important in reading.

So while children have the opportunity to learn responsibility for self-control, decision-making, and social interaction, and to learn how to solve problems in a variety of ways, the academic part of the curriculum should be reconsidered. Surely Mr. Clement's other goals could still be attained even if he made the academic content more complex and sophisticated.

Notes

1. Clifford Gertz, *The Interpretation of Cultures* (New York: Basic Books, 1973), p. 6.

2. Ibid., p. 154.

3. Stephen Pepper, *The Basis of Criticism in the Arts* (Cambridge, Mass.: Harvard University Press, 1945), pp. 6-11.

4. See Gail McCutcheon, "The Disclosure of Classroom Life" (Ph.D. diss., Stanford University, 1976); and idem, "The Use of Ethnography and Criticism as Methods for Disclosing Classroom Settings" (Paper delivered at the annual meeting of the American Educational Research Association, San Francisco, Ca., April 1976) (ERIC # ED 129 926). For a further example, see idem, "A Conflict of Interests," in *Planning and Evaluating Educational Programs,* ed. Elliot W. Eisner (New York: Macmillan, 1978).

In the following study José Rosario shapes what he calls a "developmental sociology of aesthetic meaning." This kind of sociology is concerned with how individuals acquire aesthetic perceptions, whether such perceptions differ among social classes, and how different institutions contribute to the acquisition of aesthetic meaning through the ways they distribute knowledge and socialize individuals. The study itself is the first part of a two-part investigation of how the elementary art program of an urban school system contributes to the acquisition of aesthetic meaning.

The specific strategy Rosario follows is to analyze the program as it is formally stated and its official policy and then to compare the stated principles and plans with the way they are actually translated into classroom interaction. He describes the stated principles, the specifics of the program, and the modes of transmission and evaluation adopted. Noting that the aesthetic experiences of young children are originally contextualized by the home and then gradually decontextualized through the use of language and common linguistic codes, Rosario suggests that the school serves to recontextualize aesthetic experiences through the way in which it classifies and frames aesthetic knowledge. Using Basil Bernstein's notions of "classifica-

206

tion" and "frame" (basically the degree of choice open to the student in determining the curriculum and the means by which it is learned), he suggests, further, that the specific program reflects a split between social and psychological ends. As stated and organized it reflects a highly instrumental rationality, but in practice it reflects some ambiguity and openness about the development of personal meaning. Rosario predicts what further investigation will discover about the program.

The critical focal point of the study is the "work" (Rosario's analysis of the program, or curriculum, itself), but the study also speculates on the effects on an "audience" and on how the "work" represents the somewhat indeterminate nature of the "world," which comprises the basis for aesthetic experiences. In terms of these latter focal points, the study also deals at least indirectly with how the program can be seen as embodying "metaphor," "point of view," "plot," and "theme."

The study includes the personal dimension of curriculum criticism, the basis within personal experience for the individualization of meaning; however, the dominant interests in the study are a balance between the aesthetic and the political dimensions. How is meaning developed in response to the patterns and the qualities of the external world? What are the social consequences of specific efforts to control these patterns and qualities?

10

On the Child's Acquisition of Aesthetic Meaning: The Contribution of Schooling

José Rosario

Introduction

In recent years, a number of educators have focused on what may at this point be cautiously described as children's knowledge of the arts. To be sure, the work has been fruitful and the results have been quite revealing. Briefly, we have come to know that children's linguistic codes reveal abundant use of similes and metaphors.[1] Also, we have learned that children are indeed capable of poetic use of language[2] and creative expression through the medium of painting.[3] Children, moreover, have even demonstrated an ability to recognize styles in paintings[4] and engage in art and aesthetic criticism as we "formally" know this discipline.[5] Finally, the more recent investigations of Howard Gardner and his associates at Harvard Project Zero have disclosed what may possibly be construed as cognitive stages in children's conceptions of the arts.[6] Clearly, we have begun to accumulate a significant body of knowledge regarding children's understanding of the arts as we, as adults, know them.

However, as important as this present knowledge may in fact be, there is a much more important question that remains relatively ignored. All the current investigations on children's knowledge of the arts have bypassed a crucial question: How do children come to acquire knowledge of the arts or aesthetic meaning? Consider, for example, the very recent findings of Howard Gardner. Gardner claims to have found at least three qualitatively different sets of responses among three age groups studied. There was a set of "immature" responses found among fifty-four four- to seven-year-olds, another set of "intermediate" or "transitional" responses found among fifty-one eight- to twelve-year-olds, and a final set of "mature" responses found among sixteen fourteen- to sixteen-year-olds.[7] According to Gardner, all these responses reflected conceptions and misconceptions of the arts. What Gardner failed to consider, however, is how the children came to acquire these conceptions and misconceptions. If it is true that children do in fact possess knowledge of the arts, however false this knowledge may appear from our own perspective, we should then proceed to raise the next and much more relevant question as to how it is that children come to acquire such knowledge.

The purpose of this paper is to consider this very question, although in a rather limited and specific manner. This paper actually represents the results of the primary phase of a two-phase, long-term project aimed at investigating only the contribution of schooling to the child's acquisition of aesthetic meaning.[8] I have limited the project to analytical and empirical analyses of ongoing art programs at the elementary school level. Admittedly, I have excluded at this point other contexts of schooling that undoubtedly transmit aesthetic notions in a variety of ways. The operating premise here is that one way of determining how children come to acquire aesthetic meaning is to examine sociologically how agencies of transmission, in this case the elementary school, contribute to such acquisition through forms of socialization, especially in the areas of art and aesthetic education. Schools explicitly regulate the structure of a child's aesthetic experience through modes of knowledge distribution, namely, art programs. With this in mind, I have isolated the program of art education in the Rochester City School District as the target of the project.

Analytically, I have distinguished the two phases of the project in terms of the research interests guiding each of them. During the first phase, for example, I was primarily interested in analyzing an art program as formally stated and instituted in principle—as official policy, if you will. This phase entailed an analysis of what Nell Keddie refers to as the "educationist context" as opposed to the "teacher context."[9] When examining the art program of the Rochester City School District, for example, the objective during the primary phase was to determine clearly what counted in the educationist context as aesthetic knowledge, its valid transmission, and its realization on the part of the child. In contrast, the second, ongoing phase entails an empirical investigation of how the stated principles (the educationist context) are translated into practice and situationally accomplished through social interaction in the classroom. Thus, through the latter phase, it would be possible to determine what exactly passes for aesthetic meaning during classroom interaction (the teacher context). Although there have been hints as to what passes for aesthetic meaning in the classroom,[10] there have been no attempts made to investigate systematically the transmission of aesthetic meaning in schools.[11]

To sum up, this case study summarizes the primary phase of a long-term investigation into the contribution of schooling to the child's acquisition of aesthetic meaning. First, I will proceed with a descriptive account of the program on art education designed by the Department of Arts and Humanities of the Rochester school district. The account reported here was obtained from interviews of department personnel, particularly the director, and analyses of district documents.[12] Secondly, I will follow with statements of analysis and criticism (not necessarily negative). A summation of the report and a set of concluding remarks will close the discussion.

Art Education in the Rochester City Schools: Guiding Principles, Curriculum, Transmission, and Evaluation

To begin with, the art education program in the Rochester (N.Y.) city schools is administered by the Department of Arts and Humanities of the City School District. To guide the program, this department has isolated five basic principles as operational goals.[13] These are:

1. *Self-worth.* According to this principle, art education is construed as the means through which a child can come to gain feelings of accomplishment and achievement and thereby acquire the neces-

sary competence to develop a sense of personal worth. The questionable psychological assumption underlying this principle is that self-worth is a function of highly successful and creative experiences. Thus, the principle dictates that an art program should of necessity be able to deliver such experiences to the child.

2. *Aesthetic appreciation.* This principle states that art education should seek to develop a greater refinement of tastes, sensibilities, and perceptual discrimination. Further, it calls for a broadening of the concept of art so as to include life experiences in addition to drawing, painting, and sculpture. The expectation is that through art education the child will come to acquire an appreciation of the aesthetic properties not only of art but also of human experiences.

3. *Cultural identity, dignity, and pride.* Embodied in this principle is the dictum that an art program should seek to get children to develop intergroup understanding and to acquire a sense of cultural identity, dignity, and pride through immersion in their social group's cultural and creative heritage. Any art program, according to this principle, must approach the problem of cultural identity and pride as a matter of grave concern. The built-in interest in this principle is in relating art instruction to the sociocultural needs of so-called underprivileged children.

4. *Transference.* As stated in this principle, a basic orientation of the art program is to get children to develop verbal and extraverbal skills that can then be transferred to learning activities in the cognitive domain. Implicit in this principle is a departmental interest in directing attention to the cognitive aspects of art education.

5. *Perceptual literacy.* This principle defines the art program as a concerted effort at increasing a child's range of qualitative experiences through exposure to a variety of sensory experiences. Getting the child to relate to his total environment is the overriding concern here.

We might say that the above principles constitute the basic framework of the art program. In Nell Keddie's terminology, they make up the educationist context, the theoretical and ideological matrix mentioned in conversations with teachers and department officials when they are questioned as to the guiding "philosophy" of the art program. Now, in giving substance to this operational framework, the department has built into it five curriculum areas, a mode of transmission, and an evaluative system that remains relatively vague and somewhat implicit. Let us take each of these components separately.

The department selected weaving, sculpture and construction, printmaking, painting, and work with clay as the five areas constituting the curriculum of the art program.[14] In this case, the socialization of the child into art begins with these five areas. Apparently, no justification is given for these selections. Within each area there are a number of sub-areas or topics. A breakdown of each major area with corresponding topics is given in table 1.

As to the mode of transmitting this knowledge to children, the department has established "art interest centers" in the elementary schools.[15] Specifically designed to simulate a studio, these centers include areas for painting, sculpture, collage, printmaking, construction, and ceramics. The prevailing view in the department is that perhaps the best way to respond to the interests and spontaneous choices of children is through this type of instructional design. As such, it is therefore believed to be a mode of transmission and socialization consistent with and allowing for the realization of the principle of self-worth. The argument is this: in order to promote self-worth, an art program needs to provide a higher degree of freedom and individualized attention and instruction than any other area of a child's curriculum; thus, an art interest center with built-in options and discouragement of conformity and uniformity is most suitable and highly desirable. This position of the department explains to a large extent why the socialization of the child into the area of art in the interest center is not structured to follow a sequential pattern of instruction. On the contrary, the sequential organization of subject matter is prohibited. Consequently, the child is expected literally to decide how his/her socialization into art will proceed, at least sequentially, during the elementary school years. A similar statement can also be made regarding the child's control over the timing and pacing of his/her socialization. At least in principle, the child can decide how fast and how often he/she will work on a given project. Of greater importance to the department is that the child be exposed to all curriculum areas during the elementary school experience. Whether that exposure is properly timed, adequately spaced, and sequentially organized is of less concern to department personnel, at least in principle. The reason for this lack of concern is rather simple. The consensus in the department is that systems of instructional organization and control are often too rigid, cannot be appropriately applied to art education and, more importantly, are not really essential to the successful socialization of the child into art. Indeed, what *is* essential to socialization is the child's willingness to participate in the activities of the art interest center out of personal interest and choice.

To allow for this high degree of "freedom" and individualization during transmission, the department has established criteria for limiting the size of instructional groups, defining the role of the teacher in the art interest center, and allocating time to the art program. As a matter of policy, for example, the department requires that art classes be limited to fifteen students per period. These groups of fifteen, however, need not necessarily be homogeneous in character with respect to, say, age and ability. The department in fact requests that instructional groups be composed of children varying in age, ability, and grade level.[16] Moreover, there is the requirement that teaching be patterned after the tutorial model. Even though the department recognizes that at times a need for group instruction may possibly arise (i.e., orientation lessons), the teacher is expected to be primarily responsible for establishing and maintaining a tutorial relationship with each child throughout the instructional period. Finally, teachers are required to conduct at least five instructional periods per class day. It is of considerable interest to find that the department has left it to the discretion of the principal of each school to determine, in consultation with the art teacher, the length of an instructional period. In justifying this decision, the department director argues that the principal is in the best position to determine the relative status of the art program in terms of the amount of time allocated to it. Without question, this is a matter that needs to and will be examined a bit more closely later in the discussion.

To turn now to the question of evaluation, the department's procedure for progress assessment remains somewhat unclear. There is a method of evaluation, but it consists essentially of an informal process between the art teacher and the child. The actual procedures for evaluating children, therefore, seem to vary from teacher to teacher. However, an example of a practice commonly employed is to have a child complete a "plan sheet" or "project sheet" so that: (1) his/her performance and progress in a given area may be moni-

Table 1

Rochester City School District Program in Art Education: Selected Areas and Corresponding Topics

CURRICULUM AREAS

	Painting	Clay	Weaving	Printmaking	Sculpture and Construction
TOPICS	Primary colors and creation of secondary colors through mixing	Stages of clay (i.e., slip, plastic, greenware, bisque, and glazed ware)	Strength and structure of cloth, especially the interlocking network of vertical and horizontal threads	Process of printmaking as a means of duplicating a given design or picture	Relation of sculpture to man's historical accomplishments
	Tints and shades of colors	Manipulation of clay and use and demonstration of building techniques such as pinch, coil, and slab methods	Aesthetic and functional properties of weaving as these relate to personal and environmental use	Meaning and use of the concept print in the process of printmaking	Differences between free-standing sculpture (in the round) and relief sculpture (as applied to or becomes part of relief sculpture such as the surface on a building)
	Painting techniques (i.e., wet on wet, dry brush manipulation and control of tools and materials)	Decorating techniques such as embossing, incising, relief buildup, and glazing variations	Historical and cultural origins of weaving	Methods of printmaking ranging from basic stamp printing to relief methods and stencil printing	Construction of simple forms of sculpture (from a 2D surface to a 3D) by means of varied uses of fastening, folding, scoring, and cutting
	Painting as visual record of history	Function of the kiln and the treatment of clay and glazes with intense heat	Natural and artificial sources of fibers	Repetitive use of patterns of design in forms of printmaking	"Open" linear qualities of wire, straws, reed, and toothpicks and "solid" qualities of wood, plaster, and clay
	Painting as a form of non-verbal communication	Cultural history of clay	Linguistic apparatus endemic to weaving (i.e., terms such as warp, weft, loom, and shuttle)	Variant uses for a repetitive print design or picture (i.e., a 2D design, cards, banners, textile design)	
		Aesthetic and functional significance of clay as expressive medium	Development of skills (i.e., warping and removing the weaving from the loom)		

Design of patterns through chromatic and threading variations

Construction of sculptural objects through the use of existing materials or free standing 3D objects such as boxes, tubes, cardboard or styrofoam shapes

Techniques of carving on such media as wood, plaster, paraffin, soap, and other materials

Methods and uses of various tools in sculpturing

Differences between stabile sculpture and moving sculpture such as mobiles

SOURCE. Compiled from information supplied by the Department of Arts and Humanities, City School District, Rochester, N.Y.

tored during and at the completion of a project; and (b) a record of his/her accomplishments in a given area may be kept. However, the criteria to be employed in determining a child's realization of what counts as knowledge are not clearly stated.[17] What *is* stated, at least in the educationist context, is that evaluation must be conducted in relation to the child's particular needs and that the slightest degree of expression reflecting growth must be acknowledged. How this evaluative scheme enters into the future placement of students remains relatively ambiguous. There seems to exist an informal mechanism through which the names of children isolated as possible successes in the arts are channeled to the director of the department for future placement and continued socialization in the arts. How this informal procedure actually operates in practice remains at this point only an empirical question that needs to be investigated.

Art Education in the Rochester City Schools: Analysis and Criticism

The child's aesthetic experiences at home are context bound. These reduce to what F. David Martin refers to as an "ontological sensitivity ... easily noticeable in children."[18] Gaston Bachelard wrote about the phenomenology and psychology of these early experiences in terms of the spatial intimacies that a child comes to experience when inhabiting his/her home.[19] Stated differently, for Bachelard, a child's early aesthetic experiences may be construed phenomenologically as psychological functions of a kind of "passionate liaison" that a child's body has with domestic space. At home, the child begins to decode or make sense of this aesthetic meaning, this highly bound contextual texture, through the use of certain linguistic categories. Terms such as pretty, beautiful, nice and so on are learned and used to interpret experienced qualities (or what in the home passes for aesthetic experience and meaning). This is what Wittgenstein seems to have had in mind when he commented that "if I hadn't learnt the rules, I wouldn't be able to make the aesthetic judgment. In learning the rules," he suggested, "you get a more and more refined judgment. Learning the rules actually changes your judgment."[20] These interpretive rules are implicit in and are learned through language *games*.[21] We might say, then, that there is in the home an imaginative or *aesthetic* order of meaning that tends to remain for the most part contextually bound until such meaning is decontextualized through the use of language.[22] Of course, how contextually bound this aesthetic meaning remains as the child develops is dependent upon the type of linguistic codes employed by the parents and transmitted to the child. The use of an elaborated code in the socialization of the child into the aesthetic order of meaning would most likely lead to greater decontextualization of such meaning in the home.[23] On the other hand, the use of a restricted code in the socialization of the child into this area would tend to make aesthetic meaning implicit and context bound. These notions of *aesthetic contextualization* and *decontextualization* lead us to consider a third and related notion, namely, *recontextualization*.

That is, when contrasting the school to the home with respect to the treatment of aesthetic meaning, we might say that schools, as institutions of formal learning, decontextualize and recontextualize aesthetic meaning to a greater degree than parents do at home.[24] This means essentially that schools consciously and deliberately select and extract content from orders of aesthetic meaning for purposes of transmission and social distribution. To execute this function properly and efficiently, the aesthetic knowledge ultimately selected (decontextualized) is then, as Bernstein notes, classified and framed (recontextualized). This process of classification and framing will figure later in our discussion. For now, the points to consider here are: (a) that the program in question may be construed as reflective of decontextualized and recontextualized (classified and framed) meaning; and (b) that the decontextualization (selection in current curricular terms) that a school usually makes of certain forms of knowledge for social distribution is commonly justified. Point b is the one I would like to consider and examine first.

As R. S. Peters points out, there must be reasons for featuring science, mathematics, history, art, cooking, and carpentry on the curriculum rather than bingo, bridge, and billiards. In the case of the Rochester city schools, the reasons art education is featured on the curriculum are implicit in the five guiding principles listed above. When asked to justify the current program, department personnel inevitably refer to these principles. At least at the official level, the reasons contained in these principles seem to make the pursuit of art education worthwhile. The question to raise here is whether such reasons are necessarily *good* reasons. Let us examine them and see.

Consider the reasons collectively as a single theorem: namely, socialization (initiation) into art fosters (a) self-worth, (b) aesthetic appreciation, (c) cultural identity, dignity, and pride, (d) transference of cognitive skills, and (3) perceptual literacy. This theorem binds the activity of art to an instrumental rationality (means-ends schema) that transforms it into a means for achieving psychological and social ends that are seemingly unrelated. As a result, art education, as a form of socialization, takes on therapeutic and ideological functions that tend to make it highly utilitarian and socially conservative. There seems to be an interest built into the theorem of preparing the child to lead a healthy and socially productive life rather than in socializing him/her into the area of art per se: that is, a structurally different context reflecting unique modes of ordering and experiencing personal meaning through numerous media and (even) socio-political relations.

Educators with a humanistic orientation would want to challenge the instrumentalism built into this justifying formula. The objection here would be that such a formula construes initiation into art instrumentally as a useful strategy or technique of socializing children and does not appraise art activity in terms of its intrinsic and immanent features.[25] Although at times of fiscal difficulty such an argument may appear weak to school officials, for it fails to assess the social yield to be derived from the study of art, the argument has merit and strength. The conversion of art activity into means to extrinsic ends does tend to distort the nature of the activity. The socialization into art is worthwhile not because it is a gateway to psychological stability, social respectability, and cultural pride and identity. The same argument, I suppose, can be marshaled in support of, say, history. Rather, the activity of art is worthwhile because it entails experiencing a social context in which a different mode of being is made possible through the treatment of ambiguity and ordering of objective and subjective meaning.

Further, I think the humanistic stance gains strength when we consider the possible effects that the instrumental theorem can have on the aesthetic notions the child may come to acquire in the school. Although equally if not more important, this side of the criticism is usually ignored. Yet there might be a tendency, for example, for teachers to transmit and children to acquire, through communicative patterns in the classroom, notions of aesthetic activity that are economically, therapeutically, and ideologically tinged. Moreover, if aesthetic experiences are viewed instrumentally as contexts of social preparation, we can expect to find in art classes social concerns over conformity, consensus, and social order taking relative precedence over aesthetic matters. There is now a certain amount of research lending support to these speculations. In his analysis of classroom culture and communication patterns, Jules Henry observed the manipulation of art lessons as contexts within which children were taught, among other things, to establish linkages between art and its therapeutic and economic uses.[26] During music classes, he found teachers more preoccupied with group conformity than with pitch.[27] More recently, in their investigations of classroom interaction in a kindergarten class, Apple and King note that the teacher only displayed children's artwork that conformed to her expectations.[28] Moreover, they also observed that the quality of the work was considered less important than diligence, obedience, perseverance, and participation. Although important, this research only points to a possible connection between an instrumental theorem of justification and the kinds of aesthetic notions transmitted to and acquired by the child in the classroom. The probable existence and strength of this linkage needs to be investigated much more systematically.

Besides focusing on the justification underlying the program in question, we can also isolate for analysis and criticism how the department has chosen to classify and frame (recontextualize) the art knowledge that it has selected (decontextualized) for social distribution. The concepts of *classification* and *frame* are derived from Basil Bernstein's model of educational transmission.[29] Thus, I will discuss briefly Bernstein's use of these concepts and then proceed to apply them in our investigation.

Bernstein argues that educational knowledge (socially defined public knowledge) is realized through three message systems: (1) curriculum, or what passes as valid knowledge; (2) pedagogy, or what passes as valid transmission of knowledge, and (3) evaluation, or what passes as valid realization of knowledge on the part of the student. Bernstein uses the concepts of classification and frame to determine the structure of these message systems. Classification, for example, is used to determine the basic structure of curriculum. Thus, this concept refers to the degree of boundary strength between contents. Curriculum areas may be strongly or weakly insulated from each other. Strong insulation between contents implies *strong* classification and *closed* relations between contents. These are the basic features of a *collection* type of curriculum. The different contents (i.e., history, art, mathematics, etc.) are kept apart. On the other hand, weak insulation between contents implies *weak* classification and *open* relations between contents. This is the basic structure of an *integrated* type of curriculum. The different contents are brought together and subordinated to a central idea.

Unlike classification, the concept of frame is employed to determine the structure of pedagogy. As such, it refers to the degree of control that the teacher and the child have over the selection, organization, timing, and pacing of knowledge being transmitted and received in the classroom. According to Bernstein, the degree of frame strength affects the coefficient of power in the pedagogical relationship: that is, the stronger the framing, the less control a child is bound to have over the procedures structuring transmission.

Before isolating the significance of these concepts and elaborating on their application here, it is important that we recognize three additional points. First, Bernstein argues that the strengths of classification and frames may vary independently of each other. He writes, for example, that

it is possible to have weak classification and exceptionally strong framing. Consider programmed learning. Here the boundary between educational contents may be blurred (weak classification) but there is little control by the pupil (except for pacing) over *what* is learned (strong framing). This example also shows that frames may be examined at a number of levels and the strength can vary as between the levels of selection, organization, pacing and timing of the knowledge transmitted in the pedagogical relationship.[30]

Second, classification and framing are modes of regulating the reconceptualization of orders of meaning. Third, evaluation is a function of the relative strengths of classification and frames.

The significance of Bernstein's concepts is that they allow explication of the way varying modes of curriculum organization structure, regulate, and shape the modality of socialization in contexts of schooling. Thus, according to Bernstein, variations in the strength of classifications and frames imply structural differences in socializing experiences. Consider one extreme of the continuum: strong classification and strong framing (collection type curriculum). Strong classification (high degree of insulation between contents) signifies socialization into: (a) a subject loyalty, (b) a view of knowledge as private property, and (c) "a hierarchical organization of knowledge, such that the ultimate mystery of subject (its potential for creating new realities) is revealed very late in the educational life."[31] Attention must be called to point c, for it means that the mystery of a subject is experienced only by those who reach the higher levels of schooling.

Thus, different notions of knowledge are socially distributed: knowledge as orderly and stable to some and knowledge as disorderly and permutable to others.[32] The implication of this for socialization into art is not encouraging, to say the least.[33]

With strong framing (low degree of control over the selection, organization, pacing, and timing of knowledge), socialization takes on added features: (a) the socialized is allowed no control over the selection, organization, pacing, and timing of knowledge, (b) the socialized is accorded little status and few rights, and (c) no common sense or community knowledge can enter into the socializing process —hence connections with everyday life are discouraged. Finally, under strong classification and strong framing, evaluative systems are designed to measure acquisition of *states* of knowledge rather than *ways* of knowing. As to weak classification and weak framing, we would expect the inverse of the equation to hold.

Now consider the application of Bernstein's constructs to the analysis and criticism of our own case here. We might say that the Department of Arts and Humanities of the Rochester City School District reflects strong classification and strong framing of educational knowledge. As a general rule, content areas are highly insulated from each other, and children have little control over the selection, organization, pacing, and timing of knowledge. This description certainly applies to, say, music.[34] However, it applies only in part to art education. That is, strong classification exists both internally and externally to the program. There is, however, variation in the strength of frames. At the levels of selection and organization, framing is relatively strong when compared to the weak framing present at the levels of pacing and timing. The weakest framing is present at the level of timing. While the selection and organization of curriculum areas and corresponding topics (refer to table 1 above) are handled officially by department personnel, the pacing and timing of this knowledge in the art interest center are left to students to structure. Framing is weakest at the level of timing because the department director leaves the entire matter of timing to the discretion of school principals.[35] Thus, variations in time allocations are quite common.

Turning now to how this strong classification and relatively strong framing may shape the modality of socialization into art, we can expect to find socializing experiences of the sort listed above. Specifically, we can expect to find a modality of socialization reflecting for the most part (a) initiation into subject loyalty[36] and a view of art as private property and (b) social distribution of notions picturing art as an ordered and stable system of meaning and experience. Further, we can expect to find children powerless with respect to the selection and organization of aesthetic activities and assessment procedures designed to measure the acquisition of art as a state of knowledge rather than a way of knowing. Finally, because of the weak framing present at the levels of pacing and timing, we can expect to find acknowledgment and recognition of student interests, choices, and learning styles. We have seen that, at least in principle, this is in fact the case.

There is a final and separate observation that we can note regarding the socializing consequences of the strong classification and strong framing disclosed here. The social principle or rule underlying strong classification and framing is, "Things must be kept apart."[37] Thus, when strong classification and framing is applied to art, there is interest in setting art apart and insulating it from other subject areas. But the problem that such insulation creates is not difficult to discern: the child is socialized into believing (and this happens implicitly) that aesthetic qualities and experiences are common only to art and the humanities.[38] It is possible for children to infer and acquire from these experiences that aesthetic qualities are not to be found, felt, and enjoyed in connection with other areas of knowledge. And it is also possible for them to infer and acquire the false notion that only artists are fortunate enough to experience the lived world aesthetically. Even if it is decided, as is usually the case, to broaden the concept of art and to make children conscious of the aesthetics implicit in all human experience and conduct, the high degree of insulation between art and the other areas of the curriculum may be sufficient to cancel good intentions. Thus, we are faced with quite a dilemma. While we want to declassify aesthetic knowledge, we also want to guarantee socialization into subject loyalty and identity, that is, the training of artists. It may well be that the problem posed by the strong classification and framing of aesthetic knowledge can only be resolved, even if only partially, by emphasizing the aesthetics implicit in the other areas of the curriculum.

Conclusion

In this paper, I have reported on the completion of a preliminary phase of a long-term investigation into the contribution of schooling to children's acquisition of aesthetic meaning. I described, analyzed, and criticized the educationist context, if you will, of the art education program administered by the Department of Arts and Humanities of the Rochester city schools. In this report, I also pointed to the possible relations existing between official program policies, procedures, principles of justification, and recontextualization of aesthetic meaning and the acquisition on the part of the child of certain notions of art and aesthetic meaning. To summarize, these notions may be construed as: (a) conceptions of art that are instrumentally defined and linked to therapeutic, economic, and ideological values; (b) a conception of art as private property; (c) a conception of art as an ordered and stable state of knowledge rather than a "mysterious" mode of knowing; (d) conceptions of art and aesthetic experience as processes unrelated to biography and personal meaning (since connections with everyday life are discouraged by strong classification and framing); and (e) a conception of the aesthetic dimension as a qualitative property common only to art.

In the discussion, I further noted at various points that we need to investigate these thoughts empirically, which is something I expect to do in phase two of the project. There is an additional comment. The thrust of this paper (and of the project as a whole) is to create movement toward a *developmental sociology of aesthetic meaning* that necessitates raising critically important questions. Are there social class differences in aesthetic perceptions, for example, as there are in language use? How do children come to socially acquire certain conceptions of the arts? How do social institutions (i.e., the school, the family, etc.) contribute to the acquisition of aesthetic meaning through modes of knowledge distribution and forms of socialization? This report has delineated the initial stage of a possible way of attacking the latter two questions. Analytically speaking, only the empirical testing of the strategy remains.

Notes

1. Kornei Chukovsky, *From Two to Five* (Berkeley: University of California Press, 1968).
2. Kenneth Koch, *Wishes, Lies and Dreams* (New York: Chelsea House, 1970).
3. Howard Gardner, *The Arts and Human Development* (New York: Wiley, 1973).
4. Howard Gardner, "Metaphors and Modalities: How Children Project Polar Adjectives onto Diverse Domains," *Child Development* 45 (1974): 84-91.
5. David Ecker, "Analyzing Children's Talk about Art," *Journal of Aesthetic Education* 7 (January 1973): 58-73; "Teaching Art Criticism as Aesthetic Inquiry," *New York University Education Quarterly* 3 (Summer 1972): 20-26.
6. Howard Gardner et al., "Children's Conceptions of the Arts," *Journal of Aesthetic Education* 9 (July 1975): 60-77.
7. Ibid., p. 64. For a critique of Gardner's findings, see José Rosario, "Children's Conceptions of the Arts: A Critical Review," *Journal of Aesthetic Education*, in press.
8. We might want to define aesthetic meaning here rather loosely as consisting of aesthetic notions and categories that children acquire in schools for purposes of interpreting the lived world.
9. See her "Classroom Knowledge," in *Knowledge and Control*, ed. Michael Young (London: Collier-Macmillan, 1971). As defined by Keddie, the differences between these two contexts reduce to a difference between what "ought" to take place (the educationist context) and what "is" taking place (the teacher context).
10. See Jules Henry, *Culture against Man* (New York: Vintage Books, 1965), chap. 8; "Working Paper on Creativity," *Harvard Educational Review* 27 (1957): 148-55; "Spontaneity, Initiative, and Creativity in Suburban Classrooms," in *Education and Culture*, ed. George Spindler (New York: Holt, Rinehart and Winston, 1963); "Culture, Education and Communications Theory," in *Education and Anthropology*, ed. George Spindler (Stanford, Ca.: Stanford University Press, 1955); "More on Cross-Cultural Education," *Current Anthropology* 2 (June 1961): 255-64.
11. The possible exception here is the ongoing work of Robert Witkin at Exeter and John Hayes at King's College, London.
12. Since the author was asked not to quote department personnel or district documents directly, such quotations have been avoided in this report. However, references to interviews and official documents were permitted.
13. "Goals for Art Education," Department of Arts and Humanities, City School District, Rochester, N.Y., mimeographed.
14. Drawn from mimeographed curriculum documents supplied the author by director of Department of Arts and Humanities.
15. "Elementary Art Interest Centers," Department of Arts and Humanities, City School District, Rochester, New York, mimeographed.
16. The exception to this is the "Mediaction Center" designed to improve

reading. Established in thirteen public and two parochial Title I elementary schools, these centers can accept only those students eligible for enrollment in the school's Title I (ESEA) reading program.

17. Behavioral objectives are stated, but no criteria are established for measuring their realization.

18. F. David Martin, *Art and the Religious Experience* (Lewisburg, Pa.: Bucknell University Press, 1972), p. 48.

19. See his *The Poetics of Space* (Boston: Beacon Press, 1969); and *The Poetics of Reverie* (Boston: Beacon Press, 1971).

20. Cyril Barrett, ed., *Wittgenstein: Lectures and Conversations* (Berkeley: University of California Press, 1967), p. 5.

21. Aaron V. Cicourel argues this point in his *Cognitive Sociology* (New York: The Free Press, 1974).

22. I don't necessarily want to exclude here the use of other codes, such as aesthetic forms themselves. Music lessons, for example, may figure here although the use of language may indeed be the most important code in the home. Whatever the code, the important point to note is that a code is essential for making the meaning explicit. For a discussion of the function of codes in the deciphering of aesthetic qualities, see Pierre Bourdieu, "Outline of a Sociological Theory of Art Perception," *International Social Science Journal* 20 (1968): 589-612.

23. I am using here Bernstein's conceptions of elaborated and restricted codes. Bernstein distinguishes these codes psychologically "by the extent to which each facilitates (elaborated code) or inhibits (restricted code) an orientation to symbolize ... in a verbally explicit form." See his "A Sociolinguistic Approach to Social Learning," in *Class, Codes and Control* (London: Routledge and Kegan Paul, 1971), vol. 1, chap. 7.

24. This raises a problem that we need to investigate. As Bernstein notes, "empirically the *form* de-contextualizing takes may make very different demands on different groups of children, which affects the extent to which children acquire the performances required by the re-contextualizing code" (ibid., vol. 3, p. 32). In part, the reason for this is that decontextualization rarely considers the aesthetic background of the child. Yet it is differences in experienced aesthetic backgrounds that might well explain Gardner's findings that a certain percentage of the children he studied gave supposedly correct answers to aesthetic questions posed them. At least for research, all this means is that we have to consider to what extent the aesthetic meaning transmitted in schools resembles or contrasts that which is implicit or made explicit within the family in the various social classes. In so doing, we might be able to identify any possible discontinuities between the aesthetic experiences in the home and the aesthetic experiences in the school.

25. The prototype of this argument is contained in R. S. Peters, *Ethics and Education* (Glenview, Ill.: Scott, Foresman and Co., 1967).

26. Henry, "Culture, Education and Communications Theory."

27. Henry, *Culture Against Man.*

28. See chap. 19.

29. I have drawn from his paper, "On the Classification and Framing of Educational Knowledge," in *Class, Codes and Control*, vol. 3.

30. Ibid., p. 89.

31. Ibid., p. 97.

32. This is why it is important that we investigate empirically the placement of children into art classes. In doing so, we might be able to reveal any differential treatment that may exist. It is important that we find out how children come to qualify for continued socialization into art.

33. In light of this, it is difficult to see how Marcuse's thesis of a "new sensibility" is to materialize unless schooling undergoes massive restructuring. See Herbert Marcuse, *An Essay on Liberation* (Boston: Beacon Press, 1969); idem, *Counter-Revolution and Revolt* (Boston: Beacon Press, 1972).

34. When interviewed, the director commented on the rigidity with which the music division conducted affairs. The division's use of highly formalized evaluative and screening procedures is indicative of what he meant. Of course, the division's highly structured practices point to strong feelings of specialized identity and subject loyalty, which are reflective of exceptionally strong classification and framing.

35. This no doubt was a political maneuver on the part of the department's administrative staff. Given that schools are currently facing fiscal problems, the department's strategy seems to be one of not interfering with the principal's decisions as to how his resources are to be exploited, and that certainly includes time.

36. When interviewed, the director seemed to be emphasizing the importance of getting children to behave like miniature artists, although he did mention that one of the goals was to transmit to all children a basic understanding of art without regard to the development of artistry as a unique identity. I suspect that we can expect to find the least emphasis on subject loyalty at the lowest grade levels.

37. See Bernstein, *Class, Codes and Control*, vol. 3, p. 10.

38. C. P. Snow's "Two Cultures" may be explained, if only partially, as functions of this insulation.

In this essay Francine Shuchat Shaw extensively addresses an issue raised in the preceding essay by José Rosario. Rosario has suggested that aesthetic meaning is largely individualistic, that direct efforts to prescribe aesthetic experience, therefore, violate its nature. In examining this issue at length, Shuchat Shaw suggests that prescriptive practices must also violate the nature of any specific subject matter or curricular area that includes not only aesthetic and personal dimensions, but involves expression, symbolization, or abstraction. Pedagogical practices, she asserts, are deceptive unless they are "congruent" with the curricular areas within which they are used. Congruence, in its technical sense, is basically a way of determining consistency within relationships by juxtaposing conception with practice, intentionality with actuality. It is what Shuchat Shaw describes as "an aesthetic method of inquiry for curriculum criticism."

The specific subject matter Shuchat Shaw uses to exemplify the method of congruence is a series of books by James Moffett that put forth his conception of an elementary and secondary-school language and literature curriculum, extensive examples of curricular materials, and suggestions for implementation by teachers. Using several of Monroe Beardsley's notions about aesthetic education, Shuchat Shaw points out how Moffett's work is incongruent, for the examples and suggestions are content-centered while Moffett conceptualizes students as individuals working out their own purposes and highly personal biographies. Shuchat Shaw believes students should confront their personal phenomenologies within aesthetic experience as active creator-artists, rather than as relatively passive receptors within the process of experiencing. She illustrates these ideas concretely, by describing a secondary-school film studies program, suggesting that a program consistent with the principles of congruence includes relating theory and practice, translating theory into curriculum, and integrating theory with pedagogy.

In Shuchat Shaw's view students are active participants in the creation of curricula; therefore, a curriculum can be seen in part as embodying the rhetorical conceptions of "metaphor," "point of view," "plot," and "theme" developed within the overall aesthetic experience of a student. The principal critical focal points of the study are the "work" and its existence as an expression of both the nature of the "world" and the nature of its "author." For these reasons the two dominant interests in this study are in the aesthetic and the personal dimensions of curriculum criticism.

11

In Search of Congruence

Francine Shuchat Shaw

The most natural assumption about teaching any symbol system should be that the student employ his time using that system in every realistic way that it can be used, not that he analyze it or study it as an object. . . . If such an approach seems to slight literature and language, I can only say that this is a mistake of the substantive view. A student writing in all the same forms as the authors he reads can know literature from the inside in a way that few students ever do today. . . . Most inexperienced students take all the decisions of the artist for granted . . . they see no choice, only arbitrariness or inevitability. Appreciation of form comes only with a sense of choices. . . . When you yourself invent, you see all the choices, make decisions. . . . It all begins to make sense.

James Moffett

A Story

I would like to begin with a story about James Moffett's idea,[1] as seen and told through the lens of *congruence,* an aesthetic method of inquiry for curriculum criticism.

In 1968, Moffett subscribed to blended theories of expression, human symbolization, and abstraction as conceptual bases for understanding the processes and products of discourse, art, and communication. He wished to use the common threads of these theories as a foundation for reconceiving language and literature study in primary-

and secondary-school settings, a foundation from which he might develop curricular events and instructional practices that would be congruent with these theories. Moffett's conceptual work, *Teaching the Universe of Discourse,*[2] and his pedagogical component, *A Student-Centered Language Arts Curriculum, Grades K-13: A Handbook for Teachers,*[3] were published in 1968 to represent his formulation of these ideas. From his conceptual bases, grounded in these blended theories, sprang curricular events and instructional practices that focus initially and primarily on the original creative experiences of students who are directly engaged in expressing their own biographical content, in all its dimensions, through varying forms of discourse, art, and communication, and in accordance with their own purposes. This approach reflected Moffett's apparent break with more conventional rationales and methodologies associated with initial stages of traditional language and literature study, derived from various and blended theories of impression and formalism; these focus initially and primarily on a wide range of critical activities and analytic competencies of students who encounter, experience, and react to existing substantive objects of discourse, art, and communication, the ready-made heritage of these fields, produced by others in other times and places.

Moffett subscribed to theories of expression as bases for understanding the fields of discourse, art, and communication for their capacity to correspond with his conceptual positions on several foundational curricular concerns; and, in turn, he believed that curricular and instructional translations of theories of expression would implicitly convey those conceptual positions to students as realms of meaning within educational experience. For Moffett, these theories had the capacity to recognize and support a holistic rather than fragmented conception of language and literature, their dual nature as syntactic/process and substantive/product, and the continuity and reciprocity shared by these dimensions. Further, these theories did so within an evolutionary framework corresponding in a naturalistic way with human linguistic and psychological development in the realms of symbolization and abstraction. Moffett's conception of valuable knowledge and knowing, in these fields and in general, made primary the student's subjective sources and realms of meaning as content, original processes of inquiry, syntactic manipulation and expression, symbolization and abstraction; and he made secondary the student's encounter with objective, substantive content, models and information products existing as discourse, art, and communication formulated previously by others to constitute the heritage of fields. He conceptualized the human being as "producer and manipulator of symbols"[4] through languages that must be treated as dynamic rather than static, subject to individual content and purpose rather than to conventions and standards, if they are to be functional and capable of conveying new meanings. He conceptualized the student as active rather than passive, as creator and inventor first and as receiver and inheritor second; as challenging and questioning the sociocultural milieux and political dimensions of public life rather than taking these for granted; as a responsible subject with an independent self-consciousness who reflects and acts, rather than as an object who is controlled and acted upon; as one who recognizes the difference between knowledge acquired indirectly or vicariously and understanding acquired through direct experience. Moffett held that theories emphasizing the expressive nature of the fields of discourse, art, and communication, as language systems or symbolization processes with syntactic affinities to be used in accordance with content and purpose, constituted the most appropriate conceptual bases for deriving curricular and instructional practices that might implicitly convey his positions on the human being and on valuable knowledge and knowing, in these fields and in general. In 1968 Moffett would have agreed with G. Lynn Nelson's comments in a 1974 paper, "Toward Teaching English for the Real World":

Our subject . . . is not language but *languaging*. Approaching our subject in this way, we begin to see it, perhaps for the first time, not as a subject at all—but *as a means*. This new perspective is crucial; words are no longer artifacts. . . . We must begin to fit our classrooms into this new conception of knowledge . . . we must see our primary responsibility in leading students to the discovery of words as tools by which to sculpt and resculpt raw experience in order to discover its meaning and one's own relationship to that meaning. And we must help them to see literature as another person's attempt at the same process. For what *is* man's languaging, what *is* his literature, but his attempt to sort out and to come to terms with the world of his experience and with his own place in that world. And what is the study of literature but the sharing in someone else's struggle. . . . We generally approach composition and the study of literature as if they were ends in themselves . . . as if there were something intrinsically worthwhile about the product . . . rather than the *process* of writing—the process of sorting and discovering and creating. . . . We fail to deal with it as a living example of another human's language . . . and put it in a glass case so that it can't be touched; and then we stand back with an antiseptic pointer like a curator in a museum and proceed to point out metaphors and illusions and plot development.[5]

These blended theories of expression, symbolization, and abstraction also provided support for a related set of educational aims Moffett conceived to be both foundational and transcendant in relation to those aims associated with conventional language and literature study, aims grounded primarily in theories of impression and formalism. That is, Moffett understood original acts of reflection and creative expression, of producing and manipulating content and form in purposeful discourse, art, and communication as the matrix of experience that best prepares for and informs sensitive and intelligent impressions and perceptive critical analyses of existing substantive products; and, from phenomenological and existential perspectives, Moffett understood these acts as having psychological, sociocultural, and political values for students which transcend those emerging through the more academic aims of conventional language and literature study. Moffett believed schooling ought to reflect a concern for the private subjective dimensions of the student as an individual and for the public sociocultural and political dimensions the student shares as a member of the community. He wished to return the foundational reference for the various levels of interpretational activity, which is the pedagogical process, to the student's own grounding, first to strengthen self-understanding and affirmation, and then as an antecedent to an awakened critical consciousness that perceives public shared realities fully and the individual's place in and responsibility to them. Moffett's phenomenological approach to curricula and pedagogy reflects these concerns: students always begin with an initial focus on their own characteristics, realities, and purposes, coding and decoding, disclosing and uncovering, reflecting and expressing, sharing and understanding their own content and realms of meaning in varying forms of discourse, art, and communication; juxtaposed to complement and clarify these acts is the student's subsequent encounter with existing substantive products in presentational form, which may correspond in content, form, or purpose with their own expressive acts, and to which they respond in various critical, analytic ways.

To assert his methodological priorities and the ordering of experiences in curricula and pedagogy, Moffett made an impassioned case against those barriers that conventionally come between students and their direct, original experiences of reflection and expression in initial stages of language and literature study: predetermining students' characteristics and needs, realities, perceptions, and levels of understanding; predicting and prescribing students' content and form, interests and capacities; preventing students' trials and errors by pre-teaching rules and approaches, standard definitions and problem-solving strategies, general facts and theories; textbooks and models, prepackaged materials and prestructured exercises of all sorts to stimulate and give standardized direction to initial stages of experience.

The notion of praxis is implicit in Moffett's approach, as the student's own reflection and action, integral to all expressive and analytic stages of his pedagogical process. It affirms the constant reality of change and the possibility of freedom to participate in the historical process and the shaping and reshaping of private and public life, freedom to intervene in, rather than simply inherit, the transformation of subjective and shared contexts of human experience.

This particular story was not told in 1968 when Moffett introduced his companion books, and the years that followed do not make for a supportive, enthusiastic history of an idea. His work was not carefully explored, appropriately understood, or widely appreciated for its dimension and wisdom by the educators of language and literature for whom he wrote. These educators could not sufficiently jar themselves, as Moffett seemed to do, from the more conventional traditions through which they came of age. They were stumbling with considerable misinterpretation and discomfort through our most recent bouts with student-centered, progressive, and open education in their contemporary forms; and these educators' well-documented problems with such forms became their dilemma with Moffett.

It is not surprising that the eventuation of Moffett's original idea, still to be told here, circumscribes this story to the past tense and makes for an ironic, unhappy ending. Having weathered the short outbreak of "soft" education to arrive more comfortably by 1973 in our contemporary version of a basics movement, Moffett seems to compromise and contradict the very strength of his original conceptual base and the curricular and instructional practices deriving from it. Although he insists on sustained adherence to theories of expression and the conceptual positions and aims they support, and argues against having made a foundational shift to theories of impression and formalism, Moffett seems to restore such conventional rationales to justify a near reverse of what had been described in his

1968 work; he seems to reaffirm faith in curricular events and instructional practices that focus largely on the student's encounter with preformulated materials and existing substantive products that constitute, refer to, or call forth the heritage of language and literature as fields; he maintains a deceptive, conventional faith that such events and practice have the capacity to transmit his aims and convey to students his conceptual positions on the nature of the human being and of valuable knowledge. The evidence of such restoration and reaffirmation is packaged as Moffett's and Houghton Mifflin's *Interaction Program,* an elaborate series of materials for which Moffett's 1973 edition of *A Student-Centered Language Arts Curriculum, Grades K-13: A Handbook for Teachers*[6] is written to serve as a companion and guide. Moffett comments in the revised "Preface":

> In the original introduction to this book, I said that I hoped to offer a way of teaching not incarnated in textbooks, "an alternative to the installation of a pre-packaged curriculum." I still feel strongly that organic English is killed by special books for writing, speaking, spelling, skill-building, etc., and that it is far too basic ever to be embodied in textbooks, especially those committed to this or that concept of literature or rhetoric. But I have directed a new program of school materials called *Interaction: A Student-Centered Language Arts and Reading Program* . . . this may appear to contradict the stand in this book.[7]

Moffett may be convinced that *Interaction* materials will not be used to reflect commitment to any particular conception of his fields or used to violate or contradict the theories which serve as a conceptual base for students' naturalistic evolution through discourse, art, and communication, grounded in original use and practice. However, the implications for curricula and pedagogy suggested to educators by the presence of these materials seem chillingly clear, as do Moffett's conceptual shifts with respect to the nature of the student as a human being and of valuable knowledge and knowing. Moffett describes these materials, again in the revised "Preface":

> . . . *Interaction* contains 176 paperback anthologies covering all the types of literary and nonliterary discourse discussed in this book and found in our culture . . . a multi-media independent literacy kit made up of films and games . . . eighty hours of recordings of the anthology's selections performed by professionals . . . card games . . . hundreds of unsequenced activity cards written to students and directing them how to do the assignments proposed. . . . Eighteen classroom films showing other students doing the less familiar dramatic and small-group activities . . . .[8]

The eventuation of Moffett's story portrays a familiar cluster of related discrepancies, those between theory or conceptual bases and practice, between the essential nature of a subject under study and the events or methods established for study, between educational aims and the practices developed to facilitate them, and between intentionality and actuality with respect to conceptual positions and aims conveyed and transmitted. It seems clear that Moffett's provision of an elaborate network of packaged materials, substantive products, and models will exert a conventional influence over time on the development of curricular events and instructional practices, to the extent that their use will implicitly contradict and misrepresent his original conceptual bases, negate many of his aims, and convey the reverse of his positions on the human being and on valuable knowledge and knowing. The history of Moffett's idea constitutes an exemplary story of the many ameliorative compromises and contradictions in curricula and instruction made in the name of helping "both teacher and school reorganize themselves so that innovation would have a better chance."[9] These ameliorative compromises actually function to maintain the continuity of academic, interpersonal, sociocultural, and political conventions and relationships that have become standard in North American educational settings and for which these settings are held accountable. These compromises frequently take the form of, and are believed best facilitated by, the educator's profound yet unchallenged dependence upon preformed materials which represent and extend the heritage in all its dimensions, packaged in ever-new and attractive ways to appear innovative and to conceal the tacit, comfortable consensus for conventional, academic, and content-centered priorities and relationships, and are preferably referred to as "resources" to soften or obscure their apparent conventionality in relation to conceptual advancements like Moffett's 1968 work.

Embedded in the story I have chosen to tell of Moffett's idea are various forms of discrepancy, or *congruence giving way to incongruence,* that constitute realms of meaning for educational experience; all of these might become subjects of curriculum criticism, either within the context of Moffett's own paradigm or within the context of other paradigms where such forms and realms are significant. I would like to abstract and draw critical attention to one form of congruence that frequently gives way to incongruence, in a generalized context of language and literature study, as the subject matter of this curriculum critique. I am concerned here with a method for disclosing the ways in which curricular events and instructional practices in language and literature study may or may not be congruent with theories of expression, symbolization, and abstraction, when these theories are presumed to be the appropriate conceptual base from which these aspects of pedagogy are derived. Where curricular events and instructional practices follow instead from a masked subscription to content- or product-centered theories of impression, reflecting a disjointed and imbalanced view of the dual syntactic and substantive dimensions of language and literature, out of the evolutionary context which appropriately delineates these fields first as languaging systems and symbolization processes, I am concerned with disclosing the persistent source of such misconceptions and incongruences. And finally, I am concerned with the consequences of this form of incongruence for educational experience, with the misconceptions of the human being, of these fields, and of valuable knowledge and knowing in general that may be implicitly conveyed when curricular events and instructional practices derive from product-centered theories of impression rather than process-centered theories of expression.

Monroe C. Beardsley's conception of aesthetic education has been among the most influential models of curricular/instructional environments for language and literature study; as a foundational academic tradition for conventional modes of study in these fields, through which Moffett and the majority of his readers came of age, Beardsley's model might be traced as one of Moffett's central references and a source of his and other stories of incongruence. Beardsley's model is a well-developed functional system, juxtaposing theory or conceptual bases with practice and giving structure and guidance to the practitioner's task of making decisions about the nature of curricular events and instructional practices that bring students into relation with the arts as fields of study. Beardsley's model is a general scheme that becomes particularized and adapted by those who subscribe to its conceptual foundations and aims for guidance in the design of environments specific to the various arts, typically the literary, fine, performing, and cinematic arts, in academic settings. A brief description of Beardsley's model, his conceptual bases, and the general curricular/instructional environment derived from it might serve to illuminate further the issue of Moffett's incongruence.

In a 1973 paper, "Semiotic Aesthetics and Aesthetic Education," Beardsley articulates a pertinent and clarified version of his general model of curricular/instructional environments and events for arts study in academic settings.[10] He begins with the notion, implicit in Moffett's original work, that theoretical positions about fields like the arts can and ought to serve as a significant part of the conceptual base from which decisions about educational experience are derived, and that separate and distinct theoretical positions will suggest correspondingly separate and distinct curricular directions and pedagogical practices. Beardsley expands this conceptual base, as Moffett does, to draw implications "about the appropriate ways of teaching people to understand the arts"[11] from positions on the significance of particular fields to human life and culture and from what is known about various physiological and psychological mechanisms of human learning and perceptions. However, within this three-part foundation, Beardsley finds theories of art most fertile for drawing implications about curricular and instructional matters; just as Moffett begins by subscribing to blended theories of expression, human symbolization and abstraction to draw such implications for language and literature study, Beardsley suggests that such conceptions of art, acceptable sets of propositions and assumptions about the nature and fundamental characteristics of the artistic enterprise, ought to be primary referents for designing curricular/instructional environments and events. Too, it would seem that Beardsley's initial aim resembles Moffett's of 1968 with respect to the value of conveying a holistic conception of the arts as symbolizing systems, representing and balancing their various dimensions in an evolutionary framework, through curriculum and instruction.

Beardsley does in fact derive his general model of aesthetic education from blended theories of expression, symbolization, and impression. He initially interprets the whole of the artistic enterprise in two compatible ways, in terms of the three traditional stages or components of the creative process, and in terms of the various roles assumed by individuals who are involved with each stage or component of this process. Clearly, Beardsley's holistic conception of the arts is general and basic enough to provide for the gleaning or imposing of more specific interpretations and theories of art; however, he initially seems to advocate the use of the more general view of the creative process as a reference for his model of aesthetic education. Table 1 is a visual delineation of Beardsley's conception of the artistic enterprise, defined in terms of the creative process and the roles of individuals involved with it.

Table 1
Beardsley's Conception of the Artistic Enterprise

The Creative Process: A Continuum		
Artistic Activity artist/creating	Art Product	Aesthetic Activity audience/receiving
Artist: formulates, expresses, creates, makes art product	Product	Audience: receives apprehends, perceives, engages with existing art product
Artistic Critic as Coach: addresses artist, reports on the process and recommends improvement	Product	Aesthetic Critic as Commentator: addresses the receiver, talks about the product given, assists perception and apprehension of receivers
Artistic Educator: addresses the artist, develops powers requisite for creating and producing product to be presented to receivers	Product	Aesthetic Educator: addresses receiver to develop powers requisite for receiving, perceiving, engaging with product, concerned with activities of receiving products created by others

SOURCE. This table is a graphic analogue of Beardsley's written descriptions and explanations in "Semiotic Aesthetics and Aesthetic Education," *Philosophic Exchange*, 1973, rpt. in *The Journal of Aesthetic Education* 9, no. 5 (July 1975): 48-49.

The same scheme used to delineate Beardsley's holistic and balanced conception of the arts, grounded in blended theories of expression and impression, and his primary source for drawing curricular and instructional implications, is best used to represent his model for aesthetic education. Table 2 expresses the relation between Beardsley's conceptual base and the curricular/instructional environment he derives from that base. In this model, what had been referred to as artistic and aesthetic activities and roles in relation to works of art translates into the traditional but flawed distinction between artistic

Table 2
Beardsley's Model for Artistic and Aesthetic Education

The Creative Process: A Continuum		
Artistic Activity	Art	Aesthetic Activity
artist/creating	Product	audience/receiving
Artistic Education and educative perspective	Product	Aesthetic Education and educative perspective
Artist	Product	Student
Artistic Critic as Coach	Product	Aesthetic Critic as Commentator
Artistic Educator	Product	Aesthetic Educator

SOURCE. See source note for table 1.

and aesthetic educational experiences and postures in relation to works of art. Similarly, a view of the artistic enterprise as "activity" grounded in blended theories of expression and impression becomes a view of the enterprise as "education" grounded in separated theories of symbolization and formalism, for creators and receivers respectively. The distinction is flawed because each realm of educational experience is exclusive, each derived from a different fragment of the artistic enterprise, and each confined to the perspective of those respective fragments.

Artistic education traditionally addresses the developmental activities and processes of creating, formulating, and making works of art, or creating through a form or medium of expression. As a rule, this educational realm exclusively involves the artist or creator who is engaged in the processes of intentional expression for the self and/or others; the artistic critic as coach who addresses the artist and the creating process with a view toward recommendation and improvement; and the artistic educator who addresses the artist with a view toward developing and cultivating the creative powers requisite for the process of expression.

Aesthetic education traditionally addresses the developmental activities and processes of receiving, apprehending, and perceiving intentional works of art in presentational form; these developmental activities and processes may be a wide range of critical, analytic encounters that lead to various kinds of aesthetic apprehension and understanding. Aesthetic education typically involves the student who is engaged in various processes of receiving presentational forms of art; the aesthetic critic as commentator who addresses the student-receiver in order to assist with various kinds of aesthetic criticism and analyses; and the aesthetic educator who shares the critic's responsibility with a view toward developing and cultivating the student-receiver's various critical and analytic powers requisite for aesthetic apprehension.

Conventional language and literature studies in primary and secondary settings are typically conceived as aesthetic education rather than as artistic education. In this context, the strict distinction between artistic and aesthetic education seems a valid rationale to the proponents of the tradition; as the aims seem clearly not to be artistic, the conceptual dichotomy is taken for granted for its organizational clarity, and little consideration is given to breaking it down. The imbalance begins to emerge clearly: the artist, artistic critic, and artistic educator would seem to have the advantage of focusing on the whole of the creative process, its artistic and aesthetic components, its entire evolutionary history, as creative formulation depends upon a concern with both the powers of expression and the aesthetics of presentational forms. Those engaged in aesthetic education, on the other hand, reside exclusively within the presentational realm of the creative process as receivers and apprehenders, and their critical and analytic inquiries into expressive content, form, purpose, and processes are uninformed by experience in artistic activity/education.

As the student-receiver encounters completed works of discourse, art, and communication in the presentational realm of the creative process, the conception of the nature of these fields, and by implication of valuable knowledge and knowing in general, is conveyed as substantive, fixed, and settled; it is a codified and systematic product that lies outside the student, to be discerned and acquired from a receiver's posture. The well-documented case against product-centered conceptions of knowledge, the events and methodologies that correspond to facilitate them, the sociocultural and political dimensions and relationships implicit in them, and their psychological and academic consequences surfaces from time to time through educational inquiry. Moffett's initial battle against the "substantive approach"[12] is notably followed by Paulo Freire's articulation of "banking education,"[13] and John Dewey's explication of the "scholastic method"[14] precedes both. There is reason to keep this controversy alive in our own time, to practice curriculum criticism as one means toward disclosing, supplanting, and replacing a misconception of fields in particular and valuable knowledge in general that dominates curriculum and instruction now as it did in Dewey's time:

Probably the most conspicuous connotation of the word knowledge for most persons to-day is just the body of facts and truths ascertained by others; the material found in rows and rows of atlases, cyclopedias, histories, biographies, books of travel, scientific treatises, on the shelves of libraries.

The imposing, stupendous bulk of this material has unconsciously influenced men's notions of the nature of knowledge itself. The statements, the propositions, in which knowledge, the issue of active concern with problems, are taken to be themselves knowledge. The record of knowledge, independent of its place as an outcome of inquiry, is taken to be knowledge. The mind of man is taken captive by the spoils of its prior victories; the spoils, not the weapons and the acts of waging the battle against the unknown, are used to fix the meaning of knowledge, of fact, and truth ... the same ideal has almost dominated instruction.[15]

Congruence: A Method for Aesthetic Curricular Criticism

In the first section of this essay, the method of *congruence* has been used to frame, delineate, and explore various relations among elements and realms of meaning that constitute an exemplary curricular/instructional environment. Congruence is a method for aesthetic curricular criticism that I have been developing over the past several years, and the story of James Moffett's idea demonstrates one of its applications.

In this section, I would like to attend to descriptions of the method itself, to make explicit the fundamental assumptions and aesthetic principles of congruence that have been implicit in the foregoing study.[16] I assume this meta-critical posture with several intentions: to respond to George Willis's suggestion that curricularists must be conscientious and self-observing about the development and sharing of new subjects and methodologies appropriate to curricular phenomena and inquiry[17]; to provide a companion to the foregoing study, one which will reflect on the structure of that story and illuminate the manner in which it is formulated; and finally, to make the essential processes, assumptions, and principles of congruence accessible to other curricularists for application in subsequent case studies and critiques where this method is appropriate.

Congruence is a method with which to search for the nature of relationships shared by various elements interacting in curricular/ instructional environments and events. These elements are the related levels of thought and practice which the method holds should cohere and correspond, such as in the relationship between theory or conceptual bases with respect to the subject under study and the curricular events and instructional methods developed for study of that subject; in the relationship between educational aims and the pedagogical practices developed to facilitate those aims; and in the relationship between conceptual positions with respect to the nature of the human being and valuable kowledge and the curricular events and instructional practices developed to convey those positions. The method of congruence is then concerned with those realms of meaning that pervade educational experience as a consequence of the nature of the relationships shared by these elements. For example, where the structure and substance of curricular events are congruent reflections of a particular conceptual assertion about the nature of valuable knowledge, that assertion will pervade events and be conveyed to students in both implicit and explicit ways as a realm of meaning; and the reverse, where events are not congruent translations of a particular conception of valuable knowledge, another, perhaps unintended and contradictory conception is conveyed to students as a realm of meaning.

The process of using congruence begins with a delineation and juxtaposition of, for example, a theory or conceptual base for viewing a particular field to which the author of a curricular/instructional environment subscribes and the various events and practices the author presumably derives from that base for the classroom. A second example might be the delineation and juxtaposition of an author's conception of the human being and the curricular events and instructional practices the author presumably develops to convey that conception. Theory and practice, to abbreviate, are then disclosed side by side, forming a scheme or framework for critical scrutiny with respect to the nature of the relationship they share, the degree to which these elements cohere and correspond, and the manner in which they are congruent and harmonious or incongruent and discordant.

I would like to digress briefly to provide a single, concrete reference for the reader, to delineate and juxtapose the two separate levels of related theory and practice in a cohering set of curricular events for secondary film studies, from my own experience, and adapted directly from sections of Moffett's 1968 events for literature studies. The "concept of film," as a field of study, to which the author of this environment subscribes, is grounded in blended theories of expression and impression; the author perceives the whole of the creative process of film as a languaging system, with syntactic affinities that are capable of being manipulated to convey content with purpose and meanings. The author views this process within an evolutionary framework, as a genesis involving multiple but ordered perspectives of creator and receiver, which progresses with continuity through the three traditional stages: original, intentional creative formulation, with its various internal, developmental stages of content, form, and purpose drawn from one's own realms of meaning, and with a view toward both self-expression and presentation to others; the film product as a single organic expression, with references in the creators' experiences and perceptions, and with a life of its own as new and unintended meanings are potential when all expressive elements are taken together to form the whole; and the presentation of the film product to others who experience, apprehend, and respond to content, form, and purpose, as meanings both intended by the creator and unintended but emerging from the whole from the perspective of the receivers' own experiences and perceptions.

While the author of this film studies environment must consider a cluster of aims and objectives for the development of curricular events and instructional practices, I will temporarily isolate one aim for the exemplification of related theory and practice: to convey the conception of film that has been described here. (Perhaps it is significant to note that many other aims are embedded in the one stated, and that the specific purposes for selecting this particular aim will vary widely among separate authors of film studies environments. Clearly, more specific aims, which might range from a focus on the student's technical ability to appreciation of form, may seem conceptual priorities to authors determining the more concrete nature of all pedagogical matters, and therefore seem to alter or further detail the aim that has been stated. However, I would be bold enough to support conveying the conceptual view of film I have described as an appropriate foundation and aim from which to derive pedagogy for all more specific aims, which may in fact influence a variance in emphases within the evolutionary framework or in the manners of progressing through this framework. Overriding *contextual* matters must be given priority, those of transmitting a holistic, balanced view of film as a functional languaging system which can be used with intent and choice as well as a product which can be appreciated, a view that is flexible enough for varying emphases within, or for the expression of more specific aims of authors and, more importantly, students themselves.)

The author's task of making practice congruent with theory might be described in various ways; I have preferred to conceptualize this process as *relating* the various and progressive aspects of theory and practice in search of correspondence in all dimensions, as *translating* the various and progressive aspects of theory into curricular and instructional analogues, as *integrating* all aspects and dimensions of theory and practice to form an organic whole or scheme of elements that function compatibly.

In the film studies environment, events would progress in the following general way: from the students' experiences in biographical reflection, discoursing and acting, visualizing and sounding, storyboarding and composing, all within the context of preproduction and production processes involved in the making of individual films; toward the student's completion of their own films, moving back and forth from projector to editing bench for refinements; toward student's group presentation of their films, the sharing of experiences and mutual response to meanings, aesthetics, and technique. The progression is cyclic, and all dimensions of a previous experience accrue to the benefit of a subsequent experience. This curricular/instructional framework represents a "first level" translation of theory into practice; emphases within the framework and manners of progressing through the stages in selected directions unique to each environment must be determined by the more specific aims that come into focus for authors/teachers and students as a consequence of moving through this first-level event.

The development of congruence derives from the assumption that a curricular/instructional environment or event is comprehensive and multileveled, best represented as a design of interacting elements of related thought and practice. These elements, all potential relations among them and realms of meaning embedded in them, represent variables which are more often implicit than explicit; these elements require a special framework within which their relationships might become accessible for critical scrutiny. In order to disclose these elements, ferret out their relations, and draw implications about their consequences for educational experience, the method displays the curricular/instructional environment as a multileveled scheme of theory-practice.

Much like a work of art, this scheme of presumably related elements is an organism, an organic unity, with a life of its own which may become the subject of aesthetic modes of critical inquiry. The scheme discloses a design, a concrete and symbolic representation of ideas embodied by the interacting elements taken together. Various kinds and levels of meaning may be disclosed through aesthetic analysis, meanings of individual elements, meanings embedded in the relations of elements, and meanings implied for educational experience as a consequence of these relations.

John S. Mann associates the development and use of such a scheme with the transformation of the practitioner's material into the critic-theorist's material. He suggests that the critic-theorist generalize and relate the various levels of thought and practice, both implicit and explicit, from curricular/instructional environments, engaging them in analysis of a different order than the practitioner might:

Whereas the practitioner employs his material in the context of discovering means and ends, the critic may employ the same material as data for his analysis of the designs of educational events. Where the practitioner seeks solutions to problems, the critic seeks meaning in the manner in which problems are posed and solved. Where the practitioner may customarily evaluate his practices by examining their consequences, the critic construes practice as falling in designs that may be accounted for as expressions of meaning.[18]

Mann exemplifies such a transformation of material and a shift in inquiry in the following passage; his use of this example derives from a concern with one aspect of the present study, "the various conceptions of the nature, function, source and uses of knowledge that are implicitly conveyed to students through contrasting methods of transmitting knowledge": [19]

The school practitioner seeks answers to such questions as what is known and what should be known. These questions concern the critic not because he seeks answers to them but because the fact that they are asked, as well as the processes the practitioner employs in seeking answers to them and the character of answers accepted, all constitute data for him. These fall into designs which it is the critic's task to analyze. Thus he will seek, for example, to discover what ideas about (1) the nature of knowledge, (2) the processes by which knowledge is acquired, (3) the values associated with knowledge . . . are entailed in the designs he observes. For instance, whereas the science teacher may be interested in discovering whether a pupil knows Boyle's Law or in how to get a pupil to know it, the critic is interested in discovering what meanings of "knowledge" may account for both the teacher's analysis of the problem and his teaching behavior with respect to the problem. The critic may discover, for example, that teachers vary considerably from each other and from established epistemologies in their understanding of the meaning of the scientific assertion that something is known. They vary, that is, in their understanding of the logical status of something regarded as known. And these observations in turn may account for or explain similarities and contrasts between different science instruction situations. [20]

A survey of the field of curriculum inquiry reveals that its literature is marked with inclinations toward particular modes or processes of thinking, particular perceptual frames of reference for reflecting about curriculum phenomena. Curricularists seem inclined to study dimensions and elements of phenomena through the lenses of three "interaction constructs"; that is, they look for, find, and make relationships, translations, and integrations. These constructs or tools appear and reappear throughout the literature of curriculum inquiry.

As the method of congruence asserts aesthetic standards of organic unity with which to explore and assess curricular/instructional environments, these three interaction constructs of relationship, translation, and integration become the aesthetic principles of the method. The critic looks into the scheme *with* these principles as tools for inquiry and *for* these principles in the interactions among elements.

Relationship denotes a connection among or between elements in some identifiable context, an alliance, the nature of which may vary in kind, order or level, degree or measure. Whatever the referents or components of a relationship, the context or quality they collectively form might be said to exist only as the components are taken together. Something can always be said of the bond that mediates and ties the elements in relation, that is, the elements share some common reference point. A relationship is conceived or exists, is facilitated by or is a result of likenesses or linkages in the nature, purpose of function, use, or source of the elements. The sense of relation is that something qualitative is formed, abstract or concrete, as a function of connectedness. Other words that come to mind to describe or denote relationship are correspondence, agreement, correlation, mutuality, and congruence between or among elements. The nature of relationship with regard to the scheme formed by theory and practice can be described in terms of consanguinity, organicism, a symbiosis among the two elements or levels. That is, they share an intimate, essential bond as if of the same lineage or parentage; they are interdependent, mutually influential, and their separateness in any regard is understood in relation to the function of the whole scheme.

Translation denotes a change from one form or appearance into another, a conversion from one language or set of symbols to another. With such a shift, however, the first expression and the translated construction share an essential bond; that is, a consanguine and organic relation exists between the forms. Translation is also a hermeneutic process, and shifting from a first rendering to its transformed rendering may involve interpretation of the first. The essential sameness ought to hold; however, the interpretation or translation may be a decoding, an elucidation, an adaptation, an amplification, or a general unfolding of some kind that makes the first rendering intelligible in its new form, new function, new context. Translation might occur in a number of directions, from the abstract to the concrete and the reverse, from the experiential to the material and the reverse, and so forth. Philosophical foundations translate into theory, theory into practice; both are translations or interpretations of the other, but they share essential references.

Integration addresses the entire scheme; it calls forth notions of synchronism, harmony and balance, blending and unity; integration refers to wholeness, fullness, and completeness, to holism inclusiveness, and comprehensiveness. All elements are cooperative, interwoven coefficients within the same scheme in any one particular comprehensive situation. Integration is reminiscent of synthesis, synergism, and organicism, all of which have a view to a coherent whole with congruent parts. Synthesis refers to the composing or combining of elements so as to form the comprehensive whole; synergism is the cooperative action and relation of separate but essentially interconnected parts, such that the whole is rendered more effective than if the parts were considered independently; and finally, organicism, wherein the scheme is a living process whose activities are a function of the integrated elements rather than individual fragments.

I elaborate these aesthetic principles as potential and consequential operations within curricular/instructional environments represented as multileveled schemes of related theory or conceptual bases and practice, and as operations of the critic who delineates and juxtaposes these elements to disclose congruence or incongruence, its manner and degree, its sources, and its consequent realms of meaning conveyed in educational experience.

Finally, as the method of congruence generates such disclosures, it paves the way toward post-critical tasks. Critical methods and critics must be agents of praxis, both reflection and action toward the reconceptualization of environments governed by incongruence between theory and practice.

Notes

1. James Moffett, *Teaching the Universe of Discourse* (Boston: Houghton Mifflin, 1968), pp. 7, 110.

2. Ibid.

3. James Moffett, *A Student-Centered Language Arts Curriculum, Grades K-13: A Handbook for Teachers* (Boston: Houghton Mifflin, 1968).

4. Moffett, *Teaching the Universe of Discourse.*

5. G. Lynn Nelson, "Toward Teaching English for the Real World," *English Journal* (September 1974): 48-49.

6. Moffett, *A Student-Centered Language Arts Curriculum,* 1973 edition.

7. Ibid., p. vi.

8. Ibid., p. vii.

9. Ibid.

10. Monroe C. Beardsley, "Semiotic Aesthetics and Aesthetic Education," *Philosophic Exchange,* 1973, rpt. *The Journal of Aesthetic Education* 9, no. 5 (July 1975): 5-26.

11. Ibid., p. 17.

12. Moffett, *Teaching the Universe of Discourse.*

13. Paulo Freire, *Pedagogy of the Oppressed* (New York: Herder and Herder, 1970), chap. 2.

14. John Dewey, *Democracy and Education* (New York: The Macmillan Co., 1926).

15. Ibid., pp. 219-20.

16. It should be noted that the development of congruence is still considered work-in-progress. Included in this paper are descriptions of the method's general aspects, with an emphasis on those most pertinent to the preceding study. For extended descriptions and applications of congruence, see my doctoral dissertation, *"Congruence*: A Methodology for Aesthetic Curricular Criticism and Post-Critical Theorizing; Reconceptualizing Knowledge and Methods, as Curricular Foundation, for Secondary Cinematic Arts Education" (The Ohio State University, 1976).

17. George Willis, "Curriculum Criticism and Literary Criticism," *Journal of Curriculum Studies* 7, no. 1 (May 1975). (Chapter 5 of this volume.)

18. John S. Mann, "Curriculum Criticism," *Curriculum Theory Network* 2 (Winter 1968-69), rpt. *Curriculum Theorizing: The Reconceptualists*, ed. William Pinar (Berkeley, Ca.: McCutchan Publishing Corp., 1975). pp. 141-42. (Chapter 4 of this volume.)

19. John S. Mann, "A Discipline of Curriculum Theory," *School Review* 76, no. 4 (December 1968), rpt. *Curriculum Theorizing*, p. 154.

20. Mann, "Curriculum Criticism," p. 141.

The study by Edward W. Milner consists of three parts: a description of a series of events comprising a special education curriculum; a critique disclosing forms of morality and meaning within special education and explaining how analysis of formal, efficient, material, and final causes within description can be used in curriculum criticism; and an explanation and the application of a model from theological literary criticism.

The description of the special education curriculum is in the form of a story, and the author-narrator is at once part of the action. Like all good art, the story implicitly discloses meaning, and in this sense Milner's interest is aesthetic. He artistically communicates his experiences. But the dominant interest in the overall study is personal, for the story itself becomes a disclosure of personal meaning, as do Milner's explicit critical disclosures about the curriculum and his analysis of causes and his explanation of model. For instance, Milner's analysis of formal, efficient, material, and final causes treats them much like the literary concepts of "plot," "point of view," "metaphor," and "theme." Not only are they personally experienced within the curriculum as lived, but they become personal choices made by the author of the story. The model also has a distinctly *personal dimension. It posits three world views; the Greek, in which man is a tragic figure; the Modern, in which man is sick and driven to the void; and the Judeo-Christian, in which man is a fallen creature who finds redemption. Here Milner's point is that one's world view is largely a personal matter, but that the discovery of the world view present within curriculum or critical description illuminates the discovery of causes within that work. He points out how he has attempted to embody his own Judeo-Christian world view within the story, but he encourages the reader to make a personal decision about the world view actually conveyed. In conclusion, he suggests that the kind of Whiteheadian conception of time immanent within his own world view permits events, their recollection, and their recreation all to be the curriculum. Thus, this world view in itself expands the curriculum beyond mere facts and into the personal dimension of the critic.*

The principal critical focal point in this study is the "work," but the analysis of the causes within the curriculum is done from the perspective of "author" and as a representation of "world." Within this focus the use of the model from theological literary criticism in some ways makes superfluous the critical process of judgment. Generally, as in art, skillful description leads directly to interpretations that disclose meaning, and incorporates judgments that may be more powerful than those explicitly stated. Specifically, the Judeo-Christian view itself obviates critical judgment, since morality is what Milner describes as "theonomous," a personal gift of grace. Within Milner's view, then, emphasis is on the qualities of the experienced situation. There is no logical way—nor, in fact, any necessity—of attempting to judge merely technological uses of various educational methods.

12

The Amphibious Musician

Edward W. Milner

. . . we are onely that amphibious piece betweene a corporall and spirituall essence, that middle frame that links those two together, and makes good the method of God and nature that jumps not from extreames, but unites the incompatible distances by some middle and participating natures. . . .

Sir Thomas Browne, *Religio Medici*

Introduction

The three components of the following article—special education, curriculum criticism, and theological literary criticism—were introduced to me in three different periods in my career as a teacher. I got into theological literary criticism in the early fifties. As a humanist (or more precisely as a panentheist), I refused to relinquish the Judeo-Christian heritage to the orthodox, and as a Neo-Aristotelian I refused to relinquish literary criticism to the New Critics. In the late sixties I began working in special education. Although I couldn't put my finger on the problem, I sensed that not only was the technological obsession with objectives and behaviors dehumanizing, it was not delivering the goods and services it claimed it could deliver. In the article that follows it should be clear that when I went to work on the case study (Part 1: The Story), the business of curriculum criticism had just come into my ken. Curriculum criticism suggested that the humanism I assumed was an alternative to the technology I was asked to practice. Perhaps I have built my final assumption into my work of art. We shall see. Part 2 (The Critique) skims over morals and meanings in curriculum and then, treating the story as a work in curriculum, analyzes it along literary critical lines. In Part 3 (Evaluation) a theological typology is used to raise serious questions about curriculum as a literary object. The extent to which curriculum criticism will influence special education is problematic, and I can but hope that this essay raises some of the proper questions.

Part 1. Story: A Case Study of an Amphibious Musician

There were eight children, two aides, and the teacher. The class was assembled for its juice. Not until each child had uttered a word would the teacher reward them. The bearded man sheepishly came into the room and lifted his guitar case, pointing at it. "And now," the young teacher said in a syrupy fashion, "we will have singing." The moon-shaped face on the nine-year-old became cloudy. Dirk's teeth sharpened into spear points when he grinned, and Lovell's eyes were closed. An enigmatic smile was on his face, and his hand automatically described its customary hieratic arc behind his neck and over his head and back. Helen pushed her finger farther into her eye, but the black aide gently moved it away.

Actually, the singing was done by the teacher, the aides, and the guitarist, but for each song, some gesture or word, some action, was required of the students, and as they sat in anticipation in their chairs, the teachers facilitated the appropriate moves. Lovell, however, only keened back and forth and from time to time dished up a word salad that the guitarist failed to decode.

Suddenly, in the middle of "Wheels on the Bus Go Round and Round," Lovell sang, in perfect pitch and in perfect timing, "Frère Jacques." The guitarist stopped and pulled on his beard in amazement, but he was even more astonished by the teacher and aides as they quickly returned to the second chorus of "Wheels." He did not like to indulge brats or show-offs, but this seemed *sui generis*. A unique event. Let it go on. It was the "wheels," however, that went on and on.

Later on in the day the beard came back to talk to the young teacher. "Dr. Helmet said that if it was OK with you, I might work with Lovell . . . with my guitar . . . did you notice his singing today?"

"It's echoic."

"You mean Lovell can capture words, tune, rhythm, and all and not have the slightest idea what he is saying or doing?"

"Well, I wouldn't say that unequivocally, but I think that perhaps his speech therapist would."

In the beard's fantasy he saw a tribal fire and chanting and dancing bodies round a camp fire: Whitehead's idea that singing and dancing preceded the development of language. "Well, I would like to give it a try. We will just sing with each other. I know I won't hurt him."

"He is free at 11:00 tomorrow after his rest period."

Lovell at first followed the guitarist through the door, but when the gate they encountered squeaked, he pulled back. Because other students were about to pour through the opening, the beard lifted Lovell up, balanced him on his guitar case and instrument bag, and carried him through. Lovell embraced him as though he were his mother. In fact, Lovell's mother did not quite know what to make of her blind retarded child nor of the doctor's strange-sounding diagnosis: cytomegalic inclusion disease? Taxoplasmosis? Ironically, the foreign-born grandmother did not let these foreign terms isolate her from Lovell. Rather she took his side and intervened for him when Lovell's older brother begged for attention.

The bearded and the blind made their way into a parent conference room. When the other children were brought into that room for one reason or another, neither coffee nor sugar, lamps nor magazines were safe. And a bowel movement under the chair or a bounce on the arms of the sofa ushered Adam out of the garden.

With Lovell, it was different. A persistent quietness, an ineluctable dependence. He waited for the guitar case to be opened. However, as one of the strings brushed his pants and sounded, Lovell instinctively reached out to pluck it.

The first session was an hour long. The guitarist played the nursery songs of his childhood. A few of the counting songs often sung at the Center. Show and tell pieces. Trimmed down to conceal the terrors and the grief of history. Then Lovell was given the instrument, and he played with it without a stop. He would strum and then emit his scramble of words. Strum again and repeat his atonic reflex, proprioceptively. Next he would pluck one string at a time. Then he would begin to strum and hum. To the guitarist, Lovell clearly seemed to be discriminating between one note and another, and to be structuring some sort of pattern for himself.

Every instrument other than the guitar was rejected by Lovell except the handbell. This he would use to keep in time with the guitarist. He would hum, and jingle the bell. This humming contrasted with ritual; it should generalize to the spoken dialog.

As the hour wore away, neither spoke. Merely the one would have the guitar and then the other. The guitarist was later to note in his records that the child had the musical intelligence of a first grader. He also noted the word salad, the gestures and the tics, that he thought typical of the blind, and the production of "Frère Jacques" earlier in the week.

As he moved through the literary critical categories he had adapted to his curriculum criticism, he reflected that their world was not that of the systemic modern nature. Nor was it the Greek world of tragic autonomy, the world of the mind. Rather it was the Judeo-Christian world, a boundary situation where absolutely everything is absolutely interdependent, where a friendly God sufferingly issues into the present. Mythologically, they, he and the student, were both fallen creatures, no longer protected by clichéd actions or prefabricated being.

The guitarist prepared for the next visit with Lovell by working over music that would instance various modes and moods. Also he chose music that might strike a more autonomous rather than a heteronomous note. Instead of songs that emphasized obedience and manners, he would sing songs that emphasized self-initiated action. Early in the guitarist's career as a therapist he decided that music should work its own way; it had to come from within. He might have condescended to the sick and dying, the tubercular, the emotionally disturbed, and now the retarded by singing only simple lullabies and folksongs, but, taking his chances, he decided that it was better to sing for himself, as it were, and move out of himself over into wherever it was that that other happened to be. With this disclosure model, the two could become real to each other and let the creative process between them do the healing work.

He would sing "I Can't Help But Wonder Where I'm Bound,

Where I'm Bound" because in truth he couldn't help but so wonder. He arranged both form and content for his curriculum for the day so as to imitate the Judeo-Christian action. Not the pathetic modern action of conformity, nor the tragic action of autonomy, but the redemptive action of openness. Reality would now have to give way to truth.

Lovell seemed to sense the guitar's presence before the guitarist was fully in the room. He stopped his keening and gesturing and moved toward the guitarist. The guitarist had a vision of Lovell as the "Blue Guitarist" by Picasso. Would Lovell ever grow up to cradle a guitar or indeed a woman in his arms? Or steal C.B. radios, or commit suicide, or watch World War II movies?

This eschatological note that jaded the transfiguration was matched by the sputtering and spattering of Lovell's incontinence. The effluence of every kitchen midden of the world. Why not, he thought as he changed Lovell, change a retarded child? Six years old, yes. But an I.Q. of 25 yields a mental age of one and a half. Would his children have done much better at eighteen months? This body, this diploid negligence of evolution.

Back in the conference room he tousled Lovell's hair and said, "Let's begin." That he had said something, actually said something, did not occur to him till Lovell said something also. As he was taking the triangle out of his sack of instruments, the pencil in his pocket slipped out and hit the triangle, sounding a tone.

"Hello."

The guitarist at first was delighted that Lovell had spoken. But then he saw a lonely house, silent. Only an occasional conversation on the phone. Corresponding and cohering to impoverished speech. Then, anticipating that the teacher would also dismiss this as stimulus and response, he resigned himself to his task. But then it broke over him as the smell of the Abelia would at his grandmother's: This beautiful word awoke in him the recognition that he—the great teacher stilling the choppy multitudes, the great reformer reciting his theses—he had not troubled himself to talk to Lovell. How could he have been so stupid as to overlook that? So he began to talk.

"Lovell, we will share this instrument today. You will have to go first while I set up this gear. Maybe you will want to play the triangle."

Lovell strummed the guitar as he had before, at times plucking one string, then another, then another, and humming the note of the string as he did so, at times strumming and counterpointing with his humming. Lovell shopped among the strings, marketing what he could consume most profitably.

The guitarist tried his various tunes and accepted Lovell's non-committal reaction. He offered various instruments, but they were also rejected. He turned the guitar back over to Lovell. It occurred to him that by placing the steel hammer for the triangle on the strings he could produce, as Lovell strummed, the same whining sound as the dobro, but this effect irritated Lovell. Next he tried to get Lovell himself to form a chord on the guitar.

To form the chord, he placed Lovell's strumming hand, his left hand, on the top part of the neck of the guitar and forced him to use his right hand to strum the strings. "Lovell, row the boat ashore," he sang while he guided the blind child's fingers in place to form the chord and in position to strum the string. Lovell resisted, but when they reached the chorus, he sang out "Hallelujah." The guitarist was so overjoyed at Lovell's vocalization that he greedily played the rest of the song himself while Lovell hummed in tune and vocalized.

His reaction was like that of a singer who suddenly finds some-one with whom he can harmonize. Instantly, one feels one can never be full with the singing. Incredulously he moved on, and, tentatively, Lovell moved on also, in tune.

The Dionysian communalism of frenzy later passed to the abstract individualization of Apollonian remoteness. Was vocalization caused by pain, or was the vocalization an expression of the pain? Was it the use of both hands, or Lovell's shifting from one hemisphere of his brain to another, that had caused the drift into language? He noted that he had used various modes and that these might have been aped by Lovell—blues, melancholy, joy. Perhaps Lovell had patterned himself on these modes, and thus found some affective base from which his language arose? Had his attempt to manage certain moods smacked of engineering? To what extent had play and creativity emerged rather than been imposed? He noted that words from the songs such as "boat" and "goose" and "something" and "wish" had appeared in Lovell's garbled utterances. Now here was one—alone—but in context. Was this one word the turning point in language acquisition, the "Kairos"?

William Butler Yeats's "Among School Children" crossed his

mind. The aged school inspector who falls in love with an adolescent Helen of Troy while an ancient nun explains the school's modernity. Yeats called on "gyres" and Platonic reminiscences to account mythologically for his actions (and thus made his poetry all the more beautiful/recondite). Whitehead's notion of concrescence was his mythology: all things self-caused, all things internally related, all things emerging and perishing. Yes, Lovell was, had to be, self-caused, and internally related to him.

How important is it to speak, he wondered. Must a person speak in order to be a human? How far are we permitted to "prime the pump," as it were, to engender speech? He reflected on what Lovell might be like in five years if he could verbalize. He reflected on what it must be like to be retarded and blind.

The next day he abandoned the instruments and the script and decided to move in truth and openness. He would play whatever came to mind and Lovell might use the guitar as an interest center, open and free. This was frustrating for him, for every time he began to feel his way into his particular song or style, Lovell grew impatient and seemed to demand the instrument. The day became a battle of wills. His against Lovell's. Touchy at first because of his idea of being manipulative the day before, he slowly admitted to himself that education is a matter of willpower. It begins in the training of the infant, and it is quickly etherealized, or downright denied with abstractions and rationalizations, or openly affirmed as the structure of truth, but the will is there, covertly, sometimes moving through bodily gestures, sometimes conveying the wishes of class, caste, and race. My Lord, what a topography of learning! The structure of truth had to be more embracing and widespread than the structure of language.

In the music that followed Lovell began at one point to count as he played: "One, two, three, four." This seemed to be something between the primitive enactment of a nursery rhyme and a true vocalization. He told this with gladness when he returned Lovell to the teacher. She, however, asked if this was in response to a request to count. "Did he say anything else? How long was the conversation? How much was spontaneous?"

"For Christ's sake," he thought, "she expects some goddamned oration or something." He was delighted, however, to learn that on the strength of his report the teacher was going to find an autoharp for Lovell.

He had to admit that in truth Lovell had nothing but phonology —the ability to create phonemes. No morphology—plurals or tenses; no syntax—questions and answers; no semantics—denotation and connotation. His words—"boat," "call," "come," "cut," "does," "dot," "ever," "goose," "got," "hat," "I," "let," "Lovell," "not," "of," "pet," "put," "now," "see," "sing," "the," "up"—came up indiscriminately in Lovell's glossary, were all from the songs played, and were possibly all memorized, echoic. The area of music, however, revealed generalizations, abstractions. In music, Lovell did seem to have a morphology of refrains, pluralizing them; a syntax of rhythm, question and reply in song and verse; a semantic of emphasis and timing. Time flowed through his being as it did for Rousseau or for Augustine.

The flight of being moves from truth to beauty, from what is perceived to what is valued, and so perceived again. The next day was the last. The parent conference room was not available. The recreation room across the hall stood vacant. Lovell sensed where he was. He bypassed a chair. He found the center of the room. As the guitarist warmed up, Lovell spun round and round to the rhythm. The guitarist marveled. He thought: "Do the blind get dizzy?" "Why haven't I given Lovell more room to explore?" "How perfect to let the blind dance." "Ought, ought, ought." Lovell was David dancing before the altar. The guitarist let the warmth roll over him.

He looked at the full-length mirror and saw himself watching Lovell. That was the speech therapists' mirror. The trampoline belonged to the physical therapists. Territoriality. The question surfaced. "Would creativity fit in with therapy? Openness with a baseline? Interaction with record keeping? Happiness with juice and cookies? Spontaneity with schedules? Was it fair to confront Lovell one way and then return him to the others? Like a Greek hero, left chained to his fate?"

Lovell stopped his dancing and began his strumming. He had a distinct click in his breathing. A susurrus of death? There were few utterances. Fewer self-initiated actions. Quietness now. But Lovell faced the impending separation with courage. The guitarist almost broke down and wept, for he had learned much from Lovell; felt he had imparted little.

Lovell used the handbell, keeping perfect synchronization.

> *Whenever snow falls so soft and lonely*
> *Whenever winds blow so sad and sere*
> *I think of trees lost in forest gardens*
> *I think of stones tossed by ocean waves.*

The guitarist breathed out the words, but no sounds came. Aspirants. His body shivered like labor spasms. "Think of something funny and be a man." He could not. But the feeling finally left and the sounds came. Lovell hummed, but also proceeded with caution. Something was ending.

He later was to ask the doctor if the clicking was a prosthesis. "No, probably self-initiated."

"Could he have been different if he had received early treatment?"

"No use looking down your retroscope." The words stung. The doctor, like the guitarist and the child, was an amphibian. He practiced at the boundary of his knowledge. The guitarist couldn't hate him.

Lovell patted the guitar. The cracked and faulted voice solidified. To him sounds began to reify—shapes coming like cookies—bombarding prodigiously. Whole and yoked to action and response. Did the guitar also have a friend?

Part 2. Critique: Morals, Meaning, and Curriculum Criticism

The story just presented raises several questions about morals, meaning, and curriculum criticism.[1] First, what kinds of morality are there, and is there a kind of morality appropriate for or peculiar to the retarded? Is a morality of autonomy or a morality of theonomy necessary or possible for a child who is retarded? Or should the actions of a retarded child be presumed to be premoral? Second, what kinds of meaning are there and what kind of meaning is appropriate to the retarded? Is meaning symbolic or is it only propositional? Finally, what is special education curriculum? Is curriculum criticism appropriate for special education? Would reforms effected by appropriate curriculum criticism obviate special education?

Morality

According to Paul Tillich, there are three kinds of morality: heteronomy, or morality with the law imposed from outside by others;

autonomy, or morality with the law imposed by the self, from within; and theonomy, or morality with the law-dissolving-into-grace that is within the depths of the self.[2] In the story above, the morality of Lovell appears to be heteronomous. He is compliant and receives his rules from others. In the course of the action, however, it appears that his will to be himself emerges in the context of openness provided by the guitarist. In the final part of the story, Lovell's handling the anxiety of separation comes from within. He begins to make the guitar real. He even considers that this thing, the guitar, might even have a friend (the guitarist). Lovell's action is not simply of the "good boy" or legalistic type.

The guitarist is autonomous in his morality. He desires not to manipulate his charge, he disagrees in principle with the technological model of the institution, but he tries to change it rather than to undermine it; he is fair to himself and does not allow the afflicted to undermine his artistic and religious commitments by luring him into being patronizing. His anxiety over separation from Lovell is painful but prompts him to the theonomous act of carrying his concern about Lovell to the physician in charge.

The interaction between these two characters raises the question as to whether or not there is a morality appropriate for or peculiar to the retarded. If I.Q. is the final yardstick, then it is clear that Lovell is too ignorant to have an autonomous morality. But taking our cue from Piaget's world view, where morality starts in games, the interaction between the guitarist and Lovell suggests that Lovell has a measure of freedom and creativity.[3] Our conclusion is that the action and interaction within the story reveal a world of morality like that of father-son, teacher-student, therapist-client, or friend-friend. In light of the fact that the guitarist learns from the retarded child, the moral relationship is more than a heteronomous one.

As to its appropriateness, the story suggests that morality at all levels—heteronomy, autonomy, and theonomy—is possible and appropriate, and the question then becomes, "When do the retarded have theonomous or autonomous beings with whom they can interact?" The institution that models itself on behavioristic or technological principles seems scheduled to reinforce and expect a morality of heteronomy. Arguably the self-actualizing or the humanistic model reinforces and expects a morality of autonomous dimensions. Is theonomous morality incompatible with the technological framework? If the technological model is increasingly to serve as the pattern for training the retarded, then will the self-fulfilling prophecy be that the retarded child, at best, is capable of heteronomous morality only?[4]

Meaning

What kind of meaning is there? Meaning may be connotative and denotative, but meaning of a connotative or denotative nature already has reached the propositional level. Meaning in its more pervasive sense, what Whitehead calls importance, is symbolic. It is the basic pattern, the connection given events, the referent between the causally efficacious past and future and the presentational immediacy of the present. Within my own existence, meaning is not just the song of the mockingbird, but what I make of that song; not just the struggle for survival, but what I make of that struggle; not just the suffering with death, but what I make of that suffering. Within the existence of our culture in the West, and in other cultures also, meaning is not just the dumb passage of events but the ideals that have ingressed into the events, characterizing them as drama, and the ideals that have lured the subsequent passage of events into richer concreteness. (For example, try to imagine the solution to the problem of the one and the many apart from the Old Testament drama of the Exodus.[5])

In Lovell's case we cannot write off the pattern he establishes in his strumming as merely automatic. Most of his life is predetermined, but in those instances where he is free to create, patterning sound with sense, meaning begins to emerge.[6]

Meaning, like morals, is not appropriate only to those who are not retarded. Indeed, the man in the street, and our leaders as well, often appear to be morally and cognitively retarded when we consider what they do and what they might or could do. Our regressive or retardate traits that rarely show themselves come out on occasion to cast a shadow on all that we do or have done. Such is the diploid nature of our evolutionary and evolving character.[7] In spite of our amphibious and ambiguous nature, meaning is there for everyone who seeks to make it.

Although the importance of ritual to life cannot be gainsaid, there is no denying that meaning can be expressed prematurely and become no more than a ritual. Lovell's hieratic gestures are of a low-grade level of meaning, not damaging but not retrograde. Lovell's

orchestration of the guitar (and the guitarist), the handbell, and singing was of a high grade of meaning.[8]

Special Education Curriculum

Special education curriculum is often taken from the technological model.[9] The functioning of the child is analyzed, and a baseline of his activities is recorded. Short- as well as long-term goals are
set, and objectives are prescribed. Although this method is more
humane than keeping the child in a closet, it does not follow that the
technological model of diagnosis and prescription is the only model
applicable to exceptional children, particularly if it limits morality to
heteronomy and meaning to ritual.

The model used with Lovell is similar to the self-actualizing
model. This model assumes that it is basically human to create and to
understand symbols. These symbols and actions can be feelings and
words and letters, or they can be epics and symphonies. This model
also assumes that these projections of the human spirit have a wholeness and an organic unity to them and that we get into and understand them best by looking at them as created wholes.

Let us assume, then, that in the self-actualizing model the student is able to form wholes, whether these wholes be whole and complete actions (of an autonomous nature) or whole and complete
meanings (of a symbolic nature). It is assumed then that the crea-
tions of the child are best recorded and reported by wholes (such as
the story above) that are inspired and engendered by the encounter.

The analysis of the wholeness is sometimes avoided for fear that
"we murder to dissect." But such is not the case if we consider the
millennia of art criticism that have not destroyed artistic output, but
facilitated it. The method used here is as old as Aristotle and will be
detailed later. Suffice it to say at this point that we will analyze the
story by examining its formal, material, efficient, and final causes.

The Formal Cause. The formal cause of the story is its plot or
its action. What action is imitated in the story? Does the action remain simple, or does it become complicated? Where does it become
problematic and where is it resolved? What parts (if any) of the
mimesis (or the action imitated) should be omitted to give it greater
organic unity? For example, the guitarist is "greedy" to finish the
song when Lovell enunciates the "Hallelujah." This episode for some
readers might seem to characterize the guitarist as unable to live up

to his desire to be open, to permit Lovell to be creative. Does the episode advance the action? (One might reflect thus on what part of our daily activity in the classroom really advances the basic action, and what part could easily be omitted without weakening the overall mimesis.)

In asking the question "Where does the action become complicated?" we must ask whether it was when Lovell sang "Frère Jacques," or when Lovell had his bowel movement, or when the struggle of wills took place, or at some other point?

Was the action resolved with Lovell's vocalizations, or with the guitarist's reflection, or did it remain unresolved? Is the story convincing? Is it simple or complex? If complex, is it convincingly resolved or left entangled and unresolved? Is the action Greek or Modern or Judeo-Christian? These are all formal questions.[10]

The Efficient Cause. The manner in which the story comes into being is the efficient cause. The story could have come into being in a lyrical form. It could have been written as a song about Lovell. Or it could have been an epic, with heaven and hell, past and present, gods and demons (or to be more exact, with teachers and administrators). It could have been written as a novel about the guitarist and delivered in the first person. Or it could have been written, Piaget-like, with numbered responses during numbered interviews. Or it could have been reduced to an interaction analysis grid.[11] Artistic and theological commitments have immense bearing on what style the author opts for. In the story does the angle of narration from the omniscient and the third person convey a kind of commitment to indirection and obliqueness (à la Kierkegaard), as if getting at meaning and morals directly would commit one to content and not to formal matters?

"How the story comes into being" is then the question. Should more time have been given to detailing the physical appearance of Lovell or the guitarist? Was the song (written out in full) at the end necessary as a reflection of the guitarist's inner state, or was it a purple passage? Was the author justified in switching from his (the guitarist's) stream of consciousness point of view to that of Lovell in the last paragraph? Was the flow of events mechanical or fated or open?

The Material Cause. The material cause of the case study is its words, symbols, rhythms, diction, and syntax. Lovell's monosyllabic utterances and his "Hello" are material causes of the drama. Unlike the monosyllables, however, the "Hello" additionally reveals and *is* the inner action of the hero-Lovell. Does the technological model allow words to reveal an inner action?

The drama could have been set to music (another material cause) and even recorded in rhythm and not in words. The drama could also have been painted or drawn. However, it must be said that painting favors spatial dimensions of reality, and those dimensions commit the writer to certain other aspects of reality. Storytelling commits one to a temporal dimension.[12] The drama could have been done in sculpture. In each case the formal cause might have been the same, with the material cause differing for each work, or it might be that the material cause would change the formal cause.[13]

Having said all of this, it could be argued that the stream of consciousness of the guitarist, as the material cause, is abtruse or esoteric or precious, or it could reflect real life, the life of the guitarist. Does the language of the drama capture the imagination, or does it impede the action? Does it do both? Does it put the reader to sleep? Does it get into the mind and the point of view of Lovell?

If this story were rendered in the language of the social scientist, perhaps half of it would be pared away. The part exhumed would reveal a literal but dead story. The judgment of the drama's material cause must be in these terms: Is it convincing? Is it concise? Is it vivid? Does it lend itself to making the drama a whole made object? Is the material part and parcel of world-as-machine or is it epiphenomenal of a world beyond?

The Final Cause. When we read a story, identification with a literary character leads to expectations that are fulfilled or denied. Do the words "spear points" in the first paragraph and "word salad" in the second foreshadow events to come and arouse emotions appropriate to the two characters? Is Dirk merely a stage prop or a foil for Lovell? Does the reader in his identification with the characters react with hysterics, or read Lovell as a clown or the guitarist as a buffoon? Or does he have feelings of compassion for both? Or is the work altogether unconvincing? The final cause is the feeling for which the author was shooting and with which he draws the reader into his imaginary world. Evaluation is not by test or measurement but by satisfaction of a feeling, be it nausea or pity or compassion.

Curriculum Criticism

If this digression into the four causes of the work seems roundabout, it is hoped that it will not bring the reader up too sharply to say that this analysis is curriculum criticism. In looking at the formal cause, we are inquiring about the action of the curriculum. A very real part of curriculum should be the analysis of the action, an analysis of what the learner is expected to imitate or to undertake or to perform. The reading of the mimesis may be strictly literal, imaginative, or symbolic.

The analysis of the efficient cause takes us into the manner in which the curriculum is presented, and then into the world view projected. This is the learning environment in which the action takes place. It can be organismic, where the child is at home with his feelings, or service-oriented, where the child is a passive recipient.[14] The assumption that there is only one real world and that this real world has real objects in real time and real space comes from the Modern world view, or what philosophers might call "Realism." Although this assumption may be legitimate, it does not exhaust the possible world views that might also be projected as the learning environment.

The analysis of the material cause is an analysis of the material in relation to the formal cause that it materializes. Words, sounds, colors, gestures—all materialize in space and time. The assumption that words are the only cause of curriculum is an assumption about the classroom that rules out formal causes. This rhetorical approach ultimately reduces the drama of education to didacticism.

The analysis of the final cause is an analysis of the evaluation of the curriculum. Curriculum is typically evaluated externally and objectively in terms of tests, measurement, and experimentation. But why may not feelings be placed first? What does the character feel? What does the student feel? What feeling does the drama evoke? Feelings then constitute the *eschaton,* the final judgment, required to bring the curriculum into being or to relegate it to the scrap pile of dogma and first principles. The analogy invoked here is that curriculum is like art and should be critiqued accordingly.

So viewed, the curriculum in special education should not be generically different from the curriculum in regular education. Its action is envisaged, materialized, and realized. Feelings are dramatized in the action that is imitated. As the curriculum presents an occasion for the objectification of feelings, it also is judged in terms of the satisfaction realized in this objectification.

Part 3. Evaluation: Model from Theological Literary Criticism

What model is required to make sense of the kind of analysis of morals, or mimesis (action), and of curriculum presented above? It is one borrowed from the humanities and in particular from theological literary criticism.[15] It is literary in that it deals with literature and with works of imagination. It is critical in that it criticizes whole made works of literature and imagination. And it is theological in that it posits three world views—the Greek, the Judeo-Christian, and the Modern—within works of imaginative literature. In the Greek world view, man is the aristocrat who finds himself a tragic figure in light of the enmity of the gods (or perfections). In the Judeo-Christian world view, man is a fallen creature who finds redemption within, because God is the friend. In the Modern world view, man, sick and driven, finds meaninglessness and despair and a god who is the void. This typology is humanistic because it takes the claims of competing world views seriously, but it is also humanistic because it does not retreat to a relativism that avoids all serious choices.[16] Further, this model is a heuristic one in that, once the world view presumed to be represented in the work is chosen, the typology aids as an epistemological device in the discovery of the causes within the work.

Returning to our case study, it can be seen that the typology of Greek, Judeo-Christian, and Modern can serve as a heuristic device to discover the causes of the curriculum.

The Final Cause in the Story

Is the feeling evoked by the story-case study the meaninglessness and despair of the Modern story, or is it the pity and fear evoked by the Greek story, or is it the compassion and judgment evoked by the Judeo-Christian story? In educational terminology, is the curriculum, in face of the knowledge explosion, one more nudge toward meaninglessness? Or does the curriculum bear perfections and ideals that always elude the appearances and shadows of this world? Or is the curriculum full of "surprises of grace": events that judge and also save?[17]

In the story, it could be argued that the guitarist is the Greek aristocrat whose perfections turn to condemn him: "Ought, ought, ought." It also might seem pathetic and Modern that the guitarist is despairingly trying to make an "idiot savant" out of his retarded charge. Or does the willfulness of the two characters evoke judgment; does their attempt to be human to each other arouse compassion?

The heuristic is a two-way street. One presupposes the story (in this case, the Judeo-Christian story) within the curriculum. Because of the feeling evoked by the heuristic—a combination of absorption and criticism—the reader can go on to criticize the whole made object (1) by using this insight as a way to discover other causes, and (2) by using this yardstick both to reject as intrusions those elements that do not produce the appropriate feeling and to retain as parts of an organic unity only those parts that reinforce the appropriate feeling. This kind of guiding criterion enables the reader to remember and retain much material (because it is focused and integrated), and additionally, this kind of "active" rather than "passive" reading enables the reader actively to recreate the imaginative work in his own mind.

The Efficient Cause in the Story

Assuming the third person point of view of the story as the way in which it comes into being, does the fantasy about the development of language, the reflection on the guitarist's curriculum criticism, the flashback into the guitarist's career, his *déjà vu* of Picasso's "Blue Guitarist," the image of the Abelia, his reaction to Lovell's singing, the reflection on the doctor's comments, and especially Yeats's poem, do all of these insights into the guitarist's mind serve to advance the action, and more precisely to create a Judeo-Christian character in a Judeo-Christian world? a Modern character in a Modern world? a Greek character in a Greek world? The critic may use the heuristic model as a way of discovering the answer to these questions.

Do the asides into Lovell's past strike the reader as unconvincing? Has the author cheated in putting those items into the work? Or the reflection on other children? Or the omniscient statement about beauty? Is this the guitarist or the author? To look at this from another angle, what levels of transcendence are convincing in the classroom?

The Material Cause of the Story

The sentences, the words, the metaphors may all be investigated to determine whether or not they give the work its organic unity. With the heuristic of the Judeo-Christian model in mind, the passage about the Apollonian and Dionysian dimension of the guitarist is puzzling. Does the author reveal a Greek or Nietzschean polarity that makes for tragedy? Perhaps his tortured conscience reveals a Modern mind at work? But this turn of events also leads into Yeats's poem and the guitarist's Judeo-Christian view. (Is the guitarist's world view the same as the author's?) Is the guitarist, to use Morris's terms, basically living within the realm of self-actualization? If so, what relation is there between the world of self-actualization and the tragic world? The Greek world and the world of Freud?

The Formal Cause of the Story

Does the guitarist concern himself with normality and other-directedness (heteronomy)? Does he judge the child in the light of I.Q. and inner-directedness (autonomy)? Does he look at the child as centered in a transcendent dimension (theonomy)? The answer to these questions will tell us whether the hero reenacts the action of the Modern, the Greek, or the Judeo-Christian story. But this answer then is just the beginning of the heuristic deployment of this typology to discover the formal cause of the story. Is this the Modern hero who goes from bad to worse: starts off frightened by these children and ends up engineering them in various ways? Is this the Greek aristocrat who is above all others, but for whom his own self-knowledge is missing and his fate is tragic self-discovery? Is this the Judeo-Christian character who accepts suffering as a necessary concomitant of staying in the historical process?

A similar question could be raised about the end of the story. If the story is Greek, does it need that last scene revealing the future conversation with the doctor? If the story is Modern, might not the ending have been prolonged? Does it need a more explicit resolution to be Judeo-Christian? Questions about timing and pace, recognition and discovery, are questions about the formal cause of the work, and when we tinker with the formal cause, we are asking about the basic structure. When we use the heuristic, then, we assume that we must look at the overall structure of the action to determine whether it is basically Greek or Judeo-Christian or Modern.

Conclusion

A question that may have nagged the reader thus far might run something like this: "Let me see if I understand you. You observed and worked with a retarded child, and in the process discovered a great deal about him personally and about yourself. Indirectly you also discovered something about retardation; that is, that a retarded child might have some normal functioning, in this case musical functioning, apart from his retarded functioning in other areas: memory, attention, language acquisition and so on."

My answer to that question would be, "Yes, you have gotten the point. As an amphibian, like Lovell, I learned something at the boundary of my ignorance."

"But," you might continue, "You then sat down and wrote up this series of lessons with Lovell in the form of a short story, using your imagination as well as the facts. Is this not so?"

My reply again would be, "Yes." However, I would first have to add two reservations. One, I must be fair to myself and say that I used three different observation forms (schedules, logs, and charts) as a basis for my observations and teaching and that, accordingly, my observation was not unguided or arbitrary. My assumption was that no instrument for observation is without a perspective or world view and my attempt was to state my perspective or world view (Judeo-Christian) and then from there to try to get to the facts. Second, I must say that if by "imagination" you mean a heightened form of consciousness, I would say, yes, I did use a good deal of imagination both in observing and in recording my impressions. I rounded my story off according to my world view. In short, I trust that by "imagination" you do not mean fantasy or illusion or fabrication or deceit; for I do not accept my story or any story as a falsification of reality. An approach to reality that is symbolic, rounded, and pointed is one way of telling the truth, and it is just as truthful to reality as is the natural or the social scientific story.[18] Some writers are to a greater or lesser extent aware of the world view within which they live, but all assume one or another. Occasionally, like Yeats, one has to invent one's own myth.[19]

At this point the reader may feel that my assumption is unacceptable to the logical positivists or the language analysts or the behaviorists. Perhaps this is so. If he is not troubled by this possible parting of the ways, however, he may still have another sort of reservation. "Let's assume that your story is a prehension of the truth and does point to reality," he might say. "I am still at sea, for your analysis and criticism seem—apart from being narcissistic,[20] analyzing your own story and all—to suggest that the formal work, the short story, *is* the curriculum. Now I am confused. Was the curriculum what took place between you and Lovell some time in the past? Or is the short story or case study itself the curriculum?"

I shall have to answer that this question takes us to the heart of the matter. I know it is taxing for the reader to go along with the typology of world views (though as I claim, Morris, for example, does substantially the same thing). I am also sure it is demanding to ask one to think of a short story as curriculum. But now to cap it all, the reader is asked to throw history or the time sequence to the winds. But is he? If we are proceeding according to the Modern view that reality is all "out there" and time is a matter of one irreversible bit of time following another, it is clear that we have broken step. Also, if we are proceeding according to the Greek (or indeed, Eastern) notion of time, as a cycle, our use of time is meaningless. But if, as Augustine and Rousseau and Whitehead and, indeed Lovell and myself would argue, time passes through the individual and the individual passes through time, then where indeed is the time that cannot be recreated? Although one cannot tamper with the facts, one can, by retelling and rounding the facts into a story, see facts from a new angle, see a dimension overlooked before. Conversely, one can go into the classroom (as a teacher) as though one were going into a story, and one can check his performance, the action he imitates, and the action he hopes the student will imitate, against the performance of a hero—Greek, Judeo-Christian, or Modern—that one wants to emulate. The paradigmatic figure can be a Jeremiah or an Oedipus or a Prufrock. The paradigm can be realized in the classroom. The answer to the question, then, is that all three—events, recollection, and recreation—are the curriculum.

In conclusion, the point is that the method of curriculum criticism will remain formally committed to one world view or another if the story, the criticism, and the evaluation are in the mode of that world view. My attempt here has been to render story, critique, and evaluation all from the viewpoint of the Judeo-Christian world view. It will not surprise me if one or more of these three elements are argued *not* to be Judeo-Christian, nor will it surprise me if the whole typology and method of curriculum criticism is held to be cumbersome and problematic. It is my contention that, however difficult, curriculum criticism needs to make its choices about reality (in my typology, the Greek, or the Modern, or the Judeo-Christian world views) before it tries to come to terms with morals or meaning.

Notes

1. The similarity between the position taken here and positions taken in *Curriculum Theorizing: The Reconceptualists*, ed William Pinar (Berkeley, Ca.: McCutchan Publishing Corp., 1975) and especially to John S. Mann's "Curriculum Criticism" should be obvious. Differences in approach, e.g., the use of Neo-Aristotelianism rather than New Criticism, do yield different assumptions about the formal nature of the literary curricular object.

2. Paul Tillich, *The Protestant Era*, trans. James Luther Adams (Chicago: University of Chicago Press, 1948).

3. Jean Piaget, *The Moral Judgment of the Child*, trans. Marjorie Gabain (New York: The Free Press, 1965).

4. This point is made in Michael Apple, "Common Sense Categories and Curriculum Thought," in ASCD Yearbook, *Schools in Search of Meaning*, ed. James B. Macdonald and Esther Zaret (Washington, D.C.: ASCD, 1975), p. 140.

5. Bernard Eugene Meland, *Faith and Culture* (New York: Oxford University Press, 1953).

6. See James Macdonald's article, "The Quality of Everyday Life in School," in Macdonald and Zaret, *Schools in Search of Meaning*.

7. Garrett Hardin, *Nature and Man's Fate* (New York: New American Library, 1959).

8. See James Macdonald's article, "Transcendental Developmental Education," in *Heightened Consciousness: Cultural Revolution, and Curriculum Theory*, ed. William Pinar (Berkeley, Ca.: McCutchan Publishing Corp., 1974).

9. Van Cleve Morris and Young Pai in *Philosophy and the American School* (Boston: Houghton Mifflin Co., 1976) posit a typology of models: technological, humanistic, and cultural pluralism. Both in the story and in this analysis this typology is analogous to the typology, basically Tillichean (*The Courage To Be* [London: Nisbet & Co., Ltd., 1952]), that is developed in the author's doctoral dissertation, "Myths, Morals, and Models: Implications for Special Education" (Ed.D. diss., University of North Carolina at Greensboro, 1976).

10. According to James Macdonald in "The Quality of Everyday Life in School," formal questions must be asked to achieve the "re-form" of the schools.

11. These methods may be possible, but are they any more probable than the method used in the story? Cf. James Macdonald's "Myths about Instruction," *Educational Leadership* 22 no. 7 (May 1965): 571-76, 609-17.

12. See Dwayne Huebner's "Curriculum as Concern for Man's Temporality," in Pinar, *Curriculum Theorizing*.

13. The author's choices, then, reveal, even in the innocuous area of words, deeper moral commitments. See Edward F. Kelly's "Curriculum Evaluation and Literary Criticism: Comments on the Analogy." (Chapter 6 of this volume.)

14. Macdonald, "The Quality of Everyday Life in School," p. 92.

15. The Neo-Aristotelians and the Process Theologians at the University of Chicago during and after the Hutchins era have been most influential on this

model. I refer to the unpublished Ph.D. dissertation of Preston T. Roberts, Jr., "Theology and Imaginative Literature" (University of Chicago, 1950) and R. S. Crane, *The Language of Criticism and the Structure of Poetry* (Toronto: The University of Toronto Press, 1953).

The Neo-Aristotelians argue that the plot provides the structure of imaginative literature; Roberts adds that serious plots include Judeo-Christian and Modern plots as well as Greek plots.

An interesting question beyond the realm of this paper is the correspondence between the Morris and Pai typology of technological, humanistic and cultural pluralism models, and the typology of Greek, Judeo-Christian, and Modern world views suggested here.

16. A similar line of thought is developed by Maxine Greene in her "Cognition, Consciousness, and Curriculum," in Pinar, *Heightened Consciousness*.

17. Amos N. Wilder, *Modern Poetry and the Christian Tradition* (New York: Charles Scribner's Sons, 1952).

18. I take comfort from the speech pathologist's admonition to (1) know my competency area, (2) use ignorance to motivate greater learning, (3) make the diagnosis ongoing, (4) know the normal process of language, and (5) synthesize the "facts into a working gestalt so that the data are of value." Lon L. Emerick and John T. Hatten, *Diagnosis and Evaluation in Speech Pathology* (Englewood Cliffs, N.J.: Prentice-Hall, 1974), p. 87.

19. Would it not be healthy for curriculum creators to say, like Yeats, "When I come to write poetry, I seem—I suppose because it is all instinct with me—completely ignorant"? Richard P. Blackmur, *Form and Value in Modern Poetry* (New York: Doubleday, Anchor Books, 1957), p. 67.

20. See the essay "Narcissus as Narcissus," by Allen Tate, in his *The Man of Letters in the Modern World* (New York: Noonday Press, 1955).

Madeleine R. Grumet's essay contains an elaborate conception of curriculum and curriculum criticism as well as a case study based on her involvement in a university theatre festival. The critical method Grumet describes is currere, *a term coined by William Pinar to refer to the analysis of curriculum as the individual student's own experience and use of it. In this conception, the experience of the individual is the curriculum, and the critic's task is to describe its dynamics and to disclose meaning about it. The effort to disclose personal meaning within individual experience is basically what has been described in this volume as "phenomenological," and the dominant critical interest within this essay is in the personal dimension of curriculum criticism.*

In explaining her conception of curriculum Grumet explicates an "existential aesthetic" in part derived from ideas of Sartre and Dewey. In this sense, within experience meaning is a relationship that exists between situation and action. Within a familiar situation, curriculum as new experience stands out against the ground of ordinary experience, both revealing and transforming it. Once present, however, new experience tends to sink into the ground of ordinary experience, creating a new but now familiar situation. The curriculum

274

provides a characteristic movement from familiar situation, to estrangement, to transformed situation. As aesthetic, it leads to a qualitative transformation in the way the situation is experienced, thus to the development of personal meaning. In the case study itself Grumet outlines this characteristic movement (and sometimes the lack of it) in her own experience and in the experience of university students.

The principal critical focal point is, in a very general sense, the "work," since the study analyzes the curriculum, however personal it may be. But, as Grumet suggests, within this case study "work" and "world," "author" and "audience" tend to collapse into each other. Since the curriculum is actually the inward experience of individuals, its "author," "audience," and "work" are all one, a part of (not apart from) the external "world."

As with many case studies that exemplify a dominant interest in the personal dimension, Grumet's is thick with description and with inferences about meaning. Relatively little direct judgment seems warranted. Some things happen within personal experience; others don't. Analysis and disclosure of meaning seem able gracefully to carry the weight of this form of criticism, for description is of unfolding possibilities. In this sense, both case study and curriculum as experience are rich with "theme." Written much as a story, Grumet's own account of her experience and the experience of others also embodies "point of view," "plot," and "metaphor," rhetorical devices that seem integrally connected with direct disclosure of personal meaning.

13

Songs and Situations: The Figure/Ground Relation in a Case Study of *Currere*

Madeleine R. Grumet

figure/ground—"Some of These Days"

Some of these days,
You'll miss me honey

Roquentin, the protagonist of Jean-Paul Sartre's novel *Nausea,* waits to hear the saxophone, to hear the Negress sing. He sits in the ugly cafe, dirty glasses, brown stains on the mirror. The beer in the bottom of his glass grows warm. The disc is scratched. The melody, itself, is a modest achievement. The glimpse of salvation that it offers to Roquentin cannot be attributed to the eidetic perfection of the tune, but rather to the relationship of the tune to the situation it surpasses:

I think about a clean-shaven American with thick black eye-brows, suffocating with the heat, on the twenty-first floor of a New York skyscraper. The sky burns above New York, the blue of the sky is inflamed, enormous yellow flames come and lick the roofs; the Brooklyn children are going to put on bathing drawers

I want to thank Stefan Rudnicki, William Pinar, and Bob Berky for their interest and support in both the theoretical and practical phases of this work. I also thank the students whose writings revealed their experience of that work for sharing their experience with me.

and play under the water of a fire-hose. The dark room on the twenty-first floor cooks under a high pressure. The American with the black eye-brows sighs, gasps and the sweat rolls down his cheeks. He is sitting, in shirtsleeves, in front of his piano, he has a taste of smoke in his mouth and vaguely, a ghost of a tune in his head. "Some of these days."[1]

The song, a figure silhouetted against the sweltering black heat of a summer day, falls back into the ground of Bouville and becomes the ground for the action of Roquentin, Sartre's existential dropout. "Some of These Days" is absorbed into Roquentin's situation and transfigures it. The transformation is not merely ideational, not confined to Roquentin's decision to forsake history for fiction, to draw from his existence a thing as pure and hard as the four saxophone notes. It is palpable, present in his sensations of the heat and density of the air around him: "I feel something brush against me lightly, and I dare not move because I am afraid it will go away. . . . I am like a man completely frozen after a trek through the snow who suddenly comes into a warm room."

The song played on a gramaphone in a cafe near the railroad station in Bouville, the seventh largest city in France, pervades that place, bringing resiliency to what was slimy, sodden ground. Roquentin, sated with existence, finds in the song the relationship of the existent to its possibilities, and in that tension between the factual and the possible, the impetus for his own action.

Roquentin's response to "Some of These Days" embodies both Sartre's existential aesthetic and his notion of the project: "For us man is characterized above all by his going beyond a situation and by what he succeeds in making of what he has been made—even if he never recognizes himself in objectification."[2]

I have introduced this case study with a reference to Sartre's existential theory and fiction because I intend to examine curriculum as a moving form, to catch it at the moment that it slides from being the figure, the object and goal of action, and collapses into the ground for action. That movement expresses the dynamic energy of curriculum that is realized only in the student's use of it. Curriculum, considered apart from that use as design, as a structure of knowledge, an intended learning outcome, or a learning environment, is merely a static form.

Unlike "Some of These Days," curriculum words don't brush by me lightly. They are heavy, leaden.

"Intended learning outcomes "—"intended's" airiness, swallowed by "outcomes" in a single gulp.

"Socialization"—inevitable, phase-specific liminal rituals replete with hard rock and greasy hamburgers.

Ta Da—"The Disciplines of Knowledge"—Corinthian columns, pompous but classy.

"Learning environments"—don't fence me in, piling world upon world.

Cumbersome furniture for an America on the move.

The only movement they awake in me is negation, a response not to be dismissed, for it is producing this essay. We must not rationalize the surrender of educational experience to these phrases by imagining them to be deposits in the stream of educational theory that the current will, somehow, circumvent. They clog. They occlude. In their pretentious attempt to signify the encounter of the student and the curriculum, they obliterate all that is personal in favor of what is general, all that is actual in deference to what is hypothetical, all that is moving in obeisance to all that is still.

Dwayne Huebner's address to the American Educational Research Association, "The Moribund Curriculum Field: Its Wake and Our Work" calls upon curricularists to clear the stream and to attend to the course of study, a term which is taken to include both the syllabus and the environment, but the student's participation in this course of study seems to be that of an enthralled spectator. His response to the curriculum is relegated in Huebner's scheme to the dreamy domain of the humanities where reflexivity and self-understanding dwell. I am afraid that in his eagerness to reclaim the stream, Huebner has pulled out the swimmers along with the algae and sent them to sit upon the banks. There they sit and wait for the curriculum to reach them as it is defined by Huebner: "If curriculum has any meaning left today, it is in the identification and the making present of content to persons."[3]

I propose, rather, that it is persons who are made present through their contact with curriculum. Curriculum is the process of persons coming to form, not content. Content is salient only in an idealized isolation. The gaze of the student transforms its opaque surface into a reflective one that sends back images of the student and of his situation. Then it is the student and his experience, not content, that is made present. The curriculum is transformed by the student's attention into what Sartre has called a critical mirror. The student's response to the curriculum reveals his possibilities for action within the particular domain of experience—natural, social, aesthetic—that the curriculum as content symbolizes.

figure/ground—Aesthetics and Technology

An aesthetic critique of curriculum demands that we wrest it from the clutches of the figure/ground dichotomy. We do share the propensity of animals, as Lorenz has demonstrated, for gestalt perception, the capacity for distinguishing forms experienced within a spatial and/or temporal context.[4] Nevertheless, humans, as distinct from animals, are also able to experience gestalt-free perception, a capacity for looking past the dominant figure or gestalt to the ground that surrounds it, recognizing detail that cuts across the figure/ground dichotomy as well as new configurations that violate the boundaries of the initial presentation.[5] Perhaps, then, I am not requesting the impossible when I ask that we look at both the figure and the ground, that we consider both faces, the old crone's and the young girl's, facticity and freedom, at one and the same time. I suggest that in this double vision will emerge a third form, the relation that exists between them, to be filled with human action. It is a double vision that Sartre commends when he maintains that "the most rudimentary behavior must be determined both in relation to the real and present factors which condition it and in relation to a certain object still to come which it is trying to bring into being."

This vision requires that we invest curriculum with the structure of experience that is aesthetic as well as technological. Both categories of experience are concerned with making things. What distinguishes one from the other is, among other things, the relationship of the product—the figure—to the situation from which it comes—the ground.

Technological products are designed in response to the needs experienced by individuals within a particular situation. They are fabricated to resolve a problematic situation, a need that in the empiricism of John Dewey truly resides in the situation itself. We produce the National Science Foundation and NASA for Sputnik, Title I for the "disadvantaged," Environmental Studies for the American Eagle and the Great Lakes. The Tyler rationale, framed around the "needs" of the populace, extends the ameliorative response to situation which characterizes technology into curriculum theory.[6] The product may, indeed, change the situation for which it is designed, although that change is too often inadequately imagined, recognized only when the disintegration of the ozone layer or the carcinogenic effects of red dye #2 reveal unanticipated consequences.

While the technological artifact may produce change, the change *is* designed to conform to the structure of the initial situation. Competition for the domination of outer space continues, but Friendship 7s replace Sputnik. Class distinctions continue to determine a child's grasp of social and economic power through his access to linguistic codes, but specialists are trained to wrench language from its cultural contexts, package it and ship it where it is needed. An automobile economy proceeds unchecked while environmentalists rope off breeding grounds and build treatment plants. The ameliorative approach of current educational theory, which fabricates curriculum to meet the needs of the situation, is, in its eagerness to address reality, succumbing to the technological intention to produce the pieces that will fit most comfortably into the whole.

The aesthetic response to situation is not to produce the pieces that will restore it to equilibrium but to create anew the whole gestalt. The aesthetic response does not attempt to satisfy the demands of an existing ground but posits both a new ground and a new figure distinguished from the old gestalt by their unity, a consistency that Dewey was to call "pervasive quality." Curriculum conceived in this manner is, in itself, an alternative world where content and the learning environment, as Huebner has reminded us, are fused in a relation that is consciously chosen, a work of artifice. The course of study, as I have argued in *Toward a Poor Curriculum* provides a virtual, not an actual world.[7] Its structure, even when conceived to function vis-à-vis the actual situation in a technological way, is aesthetic.

What matters most in this comparison is the function of curriculum, its impact as an agent of transformation, rather than its structure.[8] The aesthetic function of curriculum replaces the amelioration of technological function with revelation. It functions as an agent of disclosure that reveals to persons new possibilities hitherto unperceived in the ground of their daily experience. Before we examine this function of aesthetic experience as it is developed in the existential aesthetic of Sartre, Merleau-Ponty, and Heidegger, it may be pertinent to examine the distinctions between technological and aesthetic function as found in Dewey's writings on the relation of inquiry and aesthetics to situation.

figure/ground—Dewey's Theories of Inquiry and Aesthetics

Attempting to root logic and inquiry in lived experience, Dewey chose metaphors that referred to the interaction of a biological organism and the environment. Extending an ecological principle into his analysis of the genesis and development of human knowledge, Dewey conceived of inquiry as the human response to a doubtful or indeterminate situation that is to be brought to a successful resolution, reestablishing equilibrium. The *situation* is doubtful, and our response is to resolve that doubt with inquiry and action. Here is the figure/ground relation that characterizes the technological gestalt. The situation posits a need that inquiry fulfills. The figure is cut to fit the whole in the ground-patchwork.

Despite this apparent domination of situation where inquiry merely appears to develop what is latent in the natural order, bringing "determinateness" to situation and restoring its "pervasive quality," in *Logic, The Theory of Inquiry,* Dewey explicitly asserts that inquiry transforms the very ground to which, in other writings, it has appeared so subservient.

Inquiry, in settling the disturbed relation of organism-environment (which defined doubt) does not merely remove doubt by recurrence to a prior adaptive integration. It institutes new environing conditions that occasion new problems. What the organism learns during the process produces new powers that make new demands upon the environment. In short, as special problems are resolved, new ones tend to emerge. There is no such thing as a final settlement, because every settlement introduces the conditions of some degree of new unsettling.[9]

Although we have moved in this statement beyond the determination of situation to its transformation, the transformation exceeds the conscious intention of the inquirer. This intention has been to respond and minister to the doubts that exist *in situation* rather than to draw from his own experience of doubt the negation that posits and initiates a new situation. The situation is always a step ahead of Dewey's inquirer, and even if his action (in this instance, inquiry) has contributed to its quality, and even determined it, his conscious intention has been to meet the situation rather than to transform it, and as a result he is always responding to unforeseen consequences. Dewey's inquirer seems to be forever chasing his tail, meeting an endless series of problematic situations, each springing from his last achievement of equilibrium through inquiry. This inquirer is left to meet the consequences of his actions with the conscientious, if half-hearted, hospitality of the aging playboy who welcomes the children he never knew he sired.

Within the theory of inquiry, Dewey, like Piaget, has difficulty accounting for disequilibrium except by attributing it to the machinations of a capricious nature. It is not until Dewey's treatment of aesthetics that disequilibrium is seen to issue from the cultural rather than the natural order and is identified in the human impulse to negation so central to Sartre's ontology.

It is in this relation of action to situation that Dewey's writings on aesthetics diverge from those on the theory of inquiry. Art, he tells us, is the sole alternative to luck. The goods of art "are fruits of means consciously employed; fulfillments whose further consequences are secured by conscious control of the causal conditions which enter into them."[10] The artist is aware that his subjectivity transforms any objectivity that it confronts, and he integrates the consequences of his inquiry into the ground of the world that he creates. Dewey joins Sartre in the recognition that the cultural order —the order of curriculum—cannot be reduced to the natural order, that an aesthetic product is not shaped to the specifications of an external natural imperative, but contains both a new figure and a new ground. Man in a state of nature is, according to Dewey, a passive victim of cause and effect, "pulled and pushed about, overwhelmed, broken to pieces, lifted on the crest of the wave of things, like anything else."[11] This is the situation that repels Roquentin in *Nausea*. Bouville is dominated by the "given," the root of a chestnut tree, "knotty, inert, nameless."

What distinguishes the cultural from the natural order is human action, our use of what we are in the interest of what we would become. The language of cause and effect is the language of the natural order. It describes the life cycle of the chestnut root. The language of means/consequence, on the other hand, is the language of human freedom and action. Causes, consciously chosen, become the means to desired consequences. Such choices are not based on caprice, or external forces, but on human intentions, values—an interrelated system of meanings.

By asserting that a relationship of cause and effect is transformed into means-consequence when consequences belong integrally to the conditions that produce them, Dewey is bringing us beyond the determination of the immediate situation to the determination that is achieved by human reflection, "the intentional direction of natural events to meanings capable of immediate possession and enjoyment."[12]

In *Experience and Nature* Dewey maintains that the "characteristic human need is for possession and appreciation of the meaning of things...."[13] Meaning, for Dewey, is a relational structure that emerges when the implications of actions are assessed by considering their far-reaching consequences, extending them into a consideration of what Bateson has recently termed an "infinite regression of contexts."[14] The immediate situation cannot provide what in Dewey's scheme is essential to utility, "inherent place and bearing in experience." Similarly, Roquentin finds that he cannot justify his existence, discover its utility, merely by addressing himself to the immediate situation that greets him, expressed in the gnarled root, the black bark of the chestnut tree:

> Evidently I did not know everything, I had not seen the seeds sprout, or the tree grow. But faced with this great wrinkled paw, neither ignorance nor knowledge was important; the world of explanations and reasons is not the world of existence. A circle is not absurd, it is clearly explained by the rotation of a straight segment around one of its extremities. But neither does a circle exist. This root, on the other hand, existed in such a way that I could not explain it. Knotty, inert, nameless.

The cultural order offers Roquentin no more meaning than the natural one. Bouville cannot tell him how or why to live. The travels associated with his job are arbitrary, pointless, as are the social conventions that the Bouville bourgeoisie take for natural law.

But if meaning cannot be found in the existing situation, in the gnarled, obdurate chestnut roots, it is also denied to the realm of the merely possible. Roquentin cannot ignore his own experience by substituting stories about someone else's. His attempts to write the biography of a seventeenth-century nobleman fail, as does Anny's search for perfect moments that would mirror the structure of art, as does the Self-Taught Man's attempt to substitute knowledge for his own experience. An existence that has meaning requires the union of the existent to its possibles. Dewey offers us that union in art:

First then, art is solvent union of the generic, recurrent, ordered, established phase of nature with its phase that is incomplete, going on, and hence still uncertain, contingent, novel, particular . . . a union of necessity and freedom, a harmony of the many and one, the sensuous and the ideal.[15]

Both the existential theory of Sartre and the aesthetic theory of Dewey examine meaning as a relation that exists between situation and action, figure and ground. It is the conscious awareness of that relationship that transforms cause and effect into means-consequence, connects the actual to the possible, as the steamy black heat of the summer day is transformed into another existent, "Some of These Days." It is the conscious awareness of the relation of the figure, the curriculum, to the ground from which it springs and to which it returns that convinces the teacher and the student that within their experience of curriculum they can find the impetus and the energy to transform it. The relation of figure/ground is not taken for granted by the artist as it is by the technician. That relation is the very subject of his art and he addresses that relation both in the structure of the product that he makes and in the relation of that object to mundane experience.

figure/ground—An Existential Aesthetic

We cannot claim that curriculum fits the subject/figure/ground configuration that Dreyfus and Todes present as the structure of the preobjective world as portrayed in the writings of Merleau-Ponty.[16] That is a world of experience where the figure and ground are always shifting, drawing each other from concealment, but its subject has no history and no expectations, clearly not the temporal creature that we and our students are.

We also cannot identify the structure of curriculum with the objective world of science that consists of thinking subject/permanent figure/actual figure. This world is eidetic, not grounded and contingent. It is the world of theory where one figure is posited by another rather than drawn from its concealment in the ground. It is the relation of the rotation of a straight segment around one of its extremities, the circle that Roquentin can explain but that does not exist.

Dreyfus and Todes maintain that in Merleau-Ponty's *Lebenswelt* (the realm of lived experience) the structure of experience conforms to neither the objective nor the primordial structure but is a synthesis of the two.

Curriculum is a virtual figure. It requires a thinking subject, but not one who is a passive spectator to a spectacle of self-revealing figures. The student's use of the curriculum reveals more of the ground to him which he then incorporates into another figure of his own devising. The structure of aesthetic experience requires a virtual-figure/ground/personal-subject structure. It is the project of that subject who responds, acts, and chooses to transform all three terms.

First, the artist creates a new objectivity which, as I have pointed out, examines the relation of the figure to the ground by recreating and encompassing them both. Huizinga's analysis of play · as a voluntary activity set within specified spatio-temporal limits, free from material interests, supports the assertion that aesthetic activity requires the production of a new ground as well as a new figure.[17] Huizinga presents play as the prototype for religious ritual and art. In *Toward a Poor Curriculum* I included schooling within that category of ludic experience as well.[18] Painting establishes its own spatial terms, music its own temporal ones. The novel interrupts the infinite regression of contexts that confounds mundane experience by delimiting its own spatial, temporal, and social order. The novel, the dance, and the religious ritual are all forms that set out their own ground and in the process radically alter the situation as we know it in mundane experience. Recurring characteristics of the new ground provide the basis of what we call the formal characteristics of art that aesthetic criticism from Aristotle to Woolflin has attempted to specify and classify. We have seen some of this kind of aesthetic criticism in curriculum theory in the interest in describing the structure of the academic disciplines.

Dewey, unwilling to surrender aesthetics to a taxonomy of formal characteristics, expressed impatience with an aesthetic that considered a work of art a closed system, however elegant:

The presence in art, whether as an act or a product, of proportion, economy, order, symmetry, composition, is such a commonplace that it does not need to be dwelt upon. But equally necessary is unexpected combination and the consequent revelation of possibilities hitherto unrealized . . . Order and proportion when they are the whole story are soon exhausted; economy in itself is a tiresome and restrictive taskmaster. It is artistic when it releases.[19]

What is released, we learn later, is "the revelation of meaning in the old effected by its presentation in the new." What is most important for Dewey, and for this aesthetic critique of curriculum, is the relation of the artistic product to the mundane experience from which it is drawn. The relation is not merely revelatory. It is not merely experienced as insight into a preexisting situation but leads to a transformation in the way that situation is experienced. Maurice Merleau-Ponty has written that a new or created form becomes a cultural object that changes the character of the environment in which the organism feels newly adjusted.[20] It is the song that pervades the cafe, brushing by Roquentin, warming the air around him. And for Dewey too, all art is a process of transforming mundane experience: "All art is a process of making the world a different place in which to live and involves a phase of protest and compensatory response."[21] The equilibrium of the theory of inquiry concedes to the negation of aesthetics.

This is the existential aesthetic that supports the work described in the remainder of this essay. It is extended into these assertions:

1. Curriculum is an aesthetic as well as a technological product, belonging both to the cultural and natural order. As a product of aesthetic activity it creates and encompasses both figure and ground.

2. Curriculum, by providing a new gestalt, stands out against the ground of daily experience, both revealing and transforming it.

3. Curriculum, once presented, tends to sink into the ground of daily experience, to mingle with it and become confused with the natural order. This aesthetic critique requires that we acknowledge that curriculum is the world of meanings that we have devised and that as teachers and students we assume responsibility for it and for the action that it admits.

The existential aesthetic that I am presenting here scorns an idealized art that creates forms isolated from mundane experience. Even while maintaining that the cultural order cannot be reduced to the natural order, Sartre has required that the cultural order disclose possibilities for meaning and action within quotidian existence. If Roquentin writes a novel, he hopes that his readers will refer back to his existence: "Antoine Roquentin wrote it, a red-headed man who hung around cafes," just as he evokes the song writer behind "Some of These Days." It is within the relation of the new ground to the old that the meaning of the aesthetic product—its disclosure—is suggested, later to be realized in possible future actions. Rosario points to this relationship in Heidegger's existential aesthetic: "The created object sets forth the world from which it comes, against which it rests. The truth disclosed in a work of art is a tension, a conflict between an unconcealed entity and a concealed background within an 'open' field."[22] If the created object is too removed from our experience, either in its idealism or in its adherence to conventions of form and style, its meanings are exhausted in the distance that separates the new form from our actual situation.[23]

What we seek when we examine our experience of curriculum is discrepancy, a lid that won't quite fit the pot and lets a little steam escape to tell us what's cooking inside. Heidegger's example of the broken hammer is an illustration of discrepancy encountered in daily experience. We understand the structure of the tool when its function is disturbed. I understand the hammer when I, standing on my tiptoes on a ladder, trying to nail a hanging plant to a beam on the screened-in porch, work with a hammer whose head is loose and starts to wobble as I swing it toward the nail. I know the concept of the expressway when it is closed for construction and I thread my way through the local streets. Discrepancy is a result of the movement of experience from the familiar to the strange, and our subsequent awareness of the relation of the two.

First we must claim what is familiar. In our time it is no easy trick to claim our experience. When we speak about our situation, its demands, we attribute its cogency to someone else. In our society of mega-institutions it is easy to attribute our condition to "them." "They" control the rate of inflation. "They" never vacuum the lobby. "They" manufacture automobiles for planned obsolescence. "They" will never legalize abortion.

The chasm that has formed between theory and practice is reflected in the alienation of the individual from the mega-institutions that surround him. Our theory becomes a diversion, a runoff for the energy that flows into discourse because it cannot be realized in action. We are impotent, as overwhelmed by our social, economic, technological institutions as Roquentin is by the chestnut tree.

In the way: it was the only relationship I could establish between these trees, these gates, these stones. In vain I tried to *count* the chestnut trees, to *locate* them by their relationship to the Velleda, to compare their height with the height of the plane trees; each of them escaped the relationship in which I tried to enclose it, isolated itself and overflowed. Of these relations (which I insisted on maintaining in order to delay the crumbling of the human world, measures, quantities, and directions)—I felt myself to be the arbitrator; they no longer had their teeth into things. *In the way,* the chestnut tree there, opposite me, a little to the left. . . .

And I—soft, weak, obscene, digesting, juggling, with dismal thoughts—I, too was *In the way.*

By creating a cultural order as inpenetrable, unwieldy, and incomprehensible as this natural order it was designed to explain, we too are "in the way"—as awkward and impotent in the worlds we have created as Roquentin is in the one he is given.

Therefore, aesthetic critique of curriculum is micro-theory. It confines its sweep to the dimension and scope of individual experience, hoping to integrate theory and practice by making them accountable in one and the same narrative. Curriculum can only reveal to the student what is possible in his world and in himself if that student can claim what is actual in his world and in himself as his experience. Theory and practice are at odds when the former is about "them" and only the latter is about "me."

Currere, a term coined by William Pinar to refer to the analysis of curriculum derived from the student's own experience and use of schooling and the academic disciplines, requires claiming the actual situation, owning it.[24] It is what Roquentin does in that long stay in Bouville. He stays put. He attends to his current situation, the brown stains on the mirror in the cafe, the smell of tobacco, the nausea. Estrangement rests upon the familiar. We cannot be estranged from something that we have never known. In order to reap the disclosure that lies dormant within our curricular forms, we must claim them in our familiar, daily experience and then estrange ourselves from them.

Crucial to the concept of *currere* is the assertion that situation has depth as well as width. The figure/ground analogy demands a third term, the perspective from which it is viewed. And that perspective is a human one, and as such is a point in time as well as space. For us, as for Roquentin, the present situation is funded with the past. Bouville is not spread out before him, its facticity completely revealed in the street map that marks the route from the quay

to the library to the cafe. Bouville is anchored in Roquentin's expectations, the project of researching the history of the Marquis de
Rollebon, the wish to lose himself again in Anny. He may hear
"Some of These Days" many times throughout his stay in Bouville,
but he must first go for the Sunday stroll, encounter the chestnut
tree, visit with Anny, and defend the Self-Taught Man before he
hears in the tune the disclosure of his possibilities.

Curriculum is Bouville. It is the ground. It is our situation. And
the figure is my action, my novel, my song. The case study that follows charts a passage that passes through both familiarity and
estrangement as it takes us from situation to song.

figure/ground/subject—*Currere*

This case study describes an extension of this existential aesthetic into practice. *Currere* has provided a bridge to span the gap
between the insights of Dewey, of Sartre, Merleau-Ponty, and my
work with students and curriculum. *Currere* is an analysis of curriculum derived from the student's experience and use of it. It is a
process of reflection and analysis that does not focus upon the object, the figure, bent upon the revelation of its content, but it is one
that investigates the relation of subject and object, of figure to
ground, of student to curriculum. Rather than pursuing the figure-
ground analogy into the either/or dichotomies that fragment our
understanding, it is enough to say that while *currere's* emphasis is
upon the student's experience of curriculum, making that experience
the figure and curriculum the ground from which it springs, it is the
relation of the two, the margin of contiguity where one blends into
the other, that it would reveal. The private experience of public
forms is articulated in its immediacy and particularity as it exists in
the interaction of one student and his educational situation.

It is important to state at this point that this analysis of educational experience is not to be confused with the narcissism and reifi-
cation that hover around some attempts at values clarification or
research into self-concept or cognitive style. The naming of the relation of the knower to the known, of the student to his studies, is
aimed at loosening the frame of that structure rather than setting it
in concrete. By permitting that relationship to be salient rather than
focusing exclusively upon the artifact—the theorem, the play, the

Versailles treaty—or upon the student—his cognitive structures, socio-economic status, emotional needs—we may discover new possibilities for his action in the world. It is an action that he will take to heal the wound that naming creates between what is and what might be.

Case Study—The University of Rochester Theatre Festival, January 1976

The introduction of *currere* into the work of the UR theatre students was an outgrowth of my work with Stefan Rudnicki, who directed theatrical productions and taught courses in acting, directing, and dramatic interpretation on campus. I was eager to bring this work from the College of Education, where Bill Pinar and I had used it with teachers-in-training, into other disciplines of the university. I was not surprised that it was those in fine arts who had been first to recognize the relevance of *currere* to their work, being more apt than historians, chemists, or sociologists to acknowledge the impact of their own history and perspective upon what they see.

Rudnicki, working in the tradition of Brecht, Artaud, and Grotowski, was not content to produce plays merely to delight, terrify, or amuse an audience. The plays that he and his students would produce must challenge the communal myths of their audience. Actors in such a company would need to confront their own personal myths as well. Throughout the festival, the curriculum, whether it was Shakespeare's *Richard III,* a mime workshop, or a seminar, was conceived first as a critical mirror reflecting the student's experience of both the natural and cultural order, and then as the ground for his action within either or both of those domains.

This relation of theatre to dramatic literature mirrors the relation of teaching and learning to curriculum. It is well stated by Jerzy Grotowski, director of Poland's Laboratory Theatre:

The strength of great works really consists in their catalystic effect; they open doors for us, set in motion the machinery of our self-awareness. For both producer and actor the author's text is a sort of scalpel enabling us to open ourselves, to transcend ourselves, to find what is hidden within us. . . . In the theatre, if you like, the text has the same function as the myth had for the poet of ancient times. The author of *Prometheus* found in the Prometheus myth both an act of defiance and a springboard, perhaps even the source of his own creation. But his *Prometheus* was the product of his personal experience. . . . For me, a creator of theatre, the important thing is not the words but what we do with these words, what gives life to the inanimate words of the text, what transforms them into "the Word."[25]

We would not and could not tell our students what to do with the words of William Shakespeare or Samuel Beckett. (Nor can our associates tell them what to do with the words of Durkheim, Heisenberg, Rimbaud, or Lenin.) The autobiographical processes of *currere* are designed to provide a passage to agency for each student by first guiding him to claim and examine his own experience of another's words, and then encouraging him to acknowledge and develop his own response. At first, the plays of the festival, *Richard III* and *Waiting for Godot,* were salient. They were the figures that drew our attention—until they were claimed by the student and fell back into the ground, absorbed into his situation—then to be estranged in negation in favor of other words, other forms, these of the student's own devising.

There is a technological approach to theatre, and Antonin Artaud has attacked it with an inspired and eloquent fury.[26] It is one that conceives of the play as an objective entity, the "given," knotty, inert, complete, and self-contained. Technique strives to fulfill its stipulations, to meet its demands of character, setting, style. Although an effort to recreate the "authentic" Macbeth may seem as absurd as Roquentin's attempts to resuscitate the long-deceased Marquis de Rollebon, it characterizes a prevalent attitude toward curriculum. A visit to high school English classes will reveal room after room of students and teachers crammed into the awkward spaces of *The Scarlet Letter, The Odyssey,* or "Sailing to Byzantium," their own world subsumed by literary ones. Grotowski has maintained that there is no objective Hamlet, and there is no objective Hester Prynne, no objective Cyclops, no objective old men. Sartre's contention that the reader recreates what the writer discloses is demonstrated most clearly when instead of constantly circling the curricular artifact, talking about the book, analyzing it in critical papers, students recreate the text by using it as a ground for their own actions, in this case for theatre.

At the beginning of our work, the texts of *Richard III* and *Waiting for Godot* were groundless, figures out of *situ.* Our situation was neither Shakespeare's nor Beckett's. To have filled out the figure without identifying its ground in our own experience would have

been to perpetuate a theatre of dead and empty forms, the attenuated and artificial extravagances that impelled Artaud to demand
theatrical forms filled with a force akin to hunger. He demanded
"culture-in-action," forms so grounded in experience, so forceful
that they would transfigure the world just as "Some of These Days"
transfigures Bouville for Roquentin.

Artaud left us visions of a vital culture, but few means of realizing them, except to recommend the forms of Mexican religion and
Balinese theatre as models. The research and methodology of Jerzy
Grotowski have been shaped to understand and master the very relation necessary to the realization of Artaud's vision, the wedding of
force to received forms. It is an actor's method, rather than a designer's.

In curriculum theory critics of schooling and curriculum have
left us visions of alternative learning environments to replace the pretentious and empty forms of schooling scorned by Kozol, Silberman,
Holt. But by fixing their gaze upon learning environments or new
theatrical conventions, radical theorists in both theatre and curriculum persist in splitting their vision between the figure and the ground
and ignoring the third term, the subject. Producers look first at the
text of the play and then at the physical and social milieu within
which it is presented. The curriculum director or teacher looks first
at the textbooks and then at the physical and social milieu of the
school. The acting methods of Grotowski and the autobiographical
methods of *currere* are each designed to scrutinize the relation of the
figure to the ground as it is perceived from the perspective of one
individual, actor or student. Each methodology maintains that the
force and energy we seek in our educational and cultural institutions
reside within the ability of the individual to acknowledge and respond to his experience of forms rather than in the discovery and
creation of an ideal theatrical or educational world.

The play was a form, merely that. It would be our task as individuals and as a group to discover the relationship of that form to
our experience, of that figure to our ground and from that contiguity
evolve a new form that would encompass both that figure, the curriculum, and our ground, our experience. This is the first phase of
aesthetic process described earlier wherein the artist establishes a new
ground as well as a new figure, new conditions as well as new consequences. This is the created form. This is "Some of These Days"

pouring the heat and claustrophobic suffering of a city summer into its own time signature.

Throughout the weeks to follow we were to continually ask the students to examine their responses to the educational and theatrical forms that we provided. The response we sought was both communal and individual. Production of the play required that as a group, the company share its experiences. At the same time the educational significance of these events would be measured in the response of each individual student to his experience.

We formed a seminar that met weekly. The students were a varied group, over fifty in all. They ranged from freshmen and sophomores who were tentative, but eager to be exposed to an intensive program of workshops and productions, to confident upperclassmen who saw the festival as a culmination of their earlier work, to part-time students, many older, who held various jobs in the community and had joined the company for this semester only.

Our initial meetings were designed to provide some common ground for these plays by identifying the associations that occurred to us from our own experience while reading the text. Those associations that could be shared in the forms of other artifacts, plays, novels, poems, and paintings were presented to the group as contexts. For example, as contexts for *Richard III,* we listened to readings of excerpts from Eric Bentley's collection of transcripts from the McCarthy hearings, Aeschylus' *The Persians* and *Agamemnon,* attended a showing of the film *The Ox-Bow Incident,* and read selections from *Shaking the Pumpkin,* Jerome Rothenberg's collection of poetry of the North American Indians. These contexts were not presented to gain consensus but to amplify the echoes, however faint, that the themes, images, sounds of the text sounded in our shared history. I thought of this identification of contexts as a gathering of experience along a horizontal axis, a drawing out of intersubjective associations lodged within the shared social and cultural experience of the group.

In counterpoint to this group effort to claim our communal experience of the text, to make it familiar, was *currere,* a process designed to situate the plays, the seminar, the festival, within the personal history and time of the individual participants. I thought of the autobiographical process as strung out along a vertical axis of educational experience, and it was this process that I nurtured most closely.

There is a powerful communal tendency in a theatre company. The impending public exposure rapidly creates a sense of camaraderie, a society of mutual protection. In addition, there was a real need for there to be a community of players. Stefan's work in rehearsals was often conceived to heighten the ability of individuals to be sensitive to the other players, to attend to and respond to their behavior. We both agreed that fellowship could not, by itself, create either art or educational experience. So we sought the tension of the one and the many, asking each student to identify his own responses as the work progressed.

We introduced *currere* to protect the students from the curriculum. We were not merely concerned with making the curriculum, these plays, present to them, bringing these plays, or even this group, to form. As educators we were interested in bringing our students to form, not a form that labeled them, fixing them in one attitude or pose, but a form that expressed their realization of their own dormant possibilities.

Accordingly, we acknowledged that our students had not come to us as empty vessels, awaiting to be filled with experience. We asked them to claim what was familiar, to write essays that would define theatrical experience by presenting specific illustrations of it from their own biographies. These examples were not necessarily limited to stage memories. Any event, any association that the term theatrical experience brought forth was relevant. We asked the students to examine the associations they presented and to develop, if they could, some generalizations from them concerning the nature of theatre, and their own expectations. Students were reminded that in this exercise there were no experiences or assumptions that were more correct or appropriate than others. They were being asked to survey their own ground, to take stock of what they had brought with them, to articulate their expectations. By asking for this fragment of life history we were funding our scrutiny of the present situation with its endowment from past experience. Situation has depth as well as width, and just as Roquentin had carried his past into Bouville, our students had brought their own baggage to the festival, memories of make-believe games of childhood, broken ankles, bar mitzvahs, diving competitions, applauding parents, car accidents.

The tendency of some educators to dismiss such experiences as trivial ("Do you really want to read and respond to the memoirs of an eighteen year old?") revealed their own misunderstandings of autobiography, and education, as well as their contempt both for their students and probably for their own experience as well.

The value of autobiographical writing is not lodged in the revelation of startling, dramatic adventures. It is found in the interpretation of the most mundane events, a significance that evolves as these events are described. The significance of these events, it is hardly necessary to add, was not found in their promise to excite a voyeuristic reader, but in their impact upon the present assumptions and intentions of the writer.

The instructional fallacy that denigrates students' autobiographical writing subscribes to what Freire has called the banking system of education, wherein the student is merely a repository of information deposited by the instructor.[27] It is as if we had never heard of assimilation and accommodation.

By asking our students to describe their own situations, we were pursuing a theme developed in recent curriculum theory and contemporary psychological theory as well.[28] Curriculum criticism has shifted its concerns from design, a rational sequencing of materials of plan of instruction, to situation, often referred to as learning environments. The essays of Apple, Macdonald, Huebner, and Mann that appear in *Curriculum Theorizing: The Reconceptualists* as well as the 1975 ASCD Yearbook, *Schools in Search of Meaning,* aim at describing this quality of life in schools.[29] They examine a student's access to curriculum as it is influenced by his access to linguistic codes as well as by the kinds of behaviors prescribed or tolerated by those who teach in and administer schools. Learning environments are shown to vary greatly in relation to a student's age, sex, race, socioeconomic status, and ethnic ties. While Bowles and Gintis may take a long view of the impact of the economic system upon the learning environment, these others focus in upon a particular setting.[30] They may freeze a classroom in a series of still frames in an attempt to analyze the very complex assumptions and interactions and codes that determine who will learn what. Even if these analyses are extended over some time they compose a primarily synchronic view of situation, less concerned with its changes over time than in assessing the many habits of thought and action, both verbal and nonverbal, in operation at any given moment.

Added to this study of present situation is the diachronic approach provided by historians such as Cremin, Wishy, Karier et al., and Katz.[31] Their curriculum criticism traces the present situation back to its origins in the experience and interests of those who shaped the institutions that surround us today. These historical, socio-political-economic-linguistic critiques have contributed greatly to our understanding of the ways in which curriculum has been devised and the diverse influences upon the forms and patterns it assumes, as well as its translation into the daily experience contained within learning environments.

Nevertheless, despite this acute and sensitive criticism that, to borrow the phrase of Maurice Roche, looks upon "the ordinary as strange and in need of some explanation," no criticism of situation, no matter how thorough and profound, can release us from situation.[32] We are and always will be *in situ,* and every Bouville presents us with its own chestnut roots. It is the ambition of *currere* to provide students with the tools of critical reflection that they will need to transform their situations, whatever they may be, to take the objectivity that they are given and to create yet another objectivity from it. In the process of *currere, the* situation becomes *my* situation. *The* criticism that liberates must be *my* negation that arises out of *my* experience. Ultimately, only I am responsible for what I do with what I am given.

Critiques of situation present it as something that happens to students, something imposed upon them by intellectual traditions, an economic system, social biases, the physical environment. *Currere* rests upon the conviction that situations are also created by students, an approach supported by Kenneth Bowers' contention that "situations are as much a function of the person as the person's behavior is a function of situation."[33] *Currere* adds the student's perspective to this scrutiny of situation by looking at the present moment as it rests on the continuum of his educational experience, the flow of inner time that stretches from the deposits of past events to expectations and intentions flung far into the future.[34] Curriculum criticism requires, then, not only criticism of the curriculum that is spread out before us, but also criticism of the curriculum that dwells in our own habits and anticipations. Throughout *Nausea* the Bouville that we get is the Bouville that Roquentin sees. Situation is ultimately no more objective than curriculum. It is the world's answer to our question.

Each of our students brought his own question. And each question was answered by its own festival. Some of our students had difficulty in discovering their own questions, accustomed as they were to answering those of others. They had spent years learning to give the appropriate responses and now, as they worked on their essays, the nervous ones came to the office to ask, "What do you want?" Some asked with anger, some asked with suspicion, expecting a trick. The first pieces, the essays defining theatrical experience, came in motley shapes and styles. Some were stilted, hampered by reticence. Some were glib, demonstrating a facile ability to interpret everything but one's own experience. Others flowed with the energy of the story that had been waiting for years to be told. For some, theatrical experience was associated with group empathy; for others, it was related to the experience of being on display, exposed to the judgment of others. Still others saw it as an experience of emotional vulnerability. And a few relished it as an opportunity to manipulate the emotions of an audience. For some, theatrical experience was vicarious experience, therapeutic; for others, it was the fantasy of a small child. One student associated it with the concentration and control of high diving, another with the disruption of daily routine and the subsequent heightened awareness that accompanied convalescence from a broken ankle. One student, attuned to the preconceptual, offered the image of three children walking down a path in the center of the campus licking ice-cream cones.

These essays were the first step in the process of claiming familiar ground. They also served as a springboard for the process of estrangement. When I spoke of discrepancy earlier, I associated it with the juxtaposition of the familiar with the strange. It is in the tension between the two that the impetus to transform the familiar situation into a new objectivity arises. So at the same time that we sought to cultivate familiarity, we sought to create estrangement as well. Estrangement is well known to Roquentin:

By the seaside: I don't know what to do with my hand, vigorous body in the midst of this tragic relaxed crowd.

At the mirror: The grey thing appears in the mirror. I go over and look at it. I can no longer get away. It is the reflection of my face. Often in these last days I study it. I can understand nothing of this face. The faces of others have some sense. Some direction. Not mine. I cannot even decide whether it is handsome or ugly.

Roquentin's estrangement overwhelms him. It rises up as nausea between him and his existence. He cannot rush to partake of his situation, he cannot heap the food upon his plate along with the other Sunday diners of Bouville. His estrangement pervades all his experience, his appetite, his work, his friendships, even his perceptions of his own body. Yet only in its extremity is it distinguished from the estrangement that we have come to associate with the artist.

In 1917 it was Victor Shklovski (a possible source for Brecht's later formulation of estrangement, *Verfremdung*) who stated that "the procedure of art is the procedure of estrangement," "a device of making something strange," "a creative deformation."[35] Frederic Ewen takes care in his discussion of the theory of estrangement in Brecht's theatre to distinguish it from alienation, where subject and object are isolated and unrelated. Estrangement, on the other hand, implies a wrenching apart of what has been bonded together. In Brecht's theatre it is a technique used to shock spectators out of their complacent acceptance of the status quo. Brecht's own explanations of it make explicit the relation of aesthetics to praxis:

> Estrangement of an incident or character simply means taking from that incident or character that which is self-evident, known, or obvious and arousing about them wonder or curiosity.
>
> Estrangement means to *historicize*, that is consider people and incidents as historically conditioned and transitory. . . . The spectator will no longer see the characters on the stage as unalterable, uninfluenceable, helplessly delivered over to their fate. He will see that this man is such and such, because circumstances are such. But he in turn is conceivable not only as he is now, but also as he might be—that is, otherwise—and the same holds true for circumstances. Hence the spectator obtains a new attitude in the theatre, the same attitude that the man of the twentieth century has with respect to nature. He will be received in the theatre as the great "transformer" who can intervene in the natural processes and the social processes, and who no longer accepts the world but masters it.[36]

My responses to these first pieces were aimed at the cultivation of this alternate phase of aesthetic activity: estrangement. Without repudiating any of the associations that the students presented, I tried to provide an antithesis to their thesis. I did not attempt to invalidate their experience but to stimulate a dialectic that would lead them to see the limitations that accrue to our experience, the habits of seeing that prescribe the field of our vision. If a student asserted that theatrical experience was the acting out of fantasies of mastery, I indicated the possibility that this rather private conception be measured against the idea of theatre as communication between players and audience. If the concept offered was the drama of car accidents and hijackings, I asked the writer to consider the role of artifice, of action relegated to the realm of the unreal rather than the world of daily experience. If theatrical experience was identified as expression of emotion, I suggested reception of emotion. If the writer associated it with losing himself in a group project, I asked him how it differed from team sports.[37]

Some students responded to the questions I asked immediately, some later in their journals, some managed to sidestep them and, perhaps, never really heard them. I responded to the journals that the students handed in as I had to the initial pieces. The dialogue that developed varied in relation to the themes presented by each student, by his or her interest in this process and ability to write. I found in this work, as I had before, that this last factor was less significant than one would have thought. The students were asked to write about subjects on which they were conversant, their own experience. Once they could be convinced that all they needed to do was to focus on some small incident and that if they would lay it out in detail, their responses and interpretations would follow, even those students who had come to the office to tell me that they could not write, that they froze when confronted with a piece of paper, became fluent. The discipline of specificity was one that we valued not only in writing and acting, but in ascertaining one's response to any curriculum.

The journals required a biphasic process that alternated between a permissive kind of minding that focused upon images, sense memories, fragments, details of experience, and a more conceptual phase, abstract, analytical. Examples of each style are offered in the writings of one student. The first excerpt is her response to my suggestion that a theatrical experience from her childhood be rendered more specifically:

The criteria for "best" (as in our dying swan or Frankenstein play)—There were no marks, no really formal rules. We'd just each perform and the consensus would occur spontaneously. The one I remember best was the dying swan. We weren't familiar with the ballet, but we'd heard of it. I doubt if any of us had seen it, but I knew, at least, that "being a swan" was different from "being a person." I remember that one girl's version of a swan was to sprawl on her back, arms and legs out. My version, which the others liked, was to "round" myself, rather like a ballet position, one leg straight out, one tucked under, back curved, head over arms, arms out, together over legs. Interesting graphic, eh? It's interesting too, that the "best" dying swan was the more symbolic image.

But, the best Frankenstein was the girl who could do side head isolations and shift her eyes at the same time. From the sublime to the ridiculous. We were *not* intellectual.

Other games we played included acting out movies and stories (virtually memorizing dialogue), playing at being pioneers, doctors, mothers (real role-playing here with the future in mind, a little). Perhaps "real" life surprised us less because of our games.

The structure of these paragraphs illustrates the alternation of specific recollections and the comment upon them that issues from the student's conceptual present. My questions would either be designed to elicit the detailed reflections required to link past experience to present perspectives, or, once those perspectives emerged, to clarify them or suggest alternative views. Further consideration of this entry could have led us to discuss the socialization implied in each girl's version of the dying swan, a consideration of the receptiveness of children to the sway of commercial, popular imagery, relative to that of adults. We might have discussed why the writer saw one swan as more "symbolic" than the other, the multiple referents of gesture. We could, and did, go on to discuss the function of the theatre, whether it prepared one to adjust to real life or to transform it. The writings of this articulate and thoughtful student offered abundant opportunities for dialogue. I had to be careful not to inundate her by following every lead and would try to light upon the themes that seemed most important to her, themes that were threaded through her other writings as well as her day-to-day work in the festival. My question followed: "How does the adult use fantasy to transform reality, and what about the public expression of fantasy and its impact upon and reception by other people?"

And here are excerpts from her response:

I'm not convinced that we should "demand that there be some public expression to theatrical experience." Would we consider the child's open expression of his fantasies more theatrical than the withdrawn adolescent's even though the child's public act is not consciously chosen? ... I guess I can't resolve the question of which is the more theatrical, but I can consider the possibility that the more the fantasy reflects the human condition, the dramatic needs and concerns of the growing-up child-woman, the inner-life *not* stimulated by books or movies but by more original thought, the more theatrical it may be. I'm not sure, though. Is the distinction really important? In some ways the final, filled form of the adult is the outward, public expression of theatrical experience throughout growing up and being which brings me to "how does the adult use fantasy to transform reality?" Talk about nitty-gritty questions! Yeah, this is a major concern of mine, too, a theme in much, perhaps all, that I do. Once again, a question of yours has brought me back to a focus I was getting to but now I'll get there sooner. . . .

This student was a high-school English teacher. I cannot know what impact these writings had upon her work in the plays. She was an assistant stage manager in *Waiting for Godot*, and wrote a good deal of the material in the play produced by the play-writing workshop that was also part of the festival. What is important, it seems to me, is that *currere* provided her with an opportunity to respond to those aspects of the curriculum closest to her own interests, her own situation.

It may be of interest to compare her entries to those of another student, a freshman making a very tentative stab at presenting and responding to his experience:

I've never done theatre like this before. We don't just memorize what to say and where to stand. I'm actually becoming another person.

When we did the oration between Richard and Richmond, I had feelings like I've never had before. Two people I know and am friendly with were my enemies. Because of the context, I actually hated two people I like.

When Stefan stopped the scene, it was like awakening from a dream. All of a sudden I realized, "What the hell was I doing?"

It works. I am Sir Thomas Vaughn, every time I'm with the group. It's not acting. . . .

I don't know how to react to myself. Everything I wrote was a "gut reaction." I can say no more and no less. I think that's the idea behind the journals. To just stand back and see your reactions. If they look right, fine. If they look wrong, you must revise your thinking.

My response was to ask this student to talk more about the presence of the group. Why was it more influential here than in team sports, or even a classroom experience? Was he responding more strongly to certain people than others? Then I tried to correct the misunderstanding that the distanced phase was judgmental: "Rather than rightness or wrongness, you are looking for other possibilities, a chance to see your experience in a new way."

The journals were designed to provide connective tissue between inner and outer experience. We were not encouraging a total loss of self to curriculum, a loss evidenced in the willingness of the student to be Sir Thomas Vaughn. Roquentin could not *be* an adventurer, a historian. Even the actor must fill a role with his own presence, making more of it than it would make of him, not modeling himself to its figure, but using it as a ground for his own action.

The journals were the students' first line of defense against the curriculum and its pervasive agents. At the same time they were designed to diminish the distance between the student and the curriculum by highlighting points of connection. My comments were often designed to maintain a balance between these two functions and to prevent the movement of reflection between inner and outer poles of experience to circle exclusively around one or the other, mechanically tripping through the day's agenda or getting lost in a maze of introspection.

Some students found it difficult to write about their experience unselfconsciously. They would use the journals as indictments or vindications, reviewing their actions and scourging or praising themselves accordingly. In static self-portraits they would draw up a dossier of imagined sins: laziness, lack of purpose, hypocrisy, dependency, narcissistic preoccupations, that obscured their view of their daily experience. Ira Progoff has, in his extensive work with journals, noted the tendency of some writers to turn in upon their own subjectivity and move in within ever narrowing space. One student whose earlier writings were ensnared in the tangle of response turned back upon himself rather than out to the experience offered by the external world and the internal sources of his own creativity, grew to understand the balance for which we were striving as evidenced in this entry:

This handout, as I'm sure my reader is aware, is necessarily different from other journal entries. Or are you aware?

Oh, I guess you're not. . . . You haven't read my prerecorded sentiments. To speak on direct and real issues is the program here. Thus. . . .

Rehearsal progresses, continues, extends, grows. At times it is exciting, though boring and difficult at others. This we all know. I have a sense of potential, that is, I get the feeling that a public performance of the play will bring out much more that is present at rehearsal. . . .

Crew has been interesting . . . the extreme rush to complete pieces forces the joint effort to a frenzied state replete with heart-felt profanity, swollen thumbs, and fond memories . . . of a distant year and a very different vocation. Laura Mae calls my attention. There's a world to build.

At eleven the final member was nailed, and a tired cheer rose from the sawdust and nail piles where several of our noble peers were grouped. Our director's command brought the company back to matters at hand. We could not stay, but must not go. We waited.

Hot was the coffee; that retriever of morning man. I gulped it slowly, thinking solely of its therapeutic value. Would the new man emerge from the sodden ground, snow frosted ground, measured with negligent footsteps and speaking its confusion?

The chance to resolve the issue was provided by a scheduled event. Like a foghorn in a storm, the structured day compelled me. Not since grammar school had I been so sure of where I was at any certain time.

The explicit goals and techniques of the journal had been only lightly treated in our initial seminars. Whatever instruction their writing required was to emerge in my responses to each student's work, designed to correct for excesses in "objective" or "subjective" focus, specificity or abstraction. I never wrote my comments on the entries themselves, but numbered the phrases on the entry that I was to discuss in notes written on another piece of paper. Students were encouraged to write every day, but to hand in only one journal a week, so that they might develop skills of critical reflection without thinking of those skills as limited to their dialogue with me.

In addition, the journals provided a means of continuing a discussion of themes that were important in the initial pieces. We suggested to the students that the journals were also the place to record whatever relations they observed between their work within the festival and their other studies. How were the skills it demanded, the experiences it offered, familiar or strange to the chemistry major? How did the student in composition from the Eastman School of Music experience composing background music for *Richard III* in comparison to the more autonomous work that he had done in the past? How did the history major with the heavy reading schedule manage his extensive work in festival in addition to his other responsibilities? How did the high school English teacher deal with the role of assistant to a nineteen-year-old stage-manager? How did the senior with extensive experience in past productions approach a minor role that did not appear to test her talent?

The journals provided continuity, linking the student's experience of seminars, guest lectures, workshops, rehearsals, productions. Professional actors were part of the company and were working in the plays as well as in a film that was produced with the help of the students. Stefan and I were fairly satisfied that we had coordinated all the persons, the plays, the workshop in a cohesive, meaningful structure. But we knew better than to expect that this curriculum, as conceived by us, would be the curriculum perceived, let alone experienced, by the students. Each student would contribute his own organizing principles, would create his own Bouville.

Although the journals were clearly associated with the work of the theatre festival, I had shied away from enumerating the particular ways in which we hoped they would contribute to the students' work so as not to prescribe the experience they would record. Ira Progoff has commented upon a similar concern in his use of journals:

Of particular significance was the number of times when journals were used to help a person achieve a goal he had set in advance rather than to reach forward to new goals and to discover new meanings in his life. At such times when the framework of the journal was enclosed by a set of fixed attitudes, it became a static tool. Then it was used not as an instrument for growth, but for self-justification. In such contexts individuals have often employed a journal to insulate themselves against questions they did not wish to face. This use of a journal has the effect of narrowing the scope of a person's life, and of limiting rather than enlarging the possibilities of his personality. A notable contemporary exception to this is found in the *Diaries* of Anais Nin, where a person of great literary creativity used a journal also as a vehicle for her total life development.[38]

There were students with exciting creative ability, who for one reason or another—limited acting experience, a restriction on the amount of time they could devote to festival—were not given tasks that fully tapped their interest and energy. For some of those students the journals provided another outlet. One student wrote a number of mime plays and short one-act plays, as well as poems. His final review of his experience of the festival was presented in a revision of a play that he had written in the eighth grade, the recent version altered to conform to the insights that he had gained during our work. There were four or five other students whose journals regularly included poetry. The journal entry that follows illustrates one student's response to a line from *Richard III*:

Citizen 3: When great leaves fall, then winter is at hand. . . .
    She looked at me with burning, seething eyes, accusatory and full of hurt. "It's as if I am standing in the heavy winter snows, frozen and looking into your window where there is an inviting fire. You repeatedly beckon me but close yourself to me. I am left to die in the cold of winter."
    I know what she means.
    It's as if there is an OPEN sign in the window of my front door, but when anyone touches the door latch, she discovers that it's locked, and she is abandoned to the cold with shattered anticipations and disappointed expectations . . . fatal disillusionment. Better to have had a CLOSED sign in the door window than to have deceived her.
    Ah, but the tragic irony: inside my house I am consumed by my own fire.

One of the features of our curriculum that protected the journal from functioning too restrictively was the range of activity that the festival included. In addition to seminars, rehearsals, and production of the plays, the students participated in workshops, a mime workshop that ran for two weeks at the beginning of the festival and a play-writing workshop that wound it up. The mime workshop provided a physical, prereflective analogue to the written, reflective work of *currere*.

In these two-hour sessions taught by Bob Berky, mime was distinguished from the classroom version of pantomime as symbols are distinguished from signs. The gestures and movements were not studied merely to replicate behaviors lifted from the settings and props that identify them in common experience. In the effort of replication every gesture that we performed was an expression of the continuity of situation and action in human experience. The givens of the physical world, the hardness of a floor, the edge of a table, the weight of a bar, and the givens of our own bodies, their capacities for torsion, stretch, balance, were fused by our intentions into meaningful actions. Both a simple move, such as pulling a rope, or a complicated mime of finding a lost key required total awareness of the contributions of the natural and cultural orders to behavior. A movement that observed all the contingencies of the natural world and of the body but was empty of thought or feeling was lifeless and boring. A gesture that was filled with intention but oblivious of its surroundings and the mechanics of its expression was vague and silly.

If *currere* was to reveal our conceptual inclinations, intellectual and emotional habits, mime would reveal the knowledge that we have in our hands, in our feet, in our backs, in our eyes. It is knowledge gathered from our preconceptual dialogue with the world, knowledge that precedes our utterances and our stories. I had come to appreciate the importance of this work through my experiences in the workshops and acting classes of the UR Summer Theatre and had begun to use these exercises along with the written work of *currere* in my work with teachers-in-training. Mime, like teaching, was a means of filling forms, of taking the curriculum, whether it was a mime of sealing an envelope or a discussion of the Magna Carta, and filling it with our experience, bringing ourselves to form in the process. The mimes of opening a door, of lifting a weight or being a tiger could not be absently assumed, put on like the sweater I slip over my head as I review the groceries I need from the store. Both mime and *currere* require our presence. Curriculum is the situation that we must claim and make our own before we can act to realize its latent possibilities.

In addition to mime's demands that we claim the familiar, fill the forms of our daily movements and gestures with our attention, there were also demands that we estrange ourselves from habitual behavior. We would challenge our own negotiated peace with nature by studying the terms of another's agreement, mirroring his walk, his nod, his snarl. We would interrupt our patterns of movement by attempting feats of asymmetry, such as keeping one arm limp while the other is rigid.[39]

The mime workshop was very important to students. It was difficult, tiring; it demanded discipline, practice, utter concentration. It required that the student be constantly critical of his own work without being concerned about how he looked to others. Berky, a professional artist, knew the loneliness of creative achievement. He encouraged the students to develop an objective eye that would scan their behavior without issuing inhibiting judgments of proficiency. The journals reinforced this level of self-scrutiny.

It was possible for a student to conscientiously pursue all the inner work requiring concentration and imagery and not have that work manifest in his performance because he had not yet developed the requisite technical skills. This discrepancy between effort and achievement is not unique to mime but occurs in most learning situations. The journal provided a place to record one's own effort, even if it had eluded the recognition of one's instructor or peers.

Excerpts from a number of journals written during this time follow:

While doing the warmups and exercises today I realized what discipline it must take to work at this constantly, as Bob does. I have regimented other physical exercises, but this stretching and straining is really taxing. My back muscles are the most reluctant to stretch and turn me into a madman while doing the "plow."

*   *   *

I want to find a way to act that allows my body to be used correctly but still allows me to fly.

*   *   *

Tonight in mime I was told that I did a particular exercise well. Further attempts were not good at all. Suddenly the idea popped into my head—I was trying to reproduce instead of recreate.

*   *   *

This loosening up really came to me last Friday night, when Bob had us doing that walk, and falling forward and catching ourselves. I really got into it for awhile, and suddenly I felt like I was performing a mime movement. I don't know how it looked, but it sure felt great. And then I was having a blast, just breaking into laughter a few times from sheer enjoyment. I guess a lot of it was just surrendering to an idea finally and following it.

*   *   *

Stop! Where are you? Hold on to a point. Move around it, feel it, see it, hold it. Be there!

*   *   *

Everybody's been hawking imagery. You want to buy some visions cheap?

*   *   *

What happens is I imagine first, but don't really feel, for example, being pulled. Once I imagine it, I imitate what I see in my mind with my body. If I do that successfully, my body will convince my mind that I am really being pulled—I am "believing" with my hands, feet, etc. Which is terrific, when it works.

*   *   *

Be a tiger . . . so, sit down. Eyes closed. Think. Back to old movies, the zoo. Pan in. See him breathe. Feel his hot breath on my face. Feel the texture of his fur and the way it changes on different parts of his body. Pan in closer. Swing around. I am seeing what he is seeing. My feet slide neatly, snugly into his. My legs follow. My torso and arms follow suit. Only our heads are separate. A tiger with two heads . . . and one human. Finally, our eyes merge. We take in a breath through our extended black nostrils. But isn't this my daily routine?

*   *   *

This aspect of being a mime and/or an actor is rather frightening in a way. It's hard to contemplate spending years in pain, always asking the body to do a little bit more than last time, and going on even when the pain is great. It's a matter of self-discipline of course. Right now I seem to still need someone standing over me, telling me to go on when I want to stop.

*   *   *

I'm not getting up in the morning. The morning, the early sun, the dawn is my strength. Festival is Delilah; mime the scissors; I'm Samson.

Berky, a charming and persuasive teacher/performer, was also eager to protect the students from the sway of his influence. The following entry, written by a very large, heavy-set senior who had been unusually nervous about participating in the workshop describes the impact of his relationship with its instructor:

I have done work, much of it creative, innovative and valuable. Bob has seen to that.

In several weeks I have grown to know, like and maybe even love Bob Berky. At the "Hello Party" there was an illustration of this which knocked my sox off.

Near the end of the party I was standing near the stereo. Bob walked near me and behind me. Putting my hands behind my back we "slapped five." I turned around and Berky embraced me. It was an unexpected show of affection but quickly enough I had him off the ground and we exchanged words to the effect that we were grateful for each other's friendship. At that point I gave him a big kiss on the cheek, put him down, and he went on his merry way. Knocked my sox off.

It has been this which in retrospect has allowed me to deal with his mime workshop in such a way as to alleviate my fears and inhibitions. Being helped along by the comfort between Bob and me, I found the freedom to be creative, innovative and responsive to the demands of the workshop.

The Berky workshop has allowed me to become aware, for the first time in my life, of the creative potential in my all-too-suppressed body. The awareness has actually been a state of mind by which I freed myself to expressing myself in a manner I never thought I could achieve.

My response made me feel a bit like the devil's advocate. Without denigrating the contribution of this relationship to this student's experience we were as eager to prevent loss of self to instructor as we were to avoid loss of self to curriculum: "It may be useful, if you have the occasion, to think further about what it is that your relation with Berky has done for you? How can *you* do what *he* does for you for *yourself*?"

The squelch of estrangement.

In my initial meeting with the theory of estrangement, it was traveling under another name, "distancing." This concept was associated with the phenomenological practices of bracketing the natural attitude, of suspending a habitual, common-sense interpretation of experience in order to achieve a scrutiny of phenomena that would admit information generally excluded by our presuppositions. I was familiar with Heidegger's quarrel with Husserl, his contention that phenomenological reflection was too idealistic, too removed from the involvement, the care, the anguish, the expectation that are woven through our encounter with the world's events and objects. In phenomenological reflection, distancing and variations are imagined in order to *know* the actual by way of the possible. The essential form (*eidos*) of a phenomenon, whether it was an emotion of fear or the tree outside the window, would be reached when imagination had stripped it of all its contingent characteristics, leaving it only with what was essential to its identity.

Estrangement, on the other hand, researches the possible rather than the actual and wrenches the subject away from his immersion in the latter so that he may realize the former in his own action. All of this I had understood before, but it was this use of *currere* with the theatre students that revealed the awesome loneliness and responsibility that the dialectical phase of *currere* required and led me to refer to it, as I have in this paper, as *estrangement* rather than as *distancing*.

This process that called for one's own response to the curriculum to one's teachers, to one's own actions, entailed, if only for a short time, a suspension of fellowship, of comfort, of assurance of complicity—all the sweet pleasures of the familiar. It demanded a perspective that was both singular and particular, and lonely. It was the vision that we have come to associate with the artist as the outsider, a characterization common to religious ritual as well as the arts. We meet that persona in Raymond Firth's description of the spirit medium of Tikopia as living in a permanently liminal state as a marginal member of the social order whose ritual office provides him with a kind of social status that he lacks because of either personal disadvantages or undistinguished ancestry.[40] He provides alternative visions of experience that are tolerated because he is, by definition, an outsider. Tonio Kroger, Thomas Mann's young writer, provides another example of the estranged artist whose dissonant voice is acknowledged only because he lacks social clout. I, too, had seen *currere* as a shelter from the majority opinion and social hierarchy of our group and had willingly assumed the mantle of the outsider, the agent of estrangement, in order to nurture the generative tension of the familiar and the strange.

During spring vacation, which our students had spent on campus, rehearsing and building sets, their sense of affiliation intensified, as this journal entry testifies:

Spring break was like nothing I had ever experienced. Long hours, hard work, freezing conditions and group effort for a common goal characterized the week. My personal relations with members of the class grew far more familiar, and the unity which had been lacking while classes were in session was now incorporated into the experience. Without a close personal structure, including a close relationship with the instructors, our efforts would have been undirected, uninteresting and unproductive. (Whew—I found three.) Of course, the fact that we did centralize is no surprise—simply the amount of time we spent together collected us.

After spring vacation, as the plays went into production, the students' tolerance for estrangement diminished and their resistance to *currere* grew. The expression of that resistance demanded that I claim it, that I acknowledge my own response to it, for it was my situation.

It was expressed at a seminar meeting held toward the end of the vacation. One student suggested that we suspend the seminars and *currere* in favor of spaghetti suppers. Although I had spoken frequently with the students individually about the journal writing, we had not talked about the process as a group since the initial meetings of the seminar. To reclaim that evening is painful, to review their resistance and criticism without feeling denigrated almost impossible. As one might expect, those who had written most frequently and thoughtfully, for the most part kept silent. The criticisms voiced had two foci. The first was vulnerability. One student spoke of the vulnerability she experienced when she reread the thoughts she had committed to paper. What she saw there never quite measured up to her imagined self-concept. The critical mirror sent back a harsh light. For others there was too great a discrepancy between their experience and their ability to articulate it. As students used the word "vulnerable," Stefan reminded them that we had tried to cultivate vulnerability as an openness to text, to each other, that might lead us to understand why the court of Richard III was so vulnerable to his impact as well as to create an event that would reveal our own vulnerability to our audience. Rehearsals and the journals were both largely directed toward these ends, but now fatigued, yearning for closure, the students were turning in (closing down?), and vulnerability was no longer a challenging attitude of openness to experience but a threatening exposure.

The second focus of their criticism was my distance. To protect them from feeling vulnerable, I had purposely put myself out of play. Only I read the journals. I did not grade them, nor did I contribute any evaluation of their work to the formulation of their final grade for the course. My own work in the festival was located off campus, as it entailed bringing the professional staff into the local schools for performances and workshops, and thus I was not visible in that context to the students, although I led the seminars, participated in workshops, and observed at some rehearsals. While this attempt to make myself a "safe" reader was designed to remove the threat of coercive judgment, it made some students feel unsure. One was to write later:

I started hating the journal because it was so surgical, and a little too non-judgmental. I was skipping mentally all over the place and nothing was giving me guidelines that I needed. I was forced to find my own and I did—that was not pleasant although I'm glad now.

He wasn't glad then.

The students who were most vocal in their defense of *currere* that evening were the older ones, less concerned perhaps with coming to form acceptable to parents and peers and more interested in growing to new forms consonant with their own possibilities. But for some of the younger students (in my memory they are legion, though there may have been just two or three) my neutrality was intolerable.

One student demanded to know why I had not come to see him perform in a play that, though it was not associated with the festival, had figured prominently in his early journal entries. I tried to show him that I was not there to share his experience as a close friend or a parent might, to confirm or contradict it with my interpretation but to listen to his interpretation. Had I seen his play, all he would have received was my version, no more or less valid than his own. My responses to the journals were designed to be a vestigial appendage to be dropped whenever the student had internalized my half of the dialectic within himself. Perhaps the time had come, but for some students it was helpful to be heard, as one of the fiercest critics of that evening was to write:

I've become aware that alot has happened to me. Exactly why I want to write in the journal, and not just think to myself is one of the changes. I feel that somehow I'm depositing my mind politically—that wherever my entry goes—at least it goes somewhere, that somehow it meets objectivity. Even if it is a delusion, it makes me think that what I think matters.

I had taken care to diminish the transferences that might have developed had I allowed my interest in their experience and our dialogue to become too important; it was merely instrumental to the development of their own capacity to operate upon their own experience. Yet it could not be denied that my very neutrality and my careful attempts to avoid a coercive, directive voice had become the blank screen upon which their own past relationships and needs had been projected. With that realization I felt sorry for myself, victimized as I had felt during the discussion, seated in the center of a circle of students, trying to hear them and to hold off the images of the stoning scene from *Zorba the Greek* that kept coming to mind. I am compelled to relate my response to this evening, not to make you cringe (assuming that you empathize) but to acknowledge the curriculum and my students' response to it as my situation and to assume responsibility for what I may make of it.

I had offered *currere* and some had returned the gift unopened:

I grow in leaps and fits, my inside has a way of picking up what it needs and integrating. I don't want to write it down often because it's happening, that's why I dance. I try to live my life without drawn out intellectual processes. Mental analysis is another technique to be mastered and forgotten about.

And some had opened the box and put the gift up on the shelf for display but had never used it:

I guess being mature about alot of things has been a main factor in Festival. Maturity in conflict, maturity in working with a piece of art and maturity in working with other people.

And some had tried to use it but had not used the instructions and were understandably annoyed when the thing broke down:

But Festival Theatre—it meant nothing—something, somewhere went wrong—At the beginning of the semester the whole world was mine—yes—but somehow things have slipped away—So Festival Theatre is over and I'm so glad. In some ways it became a pain.

And some, and they never haunt my memory the way the dissenters do, made much more use of the gift than I had ever imagined possible as I was wrapping it for delivery:

In my view, the most appropriate play of the present historical period is the meta-drama, the play conscious of itself, if you will. The cracks in the old realism have increased with time and so theatre must take a greater reality beyond any superficial verisimilitude. The play must take itself as a play, as the interaction of real human beings, only allegedly actors. . . . Action is an integral part of the play equal to the words. Just as words in Shakespeare can produce a continuous series of images, action on the stage today can do the same. Drama becomes poetry in action, word-made flesh. . . . My dramatic view calls for the rejection of all common-sense in giving meaning to a play and in forming aesthetic premises and intuitions. . . . Ultimately any play not founded on philosophical or psychological grounds (in terms of themes and method) is invalid, trite and insulting to the intelligence of audiences. Yes, plays must captivate. But there must be a thinking, feeling willing author behind what finally occurs on stage. . . . So goodnight, ladies and gentlemen. A new phase, a new play is about to occur in my life, hopefully in the future. How about adapting Goethe's *Faust* for the stage: Here we go again. Hold on to your hats.

And from another student:

One thing that happened that I think is an outgrowth from the Festival experience, is that my interest in biology has increased! This may sound strange, but Festival made me expect more from my experience outside theatre as well as that inside theatre. I was wondering whether I could really enjoy bio research. . . . I wanted to do something interesting; not to become one of those narrow professors whose whole life is in a microscope slide. . . . At first it was hard to retain the spontaneity of improvizations in rehearsals, but once the staging became somewhat second nature, I found myself able to experiment within the bounds and regain spontaneity while working in a framework. It was like being in a dark room; at first I was afraid to move, then once I tested out the whole room and got to know it well, I could feel free to roam around fearlessly even though it was still dark . . . I started looking at biology from different angles and found that it's definitely possible to do very exciting research and remain an interesting person as well. I had thought of research as more of a job before, now it can become a stimulating way to spend my life.

Their responses are varied, and are ultimately their concern, not mine. I can only operate on my own. The plays were produced, the workshops ended and the festival receded into the past, providing me with the ground of my next project. I did not see how I could be more directive as a respondent in *currere* without sabotaging its goals, but I did resolve to be more visible—as present and as exposed in my work to my students as they were to me. Subsequently, working with *currere* with teachers-in-training at SUNY at Geneseo, I assumed a more central role, actively teaching the curriculum while at the same time engaging in the dialogue of the journals.

I can no longer relegate distancing to its comfortable place in phenomenological theory and disregard the tension that my students' response to it disclosed. I still identify that tension between the familiar and the strange as the ground for growth, and despite my own sense of vulnerability in the face of their resistance, resolve to continue to ask students to examine their experience of curriculum . . . although I often wish that I could just place "Some of These Days" on the phonograph, attribute its limitations to scratches on the record, the dullness of the needle, lecture on the history of jazz, and leave it at that.

The response of the students to *currere* was my Bouville. It was my situation and in order to transform it, I, too, had to claim it and then estrange myself from it in order to create a new curriculum. This case study of *currere* is part of that process. It is invested with Roquentin's own aspirations, voiced as he waits for the train that will take him from Bouville to Paris, where he hopes to write his book:

A book. Naturally it would only be a troublesome, tiring work, it wouldn't stop me from existing or feeling that I exist. But a time would come when the book would be written, when it would be behind me, and I think that a little of its clarity might fall over my past.

Notes

1. Jean-Paul Sartre, *Nausea*, trans. Lloyd Alexander (New York: New Directions, 1964).

2. Jean-Paul Sartre, *Search for a Method*, trans. Hazel Barnes (New York: Random House, 1963), p. 91.

3. Dwayne Huebner, "The Moribund Curriculum Field: Its Wake and Our Work" (Paper delivered to Division B, American Educational Research Association, San Francisco, Ca., April 1976).

4. Konrad Lorenz and Paul Leyhausen, *The Motivation of Human and Animal Behavior* (New York: Van Nostrand, Reinhold Publishing Co., 1973).

5. Anton Ehrenzweig, *The Psycho-Analysis of Artistic Vision and Hearing* (New York: George Braziller, 1965).

6. Ralph Tyler, *Basic Principles of Curriculum and Instruction* (Chicago: University of Chicago Press, 1950).

7. William Pinar and Madeleine Grumet, *Toward a Poor Curriculum* (Dubuque, Iowa: Kendall Hunt Publishing Co., 1976).

8. In the work of Victor Turner we find an analysis of the structure and function of ritual that is analogous to the distinction between aesthetic function and structure that I am ascribing to curriculum. He describes an Ndembu circumcision ritual, "Mukanda," in *A Forest of Symbols* (Ithaca, N.Y.: Cornell University Press, 1967) showing how ritual experience is distinguished from mundane experience by the ways in which place, action, and symbol are interrelated. Furthermore, he refers to the impact of ritual experience upon the experience of the everyday world that follows it. Another excellent study of the relation of ritual time to mundane time and the way in which ritual experience transforms mundane experience is Godfrey Lienhardt's *Divinity and Experience* (Oxford: Clarendon Press, 1961).

9. John Dewey, "The Existential Matrix of Inquiry," in *Logic, the Theory of Inquiry* (New York: Henry Holt and Co., 1938), p. 35.

10. John Dewey, *Experience and Nature* (1925; reprint ed., LaSalle, Ill.: Open Court, 1971).

11. Ibid., p. 300.

12. Ibid., p. 290.

13. Ibid., p. 294.

14. Gregory Bateson, *Steps to an Ecology of Mind* (New York: Ballantine Books, 1972).

15. Dewey, *Experience and Nature*, p. 291.

16. H. L. Dreyfus and S. J. Todes, "The Three Worlds of Merleau-Ponty," *Philosophy and Phenomenological Research* 22 (1962): 559-65.

17. Johan Huizinga, *Homo Ludens* (Boston: Beacon Press, 1950).

18. Pinar and Grumet, *Toward a Poor Curriculum*.

19. Dewey, *Experience and Nature*, p. 291.

20. Eugene Kaelin, *An Existential Aesthetic* (Madison: The University of Wisconsin Press, 1966).

21. Dewey, *Experience and Nature*, p. 294.

22. José Rosario, "Toward the Aesthetics of Existential Phenomenology:

A Disclosure Model for Curriculum Design" (Ph.D. diss., University of Wisconsin, 1976), p. 220.

23. Hence the failure of millenarian movements, as described in Kenelm Burridge's study, *New Heaven, New Earth* (New York: Schocken Books, 1969).

24. See Pinar's essay "*Currere*: Toward Reconceptualization," in *Curriculum Theorizing: The Reconceptualists*, ed. William Pinar (Berkeley, Ca.: McCutchan Publishing Corp., 1975).

25. Jerzy Grotowski, *Towards a Poor Theatre* (New York: Simon and Schuster, 1968), pp. 58-59.

26. Antonin Artaud, *The Theater and Its Double*, trans. Mary Caroline Richards (New York: Grove Press, 1958).

27. Paulo Freire, *Pedagogy of the Oppressed*, trans. Myra Bergman Ramos (New York: The Seabury Press, 1973).

28. Kenneth Bowers, "Situationism in Psychology: An Analysis and a Critique," *Psychological Review* 80, no. 5 (September 1973): 307-36; Seymour Wapner, Bernard Kaplan, and Samuel Cohen, "An Organismic-Developmental Perspective for Understanding Transactions of Men and Environments," *Environmental Behavior* 5, no. 3 (September 1973): 255-89.

29. Pinar, *Curriculum Theorizing*; ASCD Yearbook, *Schools in Search of Meaning*, ed. James B. Macdonald and Esther Zaret (Washington, D.C.: ASCD, 1975).

30. Samuel Bowles and Herbert Gintis, *Schooling in Capitalist America* (New York: Basic Books, 1976).

31. Lawrence Cremin, *The Transformation of the School* (New York: Alfred A. Knopf, 1961); Bernard Wishy, *The Child and the Republic* (Philadelphia: University of Pennsylvania Press, 1968); Clarence Karier, Paul Violas, and Joel Spring, *Roots of Crisis* (Chicago: Rand McNally and Co., 1973); and Michael Katz, *The Irony of Early School Reform* (Boston: Beacon Press, 1968).

32. Maurice Roche, *Phenomenology, Language, and the Social Sciences* (London: Routledge and Kegan Paul, 1973).

33. Bowers, "Situationalism in Psychology."

34. The work of George Willis and Anthony J. Allen, "Patterns of Phenomenological Response to Curriculum: Implications" (Chapter 3), also scrutinizes students' responses to their immediate experience of curriculum sampled at various intervals during a course. In its emphasis upon autobiography, *currere* requires that phenomenological response to immediate situation be grounded in life-history as well. Its goal is to provide data that is interpreted by the respondent as well as the researcher, and thus the data it gathers is more idiosyncratic and less generalizable than the data collected in the Willis and Allen study.

35. Frederic Ewen, *Bertolt Brecht: His Life, His Art, His Times* (New York: The Citadel Press, 1967).

36. Ibid., pp. 218, 222.

37. See "Psychoanalytic Foundations of *Currere*," in Pinar and Grumet, *Toward a Poor Curriculum*, for a more detailed description of the biphasic process of journal writing and response.

38. Ira Progoff, *At a Journal Workshop* (New York: Dialogue House, 1975), p. 25.

39. See Grotowski's assertion in *Towards a Poor Theatre* that "if something is symmetrical it is not organic" (p. 194), and the exercises that he creates to free the actor from symmetrical patterns of movement.

40. Raymond Firth, *Tikopia Ritual and Belief* (London: George Allen and Unwin, Ltd., 1967).

The essay by William Pinar is the second of the two in this volume that discuss currere, *the analysis of one's lived experience of curricula. The method requires the recollection of one's personal life in schools and provides the opportunity to ponder the future. In carefully examining past and future one can attain a new perspective, a new "biographic place" that may afford new insight about meanings, significances, and causes of action. As Pinar suggests, in examining the particulars of experience in this way,* currere *aspires to cut through to preconceptual experience, which is the basis for distinctly personal meaning.*

Pinar points out that there can be variations within the general method. However, the particular method in the case study he describes focuses on the experience of a university professor who adopts the attitude of a student in reading Sartre's Search for a Method *and who records his salient responses. These responses to a specific text reveal much of his personal and biographic movement over a period of time, including his thoughts on political and social issues. Parts of the study include illustrative passages from Sartre as well as descriptions of the specific responses themselves; other parts principally interpret and disclose meaning about re-*

316

sponses. The exercise is basically autobiographical. Search for a Method *is the course of study, the external curriculum that becomes subsumed into the experiential curriculum of its student.*

The principal critical focal point in the essay is the "audience," but, as Pinar rightly points out, there are dangers in identifying the experience of individuals with this term. "Audience" is an abstraction; it tends to eliminate specific biographic contexts. He suggests it implies too much interest in creating effects, an interest that is morally dubious. Furthermore, the manifestation of a text within the life history of an individual merges perspectives, making the four principal critical focal points one. The study, in this sense and as autobiography, is written from a distinct "point of view" and exemplifies "plot." It is rich in "theme" and contains "metaphor." The dominant interest is in the personal, in how an individual develops meaning within his inward experiential world, but not apart from the external world.

14
Currere: A Case Study

William F. Pinar

This case study has three parts. In the first I want to show how *currere* is related to, and in one sense can be viewed as a form of, curriculum criticism. In the second part I will report the study, and in the third discuss what I see as its significance.

A definitional note. As you recognize, *currere*[1] is the Latin infinitive from which curriculum is derived, and I use it to suggest a particular focus of curriculum study, a focus on one's lived experience of curricula. Instead of examining only the course of study, or one's intentions in designing the course to be run, in *currere* we focus on the running of the course. The course becomes subsumed in, though not reduced to, the experience of the runner. This runner is the teacher or the student (or whoever comes in contact with curricula), although in this present study he is a student (that is to say, he has adopted the attitude of a student), and in particular, a student of Sartre's *Search for a Method.*

Part 1

In his "Curriculum Criticism," John S. Mann begins by linking the concept of curriculum criticism with literary criticism, and with a

318

certain tradition of literary criticism—the New Criticism. He points
out that such criticism "focuses neither on the biography of the
author nor on the effect of the work on the reader, but firmly on the
literary object itself."[2] Mann then suggests that to focus on a curriculum as a literary object is to conceive of it "as a set of selections
from a universe of possibilities."[3] The function of curriculum criticism, he continues, becomes the disclosure of meaning, or the design
of selections.[4] Thus the curriculum critic "discloses meaning by explaining design."[5] The design of curriculum is not independent of
the designer; Mann calls our attention to the role of "personal knowledge" in the formulation of curriculum and curriculum criticism.[6]
The selection of content and the selection of critical focus originates
in personal knowledge.[7] And "the personal knowledge in which the
curriculum critique is grounded is principally knowledge about ethical reality."[8] Here Mann's definition of curriculum alters, or perhaps
only broadens, to include the concept of curriculum as a form of
influence over persons.[9] He discusses a curriculum as "an environing
work of art that conveys meaning."[10] (This sense of curriculum as
environment is reminiscent, as is the discussion of ethical reality, of
Huebner, but an examination of Mann's debt to Huebner is obviously
beyond the scope of this paper.) The concept of curriculum is now a
complex one; it is a literary object; it is in some sense "environing,"
in some sense a context, presumably primarily an intellectual one;
and it is influence. To capture this multidimensional nature of curriculum, Mann suggests that the curriculum critic build "disclosure
models."[11] A disclosure model is contrasted with a picturing model,
which closely resembles the phenomena it portrays. A disclosure
model bears only "certain key structural similarities to the phenomena. . . . Where the picturing model is judged for its static accuracy, the disclosure model is judged for its capacity to continue
generating new propositions that reveal the phenomena."[12] Linking
his focus on design, meaning, and influence, Mann asserts that the
"disclosures of meaning in a curriculum are disclosures about the
character of an influence."[13]

   Mann ends, then, in a different place, intellectually, from where
he began. He has moved from an identification with New Criticism,
with an emphasis "firmly" on the literary object itself, on the curriculum itself, to an emphasis on meaning, influence, and their disclosure. We have begun to move from the material embodiment of

knowledge to those living beings, that is to say, ourselves, who experience material embodiment. George Willis, in his essay on this topic, endorses this movement in its point of view. "However, if we ask the question, 'Whose meaning?' (as eventually we must), we find that the attempt to confine influences totally within the evidence provided by the 'work' itself is strictly impossible."[14] Willis goes on to suggest four focal points of curriculum criticism: the work itself, the author(s) (in this case the curriculum developers), the world, and the audience.[15] This conception usefully extends Mann's and offers the field four possible foci for curriculum research.

Some work that may be categorized under these headings has been done, of course. Illustrative of the first is Donald R. Bateman's discussion of the politics of curriculum, in which he does brief textual analyses.[16] Illustrative of the second, as Willis points out,[17] is some of the work of Decker Walker and, I would add, William A. Reid.[18] Of the third Willis says: "The question ultimately is metaphysical, but insofar as the curriculum is concerned with knowledge, it becomes for the curriculum critic an essentially epistemological one."[19] I would amend only that the epistemological concern at some levels is inseparable from psychosocial and political concerns. Some of the work of Michael Apple,[20] Dwayne Huebner,[21] James Macdonald,[22] Ira Marc Weingarten,[23] Madeleine Grumet,[24] and myself[25] are cases in point. Illustrative of the fourth is a recent paper by George Willis and Anthony J. Allen,[26] as well as the present case study.

I am uneasy thinking of this case study exclusively as a study of the audience and uneasy generally with this perspective, which is a consequence of the focus on design in the field. I will register this disquiet now.

The first objection I have to the concept of "audience" is the same one I have to much theoretical language in the curriculum field. It is its abstractness. To speak of "audience," or "learners," or, recalling Mann's essay, of "meaning" and "influence" is to speak of disembodied phenomena. Thus disembodied, the concepts become meaningless. They have reality when they occur concretely, when they refer to specific individual beings. Take "meaning," for example. A text we are examining in a seminar becomes meaningful, not in general, not to some collective entity we create when we personify abstractions like "class" or "seminar," but to individuals in individual ways. For example, Willa comprehends the dispute between Husserl and Heidegger over the utility and veracity of the "transcendental ego." But this dispute is meaningful to her only as it fits into her biographic context. She may now be aware of a certain "place," a perspective inside herself from which she observes certain of her behaviors. The concept "transcendental ego" acts first as a light in a darkened room as it allows her to become aware of that which had been only preconscious. Then the term becomes a tool; she can use it to refer to this "place," and pay attention to her experience of it. (Do I go there often? Does it feel qualitatively different from the place identified as "natural ego"? Or is this place merely an extension of the natural ego, indicative of its reflexive capacity, as Heidegger would insist?) Only if she is ready to hear these terms, only if she is sufficiently preconscious (or conscious) of these perspectives in herself can the Husserl-Heidegger dispute be meaningful to her. Otherwise, it remains interesting (or uninteresting) information, acquired (not integrated) and usable primarily in academic contexts (discussions of the history of philosophy, of themes in existentialism and phenomenology).

Take the notion of "audience." Who uses such a word? I have come to see a performance of "Uncle Vanya"; it is what I have decided to do this Wednesday night. Here I witness the dilemma of Vanya: what to do with his life, how to regard suffering, how to regard love that is unrequited. Vanya speaks to me. Because I have loved and not been loved, Vanya functions to bring my attention to my pain. Because the pain is there, on stage, in Vanya, I find it more tolerable to attend to it in myself. (Alone, the pain is too frightening to feel much of.) I am not the "audience"; I am myself; I am in biographic context, in the middle of pain and wandering. For the director or performers to think they can know their "effect" on their "audience": this is *hubris*. While we have all suffered, some have refused to suffer consciously any more, and these people refuse to emotionally accept the drama on stage. They discuss only the quality of the set and the shrewdness of this actor's performance. Others, having just overeaten, suffer in the midsummer heat, unable to concentrate on what occurs in front of them. Each responds according to his biographic situation. How can this response be anticipated in any serious way?

This anticipation is the heart of the effort at design, one focus, if not the central focus, of the field. Certainly it is Mann's interest, though it becomes distended and complex. Absorption in design necessitates putting concrete beings into abstract categories like "learner" or "audience." Become abstractions, their biographic realities are forgotten to educational researchers, who tend to view them as admittedly complex variables. Individuals become swallowed up in "learning situations" or "competencies" or the endless series of concepts current in the educational fields. This is my second objection to "audience" (which implies design, and to design, which implies audience). When one is interested in audience, one is interested in effects, and in what environing (think of Mann again) conditions can be designed to make certain intended effects likely to occur. If the curriculum theoretician has accepted this much conceptual baggage, I see only two possible destinations ahead for him. One is a kind of advertising mentality: How can I design these materials in order to make likely the teacher's facile use of them, and the students' tolerance if not enjoyment of them? How can I create a market for this skill, knowledge, or attitude? How can I persuade the audience to buy, to learn? The second possible destination is political manipulation. It differs from the first only in the motive of the designer. The advertiser usually accepts the aims of others, assumes the integrity and utility of the product, and so acts as a technician to make its dissemination effective. The politically manipulative designer is quite conscious of the origins of the product: who thought of it, for what reasons, and for whose benefit? If its intended effects serve the politically dominant classes uncritically, then the designer is said to be conservative; if the effects are somehow allied with the underclasses, then the designer is said to be radical. Both radical and conservative designers have ulterior political motives; both see "audiences"; both live in abstractions.

Because this situation is as prototypical as it is dangerous, I have worked to create a method through which the interested student (be he professor, elementary-school teacher, high-school student, curriculum specialist) may examine his experience of schools and of particular aspects of schools (a particular teacher, a certain book, a mélange of feelings regarding a particular year). The emphasis is on experience. The aspiration is to cut through the layers of superimposed thought to preconceptual experience, which is the ontological ground of all thought.[27] Only by contacting this experience, and continually reestablishing such contact, can one come to have his own thoughts. As it is, we are phantoms filled with others' thoughts,[28] dissociated from our own experience by layers of ideas we acquired in schools and out. Thus severed from our experience, we live in abstractions, identify ourselves in terms of abstractions (like social roles), and, necessarily, project such abstractions onto others. No longer do I see John, Brenda, and Betsy, but a "class," or "students." No longer do I experience my meetings with specific individuals through the medium of certain texts. Instead I teach a class with objectives in mind. I become a functionary in a bureaucratic system for which no one is responsible. This historical situation pervades not only the curriculum field, but it is here you and I live.

This method, which guarantees nothing (it is only a tool you may or may not use effectively), is the regressive-progressive-analytic-synthetic.[29] It is regressive in that it offers the opportunity to recall one's life in schools. You who read this book are probably still in school. Why is that? What is the nature of this involvement? One way to begin to answer this question is to recall and examine your past in schools. It is progressive in that it offers the opportunity systematically to ponder your future. Where does this involvement lead, psychologically, intellectually, socially? Just as dreams disclose waking reality, daydreams can serve to disclose more deeply one's psychic and intellectual investment in educational institutions. It is analytic in that this information, your remembrance of the past and meditative projection of your future, can be examined closely, comments recorded, origins uncovered, current commitments comprehended. It is synthetic in that attending to the present again, from what is now a new intellectual and biographic place, one deciphers anew its significance and sees more clearly one's next steps.

Another method, a variation of which was used in this study, is like the Rorschach test. The text becomes a kind of ink blot in that what I select as interesting, dull, instructive, or pointless is viewed as significant. It is significant because it is what I have selected out of a virtual universe of possibilities in the text. I have selected this passage (this sentence, this paragraph) and not others. Perhaps I found this part distasteful, that part fascinating. Both parts I have selected; both I experience a response to, with both there is a bond. Thus my response binds me to the text, and in this bond lies the educational significance of the text. Its philosophic significance derives from its status in the history of philosophy; its educational importance has to do with my response to it, my uses of it. Like those comprising the audience for "Uncle Vanya," each responds differently, according to his biographic situation. Perhaps one reads *Search for a Method* because a friend recommended it, and one's feeling for a friend is superimposed on the feeling in the text. Perhaps one is overfull from dinner; Sartre's urgency seems *de trop*. And possibly it is his urgency, not his philosophical and political point of view, which interests me, which draws me to him. Sartre, the writer, the one with intentions, cannot know this; like the director of "Uncle Vanya" or the curriculum designer, he is lost in abstraction and illusory omnipotence if he forgets the idiosyncratic uses readers will make of his work. That is why, in earlier papers, I have called for the death of curriculum design as an area of study. Design cannot be done. The more seriously one insists on it, the closer one inevitably moves to political manipulation and to advertising. What can be studied is individual uses of texts, of teachers, of group meetings. This study is *currere,* the running of the course.

In the present case study I have recorded the passages to which I had a noticeable response. Sometimes the reason the passage seemed important occurred to me, and to some degree I recorded these thoughts. These take on a coherence that makes it possible to speak, in a summary way, of how *Search for a Method* functioned for me when I read it on this occasion in 1974. I'll reserve discussion of its function for the third and concluding section of the paper, when I will also discuss in somewhat more detail what I see as the structural relation between reader and text. This relation, while formed with idiosyncratic content, is common to most readers and their texts. Laying bare this relation discloses the meaning of the curriculum and the character of its influence. Disclosure models, as Mann describes, built from curriculum design, are doomed to an abstraction severed from lived reality. By returning to our immediate emotional-intellectual experience of texts, teachers, and milieu, we can criticize the curriculum. I am not suggesting that we abandon Willis's four focal points. Examination of the work itself, the developers, and cultural context (the world, in Willis's scheme) will yield interesting information. But examination of the text's manifestation in the life history of the reader totalizes these three perspectives. It is where the four focal points become one: in the structural relation between he who gives life to the text by reading it, and the text which is thereby made alive. He may be a student, a teacher, author, socio-political critic; regardless of his point of view, it *is* his point of view, and point of view is his response to the text, even if this response is then superimposed on the text. By laying bare individual responses to texts, one lays bare fundamental aspects of the educational process. Thus regarded, curriculum criticism offers us significant theoretical possibilities.

Part 2

Within this variation of the method there are variations. For example, in "Life History and Educational Experience" (a current project), I took the passages to which I responded in Virginia Woolf's *The Voyage Out* and allowed them to organize themselves into themes. Illustrative themes included "relationships," "the social," "music." I wrote brief pieces regarding each theme, focusing, for example, on "The Social in *The Voyage Out.*" Then I wrote a journalistic account of my biographic situation in its concreteness; that is, where I was living, with whom, how my days were spent, what absorbed me. Then, in a final section, I compared what I had seen in the text with what I saw in my situation. The comparison disclosed a dialectical relation. What I saw in the one originated in what I saw in the other. My biographic situation was distilled in my reading of the text, and my reading of the text clearly had its genesis in my biographic situation. Examination of each revealed hitherto hidden aspects of the other.

In the present case study, written a few months earlier than the aforementioned one, I focused exclusively on my response. Pertinent aspects of my biographic situation are revealed as they surface in my response to the text. The text is Sartre's *Search for a Method*; the biographic issues stimulated are political and social ones. (Further discussion of this point is reserved for the third section.)

I have included in the text of this chapter only those passages that relate explicitly to my response. I do so for ease of reading. My initial plan was to leave all the passages that struck me in the main text, perhaps enabling the interested student to discern more completely than I the structural relation between this reader and this text, but the cohesiveness of the essay suffered. At the end of the chapter, therefore, I shall list the page and line numbers of the other passages I was particularly struck by, for those who wish to reconstruct the exercise in its entirety. For present purposes the passages remaining, over half those I was struck by, will suffice. The nature of the text under study is evident from them, and the bond between text and response apparent. The sentences in reduced type, preceded by page numbers, are Sartre's; the others are mine.*

xxxiv   . . . if such a thing as Truth can exist in anthropology; it must be a truth that has *become*, and it must make itself a *totalization*. It goes without saying that this double requirement defines that movement of being and of knowing (or of comprehension) which since Hegel is called "dialectic."

9   We are not only knowers; in the triumph of intellectual self-consciousness, we appear as the *known*.

15   Success, indeed, as an objectification, would enable the person to inscribe himself in things and finally would compel himself to surpass himself.

28   . . . existentialism has been able to return and to maintain itself because it reaffirmed the reality of men. . . . Existentialism and Marxism . . . aim at the same object; but Marxism has reabsorbed man into the Idea, and existentialism seeks him everywhere *where he is*, at his work, in his home, in the street. We certainly do not claim—as Kierkegaard—that this real man is unknowable. We say only that he is now known. If for the time being he escapes knowledge, it is because the only concepts at our disposal for understanding him are borrowed either from the idealism of the Right or from the idealism of the Left.

(I begin to realize that the split between the University and Pearl Street—where I live—between the political-social world of 1974 and spiritual development, between my "calling" and my "development," only appears to exist. One depends upon the other. To withdraw from the university would invite intellectual and psychic collapse; for to do so would be the equivalent of moving from context to vacuum. And yet this work-in-the-world is undeniably contingent upon partial withdrawal, and spiritual work. I cannot face social-political reality unless grounded in my being, unless bulwarked by glimpses of the eternal, the absolute. In this sense, I reflect my generation, and of an age glimpsed, but not yet born.)

30   Far from being exhausted, Marxism is still very young, almost in its infancy; it has scarcely begun to develop. It remains, therefore, the philosophy of our time. We cannot go beyond it because we have not gone beyond the circumstances which engendered it. Our thoughts, whatever they may be, can be formed only upon this humus; they must be contained within the framework which it furnished for them or be lost in the void or retrogress. Existentialism, like Marxism, addresses itself to experience in order to discover there concrete syntheses; it can conceive of these syntheses only within a moving, dialectical totalization which is nothing else but history or—from the strictly cultural point of view which we have adopted here—"philosophy-becoming-the-world." For us, truth is something which becomes, it *has* and *will have* become. It is a totalization which is forever being totalized. Particular facts do not signify anything; they are neither true nor false so long as they are not related, through the mediation of various partial totalities, to the totalization in process.

32, fn. 9   The only theory of knowledge which can be valid today is one which is founded on that truth of microphysics: the experimenter is a part of the experimental system.

33, 34   . . . we support unreservedly that formulation in *Capital* by which Marx means to define his "materialism": "The mode of production of material life generally dominates the development of social, political, and intellectual life."

34   As soon as there will exist *for everyone* a margin of *real* freedom beyond the production of life, Marxism will have lived out its span; a philosophy of freedom will take its place. But we have no means, no intellectual instrument, no concrete experience which allows us to conceive of this freedom or of this philosophy.

35   Why, then, are we not simply Marxists? It is because we take the statements of Engels and Garaudy as guiding principles, as indications of jobs to be done, as problems—not as concrete truths. It is because their assertions seem to us insufficiently defined and, as such, capable of numerous interpretations; in a word, it is because they appear to us as regulative ideas. The contemporary Marxist, on the contrary, finds them clear, precise, and unequivocal; for him they *already* constitute a *knowledge*. We think, on the other hand, that everything remains to be done; we must find the method and constitute the science.

65   Existentialism, aided by psychoanalysis (existential psychoanalysis), can study today only situations in which man has been lost since childhood, for there are no others in a society founded on exploitation.

66   The person lives and knows his condition more or less clearly through the group he belongs to.

71   [Referring to American sociology] Hyper-empiricism—which on principle neglects connections with the past—could arise only in a country whose History is relatively short.

72   Research is a living relation between men. . . . Indeed, the sociologist and his "object" form a couple, each one of which is to be interpreted by the other; the *relationship* between them must be itself interpreted as a moment of history.

76   ... the researcher can be "outside" a group only to the degree that he is "inside" another group—except in limited cases in which this exile is the reverse side of a real act of exclusion.

(Ready to begin part three. What interests me in this? Of course, the book's relation to philosophy, to that field's history, its relation to Sartre's work, and of course, its contents. But the student of education is also even more interested in the effect of the book upon the reader, the relation between the two. What is it that fascinates me, keeps me reading long after my eyes tire? Is it the virtuosity of Sartre's mind, its learning? The cogency of the arguments for my own situation? What is my situation? I live in what is seemingly a post-political spiritual age, yet somehow rooted in the social world of 1974—what does Sartre say of my political responsibilities? Can I know my self by inquiring into my class membership? Is my interest in self and spiritual work a "fetished interiority"?

I am not reducing Sartre to his meaning for me. Sartre is who he is, the book advances the thesis it advances, and I respect that. That is its philosophical importance. But what is its educational significance? In one sense that lies in its philosophic context, its contribution to "modern thought." But for the reader? Its educational significance has to do with the following: (a) it gives me words for what had hitherto been vague and nameless; (b) it illumines an area of my life—political aspects of my social relations—that I was not examining; (c) it therefore widens (the image I have is of a window) my intellectual "gestalt," allowing me to see more of what is at stake in the world, in my life.

To begin to understand the educational significance I must continually "remember myself," not become "absent-minded" (as Kierkegaard accuses Hegel of doing). This can be partially accomplished by returning my attention to myself and my situation. What is the context in which the reading of this book occurs? What are my motives? How do I respond to the print, to the conceptualization? What correspondences exist or do not exist between the issues comprising the book and those comprising my life? I must address myself as well as the text. I must work to awaken, to come out of myself, and converse with myself.)

89   In this sense History, which is the proper work of *all* activity and of *all* men, appears to men as a foreign force exactly insofar as they do not recognize

the meaning of their enterprise (even when locally successful) in the total, objective result.

90   Our historical task, at the heart of this polyvalent world, is to bring closer the moment when History will have *only one meaning,* when it will tend to be dissolved in the concrete men who will make it in common.

133   The object of existentialism—due to the default of the Marxists—is the particular man in the social field, in his class, in an environment of collective objects and of other particular men. It is the individual, alienated, reified, mystified, as he has been made to be by the division of labor and by exploitation, but struggling against alienation with the help of distorting instruments and, despite everything, patiently gaining ground. The dialectical totalization must include acts, passions, work, and need as well as economic categories; it must at once place the agent or the event back into the historical setting, define him in relation to the orientation of becoming, and determine exactly the meaning of the present as such.

137   The meaning of our study must be a "differential," as Merleau-Ponty would call it. It is in fact the *difference* between the "Common Beliefs" and the concrete idea or attitude of the person studied, the way in which the beliefs are enriched, made concrete, deviated, etc., which, more than anything else, is going to enlighten us with respect to our object.

139-140   Thus the heuristic method must consider the "differential" (if the study of a person is concerned) within the perspective of biography. What is involved, we see, is an analytic, regressive moment. Nothing can be discovered if we do not at the start proceed as far as is possible for us in the historical particularity of the object.

145   The sum total of these procedures—regression and cross-reference—has revealed what I shall call the profundity of the lived. Recently an essayist, thinking to refute existentialism, wrote: "It is not man who is profound; it is the world." He was perfectly right, and we agree with him without reservation. Only we should add that the world is human, the profundity of man is the world; therefore profundity comes to the world through man.

146   But the most concrete significations are radically irreducible to the most abstract significations.

146,147   It is then and only then that we must employ the progressive method. The problem is to recover the totalizing movement of enrichment which engenders each moment in terms of the prior moment, the impulse which starts from lived obscurities in order to arrive at the final objectification—in short, the *project* by which Flaubert, in order to escape from the petite bourgeoisie, will launch himself across the various fields of possibles toward the alienated objectification of himself and will constitute himself inevitably and indissolubly as the author of *Madame Bovary* and as that petit bourgeois which he refused to be. This project has *a meaning,* it is not the simple negativity of flight; by it a man aims at the production of himself in the world as a certain objective totality. It is not pure and simple abstract decision to write which makes up the peculiar quality of Flaubert, but the decision to write in a certain manner in order to manifest himself in the world in a particular way; in a word, it is the particular signification—within the framework of the contemporary ideology—

which gives to literature as the negation of his original condition and as the objective solution to his contradictions. To rediscover the meaning of this "wrenching away from toward . . ." we shall be aided by our knowing all the signifying planes which he has traversed, which we have interpreted as his footprints, and which have brought him to the final objectification. We have the series: as we move back and forth between material and social conditioning and the work, the problem is to find the *tension* extending from objectivity to objectivity, to discover the law of expansion which surpasses one signification *by means of* the following one and which maintains the second in the first. In truth the problem is to invent a movement, to re-create it, but the hypothesis is immediately verifiable; the only valid one is that which will realize within a creative movement the transverse unity of *all* the heterogeneous structures.

148, 149   We shall define the method of existentialist approach as a regressive-progressive and analytic-synthetic method. It is at the same time an enriching cross-reference between the object (which contains the whole period as hierarchized significations) and the period (which contains the object in its totalization). In fact, when the object is *rediscovered* in its profundity and in its particularity, then instead of remaining external to the totalization (as it was up until the Marxists undertook to integrate it into history), it enters immediately into contradiction with it. In short, the simple inert juxtaposition of the epoch and the object gives way abruptly to a living conflict.

(By page 156 I see I am losing myself to him. I hold myself in abeyance, in order to merge with him, see with him, as much as possible. Yet, in so doing, I forget myself, and begin unconsciously to see myself through Sartre's eyes. I become uneasy, unsettled; I feel profound, insightful, in fact superior—but it is not my profundity I feel, nor my superiority. The uneasiness confirms suspicion; it is Sartre's profundity and superiority I feel. By neglecting myself, I've given myself over to him.)

156, 157   The supreme mystification of positivism is that it claims to approach social experience without any a priori whereas it has decided at the start to deny one of its fundamental structures and to replace it by its opposite. It was legitimate for the natural sciences to free themselves from the anthropomorphism which consists in bestowing human properties on inanimate objects. But it is perfectly absurd to assume by analogy the same scorn for anthropomorphism where anthropology is concerned. When one is studying man, what can be more exact or rigorous than to *recognize human properties in him*? . . . A positivist who held on to his teleological color blindness in practical life would not live very long.

161   And if in the course of reading the book, we do not constantly go back (albeit vaguely and abstractly) to the desires and ends—that is, to the total enterprise—of Flaubert, we simply make a fetish out of the book (which often happens) just as one may do with a piece of merchandise by considering it as a thing that speaks for itself and not as the reality of a man objectified through his work.

179   Marxism will degenerate into a non-human anthropology if it does not reintegrate man into itself as its foundation.

180   It is necessary that the questioner understand how the questioned—that is, himself—*exists his alienation*, how he surpasses it and is alienated in this very surpassing.

I must read *Search for a Method* again before I write seriously about it or about me in relation to it. But, after a first reading, I can acknowledge this: my respect for the book, and for the mind that conceived it. Its clarity, scope, and pertinence are. . . .

I was dazed after reading it. It took me up, pulled and submerged me in its current and depth, then left me ashore, unable to walk. On the beach I sat for two days, unable to read or concentrate.

I had had the wind knocked out of me. I had taken the book on its own terms, that is, without clearly defined motives or intentions, without an assessment already in mind. What I brought was uncritical attention.

The attention required effort at first, as if I had to extend myself to get to the flow, to immerse myself in the current, as if it required swimming across it to get to the center and leave my own. (Not that one ever leaves one's center completely. But mind does have its characteristic ways of working, whether associatively or critically, and these ways must be put aside, poised in a sense, to follow his lead, his dance.) After twenty or so pages, it gradually took hold of me, and I went with it, without will.

What I saw in the water . . . that Sartre is convinced of the veracity of his point of view. This conviction is expressed noncognitively; it is in the weight of the words, and their movement. He understands, not only his situation, but that of the Western world as well. This—now it feels like pretension—is tempered by two points of modesty: one in the closing lines of the preface, the other in this conclusion. But if he believes what he writes about the "provisional" nature of the "solutions" he offers or his characterization of his capabilities as "modest," he forgets them in the book's center, as he reaches the middle of his argument. For, while it is an argument and by its nature admits of another perspective sufficiently threatening (not necessarily in the psychological sense) to warrant combat, it reads like a statement of fact. And I was persuaded, not really "rationally" or logically, but intuitively; his conviction entered unchallenged my defenseless (in a psychological sense) mind, partly by conceptual content (I am in deep sympathy with the existentialist aspects of his argument, and to a lesser but still significant degree, with its Marxist aspect), but more so by power and weight of the words.

That is, stripped of their denotative, even connotative meanings, they have a certain presence. They move swiftly, yet they are weighty; they feel precise, but not as if they were carefully chosen (or carelessly, for that matter); rather as if they came quickly to Sartre. It had taken years in embryo, but now that the time was proper, they came rapidly, and effortlessly, and most importantly, as truth. Not that their semantic meanings are true, in some objective, incontestable sense, but they have the force and ring of truth.

This vibration became my own, and I became it; I become meshed with the print, identified with it. Again, I am not discussing the cognitive content, the semantic point of view, but the presence of the words and the presence "behind" them. I felt a similar assurance about my own opinions superimposed upon my own intellectual gestalt. I experienced nearly absolute confidence in the legitimacy of this project, of my views on the people met here, on the necessity for remaining in the public social and political world; and as for my "dropped-out" contemporaries (who figure so prominently among my friends), well, they are simply wrong. I feel not that their points of view differ from mine (and in explicable ways given their psychological experience), but that they are wrong. That there exists, somehow in the way that this book exists, truth about the historical situation of the Western world; and that while truth is "becoming" and a "totalization," and hence is never finally known, yet it is, to a degree contingent upon our evolutionary status, *knowable*. Everything is not a matter of point of view; there is truth, and it is, to an extent, knowable. And Sartre knows it, and so do I.

Two days have passed, this sense has passed also. I am (again) persuaded that all that exists is subjectivity, and that the order of knowing that Sartre and many others claim is not objective, certainly not in this age, perhaps not in any age.

It is true, some would say, that philosophers have "resolved" the subjective-objective split and tension, and that Sartre is one of these. Yet it is not solved for me, and a transplanted, strictly cognitive solution is no solution at all. This has been one of educators' mistakes, of course: believing that puzzles such as this one can be "finished" logically, rationally, vicariously, by reading someone else's solution. But puzzles must be *lived,* and any solution that comes will be an existential one, an experienced one, not just a thought one.

So it is that I must fend off *Search for a Method,* at least its self-assuredness. I am not yet there, and the student must always travel to his own rhythm. There is always the temptation to "become one like many": to give oneself to another, to others, to make Sartre's point of view my own. One's views, one's opinions are then never entirely one's own. There is a superficial safety here; what one thinks is predicated upon authority; there is, however misconstrued, an external verification. But, while one finds a prop, one loses oneself, and one becomes, however complex, however avant-garde, an automaton, a one-dimensional presence.

There is, of course, another danger in the opposite direction, which I find common among many of my contemporaries, although hardly restricted to them. It is a refusal, rigid and seemingly final, to lend oneself to another, to give up oneself enough to attend uncritically to another. Evidently born of betrayed trust in studying, in fact in the cultivation of the intellect, one reads to pass the time, to escape in pleasantly drawn sketches of fantasy, but not to advance oneself, to conceptualize one's situation and that of the social context. It is true that, for many, the conceptual hides the *lebenswelt,* and abstraction is built upon abstraction, arresting biographic movement. It is true that these preconceptual realms are atrophied in peoples of advanced industrial nations like the United States. It is true that, given the present historical situation, it is this preconceptual dimension that must be attended to, and nurtured. And it is true that this often involves the suspension of schooling and what is known today as education.

All of this is true, as the generation born in the late 1940s and early 1950s attests. But the danger is that the mind will be abandoned, and while becoming perhaps "like children in the kingdom of God," one falls prey to abduction into political hell.

I'm not convinced that spiritual or psychic development prohibits the training and development of the mind. Certainly it prohibits idolatry of the intellect, but surely psychic evolution would welcome an assistant who describes, explains, and criticizes that evolution, perhaps helps keep it on course. Such a role for the intellect is akin to its role in some stream-of-consciousness writing, like Vir-

ginia Woolf's. It is the conceptualization of the *lebenswelt*; it is codified knowledge that never severs its relation to, in fact, its roots in,
lived experience.

Such a relation is maintained, even heightened, by continual yet
balanced focusing on it. One probes the correspondences between
Search for a Method and one's biographic situation. By attending to
the relation, to the correspondence, one observes the dialectic that is
the movement between knowledge and being. One can give oneself to
the other, to be moved downstream, to have downstream illumined,
as well as upstream. Where one has been, and where one will be are
both embedded in the present, in this experience of a text.

I'm conflicted. Is it true, as Sartre insists, that Marxism will be
surpassed only after everyone has economic and political freedom?
Or is the goal not certain economic and political circumstances but
instead individual enlightenment, proper conduct, regardless of one's
"station in life"? Or is this only a disguised apology for the comfortable? My experience says no. Yet I am attracted to Sartre's view.

12 January 1974. It is true, I'm thinking today, that at the developmental level we're now on, environmental conditions are nearly
in control, and hence the Marxist analysis, as Sartre indicates, is accurate and not surpassed. Yet, according to what I'll temporarily characterize as a biographic perspective (which later I must differentiate
from what Sartre and others dismiss as "subjective idealism"), re-
arrangement of material conditions is no final solution. (Perhaps
Sartre would agree.) It may—in fact, it will most likely—push us to
another historical point, but at that time we must begin "inner
work" in earnest. For according to this biographic view, all human
environmental structures (i.e., the means of production) are just that,
manifestations of (inner) human reality. It is true that at this historical point we are sufficiently externalized to be significantly contingent upon and formed by these manifestations, and these have developed, as it were, a "life" (or antilife) of their own, that restructuring
them would result in certain inner as well as material changes
(perhaps improvements). But because at some level human material
reality pours from internal human reality, and in fact the two are one
at some level, it is internal reality that finally must be attended to.
Thus it seems useful to me to focus on the individual and his experience of material forms, such as texts, such as curricula.

This morning, as I contemplated writing, I (again) experienced resistance. One explanation (others are the psychological—insufficient self-assurance, or the uneasiness of confrontation with a "new" field, one without precedents) is the following. Perhaps there exists a *balance* between conceptual and non- (or pre-) conceptual work, which if ignored or disrespected, pushes one more into ideation on the one hand and thoughtlessness on the other. Or into knowledge which, without roots in the preconceptual, is uprooted from experience, alienated, abstracted, or into a primitive, perhaps unconscious, experience of self and others. It is tension, this dialectic, between knowing and being that must be maintained. And such maintenance involves a certain balance.

The reading of *Search for a Method* was so intense, and my cerebral work generally so involving, that I need to dwell in the preconceptual with as little cerebral intrusion as possible for the next few days. I'll try to attend to this possible aspect of "resistance" in the future for verification.

Somewhere in his "In Praise of Philosophy," Merleau-Ponty notes that one cannot separate oneself from others in such a way as to avoid responsibility for what occurs in the public world. The actual sentence is: "While we live with others, no judgment of ours on them is possible which exempts us and separates us from them." I see I've interpreted it in a special way. Somehow I must begin to describe the relation of the individual to the collective. And it is this relation that I do not understand.

13 January 1974. Reading, skimming mostly (except for the section "Normal Appearances," which I read carefully) Erving Goffman's *Relations in Public*. It's light reading in contrast to Sartre. Certainly due to itself, its own objective weight and profundity. But due as well to its timeliness for me.

Because it doesn't speak to me in the depth of my current situation (as did *Method*; I must explore systematically matters of "speaking," "depth," "situation"; the latter Sartre uses, of course, somewhat differently) I read it curiously, with interest, but with detachment. I am able to put it aside as I wish, to take more coffee, to walk to the commissary, yet I am not bored (although at times, in the first sections, I bordered on that). I say that "it interests me," and I reflect on the strangeness of the anthropological and sociological language, amused by it (it seems so formal, even awkward, but I know it's no more so than the language my own work must seem to certain others). Its language is not my own, and the focus is not my own. It interests me, but does not speak to me; it is information acquired, but not light on my darkness.

Notes on context. Biographic. I'm twenty-six years old, and like many of my generation, have lost faith in established modes of living in this country, in achievement, competition, consumption, but I am not free of them, of course. We fight them, pretend to ignore them, live in a sense a life denied. We focus on the personal, on the spiritual, on constructing affirmative ways of conducting life. For those to whom politics remains an interest, the interest seems suspended. Nineteen seventy-three has been a year of suspension, of private pursuits, and vague awareness of politics in the distance. What my training groomed me for—"responsibility in public life, leadership"—tastes odd now, and visions of it resemble dreams—present but unreal, indicative of something deep but left unanalyzed, unconfronted. In fact the past few years I've . . . not exactly run from it, but at the least looked the other way, and that other way has to do with preconceptual matters. How I am in the present moment, what my presence is to me nonconceptually: this takes my attention. In a word, I focus on the concrete: the body, food, the feel of moving through space. I don't know what these abstractions and dreams—leadership for example—can mean for me now, what form they may take, what the nature of the future will be.

What I do think I know is that whatever future there is, is contingent upon the present. If I cannot live peacefully and understandingly in the present, I cannot hope to so live in some imagined future. So I turn to the present as I can.

This realization leads to a commitment to spiritual work. I attempt to "work on myself," to borrow technique and theory of spiritual development. I am advised to quiet the mind, to limit my intake of new information, and to work manually, to live concretely. So a split develops.

There is the university; it is conceptual work, rooted in public history, and it pulls at what I try to extinguish: striving, role-defined behavior, consumption (of information, of material goods). Yet it is my past; it is where and how I came of age. Since age six I have lived my life in schools.

There is my life outside the university, and there my friends are nonacademic, drop-outs from Yale, from Sarah Lawrence, from the state university, my kindred spirits in many ways. Yet there is a distance. They are living the life; they've left the old; they work in restaurants, as painters, as drivers of school buses; they insist they are not distant from me, and I acknowledge that this experience of distance is partly my own construction, my own psychological defense. But I insist it is in part objective; I do spend much of my working day with books, reading, studying, writing, with people who come to ask questions, who tell answers, who respond to me as "Dr." or "Professor," who respond to my position, not to me. The part of me that is employed is not the visceral, not the concrete, but the abstract and the ideational. This life involves a certain ontology, one characterized by the preeminence of the conceptual, the verbal, by role, although the physical and the sexual speak quite audibly from the background from time to time.

It involves a narrowing of focus, a following of pieces in puzzles, references to this writer, to another related one, related in a certain way for certain reasons. References connected so as to reveal aspects of a gestalt from which they come, a field of study, a discipline, and into which I attempt to pour my own gestalt. All of it is extraordinarily mental, demandingly mental, and at times so exclusively so that the surfacing of emotion, the fatigue of one's body, become quite recognizable, recalling other "parts" of myself to myself, parts that had been absent to myself and to others. I am split in my office, despite my efforts to remember the whole, be in the whole, and both the split and the forgetting of it worry me, and these preoccupations are what make me distant from my friends at home.

They deny that they live wholly, and I believe them; they suffer, and I know they do. But somehow it is different. Do they wear less on the surface? Is the wear less strong, less insistent? Somehow I experience myself as more plagued than I experience them; yes, this is it, this is what constitutes the experience of distance.

(The writing comes "furiously"—in intensity and in emotion—and it's this quality that persuades me I've penetrated a, if not the, central issue of my biographic present.)

In a certain sense the university as "place" can be said to cause this split I refer to, but in another sense it is a consequence of self. True, it is a function of training and conditioning, but those aspects of my life at the university that feel conditioned can be isolated, and I find they are peripheral. They involve a certain hurriedness, a certain mechanical quality, a certain abruptness—but only the surface of these. Deeper down they come from internalized culture, and so it is conditioning endowed with ontological status; it is presence now; I can no longer dismiss it as "conditioning." So that it seems more plausible, and certainly more profound, to say that everything observable, while of course having a relation to conditioning and to the complex stimuli of place, emanates from within. That it is manifestation, a disclosing of self, a self at once conditioned and material, and free and transcendent. So the question becomes not, How is my split and estrangement a function of present circumstances, but How is it an expression of my inner reality? How is my public personage a reflection of private self? (For Sartre and Heidegger the two are identical; they deny Husserl's imagery of a transcendental ego as well as a social ego. I think I concur absolutely, but relatively: on this level of analysis, a distinction between inner and outer, between a transcendent and public ego, is useful.)

Part 3

I am writing this third section, as I did the first, during the summer of 1976, two and one-half years after the writing of what is now the second section. The biographic issue that absorbed me then I view now as one of self-differentiation and integration. The task asked me, partly, to differentiate myself from, at one pole, my academic colleagues, and at the other, my generational and spiritual contemporaries. The integrative task was the cohering of the self-experienced-at-the-university and the self-experienced-at-home. The former was primarily an intellectual, cerebral self, the latter a physical-spiritual and primarily nonconceptual self. (This dissociation of intellect from body and spirit is, interestingly, what I still am quick to discern in others and in their work.) In the last two and one-half years there has been considerable movement on these issues, or *through* these issues. At the university, I experience still, though decidedly less intensely, a self more cerebral, more rushed, than I do at home. Yet the body is more present at the office, and my intellect more fluidly operative at home. The continuum, with intellect at one end and body-spirit at the other, is a shorter one. I experience myself as less vulnerable to my generational contemporaries *and* to my

academic colleagues. The fundamental issue (another form of which
is: what is the spiritual status of my academic work, and what is the
political status of my spiritual work) remains, but is much diminished in intensity, and other issues comprise my present.

I attribute this movement in part to conscious attention to my
experience. Correspondingly, historical movement is similarly
related, possibly causally, to conscious adherence to experience.
Sartre acknowledges this when he criticizes contemporary Marxism
for absorbing "man into the Idea." In contrast, "existentialism seeks
him everywhere *where he is.*" The concreteness of individual beings,
each with his own experience, is lost to abstractions like "class struggle," "proletariat," and "learners," "audience," even "curriculum."
The historical charge is to return, repeatedly, consciously, to one's
experience, and in experience to become increasingly conscious of it,
rendering it visible by translating it into conceptual form. For the
curriculum field this means the abandonment of "design," and a
return to "educational experience." But not to some disembodied,
free-floating substance termed "experience"; to *your* experience,
your experience of reading this now (what are you feeling? what are
you thinking?), sitting in that chair in that room with the tempera-
ture a bit cool—in short, to your experience of your bodily presence.
This is your response to the text; you are the "audience." Do you see
how impossible this conception is? You are not something general
and diffuse like "audience" or even "reader"; you are Janet, Madeleine, or Paul. You can begin to return to the concrete, to experience, by honoring that experience, by giving it time and space.
Record your response to what you read now. What does it make you
think of? These thoughts reveal, perhaps obtusely, what absorbs you
now, what constitutes, at least in part, your biographic situation,
which is distilled into your response to a text.

This is the structural relation between reader and text I alluded
to earlier. You may be pleased or alarmed, confirmed or made vulnerable by what you read. This response pours out of, as it were,
your biographic place, what you are working at now, probably what
you are committed to intellectually in the curriculum field. As you
attend to your experience of the text, the text becomes smaller in a
way; it becomes, in a sense, a pretext for attention to your own
issues. These issues, given intellectual form in, say, a critique of this
case study, become a kind of superimposition upon the text.

Such agency is illustrative of the complex nature of "influence." Recall that Mann writes of his interest in disclosing "the character of an influence"; this disclosure is a, if not the, primary function of curriculum criticism as he conceives it. "Influence" connotes an almost linear relation from A (text) to B (reader), suggesting that the text acts on and possibly transforms the reader. This is (can be— the reader must be open to transformation) accurate but incomplete. Just as importantly, we see from the present study, the reader acts on the text and transposes it into the musical key that is his biographic situation. The text can take on even an ancillary role; it served as a catalyst to the previously dormant chemical composition that was one's unconscious present. (Dormant in the sense of unconscious.) There may be a somewhat explicit conceptual link between text and response, but it seems reasonable to assume there may be only a tangential relation (from a logical point of view) between the two. Whether the relation be explicit conceptually or not, I think it is evident, cannot be adduced beforehand. To attempt to do so can only lead to blurring of the potential biographic functions of reading, studying, listening, and talking.

While my response may be philosophically irrelevant, such a judgment is pertinent itself only inside a philosophy class. Educationally the significance of *Search for a Method* is my response to it, is the way I use it to illumine my darkness, and so lighted, move into unexplored rooms, issues whose meeting, acknowledgment, and resolution depend upon resolution of the temporally and developmentally subsequent ones. Thus the personal knowledge in which "the selection of content and critical focus originates" is not "principally knowledge about ethical reality," as Mann maintains. It *is* about ethical reality, but on a deeper level it is about life history and direction, about biographic issues and movement. And so, finally, must curriculum criticism be also.

Deletions from *Search for a Method*

1. xi, lines 9-17.
2. xi, lines 20-24.
3. xviii, lines 30-35 and xix, lines 1-5, and lines 25-36.
4. xxi, lines 20-25.
5. xxii, lines 15-17.
6. xiii, lines 11-18.
7. xxviii, lines 20-23.
8. xxix, lines 26-31.

9. xxxiv, lines 25-30.
10. 9, lines 8-10.
11. 11, lines 18-28.
12. 15, lines 30-33.
13. 72, lines 25-33 and 73, lines 1-26.
14. 75, lines 8-13.

Notes

1. For background on the use of this term, see *"Currere*: Toward Reconceptualization," in *Curriculum Theorizing: The Reconceptualists*, ed. William Pinar (Berkeley, Ca.: McCutchan Publishing Corp., 1975), and "Self and Others," in *Toward a Poor Curriculum*, ed. William Pinar and Madeleine Grumet (Dubuque, Iowa: Kendall Hunt, 1976).
2. John S. Mann, "Curriculum Criticism," in Pinar, *Curriculum Theorizing*, p. 134. (This article appears as chapter 4 of this volume.)
3. Ibid., p. 135.
4. Ibid., p. 136.
5. Ibid.
6. Ibid., p. 138.
7. Ibid.
8. Ibid.
9. Ibid., p. 145.
10. Ibid., p. 140.
11. Ibid., p. 143.
12. Ibid.
13. Ibid., p. 145.
14. George Willis, "Curriculum Criticism and Literary Criticism," *Journal of Curriculum Studies* 7, no. 1 (1975): 9. (This article appears as chapter 5 of this volume.)
15. Ibid., pp. 9-12.
16. Donald R. Bateman, "The Politics of Curriculum" in *Heightened Consciousness, Cultural Revolution, and Curriculum Theory* ed. William Pinar (Berkeley, Ca.: McCutchan Publishing Corp., 1974).
17. Willis, "Curriculum Criticism," p. 11.
18. William A. Reid and Decker F. Walker, eds., *Case Studies in Curriculum Change* (London and Boston: Routledge & Kegan Paul, 1975).
19. Willis, "Curriculum Criticism," p. 11.
20. "Scientific Interests and the Nature of Educational Institutions," in Pinar, *Curriculum Theorizing*.
21. "Poetry and Power: The Politics of Curricular Development," in Pinar, *Curriculum Theorizing*.
22. "Curriculum and Human Interests," in Pinar, *Curriculum Theorizing*.
23. "Shangri-La and the Big Burger" (manuscript available from the author, School of Education, University of North Carolina at Greensboro, Greensboro, North Carolina 27412).
24. "Existential and Phenomenological Foundations of *Currere*" and "Psychoanalytic Foundations of *Currere*" in Pinar and Grumet, *Toward A Poor Curriculum*.

25. "Heightened Consciousness, Cultural Revolution, and Curriculum Theory," in Pinar, *Heightened Consciousness*.

26. See chapter 3 of this volume.

27. Maurice Merleau-Ponty, *Phenomenology of Perception* (London: Routledge & Kegan Paul, 1966).

28. See David Cooper, *The Death of the Family* (New York: Pantheon, 1971), and Friedrich Nietzsche, *The Dawn of Day*, trans. J. M. Kennedy (New York: Gordon Press, 1974).

29. See "The Method of *Currere*," in Pinar and Grumet, *Toward a Poor Curriculum*, for a more detailed description. See also Pinar, "Life History and Educational Experience," in ibid., for a comprehensive exposition.

The case study by David Jenkins describes a week-long residential course at the London Business School offered to members of industrial and business firms responsible for collective bargaining. The role Jenkins plays in evaluating the course is what he calls "participant observer"; he had paid tuition and enrolled as a student in the course, going so far as to keep his real purposes concealed so as not to "blow his cover." The criticism he writes, therefore, is very much an insider's personal perspective.

In many specifics the way the study is written reflects this perspective. Description is rich with detail and incident. Disclosure of meaning flows directly from the observations of the narrator. Judgment is relatively indirect, and when explicit, it is often understated. There are two prevailing "metaphors" in the study, drawn from the theater and from the Bible. The narrator's "point of view" is particularly important in selection of the incidents that comprise the "plot" and in his elaborately drawn characterizations of the two LBS faculty members who jointly organize and teach the course. The dominant interest in the study is personal to the extent that Jenkins is both participant in and interpreter of the action.

Both the aesthetic and the political dimensions of curriculum

343

criticism are present as well, however. Jenkins's description of the course includes a contrast between the differing intentions, content, and methods of the two instructors. In this sense the study is of the coherence of the overall form of the course. When dealing with both the intended and the unintended effects of the course on himself and other students, especially the social conceptions embodied in the course and some of the social uses to which the course might be put, Jenkins's suggestions are rather telling.

The principal critical focal points in the study are "work" and "author"—the course itself and the LBS faculty members who create it. While less emphasis is placed by the narrator on his reactions than on the course itself, the narrator also represents "audience." Several of the suggestions made within the political dimension of the study focus on how the course reflects "world."

15

Business as Unusual: The "Skills of Bargaining" Course at LBS

David Jenkins

The visitor to London Business School has an immediate impression of the theatricality of its setting. The elegant Nash façade overlooks Regent's Park at a discreet distance from London Zoo and its Snowdon bird house. Its white pepper-pot turrets crown a columned façade. Only later, viewing the flat cardboard cutout ballustrades from inside a window, does the visitor realize that the façade is a set piece of stage decor for the LBS street theater. It masks a briskly functional building. This inner sanctuary is littered with monuments of the outer magnificence, however, and the pepper-pots reappear in print, etching, and oils, alongside last year's European Executive Class, headprefects all. Yet London Business School is sufficiently nervous to call itself the London *Graduate* School of Business Studies. In one of its courses a lecturer was billed as hailing from Manchester University. She turned out to be a fresher with extremely interesting experience as an official in Clive Jenkins's white-collar union, ASTMS. Her contribution was worthy, but belied her billing.

Behind LBS is a car park that fronts a gray Victorian terrace, separate from the main building. Wooden steps offer access into this rabbit warren of Dickensian England, a maze of tiny interconnecting rooms. This is the below-stairs life of LBS, where the aspirations of

tomorrow's young turks are nurtured amid the architecture of yesterday.

The main reception area, of course, is not found among these
relatively seedy tenements. Visitors park their cars, then approach
the main building, which they enter after passing through an arched
Italianate screen. London Business School was founded in 1965 with
both government and business support to become, quite self-
consciously, a "center of excellence." Its problem isn't the excellence of the center but the centrality of the excellence.

In the main building, his carpeted and leather-chaired office
looking like a librarian's annex, his desk an issues desk piled with
recent publications, lives Andrew Gottschalk, lecturer in industrial
relations. Course brochures refer to Andrew as "a psychologist who
has specialised in industrial relations and has been closely involved in
the study of negotiating behaviour." Andrew has observed and evaluated plant productivity agreements, and most of his publications
cluster in the IR area. Although by no means innumerate, Andrew
represents a kind of literate establishment inside LBS, his approach
aspiring toward theoretical insights and shrewd practical judgment.
Andrew was director of the LBS residential course entitled Skills of
Bargaining and Negotiation. It is this short course that is the subject
of my account.

Another protagonist in our drama is Philip Boxer, director of a
computer-assisted learning unit at LBS. Philip is young, watchful,
nerve-racked, and angular as a hairpin, but quite exceptionally bright
and determined to make his mark through promoting what might,
not unfairly, be described as a "pedagogical invention." Like many
curriculum developers on short-term contracts, Philip's institutional
status is marginal. He lives with a little band of researchers high up in
the Victorian terrace, his eyrie wallpapered with computer printouts
and conceptual models. Anybody telephoning the unit cannot be put
through by the main switchboard and is told to dial a new number.
Philip enjoys music as well as cybernetics, is interested in cognitive
psychology as well as cost structures. His father is an inventive car-
toonist.

Philip's own "invention" is a package that applies computers to
management education in two ways. The first is a simulation exercise, usually known to man and computer alike as EX-SIM. This is a
simulation of a "decision-making environment" inhabited by com-

peting managers, trade union officials, and others. In the Skills of Bargaining course, EX-SIM was an exercise called *Ball Bearings Ltd.* A succession of decisions in time (called "rounds," as in professional wrestling) allows the managers to live with the consequences of their actions. The second part of the invention, which is a prime interest in this report, is a feedback process unsurprisingly called FDBACK. The purpose of feedback is to give managers access to their own and other people's perceptions of problems and events. The emphasis is on explaining concepts.

The simulation exercise and the feedback game have been tried out in a variety of institutional settings (the LBS Marketing course, the Communication course, the Unilever technical courses, the Shell course, and the Coal Board Advanced Management course as well as on the Skills of Bargaining course that I attended as participant observer).

The Skills of Bargaining course employed a variety of approaches. At its core stood the simulation exercise *Ball Bearings Ltd.,* in which students played internal roles (like production manager or skilled workers' steward) in one of four firms competing in a market. FDBACK, the conceptual game, was the geological bedrock of the course. It outcropped at several points, and was not simply tied into EX-SIM. Both EX-SIM and FDBACK require introductory and debriefing sessions, and these were conducted by Philip. Andrew's instructional role was more general, comprising a pegging out of the territory conceptually, a survey of the literature, including his own, and retrospective analysis of videotape in the CCTV suite. Andrew's talks had titles like "The Management of the Bargaining Table." In addition, a number of prestigious visitors passed through, sometimes hurrying to their next class on what seemed a round of one-off performances. These included Roger Graef with his "Space between Words" film series, Brian Towers talking of his experiences as an arbitrator in the government's Arbitration Conciliation and Advisory Service (ACAS), Professor Walter Reid discussing "inflation accounting" and the implications of the Sandilands Report for collective bargaining, Roy Moore of the Ruskin College Trade Union Research Unit offering a critique of managerial attitudes toward disclosure of commercial information in collective bargaining, and Professor Albeda giving an account of "the Dutch experience" in conciliation and mediation. (It is, of course, possible to question the overall shape of the offering. "I wonder who Walter is filling in for?" queried an inside contact of mine whose sense of anomaly tripped over the wires linking industrial bargaining with inflation accounting.)

FDBACK is an interesting element in the mixed pedagogy. What it purports to offer is a kind of formalized account of the personal constructs used by people on both sides of the bargaining table. What students actually got from FDBACK in the Skills of Bargaining course was a computer printout indicating the degree of association between concepts as used by the different negotiating parties. I don't want to say too much at this point, in the hope that readers will experience the same kind of mild confusion faced by managers when FDBACK is introduced. Suffice it to say that lying behind it is Kelly's theory of personal constructs; that it depends on using *concepts* to differentiate between previously agreed upon *elements* in a situation; and that it depends technically on the creation of concepts and elements, their ranking, and a computer printout (sometimes in the form of a dendogram, or "tree diagram") analyzing the ranking information.

There is, however, an air of mystique about FDBACK. Like most games, it is learned in play more readily than through explanation. Those who understand it technically and argue about such things as the relative merits of product-moment and rank-order correlation may fail to have any real sense of its *educational* potential; those who find it exciting in use may be puzzled by its epistemological status, particularly as claims on its behalf differ wildly. At times it is presented as a "computerized scratch pad," almost a way of allowing managers to produce collaborative doodles on their mental life. At other times it is sold hard as an X-ray photograph of particular minds at work, using Kelly's theory of personal constructs as the plate. Paradoxically, this may not matter. Like the Tarot pack, its significance depends upon *interpretation* and *use*.

This account traces the use of FDBACK in the Skills of Bargaining course. I want to look at it from two perspectives: first, as it was perceived by course members, particularly myself. (Although playing a covert role as an educational evaluator, I had full and generous access to course gossip.) Secondly I want to treat it as an arena for the clash of opposing world views, for Boxer and Gottschalk might be said to be operating conflicting pedagogies; behind the performance lies a dialectic.

The dilemma of any course using a mixed pedagogy is that the coherent assumptions of one part of a course might suddenly appear dysfunctional in another. The Skills of Bargaining course employed a bewildering variety of approaches, from straight instruction through seminar work and retrospective coaching to the "independent" learning in the games, where the conceptual structuring is done by the student himself. Such variety is welcome at one level. Students found it a pleasurable aspect of a complex and demanding course. But if we press the point a little, two radically different pedagogical styles emerge. Philip Boxer's part of the course (if it can be described thus) and Andrew Gottschalk's are visibly cobbled together out of conflicting approaches. Andrew aspires towards the Oxbridge tutor/seminar leader role. ("Learn from me," he seems to be saying.) Philip repudiates most of the advantages of ordinary introduction and explanation, sacrificing these on the altar of a purist theory of independent learning that he calls "going for broke," scarcely the motto of the natural compromiser.

Since Philip's purist theory of independent learning is the wooden horse inside Andrew's Trojan citadel, it might be useful to get some sense of the underlying rationale. Although the exact formulation has tended to shift across time as his ideas developed, Philip has returned time and time again to the 2 X 2 dichotomy as a format for mapping his choices and preferences as a teacher. In an early project document, the analysis served to characterize *student stereotypes* and ideal-typical *learning environments*. They appeared as follows:

Students	
1. Naive	2. Academic
3. Practical	4. Complex

Learning Environments	
1. Management science exercises	2. Case studies
3. Business model games	4. Projects

If I understand the project aright, by the time the Skills of Bargaining short course was given, there was a tendency to redefine the dichotomies under the influence of people like McKeon, who writes of four types of relation between knowledge and action, but also to retain the pedagogical commitment to matching "students" and "learning environments." The ideal student is complex, seeing thought and action as mutually constitutive. The ideal learning situation is the "project." ("Projects," writes Boxer, "or the meaty part of a thick sandwich course, are the most complex learning environment where the students aim to learn how to integrate process and content.")

In Boxer's 2 X 2 dichotomy (based on simple/complex and structure/function in the earlier formulations), projects (hurrah!) may be contrasted with management science exercises (boo!), which appear to be mainly discovery-based charades from which students exhume the single cognitive map embedded in the materials. Business model games (boo!) offer more opportunities for manipulative richness but are structured and defined by a model, albeit in some senses "student centered." Case studies (boo!) are seen primarily as a way of teaching a particular preselected problem-solving approach. In Boxer's scheme of things, EX-SIM and FDBACK together make up a "project." Conventional teaching does not occur in the model at all. But Elijah has to do more than bring fire down upon his educational altar. He has, in addition, to contend with the prophets of Baal. Andrew Gottschalk, too, perceived the short course as tinder for the competitive miracle. But his view of whose material was the more inflammable was quite different.

None of this was known to the little knot of middle managers who gathered in the LBS private dining room at the start of the Skills of Bargaining short course. I was there, but only because I had paid my money across the counter and was pretending to be a negotiator from the Association of University Teachers. Andrew is soon the front man, center stage, managing the student's transition into the residential short course. His performance is very professional, polished and expansive, although it is clearly and self-consciously a *performance*. Wardrobe has given him a distinctive costume (brown corduroy jacket, sunflower-yellow tie, and billowing pocket handkerchief) not too far removed from the sober suits of the middle managers, but distinctive nonetheless, the dress of one untouched by the sartorial anonymity of mid-career. Sylvia Maynard, the course registrar, is there, long haired, theatrical, and rather beautiful in a whimsical kind of way, mopping up Andrew's male-chauvinist jokes. While playing "straightperson" to Gottschalk's witticisms, she smiled ironically at his gentle jibe that linked Philip with MCPs ("Philip makes his own decisions on this one"). Boxer, too, manages a wry smile.

Andrew also offered course members the protection of a collusive relationship, coopting them into the implicit LBS conspiracy. Students were enjoined to accept the conventions of a closed group ("What goes on here is confidential to the group"). In particular, the "learning experience" of the course would be protected against the dead hand of assessment; reporting back to "the bosses" who paid up in the first place was declared unacceptable. There was a subtle redefinition of the client, as client-status shifted from the sponsoring organization to the individual course member. We were told that the important evaluation was the *student's* evaluation of his own learning. The staff, on the other hand, welcomed feedback. One manager asked, "What about him?" His boss was with him in the course (smiles all round). "Ve haf vays of dealing vif bosses," rejoined Gottschalk smartly.

The introduction to the course took place in a daze of wine and cigar smoke (later described by an unofficial LBS spokesman as a policy of "getting the buggers sloshed"). The attempt, not unsuccessful, was clearly to create group identity through conviviality, but it might also have been a way of buying into the situation some of the traditional obligations of the guest. Once the rites of passage were over, with all attendant impurities and danger, work began in earnest. Most evenings after the first one saw noses pressed to grindstones rather than hovering over brandy glasses.

On this merry occasion Andrew, who had somehow contrived to drink just enough to enhance rather than hazard his performance, represented the pedagogy of the course as governed by two principles. First, it sought to "provide learning opportunities." In relation to these the staff were cast in "learning roles," too. They were seekers rather than knowers. The second principle was incremental: "to develop skills and insights" in students of a kind that they might "take back" from the course and "implement" in their own "operational situations." Andrew, who seems a natural teacher in the sense that most people would understand that word, clearly believes, like Philip, that "skills and insights" need to be somehow lumped together. But more than Philip he is interested in how people get there; it can't be just a question of throwing students (who may, God forbid, be "academic" or "naive" or "practical" in the worst senses of these words) into the deep end of a Boxer "project." The bridge, to Andrew, is *transitional dependence*. Students must be blindfolded, led by the hand, and finally have their bandages removed in some new, faroff country. Since students who are grown ups and managers must suffer this transitional dependence, a notion was developed of the "psychological contract." The "psychological contract" is newly coined jargon for "trusting Sir," a way of handling the conditions between liftoff and escape velocity.

Andrew's contribution to the mixed pedagogy of the Skills of Bargaining short course is easy to describe. He seems uninterested in high-level abstract theorizing and opts instead for *straight exposition* of key concepts and distinctions; for example, the distinction between "distributive" and "integrative" bargaining. He is gifted at exposition and explanation (a skill surprisingly rare in teachers at any level) but clearly sees the knowledge component of the course as dormant knowledge to be handed on. It is commentary-on-the-action that Andrew finds fascinating, and a number of sessions in the closed-circuit television suite become virtual coaching sessions in his hands. He operates as a kind of licensed raconteur, swapping analyses, tips, anecdotes, and acute isolated observations, not infrequently about some point of fine detail. Many of the pre-course handouts were written by Andrew and he quoted these liberally, becoming a kind of compere of his own show. The students were quick to get the message ("Andrew, in that chapter of yours . . ."). Always he is entertaining, providing "value for money." But Andrew *never* misses an opportunity to reinforce his own image, and positively courts student dependence. The strongest possible defense of Gottschalk would be that he deals, like the Gospels, not in anecdotes but in parables. Although it's not a line I'd care to argue myself, it does have a certain zany appeal.

Examples of his encouragement of student dependence abound. Andrew was the first to abandon his lapel identification badge. During the CCTV sessions, he chose not to watch the videotape, with everybody else, on the big box. Instead he hunched in everybody's peripheral vision over the tiny producer's monitor at the front, dramatizing his separateness. On these private/public occasions he would allow (I think deliberately) a knowing smile to play about his lips as if he were some kind of connoisseur of the action. Later Andrew conducted a whole seminar against a backdrop of flickering TV screens. (I read this as a bid not to be upstaged by computer-man Boxer in preempting the high-technology environment.)

Some of Andrew's anecdotes are humorous asides ("my machine doesn't work, as Brother McGarvey pointed out to me"); others reinforce a rule-of-thumb piece of coaching ("I think that's just about the biggest sin in the book. Now I remember at Plesseys . . ."). Prescriptive, opinionated, *but committed to a point of view,* Andrew's whole use of words is to throw back at the managers a sharpened version of their own conventional wisdom, purifying the dialect of the tribe ("My scenario for disaster in that situation would be. . . ," "I am not convinced that a secretary taking longhand is a good thing. . . ," "Circulation of the minutes can become rhetorically important, a landmark in the progress of a particular steward ['I see you raised it, brother'] . . . ," "I think there is nothing worse than briefing a union official in the gangway . . ."). This is what Andrew himself, adding advice to example, calls "speaking the jargon of industry."

When, lacking contextual cues, I put in a poor performance as a shop steward in a videotaped *incident study* (playing down rather than playing up "unrest among thy members") Andrew's post-performance analysis was scintillating, fair, and (I felt) potentially useful. As a "critic of the action" at one level he is superb, although perhaps getting dangerously close at times to the view that there is a teachable repertoire of negotiating behavior. (If so, what is denied in precept is taught by example.)

The word "anecdotal" is sometimes used pejoratively. At one point Brian Towers from ACAS introduced in a talk the notion of *practice* and reminded us that it was considered the "ultimate crime" to be "anecdotal in an academic environment." Nobody laughed. Yet a harsh view would be that whereas Brian used examples to *open* reality to alternative interpretations, Andrew sought *closure* through a telling example. In a world full of pitfalls, Andrew's track record, on the basis of the anecdotes he presents, is of the guy proved right. ("So I said to him, you are paying the workers £900 per week more than you need have paid. That's all my good work down the pan. I've a good mind to treble my fee.")

Philip's pedagogical stance, as perceived by the course members, was narrowly theoretical. He was seen as a conceptual model-builder, the wizard of the blackboard, a kind of intellectual Kenwood Autochop turning the whole world to mince before your very eyes. Neither Philip nor Andrew teach by example in an action-based part of the course, say in the incident studies, the conceptual games, the simulated negotiations, or the exercise surrounding *Ball Bearings Ltd.* Philip is so hell-bent on arriving at box 4 that he relies to a dangerous extent on partial explanations (implying that it's not your secret garden unless you find it yourself). For a person whose language is complex and abstract, this provision of minimal toeholds is an extremely high risk (and Philip knows this), almost inviting students to treat him as a body-on-the-barbed-wire, over whom they climb into the exercises and projects.

The dilemmas and paradoxes run deep. Philip's box 4 ("The *dialectic* box," he will tell you firmly, communicating, like T. S. Eliot's poetry, some time before being understood) is like a bank, which will lend you money if you prove that you don't need it. As Rod Atkin—then LBS's own internal evaluator—suggested, Philip's "meta-language" (nice one, that) has a simple problem, i.e., "The ultimate dilemma of explaining conceptual frameworks to naive students." Naive students don't understand Philip, because if they did so they wouldn't be naive; and the same goes for their "practical" counterparts. In Philip's schemes, the pedagogy associated with the student-centered "dialectic" learning is clear: set up a "project," light the blue torch paper and retire. He is the bridge club secretary who wants new members to learn by playing; who wants players to exercise judgment rather than count points mechanically; who declines actually to play with them; but who, when coaxed out of his diffidence, is quite superb at analyzing hands.

Philip also refuses to ape the surface features of industrial jargon. His language is highly intelligent, if sometimes obscure, moderate in tone, and conceptually rich to an extent that places heavy demands on the listener. To the middle managers, he smacked strongly of "book knowledge." No one perceived the absurdly young-looking pink-faced Boxer as a lad whose ideas on negotiation had been forged in the cauldron of real industrial experience. Indeed, his language at times seemed tangential and elusive ("If you get yourself into an exchange situation, this is the kind of process that is going on"). Andrew's view of Philip was once condensed into three memorable words: "Bright kid, but. . . ." On another occasion Andrew summarized his partnership with Philip rather neatly: "You do, in fact, see two people there, the sublime and the corblimey [Cockney for "God blind me"]. And there are a very few occasions when I won't let Philip loose at his metalanguage level."

Because of the love-hate partnership between Boxer and Gottschalk (Philip hides his warmth for Andrew behind apparent distaste, while Andrew hides his distaste for Philip behind apparent warmth) each handles differently the ever-present LBS issue of staff credibility with middle-aged, middle-career middle managers. Andrew seeks quite early to reduce social distance by oaths, blasphemies, and a liberal use of the coarser adjectives ("so naturally I said to the lads, isn't it about time you buggers pissed off"). Philip is an earthbound spirit, a hoverer, the earnest young man at the cocktail party. He watches Andrew's extravagant chatting-up with just a hint of amused disdain, visibly keeping count of some of the most well-worn expressions. For his part Andrew generously decided to over-compensate for what he perceived as *Philip's* initial unresponsiveness, working hard on what he perceived as *Philip's* credibility problem. But Andrew's general nervousness about Philip comes through. The students ended the first evening feeling that they knew Andrew, but found it hard to place Philip. Andrew had "packed a lot of experience" into his career ("must be about in his middle thirties"). Philip was one of the new generation of "young boffins." ("He's obviously something to do with the computer bit. I wonder what that's going to be like?")

Implicit in any problem of staff credibility is the student/manager's belief that his tutors should be able to survive in his *own* world back home. Andrew produces reassuring noises while Philip doesn't. The irony is rich: Andrew shores up even as he demands dependence; Philip threatens at the very moment that he offers freedom.

And yet some exchanges had a visible competitive edge. When Philip was half-way through a rather abstract account of the difference between "operational" and "practical" (fifteen-love) Andrew jumped in with a personal anecdote, interjecting, "Now I wonder if we could take this into the industrial relations situation [neat put-down by implication]. You've got this foreman who. . . ." Before long Andrew is using the analysis to generate sweeping generalizations of the "all personnel people are seen as academic rather than practical" kind (fifteen-all). Philip loses this long volley, but then serves an ace. The words in the boxes are not "dangerous stereotypes" at all. They are merely "ways of recognizing forms of behaviors" (thirty-fifteen).

But Philip's altar for calling down the divine fire was undoubtedly the simulation exercise, EX-SIM, and the associated feedback device, FDBACK. Until this Skills of Bargaining course, the twin parts of Boxer's pedagogical invention had not been put together. This course represented FDBACK's coming of age. It was no longer somebody's party piece, but the professional conjuring trick at the heart of the event. The conceptual feedback game was to be used in a number of different contexts before integration with EX-SIM toward the end of the course. Assimilation was to be gradual, with the mechanics of FDBACK introduced in stages.

One of the incarnations of FDBACK is in an exercise called *Interview*. *Interview* was first planned as a way to "structure discussion" of a film of an industrial dispute, directed by Roger Graef in his "Space between Words" series. This immediately followed Philip's talk on "Understanding and Evaluating the Negotiator's World" on Sunday evening, which introduced the conceptual game ("We'll just teach you the mechanics of the method tonight"). Philip explained (keeping Kelly under wraps, so to speak) that the key to the method is using concepts to discriminate and using the computer to analyze ranking information ("We use the computer to process the numbers generated; OK?"). But the real purpose is said to be to "facilitate a discussion of viewpoints."

Roughly speaking, the comparison of ranking information might lead a person to say, "Funny that all the girls I think of as rich he thinks of as attractive. How come our use of different concepts discriminates among girls in a similar way?" Or else, "Funny that while both of us think power is important, in this situation we cannot agree who possesses it. I wonder if we define the concept in the same way." But the "mechanics" are not properly understood, as is clear from the questions. Philip's reply is equivocal ("This rush through has been simply necessary"). Andrew settles for round one of the "psychological contract" ("The actual task will become clearer as you go on").

The task for *Interview* is summarized in a handout that Philip distributed. The style is crisp, truncated:

As the introductory text explains, INTERVIEW is a game about exchanging viewpoints, and is designed to be played in pairs. We will be using the game throughout the week to structure discussions on a variety of topics. For the purposes of this evening we would like you to use the situation shown in the film as a topic. The 'elements' will be some of the key people in the film, and tomorrow morning you will be asked to explore each other's interpretations of what happened. Between the film and tomorrow morning at 9.30 however we would like each of you to define your own personal interpretation: choose three important concepts which describe the behaviour of the people in the film and then give each person a rating for each concept.

Seven characters were identified. During the film we scribbled enigmatic notes. ("Tucker: divisional: long sideboards: senior to Halsall." "AEU steward: fall guy?") The discussion, far from being "facilitated" by *Interview*, ran amok without it. Roger Graef was present (knowing Roger, I had a dreadful fear that he would inadvertently blow my cover), but he and Andrew were soon swapping terms like "neolithic militancy," "collusive relationship," and "negative destruction role." There was therefore an attempt to arrive at some consensus on the interests and performances of the parties before *we* tackled the conceptual game *Interview* (Andrew going in for retrospective coaching, Roger answering questions on the basis of inside knowledge). When, next day, we came to do *Interview*, it was already impossible to isolate the film from the discussion and "use the situation shown in the film as a topic."

The "elements" were previously fixed and were said to be key people in the film. One manager complained that "apart from Edwards and Roucastle all the players were bit players," so discriminating between them was pointless. But my own interest was in the exercise as the tool of the spectator rather than the participant. Hiding its ambitions, it was in service *almost as a comprehension exercise*. The student may have been free to choose concepts, but the elements (people) and the total situation (the film) were tightly defined. The road to box 4 is a long one! At this stage, too, there is no explanation offered about what is meant by concepts "differentiating."

Student: You bang it into the computer. Is that right? What does it do?

Philip: It tells how different they are in how they discriminate, how close they are to the other person's.

General puzzlement all round, but at least *Interview* had been admitted to the party. Only later would it grow in strength and become the wonder of all.

At 9:00 A.M. on Tuesday we came together to attempt the exercise *Piecework Dispute*. Although the Piecework file (like the film) was not prepared with the *Interview* exercise in mind, it is sufficiently rich to support conceptual exploration and inferences about causal models. The task was subtly contrived as one of the interim stages on the way to Philip's box 4. The intent is to bring the students gradually within the environment of an exercise (seen this way, the Graef film has them out, EX-SIM has them in, *but this exercise defines them as marginal*). The handout for *Piecework Dispute* was a twenty-three page incident study. It took me until 3:00 A.M. to get on top of it, and even then I could only survive the discussion by making constant reference to my notes. The relevance of FDBACK was said to be that it would allow us to "structure" discussion. The approach, once again, was through key concepts. We had to select "the most important determinants of each side's future actions." Although we could adopt either a union or a management viewpoint, we were told not to negotiate, but to "discuss the parameters of the dispute." A limitation imposed, which was central to FDBACK, was that *discussion of concepts had to be free of examples taken from the exercise* (i.e., terms were supposed to be defined connotatively rather than denotatively). It was through this breach in nature that ruin entered.

Let's look carefully at the instructions:

The purpose of this exercise is to develop a consensus view of an industrial relations problem—a piecework dispute. The incident, its background and the events leading up to it are described on the document in your course files. . . . Your job is to adopt either a management or a union viewpoint and to analyse the most important determinants for your side's negotiating position on that basis. You are not going to negotiate, but are going to discuss the 'parameters' of the dispute.

The INTERVIEW method will be used to structure your discussions. The elements will be the people at one of the two meetings (TGWU and AUEW) [Transport and General Workers Union, Associated Union of Electrical Workers] and the aim will be to describe the most important determinants of each side's future actions in terms of four key concepts. The conclusion to your discussion should be an agreed common set of concepts.

Several points are worth noting. The last sentence was yet more toe-dipping in the deep water of using the dendogram to generate agreed-upon, all-inclusive, explanatory concepts. Nobody was ever *asked* to do it; a cynic might infer that tuition via this final exercise was beyond the competencies of all but the most specialized audiences.

But more important to the present analysis were two other features. In the first place, the teams of students for this exercise were retained following the CCTV Incident Study, which had involved role playing, and a retrospective critique from Andrew. And as LBS antiproletarian banter includes providing store coats as costumes for managers to wear while playing out union stereotypes, there was some seething at the unaccustomed levity of the union men (the managers finding their colleagues aping union petulance even more irritating than the real thing). This meant that when we went into the *Interview* game part of *Piecework Dispute* two of the students in my group were in no mood to discuss "parameters" from a position of semidetachment. They were still seething in their store coats. The students had not managed the shift from the role play to the conceptual game. They had not managed the transition between Andrew and Philip. The second important factor was that Philip was not physically present during a crucial half hour, and the students' questions had to be fielded by Andrew.

At the end of the role playing, the discussion, the computer printouts, and the explanations, my group was left with four allegedly key concepts with which to determine the next move. (They were time, cost of settlement, new payment system, and inter-union rivalry.) It all seemed harmless enough. (Where, I wondered, was the really wild card going to come from, the concept capable of giving a new purchase on problems? We don't need a computer to tell us that different people place different values on time constraints.) There was a feeling of general tiredness, as the case study had taken until the early hours to assimilate. We had been expected to distance ourselves from our predetermined affiliations (we had, after all "picked sides") and to discuss "parameters." But what was *intended* to be a conceptual exchange (without reference to examples) was simply treated as a face-to-face confrontation:

"What do you think, brother? Should we take this one back to our members?"

"Why I chose EARNINGS is that the present system has not worked too well. What we need is a new system."

Andrew entered at this point (I waved him across but did not explain what was happening for fear of breaking cover). Andrew picked up the problem immediately, reinterpreting it through a neat but possibly misleading metaphor, the video-playback. This strengthened the link back to the earlier pedagogy ("You must leave yourself there, step back and look in"). He explained that this involved "putting oneself in the position of the other." The point of the exercise was to "learn to look at his world his way," to explore his viewpoint rather than the actual situation. "How can I do that," demanded Tim, "without reference to the situation? I don't see the point." Andrew restated the "psychological contract," insisting that the "no example" rule must be "taken on trust." It will "appear clear later." This prompted an outburst from Tim: "But we are supposed to be cast in particular roles. Hasn't emotion any part in this game? If that's what you're saying, I won't go that road with you." Andrew found a patch of firm ground by retreating to his own 2 X 2 dichotomy and gave us a punchy résumé of one of his previous analyses, describing increasing sophistication in bargaining styles, FIGHT/SELL/EXCHANGE/NEGOTIATE. He appeared to be inviting Tim to move up from fighting (although in the conceptual game he wouldn't be allowed to negotiate either!). But Tim pressed further, quite angrily. How could one pull abstract, determining concepts out of situations and treat them as if they were isolated? Andrew offered in response a *principle* and an *example*. They were interestingly unrelated. First the principle: The stepping back ought to be on the basis of general principles that determine any action. Concepts like *justice* or *fairness* would qualify. These will always be "at a high level of generality" and can be discussed in a situation-independent way. "Look," said Andrew suddenly, "it's like this guy brought in from the Yankee end of the multinational GEC. His view was that all union officials were Communists, agitators, and skivers." At this point Philip returned and put in his two pennyworth. Predictably, his handout was his Bible. Are not some concepts more salient than others as determinants of each side's bargaining position, he queried? But the words don't bite; Tim is still playing his own game: "If I may break the rules for a moment, surely Harvey isn't going to buy a pig in a poke. That's what lies behind our attitude to the new payment system." Richard makes an effort but gets it wrong: "You mean it doesn't matter a shit what's in the exercise; it's our own concepts that you are trying to get at?"

Philip strikes to break the deadlock. What we are trying to do in *Interview*, he explains, is to "take a knife to the exercise." He wants to "crash through." What are the determinants? But the group has degenerated into a touchy fragility. Tim was "up studying all night" but even then "only read the fucking thing once." He, for one, didn't "give a shit if his concepts were logical with that" (rapping the papers with his finger). *Interview* was forgotten as Kevin rescued the situation by moving back smoothly into role playing. ("As far as we in management are concerned, the maintenance of stable employment is a high priority. . . .")

Soon afterwards we broke. One of the management team offered me a quick aside; "Now we come to the impossible bit. I don't see how I can rate these concepts. I don't think this exercise has been explained at all well."

The debriefing session on *Interview* offered little improvement on Philip's somewhat minimal explanation of the mechanics. ("All the computer does is to measure similarity. If ten concepts discriminate in the same way, one basic assumption behind them is coming through.")

By midweek Philip felt that the group as a whole should revisit the 2 × 2 dichotomies, and he proposed four kinds of problem-solving strategies that were quite close to what had earlier been depicted as his "four kinds of student." Problem-solving strategies were either *operational* (he likes to get on with it), *dialectic* (he seems to be aware of what he is doing), *academic* (he prefers a more rational approach), or *practical* (he always comes up with a solution).

Soon we are presented with a *three*-category scheme; here I sit up and take notice. There is a hierarchy of sophistication in bargaining practices that goes from *fighting*, through *exchange* to *negotiation*. (Odd, I notice, how the hierarchy roughly corresponds to social class stereotypes: laborers fight, merchants exchange, and ambassadors negotiate.) But at this point Andrew leaps in to hoist Boxer with his own petard. "Let's think of it as a 2 × 2 dichotomy with a missing box," argues Andrew, assuring us that the missing word is Sell. ("Dear Rhoda," I write, sending a postcard to my mum in Cardiff, "what a mental life do these people have.") Philip accepts Andrew's interjection without demur (what he later called "defusing the short-term agenda").

There is, of course, an interesting general point to be made about the fact that union petulance (role-played by fellow managers) was one source of the irritation. The hidden curriculum of LBS might well be *management* mores and values, accepted uncritically and dignified in the story line of the incident studies (it is always the *managers* who are interested in the spirit of race legislation; the *shop floor* is where there is residual racial prejudice). Some anxiety has been expressed at LBS concerning the suitability of the learning material for a Union Officials course. ("That will show whether the system is value-free or not.") I was determined, therefore, to monitor the extent to which the LBS view of "bargaining and negotiation" on the Skills of Bargaining course appeared to be determined by a "management ideology." Certainly the managers on the course were, to various extents, locked into traditional viewpoints about workers. In the conceptual games they were inclined to see managers in negotiations exhibiting "responsibility" while unions merely "threaten" or "posture." Since the course is in effect a course for managers, one is entitled to ask a single fundamental question: where is the challenge to managerial stereotyped thinking to come from? In considering the hidden curriculum of the Skills of Bargaining short course itself, it must be said that one social mechanism deliberately employed for welding tutors and managers into a single coherent group relied to some extent on stereotyping workers as an alien group. Seemingly the shop floor is occupied by a morally diminished pigmy species properly referred to as "the lads," about whom demeaning, homely jokes, often in hammed-up regional accents, were exchanged as currency in the purchase of our own group identity. In another context this kind of attitudinal unguardedness might be labeled racist or chauvinist. A similar incident occurred in discussion following Roy Moore's talk. One of the managers took on Roy, who had been arguing for two-way disclosure of information during collective bargaining. ("Surely, Roy, you can't run with the hares and hunt with the hounds. Will management get a look at Branch Meeting minutes?") Somebody opined that if unions were to be given an educational fund the leaders would simply take off for Majorca.

The final use of FDBACK was in relation to the simulation exercise. *Ball Bearings Ltd.* is undoubtedly an interesting exercise to play, although nonmathematical participants will quickly be reduced to idiot silence by rapidly talking managers with pocket calculators. The exercise allocates interests within one of several firms competing in a market. The computer simulates production of the commodity and the cash flows. Various complications, like two production lines and two technologies, are built in. Companies buy and sell in a market, and their market share relates to the strategies they employ. The skilled and unskilled workers have their own interests at heart and will want to bleed the company as far as is compatible with keeping it going. The simulation is "white box." There are no unknown factors. Figures 1 and 2 are typical printouts.

The first few rounds were obscured by seething irritation at union obdurateness and militancy and postures were struck based on wild demands. These were met on the management side by Olympian

Figure 1

```
◆◆◆◆◆◆◆◆◆◆◆◆◆◆◆◆◆◆◆◆◆◆◆◆◆◆◆◆◆◆◆◆◆◆◆◆◆◆◆◆◆◆◆◆◆◆◆◆◆◆◆◆◆◆◆◆◆◆◆◆◆◆◆◆◆◆◆

COMPANY 1     RESULTS FOR PERIOD ENDING: 1    / 1    / 1981
◆◆◆◆◆◆◆◆◆◆◆◆◆◆◆◆◆◆◆◆◆◆◆◆◆◆◆◆◆◆◆◆◆◆◆◆◆◆◆◆◆◆◆◆◆◆◆◆◆◆◆◆◆◆◆◆◆◆◆◆◆◆◆◆◆◆◆


PROFIT AND LOSS STATEMENT                      *


SALES ON HOME MARKET AT * 1.18              450847.
SURPLUS SALES AT * .74                       65204.
                                            --------
                                            516051.

LESS MATERIALS            233137.
      LABOUR              202539.
                         --------
                         435677.
                                            --------
CONTRIBUTION                                 80375.

LESS OVERHEADS                               60000.
                                            -------

NET PROFIT                                   20375

          -----------------------------------------
```

Figure 2

◆◆

COMPANY 1   RESULTS FOR PERIOD ENDING: 1   /1   /1981

◆◆

```
                    MACHINE GROUPS
                     1         3              NET PROD.
NDS OF:
SKILL GRP 1         15         0              110.25
SKILL GRP 2          0        25              110.25
SKILL GRP 3          2         0              110.25
SKILL GRP 4          0         3              110.25

AVERAGE CYCLE DATA
TOTAL (MINS)        9.23      10.11
% DIRECT           67.22      80.76
% INDIRECT         10.02       9.15

DIRECT LABOUR COST/UNIT WITHOUT BONUS (P):
BASIC               32         32
O/T 1               43         42
O/T 2               48         47

MAX OUTPUT AVAILABLE
BASIC              173954.    264688.
O/T 1               86977.    132344.
O/T 2                   0          0

ACTUAL OUTPUT
BASIC              173954.    264688.
O/T 1                   0      31358
O/T 2                   0          0


                    SKILL GROUPS
                     1         2         3         4
RATE PAID INCL BONUS (P/HOUR):
BASIC               231       203       259       254
O/T 1               308       270       345       338
O/T 2               347       304       388       381

HOURS WORKED PER MAN PER WEEK:
BASIC                40        40        40        40
O/T 1                 0         4.74      0         0
O/T 2                 0         0         0         0
TOTAL                40        44.74     40        40

TOTAL PAY PER MAN PER YEAR (*):
BASIC              4121      3613      4612      4528
O/T 1                 0       571         0         0
O/T 2                 0         0         0         0
HOLIDAY             314       275       352       345
TOTAL             4435      4459      4964      4873
```

detachment and resorting to minor humiliating ploys ("Did you fix an appointment with my secretary, Mr. McKeown?"). But once the results were coming through, a natural competitiveness took over and some strange bargains were struck. (One work force accepted a savage wage cut and offered "industrial peace without strings for eighteen months" in an attempt to restore the firm's position.) Philip, acting as a kind of en passant confidant to several interest groups, took some shrewdly oblique lines, but always made his advice tentative ("One of the possibilities you might consider . . .").

The application of FDBACK to *Ball Bearings Ltd.* also produced key concepts that reflected the early brittleness of the negotiations. Among the words suggested were BRINKMANSHIP, FAILED COMMUNICATION, AGGRESSION, and CLOSED. First the concepts were entered at the terminal (figure 3). The dendogram or "tree diagram" (figure 4) reflected associations between concepts; these could either be turned back into the discussion or used to build

Figure 3

```
28   PLEASE ENTER YOUR PASSWORD : GAME 16

30   GAME 'COMPANY 1'

32   ENTER 4 CONCEPTS FOR MGMNT
       < AGGRESSION
34   < EMPATHY
       < CLOSED
36   < CONSTRUCTIVE

38   ENTER 4 CONCEPTS FOR UNION
       < BRINKMANSHIP
40   < FLEXIBILITY
       < HONESTY
42   < FAILED COMMUNICATION
```

Figure 4

ANALYSIS OF YOUR RATINGS SUGGESTS ASSOCIATIONS BETWEEN CONCEPTS.
STUDY THE FOLLOWING DIAGRAM OF THESE ASSOCIATIONS AND THEN ENTER
THE NAMES OF NEW CONCEPTS WHICH EXPLAIN THE ASSOCIATION BETWEEN
EACH PAIR OF CONCEPTS PRINTED BELOW THE DIAGRAM.

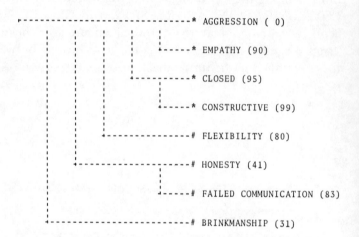

```
CLOSED AND CONSTRUCTIVE                          :  A
AGGRESSION AND EMPATHY                           :  B
B AND A                                          :  C
HONESTY AND FAILED COMMUNICATION                 :  D
C AND FLEXIBILITY                                :  E
E AND D                                          :  F
F AND BRINKMANSHIP                               :  G
```

up a cognitive map, by generating new concepts which explain the association between related pairs. Some managers remained obstinately puzzled until the very end. Others took happily to the language game, at least to the extent of playing it.

Reflecting on the computer-based elements in the course as a whole, I judge that Philip is faced with a number of choices, both at the level of personal pedagogy and at the level of course design. Alternatives include:

1. *"Going for broke."* Becoming overtly the "theorist for the course design," not a mixed-model instructor handling entry conditions into "projects." This, at an extreme, would mean seeing criticism of his own tutorial input as trivial—in the sense that it misses the nature of the "challenge of the new pedagogy." At this level the conflict escalates. It is no longer about jarring styles in a team-teaching situation, but about the new *numerate* professionalism taking on the *literate* establishment. (The *M.Sc. course* thus becomes the New Hampshire primary in Philip's bid for the White House. Of course!! Even as I write it, I know it to be true.)

2. *Cranking the engine.* Accepting responsibility for the achievement of "critical mass" both in terms of *transplanting* the pedagogy into a course (always difficult for a service enterprise) and in terms of *getting* the individual student into self-directed project-based dialectic learning. The course itself concentrated on the second—the first is ultimately political. Take the introduction to *Interview,* for example. Present policy is deeply ambiguous, comprising a written text that aspires to being minimal but sufficient, and a verbal presentation that aspired to *incompleteness* (this involves risky tradeoffs between dependence and understanding, between learning-by-being-told and learning-by-playing). But because of the credibility-of-the-tutor problem (*partial* explanation may be confused with *poor* explanation) a stunning paradox emerged. Remember it was Philip who was driven to elaborate ("The computer is used to process the numbers generated. OK?") and Andrew who played the trump card allowed by the "psychological contract" and told them to wait ("The actual task will become clearer as you go on").

3. *Coming clean.* Quite simply, this means demystifying the technology, even presenting it as a sort of juggling trick that aids "reflective thinking." Students are given no basis whatsoever for challenging

the assumptions of ratings-for-concepts and are encouraged to suppose that degree of association between two concepts can be "explained" by generating a third concept ("To get full benefit from the
game both players should now work through these associations and
create new concepts that they agree explain the associations").
Where are the good examples of this? Coming clean would seek, also,
to avoid the danger of epistemological overkill, the scorched-earth
policy that undermines the manager's view that he has at least a common-sense understanding of what using words is all about. Why not
ask managers to consider alternatives to the same end and say which
they like best (chasing some of their framing concepts through
Roget's Thesaurus? Exchanging written summaries of the axioms and
assumptions with the other side? Submitting to a tutorial grilling
from a disinterested IR counselor?). The managers on the *Skills of
Bargaining* course got something from the printouts, but in general
preferred the ordinary discourse that it fostered ("Going for broke"
might even recommend that people go back to the machine rather
than out into ordinary discourse).

4. *Back to the drawing board.* To what extent does *Interview* hold
within it an abandoned and fossilized early version of the Boxer
theory that concepts and functions have sufficient correspondence
for the exploration of a few key concepts to have a functional usefulness? Can a case be made out that regards *Interview* as having a suspect epistemology? Has the team considered hiring a philosopher of
language for a critique of the assumptions?

5. *Joining the trainer's bench.* Also, as I have said, implicit in any
problem of credibility is that LBS members of staff might be under
pressure to perform as "competence models." That is, students
should feel (as they should be able to feel of teacher educators) that
those offering advice would serve with distinction at the coalface, the
chalkface, or whatever expression depicts where the action rather
than the theory lies. Philip might choose to be dramatized differently, explicitly, as a "background strategy" man rather than as a
face-to-face negotiator, e.g., someone who could mastermind police
tactics in the London Spaghetti Restaurant Seige but who could not
be expected to haggle over the provision of chemical toilets. After
all, not all coaches are themselves exfootballers.

In spite of the dialectic elements in the short course drama, real
talent was on view. It took a whole week for the group to realize that

both Andrew Gottschalk and Philip Boxer are excellent teachers *within their chosen modes,* although in both cases one might want to say something about the mode. My only qualification is that Philip is like the classic stammerer, getting worse if things go wrong. Andrew's early warning system for this possibility is so sensitive that alarms ring at the first migrating Russian goose, and he jumps in competitively to "rescue" his colleague. It would be nice if Philip could learn to avoid slumping in despondency when this occurs. A final word about my own difficulty in maintaining a credible identity in a covert evaluation role. On Wednesday evening in the bar Kevin (a charismatic character with real-life claims to fame as the Malcolm Allison of Gaelic football) got close to breaking my cover as participant observer-evaluator. "It's funny," he said, "but your philosophy of industrial relations hasn't come through yet. You're the only course member that I can't 'place.' "

It was at the last evening's farewell dinner in Soho that my cover was finally blown. Like mountaineers who fall off cliffs on the easy route down, I had made the mistake of relaxing too much, inviting a lady to the final meal (apparently not an unobtrusive thing to do) and talking to Phil Boxer as if I knew him well (which of course I did, having been associated with him for a year or so as an independent educational evaluator). "Do you two know each other?" enquired Kevin shrewdly. To borrow Roy Lichenstein's key concept, WHAM! At the final debriefing session the following morning, which I did not attend, Philip defended having allowed me to take the course and was praised for his own courage and openness. ("That guy was asking all sorts of questions in the bar late at night," they complained.) Andrew took a hard line. To blow cover and leave him, as course director, to pick up the pieces was a "shock and a disappointment." The incident is one that I still recall with some embarrassment, and only repeat for the public record *pour montrer aux autres.* In acknowledging Andrew's directness and straight dealing I offer him, through the last paragraph of his note, the last word: "Participant observation requires immense discipline and the ability to sustain this. I feel you just ran out of both, just when it looked as if you might be achieving a minor triumph."

The case study by W. Lynn McKinney describes one of the alternative secondary schools that sprang up in urban areas of the United States during the late 1960s and early 1970s. The school, like many others, began as a reaction to perceived shortcomings in the ordinary public school system. The staff and students of the school were concerned primarily with creating a community that approximated as nearly as possible a completely participatory democracy; consequently, much time and energy were spent in creating and refining the mechanisms of governance of the school. Yet no matter how refined, these mechanisms failed to engage all students equally in the experiment in participation. While sympathetic to the impulses at work in the school, McKinney nonetheless suggests that expectations were unreasonable, that in attempting to reach what was essentially unreachable some staff and students emphasized the form rather than the substance of governance, and that the school became preoccupied with "revising the governing mechanism" instead of "deciding what sort of place the school should be." The results of this preoccupation, McKinney thinks, were basically negative, for in failing to move beyond it the school failed to perceive the possibilities in what it was doing well and failed to develop in other ways.

370

In describing events at the school over a three-year period, McKinney advances "plot." In disclosing meaning about and in judging those events, he develops a complicated "theme." He seems to suggest that human nature being what it is, people usually need optimal conditions in order to free themselves from their own preoccupations and misperceptions and to act in the best interests of themselves and others. The development of this theme and the basically negative judgment of the alternative school for failing to develop its own ideology are in part functions of the personal "point of view" brought to bear on events by McKinney. Nonetheless, the dominant interest in this study is political, for the study is predominantly an exploration of how meanings found by staff and students actually were put to use and how they could have been put to different uses. The principal critical focal points of the study are "work" and "world"; the study describes how the school and its governing mechanisms were structured and how these organizational forms seemed to reflect prevailing conditions in society that similarly influenced other alternative schools.

16

Governance and the Development of an Alternative School

W. Lynn McKinney

Introduction

This case study is devoted to the examination of governance during three school years at an alternative high school. As the external evaluator for the school, which was funded by ESEA Title III, the author observed that more effort was directed toward revising the governing mechanism than was spent on deciding what sort of place the school should be. The mechanisms that came and went were consistently in trouble.

It is argued in the study that in their general exuberance at being free of traditional secondary-school restraints and no longer serving as whipping boys for all of society and its "repressive" tendencies, the staff and a few of the students went too far in their quest for shared decision-making. At times students were dragged or shamed into attending meetings. Occasionally, elected representatives were required to check with every constituent on every issue. This happened because the governing mechanisms did not serve as means to goals or ends but as ends in themselves.

The political rhetoric of minorities and youth during the sixties centered around repression, around the centralization of power and

372

authority in the hands of ruling elites. One result of the riots and sit-ins of the sixties was that access to decision-making was extended to previously excluded groups. Student representatives were seated on search committees and curriculum committees, on advisory boards, and even occasionally on school committees.

More importantly, however, new forms of human organization became, if not significantly more numerous, certainly more visible— communes, alternative schools, encounter groups. Part of the appeal of these groups was their organization and their reliance, even insistence, upon shared decision-making. Within them, there was no such thing as being disenfranchised; it didn't matter how old one was or what kinds of experiences one had had. Everyone had feelings and opinions, and if a decision would affect an individual, he was entitled to an intense involvement in arriving at that decision. And so we saw A. S. Neill being outvoted by an involved group of children and liking it. Other educators, who saw themselves as "Neills," didn't like it nearly as much as they thought they should. Still, it was a glorious time for believing in pure equality and the goodness and rightness of man, individually and collectively.

And that is how it was at The Other School (TOS),[1] a four-year alternative high school. All decisions affected everyone, so everyone had to be involved in them. Except for enforcing the laws of the state (marijuana was quite as popular as rapping), the director of the school could do no more and no less than any teacher or any student.

We now know that such egalitarianism did not always work. People are not the same. For one thing, there were those who were ambitious and who were soon manipulating decisions and events. There were those who were impatient and could not wait for democracy to work.

These conditions prevailed at TOS, too. More important at TOS, however, was the lack of direction and development. People were not interested in governance because the government did very little that was interesting. It existed for its own sake. It was used primarily as a forum for a few actively involved individuals who saw society at large as sick and dangerous and the school as a haven.

Self-governance is generally held to be a human good, and in some societies a human right. However, not all people subscribe to all "goods." No one has the time or energy to relentlessly pursue all "goods" or virtues. It is clear that an individual who believes in a "good" can fervently want it for himself and his fellow beings, and yet spend little or no time in actively ensuring its presence or accessibility.

TOS from 1971 to 1974 was a place where these truisms were forgotten. A reaction to perceived oppression nearly resulted in a different kind of oppression, one which in some ways might have been more insidious. For, at least in the minds of many students, it no doubt aroused intense guilt feelings. An environment which was designed to be rich in opportunity nearly became rife with compulsion. And the issue at the heart of this paradox was the governance of the school.

This chapter will not trace in detail the changing structures and decisions of the governing bodies at TOS, although these are certainly dealt with. Rather, it focuses first on how the governing mechanism changed and what it did. Second, it compares some of the history of TOS governance with that of Metro High in Chicago and Home Base School in Watertown, Massachusetts. Third, it suggests how governing energy is directed. What is the source of changes in the governing mechanisms? What changes are made? And who gains satisfaction from the changes? The questions are important because limited energy must be directed toward the most important ends.

Data were collected from interviews with the TOS internal evaluator, from observation of governance meetings, from interviews of TOS students, from an excellent summary of governance events during the TOS history prepared by the internal evaluator, and from the sources cited in the text.

The Other School

The Other School was funded for three years by ESEA Title III. Designed to be a "free school" alternative to students from the four traditional high schools located in this eastern city, TOS annually enrolled approximately one hundred students. This group was selected from the roughly two hundred who applied. The drawing was done in such a way as to insure that student body reflected the population of the city in terms of race, sex, socioeconomic status, etc.

Housed in an old bowling alley, TOS provided courses in traditional school subjects but also brought in instructors to teach other courses requested by students. Programs, which were called "packages," were available in six areas, e.g., communications and performing arts. Students were required to take a workshop and a seminar in their area. Beyond these two required experiences students could select any course they wanted. State graduation requirements were adhered to, but students could be as compulsive or leisurely as they wished in completing their programs.

Many of the courses were quite as traditional in content as they were in teaching methods employed. Students were required to attend classes if they enrolled but were not required to enroll in any. Nearly all did, however. Some students took nine or ten courses for several consecutive semesters. Roughly one-half of the students each year held some sort of placement in the city as part of their programs. Students who could prove need were paid for these placements; others donated their time. These placements were arranged in order to offer students experiences which related to their "packages." For example, students in health care were usually placed with hospitals.

It "felt" different to walk into TOS than into the other city high schools. It felt different primarily because the rules were different. At TOS students were to be responsible for designing the governing atmosphere.

TOS Governance: A Brief Outline

A great deal of energy at TOS was devoted to governance. During 1971-72, the first year of the school's existence, countless meetings were held for the purposes of forming the government, of drawing up a constitution and a social contract (a statement of rules which each student was to sign). These meetings involved staff, students, and parents. Although governing documents were not ready for approval until May 1972, and did not go into effect until September 1972, there were three "official" bodies meeting during 1971-72. The staff met on a weekly basis; town meetings, which were based on the Summerhill model, were held biweekly; and the community council (the "judicial branch") met approximately biweekly. Although each of the groups represented specific groups of people, all meetings were "open" in the sense that anyone either inside or outside the school could attend. Membership on the community council and the numerous ad hoc groups that came and went was voluntary and open to anyone in the school.

The constitution of the school outlined the membership and responsibilities of the new governing bodies that began operating at the beginning of the second year of TOS. Again, staff meetings were held weekly, and so were town meetings. The advisory board (membership was voluntary) met biweekly for the first half of the year and monthly for the second half. The community review board, which only handled discipline cases, met as the need arose; two staff members and eight students were elected to membership. Parent meetings were held biweekly. Again, numerous ad hoc groups met as needed.

By December 1972, attendance at town meetings had sunk to its lowest point. Probably the major cause for this was that the meetings were boring to the students. (At the 24 October 1972 town meeting, for example, the director and one staff member argued for forty of the sixty available minutes about the optimum number of students for whom the school should provide.) As student attendance dwindled, the staff began to make more and more decisions, not necessarily in an attempt to seize power, but to insure effective work by the town meeting. A group of students felt that this was wrong and began to meet for purposes of designing a different (and perhaps "interesting") governing structure. The result of these meetings was the creation of the governing board (to replace the town meeting), which was approved and installed in April 1973.

Although meetings of both these bodies (town meeting and governing board) were open, voting at the governing board meetings was restricted to board members. These individuals (the two staff members and ten student members were either self-appointed or elected) voted the direct wishes of their constituents. Each board member was supposed to contact each of his constituents to find out how he wanted his vote cast and then was to report back the results of all such polling.

Because staff and students new to TOS in September 1973 felt that students didn't have a sufficient voice in government (this suggests that an "organic" ideology appears anew with each new cohort of students), the town meeting was readopted in September 1973.

When school opened in September 1973, the town meeting began again and met weekly for approximately one month. September meetings were devoted to discussion of a new governing form, and several proposals were put forth. There was conflict about two major issues. First, the balance of power between staff and students was debated. One student group proposed a "one man, one vote" rule, while some staff members felt that the staff, though far fewer in number, should have half the power. The second issue concerned hegemony over various kinds of issues and decisions. Since resolution of the conflict was obviously going to take time, a volunteer interim governing board served from October until December, at which time the final compromise proposal was presented and approved by two-thirds of the staff and two-thirds of the students.

The powers that the new governing board was given included (a) the hiring and firing of staff, (b) supervision of budget and finances, (c) designating building use, (d) establishing curriculum guidelines, and (e) all other powers not specifically delegated to other bodies.

Historically, some of these powers had been located elsewhere. The hiring of personnel had been done by a selection committee composed of staff, students, and parents during the first TOS year. The second year saw personnel become entirely a staff concern. This may have been the result of turmoil in the governing mechanisms. Budget had been the joint concern of the staff, the town meeting, and the community council during the first year, but only the staff was actively involved during the second year. Building use and other day-to-day affairs during the first year were the concern of the students and staff alike, but decisions were made at the town meeting (the notable exception was deciding what hours the school would be open daily). Day-to-day operations were jointly controlled by staff and students during the second year.[2] Curriculum had always been primarily the responsibility of the staff. During the spring of 1972, for example, the staff held weekly evening meetings which eventually resulted in a course package format. Students were always welcome at these meetings but rarely attended. The format was submitted to all other governing bodies in May and was approved by them. During the third TOS year the area of curriculum, however, provided the best evidence that governance at the school could be purposeful and open to input from a variety of sources.

A Curriculum Issue

There were only two issues during the first two years that staff decided on and toward which students responded unfavorably. One was the hour at which the school would close; staff held to their decision not to keep the building open in the evenings. The second issue was that of graduation requirements; this issue was resolved after the expenditure of considerable time and energy. There is simply no evidence that any other significant internal issues arose until late in the fall of 1973.

At this time a group of black students, parents, and teachers formed a group to demand that more emphasis at TOS be placed on basic skills. The group stated that the particular needs of the black students were not being met. The response of the governing mechanism was quick and decisive. A full day of classes was canceled, and meetings to discuss the demand were held instead. Student interest in and attendance at these meetings was very high. The governing mechanism which, because of a lack of crucial issues, had only been responsive to itself (by way of self-modifications) was abruptly asked to consider making a new curriculum policy. The basic skills courses that were started midway in the 1972-73 year are excellent testimony to the ability of the governing bodies to adjust policies quickly, but only after considered debate. The all-day meeting resulted in approval of the proposal; courses were quickly designed and were soon being taught. There were nine English courses, including vocabulary and spelling, functional grammar and punctuation, and reference skills; four math courses; and three science courses. Each of these courses met for an hour a day, five days a week; this was a departure from past policy when classes usually met only two or three days per week. Yet another change brought about was that only basic skills courses could meet between 9 a.m. and 1 p.m. daily. All other classes had to be held earlier or later.

The presence of a clear demand for change resulted in a fairly radical change at TOS. The governing bodies which had operated for two and a half years without a dramatic demand proved that they could be quick and decisive yet reasonable in their decision.

The sudden swell of interest in decision-making was an issue-specific event, not a sudden renaissance of the appeal of self-government. Students responded because there was an issue of importance to them; a personally meaningful decision, or one which was very important to their friends and therefore meaningful to them in a secondary fashion, was about to be made. There was a sense of purpose, of mission, which had been generally lacking.

Much of what went on in the daily routine of governing TOS

was mere formality. There normally were no "hot" issues. Clearly, the school had been well-designed as a satisfying place; had it not been, there would have been issues. The majority of governance time was spent in debating issues about the form of the governing structure. This no doubt provided some satisfaction to the adult population of TOS. They were insuring the existence of the privileges (the staff would say "rights") long denied to the students. The use of first names, the open confrontations and disagreements, the lack of a director's office all smacked of "aren't we all equal?" For a situation in which everything was ostensibly shared, however, the adults worked terribly long hours and were often quite exhausted. Something more was going on; it wasn't simply sharing. It was the adult provision to students of rights and responsibilities not often given them. The adults unquestionably experienced great satisfaction, as did the students who had an opportunity to explore and blossom.

Student and Staff Involvement

The brief overview of the changes in governance that occurred at TOS has been presented just to suggest that a great deal of time and energy was spent in governing the school. Quite clearly, at any time, the director could have been given complete authority to act as he chose. This would have violated the spirit of the school, however. Part of the reason that alternative schools are created is because of the way traditional schools are run. Many students feel (probably correctly) that "student government" in most secondary schools today is meaningless because students are given neither authority nor responsibility. Whether the reasons are based on legality, philosophy, or expediency, most high school students learn their civics from textbooks and not from shared democratic experience.

However good the intentions of a school might be in offering shared decision-making, the actual operation of government depends on the answers to several questions. First, to what extent are students willing and/or able to involve themselves in governance? How many students perceive that their contribution may be of significance? How many want to exert the necessary energy? Second, can responsibility as well as power be shared? For example, one perennial problem that all governing bodies at TOS had to face was difficulty in keeping the school clean. Many of the students were not concerned by disarray and dirt. Some staff members felt that no cleaning should be done until students finally decided that they couldn't stand the mess any longer. If the matter were that simple, there would probably be no problem. However, the school had numerous visitors, some of whom might form their opinions of the school only in regard to how clean it was. The city board of health might rightfully have become concerned. The third question that must be answered is, what is the purpose of governing? What is it used for?

The question of "governing energy" was one not of how much energy was necessary to run TOS effectively; instead, it was a question of whose energy it was and where it was directed.

During November and December of 1973, the author attended governance meetings at TOS and interviewed numerous students. With the exception of two students who regularly attended all governance meetings, none of those interviewed could describe the form of governance then in effect. The most common comment made by students was that the forms of government were coming and going so fast that they simply could not keep up. Three students stated that although the changes in governance were getting publicity, none of the changes was of much significance. "Meetings were too long; points were not made clear; too many people did not know what they wanted." Interestingly enough, opinion was equally divided about the extent to which students were involved in the changes. About half of those interviewed stated that they felt it was good that students were finally getting involved; the other half stated that apathy had never been so widespread. Both groups of students no doubt accurately reflected different aspects of reality. While few students were actively involved (thus considerable apathy existed), those who were involved were exceedingly busy. Many of the other students were taking six or seven classes and working part-time.

Some Theory and Other Examples

Initially the staff shared many of the assumptions about student participation in decision-making commonly made in the alternative schools that have been started in the past few years. Along with Metro's first teachers, we felt that the lack of student involvement in shaping decisions that affected their lives was a major cause of alienation and disruption within conventional high schools. We believed that students should be prepared to take a strong role in decision-making in their later lives. We felt that a good beginning for an effective learning program with these goals would be to eliminate the restrictive rules that generally govern students' daily behavior such as dress codes and hall passes; to allow students to select their own courses with broad distributional requirements; to involve students in the evaluation and planning of individual courses; and to involve students in making and implementing policies that would affect the entire community.[3]

This excerpt, taken from an article about Metro High School in Chicago,[4] no doubt describes the assumptions made by staff and researchers in most alternative schools. The article uses a distinction posed by Amitai Etzioni between the "instrumental" realm, the official-functions level of an organization, and the "expressive" realm, which is the personal level within an organization.[5] At both TOS and Metro, instrumental activities included the day-to-day concerns of the school such as setting school hours, allocating space within the building, dealing with the city school department, budgeting, graduation requirements, curriculum, and personnel. Expressive activities include friendships, informal "rapping," how students spend their time, and relations with the staff. In traditional high schools most of these activities are surrounded with codes of behavior, manifestations of which include hall passes, tardy slips, dress codes, the demand of addressing teachers as *Mr.* or *Ms.,* and the like.

Metro students were quite eager to have autonomy in the expressive realm; TOS students felt the same way. The right of individuals merely to hang around the school day after day was jealously guarded. TOS students during the first and second years wanted the school to be open in the evening also, not so that classes could be held there, but just so there would be a place to spend time without being hassled by anyone.

TOS and Metro student attitudes toward, and activities in, governance were quite similar. At first it was felt that the least government was the best. If the school had to have a government, it must be direct, participatory democracy; no one could represent anyone else. These student concerns clearly illustrated the lack of meaningful student experience with government. They assumed that a school could be operated without a structured form of government. They didn't realize how unwieldly a direct participation government could be. Further, their wishes and desires had been so badly represented for so long that they would not trust even their best friends to represent them. Student government at both these schools, then, quickly became the best kind of civics lesson. The making of decisions and the shouldering of responsibility for consequences are the ideal processes for educating "good" citizens and good individual decision-makers. Or so the assumption goes.

What really happened was not so ideal. Student interest in decisions in the "institutional" realm was high at first. At both Metro and TOS student attendance at the town meeting (the primary governing body) was high; however, it quickly dropped off, and only a few "regulars" could be counted on to attend. Despite the drop in attendance, the town meeting continued for some time as the major governing body. Attendance would rise sharply when well-publicized "crises" were to be discussed but would fall again quickly once the agenda returned to everyday matters. There were very few such crises.

Another example of alternative school governance is that of the Home Base School (HBS) in Watertown, Massachusetts. HBS, like TOS, began as a Title III school. HBS began with a modified version of the Town Meeting. Small groups of staff and students met, and the entire school then convened for the "presenting of issues and for sharing small group conclusions."[6] In the words of an evaluation report,

The decisions from this form of government were deadlocked so often that people lost interest and eventually tried a simplified version of the Town Meeting—with elected moderators, a published agenda, and discussion and voting on the floor of the large group, with a majority of those present and voting sufficient to carry a decision. This method also died, since students began to feel if they weren't at the meeting to register dissent, then the decisions did not apply to them.[7]

The idea that students did not consider themselves as part of the governing process unless they were in opposition to a decision which was being "imposed" on them was expressed in the Metro article, too. Student comments included, "I'm not going to spend all those hours working on that stuff. These teachers are here till six every day. They're paid to do it." And, "You go ahead and decide. Then if we don't like it, we'll be against it."

The example may not be so dramatic at TOS, but there is some evidence that the issues which generated considerable student interest were those involving outside forces impinging on previously held student freedom or responsibility. In all three of the schools there emerged a small group of students who attended all governance meetings, parent and staff meetings included. Although it is clear that they attended because of personal interest and concern, it appears as if they eventually took on some of the staff values and attitudes about governance. In all of the schools the staff began to feel that the government was not working, not because decisions were left unmade or unimplemented but because so few students were involved. It could be argued that herein lies the greatest civics lesson of all, one that dictators perhaps know best: no matter how much some people are enticed, cajoled, or badgered, they will not take an active part in the nitty-gritty business of governing. Other staff factors outlined by the Metro report also obviously affected student involvement: staff members feel ultimately responsible for the continuation of the program; staff are more experienced in the process of bureaucratic decision-making, so they tend to shape events at meetings even when students are there.[8]

For several reasons, vigorous student decision-making did not occur. Finally, it was felt that a change in the form of governance was needed to improve the situation, not because the uninvolved students were concerned but because those who were involved insisted that everyone should be involved. The next step in each case was a representative form of government based on the premise that each representative poll each of his constituents before every vote and then report back the results of that vote. But the same problems were encountered. Representatives found many students totally uninterested; these students refused to spend the time to make up their minds about issues or they were so hard to contact that representatives were forced to give up.

Until this point the narrative has suggested that the process of governance was time-consuming, even exhausting, for some people. In addition to active participation in governance, those involved were constantly "chasing" uninvolved people and debating the merits of new forms of governance. Eventually they had to write new proposals for discussion and then amend the existing constitution to transfer authority and responsibility to the new governing bodies. But, for a moment, we must digress.

Those involved with the Metro evaluation discussed at some length the "organic" notion of alternate school growth: ". . . once people are freed from the oppressive restrictions of the traditional school, a new learning community will evolve naturally as people deal with each other openly and honestly." It is a matter of "shedding" the old skin of traditional habits and attitudes, and from underneath that old skin will emerge a beautiful new man, new woman, and new community.[9] No one who has had any close contact with alternative schools will deny that in some cases new people emerge; however, a new "pure" community simply does not. It was the finding of the Metro researchers that what emerged were "those deeply ingrained patterns of thought and action of the traditional society and the patterns of functioning that govern the operation of any complex organization."[10] This is not to suggest that TOS is the quintessence of ingrained social patterns and thoughts; it is, however, to suggest (omitting the complex line of thought in the Metro article) that one manifestation of this organic ideology is the continued pursuit of 100 percent democratic participation in governance, and that this merely leads to exhaustion, not full participation. Many alternative schools have appeared to pursue participatory democracy; in fact, the pursuit has been of an ideology or perhaps just one assumption within that ideology. The pursuit, however, has been of the wrong kind of ideology.

A Retarded Ideology

During the first year of TOS's existence, there was a lot of work to be done. The structural framework had to be drawn up and put into operation. Attention was devoted to curriculum (courses to be offered), to kinds of student experience to be provided, and staff to be hired; many very practical kinds of decisions had to be made.

By the end of the third year, the school's continued existence was endangered by loss of funding from the school department. Student, staff, and parent support was quickly mobilized, and eventually the school was saved.

For the one and one-half year period between the "start-up" and the threatened demise, there were few burning issues. The basic skills curriculum is the most notable exception. What should have happened during this period of calm was the development of an ideology to define what the school was and where it was going.[11] Such an ideology did not develop to any stage of maturity. The school began as a reaction to what were seen as the bad qualities of traditional schools and the people who operated them. The three-year period that has been covered here ended with a resurgence of that same reaction. TOS felt (and with good reason) that the hope for its continued existence was a tenuous one. TOS did not work to establish itself as a focused, energetic alternative to the other city schools, however. Instead, it looked too much within itself, at its structure rather than its purpose. It continued defiantly to reassert its own perceived goodness.

A strong, healthy ideology did not develop for two reasons. First, some staff members and students did not (or could not) let it develop. Second, each entering cohort of students brought with it the spirit of negative reaction. They knew what they were escaping from but not where they were headed.

Prior to the opening of the school in September 1971, the principal hired the staff. Some friction between him and a group of interested parents developed over who had the authority to do the hiring. The principal wanted to hire individuals who had what he perceived to be the proper sympathies and attitudes toward alternative schools. While the parents did have the final say, the staff clearly reflected the principal's interests. Unfortunately, one of his interests was maintaining a "we = good, they = bad" atmosphere.

The principal's desk was located at the side of a large room; students had easy access to it and could easily overhear what was being discussed. The principal treated every communication from the city school department (the city administered the grant and TOS staff were school department employees) as an attempt to damage the school and frustrate the people there. His conversations were filled with distrustful references to an undefined "them." He actively attempted to muster school spirit by use of this ploy, and many students reacted as he hoped. An example is found in a series of "evaluation" meetings held in November 1973, roughly one-third of the way through the school's second year.

The meetings were designed to evaluate the TOS experience and to look to the future, to provide opportunity for goal-setting. In fact, the meetings consisted largely of student retelling of bad experiences in the traditional schools. It was obvious from the discussions that TOS students were having positive experiences there. Yet these experiences were described as if to affirm the essential badness of experiences in other schools. Unfortunately, this kind of talk continued to dominate discussions over the three-year period. It suggested a lack of positive direction as well as anxious self-assurance.

A viable set of beliefs does not simply emerge by asserting the antithesis of the rejected view. It needs to be worked out consciously. It needs to be shaped and reshaped in light of the realities of the school. The governing mechanisms of the school should have been the forums for developing an ideology. Efforts to use them to that end were not discernible, however. The principal, many members of the staff, and many students were content to engage in headshaking, quiet clucking, and "aren't we glad we're here and not there" sorts of talk without ever developing what "here" was all about—only what "here" wasn't about.

Yet open government was an important part of what alternative schools were all about. Governing mechanisms had to exist, and they had to be open to everyone. At TOS the mechanisms were sterile. The kinds of issues and topics which could have resulted in the growth of a positive ideology were largely ignored. The clearest issue that was dealt with was the basic skills curriculum. For the most part, however, attention was directed to the form, not the purpose. The form had to exist because it was said everywhere that it was important to students. Most of the time most of the students could have cared less.

Notes

1. Because of comments made about the school and individuals involved with it, this pseudonym will be used in the study.

2. Staff also belongs to the town meeting. Reference here is being made to staff meetings and town meetings.

3. Donald R. Moore et al., "Strengthening Alternative High Schools," *Harvard Educational Review* 42, no. 3 (August 1972): 315.

4. For a fuller description of the Metro program, see Donald R. Moore, Stephen H. Wilson, and Richard Johnson, *The Metro School: A Report on the Progress of Chicago's Experimental "School without Walls"* (Chicago: Urban Research Corporation, 1971).

5. Amitai Etzioni, "Organizational Control Structure," in *Handbook of Organizations*, ed. James G. Marsh (Chicago: Rand McNally, 1965).

6. Mimeographed history of Home Base School, p. 5.

7. Ibid., p. 5.

8. Moore, Wilson, and Johnson, *Metro*, p. 321.

9. Ibid., p. 336.

10. Ibid.

11. I am indebted to George Willis of the University of Rhode Island and to Bill Nitter of Concordia University, Montreal, for the insights they provided about the notion of retarded ideology.

The case study by Leonard Davidman is based on the author's doctoral dissertation, A Formative Evaluation of the Unified Science and Mathematics Curriculum in the Elementary Schools *(Stanford University, 1976). It uses methods of qualitative evaluation on a very large scale, to illuminate curriculum development, implementation, and dissemination in a national project. As such, it becomes something of a model of how curriculum criticism can be used to evaluate major educational programs as well as individual classrooms. The study carefully links descriptions of the project itself and of the author's techniques and assumptions with judgments about the project, thereby offering well developed justifications for the judgments rendered. The shortened study contained in this volume permits description, judgment, and justification only in condensed form, but the reader may consult the dissertation itself for their full elaboration.*

Davidman uses what he describes as "naturalistic," or non-experimental, methods of inquiry. Rather than trying to change the project or to study it according to some preconceived design, he observed the project closely over a period of time, letting central issues and specific disclosures of meaning emerge at least in part out of the diverse and extended observations of the unfolding nature of the project. Gathering and organizing data in a variety of ways have permitted him to state findings about both the strengths and the weaknesses of the project, particularly in terms of the coherence between its public and its hidden curriculum. The recommendations summarized in the study are intended specifically for educators involved in the project, for other educators developing curricula, and for educational critics.

The dominant interest in the study is political. Questions addressed either directly or indirectly include how meanings embodied in the project are intended and how they are actually put to use. A primary concern of the study is in uncovering principles which have real social consequences in terms of their use in guiding future curriculum development. The study is a chronologically ordered sequence of events and meanings written in the first person. As such, it clearly exemplifies "point of view," "plot," and "theme." Additionally, all four principal critical focal points are present. Examinations of curriculum materials, specific environments, and practical procedures focus on "work"; examinations of the origins of the project, its creators, and their intentions focus on "author"; examinations of effects on students focus on "audience"; and examinations of the relation between this project and other projects within the educational and social climate of the times focus on "world."

17

Formative Evaluation of the Unified Science and Mathematics Curriculum in the Elementary Schools: Summary and Extension of Findings and Recommendations

Leonard Davidman

Curriculum development has had a somewhat chaotic career between 1960 and 1975. In the sixties an unprecedented amount of time and energy was spent on literally hundreds of curriculum development projects, many of which operated on a national scale. In the mid-seventies this curriculum explosion, which continues to change the face of contemporary education, has been curtailed, primarily, I suspect, because of factors related to the economic recession.[1] In addition, I suspect that poor planning procedures, which characterized many of these projects, are partially responsible for the decline.

It has proved difficult for educators to create and merchandise curriculum products, even with the advantage of government and foundation grants that allowed these products a prolonged development period. While the results were often superior to what was created in the private sector, educators have encountered many difficulties as they attempted to distribute their products to school districts.

The failures and successes of these large-scale curriculum projects stimulated the curiosity of a number of educational researchers. Why did one succeed where another had failed? Were there principles that might guide the efforts of future developmental curriculum

389

projects, and might these be uncovered using naturalistic, that is, nonexperimental, methods of inquiry?[2]

In a direct way, the following chapter, which describes the author's two and a half year involvement with, and ultimate critique of, a national developmental curriculum project entitled "Unified Science and Mathematics in the Elementary Schools" (hereafter USMES) addresses such questions. I start by briefly describing (1) the USMES project and its curriculum materials, (2) my relationship to USMES prior to and during the inquiry, and (3) the reasons that prompted the inquiry. Against this background the most salient tasks, findings, and recommendations of the inquiry are enumerated and discussed. These remarks lead into a final discussion, which attempts to short-circuit a potential danger that accompanies the attempt to compress evaluative critiques that ultimately reflect on the reputations of other educators.

The Curriculum Project and Its Materials

Dr. Earl Lomon, a professor of theoretical physics at the Massachusetts Institute of Technology, has been the director of the USMES project since its inception in 1969. He became involved with this curriculum idea in 1963 when, at the invitation of the National Science Foundation (hereafter NSF), he participated in brainstorming sessions that considered the advantages of interdisciplinary science and mathematics curricula. This exposure, plus his own convictions, prompted Professor Lomon to spearhead a series of conferences that eventually led to the creation of USMES. The project, from 1969 to 1976, worked out of and under the auspices of the Education Development Center (hereafter EDC), a nonprofit educational agency located in Newton, Massachusetts. Funding for USMES, which had reached almost four million dollars by 1976, has come from a series of NSF grants. It is noteworthy that USMES/EDC (this double acronym denotes the top-level administration of USMES), which intended to culminate its national curriculum development and dissemination efforts in 1978, may have to wind down earlier because of recent restrictive NSF budgetary decisions. These important decisions were made after my dissertation was completed, and I have not been able to discern the precise reasons for this NSF move. However, anyone who has kept up with the NSF in the past two years is aware of the immense political pressure that has been brought to bear, in general, against its curriculum development, implementation, and diffusion program.

USMES's central curriculum concept is a complex teaching and learning strategy that USMES/EDC calls *real-problem-solving.* Broadly speaking, the curriculum idea is closely linked to scientific methods of reasoning and problem-solving. The concept's chief distinction lies in the assumption that students most effectively become problem-solvers in learning environments characterized by (1) carefully selected *real* problems; (2) teachers who do not dominate the students' problem-solving efforts; and (3) specific resource materials that render the real problems manageable for elementary school students.

With the real-problem-solving concept as a wedge, USMES/EDC attempted to rapidly diffuse its inquiry-oriented approach to teaching and learning on a national basis. Their major aspiration was that the real-problem-solving strategy would trigger a contagious reform movement, and with this hope in mind they made two major moves between 1969 and 1976. First, USMES/EDC designed nineteen resource notebooks to help kindergarten through eighth-grade teachers present manageable real world problems to their students. Secondly, they designed and implemented a set of workshops to train teams of teachers, administrators, and sometimes college personnel to implement USMES in their classrooms and become change agents for real-problem-solving in their respective communities. In toto, approximately five hundred teachers and administrators were trained by USMES/EDC at the several two-week workshops they ran between 1973 and 1976.

To further advance the efforts of its sixty-five change agent teams USMES/EDC created and published a set of materials that they called the USMES Library.[3] In addition to the resource notebooks mentioned, this library included:

1. The *USMES Guide,* which provides an overview of the entire project as well as descriptions of the units listed below
2. A document entitled *Preparing People for USMES: An Implementation Resource Book,* which represents an attempt to help USMES change agents plan effective workshops for other educators
3. A super-manual through which USMES/EDC intends to connect

its real-problem-solving orientation with material from other projects

4. A design lab manual, which shows teachers how to set up real-problem-solving laboratories in their schools economically

5. A set of *How To* booklets that students can consult quickly to learn the technical skills needed for successful confrontations with particular aspects of USMES problems.

The units created or modified by USMES/EDC are a varied lot.[4] By February 1976 twenty units were either completed or near completion. The titles in this group are: *Traffic Flow, Pedestrian Crossing, Lunch Lines, Dice Design, Burglar Alarm Security System, Soft Drink Design, Play Area Design and Use, Consumer Research/Product Testing, Weather Predictions, Electromagnetic Device Design, Describing People, Bicycle Transportation, Classroom Design, Designing for Human Proportions, Manufacturing, Advertising, School Zoo, Orientation,* and *Ways to Learning.*

My Relationship to USMES/EDC

My initial relationship to USMES/EDC stemmed from my position in the Department of Elementary Education at San Jose State University. Because of my interest in problem-solving and interdisciplinary education, I was asked by my department chairman, in April 1973, to become a liaison between San Jose State University, the California Suburban School District (hereafter CSSD), and USMES/EDC.[5] In this somewhat ambiguous role I attended USMES/EDC's 1973 East Lansing training workshop as a member of the CSSD USMES resource team and as a representative of San Jose State University.

Although I left this workshop disappointed with certain USMES/EDC tactics, I agreed to help CSSD's team in its 1973-74 implementation and diffusion effort as much as my crowded schedule would allow. I believed then that USMES was best understood as an attempt to reintroduce, with slight modification, the philosophical and pedagogical ideas of John Dewey and William H. Kilpatrick into the American educational sphere. As such, I considered USMES a program worthy of support. This notwithstanding, it is important to note that at this point I was not consciously an inquirer of any sort. In the main, I was a slightly pressured professor *cum* graduate student who, when possible, served as a part-time member of the CSSD implementation and diffusion team.

By May 1974, however, a change in my relationship with the CSSD change agent team and USMES/EDC was underway. Several factors contributed to this change in role. There was, to begin with, the constantly growing impression that the overall USMES/EDC curriculum development, implementation, and diffusion effort lacked coherence. This impression was triggered at the 1973 USMES/EDC workshop and nourished during the 1973-74 school year as the CSSD USMES team experienced many difficulties in their efforts at implementation and diffusion. Half the members of this team, for example, did not even set up USMES programs in their classes. A second factor was the announcement by a CSSD principal that he would set up a desirable teaching/learning environment in the 1974-75 school year. This USMES-oriented environment was designed, in May 1974, to be a self-contained mini-school in which six upper-grade teachers, three of whom were members of the original CSSD USMES team, would cooperatively teach a curriculum with a substantial USMES component. This arrangement seemed particularly suitable for an inquiry aimed at several of the questions I had begun rhetorically to ask in 1973-74.

Nevertheless, taken by themselves, these important factors would not have persuaded me to write a proposal aimed at the evaluation of the USMES/EDC program. The decisive factor was the intellectual support that several Stanford professors gave to this inquiry. Because of this supportive climate of opinion, and the perceptive student and professional debate and writing that was its mainstay,[6] I was ready to assume in May 1974 that:

1. The development, implementation, and diffusion procedures created and employed by large developmental curriculum projects were, of themselves, worthy of inquiry and description.

2. It was highly appropriate for graduate students to become *involved* with these projects as independent consultants or critics so that some form of balanced and critical record of these curriculum events might emerge from which later researchers and historians might cull generalizations.

3. The opportunity to participate, concretely and conceptually, in the initial developments of *educational criticism,* a new or at least partially new form of curriculum research and evaluation, was in itself a valid enough reason to submit a dissertation proposal.

The Inquiry's Five Basic Tasks

Armed with the above set of assumptions, I proceeded to tackle the first and most fundamental task, namely, to create a research situation in which I might think at length about selected aspects of the USMES program. Essentially, this involved persuading people in three separate educational arenas: the school of education at Stanford University, the CSSD school district, and the higher echelons of USMES/EDC. This process was not without its difficulties, but, happily, in late September of 1974 I emerged with everyone's permission to study *naturalistically* the implementation efforts of the six teachers in the USMES "pod" in Porter Elementary School. It was fully understood that my research design would be emergent, that is, once I was out in the field the set of methods and research questions outlined in the proposal would be open to modification if and when pressures arising in this real world of education made such modification necessary. This flexibility proved to be quite significant.

The second major task involved making the project manageable by limiting my field of observation. This was accomplished by drawing up a limited number of guiding questions. The guiding questions finally chosen reflected my (1) 1973-1974 involvement with USMES/EDC and CSSD; (2) analysis of the literature related to curriculum development; and (3) awareness of the type of questions that the evaluation teams at USMES/EDC and Boston University were *not* asking in their formative evaluation activities. These questions were:

1. What kinds of things, with regard to the explicit and hidden curriculum, are students learning from the USMES curriculum? (Specific attention was given here to attitudes and skills related to problem-solving.)
2. What kinds of values are implicit in the USMES materials, that is, what view of the good society, or progress, of individual responsibility and the role of the individual in society does the USMES approach to teaching and learning communicate?

3. What are the unanticipated outcomes—both negative and positive—resulting from use of the materials?

4. What happens in the classroom in which the materials are being used? To what extent are other classroom activities compatible with the expressed goals of the project?

5. How can the learning process experienced within USMES be maximized?

These five orienting questions guided my observations, interviewing, and instrument selection and construction. They were the inquiry's mast and rudder. Time and again as I stepped into and away from the ever-shifting, sometimes confusing, phenomena in CSSD a review of these questions would help me maintain focus and critical balance.

The third major task involved the selection and implementation of a set of methods designed to gather data pertinent to the above questions. Initially, the following strategies were selected:

1. Tape recordings of classroom lessons and interviews with students, teachers, and administrators at Porter Elementary School would be systematically collected, transcribed, and analyzed.

2. Selected portions of USMES projects carried out in and around the pod would be photographed and filmed.

3. A notebook containing written descriptions of USMES and USMES-related events observed in class would be developed.

4. A diary-like notebook based on rereading, analyzing, and theorizing about the first notebook's remarks plus the interview transcriptions would be kept.

5. An attitude inventory developed by Professors Krutchfield and Covington (University of California at Berkeley) would be administered to the six classes in the pod as well as a comparable group of CSSD classes.[7]

6. Selected portions of the USMES Library would be analyzed in line with guiding questions 1, 2, and 5 above.

The fourth major task involved the implementation and modification of the above strategies. In October and November 1974 several were implemented. During this period I visited the USMES pod three days a week for a total of nine hours per week. Significantly, however, by November 1, 1974, for reasons which will not be fully developed here but are detailed in chapter four of my dissertation, I found it necessary to modify the set of strategies outlined above. During the week of November 1, my thrice-weekly visits were no longer in the pod structure. By this time Steve Tam, the director of the USMES pod in Porter School, had decided to move his class out of the pod into a self-contained classroom.[8] From that point on, with regard to USMES, each pod teacher was responsible for the USMES activities of his own class.

During these first weeks of November, faced with a design-shattering move, I really needed to draw on Joseph Schwab's arts of the eclectic. Where I had originally envisioned 180 students and six teachers committed to the idea of being a USMES pod, I now had one teacher with twenty-seven students and five teachers with 150 students. A choice had to be made, and it was a difficult one because during October and November Steve Tam's room had served as the focal point for my observation. This was the case primarily because he was the director of the pod, chief of the pod's USMES program, and a man with whom I had a great deal of rapport.

In the two weeks following Steve Tam's move three important decisions were made. First, I would spend 80 percent of my field observation time in Steve Tam's classroom. Secondly, I would describe my observation in his classroom as a mini-ethnography because now, dealing with only twenty-seven students, I felt it possible to see the classroom reality from the insider's as well as the outsider's point of view. And thirdly, I would revise guiding question number five, which read, "How can the learning process experienced within USMES be maximized?" to read "How can the educational goals of USMES/EDC be maximized?"

This revision was in keeping with my decision to broaden the scope of the inquiry by including questions concerning the emergence and effectiveness of the USMES change-agent training model. Earlier, when I was writing the proposal, I decided against inquiry in this area because of time and financial limitations; but in December 1974, I concluded that a formative evaluation of USMES that totally ignored the USMES training model would be trivial. Limited though it had to be, I presumed that my inquiry would be useful if it did nothing but suggest to USMES/EDC that their training program was conceptually inadequate for the difficult task of selecting and training teams of change agents.

As one would expect, the methodological repertoire of techniques listed earlier expanded with the scope of the inquiry. To begin with, the attitude inventory that was to be administered to the six classes in the Porter School USMES pod was administered instead to the six classes taught by the original CSSD USMES resource team, as well as to a comparable group of students in six other classes. In addition, a multipurpose questionnaire was mailed to 275 teachers and administrators trained by USMES/EDC in their three major 1973 and 1974 workshops. Beyond this, the ongoing analysis of USMES resource materials was extended to include analysis of essays by USMES/EDC staff, USMES/EDC historical documents, other evaluations of USMES, and the data collected with the instruments mentioned above. The USMES/EDC historical documents, in particular, were examined for the light they might shed on USMES/EDC's early decisions regarding their change-agent training model.

To summarize, the set of strategies employed allowed me to gather and analyze data from five distinct sources. First, there was the mini-ethnography conducted in Steve Tam's classroom from October 1974 to May 1975 (three days a week—three hours a day). Secondly, there were the five remaining classrooms of the CSSD USMES resource team; data were collected in these rooms via teacher interview, attitude inventory, and some direct observation. The third source was publications written by, and communications with, USMES/EDC personnel. The ninety teachers and administrators who responded to the questionnaire comprised the fourth source. A final source of information was literature pertinent to developmental curriculum projects such as USMES.

The fifth and final task consisted of the organization, analysis, and communication of the data in the form of findings and recommendations to (1) USMES/EDC; (2) the CSSD USMES resource team; (3) educators interested in the creation and diffusion of community-oriented/problem-solving curricula; and (4) educators considering the use of naturalistic techniques in projects similar to this one.

The Findings

When a range of diverse techniques such as those listed above are applied to differing contexts, one can be fairly certain that a variety of things will be learned. In fact, the findings of this inquiry, like the techniques, are quite varied. They are particular and local as well as general and global. They concern large groups of students as well as small, six teachers as well as one. In addition, the first set of findings suggests a second group. Almost inevitably, the study of human behavior in educational settings provides implied circumstantial knowledge about these settings as well as other institutions or organizations with which the humans in question have had recent and important transactions. In other words, I am suggesting that findings about CSSD's USMES resource team reflect, in part, on the efficacy of the USMES/EDC change-agent training program.

Regarding this inquiry's findings, it needs to be stressed that, despite attempts to be dispassionate and disciplined and especially above careerism, these findings are at least partially subjective opinions, albeit of a scholarly nature. I submit that the rubric "informed speculations" suits these opinions well. Indeed, each speculation has been made more than a mere speculation by at least one scholarly strategy. Together, the two terms in the rubric are meant to denote that the findings, while more than tentative, are quite far from conclusive.

There are essentially six different findings to be presented. Before doing this, however, let me consider a methodological issue related to the *ethics* of naturalistic inquiry.

Caution in the reporting of informed speculations is highly appropriate, because in a complex inquiry such as this, where the findings may have serious political and economic implications, one needs to be particularly cautious about generalizing beyond the reach of the data. The naturalistic inquirer, more than others, must be concerned about the range of his data. However, he must simultaneously realize that there is no precise calculus to guide his judgments in these matters.

With this responsibility in mind, it is sobering to realize that a case study such as this inquiry, and certainly others that naturalistic inquirers will perform, has certain things in common with a preliminary medical diagnosis. To illustrate, consider that the short-term importance, credibility, and ultimate significance of both the diagnosis and the case study are a function of (1) the overall health of the patient or object of the inquiry; (2) the experience of the diagnostician/inquirer; (3) the quality of the overall diagnosis/inquiry; and (4) the knowledge that the patient or object of inquiry brings to the diagnosis or evaluation.

Several potential implications of this analogy are worth considering. First, the naturalistic critic, particularly if he has chosen the patient—in this case, the curriculum project—and not vice versa, has a greater responsibility than the medical diagnostician to weigh the accuracy of *public* remarks. Secondly, it is conceivable that the naturalistic critic, by over-generalizing from his data, can give the object of the inquiry, in a process similar to auto-suggestion, problems that were not there to begin with. Thirdly, in an interconnected and increasingly sophisticated marketplace of consumers and ideas, it will be the overall competence of the object of inquiry rather than the suggestion of negative symptoms that will determine the ultimate value and influence of symptoms reported by the diagnostician. In other words, I am hopeful that naturalistic findings that may be overstated, rather than contributing to unfair economic and political repercussions for the *client,* will receive eloquent rebuttals from informed defenders, rebuttals that may bring the entire discussion closer to the truth. Finally, naturalistic inquirers, to be fair to their clients, and to the new and vulnerable field of educational criticism, should design patient inquiries that produce layers of overlapping data.

Unfortunately, the above discussion does not resolve a most important and complex issue. The essence of it is this: while a case study inevitably reflects on the whole of which it is a part, the question remains as to what type of evidence, in what quantity and of what quality, will verify that a particular part is an element significant enough to allow the critic to turn from the important, but narrow, discussion of that element to the drama of the total context. I submit that the search for absolute criteria that would, in a real sense, render such decisions mechanical is aimless. In the final analysis, I believe it will be important but ambiguous qualities such as depth and interconnectedness of data, as well as the author's reputation and literary style, that will help readers determine if the critic has argued well and within the reach of his data.

With this issue explored, we are now ready to consider this inquiry's findings. These findings concern (1) the complexity of the USMES problems encountered by students in several CSSD classrooms; (2) the affective environment in several CSSD USMES classrooms; (3) the ability of the 156 students in the six CSSD USMES classes to organize their problem-solving tasks; (4) findings related to the national USMES/EDC curriculum development, implementation, and diffusion policy; (5) the lack of critical evaluation afforded CSSD USMES resource team members; and (6) the nature of the hidden curriculum in several CSSD USMES classrooms.

Finding Number One

To begin with, the vast majority of the 156 students in CSSD USMES classes were not coming into contact with problematical situations. Furthermore, in several classes this situation appeared to be influenced by the interaction of factors linked to the public nature and "realness" of the USMES units. Ironically, these qualities of the USMES units seemed to reinforce, in several USMES teachers, what appeared to be a predisposition toward the creation of teacher-dominant learning environments. In one instance, for example, the community and media awareness of the goals of one USMES class seemed subtly to create a situation in which the teacher, contrary to USMES philosophy, became widely involved in the identification and organization of the problem-solving effort.

In general, because of teacher intervention or noninvolvement with the program, the students in five of the six USMES classes did not confront problems in a manner which allowed for the possibility of short-term frustration or failure. On the other hand, as finding number two will suggest, these students, by and large, did not appear to be studying in environments designed to channel such frustrations into productive educational experiences.

Finding Number Two

This finding concerns one dimension of the affective classroom environments created by the six USMES resource team teachers. The finding essentially is this: self-report evidence gathered by the Krutchfield/Covington Attitude Inventory strongly suggests that the affective environments in three out of the six USMES classes were detrimental to the positive development of problem-solving skills and attitudes related to sharing, trusting, risk-taking, question-asking, and respectful listening. The inventory data reinforced my own impressions regarding the affective quality of these classes. These impressions resulted from observations and discussions concerning teacher expectations and efforts at reputation-building for particular individuals and, in general, disciplinary strategies employed by several of the USMES teachers, and classroom patterns of student-to-student and teacher-to-student behavior.

These areas are related. The negative patterns in each point to a fundamental lack shared by at least three of the six USMES teachers. Each, to a very large extent, lacked strategies for building effective human relationships in the classroom. In practice this meant that what happened interpersonally in the course of a school year was largely a function of the collection of behavioral patterns and reputations the students brought with them to the class. It was to this collection that the three teachers in question reacted passively. If a class was known to be rotten, it didn't improve; if a student was a sneak, he remained one; and, if a hooky player began the year with a 50 percent absence rate he ended it with a similar rate. In addition, the strategies used to control student noise level, rebelliousness, etc., were reactive and general rather than responsive and individualistic. As a group, they tended to socialize and manipulate children with boring and physically annoying tasks such as running laps or writing a particular sentence a hundred times after school. On one or two occasions the pattern was abusive to a point I found embarrassing. The strategies showed a pervasive lack of humor, imagination, and subtlety.

As indicated, on a five item subset of the attitude inventory the 156 USMES students responded in a manner that parallels and perhaps corroborates my impressions regarding three of the six USMES teachers. For example, almost 50 percent of these students indicated that (1) they were not very ready to ask questions about things they did not understand; (2) they kept ideas to themselves because they thought others might laugh at them; (3) they often had an idea for an answer that they didn't give because they were afraid it might be wrong; (4) they thought it best to make very sure an idea was a good one before suggesting it to the class; and (5) their ideas and suggestions were often not taken seriously by the rest of the class. Parenthetically, this descriptive statistical finding lends itself to various superficial interpretations when viewed in isolation. However, in the context of a naturalistic inquiry, where the time exists to use the students' anonymous proclamations as a springboard to another set of penetrating questions, the findings have a clear value.

Finding Number Three

Despite the fact that the students in Steve Tam's class had the opportunity to participate in several long-term projects such as the planting and maintenance of a vegetable garden and the development of a small notebook company, a large proportion of these students suggested, with their responses to a second five-item subset of the attitude inventory, that rudimentary organizational skills crucial to the preliminary stages of problem solving had not, in their opinion, become part of their repertoire of skills. For example, of the twenty-five responding students, 40 percent indicated that they didn't know how to get started on problems they were trying to solve; 56 percent indicated that when working on a problem they often found they hadn't paid attention to some important fact; 36 percent indicated that in solving problems they made the same kinds of mistakes over and over again; and 44 percent indicated they made up their minds too quickly about the answer to a problem and usually got rattled and confused when trying to think.

It is worth noting that the percentage patterns for the total group of USMES students was quite similar to the patterns in Steve Tam's class. For the larger group, over 50 percent of the 156 students gave incorrect answers to the items in this subset. In other words, as in the four categories above, 50 percent of these students also indicated that *they didn't know how to get started on problems they were trying to solve,* etc.

Finding Number Four

The historical aspect of this inquiry led to the uncovering of two crucial related facts. First, from its inception, USMES/EDC was committed to the notion that rapid diffusion of its concept was essential; and secondly, also from its inception, USMES/EDC considered its program, at least in part, to be a *reform* in education. Such a belief implies that before formal pilot projects and evaluation of its concepts had begun, USMES/EDC had more than a neutral, and possibly an excessively positive, attitude toward its own ideas. They chose to work with the assumption that educational research had already validated certain aspects of their real-problem-solving concept.

Given these core beliefs, several USMES/EDC curriculum decisions and behaviors become comprehensible, but not defensible. For example, USMES/EDC chose not to fully develop a set of original units to embody its *process* concepts. Rather, an attempt was made to exploit the strengths of several units previously developed, but not well disseminated, in the nineteen-sixties. In addition, USMES/EDC chose not to create a unique and various set of learning experiences for its set of two-week resource team workshops. The curriculum of these crucial workshops consisted, to a great extent, of exposure to the USMES units. It does not appear that serious thought was given to alternative strategies. The workshops were one-recipe affairs. Compounding this difficulty was USMES/EDC's failure to provide administrators with preworkshop strategies designed to inform, attract, and select the best, or near best, personnel available for resource team positions. Finally, USMES/EDC chose to proceed into its diffusion stage with a flexible, emergent perception of its curriculum materials. In my opinion, their conception was too flexible and perhaps even confused. I mean to suggest that USMES/EDC's belief that rapid diffusion was quintessential may have prompted it to move forward prematurely with a conception of itself that was too ambiguous to be fully useful. For example, the function and ultimate status of its nineteen units were not sharply elucidated during the 1973-75 period. Two different images of these units were projected simultaneously. First, there was the original image, which implied that the units were elements in an enduring USMES curriculum. This status was suggested by the number of units developed, the emphasis on exposure to the units at the resource training workshops, USMES/EDC's attempts to locate commercial distributors for its materials, and USMES/EDC's failure to suggest, at the East Lansing workshop, that the units were anything but an enduring collection. The second image came into focus during 1975 through interviews and correspondence with USMES/EDC officials. The new image suggests that the units are transitional training vehicles. The basic idea is that the units would extend the training workshops into the field by serving as field-based independent training materials for teachers. The expectation is that, after a year or two of working with such transitional units, the teachers (and students) would be capable of locating their own problems and working them through.

A change in conception such as this need not harm a developmental curriculum project's diffusion potential; after all, such projects are supposed to change in the course of their development. What is important, however, is that communication within a project's "extended family" should fully elucidate such changes. To do otherwise is to court danger with regard to a project's all-important credibility. USMES/EDC's performance in this area was uneven.

Finding Number Five

In general, USMES teachers on this resource team received little critical feedback from their administrators, or each other, regarding the quality of their USMES performance. The paucity of time spent in reflective thought contributed to the creation of learning environments that had the potential *independently* to communicate hidden learnings, learnings which are, as Kurt Lewin implied almost three decades ago, absorbed almost automatically.[9]

Finding Number Six

In Steve Tam's class the hidden learnings, that is, the unintended potential learnings that are not part of the class's conscious or explicit curriculum, often conflicted with each other. These latent potential learnings included the idea or realization that:

1. Cooperation can lead to the achievement of important personal and group goals.

2. Competitive procedures employed within a cooperative context may be a wise overall strategy in situations related to mass-production.

3. In some situations, when the chips are down, one may be forced to put friends out of business.

4. For inexplicable reasons adults—in this case, teachers—are more prone to compete than cooperate, even when competition may not be necessary or particularly productive.

5. A competitive structure that appears fair may in fact be rigged in favor of one group.

6. Individuals, even young students, can learn to contribute to large complex problems such as inflation.

7. Work is fun and satisfying.

8. Work is dull and mandatory.

9. Students, in this case sixth graders, are not mature enough to help identify their own problems.

10. The more things are supposed to change, the more they remain the same.

There were also several potential learnings not specifically related to the USMES curriculum. Of these, two stand out; first, there are unpleasant tasks in life, such as teacher punishments, which one may be forced to accept without question or protest; secondly, school is not a particularly useful place to be if you have even a mild form of a social or psychological problem.

It is difficult to assess the significance of the contradictory character of USMES/CDDS's latent curriculum. This difficulty notwithstanding, I believe it is wise to assume that the explicit, central objectives of a curriculum project will be more readily achieved when the explicit and implicit aspects of a curriculum reinforce each other. Of course, such parallelism is difficult to arrange and nearly impossible unless curriculum developers give some thought to the potential latent character of their curriculum during its initial and middle phases of development. With this desirable state of reinforcement in mind, the first set of recommendations enumerated below offers ideas that may help USMES teachers develop well-rounded learning environments commensurate with the important and ambitious citizenship goals of USMES/EDC's program.

The Inquiry's Recommendations

On the basis of the above and related findings the following recommendations, which are oriented toward three disparate groups of educators, are made.[10] Group one's recommendations address USMES/EDC specifically; they are recommended for immediate use in USMES/EDC's ongoing diffusion efforts. Group two's recommendations address a broader range of educators as well as USMES/ EDC. These recommendations are a response to the broad question: What strategies are worthy of consideration by educators interested in the creation and diffusion of community-oriented problem-solving curricula? Finally, in the closing section of this paper a recommendation of potential value to future naturalistic inquirers and educational critics is offered.

There are nine recommendations for USMES/EDC in all. First, the program should consider developing social studies essays to help the busy USMES teacher/change agent better integrate inquiry into his overall curriculum. Topics like inflation, which was selected by one of the USMES teachers studied in this inquiry, or mass production in American society, or zoos around the world, lend themselves to brief informative essays and inquiries that would effectively complement several USMES units. In a related step, I recommend using the *Bulletin for USMES Resource People* to familiarize change agents with *Three Teaching Strategies for the Social Studies*.[11] This workbook, coauthored by Bruce Joyce, Marsha Weil, and Rhoada Wald, is part of a larger collection of teacher education resource materials that are arranged for independent study.[12] The document will competently put resource personnel in touch with three useful social studies inquiry strategies. Second, in the *Teacher's Resource Book for Burglar Alarms* they should stress that a real and sustained problem with theft in an elementary school calls for, at the least, the consideration of a variety of strategies. One should not necessarily wind up building burglar alarms. Socio-drama and other values clarification techniques are pertinent here. *Role Playing for Social Values,* by Fannie R. Shaftel and George Shaftel, should be recommended reading for USMES teachers in general and for those working on the burglar alarm unit in particular.[13] Third, they should develop a pamphlet to spell out the special pitfalls that may appear in the path of a teacher who takes his students out into the real world to confront problems. Fourth, they should attempt to use the *Bulletin for USMES Resource People* to introduce resource personnel to (1) the idea of developing a *longitudinal problem-solving profile* for each student in class, and (2) descriptive techniques and forms that might facilitate the collection and analysis of such impressions and data. This recommendation has the added appeal of providing the USMES teacher with another way to spend his time constructively as the students engage a problem. Fifth, they should develop a set of broad *defining questions* to help teachers quickly identify what may be a movement away from an ideal USMES teaching posture. Questions such as the following might be included: (1) Is there psychological space for failure in my class? (2) Are my students interested in the problem? and (3) Do my students interact well in groups? The *Bulletin for USMES Resource People* or the *USMES Journal* could be used to disseminate this list of questions.[14] Sixth, USMES/EDC should encourage USMES resource people who are planning future workshops to elucidate sharply the nature of the USMES units. Seventh, in the introduction to each resource unit they should stress the importance of developing a proper affective climate to facilitate the emergence of real-problem-solving skills. They could, for example, briefly list questions to give teachers insight into the qualitative dimensions of the real-problem-solving classroom recommended by USMES/EDC.

Questions might include: (1) Do my students feel free to answer questions and make mistakes? and (2) Do my students independently choose to help one another? Eighth, USMES/EDC should consider the creation of a set of lessons that might foster the affective climates conducive to real-problem-solving and teach a class how to conduct their own community needs analysis. Finally, they should encourage teachers to use inquiry in other areas of the curriculum and to be eclectic in their choice of inquiry strategies. We should not assume that real-problem-solving is the only, or even the best, approach toward more effective problem-solving for every child. Rather, we should assume that other modes of problem-solving may serve as stepping stones to USMES real-problem-solving.

For the second group of educators there are seven recommendations in all.[15] First, plan your curriculum development program around current resources; the development and diffusion strategy should be a function of these resources rather than grandiose assumptions about the needs of the future. In particular, do not plan activities unless they can be fully evaluated within an atmosphere that allows for reconceptualization where and when it is needed. Second, be extremely cautious about the claims you make regarding problem-solving education. It is an area of education in which reliable knowledge is particularly scarce and problems of evaluation exceedingly complex. Third, build eclecticism into your design because it is conceivable, even probable, that differing types of problem-solving experience reinforce each other. Fourth, leave ample time for the crucial development period. Do not put yourself in a position where you are constantly playing catch up. Fifth, encourage your personnel to be patient, thoughtful, and flexible in their implementation strategies by modeling this behavior pattern. Appreciate that a community-oriented problem-solving curriculum that truly has young people grappling with real problems is, in a historical sense, almost counter-cultural and therefore bound to encounter serious and perhaps informed opposition. Sixth, before contacting local educational agencies, districts, universities, etc., to foster cooperative institutional relationships for the development and diffusion of your curriculum, specify unambiguous rules to govern these relationships. See Mahan for further suggestions.[16] Seventh, if you plan to train change agents to assist in the diffusion of your curriculum, conceptualize the training of these individuals as a task apart from the creation of materials for students. The learning experiences that will make teachers effective change agents are not necessarily, or even probably, identical to the set of learning experiences that will make students more effective problem-solvers.

Before I close, some thoughts about the role of the naturalistic inquirer or educational critic in projects similar to this one are appropriate. In the world of art and literature the critic almost universally works alone; his individuality is his trademark. To speak of such a critic working in a team is almost a contradiction in terms. And yet, with my dissertation behind me, I believe that a recommendation that supports the idea of, and explains the need for, a team approach to educational evaluation is highly appropriate. Such a recommendation is developed in the concluding section of my dissertation. The essence of these remarks is that it would behoove educational critics, who work, to an extent greater than their counterparts in the literary and art worlds, with projects complex in scope, flexibility, and political implication, to give serious consideration to the difficult notion of working in teams. Of course it was made clear that such an approach is not to be considered a panacea or even a necessity for all educational critics. Indeed, it is my opinion that educational critics at work on more circumscribed projects do better to work alone. Nevertheless, my experience has convinced me that, in projects similar to mine where the objectives and tactics of the object of inquiry occasionally shift and where the central questions dictate the need to observe and interview many people over an ample period of time, the advantages of a team approach outweigh the disadvantages. In short, if you are aiming your educational criticism at a developmental curriculum project, or a state board of education, or some other educational agency whose activities are diffuse and flexible rather than neat and tidy, do not work alone unless you have to.[17]

Conclusion

This report has attempted to present the fundamental facts of my inquiry. In the dissertation itself great pains were taken to substantiate and qualify assertions that, for reasons of space, were merely listed here. To a certain extent I am uncomfortable with this situation but am hopeful that readers who might, as a result of reading this case study, reach premature conclusions regarding USMES/

EDC's competence will keep in mind the exceedingly difficult economic era in which USMES/EDC operated and read more extensively in my dissertation and beyond before developing anything more than a tentative opinion.

It remains to be said that this inquiry has taught me many lessons. Certainly humility and frustration were found in this experience, but there was also a great satisfaction in working with a mode of inquiry flexible enough to fit the nooks, crannies, and changing currents of the real world of educational settings. For those who might pursue questions in this mode an extensive bibliography has been provided in my dissertation.

Notes

1. There are, of course, other factors involved. John Brademas pointed to three possible factors as he discussed the financial difficulties of the then new National Institute of Education. As possible reasons for that agency's funding problems, he suggested that: (1) many congressmen are not really clear about what research in education is and, whatever it is, are not sure that research makes any difference in improving teaching and learning; (2) the agency has not received strong backing from various professional educational groups; and (3) the Nixon administration had undermined the agency's ability to explain its programs and policies to Congress by neglecting to make crucial appointments to the National Council on Educational Research. See John Brademas, "A Congressional View of Educational R and D and NIE," *Educational Researcher* 3, no. 3 (March 1974).

2. The term *developmental curriculum project* denotes here a group effort to produce some new kind of curriculum, using experimental tryouts of preliminary materials and collecting feedback from such tryouts to be used for the improvement of the curriculum prior to its release for general distribution. The definition is Hulda Grobman's; it appears in her book *Developmental Curriculum Projects: Decision Points and Processes* (Itasca, Ill.: F. E. Peacock, 1970).

3. Attempts were made in 1974-76 to link these teams into regional networks that were supposed to carry on the diffusion effort after USMES/EDC culminated its efforts in 1978.

4. Information about these units or any other part of the USMES Library can be obtained by writing to the Education Development Center, 55 Chapel Street, Newton, Massachusetts, 02160.

5. This is a pseudonym for the school district that sponsored the USMES implementation team I worked with, and studied, between 1973 and 1975.

6. Elliot W. Eisner, "Qualitative Intelligence and the Act of Teaching," *Elementary School Journal* 73, no. 6 (March 1963); idem, "Critical Thinking: Some Cognitive Components," *Teachers College Record*, April 1965; idem, "Emerging Models for Educational Evaluation," *School Review* 80, no. 4 (August 1972); Decker F. Walker, "What Curriculum Research?" *Journal of Curriculum Studies* 5, no. 1 (1973); Decker F. Walker and Jon Schaffarzick, "Comparing Curricula," *Review of Educational Research* 44, no. 1 (Winter 1974).

7. The instrument consists of thirty-three statements that relate to problem-solving. The student is instructed that he can agree, disagree, or remain undecided about a statement. There is a correct answer for each statement. In my administration and scoring each correct answer was given three points, each undecided two points, and an incorrect answer one point. Scores for individuals were added, and means for each total group were derived.

8. "Steve Tam" is the pseudonym for the teacher whose class I observed most closely during this inquiry.

9. Kurt Lewin, "Experiments in Social Space," *Harvard Educational Review*, January 1939.

10. In the dissertation recommendations are also presented to educators considering the use of naturalistic techniques and to the CSSD USMES team. The recommendations to the latter group were made in a debriefing packet given to each member of the team.

11. The *Bulletin for USMES Resource People* is a USMES/EDC document sent monthly to approximately seven hundred people: resource team members, demonstration school principals, development teachers who have served as staff for implementation workshops, and college and other intermediate agency personnel. Because of recent budgetary cuts this publication will probably be discontinued.

12. Bruce R. Joyce, Marsha Weil, and Rhoada Wald, *Three Teaching Strategies for the Social Studies* (Chicago: Science Research Associates, 1972).

13. Fannie R. Shaftel and George Shaftel, *Role Playing for Social Values: Decision-Making in the Social Studies* (Englewood Cliffs, N.J.: Prentice-Hall, 1967).

14. USMES/EDC planned to publish an occasional journal of opinions related to USMES issues. Recent budgetary cuts have prevented the publication of this journal.

15. In the dissertation there are twice as many recommendations for this group. In particular, specific strategies for training workshops are delineated.

16. James M. Mahan, "Frank Observations on Innovation in Elementary Schools," *Interchange* 3 (1972): 2-3.

17. My entire project called for more energy and time than I had originally anticipated. In particular, I did not leave enough time for the writing phase of the project, where deadlines had to be met if my formative evaluation were to reach USMES/EDC in time to be formative. Educational critics who aspire to use ethnographic techniques would do well to read and heed the prescriptions of Rosalie Wax and Harry Wolcott, two ethnographers who have utilized such techniques in educational institutions. Their basic and important recommendation is that educational ethnographers should leave as much time for organizing and writing material as is allowed for gathering it. In addition, in his essay Wolcott discusses *ethnographic fatigue*, a topic I consider important for educational critics who are considering the use of ethnographic techniques. See R. H. Wax, *Doing Fieldwork: Warnings and Advice* (Chicago: University of Chicago Press, 1971); and H. Wolcott, "Criteria for an Ethnographic Approach to Research in Schools," *Human Organization* 34, no. 2 (Summer 1975).

The dominant interest in the case study by Thomas Popkewitz is political. Popkewitz analyzes a specific middle school and its efforts during a single year to develop and implement a program of individually guided education. Whereas a conventional assessment of the school might have employed largely quantitative measures to determine the extent to which expressed goals had been realized, Popkewitz goes far beyond the assessment of surface characteristics. Analyzing the relationship between action and the norms, beliefs, and dispositions of the school staff, he investigates the entire social structure of the school and how it functions within a self-initiated attempt at reform. He is thus concerned with the character and qualities of institutional influences on people in a social setting.

Following the introductory section the study is divided into three additional sections. The first of these sections describes essentially surface characteristics of the school and its project; the second discloses underlying meanings; and the third summarizes, amplifies, and justifies judgments rendered, explicitly stating six major implications for the problem of changing schools.

The descriptive section includes a largely chronological and topical ordering of the events of the school year. As such, it exempli-

411

fies "plot." Also included is the explanation that in developing a critique of the school the participant observer-evaluators sought descriptive and explanatory categories for their data, identified recurrent patterns and trends, and searched for appropriate metaphors. In this sense, much of the study exemplifies "metaphor" (for instance, in the section devoted to disclosure of meaning, the explanation of group consensus as representing a symbolic process). The disclosure section, of course, richly embodies "theme," as well. Whereas the author's "point of view" permeates the entire study, particularly in the concluding section it becomes entirely explicit as a means for justifying judgments. The norms suggested by Popkewitz are a function of his view. He points out that in providing individuals with ways to order and interpret the world, schools embody such things as ideologies, relationships of power, and conceptions of individual responsibility, and he insists that schools must make choices of actions available in light of political and ethical considerations. The study demonstrates how the ethical is an integral part of the political dimension of curriculum criticism.

The principal critical focal points in the study are the "work" (primarily analysis and disclosures of discrepancies between the public and the hidden agenda of the school) and the "author" (disclosures about intentions, processes of deliberation, and actions of the staff).

18

The Social Structure of Schools and Reform: A Case Study of IGE/S

Thomas Popkewitz

Introduction

The recent efforts in educational reform have given attention to the institutional nature of school life. This focus, in part, resulted from the failures of the curricular reform movement of the 1960s. The development of "new" physics, mathematics, and social science did little to instill the intellectual excitement the educational planners sought for classrooms. The failure of reform, researchers revealed, reflected the planners' lack of consideration of the social organization of the schools.[1] Curricular reforms tended to be incorporated into the existing patterns of conduct and belief. The "new" curriculum was taught just as the "old" had been.

One attempt to change the social structure of school life is the Individually Guided Education/Secondary (IGE/S) Project. The project is part of a larger effort of the Wisconsin Research and Development Center concerned with individualizing school instruction. The center's previous focus was on elementary schools, and IGE/S was

This article originally appeared as Technical Report No. 400, "Report from the Project on IGE Secondary," of the Wisconsin Research and Development Center for Cognitive Learning (Madison: University of Wisconsin, October 1976).

413

funded to extend the center's work to middle and secondary schools. The project seeks to engage school staffs in planning, implementing, and evaluating school-wide efforts to individualize instruction. School staffs are to think critically about, design, and implement alternative educational experiences for secondary students.

This paper is concerned with the impact of the IGE/S project in a specific middle school. Through the use of case study,[2] this paper examines the IGE/S intervention process to investigate how an existing educational organization incorporates proposed changes into its everyday patterns. Attention is given to the norms, beliefs, and dispositions which give direction to the actions of teachers and administrators. This level of analysis is concerned with illuminating the interpretive perspective by which individuals give meanings to the events of school life.

The analysis is in three sections. First is a discussion of the intended purposes and activities of the middle school IGE/S project. The description is concerned with surface characteristics such as what groups were formed and what programmatic changes occurred. A second section focuses on underlying meanings given to these activities. Third is a concluding section which includes recommendations.

The Middle School and IGE/S

The project's major focus of attention during the 1975-76 year was a middle school in a small city near the Madison, Wisconsin R and D Center. The school has a somewhat unusual physical location. Built at the edge of a large public park, it is bordered on three sides by a playing field, meadows, and a pond. The residential character of the school's immediate neighborhood is single-family houses, many occupied by professionals and university faculty. The school is part of a consolidated district which draws students from a nearby rural community which is more conservative than its city counterpart.

The school is moderately sized, with fifty teachers and approximately 750 students in grades six, seven, and eight. The staff consists of regular academic, related arts, and music and physical education teachers, in addition to two guidance counselors, a principal, and an assistant principal. The faculty is organized into teams of four teachers. The two sixth-grade teams function differently from the upper-grade teams, cooperatively planning courses of study in all curricular subjects. Each teacher has instructional responsibility for a specific group of children (twenty-five to thirty), like an elementary teacher in a self-contained classroom. The seventh and eighth grade teams, however, are organized by subject matter. Each team in those grades has teachers representing social studies, mathematics, science, and English. Also, the teachers belong to subject departments which cross grades. Teachers teach fifty-minute periods in their specialty and meet approximately 130 students a week.

Methodology

The project was evaluated through the methodology of participant observation, and the case study style is used to report it in order to identify and discuss the social complexities of the intervention scheme. This methodology was chosen for two reasons. First, the study is part of the developmental process of the project. The case study is to help planners make future refinements or alterations in their program. The descriptions of the school interactions can reveal purposes and consequences of action. The closeness to the events enables planners to understand why things happen and therefore reflect more critically about the effects of the intervention scheme. Second, the descriptions can be useful to others who confront similar problems about schooling. Although the knowledge gained is not causal and predictive, the emerging generalizations can help others focus upon concerns, problems, and possible unanticipated consequences in the situations they confront.

Data were collected in three ways: (1) Observations of faculty meetings concerned with IGE/S programs. Some of these meetings involved small groups of teachers planning a dimension of the "change process." General faculty meetings to discuss programs and instructional classes in which teachers were using programs developed through the IGE/S project were also observed. (2) Informal discussions with faculty about their work in the IGE/S programs. These discussions occurred throughout the school year and referred to specific meetings or issues. (3) Formal interviews with the faculty. Interviews during the school year focused upon specific activities or events such as a teacher attending a professional conference related to IGE/S. Extensive interviews were conducted at the end of the year with eighteen faculty and two administrators. These interviews were thirty to sixty minutes long. Data were collected from December to May.

Analysis of the data occurred in two interrelated stages. First, the field work sought to invent categories to describe and explain the events. While data were being collected, recurring patterns or trends were identified. Initial observations, for example, revealed an emphasis upon achieving consensus in decision-making. The category of consensus was given validity through checking other data, subsequent observations, and staff interviews.

Second, the data were reexamined after the completion of the field work. This second dimension of analysis was built upon the initial research. Here, though, the entire range of data was available for critical scrutiny. (At this point, the researcher is no longer restricted in analysis by his own participation in the events. Counter-examples to categories can be sought, validity and recurring patterns can be checked, and new relationships among the data identified.) The analysis continued into the final written stage. The search for appropriate metaphors for communicating findings was an integral dimension of the research report.

Purpose and Activities of the Project

The IGE/S project has a three-fold purpose. First, it is designated to help teachers develop individualized instructional programs. The meaning of individualized instruction is left ambiguous in the project's technical reports. It is related to a notion of continuous progress which requires that "learning activities and sequences be varied in recognition of the fact that each person has a unique pattern and rate of emotional, intellectual, and physical growth which is essentially continuous but which is likely to have high, low, and plateau periods."[3] The definition was left open to permit unique or idiosyncratic innovations. The second purpose of IGE/S is to help school staffs develop organizational patterns which are concerned with individualizing instruction. This follows from the assumption that school reform must be based upon a staff competent to initiate and sustain critical dialogs about instruction. The third purpose is to help schools employ shared decision-making as a part of their planning processes. Called an "interactive model," shared decision-making allows teachers, administrators, parents, and students to participate in the making of decisions which affect them.

To implement IGE/S programs, the project has two levels of

operation. First is the development of planning processes to individualize instruction in specific schools. It is this dimension which will be the focus of this paper. Second is maintaining a mechanism (a network of schools) by which teachers can share ideas and experiences related to individualization. The network of schools did function during the year of study but is related only tangentially to the specific work in the studied school.

The IGE/S Workshop and Task Forces

After initial contacts with the middle-school administrator, and with school board approval, the IGE/S staff organized a workshop prior to the start of school.[4] Thirty-seven teachers, two administrators, and seven parents attended six morning sessions. The focus of the sessions, identified by a prior planning group of four teachers, was "to implement a change process in the middle school." The organization of the workshop involved three parts.

First, the workshop activities were designed to have the staff obtain consensus on educational purposes of a change process. Agreement was obtained through construction of a hierarchy of purposes (figure 1). Purposes or reasons for implementing changes in the middle-school program were discussed in a morning session, and after a broad range of purposes were identified, they were arranged hierarchically. More specific purposes ("to develop communication channels between parents and staff") were placed at the top of a chart and general, more inclusive purposes ("to enhance human dignity") at the bottom. The teachers reconsidered each of the purposes and chose one as the central focus of the workshop. This purpose was "to develop a school program which develops specific competencies based upon individual needs and interests." The following workshop activities focused on that purpose to develop specific school-wide individualization strategies.

The construction of a purpose hierarchy was thought to be an important dimension of the planning process for several reasons. The agreement on purposes was to provide a single collective focus for the group and enable people with diverse ideas to agree upon a single set of purposes. The group processes in developing the hierarchy would provide a commitment to achieve the purposes. And, finally, the purpose hierarchy would provide a criterion for later decision-making.[5]

The second part of the workshop was to identify possible alter-

Figure 1
Hierarchy of Purposes (Primary Purpose Circled)

Middle School 1975-76 Change Program

To develop
communication channels between parents and staff

To develop understanding between parents and staff

To get parent involvement in decision making

To consider the teacher-advisor system

To provide individual student-teacher contact

To facilitate communication between students, parents, and teachers

To develop a sense of security and trust

To allow every child to receive attention

To allow every child to feel worthwhile

To create a positive learning atmosphere and environment

To create an open atmosphere where students want to learn

To develop a school program which develops specific competencies based on individual needs and interests

To allow the opportunity for self responsibility and commitment

To be able to express individual thoughts and feelings

To question, understand and deal with own thoughts, feelings, and actions

To have experience in taking responsibility for own actions, thoughts, and feelings

To learn how decisions (actions) affect others and self

To build positive feelings and trust about self and others

To be able to deal successfully with situations, problems etc.

To attain goals

To build self concept, feel a sense of worth, and have respect for others

To be able to interact positively and successfully with others

To have people feel good and comfortable

To have effective lifelong learning

To improve not quite the whole world

To enhance human dignity

native strategies for developing "competencies based upon individual needs and interests." Teachers brainstormed about possible more specific goals and related school programs. Among other items, teachers wanted to give attention to "developing an increased responsibility system" or introducing "more flexible scheduling." As the discussion continued, the staff formulated "We Agree" statements, which listed general, educational aims the staff would use to guide their efforts toward changing the school program. Among these was "We agree to identify and meet at least one need (skill or personal) of each student in each class." The "We Agree" statements also had concrete proposals for school-wide programs, such as "We agree to have school-wide uninterrupted sustained silent reading one period per week."

The third dimension of the workshop was to translate the purpose hierarchy and alternative strategies into a school-wide plan of action. Five tasks were identified, related purpose hierarchies constructed (see figure 2), implementation timelines constructed, and groups of teachers organized as task forces. The task forces were:

1. *USSR—Uninterrupted Sustained Silent Reading.* This task force was to implement a school period in which children could read without interruption. The purpose of USSR was, as one teacher stated, "to make kids read and to make it enjoyable."

2. *Flexible Scheduling.* This task force was to develop alternative classroom scheduling that would produce greater individualization.

3. *Club.* This task force was to organize periods in which students could pursue interests other than those found in traditional school courses.

4. *Parent Conferences.* This task force was to develop alternative forms of parent conferences to provide parents with more information about children's studies.

5. *Teacher-Adviser.* This task force was to provide a school-wide program in which teachers and students could develop closer personal relationships.

Implementation of the Task Force Plans

Approximately four to six teachers volunteered to participate in each task force. They were to plan and implement the agreed-upon programs. Each of the task forces met frequently during most of the school year, and for the first two-thirds of the year many of the

Figure 2
Purpose Hierarchy for Human Development Activities of the
Teacher/Adviser Program

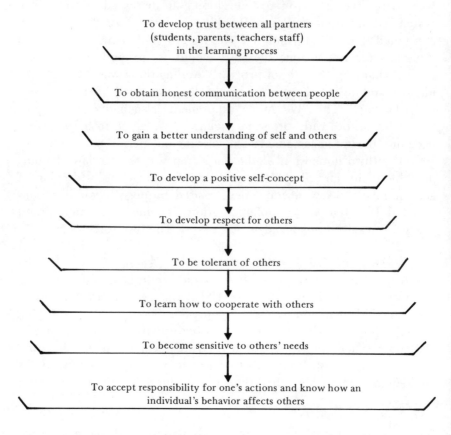

groups met once a week. The teachers involved in each group seemed eager to implement the specific program and worked hard to develop appropriate materials and procedures. The teachers involved in implementing a teacher-adviser system, for example, produced sets of materials for teachers, organized an introduction session for the entire student body, and struggled with the organizational scheduling to arrange teacher-adviser periods.

The teachers' commitment to implementing the task force objective was underscored by the scheduled time of meetings. Most schools provide little time during the day for teachers to reflect about their roles and the purposes of instruction. This middle school was no exception. The day was taken up with administrative chores, teaching classes, or grading papers. Further, the teachers' time was so fragmented that it was virtually impossible for task force teachers to meet during a regular planning period. As a result, teachers would typically set aside an afterschool time (3:30-4:15) once a week. Clubs task force, for example, might meet Mondays after school, parent conference task force on Tuesday.

Parents participated in the deliberations of two of the task forces. Four parents participated in the teacher-adviser task force, and four different parents joined the parent conference group. The parents took their responsibilities seriously, attending most meetings and participating in discussions. Parents often sought the advice of other community members and children in making decisions, which provided a different perspective on the problems under consideration. For example, one parent of the teacher-adviser committee talked to her daughter's friends about alternative approaches to forming teacher-adviser groups. This discussion was reported to the task force as part of the deliberations. Because of the purpose of the clubs task force to provide nonacademic and student-oriented activities, two students participated in that task force's discussions.

Certain results of the project can be identified even from a surface analysis. At the end of the year, the task forces had implemented some specific changes in the school program and planned others for the following year. Early in the year, a silent reading period was established. Teachers and students spent the first ten minutes of school reading a book of their choice. By spring, two fifteen-minute periods were created for a teacher-adviser system. Teachers and administrators worked with small groups of students to provide opportunities to talk in an informal, noncompetitive atmosphere. A ten-week segment of the spring term included club periods. By the end of the school year, teachers had agreed to a plan for the fall term which would increase contacts with parents. In addition, teachers had agreed in principle to a reorganization of class schedules to allow for greater flexibility. Teams of teachers were to be given three-hour blocks of time rather than fifty-minute periods. Through these less rigid block schedules, teachers believed, they could respond more adequately to demands of instruction or students' interests.

Certain workshop "We Agree" statements were not given explicit attention as the staff focused upon the school-wide task force activities. For example, teachers did agree to utilize better community resources, to teach basic language skills in all classes, and "to involve" special teachers in team meetings. Generally these individual or team-related strategies were not explicitly considered during the school year.

The role of the R and D Center staff in the school was to provide technical support. They tended to see themselves as responsible for helping the school staff identify their own priorities and find appropriate strategies. The IGE/S people provided assistance to the specific task forces, arranged for contacts with schools and professional conferences related to ideas under consideration, and helped organize school board presentations about task force efforts.

The Social Structure and IGE/S Activities

The task force activities need to be considered beyond the introduction of activities into the middle-school program. These activities existed within certain norms, beliefs which make reasonable and justifiable the various efforts for reform. Illuminating the meaning teachers give to the reform can enable us to assess more adequately the impact of the IGE/S project.

Certain underlying dimensions permeated the faculty's involvement in the task forces. For one thing, there was a concern for consensus decision-making, a concept which had been introduced in early workshop activities. During the year, the staff continued to seek changes which had a wide degree of faculty acceptance. The consensus, it will be argued, was built upon a fragile form of commitment and introduced certain organizational biases which worked against the intent of the IGE/S planners. First, the staff tended to interpret the task forces as helping to ameliorate negative student feeling toward the existing activities of instruction. Second, the implemented task force activities maintained a concern with the control and management of students. Third, the IGE/S activities had a symbolic function within the school district. Faced with possible staff reductions due to low enrollments and a low status, the faculty saw the reforms as a way of legitimizing the school program and the need for current staff allocations.

Group Consensus as a Symbolic Process

The general nature of the purpose hierarchy worked against change as it masked the conflicting ideas held about teaching. The commitment of the summer workshop was to general statements about educational purposes such as "to develop a sense of security and trust," "to allow every child to feel worthwhile," or "to develop specific competencies based upon individual needs and interests." The purposes provided emotive symbols which condensed the feelings, hopes, and desires of many who are associated with schools. The abstractness of statements made them highly appealing, and few could disagree.

The ambiguity of the purpose statements permitted teachers with diverse beliefs and practices to accept the purposes without contradiction. Some teachers saw their work as subject-centered; others focused upon psychological characteristics; still others wanted a problem-solving orientation to education. While more will be said about teaching perspectives later, the idea of "individual needs" can illustrate a function of ambiguity. Some subject-centered teachers give diagnostic tests in reading or social studies to identify some missing knowledge which a teacher decides a student should know. The lack of knowledge becomes a "need," and a "prescription" such as doing a workbook page is devised to meet it. Another teacher is concerned with the "need" of a child to learn how to solve social problems. This teacher meets students' "needs" by creating opportunities for students to develop their own curiosities and seek answers from many different sources. The process of inquiring becomes important, not the learning of a discrete skill or fact.

The purpose hierarchy enabled those two types of teachers to accept the statements of faculty goals without providing concrete referents by which to judge the assumptions and implications of their specific teaching actions. Each teacher is concerned with "needs." Yet each has a different conception of teaching, what learning means, and what the roles of student and teacher should be.

The staff was able to ignore the deep ethical and political issues embedded in educational choices.[6] At its most fundamental level, schooling is the attempt to provide individuals with ways to order and interpret their social world. Implicit in the formation of consciousness are values, attitudes, and ideologies as well as subject-matter. Curricular approaches contain conceptions of individual responsibility and power, of appropriate relationships between people and social institutions, and of the role of the school within a larger economic and social system. The political and ethical choices implicit in the faculty's actions remained hidden through the abstraction of the hierarchy.

The lack of substantive commitment compelled the task forces to devise strategies which would reduce sources of contention or opposition. Each group of teachers had the task of translating the general purpose into specific forms and concrete actions. This would of necessity challenge the particular life space of the staff, yet the task forces had no mandate related to a particular vision of educational affairs. The process of change avoided the implications of the staff's conflicting views of education. As a result, the work-a-day activities of these task groups focused upon identifying a course of action which would accommodate the diverse views of the many faculty members.

A course of least resistance was devised as the task forces' strategy. Least common denominators were sought in programs. Task force discussions were dominated by compromises designed *not* to challenge taken-for-granted rules of the school. Contrary to the intention of the IGE/S project, the consensus was built upon the pragmatics of reducing substantive dialogs and possible conflict.

One approach to gaining program acceptance was not to challenge vested interests. At a meeting of the flexible scheduling task force, for example, a physical education teacher reacted strongly to a suggestion of using the gymnasium for large-group instruction: It would interfere with the current schedule of classes. Eventually the subject was dropped and the staff focused upon other areas of the school. The teacher-adviser task force provided two fifteen-minute periods for advising by reducing the passing time allotted between classes. The teachers realized the period was too short for discussions between teachers and students, but the proposal was accepted because the teachers realized the academic teachers would not approve time being subtracted from their regular instructional periods. As one teacher commented at a teacher-adviser task force meeting: "People will fight about taking the time from their period and we should not have conflict. We don't want people to be negative about the scheduling, so we have to find a way that makes everybody happy" (Observation).

Teachers also sought to prevent the task force proposals from challenging existing work duties or relationships. The notion of flexible scheduling, for example, was developed around rigid organization scheduling which had specialists (foreign language, music, art) moving between teaching at the high school, middle school, and elementary school. There was a reluctance to make new demands upon teaching. A teacher-adviser meeting discussion, for example, focused on the use of cross-aged grouping. A parent thought that groups of children of different ages could help develop a more total sense of community in the school. The teachers disagreed, citing the additional burdens it would demand of teachers. These burdens, they felt, would not be acceptable to the faculty.

Parent: I want it to be like a family and maybe this would be interage grouping so that kids can help, like peer teaching can help students adjust to problems at school. For example, my seventh grade daughter could help a sixth grader.

Teacher #1: The problem is adjusting to the pattern of scheduling in the school. It's more intricate to do cross-age planning, you need more planning to get an interage grouping.

Teacher #2: If you separate the kids who are in different grades, as you would in interage grouping, it's messy. You have the same period every week and you begin falling behind. Teachers are not going to be able to give the same work. (Observation)

The fragile nature of the staff consensus produced tensions within task force deliberations. Teachers expressed reservations, frustration, and anxiety about the level of the actual agreement reached with the staff. There was continual mention of the need to take concrete parts of a program to the faculty for a "We Agree" statement. The "We Agree" statement provided the group with a sense of security that the staff would allow them to proceed. A teacher-adviser group meeting prior to the winter recess, for example, reflected the continued questioning teachers had about the staff's acceptance of their efforts.

The guidance counselor suggested "a new 'We Agree' statement needed to be formulated, one which would establish that the staff agreed to the procedures that were set out in the in-service." . . . . The guidance counselor remarked that the sixth grade teachers did not want to participate because they already know the children. The sixth grade teachers work with only thirty children, have a homeroom, and they know the children fairly well. (Observation)

The problem of using the IGE/S procedures for providing direction was discussed during the interviews. Some teachers found the purpose hierarchy too abstract and nonsequential to guide action.

It might be a really nice technique to get people involved and get them stirred up, talking and thinking, but when you go to write an outline of the program or you set up the goals of the program, throw it away. . . . I would not really understand how one level led to the next and how you could take that hierarchy and go. (Teacher interview)

The vagueness of purposes was reflected in teachers' thoughts about the "We Agree" statements. Many of the initial ideas were highly general, teachers said, and not helpful when considering the concrete substance the task forces proposed. Teachers thought the proposals had to be considered on their specific merits and not on their nebulous relationships to a purpose.

Some teachers also viewed the outward search for consensus as serving the political function of legitimizing directions sought by the administration. At certain times, one teacher argued, "When it was likely a 'We Agree' statement could be achieved, a vote was taken. At other times, when disagreement appeared, there would be no 'We Agree' statement and they would go on and on with this 'We Agree' until the thing was accomplished." Another teacher thought the "We Agree" statements served as a public relations device within the school district. (More will be said about this later.)

I am a little bit disgusted with the fact that it has gotten away from the "We Agree." It is being more or less pushed at us so it is mostly been for their benefit up there, just to say, "Hey, we're doing some new things." Now I don't know if they're under the gun from the Superintendent saying: "Hey, we want to see some improvements in that school or curriculum" or whatever. (Teacher interview)

To summarize, the search for consensus had a particular meaning within the middle-school context. The constructing of purpose hierarchies and "We Agree" statements permitted the staff to believe they had general agreement on the changes. However, this agreement was largely symbolic. The efforts to implement concrete changes in programs produced sources of opposition as the proposals challenged specific rules and vested interests in the school. The task forces chose to maintain staff commitment by not challenging the specific motives and intentions guiding the day-to-day activities of the school. It is to these motives and intentions we now turn our attention.

Making Existing Practices Reasonable

One of the major innovations of the school year was the introduction of teacher-adviser groups. Teachers and parents suggested that children needed to develop a more trusting and personal relationship with adults in the school. Further it was reasoned that the large classes (twenty-five to thirty) plus a teacher's large number of classes (five per day) made this personal contact difficult. Teachers argued, correctly I think, that successful teaching depends upon an atmosphere of mutual trust and respect.

The problem, however, could be understood from a variety of perspectives. First, one could say that there is something wrong in the patterns of interaction between professionals and students in each class. Different instructional strategies and conceptions of curriculum could be devised to deal with the problem. Second, a teacher might say it is difficult to develop trust and respect when meeting 125 students a day. The problem of scheduling, moving, and controlling so many children mitigates against any sustained involvement among faculty and students. A strategy could be sought to reorganize school groupings to involve smaller numbers of students with faculty. In addition, different expectations and patterns of interaction within any one class could be explored to promote mutual respect, trust, and intellectual pursuits. Both alternatives stress the general institutional character of the problem by focusing upon structural qualities of schooling. A third type of approach focuses upon the students as the problem. The goal is to make students believe the school is a better place while not altering in any fundamental way the conditions in which students work. Innovations function to make existing routines and regularities seem more palatable to students. An analogy in industry is the introduction of better lighting or more coffee breaks to increase production without considering the social and ethical implications of the assembly line itself.

It is the third approach which characterized the staff's use of the task forces. Teachers generally treated their involvement in the

IGE/S project as a way of making reasonable the ongoing activities, priorities, and assumptions of their teaching. Many teachers defined the issue of educational reform as eliminating a feeling of mistrust and alienation among students. Children were seen as having a neutral or negative attitude toward school. Things were stolen. Vandalism occurred. Drugs had been used. Behind the task forces' efforts was a desire to help students develop better attitudes toward "what teachers were doing, to try harder, to do better."

The staff was concerned about improving relationships between students, and between teachers, and hopefully, having a more positive atmosphere within the school. A lot of negative things have happened in the past. There's been a lot of vandalism, students seem very negative toward school. The school has received a lot of pressure from the community because the middle school is viewed as not a real desirable place for students to be in at times. They feel that the climate is bad. There are drugs. (Teacher interview)

The effort to eliminate student alienation produced a basic dichotomy between IGE/S activities and the regular school program. The teacher-adviser system, USSR, and clubs, for example, were defined as "human development" activities. They could provide limited situations within the school day for personalized contacts with students. The human development activities were thought of as separate from the "academic" but helpful as a mechanism for gaining student acceptance of the regular school programs. This distinction between academic and human development was explained by a guidance counselor considering the purpose of teacher-adviser systems.

Q: I'm still not clear about the distinction you are making between academic and teacher-adviser system.

A: Well, the difference is that academic is concerned with what the student does. The TA counseling is concerned with who the student is. Academic work is concerned with motivating kids to work, to help them adapt to programs, to keep students informed, to help them with their habits of study, to meet with students about evaluating their course work and monitoring what they're doing in the subject-matter. TA, on the other hand, is concerned with human development. I see the pattern as the growth of a total person and how they come across to others and relate to others. It's concerned with interpersonal relations and the perceptions that others have. (Interview)

Another faculty member also saw the personal development emphasis as important to the task force work.

I think they meant social needs, interactions between students, having positive relationships between students and teachers, and then, through that, the students would be happier and more fulfilled, and also meeting their needs academically, but I don't think that there was a real academic thrust at all. It was more social, meeting social needs and personal needs. (Teacher interview)

The dichotomy enabled many teachers to view the problem of trust and respect as unrelated to their everyday activities. In discussing the assignments to teacher-adviser groups, one teacher suggested the classroom teachers "had responsibility for reporting on students' work and therefore would not be trusted." Another teacher justified separate teacher-adviser periods by saying, "We have fifty minutes in academics and can't squeeze in the TA as a teacher. It's neat to know children. The buses leave at 3:00 and there is no way of getting to know them except through a TA period." During an inservice meeting, a question was raised about whether the adviser (teacher) be called by a first name. After a few comments, it was suggested, "Well, they could do it only in here, and then when they go out they start calling teachers by their last name." Trust was on the agenda only for the group meeting.

Other task force work also reflected a view that the reforms were separate from, yet supportive of, regular school activities. Some teachers saw the reorganization in flexible scheduling as a more efficient way of conveying the existing lessons. One teacher suggested flexible scheduling would enable him to teach one lesson to 120 students rather than repeat it four or five times. Clubs were thought of as a form of play, distinct from learning activities of the school. Parent conferences were to provide a more effective way to convey information to parents. Few teachers felt that more communication with parents in a dialogic way would affect what and how to teach.

Control as a Factor of Reform

A major dimension of the staff's involvement in the task groups was the legitimation of existing forms of school control. The fact that control was a factor is of no surprise. Since institutionalized actions contain regularized patterns of conduct, forms of social control are inevitably created. The important question, therefore, is the nature of that control. Much of the middle school staff activity gave credence to a professional control over the ideas and social relationships of students. This control orientation was reflected in teaching perspectives and discussion about strategies of reform.

At least three perspectives to teaching existed among the middle school staff: subject matter, human development, and problem-solving. While no one teacher would fit all the characteristics of an ideal type, the three categories provide a way of thinking about the variation. The sets of beliefs about teaching and curriculum guided the teachers' interpretation of the proposed reforms and gave direction in finding solutions to educational problems.

The dominant faculty perspective was the subject-matter orientation. The teachers in that group believed there exists a specified, limited body of knowledge to be imparted to students. Knowledge is treated as an "object" or "thing" that is given to individuals. Students are to master the teacher's predetermined facts or generalizations. Most often, the teachers justified this learning by saying "students need this information for the next grade" or "it will be required when they get into high school."

Testing and grading is an important dimension of subject-centered teaching. The test validates the student success in knowledge acquisition. Although teachers often referred to important non-testable aspects of teaching and learning, much of their time was taken up with making, giving, and scoring tests. Achievement was defined in precise scores, such as sums of correct answers on quizzes. During the year many teachers were observed working with tests during periods assigned for class preparation. Teachers paid careful attention to test scores and entered them in a specially designed booklet. One team meeting, for example, centered entirely upon these booklets. The team had to decide which students performed well enough to get end-of-year awards. Teachers summarized the test scores written for each student, compared the scores with team members, and then made a decision on who would be given a scholarship award.

Individualization to the subject-centered teacher meant devising strategies which would enable students to master the content. Packets of materials were to be created by which students would pace themselves through a given program.

An individualized math program to me would mean, there is some structure provided to the student. In the sixth grade we have addition, subtraction, division, etc., fractions, percent measurement. Okay, we find out where the student should be working, or what he has mastered right now. If he has mastered addition, subtraction, division, fine, then he starts in fractions, works through various levels, and we allow him to progress at his own pace. That's what individualized means to me. (Teacher interview)

The subject-centered perspective was supported by and supportive of the existing school organization. Much of the organization of teachers and students concerned the control and ordering of people. Time in school was divided according to subject-matter specialties. Teachers were classified by content they were to make available to students. Evaluation was determined by seemingly precise number systems. Further, each teacher was assigned to convey the appropriate knowledge to 125 students. Time became a precious commodity to be used correctly. There were so many minutes to learn history or French and to pass between classes. French, band, and music teachers moved between district schools to their allotted places and periods. The carefully orchestrated movement was an important part of both the teachers' and students' day. Each had to move "purposefully." The student was to get to his desk and sit quietly. The teacher was to ensure an orderly transition of students from one place to another.

It was the subject-matter specialists who reacted most strongly to proposals which would limit the time of teaching periods. The fifty-minute period, they argued, is barely enough time to present all the knowledge students need. To take away time for nonacademics posed an unwarranted restraint upon their teaching.

I guess I feel right now that I only have these kids for 50 minutes a day and trying to cram reading, writing, spelling, and literature into one fifty-minute period and for 180 days; trying and expecting these kids to really improve. I'm really having a hard time—there are so many things this year that I never got into because there just wasn't the time. (Teacher interview)

The subject-matter teacher believed obeying directions was integrally related to learning content: "Kids have to learn. You can't let the kids take the period to play. You need to slap their hands when they misbehave. Time is a valuable commodity in school." Discipline means to sit quietly in classrooms, to move quickly and in orderly fashion through halls, and to complete assignments neatly and on time; to have self-discipline is viewed as having potential for achievement.

The discipline-centered teachers tended to separate the staff according to their control or their laxness. Exerting tight control, a teacher argued, was a "professional approach" to teaching. The teacher's approach "has a tremendous influence on the kids. I think that there are some people who are tougher staff members and there are those who are pushovers, where students can go and weasel out of something."

The "pushovers" were the "human development" teachers, a second teaching perspective. These teachers focused primarily on student feelings and the psychological effects of teaching and learning. The problem of teaching is seen as "the growth of a *total* person and how they come across to others and relate to others." The human development teacher gives attention to the interpersonal relationships in school, and content learning is secondary to development of a "warm, trusting" relationship. These teachers viewed subject-matter teachers as "traditional" and "fearful" of the risk involved in taking a human development approach.

To the human development teacher, individualization is establishing an atmosphere in which students work in small groups to explore attitudes, feelings, and values: "It is a way to talk with kids and how they're doing in school, relating more to their individual needs, and dislikes and values, their attitudes towards teachers" (Teacher interview).

A third perspective on teaching can be called "the problem solver." This teacher was typically concerned with an interrelation of subject matter and the psychological atmosphere in the classroom. The problem-solving teacher would view the teacher-adviser system as psychologically important. It allows students to feel less constrained in their interactions with teachers and should be incorporated into regular classroom activities. However, students' tasks in school are not only psychological. There are materials students should be acquainted with and books to be read. The ideal of the problem-solver teacher is to have children develop questions which they investigate in search of answers. Individualization is a form of scholarship in which individuals explore personal curiosities. As one teacher reported, this type of individualization doesn't happen often enough.

Q: Can you provide an illustration of individualized instruction?

A: The advanced student might get a chance to do some research on his own, into specific interests that he had about that continent or that country, or he might, if he had, you know, in the community there were people who had either visited that area or had pictures or mementos or that sort of thing and they could do some kind of research or go and talk to that person. That happened a couple of times. (Teacher interview)

The subject-centered belief was dominant in the school, and it was from that orientation system that the IGE/S reorganizations were seen. Teachers considered many of the task force proposals in relationship to the order and discipline requirements of the school, wanting to ensure that reforms would not disrupt established routines or provide students with freedoms "they were not ready yet to handle." During a teacher inservice meeting held to explain the teacher-adviser system, for example, some teachers reacted strongly against the possible chaos resulting from group dynamics approaches. After observing a group dynamics exercise in which each member's name was repeated three times, a teacher responded that the approach was too lax: "What happens if kids go bananas? What do we do?"

Sometimes the reforms were used to root out parts of the school day which teachers felt were troublesome. Passing time was one of the disturbances. Students had five minutes between periods. It was here students became unruly and posed "problems." One way to reduce the possibility of trouble was to ensure that students' movement through the halls was "purposeful, for it can be clocked at two or three minutes." With this in mind, reducing passing time to three minutes to provide for teacher advisory periods seemed a reasonable solution.

The problem is too much time between classes. There is five minutes passing time. We should cut it to three minutes. That would give us six minutes a day, thirty minutes a week for the student and counseling. That would eliminate, most importantly for me, the problem of the hall for the eighth graders. That is an unruly time. (Observation)

The consensus brought about by the IGE/S processes worked against change. The school's new purposes were phrased so abstractly that everyone could agree, but the agreement only masked the different ideas by which teachers chose. The search for consensus also had to get people in a mood to accept the proposals of the task forces, which led to a strategy of avoiding conflict and confrontation. The resulting consensus introduced an organizational bias which supported the subject-matter perspective and its related emphasis upon control and discipline.

Why Allow Outside Intervention? The External Politics of a School

Why does a school agree to have outsiders intervene in its internal policy matters? The avowed intention of the IGE/S staff was to change the ways in which people worked in the school. They sought a shared decision-making process which would alter the status of teachers, principals, and to some extent, parents. Further, the IGE/S staff itself was a new source of outside influence in school affairs. The history of institutions suggests that such challenges to the status quo would produce resentment and hostility. Organizations tend to be self-protective and to maintain their members' prerogatives, status, and privileges.[7] To answer the question about why the project was accepted, we need to turn to the middle school's relationship within the school district.

The middle school's agreement to work with the IGE/S project was related to two district-wide problems the school was having. First, the district had declining enrollments. The following year the sixth and seventh grades were to be reduced by one-third, causing staff cuts. The introduction of IGE/S into the middle school, the principal reasoned, would serve political as well as educational purposes. The IGE/S program would provide leverage with the superintendent and school board in maintaining staff. Administrators and teachers saw the project as providing an argument against cutbacks by giving evidence of the innovative quality of the staff.

But when IGE/S, but when something from outside can come in, come into a school and the principal can take something to the board of education and say "Look, we had the University come in here, the R & D Center, and developed IGE/S. Look, first you've got the University, the R & D, then you've got IGE/S. You've got impressive sounding things right away. Say "We've had them come in, they've set up programs and this is what we're doing." (Teacher interview)

A second political aspect of the case was related to the intra-district rivalry between the middle and high schools. Many of the middle-school teachers viewed their school as a "stepchild" in the district. They complained that the high school principal was very aggressive and maintained his programs at the expense of other district schools. Recent budget cuts, for example, had not affected the high school. Further, middle-school teachers felt the high school staff and superintendent saw their school as having no identifiable focus and the middle school staff as second-rate teachers who created remedial problems the high school staff had to correct. The IGE/S program, teachers argued, could provide the middle school with an identifiable focus and credibility within the district.

It seems like new programs can come out of the high school, for example, and they get zapped up—those are terrific. But they come out of middle school and it seems like they never get off the ground for one reason or the other. So whenever you have something come in from the outside, like IGE/S, Mr. Superintendent and the board can look at it and say, "Hey, look it, this is coming from the University. Boy, they must be doing something over there." (Teacher interview)

The legitimizing function of the IGE/S project manifested itself within the school in different ways during the year. Often task force discussions gave attention to ways of publicizing the activities. Efforts were made to have the local newspaper and school newsletter publish accounts of task force activities. Further, each task force presented its specific proposals to the board of education. These presentations, it was hoped, would keep the board acquainted with and supportive of the staff activities. Discussing the successes of USSR, the reorganization plan of flexible scheduling, or the introduction of TA periods provided the board with tangible evidence of the staff's ongoing efforts.

The staff viewed the board presentations as public relations. A teacher-adviser group preparation for a board meeting, for example, was concerned with providing the minimal information required to make the board members aware of their activities.

The leader of the group was nervous about preparing materials and making a presentation to the board. After much debate about what to include in the presentation, the group decided to give few materials. An administrator suggested the group leader make a very general statement and that "probably is all that is required." It was also suggested that parent members of the group attend to give moral support. It became clear, however, that the presentation to the board of education had no function except for "information." (Observation)

Parent participation was, in part, related to the staff's need for acceptance. They could provide recognition and support from the community. The district administration, and, the teachers reasoned, board members and the superintendent would look more favorably upon the teachers' proposals if parents joined in the presentations.

Implicit in the preparation for the board meeting was the lobbying with the school superintendent. The superintendent had been in the district for a number of years and seemed to establish priorities with or without the consent of the principals. This political reality became an important dimension in deciding upon an approach to flexible scheduling: "Before we start our meeting, I want you to know that the superintendent sets priorities with or without consultation with the principal. The principal then informs other administrators in the school. The IGE/S staff should be aware of the power hierarchy as we proceed to talk about flexible scheduling" (Administrator interview).

Later that year, the same administrator talked about the IGE/S project giving the necessary visibility to the superintendent: "For the first time I think he is impressed with what the staff is doing. The superintendent is a high school man, and," added the administrator, "he has often overlooked the middle school's accomplishments."

As the spring semester began, the administration sought to use the IGE/S project as political leverage to argue against possible staff reductions. At a February meeting of the flexible scheduling group, the staff began to prepare for a board meeting in which a plan would be presented. In the back of everyone's mind was the staff reduction (two to six teachers) for the fall term. Teachers and administrators argued the adoption of flexible scheduling would require the same staffing as this year. At a March staff meeting, the principal again echoed these thoughts: "Well, we can take the initiative *away* from the school board by proposing block scheduling. But I need a commitment from the staff."

When it became obvious that there would be staff reductions, many of the staff became hostile to the IGE/S project: "If teachers are cut," one suggested, "there should be no IGE/S program." While the ability to implement a more flexible schedule or other aspects of the IGE/S program were unrelated to the reduction of the staff, the faculty reaction was related to the political function of the project. Teachers had believed the project would prevent teacher cuts, and when it did not serve that function some considered it a liability.

I'm very disillusioned with our board, with all that we've been knocking ourselves over backwards as far as I'm concerned, trying to get all this done, and
about all we got from it was a slap in the face, and staff cuts and a whole bunch
of shit firstly, so no, I don't think IGE/S has helped us relate to the board one
bit. I'm very bitter. (Teacher interview)

Conclusions

The IGE/S involvement in the middle school did produce certain school-wide programmatic changes. Through the task force activities, the staff engaged in discussions about educational purposes and
school programs. The "purpose hierarchies" and "We Agree" statements started the staff thinking about the relationship of educational
purposes to school practices. The staff accepted the task of designing
and implementing new school-wide programs; teacher-adviser system,
clubs, and an uninterrupted silent reading period were made part of
the school program. Preparations to introduce changes in parent conferences and a more flexible scheduling of classes were made for the
following year. In addition, parents and, in one instance, students
participated in the planning process.

At a deeper interpretive level, the basic teaching assumptions of
the middle-school staff remained unchallenged. The change strategies
supported existing dispositions toward education. School was seen as
a problem of gaining control and discipline so students would ac-
quiesce to the authority of professionals. Teachers saw the task force
activities as separate from their academic task but as a way of making
the control and discipline of school seem psychologically appealing.
The task forces functioned externally to legitimate the school program within the larger community.

The conservative direction of the reforms was in part an unintended consequence of the project strategy for staff consensus. The
workshop approach sought to gain a general commitment to change.
The statements of purpose and subsequent "We Agree" statements,
however, were abstract and general and appealed to people with
many teaching perspectives. The statements' implications for teachers' conceptions of their professional tasks and organization of their
work were not examined critically. The generality of the statements
enabled the staff to maintain their current beliefs without posing any
contradictions.

The vagueness of staff commitment influenced the task force

actions in two ways. First, it was assumed the problems of educational purpose were solved. The purpose hierarchy gave teachers a false sense of commitment and allowed them to ignore the deep political, ethical, and social questions involved in defining purpose. Individualization became a slogan which had little concrete reference to school activities. The task of the faculty became technical: "Let's get the job done." Teachers tended to ignore the disparate reasons people gave for accepting the proposed changes. The search for change became a search for a set of procedures acceptable to the staff.

Second, the reduction of conflict among staff members was a major consideration in task force deliberation. Since faculty commitment was built on a precarious foundation, the task forces needed to find a least common denominator in implementing proposals. Procedures were devised for the teacher-adviser system, flexible scheduling, or parent conferences that would not infringe upon existing school rules or customs. The vested interests and existing school priorities were taken for granted.

The search for a common denominator introduced an organizational bias. The dominant teaching perspective—subject-centered teaching—was given further credence. The task force activities were thought of as providing the psychological conditions in which the existing approaches would seem reasonable to both students and community. Many faculty hoped that through human development techniques, students would be more accepting of the "real" work of school. This perspective defined the teacher as a knower and teaching as the problem of control. The task of teaching was to distribute knowledge to the benighted.

At the end of the year, the IGE/S approach had produced no rationale or coherent curriculum plan for school-wide individualization of instruction. Teachers and administrators became involved in the planning process without considering curricular problems. In part, curricular design can be viewed as having substantive issues independent of a planning process. Curricular issues, however, were not addressed.

What are some of the implications of these findings for the problem of school change?

First, the problem of change should be considered, in part, a political process. There is an interplay between the teachers' beliefs and the organizational structure of work in schools. The subject-centered perspective is related to a school organization which fragments knowledge into "objects" to be learned, defines professional status and privilege through the structure of school activities, and so on. To make the teaching perspective problematic is to challenge not only one view of the world but the vested interests which are legitimated by the view. To have done so in the middle-school situation, the staff would not only have had to question their own ideas about teaching but the nature of appropriate power for principal and teachers in controlling the knowledge and social arrangements of students.

Second, the notion of technical assistance needs to be reconsidered. "To start where a school is" cannot mean to imply existing practices are reasonable and to provide a staff with help clarifying their own purposes and strategies. The belief that a school staff can identify and plan to alter its own assumptions and power arrangements seems to belie experience. A planning approach, therefore, must provide a critical dialog about the priorities and underlying characteristics of institutional life. This entails considering the moral responsibilities of teaching *in a context of social action.*

The role of the intervening agent should be to stimulate and encourage a dialog. This function is as much educational as instrumental. Curricular issues must be given explicit attention. The direction of the dialog should be to have a staff consider the interplay of curriculum, organizational structures, and ethical choice. The dialog, I believe, should not be to impose but to develop a professional consciousness in which people in the context of schools can become more enlightened about the consequences of their actions. As Dewey commented, it is out of understanding the problem that we evolve methods. Problems of curricular design and methods of school change are dialectically related.

Third, the separation of affective and cognitive dimensions misconstrues the nature of social action. The human development focus posited a psychological orientation to the problem of change. It assumed that values and feeling are independent of the social or objective conditions of school life. In fact, this belief is not supported. Embedded in the regularities and assumptions of school are values and dispositions to guide action. The social and subjective dimensions of schooling are intertwined and gave meaning to the club, teacher-adviser, or flexible scheduling task forces.

One might ask, why do educators separate the affective and cognitive dimensions of social affairs? First, it does seem commonsensical. The complexity of human activities, we believe, compels us to make distinctions between valuative and factual knowledge. Analytically, the dichotomy is false. Our most cognitive knowledge—social theory, for example—contains emotions, attitudes, and dispositional stances toward the social world.[8] In this specific study, different teaching perspectives found in the middle school contained not only facts about instruction but also values about how one should act toward children. Second, reformers may think if you can get teachers to develop accepting attitudes toward change, institutional change will follow. The empirical evidence in this case suggests this does not work. The focus on psychological dimensions produced a conservative response. Students' feelings were manipulated to develop acceptance about the existing structure of school.

Fourth, as schools currently exist, there is little or no time for reflection or critical analysis. The middle-school teachers had their days filled with the ordinary routines and regularities of school. Meeting after school for task force matters tended to rush discussion. Part of the problem of change becomes how to make the regular school day a period of reflective activity for teachers as well as students. The problem is not setting aside a period such as was done for the teacher-adviser system, but creating a community discourse. The ability to critically reflect must be imbued in all activities of *both* professionals and students in a school.

Fifth, the power of the superintendent and principal in deciding school matters needs to be considered. The middle school was hierarchically organized, and these administrators had power in the determination of a situation even though they often were not present in decision-making. These people need to be committed to change and understand the ideological and political implications of that commitment.

Sixth, schools are dynamic social contexts. The planning approach must be able to respond to unanticipated events, human ambiguities, the particular conditions of the setting, and the politics involved in substantive change. The planning process cannot be "packaged" into "models" which define human action as linear or additive.[9] The process is dialectical and related to dealing with the motives and actions of people in the contexts of their work.

Notes

1. See Seymour Sarason, *The Culture of the School and the Problems of Change* (Boston: Allyn and Bacon, 1971).

2. For discussion of this case study approach to educational evaluation, see Thomas S. Popkewitz and Gary Wehlage, "School Evaluation and Institutional Life" (Paper delivered at the annual meeting of the American Educational Research Association, Washington, D.C., April 1975); and B. Robert Tabachnick, "Problems in Describing Events within Teacher Education" (Paper delivered at the annual meeting of the American Educational Research Association, San Francisco, Ca., 1976).

3. Patrick W. Struve and James A. Schultz, *Planning and Managing the IGE/S School*, Theoretical Paper No. 65 (Madison: Wisconsin Research and Development Center for Cognitive Learning, 1976), p. 6.

4. The research began in the winter, and the account of the workshop is reconstructed from documents produced during that time and through discussions with participants.

5. Much of this is discussed in Struve and Schultz, *Planning and Managing the IGE/S School*.

6. For a discussion of the ethical and political issues involved in educational choices, see Michael W. Apple, "Commonsense Categories and Curriculum Thought," in ASCD Yearbook, *Schools in Search of Meaning*, ed. James B. Macdonald and Esther Zaret (Washington, D.C.: ASCD, 1975).

7. Howard Becker, *Sociological Work, Method, and Substance* (Chicago: Aldine, 1970).

8. Michael W. Apple and Thomas S. Popkewitz, "Knowledge, Perspective, and Commitment: An Essay Review," *Social Education* 35, no. 7 (November 1971).

9. Thomas Romberg, "Problems of Analyzing Dynamic Events in Teacher Education" (Paper delivered at the annual meeting of the American Educational Research Association, Washington, D.C., April 1975).

The essay by Michael W. Apple and Nancy King exemplifies a dominant interest in the political dimension of curriculum criticism. Not only does the essay describe, disclose meaning about, and judge the opening weeks of a particular kindergarten class as the children are socialized into some common meanings of life in schools, but the essay also provides a well developed explanation of the relationship between schools and the larger society. Especially in this latter sense, the essay presents a well developed concept of the political dimension of curriculum criticism as well as being a particular case study. Specifically, the authors treat schools as "institutions that embody collective traditions and human intentions that are the products of identifiable social and economic ideologies." The critic's basic task thus becomes the locating of school experience within the complex totality of which it is a constitutive part. In increasing understanding about the relationship between ideology and school knowledge the critic increases understanding about both the larger social collectivity and the schools.

In so treating the schools Apple and King carry out several specific tasks: description of the historical process by which social meanings became school meanings, empirical documentation of the

442

pervasiveness of these social meanings within the particular kinder-garten classroom, and suggestion about whether piecemeal reform of schools can succeed. They point out how the curriculum field has historically been concerned with social control and how this concern shaped the "hidden curriculum" of modern schools. The schools are intended primarily to create a normative consensus and economic ad-justment within American society. The kindergarten described carries out this intention through use of praise, rules governing access to materials, control of time, control of emotionality, and meanings attached to work. Basically, Apple and King assert that life in this kindergarten is very much like industrial life and that given what society seems to want from the schools, the kindergarten teacher can be regarded as highly successful in so socializing children. The au-thors suggest that the qualities of life in schools can be understood only within the external social and economic context within which schools exist.

The descriptive and interpretive parts of the essay emphasize "point of view" and "theme." "Metaphor" is also used, as in the direct comparison of school life to industrial life. The analysis of the meanings of education within past and present American society provide substantial justification for the judgments of the authors. The principal critical focal points of the essay are the "work" and the "world." In analyzing a particular classroom as a reflection of the whole society and in pointing out how the analyses may be general-ized to other classrooms, the authors elucidate a specific relationship between "work" and "world" exemplifying the political dimension of curriculum criticism and qualitative evaluation.

19

What Do Schools Teach?

Michael W. Apple and Nancy King

Schooling and Cultural Capital

One of the least attractive complaints about schools in recent years has been that they are relatively unexciting, boring, or what have you, because of mindlessness.[1] The basis of this argument is that schools covertly teach all those things that humanistic critics of schools like to write and talk about—among them, behavioral consensus, institutional rather than personal goals and norms, alienation from one's products—because teachers, administrators, and other educators do not really know what they are doing. Such a perspective is misleading at best. In the first place, it is thoroughly ahistorical. It ignores the fact that schools were in part designed to teach exactly these things. The hidden curriculum, the tacit teaching of social and economic norms and expectations to students in schools, was not as hidden or "mindless" as many educators believe. Such a perspective also ignores the critical task that schools, as the fundamental set of institutions in advanced industrial societies, do perform in order to certify adult competence, and it pulls schools out of their

---

This article originally appeared in *Humanistic Education: Visions and Realities,* ed. Richard H. Weller (Berkeley, Ca.: McCutchan Publishing Corp., 1977).

setting within the larger and much more powerful nexus of economic and political institutions that give schools their meaning. That is, schools seem to do what they are in fact supposed to do, by and large, at least in terms of roughly providing dispositions and propensities that are quite functional to one's later life in a complex and stratified social and economic order.

While there is no doubt that mindlessness does exist outside Charles Silberman's mind, neither it, nor venality, nor indifference are adequate descriptive devices in explaining why schools are so resistant to change or why schools teach what they do.[2] Nor is it an appropriate conceptual tool for use in ferreting out what exact kinds of things are taught in schools or why certain social meanings and not others are used to organize school life. Yet it is not just the critics of schools who tend to oversimplify their analysis of the social and economic meaning of schools.

All too often the social meaning of school experience has been accepted as unproblematic by sociologists of education or as merely engineering problems by curriculum specialists and other programmatically inclined educators. The curriculum field especially, among other educational areas, has been dominated by a perspective that might best be called "technological" in that the major interest guiding its work has involved finding the one best set of means to reach prechosen educational ends.[3] Against this relatively ameliorative and uncritical background, a number of sociologists and curriculum scholars, influenced strongly by the sociology of knowledge in both its Marxist or "Neo-Marxist" and phenomenological variants, have begun to raise serious questions about this lack of attention to the relationship of school knowledge to extraschool phenomena. A fundamental basis for these investigations has been best articulated by Michael F. D. Young. He notes that there is a "dialectical relationship between access to power and the opportunity to legitimize certain dominant categories, and the process by which the availability of such categories to some group enables them to assert power and control over others."[4] In essence, just as there is a relatively unequal distribution of economic capital in society, so, too, is there a similar system of distribution surrounding cultural capital.[5] In advanced industrial societies, schools become particularly important as distributors of this cultural capital and play a critical role in giving legitimacy to certain categories and forms of knowledge. The very fact that certain traditions and normative "content" are construed as school knowledge is prima facie evidence of perceived legitimacy.

The argument in this presentation is that the *problem* of educational knowledge, of what is taught in schools, has to be considered a form of the larger distribution of goods and services in a society. It is not merely an analytic problem (What shall be construed as knowledge?), nor exclusively a technical consideration (How do we organize and store knowledge so that children have access to it and can "master" it?), nor solely a psychological concern (How do we get students to learn X?). Rather, the study of educational knowledge is a study in ideology, the investigation of what is considered legitimate knowledge (be it knowledge of the logical type of "that," "how," or "to") by specific social groups and classes, in specific institutions, at specific historical moments. It is, further, a critically oriented form of investigation in that it chooses to focus on how this knowledge, as distributed in schools, can contribute to cognitive and dispositional development that strengthens or reinforces existing and often problematic institutional arrangements in society. In clearer terms, the overt and covert knowledge found within school settings and the principles of selection, organization, and evaluation of this knowledge are valuative selections from a much larger universe of possible knowledge and collection principles. As valuative selections, they must not be accepted as given, but must be made problematic—bracketed, if you will—so that the social and economic ideologies and the institutionally patterned meanings that stand behind them can be scrutinized. It is the latent meaning, the configuration that lies behind the commonsense acceptability of a position, that may be its most important attribute. And these hidden institutional meanings and relations[6] are almost never uncovered if we are guided only by amelioration. As Daniel Kallós has noted recently, there are both manifest and latent "functions" of any educational system. These functions need to be characterized not only in educational (learning) terms but, more importantly, in politico-economic terms. In short, discussions about the quality of educational life are relatively meaningless if the "specific functions of the educational system are unrecognized."[7] If much of the literature on what schools tacitly teach is accurate, then the specific functions may be more economic than "intellectual."

The focus here is on certain aspects of the problem of schooling and social and economic meaning. Schools are viewed as institutions that embody collective traditions and human intentions that are the products of identifiable social and economic ideologies. The starting point might best be phrased as a question: *Whose* meanings are collected and distributed through the overt and hidden curricula in schools? That is, as Marx was fond of saying, reality does not stalk around with a label. The curriculum in schools responds to and represents ideological and cultural resources that come from somewhere. Not all groups' visions are represented and not all groups' meanings are responded to. How, then, do schools act to distribute this cultural capital? Whose reality "stalks" in the corridors and classrooms of American schools? The concern here is, first, to describe the historical process through which certain social meanings became particularly *school* meanings, and thus now have the weight of decades of acceptance behind them. Second, we shall offer empirical evidence of a study of kindergarten experience to document the potency and staying power of these particular social meanings. Finally, we shall raise the question of whether piecemeal reforms, be they humanistically oriented or other, can succeed.

The task of dealing with sets of meanings in schools has traditionally fallen to the curriculum specialist. Historically, however, this concern for meaning in schools by curriculum specialists has been linked to varied notions of social control. This should not be surprising. It should be obvious, though it usually is not, that questions about meanings in social institutions tend to become questions of control.[8] Forms of knowledge—both overt and covert—found within school settings imply relations of power and economic resources and control. The very choice of school knowledge, that is, the act of designing school environments, consciously or unconsciously reflects ideological and economic presuppositions that provide the commonsense rules for educators' thoughts and actions. Perhaps the link between meaning and control in schools can be made clearer by a relatively brief account of curricular history.

Meaning and Control in Curricular History

Bill Williamson, a British sociologist, argues that men and women "have to contend with the institutional and ideological forms of earlier times as the basic constraints on what they can achieve."[9]

If one takes this notion seriously in looking at education, what is both provided and taught in schools must be understood historically. Speaking specifically about schools, Williamson notes: "Earlier educational attitudes of dominant groups in society still carry historical weight and are exemplified even in the bricks and mortar of the school buildings themselves."[10]

If we are to be honest with ourselves, the curriculum field itself has its roots in the soil of social control. From its beginnings early in the twentieth century, when its intellectual paradigm took shape and became an identifiable set of procedures for selecting and organizing school knowledge, a set that should be taught to teachers and other educators, the fundamental consideration of the formative members of the curriculum field was that of social control. Part of this concern for social control is understandable. Many historically important figures who influenced the curriculum field (such as Charles C. Peters, Ross Finney, and, especially, David Snedden) had interests that spanned both the field of educational sociology and the more general problem of what should concretely happen in school. Given the growing importance of the idea of social control in the American Sociological Society at the time, an idea that seemed to capture the imagination and energy of so many of the nation's intelligentsia, as well as powerful segments of the business community, it is not difficult to see how it also attracted those people interested in both sociology and curriculum.[11]

Interest in schooling as a mechanism for exerting social control did not have merely sociological origins. Individuals who first called themselves curriculists (men like Franklin Bobbitt and W. W. Charters) were vitally concerned with social control for ideological reasons as well. Influenced strongly by the scientific management movement and the work of social measurement specialists[12] and guided by beliefs that found the popular eugenics movement a "progressive" social force, these men brought social control into the very heart of the field that was concerned with developing criteria to guide selection of those meanings students would encounter in educational institutions.

This is not to say that social control in and of itself is always negative, of course. In fact, it is nearly impossible to envision social life without some element of control, if only because institutions, as such, tend to respond to the *regularities* of human interaction. What strongly influenced early curriculum workers was a historically specific set of assumptions, commonsense rules, about school meanings and control that incorporated not merely the idea that organized society must maintain itself through the preservation of some of its valued forms of interaction and meaning, which implied a quite general and wholly understandable "weak" sense of social control. Deeply embedded in their ideological perspective was a "strong" sense of control wherein education in general and the everyday meanings of the curriculum in particular were seen as essential to the preservation of the existing social privilege, interests, and knowledge of one element of the population at the expense of less powerful groups.[13] Most often this took the form of attempting to guarantee expert and scientific control in society, to eliminate or "socialize" unwanted racial or ethnic groups or characteristics, or to produce an economically efficient group of citizens in order to, as C. C. Peters put it, reduce the maladjustment of workers to their jobs. It is this latter interest, the economic substratum of everyday school life, that will become of particular importance when we look at what schools teach about work and play in a later section of this presentation.

Of course, neither the idea of nor an interest in social control emerged newborn through the early curriculum movement's attempts to use school knowledge for rather conservative social ends. Social control had been the implied aim of a substantial number of ameliorative social and political programs carried out during the nineteenth century by both state and private agencies so that order and stability, and the imperative of industrial growth, might be maintained in the face of a variety of social and economic changes.[14] Walter Feinberg's analysis of the ideological roots of liberal educational policy demonstrates even in this century many of the proposed "reforms" in schools and elsewhere latently serve the conservative social interests of stability and social stratification.[15]

The argument presented so far is not meant to belittle the efforts of educators and social reformers. Instead, it is an attempt to place the current arguments over the "lack of humaneness in schools," the tacit teaching of social norms and values, and similar considerations within a larger historical context. Without such a context, it is impossible to understand fully the relationship between what schools actually do and an advanced industrial economy. The best example of this context can be found in the changing ideological functions of schooling in general and curricular meanings in particular. Behind much of the argumentation about the role of formal education during the nineteenth century in the United States were concerns about the standardization of educational environments, the teaching through day-to-day school interaction of moral, normative, and dispositional values, and economic functionalism. Today these concerns have been termed the "hidden curriculum" by Philip Jackson[16] and others. But it is the very question of its hiddenness that may help us uncover the historical relationship between what is taught in schools and the larger context of institutions that surround them.

We should be aware that historically the hidden curriculum was not hidden at all; instead, it was the overt function of schools during much of their existence as an institution. During the nineteenth century, the increasing diversity of political, social, and cultural attributes and structures "pushed educators to resume with renewed vigor the language of social control and homogenization that had dominated educational rhetoric from the earliest colonial period."[17] As the century progressed, the rhetoric of reform, of justifying one ideological position against that of other interest groups, did not focus merely on the critical need for social homogeneity. The use of schools to inculcate values, to create an "American community," was no longer sufficient. The growing pressures of modernization and industrialization also created certain expectations of efficiency and functionalism among certain classes and an industrial elite in society as well. As Elizabeth Vallance puts it, "to assertive socialization was added a focus on organizational efficiency." Thus, the reforms having the greatest effect on school organization and ultimately the procedures and principles governing life in classrooms were dominated by the language of and an interest in production, well-adjusted economic functioning, and bureaucratic skills. In this process the underlying reasons for reform in a modern industrial society slowly changed from active concern for valuative consensus to a recognized need for economic functionalism.[18] But this could only occur if the prior period, with its search for a standardized national character built in large part through the characteristics of schools, had been both perceived and accepted as successful. Thus it was that the institutional outlines of schools, the relatively standardized day-to-day forms of interaction, provided the mechanisms by which a normative consensus could be "taught." And within these broad outlines, these behavioral regularities of the institution if you will, an ideological set of commonsense rules for curriculum selection and organizing school experience based on efficiency, economic functionalism, and bureaucratic exigencies took hold. The valuative consensus became the deep structure, the first hidden curriculum, which encased the normative economic one. Once the hidden curriculum became hidden, when a uniform and standardized learning context became established and when social selection and control were taken as given in schooling, only then could attention be paid to the needs of the individual or other more "ethereal" concerns.[19]

Thus it was that a core of commonsense meanings combining normative consensus and economic adjustment was built into the very structure of formal education. This is not to say that there have been no significant educational movements toward, say, education for self-development. Rather, it would appear that behind preferential choices about individual needs there is a more powerful set of expectations surrounding schooling that provides the constitutive structure of school experience. As a number of economists have recently noted, the most economically important "latent function" of school life seems to be the selection and generation of personality attributes and normative meanings that enable one to have a supposed chance at economic rewards.[20] Since the school is the only major institution that stands between the family and the labor market, it is not odd that, both historically and currently, certain social meanings that have differential benefits are distributed in schools. But what are these particular social meanings? How are they organized and displayed in everyday school life? It is these questions to which we shall now turn.

Ideology and the Curriculum in Use

The larger concerns with the relationship between ideology and school knowledge, between meaning and control, of the prior section tend to be altogether too vague unless they can be seen as active forces in the activity of school people and students as they go about their particular lives in the classroom. As investigators of the hidden curriculum and others have noted, the concrete modes by which knowledge is distributed in classrooms and the commonsense practices of teachers and students can illuminate the connection between school life and the structures of ideology, power, and economic resources, of which schools are a part.[21]

Just as there is a social distribution of cultural capital in society, so, too, is there a social distribution of knowledge within classrooms. For example, different "kinds" of students get different kinds of knowledge, as Nell Keddie so well documents in her study of the knowledge teachers have of their students and the curricular knowledge then made available to the students.[22] While the differential distribution of classroom knowledge does exist and is intimately linked to the process of social labeling that occurs in schools,[23] it is less important to this analysis than what might be called the "deep structure" of school experience. What underlying meanings are negotiated and transmitted in schools behind the actual formal "stuff" of curriculum content? What happens when knowledge is filtered through teachers? Through what categories of normality and deviance is knowledge filtered? What is the *basic and organizing framework* of normative and conceptual knowledge that students actually get? In short, what is the curriculum in use? Only by seeing the deeper structure does it become obvious that social norms, institutions, and ideological rules are ongoingly sustained by the day-to-day interaction of commonsense actors as they go about their normal practices.[24] This is especially true in classrooms. Social definitions about school knowledge, definitions that are both dialectically related to and rest within the larger context of the surrounding social and economic institutions, are maintained and re-created by the commonsense practices of teaching and evaluation in classrooms.[25]

We shall focus on kindergarten here because it occupies a critical moment in the process by which students become competent in the rules, norms, values, and dispositions "necessary" to function within institutional life as it now exists. Learning the role of student is a complex activity, one that takes time and requires continual interaction with institutional expectations. By focusing on both how this occurs and the content of the dispositions that are both overtly and covertly part of kindergarten knowledge, it is possible to illuminate the background knowledge children use as organizing principles for much of the rest of their school career.

In short, the social definitions internalized during initial school life provide the constitutive rules for later life in classrooms. Thus, what is construed as work or play, "school knowledge" or merely "my knowledge," normality or deviance are the elements that require observation. As we shall see, the use of praise, rules governing access to materials, control of both time and emotion—all make significant contributions to teaching social meanings in school. But as we shall also see it is the meanings attached to the category of work that most clearly illuminate the possible place of schools in the complex nexus of economic and social institutions that surround us all.

Kindergarten experience serves as a foundation for the years of schooling to follow. Children who have attended kindergarten tend to demonstrate a general superiority in achievement in the elementary grades over children who have not attended kindergarten. Attempts to determine exactly which teaching techniques and learning experiences contribute most directly to the "intellectual and emotional growth" of kindergarten children have, however, produced inconclusive results. Kindergarten training appears to exert its most powerful and lasting influence on the attitudes and the behavior of children by acclimating them to a classroom environment. The children are introduced to their roles as elementary school pupils, and it is the understanding and mastery of this *role* that makes for the greater success of kindergarten-trained children in elementary school.

Socialization in kindergarten classrooms includes the learning of norms and definitions of social interactions. It is the continuous development of a working definition of the situation by the participants. In order to function adequately in a social situation, those involved must reach a common understanding of the meanings, limitations, and potential the setting affords for their interaction. During the first few weeks of the school year, the children and the teacher forge a common definition of the situation out of repeated interaction in the classroom. When one common set of social meanings is accepted, classroom activities proceed smoothly. Most often these common meanings remain relatively stable unless the flow of events in the setting ceases to be orderly.

Socialization is not, however, a one-way process.[26] To some extent, the children in a classroom socialize the teacher as well as becoming socialized themselves, but children and teacher do not have an equal influence in determining the working definition of the situation. On the first day of school in a kindergarten classroom, the teacher has a more highly organized set of commonsense rules than the children do. Since the teacher also holds most of the power to control events and resources in the classroom, it is his or her set of meanings that is dominant. This does not mean that teachers are free to define the classroom situation in any way they choose. As we saw earlier in this presentation, the school is a well-established institution, and it may be that neither the teacher nor the children can perceive more than marginal ways to deviate to any significant degree from the commonsense rules and expectations that set the school apart from any other institution.

The negotiation of meanings in a kindergarten classroom is a critical phase in the socialization of the children. The meanings of classroom objects and events are not intrinsic to them, but are formed through social interaction. As with other aspects of the definition of the situation, these meanings may shift initially. At some point, however, they become stable, and they are not likely to be renegotiated unless the orderly flow of events in the classroom is disrupted.

The meanings of objects and events become clear to the children as they participate in the social setting. The *use* of materials, the nature of authority, the quality of personal relationships, the spontaneous remarks, as well as other aspects of daily classroom life, contribute to the children's growing awareness of their roles in the classroom and their understanding of the social setting. Therefore, to understand the social reality of schooling, it is necessary to study it in actual classroom settings. Each concept, role, and object is a social creation bound to the situation in which it is produced. The meanings of classroom interaction cannot be assumed; they must be discovered. The abstraction of these meanings and the generalizations and insights drawn from them may apply to other contexts, but the researcher's initial descriptions, understandings, and interpretations require that social phenomena be encountered where they are produced, that is, in the classroom.[27]

By observing and interviewing the participants in one particular public school kindergarten classroom it was established that the social meanings of events and materials became fixed remarkably early in the school year.[28] As with most classroom settings, the socialization of the children took overt priority during the opening weeks of school. The four most important skills the teacher expected the children to learn during those opening weeks were to share, to listen, to put things away, and to follow the classroom routine. It was her statement of her goals for the children's early school experiences that constituted the definition of socialized behavior in the classroom.

The children had no part in organizing the classroom materials and had little effect on the course of daily events. The teacher made no special effort to make the children comfortable in the room or to reduce their uncertainty about the schedule of activities. Rather than mediating intrusive aspects of the environment, she chose to require that the children accommodate themselves to the materials as presented. When the noise from another class in the hallway distracted the children, for example, the teacher called for their attention, but she did not close the door. Similarly, the individual cubbies where the children kept their crayons, smocks, and tennis shoes were not labeled although the children had considerable difficulty remembering which cubby was theirs. Despite the many instances of lost crayons and crying children, the teacher refused to permit the student teacher to label the cubbies. She told the student teacher that the children must learn to remember their assigned cubbies because "that is their job." When one girl forgot where her cubby was on the day after they had been assigned, the teacher pointed her out to the class as an example of a "girl who was not listening yesterday."

The objects in the classroom were attractively displayed in an apparent invitation to the class to interact with them. Most of the materials were placed on the floor or on shelves within easy reach of the children. Opportunities to interact with materials in the classroom were, however, severely circumscribed. The teachers' organization of time in the classroom contradicted the apparent availability of materials in the physical setting. During most of the kindergarten session, the children were not permitted to handle objects. The materials, then, were organized so that the children learned restraint; they learned to handle things within easy reach only when permitted to do so by the teacher. The children were "punished" for touching things when the time was not right and praised for the moments when they were capable of restraint. For example, the teacher praised the children for prompt obedience when they quickly stopped bouncing basketballs after being told to do so in the gym, but made no mention of their ball-handling skills.

The teacher made it clear to the children that good kindergartners were quiet and cooperative. One morning a child brought two large stuffed dolls to school and put them in her assigned seat. During the first period of large group instruction, the teacher referred to them saying, "Raggedy Ann and Raggedy Andy are such good helpers! They haven't said a thing all morning."

As part of learning to exhibit socialized behavior, the children learned to tolerate ambiguity and discomfort in the classroom and to accept a considerable degree of arbitrariness in their school activities. They were required to adjust their emotional responses to conform to those considered appropriate by the teacher. They learned to respond to her personally and to the manner in which she organized the classroom environment.

After some two weeks of kindergarten experience, the children had established a category system for defining and organizing their social reality in the classroom, but interview responses indicated that the activities in the classroom did not have intrinsic meanings. The children assigned meanings depending upon the context in which each was carried on. The teacher presented the classroom materials either as a part of instruction, or, more overtly, she discussed and demonstrated their uses to the class. This is a critical point. The use of a particular object, that is, the manner in which we are predisposed to act toward it, constitutes its meaning for us. In defining the meanings of the things in the classroom, then, a teacher defines the nature of the relationships between the children and the materials with contextual meanings bound to the classroom environment.

When asked about classroom objects, the children responded with remarkable agreement and uniformity. The children divided the materials into two categories: things to work with and things to play with. No child organized any material in violation to what seemed to be their guiding principle. Those materials which the children used at the direction of the teacher were work materials. They included books, paper, paste, crayons, glue, and other materials traditionally associated with school tasks. No child chose to use these materials during "play" time early in the school year. The materials which the children chose during free time were labeled play materials or toys. They included, among other things, games, small manipulatives, the playhouse, dolls, and the wagon. The meaning of classroom materials, then, is derived from the nature of the activity in which they are used, and the separate categories for work and play emerge as powerful organizers of classroom reality early in the school year.

Both the teacher and the children considered work activities more important than play activities. Information which the children said they learned in school was what the teacher had told them during activities they considered "work." Play activities were permitted only if time allowed and the child had finished the assigned work activities. Observation data revealed that the category of work had several well-defined parameters that sharply separated it from the category of play. First, work includes any and all teacher-directed activities; only free time activities were called "play" activities by the children. Activities such as coloring, drawing, waiting in line, listening to stories, watching movies, cleaning up, and singing were called "work." To work, then, is to do what one is *told* to do, no matter what the nature of the activity involved. Second, all work activities, and only work activities, were compulsory. For example, children were required to draw pictures about specific topics on numerous occasions. During singing the teacher often interrupted to encourage and exhort the children who were not singing or who were singing too softly. Any choices permitted during work periods were circumscribed to fit the limits of accepted uniform procedure.

During an Indian dance, for example, the kindergarten teacher allowed the "sleeping" children to snore if they wanted. After a trip to the fire station all of the children were required to draw a picture, but each child was permitted to choose whatever part of the tour he liked best as the subject of his picture. (Of course it is also true that each child was required to illustrate his favorite part of the trip.) When introducing another art project, the teacher said, "Today you will make a cowboy horse. You can make your horse any color you want, black or gray or brown." At another time she announced with great emphasis that the children could choose three colors for the flowers they were making from cupcake liners. The children gasped with excitement and applauded. These choices did not change the fact that the children were required to use the same materials in the same manner during work periods. If anything, the nature of the choices emphasizes the general principle. Not only was every work activity required, but every child had to start at the designated time. The entire class worked on all assigned tasks simultaneously. Further, all of the children were required to complete the assigned tasks during the designated work period. In a typical incident that occurred on the second day of school, many children complained that they either could not or did not want to finish a lengthy art project. The teacher said that everyone must finish. One child asked if she could finish "next time," but the teacher replied, "You must finish now."

In addition to requiring that all the children do the same thing at the same time, work activities also involved the children with the same materials. During work periods the same materials were presented to the entire class simultaneously. All of the children were expected to use work materials in the same way. Even seemingly inconsequential procedures had to be followed by every child. For example, after large-group instruction on the second day of school, the teacher told the children, "Get a piece of paper and your crayons, and go back to your seats." One child, who got her crayons first, was reminded to get her paper first.

The products or skills which the children exhibited at the completion of a period of work were also supposed to be similar or identical. The teacher demonstrated most art projects to the entire class before the children got their materials. The children then tried to produce a product as similar to the one the teacher had made as possible. Only those pieces of art work that most closely resembled the product the teacher used for demonstration were saved and displayed in the classroom.

Work periods, as defined by the children, then, involved every child simultaneously in the same directed activity with the same materials to the same ends. The point of work activities was to *do* them, not necessarily to do them well. By the second day of school, many children hastily finished their assigned tasks in order to join their friends playing with toys. During music, for example, the teacher exhorted the children to sing loudly. Neither tunefulness, rhythm, nor purity of tone and mood were mentioned to the children, or expected of them. It was enthusiastic and lusty participation that was required. Similarly, the teacher accepted any child's art project upon which sufficient time had been spent. The assigned tasks were compulsory and identical, and, in accepting all finished products, the teacher often accepted poor or shoddy work. The acceptance of such work nullified the notion of excellence as an evaluative category. Diligence, perseverence, obedience, and participation—behaviors of the children, not characteristics of their work—were rewarded. In this way the notion of excellence became separated from the concept of successful or acceptable work and was replaced by the criteria of adequate participation.

The children interviewed in September, and again in October, used the categories of work and play to create and describe their social reality. Their responses indicated that the first few weeks of school were an important time for learning about the nature of work in the classroom. In September no child said "work" when asked what children do in kindergarten. In October half of those interviewed responded with the word "work." All of the children talked more about working and less about playing in October than they had in September. The teacher was pleased with the progress of the class during the first weeks of school and repeatedly referred to the children as "my good workers."

The teacher often justified her presentation of work activities in the classroom in terms of the preparation of the children for elementary school and for adulthood. For example, she believed that work activities should be compulsory because the children needed practice following directions without exercising options as preparation for the reality of adult work. The children were expected to view kindergarten as a year of preparation for the first grade. In stressing the importance of coloring neatly or putting pictures in the proper sequence, the teacher spoke of the necessity of having these skills in first grade and how difficult it would be the following year for children who were inattentive in kindergarten. The children were relatively powerless to influence the flow of daily events, and obedience was valued more highly than ingenuity. Again, this atmosphere was seen as an important bridge between home and future work situations. The teacher expected the children to adjust to the classroom setting and to tolerate whatever level of discomfort that adjustment included.

Thus, as part of initiation into the kindergarten community, young children also receive their first initiation into the social dimension of the world of work. The content of specific lessons is relatively less important than the experience of being a worker. Personal attributes of obedience, enthusiasm, adaptability, and perseverence are more highly valued than academic competence. Unquestioning acceptance of authority and the vicissitudes of life in institutional settings are among the first lessons learned in kindergarten. It is in the progressive acceptance as natural, as the world "tout court," of meanings of important and unimportant knowledge, of work and play, of normality and deviance, that these lessons reside.

Beyond a Rhetorical Humanism

As the late Italian social theorist Antonio Gramsci argued, the control of the knowledge-preserving and producing sectors of a society becomes a critical factor in enhancing the ideological dominance of one group of people or class over less powerful groups of people or classes.[29] If this is so, the role of the school in selecting, preserving, and passing on conceptions of competence, ideological norms and values, and often only certain social groups' "knowledge"—all of which are embedded within both the overt and hidden curricula in schools—is of no small moment.

At least two aspects of school life serve rather interesting distributive social and economic functions. As the growing literature on the hidden curriculum and the historical and empirical evidence provided here seek to demonstrate, the forms of interaction in school life may serve as mechanisms for communicating normative and dispositional meanings to students. Yet, the body of school knowledge itself—what is included and excluded, what is important and what is unimportant—also often serves an ideological purpose.

As one of this paper's authors has demonstrated in an earlier analysis, much of the formal content of curricular knowledge is dominated by a consensus ideology. Conflict, either intellectual or normative, is seen as a negative attribute in social life.[30] Thus, there is a peculiar kind of redundancy in school knowledge. Both the everyday experience and the curricular knowledge itself display messages of normative and cognitive consensus. The deep structure of school life, the basic and organizing framework of commonsense rules that is negotiated, internalized, and ultimately seems to give meaning to our experiences in educational institutions, appears to be closely linked to the normative and communicative structures of industrial life.[31] How could it be otherwise?

Perhaps we can expect little more from school experience than what has been portrayed here, given the distribution of resources in the United States and given the wishes of a major segment of the citizenry. Nor can one dismiss the hypothesis that schools actually do work. In an odd way they may succeed in reproducing a population that is roughly equivalent to the economic and social stratification in society. Thus, when one asks of schools, "Where is their humaneness?" perhaps the answers may be more difficult to grapple with than the questioner expects.

For example, one could interpret this presentation as being a statement against a particular community's commitment to education or as a negative statement about particular kinds of teachers who are "less able than they might be." This would, however, be inaccurate. The city in question is educationally oriented. It spends a sizable proportion of its resources on schooling and feels that it deserves its reputation as having one of the best school systems in the area, if not the nation.

Just as important, we should be careful not to view this kind of teacher as poorly trained, unsuccessful, or uncaring. Exactly the opposite is often the case. The classroom teacher who was observed is, in fact, perceived as a competent teacher by administrators, colleagues, and parents. Given this, the teacher's activities must be understood not merely in terms of the patterns of social interaction that dominate classrooms, but in terms of the wider patterning of social and economic relationships in the social structure of which he or she and the school itself are a part.[32]

When teachers distribute normative interpretations of, say, work and play like the ones we have documented historically and currently here, one must ask, "to what problems are those viable solutions for the teacher?"[33] "What is the commonsense interpretive framework of teachers and to what set of ideological presuppositions does it respond?" In this way we can situate classroom knowledge and activity within the larger framework of structural relationships which, either through teacher and parent expectations, the classroom material environment, the focus of important problems, or the relationship between schools and, say, the economic sector of a society, often determine what goes on in classrooms.

This work alone will not confirm the fact that schools seem to act latently to enhance an already unequal and stratified social order. It does, however, confirm a number of recent analyses that point out how schools, through their distribution of a number of social and ideological categories, contribute to the promotion of a rather static framework of institutions.[34] Thus, our argument should not be seen as a statement against an individual school or any particular group of teachers. Rather, it suggests that educators need to see teachers as "encapsulated" within a social and economic context that by necessity often produces the problems teachers are confronted with and the material limitations on their responses. This very "external" context provides substantial legitimation for the allocation of teachers' time and energies[35] and for the kinds of cultural capital embodied in the school itself.

If this is the case, as we strongly suggest it is, the questions asked should go beyond the humanistic level (without losing their humanistic and emancipatory intent) to a more relational approach. While educators continue to ask what is wrong in schools and what can be done (Can your problems be "solved" with more humanistic teachers, more openness, better content, and so on?), it is of immense importance that we begin to take seriously these questions: "In whose interest do schools often function today?" "What is the relation between the distribution of cultural capital and economic capital?" "Can we deal with the political and economic realities of creating institutions that enhance meaning and lessen control?"

Rachel Sharp and Anthony Green summarize this concern about a rhetorical humanism rather well:

... [We] want to stress that a humanist concern for the child necessitates a greater awareness of the limits within which teacher autonomy can operate, and to pose the questions, "What interests do schools service, those of the parents and children, or those of the teachers and headmaster?" and "What wider interests are served by the school", and, possibly more importantly, "How do we conceptualize 'interests' in social reality?" Therefore instead of seeing the classroom as a social system and as such insulated from wider structural processes, we suggest that the teacher who has developed an understanding of his [or her] location in the wider process may well be in a better position to understand where and how it is possible to alter that situation. The educator who is of necessity a moralist must preoccupy himself with the social and [economic] preconditions for the achievement of his ideals. Rather than affirming the separation of politics and education, as is done within commonsense liberal assumptions, the authors assume all education to be in its implications a political process.[36]

Thus, to isolate school experience from the complex totality of which it is a constitutive part is to be a bit too limited in one's analysis. In fact, the study of the relationship between ideology and school knowledge is especially important for understanding the larger social collectivity of which we are all a part. It enables us to begin to see how a society reproduces itself, how it perpetuates its conditions of existence through the selection and transmission of certain kinds of cultural capital upon which a complex yet unequal industrial society depends, and how it maintains cohesion among its classes and individuals by propagating ideologies that ultimately sanction existing institutional arrangements that can cause unnecessary stratification and inequality in the first place.[37] Can we afford not to understand these things?

Notes

1. Charles Silberman, *Crisis in the Classroom* (New York: Random House, 1970).

2. Herbert Gintis and Samuel Bowles, "The Contradictions of Liberal Educational Reform," in *Work, Technology, and Education*, ed. Walter Feinberg and Henry Rosemont, Jr. (Urbana: University of Illinois Press, 1975), p. 109.

3. That this is not merely an "intellectual" interest, but embodies social and ideological commitments, is examined in greater depth in Michael W. Apple, "The Adequacy of Systems Management Procedures in Education," in *Regaining Educational Leadership*, ed. Ralph H. Smith (New York: John Wiley and Sons, 1975).

4. Michael F. D. Young, "Knowledge and Control," in Young, *Knowledge and Control* (London: Collier-Macmillan, 1971).

5. John Kennett, "The Sociology of Pierre Bourdieu," *Educational Review* 25 (June 1973): 238.

6. On the necessity of seeing institutions relationally, see Bertell Ollman, *Alienation: Marx's Conception of Man in Capitalist Society* (New York: Cambridge University Press, 1971).

7. Daniel Kallós, "Educational Phenomena and Educational Research," report from the Institute of Education, University of Lund, Lund, Sweden, p. 7.

8. Dennis Warwick, "Ideologies, Integration and Conflicts of Meaning," in *Educability, Schools and Ideology*, ed. Michael Flude and John Ahier (London: Halstead Press, 1974), p. 94. See also Michael W. Apple, "Curriculum as Ideological Selection," *Comparative Education Review* 20 (June 1976).

9. Bill Williamson, "Continuities and Discontinuities in the Sociology of Education," in Flude and Ahier, *Educability*, pp. 10-11.

10. Ibid.

11. Barry Franklin, "The Curriculum Field and the Problem of Social Control, 1918-1938: A Study in Critical Theory" (Ph.D. diss., University of Wisconsin, Madison, 1974), pp. 2-3.

12. Ibid., pp. 4-5. It should be noted here that scientific management itself was not necessarily a neutral technology for creating more efficient institutions. It was developed as a mechanism for the further division and control of labor. This is provocatively portrayed in Harry Braverman, *Labor and Monopoly Capital: The Degradation of Work in the Twentieth Century* (New York: Monthly Review Press, 1975).

13. Ibid.

14. Ibid., p. 317.

15. Walter Feinberg, *Reason and Rhetoric: The Intellectual Foundations of Twentieth Century Liberal Educational Policy* (New York: John Wiley and Sons, 1975).

16. Philip Jackson, *Life in Classrooms* (New York: Holt, Rinehart, and Winston, 1968).

17. Elizabeth Vallance, "Hiding the Hidden Curriculum," *Curriculum Theory Network* 4 (Fall 1973-74): 15.

18. Ibid.

19. Ibid., pp. 18-19.

20. Gintis and Bowles, "Contradictions of Liberal Educational Reform," p. 133. These normative meanings and personality attributes are distributed unequally to different "types" of students, often by social class or occupational expectation as well. Not all students get the same dispositional elements; nor are the same meanings attached to them by the distributor of cultural capital. See ibid., p. 136.

21. See, e.g., Michael W. Apple, "Ivan Illich and Deschooling Society: The Politics of Slogan Systems," in *Social Forces and Schooling,* ed. Nobuo Shimahara and Adam Scrupski (New York: David McKay, 1975), pp. 337-60; Michael F. D. Young, "An Approach to the Study of Curricula as Socially Organized Knowledge," in Young, *Knowledge and Control,* pp. 19-46.

22. Nell Keddie, "Classroom Knowledge," in Young, *Knowledge and Control,* pp. 133-60.

23. Michael W. Apple, "Common Sense Categories and Curriculum Thought," in *Schools in Search of Meaning,* ed. James B. Macdonald and Esther Zaret (Washington, D.C.: ASCD, 1975), pp. 116-48.

24. This, of course, is a fundamental tenet of ethnomethodological studies as well. See Peter McHugh, *Defining the Situation* (Indianapolis, Ind.: Bobbs-Merrill Co., 1968); *Ethnomethodology,* ed. Roy Turner (Baltimore: Penguin Books, 1974); Aaron Cicourel, *Cognitive Sociology* (New York: Free Press, 1974).

25. For further explication of this point, see Basil Bernstein, "On the Classification and Framing of Educational Knowledge," in Young, *Knowledge and Control,* pp. 47-69.

26. Robert MacKay, "Conceptions of Children and Models of Socialization," in *Recent Sociology,* no. 5, *Childhood and Socialization,* ed. Hans Peter Dreitzel (New York: Macmillan, 1973).

27. An excellent treatment of this "ethnographic" tradition can be found in Philip E. D. Robinson, "An Ethnography of Classrooms," *Contemporary Research in the Sociology of Education,* ed. John Eggleston (London: Methuen and Co., 1974), pp. 251-66.

28. For a more complete discussion of this research project, see Nancy R. King, "The Hidden Curriculum and the Socialization of Kindergarten Children" (Ph.D. dissertation, University of Wisconsin, Madison, 1976).

29. Thomas R. Bates, "Gramsci and the Theory of Hegemony," *Journal of the History of Ideas* 36 (April-June 1975): 360.

30. Michael W. Apple, "The Hidden Curriculum and the Nature of Conflict," *Interchange* 2, no. 4 (1971): 29-40.

31. Habermas's arguments about patterns of communicative competence in advanced industrial "orders" are quite interesting as interpretive schemata here. See, for example, Jürgen Habermas, "Towards a Theory of Communicative

Competence," in *Recent Sociology*, no. 2, *Patterns of Communicative Behavior*, ed. Hans Peter Dreitzel (New York: Macmillan, 1970), pp. 115-48; Trent Schroyer, *The Critique of Domination* (New York: George Braziller, 1973).

32. Rachael Sharp and Anthony Green, *Education and Social Control: A Study in Progressive Primary Education* (Boston: Routledge and Kegan Paul, 1975).

33. Ibid., p. 13.

34. Ibid., pp. 110-112. See also the provocative analysis found in Basil Bernstein, *Class, Codes, and Control*, vol. 3, *Towards a Theory of Educational Transmissions* (Boston: Routledge and Kegan Paul, 1975).

35. Sharp and Green, *Education and Social Control*, p. 116.

36. Ibid., p. x.

37. Ibid., p. 221.

Comments

Chapters 20-22 are observations about some of the issues raised and the case studies included in the preceding sections of this volume. Chapter 20 presents a critique of traditional forms of educational research and evaluation and a view of the relationship between education and society. Chapter 21 comments specifically on a number of the foregoing case studies from still another perspective on education and society. Chapter 22 enlarges on preceding discussions about the functions of criticism and the critic.

In his essay Daniel Kallós does not comment directly on the specific case studies in this volume. Instead, he develops a position about the nature of education in modern society that provides both an overview of many salient issues confronted by case studies and a framework within which such studies can be considered. In so doing, he brings substantial international perspective to his subject matter, commenting specifically on developments in the Federal Republic of Germany, France, Sweden, and the United States.

The position Kallós develops is basically Marxist. He analyzes the function of schooling in capitalist countries, asserting that the schools act primarily as an ideological apparatus of the state in reproducing prevailing economic, political, and social relations. Since these relations are in the interest of the dominant class, schools work against the real interests of most students. In this light there are three principal problems with "traditional" educational research and curriculum evaluation. First, most research and evaluation activities are "commissioned" by the state; that is, they are dependent on state support, and divergent views are thus indirectly suppressed. Second, in attempting to be "scientific" and to act as an integral part of "rational" educational planning, most such activities become pre-

occupied with technological effects on practice. Third, in being based on comparison between "expected" and "observed" outcomes, such activities promote only "predetermined" knowledge, values, and skills. Kallós asserts that educational research and curriculum evaluation must instead be "structural"; they must explain the causes of prevailing educational practices by relating curricula to the structure of the school system and the structure of the school system to the structure of society. Ultimately, any analysis of schooling must be based "on a concrete analysis of the class structure within the country in question." Kallós provides examples of the kind of concepts useful in such an analysis and concludes by suggesting that even Schools in Search of Meaning *(the 1975 ASCD Yearbook, widely regarded in the United States as largely Marxist in orientation) falls considerably short of being Marxist curriculum evaluation, most of its writers adopting a "subjectivist" position.*

The position Kallós develops leaves the case studies in this volume in a curious kind of limbo. On the one hand, they clearly do not partake of the principal problems Kallós ascribes to traditional studies. None is in any pejorative sense "commissioned." None adopts a narrowly "scientific" paradigm or leads toward technological control. In fact, all at least implicitly (and most, explicitly) reject the notions of control and of evaluation in terms of fit between anticipated and achieved outcomes. On the other hand, none (with the possible exception of chapter 19) engages in the kind of "structural" analysis Kallós thinks essential to curriculum criticism. From a Marxist point of view, then, the kind of aesthetic, personal, and even political studies in this volume are not offensive, but they are not exactly inoffensive either. Perhaps Kallós's attitude toward them can be summarized by his sentence, "A critical approach misses its target if the critique is aimed at unimportant or insignificant aspects of the object under scrutiny."

Now, whether these case studies deal with the "unimportant or insignificant," and thus inadvertently work in the interest of "the dominant class," is something readers will decide for themselves in light of a great many considerations, only some of which are dealt with in this volume. While the volume does supply a number of answers to questions about the value of the critical approaches it exemplifies, several points may still be worth mentioning briefly here. Even when one fully accepts Kallós's position, at the very least the case studies do not preclude analyses of society. In fact (and this does depend on the importance and significance of what they scrutinize), since neither aesthetic nor personal reactions occur apart from a social context, studies of them may serve to stimulate, to direct, or to refine social and political studies. Heightened cognizance of the aesthetic and the personal dimensions of experience may thus act as a catalyst to a kind of general critical consciousness and, in this sense, be both logically and psychologically prior to political or social awareness. One might speculate, then, that attention to the quality of lived experience is as powerful a way of reforming the political and redistributing the material aspects of society as attention to the political and the material is of improving the qualities of living.

Daniel Kallós's essay causes one to consider where to begin.

20

Notes on Schooling, Curriculum, and Teaching

Daniel Kallós

Introduction

The famous Gotha program of the German Social Democratic party contained a paragraph demanding universal and equal elementary education by the state. Commenting on that part of the program, Karl Marx asked:

Equal elementary education? What do these words suggest? Is it believed that in present-day society (and it is only with this one has to do) education can be equal for all classes? Or is it demanded that the upper classes also shall be compulsorily reduced to the modicum of education—the elementary school—that alone is compatible with the economic conditions not only of the wage workers but of the peasants as well?[1]

I have chosen these classic words to begin this paper because the questions asked by Marx in 1875 are still with us, even though present-day society is different from Germany in 1875. But it is still obviously presumed that a school system within a capitalist society may provide children with equal opportunity, or at least that the school should strive in that direction. And even though "equal elementary education" has been achieved—at least on paper—in the industrialized capitalist countries, classes still remain.

Books like those of Bowles and Gintis or Carnoy and Levin have recently presented rather strong evidence that schools in present-day society aid in the reproduction of inequality.[2] This is considered a mark of failure by some of the modern critics of schools. Carnoy and Levin express the problem in the following way:

> Why did education fail, and can it succeed in eliminating poverty and in achieving other "desirable" social changes? In our view the schools of a society serve to reproduce the economic, social, and political relations, and the only way that schools can change these relations is through their unforeseen consequences rather than through planned and deliberate change. In this sense we argue that a society based on largely unequal positions of power, income and social status among adults, will not be able to alter those relations through schools. To the contrary, the schools will tend to reproduce the inequalities in order to contribute to the legitimation of adult society.[3]

The questions asked by Marx and modern statements like that of Carnoy and Levin are not, however, in harmony with the dominant tendencies of current pedagogical research in the Western world. Nor are they in harmony with "popular" critical examinations of schools and curricula (e.g., Postman and Weingartner).[4] The mainstream of pedagogical research and debate uses other points of departure. If we study attempted reform (or change), we see that schools and curricula are regarded by many as malfunctioning. In one way or another this malfunctioning is regarded as an abnormal state of affairs that can be corrected through rational decisions based on scientific research. The task of educational researchers is not only to detect and describe this state of affairs but also to provide the remedy. Even if this "model" is not explicitly used, it is assumed that reform (or change) which will alter the situation more or less fundamentally is possible within present-day society. Judging from the extent of the literature, there seem to be almost endless possibilities within the society, according to the adherents of the dominant modes of discourse. And there is always at least one classroom (or one school) which can be offered as proof: Change is possible! But careful case studies (often conducted over an extended period of time) tend to paint a more complicated picture.[5] What may appear as profound change may in the last analysis turn out to be an example of stability.

Any study of schooling or curriculum must rest upon some kind of theory concerning the function or meaning of schooling. This is perhaps especially true if the case study approach is used. In such instances the researcher must be able to classify his case; it must be an example of something. A critical approach misses its target if the critique is aimed at unimportant or insignificant aspects of the object under scrutiny. One of the major fallacies of curriculum critique is that it seems to start from the assumption that schools actually are institutions promoting equality, cooperation, creativity, and opportunities for all students to develop maximally. If schools do not do this, it is not enough just to attribute the failure to cultural lag, malfunctioning, or any other such "explanation." A more basic question must be asked: Can the definitions of schooling offered by the schools be taken as a starting point for an analysis of schooling and curriculum? A growing number of researchers have answered this question in the negative. For example, Feinberg and Rosemont, in their introduction to a volume of dissenting essays on American education, state:

> most educational critics have assumed and/or argued that the schools have failed in carrying out their mission, and that therefore education was in need of radical change. The present volume, on the other hand, rests on the contrary assumption that the schools have succeeded well in their task, and that therefore it is society that is in need of radical change.[6]

But if the common views are refuted it is still necessary to discuss and analyze schools and curricula as they are; research cannot wait for profound structural change to occur.

But one is, of course, doomed to failure in explaining or understanding anything that goes on in a classroom if one starts with the assumption that the teaching process is a more or less perfect instrument for transmission of a maximum amount of knowledge to as many students as possible. The situation may become even more difficult if one perceives the curricula and teaching processes as instruments constructed rationally and deliberately in accordance with some stated objectives. This is due to a rather simple fact. The inner work of schools, as this is performed by teachers and students within the classroom, fulfills a number of mutually dependent functions at the same time. These functions may only be combined with one another in such a way that they mutually constrain and determine each other. The school does not offer to the majority of pupils the possibility of further development of knowledge and skills adapted to their prior experiences or to their future objective interests. Instead, it offers them a preselected and predetermined body of knowledge, values, and skills that in principle are derived from the interests of a dominant class. This knowledge in its turn represses and is a substitute for this knowledge needed by (or in the objective interests of) the majority of students. Traditional research on teaching considers effective any instructional procedure (or any curriculum) that promotes learning of this predetermined kind. The effectiveness is in reality the result of a cultural struggle or, rather, the result of a resocialization. At the level of the compulsory school it could furthermore be noted that the socializing function is probably more important than the promotion of subject-specific knowledge. This is primarily due to the objective functions of the compulsory school within the societies of advanced capitalism. The social division of labor within class society does not require that the majority should be bearers of the dominant culture, but it does require that everyone should be an active or passive bearer of a behavioral pattern and its complementary norms, attitudes, and values. On the other hand, the school must also use a major part of the available time for the purpose of establishing and maintaining its own inner work and fulfilling its different functions through the establishment of social control. This is important not only for the school itself but also for the future work of its pupils. Within the framework of a certain curriculum—within the space offered by time and resources, by the social relations between teachers and students, by the marking (or examination) system in existence, and by the social composition of the class —all this is inevitable. It is not due to inadequate behavior on the part of those involved, or to flaws in the administrative planning of the schools. With certain variations, all those involved execute functions of which they are not the masters, because these functions are determined by the superordinate structures of capitalist society, structures partly outside the explicit consciousness of those involved, and definitely outside their scope of action.[7]

The School as an Ideological State Apparatus

In the preceding section, I have tried to provide a background for the study, analysis, and discussion of schooling, curriculum, and instruction. In order to elaborate further on the issues raised in the introduction, at least a few paragraphs should be devoted to the question of the functions of schooling in advanced capitalist societies that transcend the notions presented so far.

During the 1960s and 1970s, a renewed interest in the study of education has become evident among those who, somewhat inadequately, may be called Marxist scholars. At least two major and different positions or lines of analysis exist. On the one hand, a number of economists, primarily in the Federal Republic of Germany (FRG), have tried to reestablish a critical political economy that would also include the educational sector.[8] These approaches to determining the role and function of the educational system (or parts of it) within society tell us something about the general economic causes for expansion and crisis within the educational system. They also represent a powerful challenge to the dominant mode of reasoning within the field of the economics of education.

However, the educational system also fulfills ". . . crucial functions on the symbolical-ideological level that serve to support the reproduction of economic and legal-political power relations in the society."[9] This notion brings us to the second perspective, developed mainly in France. In education, the work of Bourdieu and Passeron may be regarded as a forerunner in its break with the almost absolute dominance of the social-liberal models.[10] It is, however, mainly the writings of Althusser, Baudelot and Establet, and Poulantzas that have advanced this discussion.[11] In a now-famous and oft-quoted paper Althusser discusses the school as the ideological state apparatus that plays a central part in the reproduction of the relations of production. Althusser advances the thesis that

the Ideological State apparatus which has been installed in the *dominant* position in mature capitalist formations as a result of a violent political and ideological class struggle against the old dominant ideological State apparatus, is the *educational ideological apparatus.*[12]

Although Althusser notes that this thesis may sound paradoxical, he nevertheless maintains that

behind the scenes of its political Ideological State apparatus, which occupies the front of the stage, what the bourgeoisie has installed as its number one, i.e., as its dominant, ideological State apparatus is the educational apparatus, which has in fact replaced in its functions the previously dominant ideological State apparatus, the Church. One might even add: The School-Family couple has replaced the Church-Family couple.[13]

Each of the state's ideological apparatuses contributes in its own way to the reproduction of the relations of production. In 1971 Baudelot and Establet published their book *The Capitalist School in France* (*L'ecole capitaliste en France*). In this book, which led to a vigorous debate, they empirically and theoretically tried to demonstrate that the unified school system in fact comprises two separate systems that correspond to the two antagonistic classes in French society—the bourgeoisie and the working class. According to Baudelot and Establet, the common notion presented by the school itself, i.e., that students who differ in social background or intelligence may reach different levels within *one* school system, must be rejected. There are *two* schools within the school, hidden behind a number of options within the comprehensive school system. The authors try to demonstrate this fact statistically by pointing to, for example, the small and insignificant number of crossovers between the two systems and by establishing the existence of different pedagogical practices within the separate parts.

The division between the two systems is clearly related both to social class and the positions within the social distribution of labor to which they lead. It is especially important to note that the two essential systems are located on the side of mental labor and on the side of manual labor. Thus the two systems reflect the separation between mental and manual categories. This separation is further reflected in the contents and in the pedagogy of the two systems. Poulantzas regarded the reasoning about the two systems as basically correct, but added that

the "bipolar" division involved here is a tendential one, and takes specific forms for the various social classes affected. This is where the argument of these writers seems to fall short. Their conclusion directly leads them to obscure the specific place of the new petty bourgeoisie in the educational apparatus.[14]

Poulantzas argues convincingly that we cannot discard the "third system" that is specific to the new petty bourgeoisie. He maintains that a whole series of indices points to the existence of a specific education for the new petty bourgeoisie. His arguments lead him to the conclusion that the educational apparatus

plays a quite specific role for the new petty bourgeoisie, directly contributing to reproducing its place in the social formation. This is directly reflected in the role that this apparatus plays in distributing agents among places of the social classes, a role which is very important for the new petty bourgeoisie, while it remains a secondary one for both the bourgeoisie and the working class. The agents of these two basic classes, or alternatively their children, are not themselves distributed by the educational system in any literal sense, or rather they are distributed while remaining in the same place, everything happening as if they were bound to these places, with the school simply sanctioning and legitimizing this connection.[15]

Poulantzas also questions the notion that the school is the dominant ideological apparatus of the state in the capitalist mode of production ". . . as far as the reproduction, distribution and training of agents is concerned. . . ."[16] He notes that the dominance of any one apparatus is dependent on the class struggle in specific social formations. He furthermore states that the dominant apparatus may vary even within a particular social formation. The educational apparatus is, according to him, the dominant apparatus for the petty bourgeoisie in France, but it is not so ". . . for the working class, either in France or in the other capitalist countries. It would seem in fact that for the working class, this dominant role falls directly to the economic apparatus itself, to the 'enterprise.' "[17] This does not, of course, mean that schools are "unimportant" from the perspective of the working class. The capitalist school emphasizes and qualifies mental labor, while at the same time it disqualifies manual labor. To the majority of the working class, the school teaches ". . . the veneration of a mental labour that is always 'somewhere else.' "[18]

Although the school cannot provide the worker with sufficient technical or professional skills (manual labor), it is fully equipped to train the new petty bourgeoisie. The relative dominance of the new petty bourgeoisie within the school system is also reflected in educational research. Using Sweden as an example, I have described the current situation as an example of a "rose-coloured wave in Swedish pedagogy."[19] Basil Bernstein in a recent important paper described and analyzed the emergence of a "new" pedagogy, which he called "invisible" from the point of view of the child.[20] This presumably nondirective pedagogy is, in his opinion, really well-defined and well-rooted in the need for internalized social control in societies of advanced capitalism, and is supported by a growing "new middle class" for which this ideology constitutes its subculture in both professional and private life.

In this section I have tried to emphasize and illuminate some aspects of the educational system as an ideological apparatus of the state. It should finally be pointed out that ideology within a society is not shaped by the school or any other ideological apparatus. Concrete processes and power relations at all levels of society determine how ideology and symbolic relations are formed, maintained, and changed. It is a common misconception that the schools bear the responsibility for the origin, shaping, and upholding of existing ideas and values in society. On the contrary, it is the task of the schools to cultivate and disseminate these ideas and values.

On Research of Schools and Curricula

Gintis wrote that reformers commonly err in treating education as if it existed in a social vacuum.[21] This may or may not be true. But it is certainly true that the relations between school and society are neglected by educational researchers. In the preceding sections the school has been identified as an ideological state apparatus and as such has been related to the characteristics of the societies of advanced capitalism. I used excerpts from texts by Althusser and Poulantzas to articulate this thesis. It should, however, be understood that these authors are not primarily interested in education or schooling. It is within an analysis of the state and of the class structure of contemporary capitalism that Poulantzas discusses the important role of the school as an ideological apparatus of the state.[22]

The close examination of the educational system as an ideological apparatus of the state is an important task for educational research. Generally speaking, it may be said that the task of educational research is to describe and analyze the educational practices prevailing in the society and to work out theories which can explain the causal relationships giving rise to such practice. The immediate causes are, in their turn, rooted in the overall structure of the society. The task of educational research also includes the critical examination of existing descriptions, analyses, and explanations.

What is suggested here is that any analysis of educational practice must be carried out from the perspective of its structural determinants. This means that, for example, curricula and instructional processes must be related to the school system to which they belong, and the school must in its turn be assessed in relation to the structure of the society in question. Educational researchers in the United

States (and in Sweden) have in most instances chosen an almost opposite route. Curricula and instructional processes are linked to learning, and their analysis is accordingly carried out in terms of intentions, teacher behavior, etc. It is virtually impossible—as history has demonstrated—to reach any valid conclusions about the objective functions of the processes of education if we use the level of curriculum and instruction as a starting point. In the preceding sections I have presented some of the arguments supporting this view.

Curriculum studies based on the perspective adopted here cannot be primarily normative. They cannot focus primarily on *how* a curriculum should be constructed or developed, but must map out and explain the determinants of the curriculum. One important issue is thus the question of *why* a certain type of curriculum becomes necessary under a certain set of circumstances. I do not imply that curriculum research has neglected this question completely, but I certainly imply that the traditional answers have been very limited in scope. Curriculum is typically regarded as an answer to certain demands in the society. *Why* these demands dominate or *why* certain groups in society at a certain point in history are in the position of exerting an influence on the curriculum are questions rarely asked in traditional curriculum research.

On the other hand, the perspective adopted here makes it possible to go beyond traditional curriculum criticism. Such criticism has mainly been concerned with the realization of certain objectives (explicitly stated in, e.g., a curriculum guide or objectives that the critic would like to see realized). At best such a critique may expose the myths of schooling as discrepancies between explicitly stated objectives (intentions) and outcomes, for example. This is in essence what Bourdieu and Passeron and Bowles and Gintis have done in the area of equal opportunity.[23] Bourdieu has neatly summarized one of the conclusions:

Indeed, among all the solutions put forward throughout history to the problem of the transmission of power and privileges, there surely does not exist one that is better adapted to societies which tend to refuse the most patent forms of the hereditary transmission of power and privileges than that solution which the educational system provides by contributing to the reproduction of the structure of class relations and by concealing, by an apparently neutral attitude, the fact that it fills this function.[24]

But the fact that it is possible to demonstrate over and over again that children from different social classes have different educational

futures is not enough. It demonstrates only that the child inherits the
social class of his father and that the school is an intervening institution. But even if it were possible to identify some of the mechanisms
used by the school in this process—e.g., in terms of the language used
in the school in relation to prior experiences of the child—it still
would not be enough. The common "explanation" behind the outcomes described by Bourdieu above is that the ultimate cause of
"failure" or "success" in school must be traced back to earlier experiences. However, Baudelot and Establet have pointed out that it is
necessary to go beyond "regressive, chronological, and individual"
explanations in attempts to analyze how schools contribute to the
reproduction of class and class relations in society.[25] What studies of
the kind mentioned above demonstrate are some of the effects of a
class society. But what is important is that classes and class relations
are reproduced, not that individuals inherit a position. The process of
reproduction of classes is the fundamental process. In accordance
with Baudelot and Establet it should be emphasized that classes cannot be reduced to a number of social attributes characteristic of different individuals. The analysis cannot stop in front of the school, so
to speak, but must also take into account the contradictions within
the school.

As an ideological apparatus of the state the educational apparatus must inculcate bourgeois ideology in such a way that two objectives are reached. According to Baudelot and Establet this means
that all pupils must learn this ideology and how its modes of expression and conceptions are used. Additionally, the contents and effects
of a proletarian ideology must be suppressed wherever they appear so
that they can be subjected to a bourgeois ideology appearing as a
distorted petty bourgeois variant. As an ideological apparatus of the
state, the educational apparatus simultaneously divides and selects
the students *and* inculcates a specific ideology in two antagonistic
versions (i.e., an explicit inculcation of bourgeois ideology and the
suppression and distortion of a proletarian ideology). But this
process is not smooth and effortless. The educational apparatus is
characterized by contradictions, and struggle and various forms of
opposition are clearly visible within it.

The analysis of curricula and the practices of the educational
apparatus within the perspective outlined in this paper thus tran-
scends traditional curriculum criticism. The traditional vocabulary,

which uses words like learning, development, failure, normal, etc., implies a denial of the contradictions; i.e., a denial of the class struggle that manifests itself within the educational apparatus. As an ideological apparatus of the state, the school is an instrument of the ideological class struggle of the state directed *against* the proletarian ideology that exists outside the school among the workers and in their organizations.[26]

At this point it is possible to become quite explicit. Current research on schooling, curricula, and teaching legitimizes existing practices and obscures the actual state of affairs. This is primarily because most educational research is done by academically trained people with access to economic resources who are institutionally more or less clearly attached to the state apparatus and, thereby, to the ruling class. Opportunities for genuinely critical research are rare. In Sweden approximately 60 percent of all funds for educational research are administered by the National Board of Education (NBE). This means that

assignments are mainly given to researchers who agree with the basic view of the NBE. . . . Research which is critical of the NBE's basic view is not supported; it is quickly checked. This is certainly not done intentionally—there have been cases of support being awarded to critical research. The main impediment lies in the fact that critical research cannot be integrated with the top priority problem areas, and also in the fact that there are so few bodies apart from the NBE which can provide financial resources for research of this kind.[27]

At the same time it is quite clear that research within the Marxist tradition of historical materialism is not in harmony with the political interests of the class that dominates the funding agencies, the universities, and the teachers colleges. Nor could that harmony exist in the societies of advanced capitalism. The remnants of so-called academic freedom are constantly threatened and must constantly be defended even against those who on solemn occasions pay lip service to ideals which in practice they rarely uphold.[28]

The "rational view" of educational planning implies that decisions concerning education, curricula, and instruction are to be based on research. Questions are asked by so-called decision-makers, and the researchers try to provide the answers.[29] In reality this is, of course, almost never true. Even an immanent critique would quickly discover the fallacies in such a view of the relation between research and educational practice. One of the prime functions of educational research is to legitimize existing practices and to uphold the myths of schooling and the illusion of the potential for radical change within the educational apparatus.

In an era when signs of crisis within the society are constantly visible as crises within the schools, educational researchers have had little success in providing the solutions asked for. The legitimizing capacity of the educational research community is being questioned (witness the decrease in funding, etc.). Educational researchers have responded to this in different ways. Where quasi-experimentation, behavior, and statistics had flourished, discussions arose about symbolic interactionism, phenomenology, humanistic psychology, Piagetianism, hermeneutics, critical theory, action research, ethno-methodology, and even neo-Marxism. It was, of course, easy to prove that these "isms" were at least fifty years old. But what difference did that make when they seemed new to many research workers? The true problems of educational research could be transformed into questions concerning an illusory choice between theories and/or methods. This means that ". . . one rationalizes knowledge in detail (method)—and is defenseless against the historical irrationality of the aims and purposes to which it is subservient."[30] But what is thus supplied is still an ideological defense for the established society.

Curriculum Criticism and Evaluation as Examples

Several of the issues raised in the preceding sections may be illustrated at a more concrete level if a typical educational research activity is chosen as an example. Curriculum evaluation will be used as such an example in this section.

Within educational research the study of curriculum has a long history. One of the weaknesses of the field is its lack of theoretical underpinnings—a weakness it shares with many other areas of educational research.[31] Curriculum evaluation is, however, of more recent origin, although informal evaluational activities have also been carried out in relation to curricula for a long time.

We may trace two interdependent lines in the development of curriculum evaluation. This field is firmly embedded both in the development of curriculum research *and* in the development of educational evaluation. Today, evaluation plays a prominent role within educational research, although its peak has probably been reached.

Evaluation of curricula and instruction has furthermore probably been scientifically influenced more by educational measurement than by curriculum theory and research.[32] The area of educational measurement, which has in practice consisted mainly in the development of instruments and techniques to measure characteristics (traits) and achievement of students, has played an important part in the establishment of educational research as a scientific endeavor. It is also an area where notable success has been registered, if success is defined in terms of effects on practice. The instruments developed have been used to select students, to grade them, to place them in different educational environments, etc. Intelligence tests, for example, have from the very beginning fulfilled the important function of contributing to a quasi-scientific legitimation of profoundly undemocratic educational practices.[33] Achievement tests have in their turn been used to ensure control of and domination within the school, and as means for selection.[34] The practitioners of educational measurement provided instruments and techniques to be used in the assessment of input and output characteristics of students. They have provided instruments for measurement of the essential components in the evaluation equation.

After World War II the educational apparatus in advanced capitalist societies was expanded. This period of growth, when the solution to educational problems seemed to be simply increased investment in the educational sector, was quickly followed by a phase of rationalization. Allocation of scarce resources and demands for improvement of efficiency became prominent issues. At the same time, discontent grew. Some of the myths of education were openly challenged. By the 1960s what may even be referred to as a crisis began to occur within both the educational apparatus and educational research.

Within the paradigm of rational decision-making that had been established it became increasingly important to justify existing practices and suggested change through the use of information gathered scientifically. The field of educational evaluation gained momentum, as is reflected by the increase in funding. Educational evaluation as a research activity could be superficially regarded as an almost pure example of applied or decision-oriented research.[35] The fact that most curriculum evaluation studies are examples of commissioned research could be used to support this statement.

A study of the literature concerning curriculum evaluation, however, quite clearly demonstrates that it cannot be regarded as a straightforward application of theories, principles, concepts, and methods borrowed from the scientific study of education and applied to particular issues. Furthermore, there is a marked tendency to try to establish curriculum evaluation as a special branch within the discipline of education. Quasi-theories concerning curriculum evaluation are presented, and in many instances curriculum evaluation studies are judged as scientific research and not primarily as the activity of a trained researcher using the tools and tricks of his trade to obtain certain information.

In order to understand the field of curriculum evaluation the origins of the field should be explored in detail, but not as problems within the scientific discipline of education. Curriculum evaluation has been established as a field by those agencies that commission evaluation studies. This does not imply that curriculum evaluation studies do not provide researchers with information which can be used for scientific purposes. But it implies that the general study of the effects (or outcomes) of educational practices (including curricula) cannot be regarded as identical with those activities that are labeled evaluation. The scientific study of the results of the practices of the educational apparatus is—as already indicated—an important and integral part of educational scientific research.

All traditional curriculum evaluation studies seem to involve a comparison between "expected" and "observed" outcomes. But if the term "expected" is discussed scientifically and critically, the limits of commissioned research are exceeded. This means that when "objectives," "intentions," and "expectations" are regarded in their context, i.e., as expressions of an ideological apparatus of the state, the field of curriculum evaluation disintegrates. At one point in the analysis, evaluation encompasses *everything* or *nothing*.

Disputes within the field of curriculum evaluation are thus not to be regarded as examples of particular scientific issues in an area in which problems are defined by those agencies that commission research, but instead as yet further indications of a crisis within the scientific discipline of education. At a general level this crisis is related to the political and economic conditions of research. At a more specific level the problem must be discussed in terms of the relations between educational research and educational practice. The problems within the field of curriculum evaluation are thus expressions of issues of a more fundamental nature.

The crisis in educational research appears to be located within the domain of theory of science. The lack of compatibility between theory and practice is accordingly ascribed to a poor choice among existing schools of meta-science. Dunkel has argued that the "narrow view of science" is a poor choice as a basis for educational research.[36] But he was unable to demonstrate why this narrow view dominated the scene for a considerable time and still does. The alternative choices commonly proposed do not imply a break with the views under discussion, nor do they challenge the basic assumptions concerning the nature of the phenomena under study. Most proposed alternatives are well within an idealistic frame of reference (as opposed to a materialistic one). The issue of meta-theory and of a theory of education is furthermore transformed into a debate over methods. When this happens, shifting between qualitative data and quantitative data does not alter much. Approaches such as those labeled "illuminative," "portrayal," "responsive," "narrative," or "critical" all seem to fall well within tolerable limits, i.e., within the borders of the dominant ideology.[37]

The particular aspects of many of these allegedly new approaches must be studied in relation to the specific characteristics of the societies from which they emerged. In Sweden such tendencies as those mentioned above seem to correspond with the emergence and increased importance of a new petty bourgeoisie.[38]

If the theses put forward by Althusser and by Poulantzas concerning the school as an ideological apparatus of the state are basically correct, this also implies that a number of concepts commonly used in educational literature are completely insufficient for an analysis of schooling, curricula, and instruction. A criticism of curriculum that limits itself to the use of common educational terminology will accordingly never transcend the limits of an immanent critique. Baudelot and Establet provocatively state that what goes on within the comprehensive school has absolutely nothing to do with pedagogy, children, instruction, etc. They consider such concepts to be a kind of "mask" that serves to hide what is really taking place in the school. Baudelot and Establet point out that in order to describe the schools and what happens there, it is necessary to introduce new concepts, at least at the level of description: for example, "social class," "inculcation," "submission," "exploitation," "ideological dominance," "conditions of production," etc. That is, such description must employ concepts and terms from the Marxist tradition of analysis of the world.

At a superficial level it is possible to reach a consensus concerning the nature of schools, curricula, and teaching. Many would agree that there is a relation between schooling and society. Some would even admit that we live in a class society and that this fact is mirrored in the educational apparatus. But this does not mean that there is agreement when these concepts are defined within a Marxist tradition, nor when the consequences of such a perspective are involved.

As the work of Baudelot and Establet in France has demonstrated, it is necessary to base an analysis of schooling and curricula on a concrete analysis of the class structure within the country in question. At a certain level of discourse this means that our evaluation and criticism of schools and curricula must be specific and concrete. As Marx noted in 1875, it must be related to society as it is.

Some Final Notes

I have already noted that the scientific study of curriculum within the realms of the dominant mode of inquiry has several shortcomings. Critical views on schooling and curriculum are, however, beginning to emerge in the United States. A recent and important collection of essays entitled *Schools in Search of Meaning,* edited by Macdonald and Zaret, is a good example of this trend. In the introduction, the authors note that their attempts to utilize "class interest in educational criticism is not the first such attempt" in the United States, and refer the reader to work by Counts and Childs, among others. In defining their own position the authors state that

It would be less than accurate to suggest that the writers . . . are clearly unified in their definition of "class" and "class interest." It is certain, however, that we all conceive "class" to denote a sociological and political reality, and believe that an analysis along the lines of this reality, however defined, is the only way in which the activities and meanings of schooling can be made to make sense. The critical questions which will run through the writing here are, "In whose interest is it?" and "Who decides?" The answers to these questions outline different, but largely overlapping, notions of what classes exist in our society and how the interests of those classes work themselves out in public schooling.[39]

The writers' lack of unity in their definitions of "class" and "class struggle" is also evident from the texts themselves. The fact that most of the writers do not accept a Marxist concept of class is clear from the essentially subjectivist position revealed in the two questions posed, "In *whose* interest is it?" and *"Who* decides?"[40]

The important issue is not hidden in the answers to the questions "Who has power?" and "How much power?" If we approach the problem of power within the tradition of historical materialism, another set of questions emerge, which can be contrasted to the essentially subjectivist approaches mentioned above (whether these approaches materialize themselves in the adoption of an elitist position or a pluralistic position). "What kind of power is executed and how?" is the basic question to be asked.[41] This means that we ask questions concerning the society, and because power within society is concentrated in the state, questions concerning the role of the state in the reproduction and change of the society must also be answered. As Therborn points out, it is necessary to analyze the nature of state power and the ruling class in such a way that the blind alley of subjectivism is bypassed. This might be achieved if we were to study the objective effects of the state's interventions in the (re)production of a given mode of production.[42] This, then, is a concrete task for the educational researcher investigating schooling and curricula in present-day society. The analysis of the educational apparatus as an ideological apparatus of the state may also be regarded in this perspective.[43]

Notes

1. Karl Marx, *Critique of the Gotha Programme* (1875; rpt. ed., Peking: Foreign Languages Press, 1972).

2. Samuel Bowles and Herbert Gintis, *Schooling in Capitalist America* (New York: Basic Books, 1976); Martin Carnoy and Henry Levin, *The Limits of Educational Reform* (New York: McKay, 1976).

3. Carnoy and Levin, *Limits of Educational Reform*, p. 4.

4. Neil Postman and Charles Weingartner, *Teaching as a Subversive Activity* (Harmondsworth: Penguin Books, 1971).

5. See, for example, W. Lynn McKinney and Ian Westbury, "Stability and Change: The Public Schools of Gary, Indiana, 1940-1970," in *Case Studies in Curriculum Change*, ed. W. A. Reid and D. Walker (London: Routledge and Kegan Paul, 1975), pp. 1-53.

6. Walter Feinberg and Henry Rosemont, Jr., "Introduction" to *Work, Technology, and Education*, ed. Feinberg and Rosemont (Urbana, Ill.: University of Illinois Press, 1975), p. 12.

7. S. Callewaert and U. P. Lundgren, "Undervisningsforskning och social reproduktion" [Research on teaching and social reproduction], in *Jämlikhets-*

myt och klassheravälde, ed. S. Lundberg et al. (Lund: Cavefors, 1976), pp. 64-96; D. Kallós and U. P. Lundgren, "Lessons from a Comprehensive School System for Curriculum Theory and Curriculum Research," *Curriculum Studies* 9, no. 1 (in press).

8. See, for example, E. Altvater and F. Huisken, eds., *Materialien zur politischen Ökonomie der Ausbildungssektors* (Erlangen: Politladen, 1971); F. Huisken, *Zur Kritik bürgerlicher Didaktik und Bildungsökonomie* (Munich: List Verlag, 1972); R. Heinrich, *Zur politischen Ökonomie der Schulreform* (Stuttgart: Europaische Verlagsanstalt, 1973).

9. B. Berner, S. Callewaert, and H. Silberbrandt, eds., *Skola, ideologi och samhälle* [School, ideology and society] (Malmö: Wahlström and Widstrand, 1977). (Our translation.)

10. P. Bourdieu and J.-C. Passerson, *La reproduction* (Paris: Les Editions de Minuit, 1970); see also P. Bordieu, "Cultural Reproduction and Social Reproduction," in Richard Brown, ed., *Knowledge, Education, and Cultural Change* (London: Tavistock, 1973), pp. 71-112. *La reproduction* is available in English as *Reproduction in Education, Society, and Culture* (London and Beverly Hills, Ca.: Sage Publications, 1976).

11. Louis Althusser, "Ideology and Ideological State Apparatuses," in Althusser, *Lenin and Philosophy, and Other Essays* (New York: Monthly Review Press, 1971), pp. 127-86.

12. Althusser, "Ideology," p. 152. The main distinction made by Althusser is between the "repressive state apparatus" and the "ideological state apparatuses." According to Althusser, the ideological state apparatuses are distinguished from the repressive state apparatus by the fact that the former function by ideology, while the latter functions by violence. Just as it is important to note that the repressive state apparatus may function secondarily by ideology, so also is it important to note that for their part

the Ideological State Apparatuses function massively and predominantly by *ideology,* but they also function secondarily by repression, even if ultimately, but only ultimately, this is very attenuated and concealed, even symbolic. (There is no such thing as a purely ideological apparatus.) Thus the Schools and Churches use suitable methods of punishment, expulsion, selection, etc. to "discipline" not only their shepherds, but also their flocks. The same is true of the Family . . . (p. 145).

Nicos Poulantzas, in *Classes in Contemporary Capitalism* (London: New Left Books, 1975), states

The principal role of the state apparatuses is to maintain the unity and cohesion of a social formation by concentrating and sanctioning class domination, and in this way reproducing social relations, i.e. class relations. Political and ideological relations are materialized and embodied, as material practices, in the state apparatuses (pp. 24-25).

He furthermore adds:

It remains none the less true that it is class struggle that plays the primary and basic role in the complex relationship between class struggle and apparatuses, and this is a decisive point to note, given the errors of numerous present-day arguments on these questions. The apparatuses are never anything other than the materialization and condensation of class relations; in a sense, they "presuppose" them, so long as it is understood that what is involved here is not a relation of chronological causality (the chicken or the egg). Now according to a constant of bourgeois ideology in the "social sciences," which might be loosely referred to as the "institutionalist-functionalist" current, it is apparatuses and institutions that determine social groups (classes), with class relations arising from the situation of agents in institutional relationships. This current exhibits in specific forms the couple idealism/empiricism, in the specific form of humanism/economism, both of which are characteristic of bourgeois ideology (pp. 25-26).

13. Althusser, "Ideology," pp. 153-54.
14. Poulantzas, *Contemporary Capitalism*, p. 260.
15. Ibid., p. 269.
16. Ibid.
17. Ibid., p. 270.
18. Ibid., p. 266.
19. S. Callewaert and D. Kallós, "The Rose-Coloured Wave in Swedish Pedagogy," *Educational Studies* 2: 179-84.
20. Basil Bernstein, "Class and Pedagogies: Visible and Invisible," *Educational Studies* 1: 23-41. Bernstein has recently expanded the views put forward in the paper mentioned here. He has attempted to relate the occurrence of new forms of pedagogy more directly to the relations between education and production. See Basil Bernstein, "Aspects of the Relations between Education and Production," in idem, *Class, Codes and Control*, 2d ed. (London: Routledge and Kegan Paul, 1977), vol. 3, pp. 174-200.
21. Herbert Gintis, "Towards a Political Economy of Education: A Radical Critique of Ivan Illich's *De-Schooling Society*," *Harvard Educational Review* 42, no. 1, pp. 70-96.
22. Earlier writings by Poulantzas also contain important discussions concerning the state and state apparatuses (e.g., *Fascism and Dictatorship* [London: New Left Books, 1974]). Both Althusser and Poulantzas refer to Antonio Gramsci (*Selections from the Prison Notebooks* [London: Lawrence and Wishart, 1971]) and his attempts to discuss not only the repressive state apparatus but also the ideological state apparatuses "on the basis of his experiences as a proletarian leader" (Poulantzas, *Fascism and Dictatorship*, p. 299). The work of Gramsci, Althusser, and Poulantzas should furthermore be regarded as Marxist; i.e., they follow the tradition established by Marx, Engels, and Lenin. I mention this because I tend to agree with Paulston's assessment of the influence of Marxist views within educational literature in the United States: "In the United States . . . Marxist perspectives on social and educational change have been largely rejected and/or ignored" (Rolland G. Paulston, *Conflicting Theories of Social and Educational Change: A Typological Review* [Pittsburgh, Pa.: University Center for International Studies, University of Pittsburgh, 1976], p. 26). It is perhaps significant that to the best of my knowledge none of the works *directly* concerned with education in contemporary Marxist literature in Germany or France have been translated into English.
23. Bourdieu and Passeron, *La reproduction*; Bowles and Gintis, *Schooling in Capitalist America*.

24. Bourdieu, "Cultural Reproduction," p. 73.

25. C. Baudelot and R. Establet, *L'ecole capitaliste en France* (Paris: Maspero, 1971).

26. Ibid.

27. K.-G. Ahlström and E. Wallin, "Effects of Commissioned Research," in *Educational Research and Development at the NBE,* ed. B. Estmer (Stockholm: LiberLäromedel, 1976), pp. 83-87.

28. The situation in the Federal Republic of Germany may be mentioned as a pertinent example of threats to the freedom of inquiry. The so called *Berufsverbote* (Ban on Professional Employment) and similar measures strongly reminiscent of the McCarthy era in the United States seriously affect research in the social and behavioral sciences. Hundreds of thousands of civil servants have been examined as to their political views and activities. Several have been banned from carrying out their chosen profession. See *Ban on Professional Employment in the FRG: A Juridicial and Political Documentation* (Frankfurt: Institut für Marxistische Studien und Forschungen, 1975).

29. See, for example, S. J. Eggleston, "The Process of Curriculum Change," *Paedogogica Europaea* 6: 11-18.

30. C. Marzahn, "Zur Beduetung der revolutionären Pädagogen für die Rekonstituierung einer marxistischen Erziehungstheorie und Praxis heute," *Erziehung und Klassenkampf* 1, no. 1, p. 32. (Our translation.)

31. D. Kallós and U. P. Lundgren, *Curriculum as a Pedagogical Problem* (Stockholm: Department of Education, Teachers College, 1976); idem, "Lessons from a Comprehensive School System."

32. See, for example, J. C. Merwin, "Historical Review of Changing Concepts in Evaluation," in *Educational Evaluation: New Roles, New Means—The 68th Yearbook of the National Society for the Study of Education,* ed. Ralph W. Tyler (Chicago, Ill.: University of Chicago Press, 1969), pt. 2, pp. 6-25.

33. See, for example, Brian Simon, *Intelligence, Psychology, and Education: A Marxist Critique* (London: Lawrence and Wishart, 1971).

34. See, for example, S. Kvale, *Prüfung und Herreschaft* (Weinheim and Basel: Beltz Verlag, 1972).

35. Lee J. Cronbach and Patrick Suppes, eds., *Research for Tomorrow's Schools* (New York: Macmillan Co., 1969).

36. Harold B. Dunkel, "Wanted: New Paradigms and a Normative Base for Research," in *Philosophical Redirection of Educational Research—The 71st Yearbook of the National Society for the Study of Education* (Chicago, Ill.: University of Chicago Press, 1972), pt. 1, pp. 77-93.

37. The widely published Cambridge Manifesto may be mentioned as another pertinent example. See "The Cambridge Manifesto," *SRIS Quarterly* 6, no. 2, p. 17.

38. Callewaert and Kallós, "The Rose-Coloured Wave."

39. James B. Macdonald and Esther Zaret, eds., *Schools in Search of Meaning* (Washington, D.C.: ASCD, 1975), pp. 10-11.

40. The chapters in the volume edited by Macdonald and Zaret (see n. 39) are also different in relation to the issue of subjectivism. The perspective developed by Mann in his chapter and the issues that he raises are in my opinion the most fruitful ones for further work in the area of curriculum analysis. See John S. Mann, "On Contradictions in Schools," in Macdonald and Zaret, *Schools in Search of Meaning,* pp. 95-115.

41. G. Therborn, "Vad gör den härskande klassen när den härskar?" [What does the ruling class do when it rules?] *Häften för Kritiska Studier* 9, no. 4, pp. 4-31.

42. Ibid., p. 24.

43. The discussion concerning the educational apparatus as an ideological apparatus of the state has recently been taken up in Great Britain. Thus Erben and Gleeson have published a critical review of the paper by Althusser which I have referred to. (See M. Erben and D. Gleeson, "Education as Reproduction: A Critical Examination of Some Aspects of the Work of Louis Althusser," in *Society, State, and Schooling*, ed. Michael Young and Geoff Whitty [London: The Falmer Press, 1977]). These authors have, however, not taken into account the French discussion of Althusser's position. They state that Althusser fails ". . . to take into account possibilities for dynamic change within situations themselves" (p. 89). They furthermore hold that "It is one thing to describe education as reproduction, but it is another to explain this phenomenon as transcendable" (p. 89). Although the essay by Althusser may be somewhat overrated, it still has been extremely powerful in stimulating Marxist debate concerning the ideological apparatuses of the state. That debate has by far transcended the rather simple criticism of Erben and Gleeson.

The essay by Michael W. Apple is a direct comment on many of the case studies in this volume. From his own position about the value and the uses of qualitative curriculum evaluation, Apple points out what he considers to be the strengths and the weaknesses of those specific studies which were completed prior to his writing.

He suggests that in general they seem to be a response to two deficiencies in the dominant kinds of educational research: the failure to attend to the actual processes of education and the positivistic assumption that values cannot enter meaningfully into propositions about real things. While most sympathetic to this response and even personally identified with the authors of several studies, Apple offers his own criticisms in the spirit of shared inquiry necessary to maintain and to advance the field. His most basic concern is that in revealing the dynamics of specific educational situations, qualitative studies run the risk of not fully interpreting the connections with the social, political, and economic world in which educational processes are embedded. Despite real advantages, the general form which qualitative studies take (especially the more artistic and personalistic studies) contributes to this risk.

Still, the principal value of such a form may be that it causes

*reconsideration of ordinary perceptions and procedures and illumi-
nates the individual human concerns which give meaning to political
action. As Apple asserts, ". . . there is something of a logical progression from aesthetic awareness to politico/economic understanding."
Thus, although he has some reservations, Apple suggests that, especially taken as a group, the studies signal some real progress in curriculum evaluation, and to maintain this progress the authors must continue "to pass from the psychological to the social, and from the
social to the politico/economic, and then dialectically 'back' to the
individual."*

*Both in developing his position and interpreting specific studies
Apple raises any number of issues which will cause the reader of this
volume considerable reflection. Among his most interesting points
are the ideas that in emphasizing individual experience the literary or
personalistic form could actually lead to "ideological hegemony,"
noncoercive control through the individual's internalization of prevailing norms, values, and categories of thought; that in modern society the idea of being an individual receives great emphasis, but the
emphasis is usually on being an individual unconnected with concrete
social, economic, and political realities; and that emphasizing experience tends to confound educational experience with "everything we
do," making values relative and tending to preclude "serious ethical,
political, or even aesthetic dialogue." These are powerful ideas,
powerfully stated.*

*In reflecting on them the reader should also consider that the
curriculum field generally and curriculum evaluation in particular
have virtually no tradition which deals at all adequately with individual experience. Almost nothing is really known about how individuals constitute meaning within educational contexts, which are,
after all, part of broader social contexts. Lacking such a tradition and
body of knowledge, curriculumists historically have succumbed to
ideologies that have emphasized group norms, collective reactions,
and social control. In this light the case studies in this volume may be
seen as a contribution to this missing tradition.*

*The form many of these studies take may also be seen as a way
of investigating what all kinds of individual experience—educational
and otherwise—have in common. Knowing something about these
commonalities may be a rather important step toward knowing how
individuals are in fact connected with educational and social con-*

texts. (Even those studies which tend most to report and least to interpret experiences describe specific contexts as well.) Studying individual experience may therefore also be a way of studying both commonalities and differences in experiences within social contexts. Perhaps ironically, such studies may thus provide a rather important basis for defining values and for establishing dialogue, and the general form in which they are embodied may thus also be considered a powerful way of commenting upon the structures of the individual's external social world.

Apple's essay throws these issues into sharp relief.

21

Ideology and Form in Curriculum Evaluation

Michael W. Apple

On What Is Lost in Educational Research

In order completely to comprehend a set of studies like those in this volume, the reader must see them as "cultural products." He or she must encase their internal structure and arguments within wider issues. An explanation of this kind of work needs at least in part to go beyond the individual authors to what might be called the collective consciousness that they reflect.[1] In essence, we must look at the *form* of qualitative studies, not merely at the content. Why do they take on so much importance today? To what are they a response?

They seem to be a response to two kinds of conditions surrounding education. The first is a set of intellectual claims about research. With Philip Jackson and others, they reject as relatively unsophisticated the input/output or econometric styles that dominate educational research, where one measures beginning and end but pays little attention to the very process of education. What actually happens in classrooms, the curriculum-in-use, is ignored.[2] They also seem to be arguing, and rightly so, that in the investigation of social life there is a dialectical interplay between the values and perspectives of the investigator and the "facts out there" to be investigated

495

or evaluated. This involves a rejection of the positivistic claim, found most fully in the early Wittgenstein and the logical atomists, that one can only make meaningful propositions about facts. Values cannot meaningfully enter into these propositions. They lie outside the world of sensible conversation about the real nature of things.[3]

While this positivistic claim has been rejected in philosophy for decades, the "science" based on it still dominates a good deal of educational research.[4] All too many educational evaluators still assume that the ideal of their work is the elimination of any consideration of values that might "pollute" their investigations. Thus, the world of facts is one which excludes, within the body of one's analysis, considerations of justice, of ethical responsibility, of economic inequalities, of aesthetic or personal knowledge. While any serious appraisal of the practice of science reveals the complex blend of the technical with the aesthetic, the impersonal with the personal, somehow this appraisal has been lost on many members of the educational community.

Besides these conceptual questions about the nature of educational evaluation and research, the authors of these studies are responding to something else—the flattening of everyday reality. They seem to be groping—some more successfully than others—for a personal, political, and social awareness, for a way to counterbalance the anonymization of social life in advanced industrial societies like our own. There seems to be a growing recognition that with the increasing rationalization and bureaucratization of people's lives, something essential has been lost. Perhaps this something is our sense of being a self; or perhaps what is missing is our ability to argue the serious ethical, political, and economic ramifications of our actions in an unequal society. Perhaps the missing element is seen in our propensity for process/product and instrumental reasoning in our day-to-day lives, a form of reasoning so clearly exemplified in curriculum by the "Tyler rationale." It may in fact be a combination of all these things and more. But the attempt to regain a certain human element comes through fairly clearly in these investigations.

Because of my own belief that we have indeed lost the "communicative competence" to argue competing ethical and political positions, and that the social and economic structures that organize our lives have contributed to this loss, I find all of these studies interesting. They all speak to the growing commitment in educational evaluation to recapture real human experience and give it an epistemological warrant. Yet with this said, I shall be somewhat critical of a number of these studies, some for their overt methodological errors and others for the tacit ideologies that lie behind them.

Before I begin this criticism, though, a few points should be laid out. Many of the individuals whose work is presented in this volume are less than anonymous to me. More than one has studied with me. This very familiarity may make my response seem unkind to some of them. After all, it might be asked, how can you be critical of people who are pursuing a path you have been identified with? Shouldn't you do everything possible to support them, to fend off criticism of their work? Well, yes and no. The activity of qualitative evaluation, of differing forms of curricular criticism, if you will, is exceptionally important. But it also must be open to argument, especially from those who share its orientation. As I have argued elsewhere, why should we assume that educational issues are any less difficult to grapple with than those of physics, ethics, or aesthetics?[5] They are not easy; they require serious and extensive analysis, not easy biographical or quasi-scientific slogans. Thus, while my comments here may seem a bit harsh in places, they are guided by a sense of shared searching. They embody a perspective of collective commitment to, and hence collective criticism of, each other's work. Only through such criticism can we grow.

Obviously, the quality of these case studies varies considerably. Some are exceptionally insightful; others provide little more than a scholarly gloss on simplistic assertions about how to make classrooms more "affective" places for children. I think this variation in quality is to be expected. Qualitative studies *are* rather new to current educational scholarship. These initial studies need to be looked at as something propaedeutic to a more sophisticated stage of analysis that will, no doubt, provide an even more potent set of approaches for illuminating classroom life.

I have chosen to focus most extensively on the logical and political strengths and deficiencies of these studies. Because of this orientation, many of my comments will delve deeper into the more "subjectivistic" or quasi-phenomenological evaluations than into those which are more ethnographic in nature. This is primarily because I trust that many readers have some insight into what ethnographic or anthropological case studies are about. As we shall see, the lack of familiarity may present a few problems with some of the other forms of analysis. I shall devote considerable attention to the subjectivistic (I do *not* mean this at all negatively) studies for another reason. They provide an archetype for the individualistic political and economic position that lies at the root of a part of the sense of loss I mentioned earlier.

Logic and Politics in Case Studies

A fruitful way of looking at qualitative models of educational inquiry is to think of them in somewhat Wittgensteinian terms. It is not merely that the language systems of the "quantitative" and the "qualitative" are different ways of describing events. They may be, of course. But these different language games are different modes of existence. Their meanings are tied to ways of both *attending to* phenomena and *interacting with* them. Thus, to be concerned with the qualitative is to embrace a "form of life" that attempts to rescue human meanings and intentionalities from their status as mere epiphenomena in quantitative inquiry.[6] In this, it is as close to poetic understanding as it is to science.

Jacob Bronowski catches part of the formal difference between scientific and aesthetic or poetic understanding.

I am asserting that a poem informs us in a mode of knowledge that is many-valued, and that a scientific paper instructs us in a mode of knowledge that is single-valued. This says something quite different from the traditional assertion . . . that the language of poetry is ambiguous and personal and intense, and the language of science is exact and impersonal and general. Indeed . . . it is not true that science, as a language of thought, is free from ambiguities. It could not be imaginative if it were; it would be closed and dead. In all living language, the human mind plays with and explores the ambiguities that lie hidden in every general idea—that is, in every word. The difference lies elsewhere, in the different endeavors of science and literature. The scientific experiment is planned to be critical, so that we may have grounds for preferring one action to another. The experiment of literature parades its alternatives so that we may steep ourselves in them, and learn to know ourselves and others together.[7]

Thus, for Bronowski, the poetic form enables us to dwell in the ambiguities of the human condition. It is not there to resolve ambiguities by making "critical and decisive tests between alternatives." Rather it aims to enlarge and sharpen our sensitivity to the contraries of the "human predicament."[8] Thus, if we are to understand the depth of the experience of being a student, enlarge our perception of the relations people have to their environment, and ultimately enhance the inquirer's sensitivity to the uncertainties and *density* of educational activity, we need to blend these two perspectives together. As we see in this volume, the case study provides a format for enclosing and working within the tension that exists between these two forms of understanding.

The case study does have a few logical and political difficulties, though, that I want to note here. The logical difficulty usually involves the argument that case studies are exactly that; they provide little generalizability. The political problem involves the case study's lack of connectedness with the economic or social forces external to the individual case. That is, the case study does not usually employ what Ollman has called relational analysis.[9] Both are real issues, it seems to me, though the former seems less of a problem than the latter.

Logically, there is not much more difficulty in using case studies to generalize to other particular situations than in employing larger, more statistically complex studies. Both are useful for illuminating the particulars of any given relatively complex educational setting, but the same difficulty confronts each. There is a problem in trying to take a single case and "write it large," to make it explain a number of other settings. However, and we often forget this, conceptually it is just as difficult to take the "facts" gathered from a huge sample and use them to unpack the nexus of factors that go into any single case. Therefore, the argument over generalizability is not necessarily a telling one. It is a two-edged sword that needs to be applied in both large-scale and case study approaches. In view of this, the political issue is more interesting to me here.

Part of the very logic of the case study as a qualitative form presents a strength and a weakness. The strength lies in its depth, its ability to enable inquirers and readers to sense the framework and texture of meanings and events as they are built and as they interact in one specific setting. Yet because of the focus on specificity, one tends to be pulled away from seeing the connections these events and meanings have with real forces and institutions "outside" the setting. This failure to search for connections between the dynamics within one particular case study and the larger configuration of economic, political, or even cultural institutions is a weakness in nearly all of these studies.

Rosario comes closest to realizing this in his analysis of the social distribution of aesthetic meanings in the school system on which he focused. Here he expressly grounds himself in a tradition that links the quality of school experience to the larger question of how and why particular kinds of meanings are preserved and distributed in society. Since he relies heavily on Bernstein, the weaknesses of Bernstein (and of course the strengths) are his as well.[10] But Rosario understands that case studies are case studies of *something*, not merely interesting slices of life. He is aware that in order to make sense of his findings about the distribution of aesthetic knowledge, he has to relate them to the more critical question of "whose knowledge gets into schools?" It is this realization that makes his research more important than he may yet realize. Given the fact that he is in the initial stages of his research and interpretation, one can hope that this larger political question will become a more constitutive part of his analysis. My only suggestion here would be that he inquire further into the possible *economic* reasons behind two things: (1) why schools distribute the kinds of aesthetic knowledge they do; and (2) why technical knowledge (defined as efficient means to reach prechosen ends) is seen as more powerful than aesthetic knowledge in advanced industrial economies.[11]

Davidman's study provides a case in point of the difficulties of overcoming that odd mixture of logical and political problems in qualitative research. One would want to applaud his effort to blend his experiences as an evaluator with the evaluation of the curriculum project itself. Yet we really have little warrant for accepting his conclusions. For example, he certainly understands the problem of insufficient grounds for general conclusions when he notes that he simply did not have space to do more than merely list his findings. However, while this approach is understandable, his findings are not really situated; they are vague at best. He lists "hidden learnings" that occurred in classrooms, yet what these actually mean are never quite clear. He gives the reader a cookbook variety of strategies for curriculum improvement that also seem to have no other warrant than personal or ideological choice.

Let me be specific here. One of his suggested recommendations is for the curricular materials (the *Teacher's Resource Book for Burglar Alarms*) to stress a variety of strategies for dealing with the problem of theft. Sociodrama and value-clarification techniques are among the added suggestions. By this does he mean that the curriculum should include alternative activities (but why these particular ones?) so that students can understand better? Or, does he mean that the question of theft is an ideological one? (e.g., Do not ask how to prevent theft, but instead ask, say, that given the unequal distribution of goods and services in the United States, why don't more people steal?) Again the suggestions for large-scale curriculum reform seem to have been generated less from his interesting naturalistic account than from that eclectic bag of tricks most decent educators carry around with them. This is not to say he is necessarily wrong. In fact, his research is better than a number of more conventional input/output studies that could be named. The problem lies in the lack of clarity of both his own ideological or political position (and again his failure to situate the economic and behavioral exigencies of schools back into our society) and his logical warrant for suggesting specific ameliorative practices to "solve" the problems he identified.

The logical issue is less of a concern in McCutcheon's investigation, perhaps because its boundaries are more limited than Davidman's. At the least, as reported here, her study seems stronger (again perhaps because space considerations weighed more heavily in reporting Davidman's study). She seems to grasp intuitively that curious interplay between the poetic and scientific that Bronowski so nicely articulated. McCutcheon also writes well, which brings out some of that density of personal and environmental interaction that is too often missed in curricular inquiry. Even with these very evident strengths, she is also subject to one of the major dilemmas of case studies. She does not provide a relational analysis. Mr. Clement's fourth grade sits isolated from the history of the institution and from the world outside of it.

For instance, from the example she gives, one would guess (though I may be wrong) that these children and this teacher are more "middle class" than not, with that class's fears, hopes, dreams, ideology, and so forth. In order to understand what classrooms of this kind do, one would have to connect the types of activities, knowledge forms, and the dispositions and propensities taught overtly and covertly, to the structure of opportunities available to this socioeconomic class in the larger economic arena.[12] One would need to know why this particular knowledge is taught in this particular way to this particular group of children. The study would be even more valuable if it were situated within the expectations that the

community, the school, and the marketplace had of the economic
and social roles these children were to perform when they grew up.[13]
It would need to see classroom activity as representing the forms of
economic and social interaction "expected" (that is, made structurally necessary) by the rather powerful institutions that give schools a
major reason for their existence.

My point here is that school experience, even when poetically
or ethnographically recounted, does not exist in a vacuum. As King
and I argue in our paper (chapter 19 of this volume), we need to see
teachers and curricula "as encapsulated within a social and economic
context that by necessity often produces the problems teachers are
confronted with and the material limitations on their responses." As
we note, "This very 'external' context provides substantial legitimation for the allocation of teachers' time and energies and for the kind
of cultural capital embodied in the school itself."[14] I do not want to
take an overly deterministic position here; however, to assume that
even individual teachers exist unrelated to larger structural forces
that in part determine their sense of appropriate school experience,
teacher role, etc., is merely to continue education's long history of
blaming the victim. If our problems were merely those of getting
individual teachers to "act better," these problems would have been
solved years ago.

Obviously no one case study can do all of these things thoroughly. What I want to argue here, however, is that if we truly want
to grapple with the larger meaning of the activities McCutcheon and
others so clearly document, we may need to go beyond the personal
interpretations of the actors involved. This need to go beyond the
subjective interpretations of individual actors at times will become
even more important when we look at the studies by such people as
Pinar and Grumet in the next section of this chapter. But before we
do that, I want to single out one more of the ethnographically
inclined qualitative evaluations for comment, Popkewitz's interesting
and sometimes insightful investigation of Individually Guided Education.

Popkewitz has worked hard at developing the tools of qualitative evaluation and has in the past contributed to our understanding
of the politics of technical reforms in education.[15] He has a fairly
firm grasp on most of the issues raised by case study procedures.
While more sophisticated than some of the other contributors about
the political and logical problems I have discussed here, Popkewitz

falls prey to a similar pitfall when he evaluates IGE within a predominantly educational framework. While this is certainly useful, he does
not go far enough in asking *why* this particular type of reform is so
popular now. Why do educators, funding agencies like the Office of
Education (and industry as well, one would guess), respond positively
to something that incorporates a technical adaptation of systems
analysis, a vision of teaching that often can isolate students from
each other, and so on? Why is the language of individualization such
a powerful emotive force in the rhetorical arsenal of education?

Many "reforms" of this type can be seen as symptoms of a
more general set of problems. First is one that Popkewitz recognizes,
and one that I have talked about at length elsewhere, the lack of neutrality in supposedly technical reforms such as systems management,
behavioral objective based curriculum programs, and so on.[16] It is the
case that administrative curricular reforms like systems management
procedures have "systematically" covered ethical and political positions. They have transformed difficult moral choices into technical
ones and have tended to centralize control within institutions so that
power is not shared to any significant extent. However, only when
we can see such educational reforms as reflections of similar procedures that have had such a long history in industry—where they have
been used to control and manipulate blue- and white-collar workers
and "professionals"—only then can we begin to understand part of
their social control function in education.[17] What Popkewitz gives us
is valuable. He nicely captures the latent activity, both linguistic and
interpersonal, that underlies IGE as a reform. His account is still primarily an internalist account, though. It does not tie specific educational reforms such as IGE to their educational or economic history;
nor does it inquire into the latent function of the language of individualization as a rhetoric of social control.[18] Thus, once again, though
it is a stronger study in this regard than many of the others, there is a
failure to go the next step, to follow the logic of one's conclusions as
far as one might. Part of this failure—one common to many of these
studies—can be explained by the training most educators receive in
the United States. Many people now engaged in qualitative research
have had to learn how to do it themselves. There is little cumulative
research as yet, so the questions one asks will tend to be descriptive,
taxonomic, and internalistic merely to establish a base upon which to
stand. Another reason is probably just as important, if not more so.
This has to do with the politics of knowledge distribution. The tools

and traditions of a critical "externalist" analysis of schools—that is, the evaluation of school experience that relates the day-to-day life in classrooms to the unequal economic and social relations and unequal control of institutions outside it—is usually unavailable to educators. These traditions (call them neo-Marxist, critical theory, the study of political economy, or other terms) may be fundamental to our understanding of why certain "reforms" are proposed in schools and what actually happens to them. But one often has to master these tools and traditions on one's own, too. This situation is a bit odd and points once more to the ahistorical nature of education. Anyone familiar with the work of, say, George Counts knows the influence that these kinds of economic and social perspectives had on curriculum work in earlier periods of educational history.[19]

I could obviously go on talking about the need for a more thoroughly relational analysis. Instead, let me suggest that one of the better places to turn for substantive arguments concerning a relational evaluation of educational settings is not found in this volume, though Rosario and Popkewitz seem to see the issues more clearly than some of the others. Sharp and Green's analysis of three "open" classrooms in England, though not without its methodological problems, provides an insightful example of the arguments for such a political and theoretically grounded study.[20]

So far we have examined the interplay of the logical and the political in some of the case studies found here. I have tried to caution against both going too far beyond one's warrant and not going far enough in one's political or economic analysis of the setting being examined. Another caution is necessary, however. This involves deciding what is to count as an appropriate form for describing educational events. Given our dissatisfaction with traditional quantitative research, how do we judge the worth of the welter of qualitative forms now being proposed to evaluate and criticize curriculum? Is every form as valuable as the others? With these questions in the forefront, let us turn now to a discussion of the more personal styles of curricular evaluation.

Ideology and Form in Curriculum Inquiry

As I noted earlier, a good deal of the impetus behind qualitative evaluation is the restoration of the person (both that of the investigator and the people being "studied") in educational research. In other fields there is a long, and quite sophisticated, history that speaks to these concerns. For example, phenomenology, in both philosophy and psychology, has provided one such person-oriented tradition. This tradition, especially in philosophy, is not something one picks up overnight. It is serious business and requires just as much hard work to understand and use as do other philosophical or empirical approaches. We should not assume that the switch from the quantitative to the person-oriented means there is less need for precision and discipline. Quite the opposite is the case. Though it may require a somewhat different kind of precision, the qualitative in no way replaces the need for conceptual sophistication. (It is probably silly, as well, to make hard and fast distinctions between the qualitative and the quantitative. Both interpenetrate each other. The same should be said about objective vs. subjective, of course.)

Because of this, there is a very real danger we must be cautious of. Since curriculum scholarship does not have a long tradition of qualitative, and especially phenomenological, inquiry, we can have a tendency to accept just about anything that labels itself as such. If one's footnotes are filled with quotes from Husserl, Heidegger, Merleau-Ponty, or Sartre, then the reader usually has no choice but to assume one possesses expertise. Given his or her lack of familiarity with its language and conceptual apparatus, the reader has no reservoir of background knowledge with which he or she can evaluate the "phenomenological" contribution. This is less of a problem with statistical research in curriculum. Most educators can read tables. They are able to interpret reliability coefficients and can usually make a choice between when to use an r^2 or beta weight. Thus, their own evaluation of whether or not a paper contributes to the progress of the field is informed by a wealth of practical and theoretical background. I would be the first to admit that this background may often represent a vision of science as mere technical manipulation; however, at the very least, even if on a relatively superficial level, the reader is usually able to decide if a paper makes empirical sense.

Can the same be said for the more phenomenological forms? I think not. For this very reason, we need to be very cautious about being too accepting, too eager to embrace alternative forms of curriculum inquiry. In order to judge their worth honestly, what is required is a serious investigation of the disciplines from which they borrow their language. Though the educators who practice what is called, for want of a better name, experiential research seem to us to be sensitive and good people, we have a history of jumping on bandwagons *before* we find out if the wagon has all its wheels.

Do not interpret these remarks as an argument for the traditional positivistic methodologies and concepts that have dominated curricular and more general educational thought and action for so long. These concepts and procedures have, in fact, led to few cumulative results, are often conceptually weak, and have tended to be economically and politically conservative in practice. However, it is just as problematic to be uncritically accepting of "subjectivistic" models as it was and is to be less than critical about "scientific" concerns. The real problem is our inability to maintain an ongoing critical posture in the field. It is possible to argue, in fact, that such a critical posture is the real measure of a field's rationality and maturity.[21]

While I agree with a significant portion of the phenomenological program and have, in fact, been trained in it since I studied with Huebner, I want to offer some criticisms of its orientation here. In this section my major questions will be less of a logical nature and more overtly political. I want to examine closely the following issue. What are the possible ideological functions of a focus on "private" experience? At the same time that such people as Pinar, Grumet, Shuchat Shaw, and others attempt to free the individual by giving him or her tools to describe personal experiences, is there a contradiction built into their wholly meritorious aim?

To begin with, I am again as much concerned with the *form* that these personal analyses take as with their content. The somewhat autobiographical form of the "phenomenologists" is an attempt at something like art. It tries to give us an experience of a unique situation as seen through the eyes of the real people who lived it. This is not to be treated lightly. Done well, as some of these studies are, it can be a powerful way of illustrating what Bronowski called the contraries of the human predicament. The form can do something else, however. With the cultural critic Georg Lucács, I want to argue that "the true bearers of ideology in art are the very forms, rather than the abstractable content, of the work itself."[22]

As we have seen, the forms available to articulate our curricular concerns are varied. They range from the naively behavioristic and process/product mentality to the subjectivistic language of educators such as Pinar and others. Neither of these positions is neutral. The first has tended to function as a mechanism of control. While it has wanted to pose as a "science," it is also just a bit too naive about what good science looks like.[23] The latter, more subjectivistic position, though certainly less concerned with the problem of control, needs to be analyzed ideologically as well. It too may serve important social and economic functions.

As Raymond Williams has persuasively said, forms are better thought of as "structures of feeling," sets of "received" ways of perceiving and responding to reality. They have social roots, ties to existing social relations, which penetrate symbol, fantasy, imagination, and personal perception.[24] I do not want to take a vulgar Marxist perspective here by arguing that the language or forms we use to describe, criticize, or evaluate curriculum are through and through conditioned by an economic structure. Rather, I do want to argue that these forms are complex entities that need to be understood by their *use*. One of these uses is ideological. By choosing a literary form (and this is in fact what the phenomenologically oriented curriculists have chosen) one is also choosing a set of meanings that are in part a response to specific structural conditions pervading a society. This will be especially evident in the autobiographical curricular forms I shall talk about.

In describing the way Marxist criticism examines the relationship between ideology and, say, literary form, Eagleton provides some hints as to my meaning here.

Form, I would suggest, is always a complex unity of three elements: it is partly shaped by a "relatively autonomous" literary history of forms; it crystalizes out of certain dominant ideological structures . . . ; and . . . it embodies a specific set of relations between author and audience. It is the dialectical unity between these elements that Marxist criticism is concerned to analyze. In selecting a form, then, the writer finds his choice already ideologically circumscribed. He may combine and transmute forms available to him from a literary tradition, but these forms themselves, as well as his permutation of them, are ideologically significant. The language and devices a writer finds to hand are already saturated with certain ideological modes of perception, certain codified ways of interpreting reality; and the extent to which he can modify or remake those languages depends on more than his personal genius.[25]

The saturation of our very modes of perception and articulation is an important point here. The argument is, in essence, something like this. Economic modes tend to "duplicate" themselves structurally in individual and social consciousness.[26] That is, the everyday relations among men and women in general, and in more specific things like education, tend to be strongly influenced by the economic structures of a society. The forms of literature, the tools of languaging, stand in a similar though more complex relationship to the social structure. While not mere reflections of a social order, these forms of human inquiry both articulate concerns and orient one toward issues that are not ideologically neutral, especially when they are used in policy-oriented fields such as curriculum. The individual is "free" to choose, but the forms available and the uses to which these forms are put cannot be seen as disembodied, as unrelated to the kinds of consciousness "required" of people who live in a stratified society like our own.

There is, in the phenomenological and personal styles of curricular evaluation, a peculiar kind of danger in addition to the lack of familiarity that I mentioned earlier. And it has to do with the evaluators' very choice of particular literary forms. The problem is one that these thoughtful individuals are undoubtedly aware of, but one that they have yet to address in a consistent fashion. The danger I wish to point to is perhaps best described in Gramsci's notion of *ideological hegemony*. In any society, but especially in advanced industrial economies, the control of people is not necessarily done through the use of force. Noncoercive control—hegemony—is exercised more commonly. The internalization of particular dispositions, propensities, norms, values, and basic categories of thought makes overt control less necessary. Popular and elite culture—mass media, books, drama, other literary forms which channel our perceptions of imaginative possibilities—all play an important part in the creation and recreation of this hegemony. One of the major categories of thought that economic control requires in our society is that of the *private individual*. The internalization of a perspective that isolates the individual from his or her real economic or cultural relations with other people may be a help in describing educational experience (we do in fact experience ourselves as isolated, and *that* is exactly the point). It may also represent an ideological configuration through which people are separated and controlled.

We must begin to think about how we learn the idea that people are unattached, that one has private experience that is totally unconnected to structural phenomena "outside" us. It is basically incorrect to argue that all thought, creative or otherwise, can be reduced to being mere reflections of economic and social conditions. However, the basic outlines, the thematic possibilities we seize upon, are strongly related to the control of social and economic institutions. We think in certain ways partly *because* of the kind of society we live in and the position we hold in it.[27] In more philosophical terms, one cannot divorce biography from history.

The individualistic position in curriculum evaluation, with its focus on the "growth" of each specific person, fails to appreciate the ways in which a model of thoroughgoing individualism is itself symptomatic of the problem. Its psychologistic solutions—understand your own "internal" makeup, delve into your private experience—speaks less to alleviation of the lack of humaneness in our institutions than it does to the privatization of human experience. Emphasis on the private self, who always stands back to reflect on his or her experience, though certainly not unimportant, does not speak forcefully enough to the ability of a complex and stratified society to penetrate our very ways of experiencing and thinking.[28] To the extent that we speak primarily in individual terms, we obscure the possibility that the problems we face are of a collective, more structural sort.

Thus, part of the individualistic emphasis in the existential and phenomenological papers in this volume reflects concerns that have economic and political roots. Focus on one person's consciousness is quite functional to a society that depends on privatized individuals. The concern with each person as a solitary unit should not be debunked. It is surely better than having no real concern for the actual people who live in our schools and other institutions. On the other hand, its contradiction is that it is a symptom of our inability to see each individual as existing in relation to others. It speaks to our loss of community, to our lack of understanding of collective commitment.[29]

I can appreciate part of the program behind the work of those who want to focus on individual experience. They seek to recapture the biographical roots of knowledge, to make disparate disciplines whole again, by enabling people to integrate their experiences into their selves. This marks, in fact, the beginnings of political awareness. For it is the case that the very fragmentation and division of intellectual and other labor in universities, factories, and elsewhere contributes to the fragmentation of one's understanding of social and political life. However, the personal case studies, unless done exceptionally carefully, remain by and large on a relatively simple level if they do not recognize that their own biographies, like the classroom situations described earlier, are situated ones.

Just as it is necessary to break down the distinctions between sociology, psychology, politics, and economics if we are to gain a more serious appraisal of the political economy of our society, so too is it essential to see the connections between individual biography and social and economic history. This is not to recount that odd conception of history that states that without a knowledge of history we are condemned to repeat the past. Rather, my point here is to argue for a sense of personal "groundedness." We need to place our curricular inquiries in a clearer sense of what has gone on before. We must not only see the social components of being an individual, but the *social and historical* roots of the symbolic and significative forms we use to interpret our interaction with other people (partly missing in Grumet's interesting work) or with curricular phenomena like texts or books (partly missing in Pinar and Shuchat Shaw).[30]

When we speak of the individual, we are employing concepts filled with historical meaning. The very notion of the individual embodies particular interpretations of our experience. These interpretations gained currency at a specific point in time; before that, perceptions were quite different. Yet today, the idea of each of us as an individual whose concrete experience has no real connection to his or her social past or social class has established itself as nearly an absolute in our minds.[31] Before the growth of modern industrial economies, the person was thought of as inseparable from his or her social rank. With the growth of the industrial state and the increasing division of labor, people began to see the individual in a totally different way. The individual was the source of economic activity. Freedom became associated, in essence, with free enterprise. There is no doubt that this changed emphasis on the individual led to the liberation of many people from arbitrary political systems. Yet today the interpretation of the individual as a person who is free and unattached, who does not exist, at root, in a series of social and economic relationships, is quite misleading and may have gone too far.[32] The focus on the unconnected individual, with his or her personal experience as the metaphor for educational inquiry, is not an accurate assessment of one's real position in a society.

Let me give two concrete examples I have used elsewhere of the way our basic categories and forms of thought are partly economically related. Apple or Pinar want to read a book by Merleau-Ponty. We sit down in a chair and turn on a light so that we can interact with the meanings the author has put down on paper. However, turning on that light is more than getting better illumination so that we avoid eye strain. It is also a social relation (albeit a relatively anonymous one) with the other individuals who produced both the lamp and the power it uses. My individual freedom to read in comfort is conditional. It depends on the economic activity of others. In this way, even seemingly inconsequential everyday happenings are really relations between concrete groups of people, relations that are highly dependent on how a given society is organized and controlled.[33]

Raymond Williams gives a similar example of how our commitment to the categories of individualism distorts our understanding of our dependence on, and our relations with, others. He points out that the dominance in our thought of what he calls the bourgeois individual performs an economic function.

I remember a miner saying to me, of someone we were discussing: "He's the sort of man who gets up in the morning and presses a switch and expects the light to come on." We are all, to some extent, in this position, in that our modes of thinking habitually suppress large areas of our real relationships, including our real dependence on others. We think of my money, my light, in these naive terms, because our very idea of society is withered at root. . . . In a society whose products depend almost entirely on intricate and continuous cooperation and social organization, we expect to consume as if we were isolated individuals, making our own way. . . . Unless we achieve some realistic sense of community, our true standard of living will continue to be distorted.[34]

Now I want us to think of the subjectivistic form of curriculum inquiry in a similar way. It is saturated with the positive and the negative. It speaks to our need for individual freedom, yet it neglects to tie that experience to its concrete social relations beyond that one individual. It embodies the self as something like the classical novelistic hero, without inquiring deeply enough into the economic functions of such a conception of self.

We can see this more clearly, perhaps, if we think of the similarities between the phenomenological as a literary form of curriculum work and, say, that of the novelistic form and its hero I just mentioned. One of the major themes of the literary productions of bourgeois life is that of the individual, the problematic hero, attempting to define himself or herself. In fact, the literary form of the novel was developed precisely on "the opacity of social life and the individual's difficulty in orienting himself and giving his life meaning."[35] While a bit reductive, it is helpful to think of the novel as in part representing an aesthetic response to the "liberal" revolt of the growing middle class and the economic necessity of freeing the individual so that the commercialization of society and the accumulation of individual wealth could proceed at a more rapid pace. As a form of both elite and popular culture, the novel provided avenues for individual aesthetic excellence. But it is quite possible that it also helped reproduce a cultural configuration that was linked to an unequal set of structural arrangements in society.

Compare the individualistic thematic structure in the novel with that found in the plays of Sartre and Genet as these literary artists moved from the individual perspective of existentialism to a clearer recognition that social change requires collective political action. Once the problem became structural, once Sartre and Genet became aware that a focus on one's own phenomenological experience was relatively one-sided and both ahistorical and apolitical, they began to change literary forms. Individuals are important, yes, but for Sartre and Genet what is required are individuals who affiliate themselves with a larger movement to restructure the institutions that lead to the lack of human sensitivity in our lives. The choice of literary form to articulate this, though not necessarily always conscious, becomes quite critical, obviously.

Lucien Goldmann makes this point about Sartre and Genet clear.

A first common element distinguishes them from all the rest of contemporary literature: the characters are collective. There are no individual characters, except to some extent Said in *The Screens*; but he is defined in relation to collective forces and, in addition, is not entirely individual in that he is part of a group formed by himself, his mother and his wife Leila. In *The Maids* there are Monsieur and Madame on the one hand, Solange and Claire on the other; in *The Balcony* there are the characters of the balcony on the one hand, and on the other the rebels and the populace who come to the house of illusions; in *The Blacks* there are the Blacks and the Whites; in *The Screens* there are the colonists, the rebels, and the dead, not to mention the army and the prostitutes. Clearly, insofar as the historical action forms the theme and problematic of a work, the forces acting are not individuals but groups, since individual time is only biographical whereas historical time is that of groups. . . .What are the relations between these collective characters? At least for the first three of these plays and to some extent for the fourth, the subject is the opposition, the conflict between the dominated and the dominators, with the dominated assuming a different face each time (the Maids, the Blacks, the populace and the rebels in *The Balcony*, and the colonized people; to whom are opposed Monsieur and Madame, the Whites, the powers of the balcony, the colonists or the victorious group of colonial rebels in *The Screens*).[36]

To heighten the importance of individuals "acting" together, so that even in the theater, as in real life, one reconciles the dialectical interplay between individual and social existence, Genet has the actors raise the masks they are wearing in *The Blacks* in order to appear as actors again. They "explain their solidarity with those playing the role of the dominated."[37] Notice, hence, how the very choice of form can heighten certain ideological elements. It creates a horizon against which we experience the aesthetic elements.

It is the lack of this realization in practice that is part of the problem in some of the phenomenological studies. Like some aspects of early novels, the literary form used by some of the overly subjectivistic educators may heighten our appreciation of individual meaning. However, at least in Pinar's case, in both his general arguments and the analysis of his private experience which are found in this volume, it does not go beyond the isolated individual. Nor does it sufficiently recognize the ideological and economic function such a form may play in the mental reproduction of our relatively unequal society. Its very form contributes to these dilemmas.

Grumet comes a bit closer, I think, to a realization of the problems. She obviously sees personal understanding as an intersubjective process that is often dependent, in the microcosm she reports, on group interaction, past histories, and the structure of power within a situation. She is also obviously quite technically sophisticated and talented in the techniques of drama herself. Perhaps because her description of the dramatic production is sensitive to many of the elements that went into her experiences, it seems stronger than, say, Pinar's reporting of his own thoughts when reading a text.

Notice I did not call Pinar's account a description. His method is certainly an interesting one and does enable a person to attempt to grasp an experience retrospectively (and introspectively). It is somewhat limited in its ability to make these experiences sensible, though. In the formal philosophical sense of the word, Pinar's approach does not go far enough in making his reports *meaningful*. They are not adequate descriptions.

Let me be more specific here. We may want to look at the language form of this kind of analysis as less descriptive than it is affiliative. The reports Pinar gives are neither more nor less descriptions than those of a "patient" telling a psychoanalyst his or her remembrances of past actions. The memories may be interesting (and Pinar's are), but they are given their warrant and their meaning by the interpretative schema that the psychoanalyst "gives" to the patient or that they build together. It is only when these memories are no longer merely subjective or random, but are put together coherently, that these memories "make sense." The sense lies in the underlying patterns in the person's experience, not necessarily in the individual memories themselves. The scattered notes and remembrances of Pinar are exactly that—scattered. They *denote* thoughts and feelings, but they *connote* little as they stand now. They have too little coherence. There are no interpretive schema visible; hence, the memories are not described meaningfully. I do not think Pinar's thoughtful work necessarily precludes this, but this is a problem which demands more careful scrutiny.

If Pinar's words are not sensible (again in the formal use of the word) descriptions, what are they? They function less as a communicative form than as an affiliative one. They give writer and reader a feeling of connection. The words call forth "emotive" responses, perhaps a feeling of oneness with each other and the early existential tradition. This feeling can be, oddly, the first step toward ending the isolation of individual experience that I mentioned as a serious problem in the phenomenological approach. I do not think it is enough to overcome the political logic of the form itself, however.

This affiliative function is not unimportant, of course. As Huebner and I have argued, in order to be effective, curricular language must create bonds between people so that coordinated educational action can go on.[38] Unfortunately, the forms through which we articulate our curricular criticism, even of a qualitative sort, must do more than this. This is especially critical if the individualistic form serves to affiliate people with an apolitical style of existentialism.

For example, as I noted, in many of the recent evaluations of personal curricular experience, there is a reliance on Sartre, on Merleau-Ponty, etc. Yet the analyses are too often devoid of the politics which gave existential commitment its meaning to these people. Sartre, himself, points to the utter importance of combining existentialism with, in his case, an overtly Marxist politics. The former could help us clarify our individual lives, but the latter could give us a past. As a form, the political and economic analysis could situate our lives and give them coherence and meaning, could give them a history.[39] This was the answer of Sartre and others to the problems I have raised about the subjectivistic orientation in curriculum inquiry. Thus, Sartre's "search for a method" is a search that seeks to combine existential sentiments with a program for political action that might realize these sentiments in real life. (I am a self; but I am also a member of a class. I am an individual; but my very perception of this fact and my day-to-day life are related to the unequal economic and social structures that help to create this perception and this life. Hence, I cannot remain isolated. I must commit myself to organized action.) Sartre's individual perceptions are made sensible. They become coherent because he interprets these thoughts in other than individualistic categories. This is his way of going beyond the ideological saturation of his previously accepted form. His "method" does not remain, as it is too easy for some of the phenomenologically inclined curriculum workers to do, on the level of the reporting of one's thoughts.

The relationship between ideology and form is obviously a complex one in terms of the hidden economic function of the category of private individual experience. Because of this I want now to note one other area that curriculum critics need to think further about. The focus on unconnected "experience" performs another function that can have social and economic consequences. In its own peculiar way it also flattens reality as much as the scientistic work it seeks to replace. Like the positivists before it, it can defuse political and economic debate. Here Pinar's arguments can serve as a case in point again, though I do want to caution against assuming that this makes his work inconsequential.

Pinar argues that the fundamental category of a curriculum theory worthy of its name is "experience." However, if curriculum theory (and one would assume curriculum evaluation and criticism) is to concern itself only with experience, then it becomes identical with everything we do.[40] There can be little serious ethical, political, or even aesthetic dialog. All things are equal; all values are relative; all possibilities are the same; everything we do is an experience. This is not to say that a focus on one's personal experience is, in principle, not helpful, though I have claimed that it may be as much an economic category as it is an educational one. However, once again, experience must be valued in specific ways if it is to be differentiated from the blooming, buzzing confusion of one's interaction with the world. It must be interpreted not merely biographically, but educationally, socially, and politically as well, if it is to be evaluated at all. There can be no debate about the value of any curricular activity if the mere fact that it is "experience" (a concept that has such a penumbra of vagueness as to be less useful than one might think) is all that is necessary.[41]

From Poetics to Politics

I do not want to be too negative toward these kinds of personal studies. While they may be ideologically problematic, and may be somewhat inadequate in finally reaching all of their goals or in really proving their assertions, they do other useful things. They are art forms. As such, they need to be valued as that as well. Just as one prizes the aesthetics of, say, a collage, so one can appreciate the "collage of thoughts" of educators like these. They are there. It might destroy their aesthetic qualities to talk only of their use value.

Shuchat Shaw's aesthetic analysis of Moffett does point to one use of aesthetic forms of curricular criticism. Its simultaneous focus on cinematic production, where there is a dialectical relationship between filmic art, material resources, individual production, environmental form, and interpersonal action, is a bit convoluted but actually necessary. While it only occasionally notes the impact of political and cultural forces outside of the educational environment, and even then as almost an afterthought, its method at least points the way to the importance of an aesthetic rendering of the components of a curricular environment. There is some conceptual confusion, though, and some questions this reader would like clarified. For instance, what is meant by "conceptual base"? Are aesthetic theories free-floating or, as Raymond Williams asserts, are they social productions as well as aesthetic productions? What is the concrete relationship between the aesthetic ideas *made available* through cultural institutions (schools, museums, mass media) in a given society and the structure of social and economic institutions which organize and control this availability?[42] Some of these questions could be best dealt with by combining Rosario's and others' more sociological approach with the more properly artistic appraisal of Shuchat Shaw. In fact, I see the combination of these two types of forms in general as critically important for further curriculum work.

Let me be more specific here. I have criticized the style and form of the individual-centered evaluations, but such work needs to go on, if only to preserve the tradition of aesthetic understanding in education. However, something else makes this style of criticism important, *if* one is cognizant of its inherent logical and ideological problems. Aesthetic and qualitative criticism is of no small moment, not just because, as Willis has noted in his Introduction and as I have noted here, it allows us to see the qualities of educational interaction in ways too often missed by more positivistic inquiries. It also does something else. With all the problems of case studies, with all of the contradictions within phenomenological and individualistic forms, they provide one means by which we can distance ourselves from the comforting illusions of commonsense perceptions. By pointing to alternative conceptions of our activities, by giving us new horizons against which we can value our curricular structures, aesthetics especially discloses the very possibility of difference. It allows us to see that things could be other than they are by showing the determinate *limits* of our accepted procedures.

All of this has been said before by curriculum workers like Huebner and Eisner. Yet this interpretation of the function of aesthetic and qualitative criticism is still only partially accurate. It does not go far enough in interpreting the political role of "poetic" understanding. While it is not naturally preordained that aesthetic analysis will help one to see many of the political and economic roots of our curricular and more general educational issues (after all, Ezra Pound was a superb poet, but his politics were of the worst sort), I do want to assert that there is something of a logical progression from aesthetic awareness to politico/economic understanding.[43]

This needs some explaining. Once an educator "schools" him- or herself in qualitative forms, once the very possibility of something akin to aesthetic perception is recaptured, one must begin to inquire into the problem of *why* it was missing in the first place. Why is it that particular types of evaluation and criticism, specific forms, dominate educators' perceptions? How and why have the ways educators describe and evaluate their actions come about? Why do they resist change?[44] It seems to me that there are not merely conceptual questions. These kinds of issues are more properly the subject of an economic and political, which is to say relational, analysis. If aesthetic and qualitative understanding of curricular events is in fact possible (as these studies demonstrate) and is indeed desirable as a counterbalance to the reductive forms of evaluation so popular in education, then it makes sense to inquire into the social and economic conditions required for its development. This also requires that we see qualitative evaluation as an important step on the way to a more mature political understanding. But this political understanding itself must *not* lose sight of the concern for poetics and for the real person who gives meaning to that political action.

Therefore, we need to preserve the intent of many of the people whose studies appear in this volume. At the same time, though, we must sometimes criticize the forms they employ to articulate this intent, their choice of methods, and perhaps their tacit ideological affiliations. But we should be wary of *ad hominem* debate. All of these people are committed to bringing living, breathing, thinking human actors back into curriculum evaluation. Each of them has an obvious and strong interest in finding ways to illuminate the complexity of life in classrooms. And each of them provides one tool which, when used thoughtfully and in combination with the others, might help in this illumination. Thus, there is more than a kernel of truth in the position advanced by many qualitatively oriented inquirers that human action cannot be properly identified, described, or understood unless the inquirer takes certain things into account. Intentional descriptions, the meaning such action has for the actors involved, the ways people interpret their own and others' actions, all of these help *constitute* human interaction. Without them, there could be no action at all. As the late Alfred Schutz and others so clearly recognized, "any conception of what is strictly speaking empirical or observable that excludes this dimension of human life, or simply relegates it to the realm of subjective opinion, is emasculated or epistemologically unwarranted."[45]

This is a limited program, however, if it does not also realize that there may be external *reasons* for thinking as we do. Socioeconomic forms may also constitute our consciousness, may make even the most personal of our dispositions, meanings, and basic categories perform functions that contradict our very desire to be a self.

Thus I am asking the authors of these studies to traverse a rather thorny path that is filled with very hard personal decisions. If their work is to make the fullest possible sense, they need to pass from the psychological to the social, and from the social to the politico-economic, and then dialectically "back" to the individual.[46] For all of these are embedded within the other. They do not exist separately, but in continual interpenetration and relation.

I have been somewhat critical of a number of these studies, often because they claim too much beyond what is obviously valuable in each of their investigations. All of them do succeed partially. The phenomenological studies (Grumet's and others) do help render the meaning of concrete curricular situations to the real individuals who experienced them. The essays on what went on in classrooms or in curriculum projects, such as, among others, McCutcheon's, can give us a greater sense of the richness of classroom life than evaluators have had before. This will undoubtedly enable us to understand those contraries of the human predicament and perhaps help us to make more knowledgeable curricular decisions. The evaluations of both the distribution of aesthetic knowledge and of IGE take a step in bringing us closer to a clearer political awareness if they had been taken just a bit further than their authors have gone.

When all of these kinds of studies are put together, one gets a sense of progress, flawed in certain crucial respects, but progress nevertheless. Such movement is not unimportant. Perhaps the arguments I have offered here may help point to the paths this movement might take if it is serious about finding the roots of the loss to which it wants to respond. At the least, the arguments might make us check the wheels of the wagon we will use to make the trip.

Notes

1. Lucien Goldmann, *Cultural Creation in Modern Society* (St. Louis, Mo.: Telos Press, 1976), p. 15.

2. Philip Jackson, "Naturalistic Studies of Schools and Classrooms," in *Educational Evaluation: Analysis and Responsibility*, ed. Michael W. Apple, Michael J. Subkoviak, and Henry Lufler, Jr. (Berkeley, Ca.: McCutchan Publishing Corp., 1974), pp. 83-96.

3. Richard J. Bernstein, *The Restructuring of Social and Political Theory* (New York: Harcourt Brace Jovanovich, 1976), p. xxiii.

4. J. O. Urmson, *Philosophical Analysis: Its Development between the Two World Wars* (London: Oxford University Press, 1956), p. 246.

5. Michael W. Apple, "Making Curriculum Problematic," *Review of Education* 2 (January-February 1976): 67.

6. See the discussion of Wittgenstein's vision of social science in Albrecht Wellmer, *Critical Theory of Society* (New York: Herder and Herder, 1971), pp. 26-30.

7. Jacob Bronowski, *The Identity of Man* (New York: The Natural History Press, 1966), p. 65.

8. Ibid., pp. 49, 86.

9. Bertell Ollman, *Alienation* (London: Cambridge University Press, 1971).

10. For an analysis of these strengths and weaknesses, see Michael W. Apple and Philip Wexler, "Cultural Capital and Educational Transmissions," *Educational Theory*, in press.

11. Cf. Walter Feinberg, "A Critical Analysis of the Social and Economic Limits to the Humanizing of Education," in *Humanistic Education*, ed. Richard Weller (Berkeley, Ca.: McCutchan Publishing Corp., 1977).

12. See Basil Bernstein, *Class, Codes and Control*, vol. 3, *Towards a Theory of Educational Transmissions* (London: Routledge and Kegan Paul, 1975), and Samuel Bowles and Herbert Gintis, *Schooling in Capitalist America* (New York: Basic Books, 1975).

13. James E. Rosenbaum's study of tracking is interesting here. See his *Making Inequality* (New York: John Wiley and Sons, 1976).

14. This argument is significantly expanded in Rachael Sharp and Anthony Green, *Education and Social Control* (London: Routledge and Kegan Paul, 1975).

15. Thomas Popkewitz, "Reform as Political Discourse: A Case Study," *School Review* 74 (September 1975): 43-69.

16. Michael W. Apple, "The Adequacy of Systems Management Procedures in Education," in *Regaining Educational Leadership*, ed. Ralph Smith (New York: John Wiley and Sons, 1975), pp. 104-21.

17. Harry Braverman, *Labor and Monopoly Capital* (New York: Monthly Review Press, 1974).

18. Cf. Michael W. Apple and Barry Franklin, "Curricular History and Social Control," in *Community Participation in Education*, ed. Carl Grant (Boston: Allyn and Bacon, 1978). For further discussion of the language of individualization, see Ian Hextall and Madan Sarup, "School Knowledge, Evaluation and Alienation," in *Society, State and Schooling*, ed. Michael Young and Geoff Whitty (London: The Falmer Press, 1977).

19. This is not to say that Counts himself always carried his analysis to its logical conclusion. Furthermore, his political commitments became quite mercurial. See, e.g., Walter Feinberg, *Reason and Rhetoric: The Intellectual Foundations of Twentieth Century Liberal Educational Policy* (New York: John Wiley and Sons, 1975).

20. Sharp and Green, *Education and Social Control.* See also Michael W. Apple, "Power and School Knowledge," *Review of Education* 3 (January-February 1977): 26-49.

21. Stephen Toulmin, *Human Understanding*, vol. 1, *The Collective Use and Evolution of Concepts* (Princeton, N.J.: Princeton University Press, 1972), p. 84.

22. Terry Eagleton, *Marxism and Literary Criticism* (Berkeley, Ca.: University of California Press, 1976), p. 24.

23. For an examination of the social control function of "a science of education," see Apple, "The Adequacy of Systems Management Procedures in Education," and Apple and Franklin, "Curricular History and Social Control."

24. Eagleton, *Marxism and Literary Criticism*, p. 25.

25. Ibid., pp. 26-27.

26. Goldmann, *Cultural Creation*, p. 14.

27. Peter Berger and Thomas Luckmann, *The Social Construction of Reality* (New York: Doubleday and Co., 1966). See also, Raymond Williams, "Base and Superstructure in Marxist Cultural Theory," in *Schooling and Capitalism: A Sociological Reader*, ed. Roger Dale et al. (London: Routledge and Kegan Paul, 1976), pp. 202-10.

28. Sharp and Green, *Education and Social Control*, p. viii.

29. I have described this problem in greater detail in "Humanism and the Politics of Educational Argumentation," in Weller, *Humanistic Education*, pp. 315-30.

30. Goldmann, *Cultural Creation*, p. 7.

31. Raymond Williams, *The Long Revolution* (London: Chatto and Windus, 1961), p. 72.

32. Ibid., pp. 75-78.

33. Michael W. Apple, "Power and School Knowledge."

34. Williams, *The Long Revolution*, pp. 298-99.

35. Goldmann, *Cultural Creation*, p. 43.

36. Ibid., pp. 64-65.

37. Ibid., p. 69.

38. Dwayne Huebner, "The Tasks of the Curricular Theorist," in *Curriculum Theorizing: The Reconceptualists*, ed. William Pinar (Berkeley, Ca.: McCutchan Publishing Corp., 1975), pp. 250-70 and Michael W. Apple, "Ideology as Rationality," *Educational Theory* 26 (Winter 1976): 121-31.

39. Cf. Jean-Paul Sartre, *Search for a Method* (New York: Vintage Books, 1963), and Fredric Jameson, *Marxism and Form* (Princeton, N.J.: Princeton University Press, 1971), chap. 4.

40. Raymond Williams, *Culture and Society* (New York: Harper and Row, 1966), p. 256.

41. The work of both John Dewey and Alfred Schutz would be helpful here in unpacking the complex meaning we might intuitively associate with the term "experience."

42. This is clearly a very knotty issue concerning the relationship between economic capital and cultural capital as well. As I mentioned earlier, I do not want to reduce art to a mere question of social function. Some facets of this issue, especially involving literature as art and as an aspect of the cultural reproduction of class relations, are usefully laid out in Terry Eagleton, "Criticism and Politics: The Work of Raymond Williams," *New Left Review* 95 (January-February 1976): 3-23. See also Anthony Barnett, "Raymond Williams and Marxism: A Rejoinder to Terry Eagleton," *New Left Review* 96 (March-April 1976): 47-64.

43. Eagleton, *Marxism and Literary Criticism*, pp. 18-19.

44. Geoff Whitty, "Sociology and the Problem of Radical Educational Change," in *Educability, Schools and Ideology*, ed. Michael Flude and John Ahier (London: Halstead Press, 1974), p. 125.

45. Quoted in Richard Bernstein, *Restructuring*, p. 231.

46. Jameson, *Marxism and Form*, p. xiv, and Ollman, *Alienation*.

The essay by David Jenkins and Bridget O'Toole could plausibly have been placed in the "Concepts" section of this volume, since it develops its own view about the nature of curriculum criticism. It has, however, been located in the "Comments" section primarily to provide a retrospective look at many of the basic issues this volume has dealt with, including how approaches to them have been embodied in the case studies.

Jenkins and O'Toole are concerned with exploring the analogy between literary criticism and curriculum criticism, and in doing so they reiterate a number of topics considered earlier in the volume (especially in chapters 5 and 6). But in a more general sense their exploration is of any form of criticism, be it in the arts generally or in education specifically. For instance, the same relationships obtain among any object of criticism, the critic, and the criticism itself. The discussions at times focus on such basic relationships themselves and at other times on how the relationships apply to the educational critic. To illustrate the position they develop, the authors include within the essay a short piece of educational criticism upon which they comment. They correctly contend, "In this and other ways the paper offers in a sense a British perspective on some of the issues behind this volume on curriculum criticism."

More than just providing a British perspective on issues, however, Jenkins and O'Toole also describe the British equivalent of the movement in the United States for qualitative evaluation. The British movement is most frequently described by the phrase "illuminative evaluation," which, the authors suggest, covers a variety of methodologies. What these methodologies have in common is that they "offer an interpretative description of an educational program in action." The methodology which the authors subscribe to, analogous to methodology in literary criticism, is one of many strands within the general movement in Britain.

In terms of movement, of issues, and of specific methods, Jenkins and O'Toole provide a carefully worked out basis from which the preceding chapters in this volume may be analyzed and appraised.

22

Curriculum Evaluation, Literary Criticism, and the Paracurriculum

David Jenkins and Bridget O'Toole

Their thoughts are often new, but seldom natural; they are not obvious, but neither are they just; and the reader, far from wondering that he missed them, wonders more frequently by what perverseness of industry they were ever found. The most heterogeneous ideas are yoked by violence together; nature and art are ransacked for illustrations, comparisons, and allusions; their learning instructs, and their subtilty surprises; but the reader commonly thinks his improvements dearly bought, and, though he sometimes admires, is seldom pleased.

Dr. Johnson, *The Life of Cowley*

Inclusive Angles: The Parallel with Literary Criticism

This paper is based on a view that is gaining ground among curriculum evaluators, i.e., that they may learn something by pursuing parallels with literary criticism.[1] Yet to some the analogy will appear contrived and pretentious rather than witty, practical, or illuminating. The "perverseness" identified by Dr. Johnson in the wit of metaphysical poets is always a potential trap to those whose argument is based on extended analogy. The counterplay comes from Dr. Johnson himself: "if their conceits were far-fetched, they were often worth the carriage." Our purpose is to explore some of the concepts and dilemmas familiar in the world of the literary critic, to see

524

whether they offer the educational evaluator an extension of his vocabulary.

Some of the concepts, like paradox, ambiguity, the relation of writer to his audience, narrative point of view, the intentional fallacy, and the sociological aesthetic appear to suggest a parallel configuration of certain problems between the two disciplines. But exploration in this area is relatively new; it is probably wise to proceed cautiously, press the analogies, and see to what extent we still feel comfortable with them.

It is common gossip among curriculum evaluators that psychometric approaches to evaluation are currently being usurped by "alternative" models.[2] Not all of these young pretenders welcome the label "alternative," contaminated as it has been by such expressions as "alternative society" and "alternative medicine." Yet change is certainly in the air. Malcolm Parlett and David Hamilton polarized the trends into competing paradigms and popularized the fashionable umbrella term "illuminative evaluation."[3] At its crudest, illuminative evaluation seeks to offer an interpretative description of an educational program *in action,* perhaps getting close to what Bob Stake called "portrayals."[4] The illuminative tradition is not, however, premised on a standard methodological package. Not only do such evaluations require a kind of "situational morality," adaptive to the exigencies of particular situations; illuminative evaluation is also itself something of a rag-bag, a loose eclecticism containing a number of (sometimes conflicting) inspirations.[5] Among the influences conventionally cited are participant observation, ethnographic fieldwork in social anthropology, client-centered therapy, bidding in card games such as bridge, legal advocacy, investigative journalism, the so-called new journalism, and literary criticism.[6] In addition, of course, Her Majesty's Inspectorate tell us it is what they've been doing all along. Literary criticism, then, is just one of a large number of the strands making up illuminative evaluation.

At the risk of self-indulgence, some of the dilemmas faced by evaluators aspiring toward a "literary critical" approach will be explored in part by considering the work of one of the authors in evaluating the Schools Council *Integrated Studies Project* and the DES-funded *National Development Programme in Computer Assisted Learning.*[7] In this and other ways the paper offers in a sense a British perpsective on some of the issues behind this volume on curriculum criticism.

In this paper we put forward two claims, one "weak," the other "strong." The weak claim, all but conceded in principle by the evaluation fraternity, although needing to be fleshed out in practice, runs something like this: there is a suggestive parallelism of critical issues and ideas between literary criticism and curriculum evaluation, but the inspiration is likely to be both general and diffuse. The strong claim is that there is considerable untapped potential in a thorough-going and explicitly literary-critical stance. Although only one strand within illuminative evaluation, this approach might at times break away from its backing group and go solo. Whether such up-front exercises would need to advertise themselves on public hoardings like Elliot Eisner's "curriculum connoisseurs" is an issue that requires some examination, and not only because educational wine tasters may be inhibited from public use of the spittoon.[8]

Where to begin? David Lodge, in "Literary Criticism in England in the Twentieth Century," offers, as a British head-teacher might say, a school of literary criticism streamed into three broad bands.[9] The top stream, so to speak, are those literary critics who have been selected academically. They live in ivory or red-brick towers, preserve the authority and mystique of their own endeavor, and act generally as mediators in a game of public reputation. The very presence of these academic critics is an implicit denial of the possibility of a self-explaining culture.[10] Everything is to be judged by the standards of the best, and a European super-league of standard authors is imposed as an act of cultural solidarity.[11]

The second stream are those who would be described by our headmaster as of a more practical bent. These writer-critics perceive criticism as a second-order activity, a byproduct of the artist's quest for the aesthetic principles underlying his own art. T. S. Eliot, for example, frequently discusses other poets and dramatists in terms of their influence on his own work.[12] Such critical endeavor can at one level become a self-justifying attempt by the creative writer to determine the taste by which he is to be enjoyed. This dilemma is not altogether avoided by the present writers.

One interesting tendency among the creative writers-as-critics is that their works of criticism take on some of the characteristics of creative writing. The old jibe that critics are "failed novelists and poets" is a powerful one. Similarly, curriculum evaluators may be tempted to impose an imaginative order on complex and sometimes intransigent material. There is a general point here. The boundaries between literature and literary criticism have been partly eroded.[13] Our own approach in this paper, although mainly concerned with the parallelism between curriculum evaluation and literary criticism, cannot help dealing with the possibility that evaluation reports, "critical" or otherwise, may themselves evidence a literary style.

The third kind of critic belongs to a remedial stream; he is not allowed to enter for public examinations, but is kept busy with various projects. Lodge labels him "freelance" and "journalistic." In one sense he is part of the literary social establishment, but his products are sold in the marketplace. At best his activity is broadly consumer-related: he seeks to defend a reasonably educated audience "against the pedantries of academia and the subversions of the *avant garde.*"[14]

It is easy to point to suggestive parallels within the world of curriculum evaluation. Certainly psychometric evaluation has been "academic," methodologically pure, prestigiously related to the dominant experimentalist paradigm, and university based.[15] But illuminative, even literary-critical, evaluation might be "academic" too. One recalls the different claims made to authority by the evaluators, ranging from Michael Scriven's view that the evaluator is required to judge by virtue of the likelihood that his grasp of the educational program under review is at least as reliable as anybody else's, to Bob Stake's view that the evaluator should refrain from making explicit recommendations, and should *process* judgments rather than *make* them.[16] Indeed, it is at least arguable that Elliott Eisner's notion of "curriculum connoisseurship" is an attempt to hold on to the autocratic stance alongside the literary style. (We use the term "autocratic" in the sense suggested by Barry MacDonald in his political classification of evaluation activity.)[17]

The possibility of a "practitioners' evaluation" similar to the creative writer's own excursions into literary criticism is an attractive one to many curriculum developers and teachers. Expert "outside" evaluation (even if the "connoisseurs" are in some way culturally authenticated rather than self-styled) raises legitimate suspicions about novel doctrines of accountability. One position that might seem at least initially attractive is that of Lawrence Stenhouse.[18] Stenhouse advocates formation of a community of teacher-researchers, exhuming the underlying assumptions of their own teaching and testing the effects of trying out in classrooms views *that just happen to be their own.* As with the creative writer/critic, the canons of criticism derive from the first-order activity, not the second. Thus Stenhouse sees curriculum evaluation (in his version subsumed under curriculum research) not as criticizing practice by reference to theory, but as chastening theory by confronting it with professional judgment on what is possible. John Elliott has recently argued that the practitioner-evaluator model erodes previously held notions of accountability.[19] Any socially just view of teachers' accountability now includes the right to self-adjudication. Public reputation can be quirky, particularly for an innovator. Gerard Manley Hopkins held onto his poetic integrity in the absence of general acclaim by regarding Christ as the only just literary critic.

The journalistic model, with its emphasis on hit-and-run fieldwork, cryptic presentation, and narrative strength, has also been endorsed by the evaluation community. Rob Walker of the Ford SAFARI project, for example, admits explicit allegiance to Tom Wolfe and the "new journalism."[20] Tom Wolfe sees the new journalism as employing literary devices of the kind that "gave the realistic novel its unique power." His four "devices" (scene-by-scene construction, the use of dialog, the representation of events as seen by a third party, and the inclusion of descriptive detail) provide a *vade mecum* for the SAFARI reporter. A not atypical detail from a Walker report reads: "A girl came up behind and greeted the teacher very loudly with 'Hey Bummer, had any good ones lately?' To which he replied, 'No, I can't get a look-in anywhere since you put the word round about me!' then turned to the visitor and said, 'We call him Bummer, you know, because he is queer.' "[21] But the literary evaluator is in danger of becoming caught in a persistent antinomy between his twin roles of novelist and critic. This is one area in which educational evaluation and research, anxious not to foul its own nest, would not find it easy to go along with Tom Wolfe's bald assertion of the arrogance of the writer: "A writer needs at least enough ego to believe that what he is doing as a writer is as important as what anyone he is writing about is doing . . . therefore he should not compromise his own work."[22]

Commonsense Threats to the Analogy

Before taking a closer look at recent issues in literary criticism as a source of suggestive leads, we first turn to face some obvious problems that might undermine the credibility of the parallel and, consequently, the value of the inspiration. This section, therefore, might be called "common-sense threats to the analogy." The first threat that we might consider is a strong one, the simple assertion that educational programs are not works of art at all, nor even cultural artifacts; typically a curriculum implementation does not exist in a preserved form and offers no lasting "alms to oblivion." It thus does not merit the attentions of literary criticism, which activity is in part an adjudication of a claim to cultural survival.[23] Such a view might partially be answered by pressing the analogy with drama. Plays come alive in the theater, and the text (although it remains eligible for study by the academic critic) is little different from an unperformed musical score. Francis Link makes an identical point in describing *Man: A Course of Study,* which one would be forgiven for supposing to be the packaged course par excellence, as an "unfinished curriculum."[24] But this response by those defending the analogy would be an over-nervous one. The general shakedown in the rigid assumptions about what constitutes art has certainly admitted ephemera, and (in the case of pop art) a new willingness to see significance in the ordinary and the everyday.

But the point may be pressed in other ways too. Those who see teaching as an art rather than a science may legitimately seek exploration of its underlying heuristics, and not just as a performance made up of a public repertoire of composed behavior. Recent developments in evaluation technology (e.g., film-based documentary, videotaping, tape-recorded interviews, photographic analysis, descriptions aimed explicitly at offering "surrogate experience," etc.) might be said to have closed the gap between the implemented curriculum as preserved art form.[25] But the distinction between the two disciplines is critical for another reason. Our capacity to adjudicate the second-order activity of literary criticism is dependent to some extent on having *independent access* to the work under scrutiny. To have the criticism without the creative work is by some considerations absurd. Yet educational evaluations not infrequently offer critical appraisal in the absence of parallel access to "the work" itself. Minimally this forces the evaluator to separate his evidence from his interpretations; it has led some toward the kind of portrayal that acknowledges the multiple perspectives of those in and around the program.[26] But the objection remains a strong one.

A second line of attack might be developed using some notion like "equality of endeavor." By this we mean that typically in literary criticism the very best criticism is done by people with minds matching in subtlety that of the artist. Now if we see education as fighting its battles as much against absurdity as ignorance or if we acknowledge even the routine humiliations of the classroom (Readers, we *partook* of them!), then there may be an aesthetic objection to bringing a whole critical apparatus to bear upon institutions that contrive at one and the same time to be both preposterous and unremarkable. At worst, evaluations might become "camp" in the sense that the word was used by Susan Sontag.[27] "Camp" is a capacity for making bad art (like *Batman* comics) into a source of refined pleasure. The awfulness of the original is defeated by a contrived shift in taste. An example of camp in an evaluation report is found in *Saved by the Bell,* an account of Mr. Bondine's integrated studies lesson at Hardacre Lane High School:

"Right! Oliver Twist!"

The books are duly handed out by monitors. The books themselves are tatty, one-between-two. Interest is low. Bondine offers an option. Would the class like to read the play of "Oliver Twist" aloud or dramatise the story? There is a chorus in favour of reading aloud, although the alternative is kept attractively open (wouldn't you prefer . . .). The result of the vote is greeted with applause.

At this point Bondine passes by your observer. A quick move into literature, he explains. This lapse in confrontation causes the class to renew private conversation. Two lads in the far corner (one recently absent) are talking about the fish floating dead in the green water of one of Bondine's tanks. It was later explained to me that the fish had terminated a project on "fish" and initiated one on "death and decomposition."

"You! What are you talking about?"

The boy (with genuine feeling), "The fish, sir! The fish. It's dead!" (Chorus: "Didn't you know that!") Bondine follows "the flow of interest."

"It's stopped breathing hasn't it? but we don't want to go into the circulation of the blood just now." (A little puzzling this; but evidently one of those opportunist moments through which it is legitimate to digress in quest of clarity.)

"Could a really clever scientist bring that fish back to life? It's dead." (Chorus of doubt. DRJ wonders about the question as put. Just what would count as evidence?)

"What is the most important . . . What do we associate with the brain?" (Continued puzzled responses.)

"What, so we are told, is the state of—the difference—so we are told, between man and, you know that, the animals?"

"It's bigger, sir" (ventured one lad).

"It's bigger, yes there is that."

The next tactical target in the drift of the lesson was the "soul," or perhaps it was a target before, lost in the previous exchange. As before the method was the dialogue. The idea has to come from the pupils, with Bondine as a kind of mental sheep dog, leading them towards the right pen.

"Coming back to this death business. What happens to fish when they die?" (A sudden dart; the stabbing finger)—"You!"

Girl: "They rot away, sir."

"They rot away! Nothing else? You!"

Boy: "They sink to the bottom, sir." (Evidently they needed more direct clues.)

"Anybody here . . . How many think there is something after death?" (Pupils reconsider briefly their own theological position, Bondine declaring that they are free to decide themselves on this private matter.) Then comes the naming of parts.

"You. Master of the workhouse. . . ." (At this point my eye caught the blackboard, on which Bondine had written from time to time the odd key word. It read: "BRAIN HEAVEN HELL SHEEP INDUSTRIAL REVOLUTION FISH." I wondered whether in any sense it could be cited as a testimony to integration.)[28]

One of the more powerful arguments to come out of "practitioners' evaluation" makes opposite assumptions about the direction of the imbalance: that it is the evaluator who has problems of adequacy. Academic evaluators cannot be "trusted to understand" the world of schools and classrooms, and actually need to be protected against inadequacies in their tacit knowledge.[29] Just as Stouffler et al. found in *The American Soldier,* the norms of the combat troops (organized around veteran talk) allow the norms of the transit camp (full of the "young officer" breed) to be defined as hypocritical.[30]

A final objection to the literary criticism analogy might be that there are inadequate public criteria, using a literary-critical approach, for judging how worthwhile a program of study or an educational innovation is. We return to this theme later. Suffice it to say at the moment that literary criticism is still grappling with this issue, which is difficult to resolve in either field. Some of the arguments offer highly suggestive lines for the curriculum evaluator.

The Hidden Curriculum

There are, by way of counterweight, arguments that can be pressed in the opposite direction. One of the tasks of literary criticism is to develop methods of understanding and assessing material which has the complexity and unpredictability of life itself with all the added interest and problems created by the use of formal structures. Such a discipline must inevitably develop a vocabulary and concepts which are of value to the curriculum evaluator, particularly, we feel, in dealing with the complex nature of the "hidden curriculum." It is no accident that the word "evaluation" is of central importance in both areas. We have already suggested that the theatrical metaphor is a particularly instructive one. Role theory itself began as a migrating concept that entered sociology from theater studies, concerned with the way in which public performances are constrained and allowed by socially construed expectations. Curriculum evaluation is also in the business of interpreting performances, addressing general cultural questions like "What are the ceremonies and rituals of life in schools *actually worth?*" To some extent this interest in the nuances of a school's curriculum subculture may suggest that the evaluator is more interested in the "real," hidden curriculum than the "pretend," formal one. A recent paper by David Hargreaves, "Power and the Paracurriculum," vivifies the political content of this shift in interest.[31] Hargreaves offers the term "paracurriculum," which we have borrowed for the title of our paper, partly to suggest that it lies alongside the formal curriculum and interpenetrates it, and partly to get over the problem that the "hidden" curriculum, albeit unacknowledged, is increasingly open to public discussion ("from whom is it now hidden?"). The paracurriculum of an institution is accessible to the participant observer and lends itself to in-depth narrative exposition. An analogy might be the use in dramatic criticism of the idea of the "subtext."[32] The real life of a play is seen as going on as much in what is not said as in the actual words of the dialog. It is one task of the producer to understand and make sure the actors understand the rich and complex life of the subtext, the underlying tensions, sympathies, impulses, of which the dialog is only a partial reflection. One canonical inspiration has been Erving Goffman, whose field-work at St. Elizabeth's was an attempt to "try to learn about the social world of the hospital inmate, as this world is subjectively experienced by him." Goffman could be talking about the realistic novelist or the curriculum evaluator when he writes:

It was then, and still is, my belief that any group of persons—prisoners, primitives, pilots or patients—develop a life of their own that becomes meaningful, reasonable, and normal once you get close to it, and that a good way to learn about any of these worlds is to submit oneself in the company of the members to the daily round of petty contingencies to which they are subject.[33]

Hargreaves develops a concept of the paracurriculum that not only builds up a consistent subculture through the "daily round of petty contingencies" but also allows the possibility of ideological analysis, for example, the Marxist account of contemporary schooling put forward by Bowles and Gintis.[34] (This paracurriculum "operates . . . through a close correspondence between the social relationships which govern personal interaction in the work place and the social relationships of the educational system.") Jules Henry sees the paracurriculum as training for a future life "not because it teaches the 3R's (more or less), but because it instils the cultural nightmare fear of failure, envy of success and absurdity."[35]

Although the authors of this paper part company with Hargreaves in his broad view that the paracurriculum might be systematically evaluated within existing social scientific paradigms ("for some, this will mean presenting the claims in some falsifiable form and subjecting them to empirical text") and prefer his alternative suggestion that "some kind of illuminative evaluation" might be attempted, it is one area of curriculum where we would press the strong argument— that an explicitly literary-critical style of evaluation would take us closest to the essential meanings involved.

But there are other reasons for pressing the theater analogy. Elizabeth Burns, in "The Sociology of the Theatre," reminds us of the "theatricality of ordinary life" in settings such as the school, in which participants typically "resort to a special grammar of composed behaviour."[36] The idea of the theatricality of everyday life takes the dramatic critic close to the work, clearly "literary" in style, of symbolic interactionists like Erving Goffman. Goffman's chapter on "The Underlife of a Public Institution" is in effect an explication of the hidden curriculum of a mental hospital, the environment-as-experienced together with the adaptations and self-presentations needed to cope with it.

"Ghost Writing" and Ghoul-Free Evaluation

One objection that might be sustained against the argument of our paper to this point is that it misconstrues the nature of curriculum and proposes instead a kind of literate social anthropology of schooling, treating the ordinary as exotic instead of the exotic as ordinary. There is a problem here, but not an insuperable one.

Admittedly a part of the psychometric inheritance was a narrow definition of curriculum; it was often seen as little more than a statement, in behavioral terms, of the learning that teachers intended the course to bring about.[37] "Curriculum" thus belonged to the world of stated intentions, not the milieu of school-as-experienced. Indeed, it was seen as almost illicit to show much interest in classrooms, rather like stimulus-response psychologists who treat the mind as a black box. In retrospect it seems surprising that the evaluation tail had been allowed without challenge to wag the curriculum dog. But by the time of Bob Stake's "Countenance" paper it was at least possible to take a broader view of what is eligible for collection as evaluation data.[38] "Curriculum" included the intentions, the transactions of the classroom, and the effects (including student learnings). But the evaluation community had hardly gotten used to this new freedom before the data base began to contract again, the contraction coming from an unexpected quarter.

Arguments were suddenly put forward by Mike Scriven for a style of evaluation which he christened "goal-free evaluation" (GFE).[39] This development in curriculum evaluation has a parallel in one very important trend in twentieth-century literary criticism. The main idea behind goal-free evaluation is the view that an evaluator needs to study a program's effects unhampered by contact with the rhetoric of intent produced by the program builder, be he curriculum developer or teacher. Scriven writes:

It seemed to me, in short, that consideration and evaluation of goals was an unnecessary but also a possibly contaminating step. I began to work on an alternative approach—simply the evaluation of actual effects against (typically) a profile of demonstrated needs. This is close to what the Consumer's Union actually does. I call this goal-free evaluation (GFE).[40]

GFE has parallels in a number of fields. Perhaps part of its inspiration derives from "double-blind" designs in experimental research (in such designs neither the subject nor the experimenter knows which group is the experimental group and which the control). But a stronger analogy is with the notion of the "intentional fallacy" in literary criticism. This addresses a pervasive critical dilemma—the need to adjudicate for or against the relevance of biographical data or information alleging the *intentions* of the artist. Most contemporary critics are inclined to assert the essential *autonomy* of a work of art.

The play or poem or novel is treated as an "aesthetic monad"; once launched, it leaves the author behind on the slipway, so to speak, and makes its own independent way in the world.[41] A paper by William K. Wimsatt and Monroe Beardsley expresses this stance; the issue is one of *criteria for judgment* (though literary biography may be interesting for other reasons): "The desire or intention of an author is neither available nor desirable as a standard for judging the success of a work of literary art."[42] The implications of this position for literary criticism are far-reaching. At its most extreme the idea of the entirely self-contained artefact implicitly denies the claims and responsibilities of the author. Almost certainly educators would find this hard to adopt as a down-the-line ideological position. The GFE blinkers may be worn for a particular race, but they are not usually seen as obligatory. Nevertheless, GFE is an appropriate manifesto for those whose interest is more illuminative or interpretative than that proposed by Scriven himself in his no-nonsense Goal Free Checklist.[43]

But the task of criticism is itself surrounded by ambiguity and mystery. At one level, of course, it is what people choose to write in response to a work of art. But this leaves many questions unanswered. Does the literary critic (or the curriculum evaluator) have a describable social role? Who are his audiences?[44] Are there any standard procedures that may be pressed into service in defining his scope? Are critics and evaluators in some special sense cultural mediators? Attempts to answer this kind of question are more likely to be found among academic critics than elsewhere.

In 1924, I. A. Richards wrote one of the seminal texts in quest of a defensible formal and moral literary criticism. *Principles of Literary Criticism* castigates the extant critical tradition as one made up of "conjectures, admonitions, acute isolated observations, brilliant guesses, oratory, confusion, dogma, prejudices, whimsies, genuine speculation and sundry stray inspirations."[45] It is an account that could stand for the current state of illuminative evaluation, give or take a few strong themes like narrative description and progressive focusing on key educational issues. John Crowe Ransom takes the same astringent line in "Criticism Inc.," excluding from true criticism things like personal registrations, synopsis or paraphrase, historical studies, linguistics studies, and moral studies.[46]

What Ransom proposes in their place is an alternative critical task, central to which is a study of "the Tropes, fictions and inventions by which a work of art secures aesthetic distance and removes itself from history." Thus the critic turns his attention to the formal characteristics of a work of art. The curriculum too, is partly a formal matter, involving ritualistic and symbolic expressions. Hargreaves includes a nice example of symbol study from a postgraduate thesis by one of his ex-students:

Court etiquette long decreed that the Sovereign alone should occupy a chair, other persons present being seated on stools. This usage was governed by rigorous court etiquette right down to the early Georgian period. It is this symbolism which seems to have ossified in many of the public schools, where the great chair is retained and the headmaster sits alone on the stage. It has diffused more widely. In the majority of the schools in this study, the head teacher continued to take assembly alone. Sometimes there are three chairs rather than one. This may be related to the arrangements in the House of Lords, where there are thrones for the King and Queen at the centre and for the heir apparent at the side. But besides being a symbol of regal authority, the chair has also, as the throne of God, been the symbol of divine authority, so there may be some trinitarian flavour about this triple arrangement. . . . Since "chairs" are also offered to professors, the chair can also symbolise academic authority and it begins to emerge that the great chair, long used in schools, and retained in many, is a ritual symbol with a high degree of ambiguity which can supply rich associative links of a generalised character and permit a transition between levels of meaning. When the head of one public school was asked who sat in the three big leather chairs at the front of the stage, he looked the investigator straight in the eye and replied "I do" in a tone which combined the authority of holy trinity, demonic trilogy, male triad and Goldilocks legend.[47]

The question of interest to the evaluator is what this kind of analysis might lead to. Some evaluators may stay with Ransom at the level of simple recognition of these formal characteristics, others may go on to ask what the rituals and ceremonies of our social life are actually *worth*.[48] Ransom sees a poem as "nothing short of a desperate ontological or metaphysical manoeuvre." This rather complex but compelling phrase springs in the first place from an acknowledgment of the writer's *struggle* in creating a work of art. A poem is redeemed out of chaos; while writing, the poet fights to maintain the poem's integrity against irrelevancies. There are two senses in which the curriculum might be said to engage in similar ontological and metaphysical maneuvering. The individual lesson, both in its content and its subject matter, is a *realization of what it is,* against all the threats of what it might have been; it requires that evaluators describe it in such a way that its ontological and metaphysical status is recognized.

A more fanciful extension of Ransom's idea is to the subject structures and curriculum strategies themselves, which engage over a longer period of time in making metaphysical bids through their implicit epistemologies.[49] A number of teaching strategies contain assumptions about the knowledge domain being studied and how competent performance is to be recognized. As one moves from the objectives and learning experiences of a behavioral technology (e.g., stimulus-response learning in a simple teaching machine) to what Gordon Pask has called "conversational learning," it is possible to chart increasingly liberal assumptions in the way in which the student and the knowledge structure are represented and understood.[50] For example, the student might be treated no longer as a "simple adaptive device" or even as a "restricted problem solver" but as a person able to "select his mode of attack." According to Pask these facets of a curriculum strategy are "formal" to the extent that they can be expressed in the formal language of *systemics*.[51] But they also have a concrete reality, since Pask defines *curriculum* simply as a teaching strategy. The formal aspects, too, may be inferred analytically from the practices, in which they will be sustained by something akin to Ransom's "Tropes, fictions and inventions." A curriculum may also be described in a way that removes it from history and gives it pedagogical distance. But in some sense this approach to curriculum evaluation takes away from the "Tropes, fictions and inventions" of a single work in the direction of genre studies, or the theory of modes, which involve the kind of critical facility that allows *Anna Karenina* to be conceived of as a bourgeois epic, or Fielding to describe *Joseph Andrews* as a "comic epic in prose."

All Along the Watchtower: Narrative Perspectives

Another literary critical concept offering guidelines to the educational evaluator is "narrative point of view." Point of view is perhaps *the* fundamental device of the novel. There is sufficient similarity with problems associated with the location of the observer in *participant observation* research (Colin Bell: "The social position of the observer determines what he is likely to see") for the parallel to be cited, but its real significance to the curriculum evaluator lies elsewhere.[52] The term "point of view" has particular relevance to the methods of the curriculum evaluator rather than to the curriculum itself. It is a term likely to be of use to the meta-evaluator, whose job it is to criticize the critics. To the novelist, "point of view" might get tied in with the possibility of "omniscient authorship," that is, the writer may allow himself to be both the creator of the artefact and the moral interpreter of his own fiction.[53] But the issue is more complicated than anything encompassed within that possibility. Raymond Williams has suggested that there are three ways of relating words and ideas: propagandist fiction, made up of things like tracts and improving stories of the Sunday School Prize variety; works that in some sense embody ideas; and works in which ideas are argued out or discussed.[54] This three-fold division holds broadly true both for educational schemes and for curriculum evaluation reports. The point of view taken by the writer must be acknowledged, but will not in any facile sense determine the point of view taken by the critic. But even here a sharper distinction is needed. *Narrative* point of view is embedded in the tone and substance of the novel as well as its moral sequences. A nice exposition of this point is found in D. W. Harding's "Regulated Hatred in the Work of Jane Austen."[55] Harding argues that the "unexpected astringencies" in the work of Jane Austen ought not to be interpreted as lapses in the tone of middle-class gentility, but given due weight as part of the narrative point of view.

This account poses some problems for the illuminative evaluator. He may wish to repudiate a judgmental responsibility, preferring instead to collect the opinions of participants in and around the program. Even if, like the UNCAL team,* he formally eschews making recommendations, he may not, if he uses narrative description, altogether avoid "point of view."[56] Implicit judgments are inextricably bound into narrative technique. Indeed, one of the dilemmas facing the UNCAL team is whether it is possibie to combine a "portrayal" style of evaluation with a commitment to the role of the evaluator as "honest broker," simply reflecting the multiple perspectives that different participants bring to complex situations under review. Levine takes a somewhat different line, arguing that since reports increase in power when organized around a point of view, the best way of "testing the inferences that are derived from natural field situations" may

*UNCAL (an acronym for Understanding Computer Assisted Learning) is a team carrying out an independent educational evaluation of the British *National Development Programme in Computer Assisted Learning.* It is directed by Barry MacDonald of the Centre for Applied Research in Education, University of East Anglia, Norwich.

be to set up opposed arguments and counterarguments.[57] These might take the form of an *advocate's statement* and an *adversary's statement*. The analogy is legal rather than literary, but that did not stop Bob Stake and Craig Gjerde trying it out in their *T-City Report*.[58]

When an evaluator is faced with both a program and an institution that relate words to ideas in the manner described by Raymond Williams as "propagandist fiction," and he is himself concerned, say, with the *political* problems surrounding the institutionalization of a high-technology innovation, the narrative account is likely to read something like the following, written by Ernie House about the arrival of PLATO (an advanced computer based educational system developed by the University of Illinois) at "Muslem College":

Muslem College lies along the Truman Expressway, a sleek black building two blocks long, in the middle of the West Side ghetto. Across the expressway it faces off against County Hospital and the massive medical complex. The area is one of the roughest in the city. No nurse can travel the underway passage to her quarters without a guard. During the King riots, this was the worst-hit part of Chicago.

Sitting in the midst of this decay is the beautiful black building of Muslem College designed by Mies van der Rohe. In front three enormous sixty-foot flag poles fly the American flag, the white Illinois flag and the Black Liberation flag, the latter strikingly dissonant with its thick black, green and red bars. When the building was dedicated, James Garvey, the President, explained for television why the Black Liberation flag flies there: "At one time you couldn't fly the American flag in this neighborhood. Now you can."

Both at the parking lot and at the doors one must stop for security guards wearing black uniforms with orange Muslem insignias on the sleeve. All are reportedly former convicts. Inside, the building is handsomely furnished with heavy oak furniture and African art. In the lobby sits a black Oldsmobile dating back to the 1950s—an assassinated martyr's car. . . .

Garvey claimed that people were out to get him. Others claimed he had strong paranoid tendencies. Whether a self-fulfilling prophecy or not, in December 1972, a month after the arrival of the first PLATO terminals, irregularities were found in the financial books, Garvey resigned. . . .

And a little later in the report:

A smaller, older (around thirty) and more experienced group within the Learning Resources Center was the tenured, contract faculty. They had been around Muslem a little longer (three to five years) and could best be described as cynical, wary, and weary. They had seen the "innovations" come and go and, as one put it, "Muslem blew the groundwork for PLATO." Like everything else in the school, in their view, PLATO had been crammed down teachers' throats and would not receive a fair trial, they felt. Instead of being soft-pedaled as a supplement, which it might be good for, it was being forced on everybody.

According to the tenured faculty, the non-contract people were so enthusiastic because they had no choice. They had to reflect the administration line or
be fired.[59]

In effect what House is doing is writing an alternative to the official
account, while himself adopting a narrative stance. But the curriculum evaluator may in general see himself faced with a choice between
description and analysis, literature and criticism. Our case study of
the London Business School's Skills of Bargaining course attempts to
hold a narrative line side by side with an analysis, which is itself elaborately metaphorical, of the hidden curriculum, for example in seeing the competing pedagogies within the single course as a kind of
rerun of Elijah versus the prophets of Baal.[60] There is some tension
between the styles of reportage involved. This is because "thick-
description" often finds itself uneasily on the boundary between the
literary and the literary-critical. Elliot Eisner himself, it must be remembered, came to his present position obliquely, first arguing for a
distinction between "instructional" and "expressive" objectives (i.e.,
open-ended tasks in which no "correct response" can be anticipated),
and only later wondering whether whole educational programs might
not be evaluated as expressive products.[61]

Miss Jean Brodie's See-Through Blouse: Flat and Round Portrayals

Another central interest of the critic of fiction or drama is, of
course, the presentation of character. The parallel activity in curriculum evaluation is the portrayal of persons in evaluation reports. But
there are implicit ethical problems which have been explored interestingly by Rob Walker and more recently by Barry MacDonald.[62]
MacDonald's paper "The Portrayal of Persons as Evaluation Data"
arose in part from the experiences of directing the UNCAL evaluation. One of the thrusts behind Bob Stake's recommended "responsive evaluation" is that evaluators should respond to questions raised
by decision-makers, or, as Ernie House once put it, should "match
their vocabulary of action." Yet the DES-dominated Programme
Committee became distinctly unhappy about UNCAL reports portraying individuals. ("Rigid with innuendo," snapped one critic.)
MacDonald writes:

The focus on personalities and their influence on events was a realistic recognition that the personal dimension is never ignored by the decision-maker if information about it is available. It was an attempt to close one particular gap in the evaluation data. Yet that effort was heavily criticised. Could it be that the portrayal of persons, far from rendering those persons vulnerable to greater external control, in fact erodes that control by introducing into personnel evaluation an element of public answerability?[63]

The kind of writing that occasioned the criticism sprang from the view that innovations are prone to personality-dependence, not least in their ad hoc working arrangements. One account of a project director ran as follows:

There is a consensus view of Harry McMahon, relatively unchallenged, that points to his openness, his dedication, his ability to "think big," and a track record that suggests high levels of competence and reliability. If the National Programme had an Alf Ramsey as evaluator he would doubtless declare McMahon's "work rate" to be highest of them all. But some are perplexed by his talkativeness, his over-watchfulness in situations, a calculating quality that does not escape an element of self-regard, and the fact that he can be a little overwhelming (if not manipulative). But McMahon is also valued differently by different people and the accounts picked up by UNCAL have varied from near-adulation to indifference. Colleagues trying to bring order to these differences have been tempted to see Harry as "upward-orientated," more concerned to win approval of those above him than the respect of those below. At one extreme he has been suspected of male chauvinism, but there was insufficient evidence to make the charge stick. It could amount to as little as a tendency for Harry, finding himself surrounded by female aides, to exaggerate his disposition to delegate *responsibility* rather than *authority* and to appear "hovering" around everybody else's work situation ("short term contract people need support," explains McMahon). What is ungrudgingly agreed by Harry's admirers and detractors alike is his talent for organisation, his meticulous concern for details and capacity for sheer hard work. His colleagues judge him as "unrivalled" in committeemanship, although inclined to play the system a little unashamedly. He is also patently ambitious ("You can almost *smell* the ambition"). His success in Committee is not always fully acknowledged, particularly by those who attribute more success to the organ grinder than the monkey, and dismiss McMahon easily as "Skilbeck's man." Some remember the time when McMahon with Skilbeck's approval went around asking people if their undergraduate courses were really necessary.[64]

But this kind of writing presents serious difficulties. Informal discussion of the merits of particular individuals ("What do we know about Clements? Sound man?") is commonplace in bureaucratic organizations, but not openly acknowledged in the way that a written account forces. The problem, however, for the evaluator aspiring to a literary or literary-critical style may be posed differently. Can cryptic pen-portrayals of individuals get close enough to their full, rounded uniqueness as people for the human perspective to be defensible? E. M. Forster in *Aspects of the Novel* distinguishes between "flat" and "round" characters in fiction.[65] Flat characters are humorous types of caricatures constructed around an idea or quality. Round characters partake of a full imaginative and moral existence. It seems unlikely that the curriculum evaluator will ever compete with the novelist in sheer roundness of characterization. Perhaps the best he can hope for is a few well chosen suggestive phrases held together by a narrative viewpoint, or some sense of an issue that can be sharply personalized (art teaches by example). If so, he is closer to the world of the theater critic than the world of the novelist, and his ethical dilemmas, vis à vis his responsibility to the subjects of the study, are increased rather than diminished.

There is one further paradox that the curriculum evaluator may need to face. The kind of "character analysis" associated with the work of people like A. C. Bradley in Shakespearean criticism has for some time been on the wane.[66] Academic drama critics have shifted their interest toward other concerns that may appeal to the illuminative evaluator: underlying themes, patterns of imagery, and the play as an arena for a dialectic of alternative world-views. In short, plays are treated as aesthetic monads rather than as slices of life.

Real people subjected to outside appraisal because of their involvement in educational programs may well wish to argue that the evaluator's interest in them should be confined to their public performance. That is, they may be brought within the illuminative evaluator's interest in the theatricality of educational situations, but not within his general interest in Homo sapiens and what makes him tick. The adjudication of relevance is not clearcut. Could it be of interest that a maths adviser is a deacon in a local evangelical church? that a curriculum coordinator for a national project has illusions of grandeur that lead to his keeping a file of current rates for private helicopter hire? that a teacher opposing an innovation in a school was recently turned down for internal promotion? Just to read the short extract above from Ernie House is to realize that his net of relevance for the inclusion of biographical information is cast widely.

But Bradley also suggests explicit modes of attack that an evaluator may employ. When we wrote a "pathological" account of a failed innovation recently, we employed Bradley's mechanical tragic sequence of "character, deed, and catastrophe," pointing to tragic flaws in the performance of named participants, although conscious of and sympathetic about the situational traps in which they found themselves.[67] There was strong hostility to the report, and we were unable to negotiate its full release, even to a limited audience. Although this may be in part a failure in the social skill of the evaluator, there is a general problem of pressing new styles of evaluation without creating the taste by which they are enjoyed. By way of contrast one may cite lampooning cartoons which the victim-politicians simply frame and hang on their drawing-room walls.

Stylistic Devices

One final area for our comparison between literary criticism and curriculum evaluation is the matter of style. At its simplest, the illuminative evaluator employing literary or literary critical models may feel more free to attempt the elegant turn of phrase, unembarrassed by his abandonment of a careful referential language for a more personal one. Not only is style a writer's cutting edge, it is where the cold is most felt, if one allows Graham Greene's observation that "there is a splinter of ice in the heart of every writer." The unkind phrase, the quip, the deadly observation: all these enter the armory of the literary evaluator, however much he may prefer to be the sort of critic possessing tact, understanding, artfulness, and sympathy to the author and the work. When *The Guardian* reviewed Angela Pope's film depicting life in an Ealing (London) comprehensive school, one shot of a teacher entering a class with unruly kids was described as showing the teacher floundering "like a non-swimmer in heavy surf."[68] Such telling phrases have the twin qualities of imaginative immediacy and a curious undeniability.

We shall be talking in this section both about the style of the work to which the critic is attentive and the style adopted by the critic. To the curriculum evaluator this problem can be rephrased, as "style" in an evaluation report is more *literally* present although no more pervasive than is "style" in an educational setting. As well as using, say, highly metaphorical language himself, the illuminative evaluator in this tradition may be engaged in analyzing the imagery and symbolism of the institution. Much of this, as Hargreaves and others have shown, makes up the hidden curriculum or paracurriculum of the school. The questions addressed will include the following: What is the metaphorical content of the teacher's language? What kind of examples does he give? What imagery underpins curriculum planning? What makes up, in Goffman's term, the "underlife" of the institution, and what are its symbolic constituents?

The task of exploring the imagery of schooling is directly analogous to the image-tracing of such literary critics as G. Wilson Knight and Caroline Spurgeon, in which work the basic assumption is made that access to the deepest significance in a Shakespearean play is yielded through an analysis of its patterns of imagery.[69] In the extract below from an evaluation of the *Keele Integrated Studies Project,* image-tracing takes precedence over narrative account. The quest is less for surface features than underlying preoccupations or themes. Lying behind the imagery of the curriculum that a teacher builds into his public performance will be his own "self-image" as a teacher. This term has more literary connotations and implications than are usually acknowledged.

Another aspect of style likely to be employed by the illuminative evaluator comes out of his taste for anomaly. Words like wit, irony, humor, paradox, and ambiguity have been steadily moving nearer the center of the literary critical tradition. Literary critics in the first half of the twentieth century have been especially preoccupied with such concepts, reflected in a keen appreciation of seventeenth-century metaphysical poetry (which is one reason why we began with Dr. Johnson). The essays of T. S. Eliot, and William Empson's *Seven Types of Ambiguity,* have been particularly influential here.[70] One nice point for the illuminative evaluator exploring the parallel is that the literary critic acknowledges that teasing out ambiguities is not always confined to those effects intended by the author, but may also extend to an analysis of the complexities, inconsistencies, and even obscurities found in a flawed work of art, even a flawed masterpiece. Many of the ambiguities, ironies, and paradoxes of the curriculum/paracurriculum are in an identical sense unintended or unacknowledged.

This is not to say that curriculum evaluators will use irony in any consistently debunking way, restoring "discrepancy evaluation" in another guise.[71] It would take a very bold evaluator indeed to go beyond incidentally insightful humor (which increasingly is creeping into curriculum evaluation reports) to formal comedy, or what Northrop Frye in his theory of modes calls a "catharsis of sympathy and ridicule."[72] There is a connection here too with the allegation that the paracurriculum teaches "absurdity," although that term could be equally a part of a tragic resolution, which Frye calls a catharsis of pity and fear.[73].

One general question for both the writer and the critic, both the teacher and the educational evaluator, is whether imaginative orders have been imposed rather than identified. Are wit, paradox, and ambiguity, or the "lessons" of obedience and absurdity, "really" in the curriculum/paracurriculum, or are they just the inventions of the observer?

Irony, ambiguity, and paradox all rely to some extent on a persistent antinomy between statements that embody conflicting standards. These are interesting to anybody concerned with the internal logic of educational proposals and suggest themselves as rhetorical devices that may form part of the style of the critic. A seminal paper on paradox is Cleanth Brooks's "The Language of Paradox."[74] Brooks begins by castigating as prejudice the tendency to regard paradox as intellectual rather than emotional ("paradox is the language of sophistry, not the language of the soul"). The paper is largely concerned with a close examination of Donne's *The Canonization,* a poem of complex metaphorical wit. Donne treats profane love as if it were divine: lovers each have their "hermitage" in the body of the other, and can thus cunningly argue a title to sainthood. Paradox is hard, bright, witty, but also subtle and emotionally serious. It is not difficult to see pervasive paradoxes in education. For example, as a rule teachers ask questions only when they know the answers.[75]

In the following excerpt many literary devices are used, perhaps a little too self-consciously. The evaluator is monitoring various interpretations of the Keele-based Schools Council *Integrated Studies Project* held by its trial teachers, and expressing these in terms of nine guiding metaphors. The excerpts are from three of these guiding metaphors: the project as agitation or distress, the project as salvation, and the project as theater.

Troubled waters: The project as agitation or distress

Mr. Larchwood: What did Mr. Pickford really mean when he said it all starts with you?

Pupil: Voting. We chose.

Mr. Larchwood: Yes, that's what I think he meant. Anybody over 21 may vote. It may come down to 18.
Mr. Pickford: There are some exceptions, Mr. Larchwood.
Mr. Larchwood: Exceptions?
Mr. Pickford: Yes, Mr. Larchwood. Have you any first-hand knowledge of them?
Mr. Larchwood: Lunatics?
Mr. Pickford: And felons actually undergoing a prison sentence.
Mr. Larchwood: Mr. Pickford has just given you the answer, I'm sure.
Mr. Pickford: Yes, Mr. Larchwood, I've a real live lord living next to me.
Mr. Larchwood: (interrupting) Just a quick point about the date of the general election. . . .

What is functional in one context may be dysfunctional in another. In spite of the felt obligation to assent to a rhetoric of collaboration, the truth is that internal tensions within teams of teachers are unremarkable and normal. The competitive edge in the above example is readily visible. The analogy is with tag wrestling, or a tennis match in which the children are spectators while the teachers score off each other. Team teaching is an institutional apparatus that threatens privacy. It also exposes teachers to a second audience of potentially critical colleagues. . . Many teachers expressed nervousness about the presence of other teachers. . . .

The issue of team "leadership" is also a problem, linked as it is to the career structure of the profession and the possibility of "departmental overlordships," as one feudally minded trial school teacher put it, in Humanities. In one school a rhetoric of democracy masked real differences and policies. In another a trial school teacher could not bring himself to use the name of her more dominant adversary, directing all her criticism at an abstract entity called "the leader" ("The problem with the leader is that she has no time to listen"). In front of the integrated studies pupils they simulated unity and called each other by Christian names. The headmaster of the leader's school believes that leadership emerges naturally, like in the Tory party. Except his, of course.

But our guiding metaphor of troubled waters draws attention to the uncertainty, which is often valued for its own sake. The crowning glory of the Keele project was that it offered its imprimatur on the ensuing chaos, creating the taste by which it was enjoyed. Most appropriate garb for the curriculum visitor is a combat jacket and a floral tie.

The gift of grace: The project as salvation

In spite of the self-help rhetoric of grassroots curriculum development, many teachers welcomed the project as a kind of act of grace. Few teachers in fact had this response, but those that did had it in full measure (not only life, but life more abundant!). As a response it is curiously ambiguous. The teacher admits weaknesses, expresses belief, and is rewarded not only with assistance, but the certainty of belonging to the elect. The underlying metaphor is one more naturally embedded in nonconformist theology. Only sinners achieve salvation. Statements of profound inadequacy ("We're just groping in the dark") become closely associated with a feeling of being in the van of educational progress. . . .

New props for identity: The project as theatre

"If you've got a class, you're teaching. If you've got any other audience, you're performing. If you've got other members of staff, just as if parents came in on an open evening, well, that's a performance. Even if you are giving a demonstration of how you teach, it's still a performance."

Within our fifth guiding metaphor the teacher is able to see the curriculum project quite simply as a theatre and a collection of props. He is an actor, and by manipulating the props can reconstruct his own professional identity. He may be seeking personal or political visibility or he may see contact with a Schools Council curriculum project as having career significance. Often this aspiration was quite explicit. ("When I move from here I hope my time with the Keele project will allow me to get a head of Humanities in another school.") For the subject for integrated studies, there may be a dilemma. He suspects that integrated studies is seen by headteachers as low-status knowledge, but believes that this is more than compensated by the value of the public label that reads "curriculum innovator." This lapel badge of the innovator is the most glittering bauble that a project can offer, which is why trial school teachers at a Keele project diffusion conference complained bitterly when an administrative oversight prevented the allocation of three bubbles of identity, so that trial school teachers were indistinguishable from "interested others". . . .

But how are these stars and badges allocated? There are two traditions, reflecting two different kinds of political aspiration. The first tradition is the war medal, the second tradition is the badge of the sheriff's deputy.

The war medal rewards past achievement. It is set firmly within the grassroots tradition. The project's task is to articulate and spread "good practice" within schools. Its first task, therefore, is to select those schools where good practice is already rooted. . . .

Not so the badge of the sheriff's deputy, which indicates future responsibility. The star suggests a delegated task ("We realized what a difficult assignment the Keele project was giving us"). The war veteran may swap the anecdotes of classroom survival, but the sheriff's deputy saddles up his horse. He is culturally obliged to express routine modesty and doubt, but is expected to bring his man home in the end.[76]

One danger of this kind of writing in evaluation reports is a preoccupation with the surface texture of events and an over-awareness of style. There are also some ambiguities of tone, an uncomfortable mixture of the serious and the flip, and a weakened sense of the way in which a potential audience might put the report to practical use. But there is also the need for the evaluator to consider the locale of the action, to acknowledge that the figures are in a physical, cultural, and ideological landscape. Schools are places where alternative policies compete for attention: where things are learned by indoctrination and institutional seepage as much as by curiosity and investigation. The curriculum evaluator needs to be aware of the different social forces at work on the curriculum, both those contained within it and those exerting their subtle or insidious pressures from the world outside. Literary criticism, particularly in the Marxist tradition, has long talked of the "social context" of a work of art. Lucien Goldmann argues that in addition to a "literary aesthetic" concerned with the artistic devices used by the writer, the critic needs a "socio-logical aesthetic" which would bring out the relationship of an exist-ing "world vision" to "the universe of characters and things created in a particular work."[77] This is broadly similar to learning milieu theory as explicated by Malcolm Parlett and built into his evaluation report *A Study of Two Experimental Programs at MIT*.[78]

Noseprints on the Glass

Conclusions to a paper of this kind are necessarily tentative, but perhaps five might be canvassed:

1. In spite of the violent yoking of the analogy, it seems clear that a number of the parallels between literary criticism and illuminative evaluation are instructive ones, although (to use an image from chess) some of the resulting positions are a little wild. Whether they should attract the chess commentator's rubric (!?) or (?!) is at times a matter of fine judgment.

2. The inspiration is likely to remain diffused, not least because aspects of the comparison pull in different directions. The influence of Marxist literary criticism would take an illuminative evaluator to practices removed from those he would consider if enchanted by the notion of the aesthetic monad.

3. Central to much twentieth-century literary criticism is the idea that the work of art must be its own justification, not leaning for support on the intentions, explanations, or excuses of either artist or commentator. There is even the notion that the final effect of the work may be at odds with the declared aims of the artist. In assessing the curriculum, evaluators might find it useful to bear in mind the dictum of D. H. Lawrence: "Never trust the artist, trust the tale."[79]

4. Literary-critical approaches to curriculum evaluation are appro-priate both for the formal curriculum and the paracurriculum, but they are of special relevance to the paracurriculum, which is less accessible to conventional techniques.

5. Finally, a leaf might be taken from another book. In participant observation research the advantages of getting a participant to ob-serve are different from those associated with getting an observer to participate. Let teachers and other practitioners join professional evaluators in a joint activity stripped of its protective mystique. But

let also poets, novelists, critics, and reviewers follow their ideas across the boundary and actually take part in curriculum evaluation alongside the educators. It would be several glorious years before the illuminative tradition recovered from the shock.

Notes

1. See especially Edward Kelly, "Curriculum Evaluation and Literary Criticism: Comments on the Analogy," in *Curriculum Theory Network* 5, no. 2 (1975): John S. Mann, "Curriculum Criticism," *Curriculum Theory Network* 2 (Winter 1968-69); and Robert Stake, "Analysis and Portrayal" (Paper prepared at the Institute of Education, University of Goteberg, 1975). (The Kelly and Mann articles appear as chaps. 6 and 4 of this volume.) In England one paper of general but seminal effect was Richard Hoggart's "The Literary Imagination and the Study of Society" (Paper delivered to the Sociology Section of the British Association, Leeds, 1967).

2. This tradition perhaps began with Ralph Tyler's *Basic Principles of Curriculum and Instruction* (Chicago, Ill.: University of Chicago Press, 1949), and has been best expressed recently in James Popham's *Educational Evaluation* (Englewood Cliffs, N.J.: Prentice-Hall, 1975). A critique of this approach can be found in Michael MacDonald Ross, "Behavioural Objectives: A Critical Review," in *Curriculum Design*, ed. Michael Golby, Jane Greenwald, and Ruth West (Bletchley: Open University, 1975).

3. See Malcolm Parlett and David Hamilton, "Evaluation as Illumination" (Occasional paper no. 9, Centre for Research in the Educational Sciences, University of Edinburgh, 1972).

4. Robert Stake, "An Approach to the Evaluation of Instructional Programs: Program Portrayal vs. Analysis" (Paper delivered at the annual meeting of the American Educational Research Association, Chicago, 1972).

5. A number of the methodological underpinnings of illuminative evaluation are brought together and discussed in David Hamilton et al., *Beyond the Numbers Game: A Reader in Curriculum Evaluation* (New York: Macmillan, 1977).

6. For participant evaluation, see Louis Smith, "Integrating Participant Observation into Broader Evaluation Strategies," in Hamilton et al., *Beyond the Numbers Game*. For ethnographic fieldwork, see Center for New Schools, "Ethnographic Techniques in Educational Research," in idem. For client-centered therapy, see Donald Moore, "Strengthening Alternative High Schools," *Harvard Educational Review*, Fall 1974; and Center for New Schools, "On-site Technical Assistance as a Facilitator of Educational Change: A Comparative Study of Five Technical Assistance Groups" (mimeo). For bidding in card games, see Michael Scriven, "Prose and Cons about Goal-Free Evaluation," *Evaluation Comment* 3, no. 4 (1972); and idem, "Current Problems: Philosophy and Practice of Evaluation" (ETS Product Evaluation Pool, occasional paper, private circulation). For legal advocacy, see "Adversary's Statement" and "Advocates Statement," in Robert Stake and Craig Gjerde, *T-City Report* (Report of the 1971 Session of the Twin City Institute for Talented Youth at Macalester College, St. Paul, Minne-

sota, 1972). See also Rob Walker, "Stations" (Paper delivered at the annual meeting of the American Educational Research Association, San Francisco, Ca., 1976).

7. See Marten Shipman, *Inside a Curriculum Project* (London: Methuen, 1974); David Jenkins, "The Keele Integrated Studies Project," in *Evaluation in Curriculum Development: Twelve Case Studies* (Schools Council, 1973); Richard Hooper, "Two Years On C.E.T."; and Barry MacDonald, David Jenkins, David Tawney, and Stephen Kemmis, "The Programme at Two" (Norwich: University of East Anglia, UNCAL, 1975). UNCAL reports are governed by complicated rules for release of data, so at the time of writing this one is not generally available.

8. See Elliot Eisner, "The Perceptive Eye: Towards the Reformation of Educational Evaluation" (Invited address to Division B, Curriculum and Objectives, annual meeting of the American Educational Research Association, Washington, D.C., 1975).

9. See David Lodge, "Literary Criticism in England in the Twentieth Century," in *The Twentieth Century*, ed. Bernard Bergonzi, vol. 7 of *History of Literature in the English Language* (London: Barrie and Jenkins, 1970).

10. George Watson points out in *The Literary Critics: A Study of English Descriptive Criticism* (London: Chatto and Windus, 1964), that as criticism becomes less technical it becomes more value-laden. Critics, then, are increasingly cultural middlemen.

11. Educational programs may be judged according to current practice or according to on-site improvements. The hard-line criterion of excellence is not the only one.

12. See, for example, T. S. Eliot's essay on Baudelaire in his *Selected Essays* (London: Faber and Faber, 1951).

13. See, for example, Leslie Fiedler, *Love and Death in the American Novel* (New York: Stein and Day, 1966), which at times appears to be closer to fiction than to literary criticism.

14. Lodge, "Literary Criticism in England."

15. See E. P. Willems, "Implications of Viewing Educational Evaluation as Research in the Behavioural Sciences," in *Readings in Curriculum Evaluation*, ed. Peter Taylor and Doris Cowley (Dubuque, Iowa: W. C. Brown, 1972).

16. This is a reasonable inference from Michael Scriven's writing. See the Scriven anthology in "Five Advocates of Change," in Hamilton et al., *Beyond the Numbers Game*; and Robert Stake, "The Countenance of Educational Evaluation," first printed in *Teachers College Record*, no. 68 (1967), now much anthologized.

17. See Barry MacDonald, "A Political Classification of Evaluation Studies," in Hamilton et al., *Beyond the Numbers Game*.

18. See Lawrence Stenhouse, *An Introduction to Curriculum Research and Development* (London: Heinemann Educational, 1975).

19. See John Elliott, "Preparing Teachers for Classroom Accountability," mimeographed (Cambridge Institute of Education, 1975).

20. SAFARI, an acronym for Success and Failure and Recent Innovation, is a Ford-sponsored evaluation of the medium-term effects of Schools Council curriculum projects. It is directed by Barry MacDonald at the Centre for Applied Research in Education at the University of East Anglia. Rob Walker developed the "new journalism" ideas in discussing SAFARI at the Cambridge Conference

on Case Study in Educational Research and Evaluation, 1975; see Tom Wolfe, *The New Journalism* (London: Pan, 1975).

21. A SAFARI report by Rob Walker cited in Barry MacDonald's "Portrayal of Persons as Evaluation Data," SAFARI papers (in press).

22. Wolfe, *New Journalism.*

23. In the work of both T. S. Eliot and F. R. Leavis, there is a preoccupation with evaluating and reevaluating the literary tradition; see Eliot, "Tradition and the Individual Talent," in *Selected Essays*; and F. R. Leavis, *The Great Tradition* (1948; rpt. ed., New York: New York University Press, 1963).

24. See Frances Link, *"Man: A Course of Study*: Getting Innovation Curricula into the Bloodstream of American Education," mimeographed (Private circulation, 1973).

25. See John Elliott and Clem Adelman, "Reflecting Where the Action Is: The Design of the Ford Teaching Project," *Education for Teaching*, 1973, p. 92.

26. See Stephen Kemmis, "Telling It Like It Is: The Problem of Making a Portrayal of an Educational Program," in *Handbook of Curriculum*, ed. Louis J. Rubin (Boston: Allyn & Bacon, 1977).

27. See Susan Sontag, "Notes on Camp," *Partisan Review* 31, no. 1 (Winter 1964). A nice summary of this concept by David Lodge is to be found in his *Twentieth Century Literary Criticism: A Reader* (London: Longmans, Green, 1972).

28. A longer extract from "Saved by the Bell" is included in Hamilton et al., *Beyond the Numbers Game.*

29. For a discussion of "tacit knowledge" in case study, see Clem Adelman, David Jenkins, and Stephen Kemmis, "Rethinking Case Study: Notes from the Second Cambridge Conference," *Cambridge Journal of Education*, 1977.

30. See Samuel A. Stouffer et al., *The American Soldier*, 2 vols. (New York: Wiley, 1965).

31. See David Hargreaves, "Power and the Paracurriculum," mimeographed (University of Manchester, 1977). Hargreaves presented the paper to the 1977 Conference of the British Association for the Study of the Curriculum at Durham.

32. See Konstantin Stanislavski, *Building a Character*, trans. E. R. Hopgood (London: Reinhardt, 1950).

33. See Erving Goffman, *Asylums: Essays on the Social Situation of Mental Patients and Other Inmates* (New York: Anchor Books, 1968).

34. See Samuel Bowles and Herbert Gintis, *Schooling in Capitalist America* (London: Routledge and Kegan Paul, 1976). Considerable interest, even controversy, was caused recently in Britain by the Marxist interpretations underlying a number of papers in the Open University *School and Society* course readers. See Roger Dale et al., eds., *Schooling and Capitalism* (London: Routledge and Kegan Paul, 1976).

35. See Jules Henry, *Culture Against Man* (Baltimore, Md.: Penguin, 1966).

36. See Elizabeth Burns, "Conventions of Performance," in Elizabeth Burns and Tom Burns, *Sociology of Literature and Drama* (Baltimore, Md.: Penguin, 1973).

37. See Elliot Eisner, "Educational Objectives: Help or Hindrance?" *The School Review* 75, no. 3 (Autumn 1967).

38. See Stake, "Countenance of Educational Evaluation."

39. See Scriven, "Prose and Cons," and idem, "Goal-Free Behavioural Objectives?" in Hamilton et al., *Beyond the Numbers Game*. See also Daniel Stufflebeam, "Should or Can Evaluation be Goal-Free?" *Evaluation Comment* 3, no. 4 (December 1972).

40. Scriven went on to produce the "GFE Manifesto," which elaborated this profile of demonstrated needs. Scriven's product checklist is "lethal," because it is conceived not in terms of *desiderata* but *necessitata*. Failure on any count absolutely disqualifies the product. It's a long way from the literary critical tradition.

41. For a discussion of this concept, see Arthur George Lehmann, *The Symbolist Aesthetic in France, 1885-1895*, 2d ed. (Oxford: Blackwells, 1950).

42. See William K. Wimsatt and Monroe Beardsley, "The Intentional Fallacy," in Lodge, *Twentieth Century Criticism: A Reader*. Other essays discussing this critical question are to be found in the same collection.

43. Michael Scriven's full checklist is found in "Evaluation Perspectives and Procedures," chap. 1 of *Evaluation in Education*, ed. W. James Popham (Berkeley, Ca.: McCutchan Publishing Corp., 1974).

44. See Barry MacDonald, "Briefing Decision Makers," in *Towards Judgement: The Publications of the Evaluation Unit of the Humanities Curriculum Project*, ed. Donald Hamingson (Occasional paper no. 1, Centre for Applied Research in Education, University of East Anglia, Norwich, England, 1973).

45. See I. A. Richards, *Principles of Literary Criticism* (London: Kegan Paul and Co., 1924).

46. See John Crowe Ransom, "Criticism Inc.," *Virginia Quarterly Review*. Reprinted in Lodge, *Twentieth Century Criticism*.

47. See Kathleen Evans, "The Symbolic Culture of the School" (M.A. thesis, University of Manchester, 1971).

48. A sensitive approach to this question can be found in Fred Inglis, *The Englishness of English Teaching* (London: Longmans, Green, 1961).

49. However, the "bids" will be read differently according to the basic stance taken on the epistemological status of curriculum subjects or strategies. Two statements of opposed position are found in Paul Hirst, "Liberal Education and the Nature of Knowledge," in *Philosophical Analysis and Education*, ed. Reginald D. Archambault (London: Routledge and Kegan Paul, 1965); and Michael Young, "On the Politics of Educational Knowledge: Some Preliminary Considerations with Particular Reference to the Schools Council," *Economy and Society*, 1972, p. 125.

50. See Gordon Pask, "Teaching Strategies: A Systems Approach," Unit 9 of Open University course E283, *The Curriculum, Context, Design and Development* (1972).

51. Ibid. A paper by Michael MacDonald Ross exploring the problems of a "satisfactory syntax of knowledge," entitled "The Problem of Representing Knowledge," was delivered at the Structural Learning Conference in Philadelphia, Pa., 1972 (Mimeographed, Open University).

52. See Colin Bell, "A Note on Participant Observation," *Sociology*, no. 3 (September 1969).

53. Twentieth-centurh novelists, beginning with Conrad and Ford Maddox Ford, frequently explore the possibilities of a limited or unreliable narrator.

54. See Raymond Williams, "Dickens and Social Ideas," in *Dickens: 1970 Centenary Essays*, ed. Michael Slater (London: Chapman and Hall, 1970).

55. See Denys Wyatt Harding, "Regulated Hatred: An Aspect of the Work of Jane Austen." This paper first appeared in *Scrutiny* 8, no. 4 (March 1940), and is reprinted in Lodge, *Twentieth Century Criticism.*

56. David Jenkins, Stephen Kemmis, and Rod Atkin, "UNCAL: An Insider's Critique," in *Safari Papers 2: Theory into Practice*, ed. Nigel Norris (Occasional paper no. 4, Centre for Applied Research in Education, University of East Anglia, Norwich, England).

57. M. G. Levine, "Scientific Method and the Adversary Model: Some Preliminary Suggestions," *Evaluation Comment* 4 (1973).

58. Stake and Gjerde, *T-City Report.* Extracts from this report are included in Hamilton et al., *Beyond the Numbers Game.*

59. See Ernest House and Craig Gjerde, "PLATO Comes to the Community College," in *The Politics of Educational Innovation*, ed. Ernest House (Berkeley, Ca.: McCutchan Publishing Corp., 1974).

60. Chap. 15 of this volume.

61. See Elliot Eisner, "Instructional and Expressive Objectives: Their Formulation and Use in Curriculum," in *Instructional Objectives*, ed. W. J. Popham (AERA monograph series on curriculum evaluation, no. 3), p. 3. See Elliot Eisner, "Emerging Models of Educational Evaluation," *School Review* 70 (1972).

62. See Rob Walker, "The Conduct of Educational Case Study: Ethics, Theories and Procedures," in SAFARI Interim Papers, *Innovation, Evaluation, Research, and the Problems of Control* (Norwich: University of East Anglia, 1976).

63. See MacDonald, "Briefing Decision Makers."

64. From an UNCAL report of a computer-managed learning project in the New University of Ulster (not generally available).

65. See E. M. Forster, *Aspects of the Novel* (London: Arnold, 1927).

66. The reaction of this kind of character analysis in drama was neatly summed up in an essay by Lional Charles Knights, with a tongue-in-cheek title lifted straight from Bradley himself, "How Many Children Had Lady Macbeth?" in *Explorations* (London: Chatto and Windus, 1946). But for a novelist's reaction against this trend, a plea for the restoration of the importance of character in fiction, see Iris Murdoch's essay "Against Drynesse," which first appeared in *Encounter*, January 1961; reprinted in Malcolm Bradbury, *The Novel Today* (Manchester: Manchester University Press, 1977).

67. See A. C. Bradley, *Shakespearean Tragedy*, 2d ed. (London: Macmillan, 1960).

68. The response to Angela Pope's film is an example of classic problems of justifying documentary treatment in the absence of endorsement by the subjects of the study.

69. See G. Wilson Knight, *The Wheel of Fire* (London: Methuen, 1949), and *The Imperial Theme* (Oxford: Oxford University Press, 1931); see also Caroline Spurgeon, *Shakespeare's Imagery and What It Tells Us* (Cambridge: Cambridge University Press, 1961).

70. See Eliot, *Selected Essays*, and William Empson, *Seven Types of Ambiguity* (London: Chatto, 1930).

71. See Malcolm Provus, *Discrepancy Evaluation* (Berkeley, Ca.: McCutchan Publishing Corp., 1971).

72. See Northrop Frye, *Anatomy of Criticism* (Princeton, N.J.: Princeton University Press, 1957).

73. See Henry, *Culture against Man*, and Martin Carnoy, *Education as Cultural Imperialism* (New York: McKay, 1974).

74. See Cleanth Brooks, "The Language of Paradox," which was subsequently revised slightly as the first chapter of *The Well Wrought Urn: Studies in the Structure of Poetry* (New York: Harcourt Brace Jovanovich, 1947).

75. See Jules Henry, "Docility, or Giving Teacher What She Wants," *Journal of Social Issues* 11 (1955).

76. See Shipman, *Inside a Curriculum Project*.

77. See Lucien Goldmann, "The Moral Universe of the Playwright," in *The Hidden God*, trans. Philip Thody (Atlantic Highlands, N.J.: Humanities Press, 1964); reprinted in Burns and Burns, *Sociology of Literature and Drama*.

78. See Malcolm Parlett, *A Study of Two Experimental Programs at MIT* (Cambridge, Mass.: MIT, 1972). Extracts from the MIT report are included in a section entitled "Evaluation as Vivisection," in Hamilton, et al., *Beyond the Numbers Game*. It is also included in Curriculum Evaluation, units 19 and 20 of Open University course E203, *Curriculum Design and Development*.

79. D. H. Lawrence, *Studies in Classic American Literature* (1923; rpt. ed., New York: Viking Press, 1964).